ADVANCE PRAISE FOR

Bangladesh: Political and Literary Reflections on a Divided Country

"A pictorial and factual picture of Bangladesh bogged down in the swamp of distortions and deviations perpetrated by a corrupt Awami one-party rule and its police and judicial tyrannies."

— *Syed Serajul Islam, Distinguished Professor and former Chair of Political Science, currently Director of Criminology Program, Lakehead University, Canada.*

"The result of extreme hard work for a number of years, this volume basically refutes the one-sided rhetoric of the government machinery in Bangladesh. Well-written and well-argued, it exposes the despotic and fascist nature of the current regime with sufficient convincing details. The publication is a timely reflection of the current regime's authoritarian rule in Bangladesh. I am sure it will find a good market worldwide."

—*Abdullah al-Ahsan, Professor of History and Civilization, IIU Malaysia*

"Q M Jalal Khan made a serious intellectual effort to uncover the truth and justice behind Bangladesh being ruled by a brutal regime. Although politically sensitive (as it contests the current regime widely known for trampling democracy and for massive human rights abuse), Khan's work is a phenomenal contribution and hence is likely to have a wide marketability."

—*Md Saidul Islam, Professor of Sociology, Nanyang Technological University, Singapore*

"Highly recommended to readers, this book by Q M Jalal Khan makes a significant contribution to studies in Bangladesh politics. Using Western literary and historical references, Khan boldly exposes the cruel, fascist character of the despotic ruling party that has virtually killed the future of democracy by changing the electoral policies to secure its hold on political power forever. To the best of my knowledge, no other publication has thus far so eloquently addressed the systematic campaign of terror and torture that the current ruling party of Sheikh Hasina, the Awami League, is inflicting upon the opposition political groups. The manuscript cogently tackles many related issues debated in the political circles of Bangladesh and will certainly appeal to readers not only within Bangladesh but also in South and Southeast Asia. It will also intrigue the global crowds concerned about democracy and human rights anywhere in the world. By publishing the book, the publisher has given a voice to an overwhelming majority of the people of Bangladesh whose political and civil rights have been rendered null and void by the ruling Awami party. Just on this count alone, I believe, Khan's book merits a wide readership home and abroad."

—*Mohammad A. Auwal, Professor of Communication Studies, California State University, Los Angeles*

Bangladesh

This book is part of the Peter Lang Politics and Economics list.
Every volume is peer reviewed and meets
the highest quality standards for content and production.

PETER LANG
New York • Bern • Berlin
Brussels • Vienna • Oxford • Warsaw

Q M Jalal Khan

Bangladesh

Political and Literary Reflections on a Divided Country

PETER LANG
New York • Bern • Berlin
Brussels • Vienna • Oxford • Warsaw

Library of Congress Cataloging-in-Publication Control Number: 2017035871

Bibliographic information published by **Die Deutsche Nationalbibliothek.**
Die Deutsche Nationalbibliothek lists this publication in the "Deutsche Nationalbibliografie"; detailed bibliographic data are available on the Internet at http://dnb.d-nb.de/.

ISBN 978-1-4331-4613-8 (hardcover)
ISBN 978-1-4331-4824-8 (ebook pdf)
ISBN 978-1-4331-4371-7 (epub)
ISBN 978-1-4331-4957-3 (mobi)
DOI 10.3726/b11672

The paper in this book meets the guidelines for permanence and durability of the Committee on Production Guidelines for Book Longevity of the Council of Library Resources.

29 Broadway, 18th floor, New York, NY 10006
www.peterlang.com

Printed in Germany

This book is dedicated to:

- The illumining and illuminating memory of the great and glorious President Ziaur Rahman (1936–1981), declarer of the independence of Bangladesh and founder of the popular and patriotic Bangladesh Nationalist Party (BNP), who was at the forefront of both the emergence and existence of Bangladesh—first in March 1971 and then in November 1975; and who, in light of his numerous milestone contributions, his incandescent collective vision, and his vigorous pursuit of lofty national goals and ideals, may be regarded as হাজার বছরের শ্রেষ্ঠ বাংলাদেশী (the greatest Bangladeshi ever, of a thousand years);
- the three-time former Prime Minister and BNP Chair *DeshNetri* Begum Khaleda Zia, who, of stunning beauty and majestic stature, has been living a politically fighting but personally lonely life since the prime of her youth following the assassination of her husband Zia;
- the young and exiled Tarique Rahman, who, though of a beautiful mind and a heroic stock, was served with a crippling and debilitating physical punishment by the notoriously malicious and malignant *Uddins* in 2007, both the mother and the son forced to live far apart from each other, long suffering, yet uncompromising Promethean victims of all-out Awami venom and vitriol;
- the memory of Tarique's younger brother Arafat Rahman Koko, who died in exile too young and whose premature death was probably hastened by the same lowly political vendetta;
- the remarkably resplendent Tarique's wife Zubaidah Rahman; and Koko's young and lonely widow, equally radiant Sharmila;
- the brave and brilliant Mahmudur Rahman, until recently, a long prisoner of conscience;
- the abominably abducted and shockingly stranded and exiled BNP leader Salahuddin Ahmad;
- the long confined and long incarcerated BNP leader Lutfuzzaman Babar, who had a distinctive and individual style of his own, regardless of whatever his নিন্দুক/ critics claim him to be by way of their নিন্দা / destructive and mischievous criticism of him;
- the once confined Mahmudur Rahman Manna, one of the most assertively spoken and patriotically inspired politicians;
- the memory of the trio: former Prime Minister Kazi Zafar Ahmed; journalist and columnist Sadeq Khan; and the political commentator Dr Piash

Karim, who were all loud and outspoken against the Awami extremes and excesses of political violence, vengeance, and vandalism;

- the memory of all the known and unknown multitude, in millions and more, who died brutal and bestial deaths during the liberation war and then in tens of thousands due to the bloody Awami paramilitary forces [রক্ষীবাহিনী], the devastating Awami famine of 1974, and the frequent floods and cyclones, followed by thousands in death, disappearance, and abduction either due to or with connivance of the cruel Awami police, especially since the Awami লগি ও বৈঠা horror and terror of October 2006, through the Awami murderous গুম ও খুন and bombs and burns and boots and bullets, from 2009 onward, including the BDR massacre of February 2009 and the Hefajote massacre of May 2013, through the odd, occult, eerie, and weird (উদ্ভট and অদ্ভুত), hecatine black Awami farce of January 5, 2014, till today; and, finally, the thousands of children and adults senselessly and mercilessly killed by savage anthropoid animals, politically attached or not;
- the treasured memories of my parents; and their three young grandchildren—Saiaz, Meehan, and O'Ami, all born and living abroad (North America).

Lines for Sharmilah, Zubaidah, and Tarique

(These lines form the second part of my poem, "Beauty of that land: the reverse," yet to be published in full.)

The greatest beauty of that land lies, however,
Not in the too idealistic souls'
Too simple neutrality,
And their third option advocacy,
But in the new and reformed and trusted views
Of many a leader out of power
United under one common banner,
(Reform being better than radical leveler),
And their enlightened strategy,
Tolerance and repentance as necessary,
On which has missed out, miserably,
The ruling party.

Drowned in mayhem,
Drenched in partisan divide,
Drunk in power,

Corruption-ridden, clearly,
The regime has paved the way for
The opposition's winning popularity.

The nation can't wait for you, Tarique,
Orphaned early, a boy tender
Born of a heroic stock
Bereft of parental love and care,[1]
But then from a certain height
A beacon to the befitting subject
Of জাগো and হুশিয়ার সাবধান musica fair.[2]

The young man of broken bones
In their dark prison,[3]
Beleaguered, bedeviled
Now in long exile in Brutus's Britain,
Albion of white English cliffs
And London Bridge that never fell down.

Forced to be away—
As were many in history there
(Aeneas, Thucydides, Hobbes, Charles II, Gibbon, and Voltaire),[4]
From the wrong-headed, listless terrors, at home—
Her ladyship's land's ready for you
(Our Prince Hal and Henry V of England,
And the misleading figures of Falstaff discarded),
And your leadership to overwhelm
And to be at the helm.

And yours, too, the radiant Sharmila,
And, certainly yours,
The remarkably resplendent Zubaidah,
All three scoring high in your
Sane, sound, and steadfast ways.

Contents

Notice to the Reader and Putting the Bartlebys on Notice

One aspect of this book is the integration and interweaving of Western literary references with the political, historical, and cultural context of the divided Bangladesh—more intensely divided than Donald Trump's America, as bitterly divided as the other modern autocratic and authoritarian countries in the world, starting with Franco's Spain in the 1930s, on to today's Egypt, Sudan, Syria, Zimbabwe, Venezuela, Vietnam, and Cambodia, among others. The literary references that occur throughout provide a new dimension to this South Asian country-specific political book. I am, therefore, pleased to present the reader, in this notice, with a preliminary idea of the telescoping of the literary and the political that appears in the volume as one of its marked stylistic features to reinforce the themes concerning the rein-less Awami reign drifting far away from the dream of "Cloud Nine," let alone the higher "Cloud Eleven" democracy, immersing itself into its deep-dug dictatorship and increasingly silencing political dissent to establish its titanic tyranny.

The Hasina regime and its Awami party are far drifting in "the foam/ Of perilous seas, in faery lands forlorn," showing no charm whatsoever, as the English Romantic poet Keats's Nightingale does, to open the political "magic casements" for democratic peace, harmony, and stability in Bangladesh. Writer and researcher Mohiuddin Ahmad is clear about the Hasina regime's false cover of highly defective, one-sided, and jaundiced material development to justify its Machiavellian pursuit of all nefarious and crooked means to stay in power: "দেশটা ওপরে ওপরে ফুলেফেঁপে উঠেছে। চওড়া সড়ক, লম্বা সেতু, বিশাল বাজেট দ্যুতি ছড়াচ্ছে। ভেতরে ঘুণ ধরেছে, ক্রমাগত ক্ষয়ে যাচ্ছে। একটা সময় আসবে, যখন প্রশ্ন উঠবে, তাহলে আমরা স্বাধীনতা চেয়েছিলাম কেন? কেন লাখ লাখ মানুষ জীবন দিলেন, সম্ভ্রম হারালেন? কেন?"[5]

This alerting notice has in fact been triggered by the latest fuss and fanfare in the politically suppressive and democratically declining Bangladesh, the noisy whoopla being in existence for the last ten years. There is no end of farcical charades and masquerades in this class-ridden country of fantastic সাগর চুরি পুকুর চুরি / sea-and-swamp big corruption and exploitation. The latest farce in the series, especially after the sham and mock election on the coal-black January 5, 2014, was the search within the already unnecessary and superfluous search (similar to the story within the story, subplot within the plot in a literary work) for what finally turned out to be a foregone conclusion: yet another predetermined pro-Awami Election Commission (EC), to be only nominally in charge of what are extremely important and crucial elections, especially the national/parliamentary ones, that make the change of government and thereby the transfer/transition of power possible.[6]

Practically, it is the brutally biased and purely partisan Awami government that remains in charge of the "do or die" elections. That it was a preplanned EC is proved by the disputable choice of the new EC Chief, AKM Nurul Huda, who was recommended through a secret arrangement and understanding by Hasina's political allies: controversial H M Ershad and the equally controversial, small, and negligible religious sect called *Tarikat Federation*, who are a religious grave-specific and grave-centered (মাজার-কেন্দ্রিক, rather than mosque-centered) offshoot, consisting of মাইজভান্ডারি বাবাজান হুজুর কেবলা পীর ও মুরিদ community. That it was a preplanned EC is also proved by Nurul Huda's own words as well as the doubtful haste and hurry with which the new Commission was announced by the government.[7]

New Chief Election Commissioner (CEC) AKM Nurul Huda may not be different in his personal biases and preferences than the former CEC ATM Shamsul Huda, both still viewed to be far from at least commendable, if not total, impartiality and objectivity. Justice M A Aziz, who was CEC for a year and a half only, was unfortunately a scapegoat for no fault of his and was blamed for no good reason, the fact being that there were no elections held during his short tenure. Honest and innocent as he was, Aziz was way better than Shamsul Huda and way, way, way better than Rakibuddin Ahmed.

If (1) the 19 local (Upazela and Poura-shava) elections of March 5, 2017, (2) the Comilla City Corporation election of 30 March, (3) the information of about 10 lakh voters missing from the EC server, (4) the internal EC staff transfer without the knowledge and unanimous consent of all the Election Commissioners, and, most importantly, (5) the EC roadmap in preparation for the next general election make for an owlish and ominous harbinger, as written about by Stalin Shorkar, the new EC under Chief Nurul Huda may be heading toward yet another round of dull disaster.[8]

The EC seems to be as perplexed and retarded in its noble effort as John Keats's "dull brain"—burdensome knowledge of physical reality—"perplexes and retards" his upward flight in soul and imagination to the nightingale singing in the forest. Claiming, without feeling sorry for the Commission's alleged failures, that those elections (#1 and #2 above) were hundred percent clean, fair, and smooth, Chief Huda was speaking in the same loyalist language as his immediate predecessor Rakibuddin, not as a CEC with a strong backbone of his own. In his being hopelessly unprofessional and unprofessionally loyal to the Hasina regime, Rakibuddin may be regarded as one more *Uddin* added to the 2006–2008 trio or tetra of *Uddins*, all known for their well-earned disrepute. Trump accused Hillary Clinton and Barack Obama and the media of being "fake," "crooked," "inefficient," and "low." One wonders how he would have described the contestable and controvertible "penta" of *Uddins*, had they been in the leading positions of his country to fight against.

Despite many serious complaints of irregularities (without which the opposition BNP candidate would have won by a landslide in Comilla, for example), not only did CEC Huda let them go unaddressed but also dismissed and downgraded them as only a few isolated incidents. Why should there be even one incident (not accident), one instance of rigging, and one case of stuffing boxes with false and fake ballots, like why should there be even one shooting, one death, one abduction, one assassination, whether in the capital or the countryside, connected or isolated?

The few and far between BNP wins, at the chosen and selective mercy of the repressive Hasina regime, can be read as a trap for the BNP. The neo-and-near-fascist stratagems of the regime would like to coax the BNP into the upcoming general elections, which it wants to hold under its highly coercive police and civil admin control and under its loyal, so controversial Huda Commission. The latter is using the scattered and isolated BNP wins as a so-called neutrality card to increase its so-called credibility, however dubious that may be, and lure the BNP into the parliamentary elections, which, as the game-changer big jumbo jackpot—তালগাছ—the vehemently bellicose, belligerent, and BNP*hobic* Sheikh Hasina wants to carry. If successful, that would enable her to grab the state power to form the third corrupt and consecutive government, after the questionable first and detestable second.

That the Hasina regime would never allow free and fair elections at the national তালগাছ level is being demonstrated by the fact that her police, in plain-clothes or otherwise, various clandestine forces with or without her knowledge, Gopal/Gopali gangs and gongs, and their well-protected hoodlums and hooligans, mischievously and maliciously, continue to arrest, abduct, kill, and imprison the BNP leaders and activists, day in and day out.[9] That Hasina would never allow inclusive and impartial elections is being demonstrated by her ever denying the rights of the opposition to hold public meetings in public squares, while she has been going around holding public meetings everywhere and actively campaigning for her party, all at the expense of the public exchequer and all at the demolition of the political and democratic freedoms of the opposition BNP.

That the Hasina regime would never allow credible and participatory polls in a level (plain)-playing field is being demonstrated by its continually firing the elected BNP mayors and filing politically cooked lawsuits against them, ruining their careers and keeping them running from court to home and back. The regime's evil intention manifests itself when it makes clear that it would like to stay for four or five consecutive terms and then forever. The regime has been cynically acting according to the rural countryside story of jealousy and malignity that goes like this: "You're a poor dull boy. It's worthless for you to go to school. You won't do well and you won't pass. Even if you pass, you won't be accepted for college. In case you pass college, you won't get a job. If there's a job for you, you'd be kicked out no sooner than you get it."

The Nurul Huda Commission is yet to rise over the "lovely, dark and deep" attractions of the Hasina regime and yet to keep the "promises" that Chief Huda made at the beginning. He has long electoral miles to go to earn the public trust before he goes to "sleep," meaning rest and retirement (to echo Robert Frost).

Otherwise, in all likelihood, the new EC, as complained about by the BNP, is going to turn into another Rakib-মার্কা EC (the immediate past EC, the worst of its kind Bangladesh has ever had—sadly soft and spineless—that, instead of being strong and independent, as the Constitution clearly mandated the Commission to be, served at the pleasure and satisfaction of the Hasina regime and delivered the election results accordingly, with only a few accidental or intentional exceptions, to be used as a cover for the so-called, already traded, compromised, and sold-off neutrality). Despite having broad Constitutional powers and being responsible under oath to act independently and judiciously and to be fair and equal to all the stakeholders, the Rakib Commission was garishly happy to play as a tool of the Hasina regime, so much so that it was closely akin to the American Novelist Herman Melville's deluded Wall Street scrivener Bartleby.

The said Commission would constantly shy and shirk away from doing its job. It would be glad and gleeful to stay put to its inertia and be carefully careless to refrain from being assertive and taking any initiative, for long five years, by virtually meaning to say what Bartleby so famously says, "I would prefer not to," thereby leaving all the benefits and advantages that accrued from the Commission's passivity and inaction to the ruling Awami League (AL), the party of Hasina. Its full and complete loyalty to the League must have been in full and complete violation of the spirit of the oath its members took. (What's the point of taking the oath in Bangladesh when there are all sorts of moral and political deviations and deprivations taking place to let the majority or the overall national and democratic interests go awry and sundry, sore and sordid? Is it all a photo opportunity? A redundant, decadent, and supercilious showoff?)

Again, exactly like Bartleby, the members of the last (Rakib) Commission, according to common public perception, must have been suffering from a kind of clinical disorder and psychological depression, out of their blind, uncritical, and unconstitutional allegiance to the AL and its Hasina government. Can they one day stand trial, despite whatever constitutional impunity they may have?

No wonder, all the fair-minded, neutrally inclined, and well-respected observers and commentators, such as Dr Akbar Ali Khan, Dr Asif Nazrul, and Dr Syed Anwar Hussain, hold the succeeding, newly formed EC, suspiciously formed so swiftly and speedily (all probably having been set previously), to criticism and ridicule as they also held the previous ones, all for being weak, timid, and cowardly, afraid of exercising their constitutional powers and being HMV (Her Majesty's Voice).[10] It is not surprising that one bold and impartial journalist and TV anchor of fair and fine talk, Mahmud Bin Feisal of SATV, dismissed the new EC as consisting of all *Gopals*, a disgraceful and derogatory term for those who are hopelessly servile and slavish to a government, especially the present Hasina-led Awami government, as people in general also love to stigmatize such Commissions as being this or that মার্কা /marked Commission, after the name of whoever was the Head of the Commission?[11]

It was a disputable search for the controversial search committee for, as has just been said, yet another prearranged commission, considering (1) the last ten years of regressive and retrograde political history of Bangladesh under this regime and the two years of the military-backed interim government before; (2) the haste and hurry, within just over an hour after it had received the search committee recommendation, with which the regime decided upon and declared the commission members, about ten days in advance of their taking oath of office; and (3) the fact that the majority of the finalists and the finally successful names came from the regime's very small and inconsequential allies, with most of them bearing the mark of not so clean associations, having largely been Awami beneficiaries and holding Awami leanings and leniencies. The whole process was thus all "struts and frets [...] full of sound and fury/signifying nothing," to take the phrases from Shakespeare's Macbeth, who thus expresses his realization of the petty and idiotic vanity and emptiness of his otherwise action-packed and ambition-filled life at the end of the play.

If morning shows the day, why should the high-sounding yet partisan Presidential Search Committee and the Presidential EC be an exception? After a long-winded eyewash or showoff dialogue of dozens of political parties, some of which is as fabulously big as some are microscopically small, with the figurehead president, it all came down to an all pro-Awami select committee of five, far from being a balanced and bipartisan one, let alone a fair and neutral one. Didn't the President, precisely similar to the biased and partisan precedent set by his predecessor, find even a single individual considered fair and neutral, like the widely acceptable and twice recommended former Secretary Ali Imam Mazumder, to head the 5-member committee to make a real difference? Forget about the far cry of looking for one even remotely sympathetic to the popular opposition BNP from the population of 160 million to head the much hyped 5-member committee, many members of which had actually Awami favors and blessings that were expeditiously but cynically programmed and manipulated through the small and inconsequential Awami allies?

Why did the majority of them, especially the chief, have to be of pro-Awami badge and background, directly or indirectly, if the polls were "promised" to be free and fair at all? As the nation's ill luck would have it, President Abdul Hamid was not able to come out of the narrow vision of his purely partisan and endlessly circuitous loyalties. So, as one helplessly holding the merely ceremonial guardian position, President Abdul Hamid pitiably failed to become a bipartisan and above the partisan unifier president and lost a rare opportunity to present himself as president and pave the way for enlightened public discourse in a moment of utmost necessity and utter democratic crisis that his country, their country, and our country—ultimately and simultaneously one and the same country—was unprecedentedly facing.

So here I go connecting and correlating literature and politics, as I have just done above, sometimes by way of similarity, sometimes by contrast. At the satanic prospect of embracing the mythologically most beautiful woman on earth, that is, Helen, or actually her deceiving phantom, English dramatist Christopher Marlowe's tragic Dr Faustus is effusively saying "all is dross that is not Helena." Similarly, Bangladesh's Sheikh Hasina (forcibly hanging on through her police/ RAB) and her farcically ruling AL think that nothing is worth anything that does not belie, behoove, and conform, even remotely, to the closet and carbuncle of their autocratic and despotic rule and their narrowly one-sided and myopically short-sighted frame of views.

Of the endless number of excruciatingly painful, biased, and discriminatory stories that keep occurring daily, only a few of them say it all about the dictatorial and totalitarian designs of the Hasina regime. One is of the long suffering, long harassed, and long humiliated Begum Khaleda Zia, the most popular political leader of Bangladesh; another is the similar story of the thousands of long-persecuted, beleaguered, and bedeviled leaders, workers, and followers of her party, BNP; and yet another is of her former cabinet minister, editor of the now suppressed popular daily *Amar Desh*, a public intellectual, and a media personality, Mahmudur Rahman, who, as a national treasure and a national hero, was a prisoner of conscience for many years, a heavy price he paid for his freedom of speech under what he describes as a fascist government, for the toppling of which he is openly calling for a mass upheaval, a mass uprising.[12]

One of Portia's boxes (in the casket scene of Shakespeare's *The Merchant of Venice*) containing a written scroll reads: "All that glitters is not gold." Similarly, all that is claimed by Hasina to be glittering and shining in the name of the so-called development is not actually golden. It is all class-ridden and corruption-ridden, causing more and more economic divide and disparity, poverty-stricken slums, traffic congestions, bank and business lootings, share market scams, and black market smugglings, all in millions and billions, all to the big benefit of the AL and their allies, followers, affiliates, associates, and loyalists.

Marcellus, one of the palace guards in *Hamlet*, says to Horatio, at the beginning of the play, "Something is rotten in the state of Denmark." So is in the state of Bangladesh, making many to soliloquize, as Hamlet does, "To be, or not to be …," all being in the dark and insecure and frightening atmosphere of unending police violence and state terrorism let loose mainly on the people of democratic dissent, with thousands and thousands, including all the opposition political leaders, detained, remanded, and thrown into jail. Given the bloody chaos, waves of fear, violent murders, cruel conspiracies, deadly disappearances, and hard moral reversals, it takes no time to apply to the situation in Bangladesh the weird sisters' formula of "fair is foul, foul is fair" found in the opening scene of *Macbeth*.[13]

Probably no other country is as full of sham and shallow political theaters, masques, and pantomimes as Bangladesh, staging up and staging down the different scenes of the Hasina-directed political play in different ways, but nothing in a free and frank and fair way, all being in the way of the narrow and naked interest of the ruling clique and coterie, more so than ever, under the currently ruling and democratically illegitimate Hasina, who, from the point of view of a clear and absolute majority, is defiling and devouring everything possible to feed and fatten her personal and political ego, to the detriment of what is quintessentially, most conspicuously and most consequentially the lifeline of democracy and democratic culture and environment—transparency, accountability, and free and fair polls. Destruction and displacement of the freedom of choice and the people's vote and voice have become the hallmark of her rope-less and rein-less reign, which is not possible in a country of democratic openness and fairness with both rein and rope.

Sheikh Hasina is able to do all she wants and wishes to do with the help of her police/RAB and other agents and accomplices in her governing regime and her party. The police/RAB are the main players on the stage that she has maliciously and malevolently set up in pursuit of her personal and political goals, the cast of the minor characters being members of the civil bureaucracy and civil administration, along with a few greedy very small parties, too small to be named, headed by individuals of no real following. All the wings and feathers and branches of the state are used in a purely partisan way. Not even a divinely appointed and/or anointed King or Queen, Tsar or Tsarina, Kaiser or Kaiserin would be able to do what Hasina can do at the stroke of a pen or a word of mouth, in her sole and solo female version of "let it be and it is."

Some low comedy scenes of raw and raucous humor but affecting the course of national events and their final outcome, as in the English Elizabethan/Renaissance plays of fools, jesters, and entertainers, include, among others, those of (1) Sheikh Hasina's fishy and dirty tricks in connection with the repeatedly ripped and revised constitution and the interim CTG system; (2) the constantly fluctuating and fickle-minded, yet Hasina's once enemy now a close crony, former President Ershad (satirically and sarcastically called CMLA, "Cancel My Last Announcement," and by many other distasteful and dishonorable names for his antics related to his on-again off-again unreliability and untrustworthiness, both in his personal love life and political/public life, including the one called বিশ্ব বেহায়া given him by artist Kamrul Hasan in the last year of his rule, 1990); (3) Ershad cum-and-versus his wife Rawshon, both often locked in a tenuous and strained relationship, to be periodically reconciled by comical political and domestic marriages of convenience; (4) the mock-heroic দিদি ও দাদাগিরি visit of the Indian emissary Sujata Singh to Ershad days before the phony, fraudulent, and the opposition-boycotted nonelection of 5 January (blacker than black, perhaps the blackest and most bogus day in the history of Bangladesh) and the intervention of দিদি Singh's Indian government in the affairs of Bangladesh run by India's too friendly Hasina government (to use that mild euphemism for what is described by critics as a stooge or puppet); (5) Indian Ambassadors' visits of "insidious intent" to different police academies in Bangladesh; (6) the highly disreputable and disastrous Rakib-মার্কা EC; (7) rubber stamp parliament; and, finally (8) sections of pro-Hasina interest in the judiciary, media, civil service, and civil society. Some of these coarse and jarring scenes and acts have been nicely touched upon by journalist Minar Rashid.[14]

All this is/was possible in the country of all possibilities, Bangladesh, suffering from too many cons and phonies in terms of the destruction of the spirit of independence, freedom of speech, democratic tolerance, economic equality, social justice, human dignity, rule law, and good governance, all shrunk, squeezed, diminished, and degenerated, to the point of being nil, especially for the popular opposition BNP, especially under the present Awami government, which is being shielded and sheltered by the neighboring India in the latter's selfish and hegemonic interest. It is a government that kills and jails and kidnaps its own people, sometimes for no reason and sometimes for the slightest and flimsiest of social media criticism against its own fellows and followers, be they politically and financially corrupt black cats or wrongheaded leaders.

Billionaire New Yorker Michael Bloomberg and the former Republican Presidential candidate Mitt Romney of Massachusetts described Trump, before he became President, as a con, a fraud, and a phony. There is no dearth of such people in Bangladesh, which is also full of (Shakespearean?) fools and clowns, otherwise quite wise and reflective, as poet Abu Shahriar is known to have once described the dramatic culture figure Aly Zaker to be one such:

> "সর্বপ্রকার বিচারে মনুষ্যত্ববোধবিবর্জিত সেই ভাঁড়শ্রেণীর লোকটিকে ইদানীং 'আলোর পথযাত্রী', 'আলোকিত মানুষ', 'আলোয় ভুবন ভরা', ইত্যাদি তকমা গায়ে এঁটে তেলতেলে হাসিমুখে যত্রতত্র অনুষ্ঠান করতে এবং ঘুরে বেড়াতে দেখা যায়॥"- আবু শাহরিয়ার (কবি)/ বালুকাবেলায় ॥ [পার্ল পাবলিকেশন্স - ফেব্রুয়ারি, ২০০৯ । পৃ: ১৫/৩১-৩২/৬১-৬২/৭০][15]

All the national institutions—from the office of the titular president to the fearful and frightening police (who are a reincarnation of the Awami Rakkhi-Bahini of the mid-1970s), from the Prime Minister's office and residence গণভবন to the figurehead President's office and residence বঙ্গভবন, from the national parliament to the local council পৌরসভা, from the courts and the clubs to the commissions and the corporations, from the civil admin to the media, from the banks and boards to the federations and directorates—have been "franchised" as no more than an outfit of party loyalists, sycophants, flatterers, and miscreants. All institutions are suffering from eroding trust, independence, and confidence. All this is taking place by way of boring political camouflage and dreary diabolic criminalization, of the nature of "a tedious argument/ Of insidious intent," to quote a trope from T S Eliot's *The Love Song of J. Alfred Prufrock*. The entire spectra of the beaten and blunted political opposition have been "etherized, like a patient, upon a table," again, with a small change in word order, of course, from Eliot's *Love Song*.

One tactic/strategy of the dictatorial regime is: allow "them"—the other—some, not more than some freedom to talk on the public/mass media, print or electronic, in criticism of "us" as a way of limited ventilation of "their" emotions, but don't allow "them" any street action, which should solely belong to "us" and all election results have to be on "our" side, in "our" favor. No protest, no demonstrations, no meetings, no assemblies, no rallies, no celebrations by the opposition are to be tolerated, just as no such popular and plebian outburst is allowed by the Pompey supporting aristocratic patricians to mark the triumphal return of Pompey's rival Julius Caesar, even though that would coincide with the pagan Lupercal holiday, as it is seen in the very first scene of that play by Shakespeare. No opposition win in the election is to be allowed to stand and, if there are any wins anyway, those wins are to be snatched away and the such elected representatives, instead of being allowed to function, are to be charged with petty, paltry, flimsy, fishy, and made up offences to be arrested and put in jail. All images of the opposition leaders, dead or alive, are to be vandalized and removed the way Caesar's images are dislodged and taken down, again as seen in the same first scene.

On the one hand, the Hasina-led AL is intransigent and recalcitrant, and, on the other, it is also paranoid, hypochondriac, and schizophrenic. It has been chronically suffering from a deep and dark sense of BNP*hobia*, just as the Nazis were suffering from anti-Semitic Judophobia. Similarly, Narendra Modi's India, Trump's America, Geert Wilders's Netherlands, Marie Le Pen's France, Matteo Salvini's Italy, Gabor Vona's Hungary, Frauke Petry's Germany, and Nigel Farage's England are unnecessarily suffering from Islamophobia. The Awami-Hasina regime's ballistic bulldozer and bombastic steamroller have successfully tamed and domesticated the opposition BNP into a rudderless and leaderless party, reduced to the status of the locally bred political *Rohingyas*, left in weary and dreary doldrums. The Awami way of liquidating the opposition BNP is the same as the Pakistani way of leaving Bangladesh free of academic intellectuals on December 14, 1971. It is the same way as many Awamis themselves wanted to render their own country devoid of top political leaders on August 15 and November 3, 1975.

There is a commonality between the two first parties—the Awamis and the Pakistanis—the latter having played in 1971 and the former now playing the same role to realize their dark intent of dictatorial suppression, oppression, and repression. Shouldn't any government whose history is one of deadly *Rakkhi-Bahini* locusts descending down on the people of Bangladesh with dire consequences, গুম ও খুন (abductions and assassinations), হামলা ও মামলা (attacks, accusations, and penal persecutions) and jail and *zulum* জুলুম (imprisonment and incarceration) have its moral and political rights eroded and evaporated? Doesn't any government whose history is one of tons of heinous and horrible crimes against humanity and human rights abuses in a neo-and-near-and-more-than-partially fascist manner have to think twice before it talks out loud about 1952 and 1971?

Why should a leader who lived in great comfort under the generous care of the Pakistanis (receiving 1,500 taka per month, in addition to all other expenses and services, including the safety and security provided by them and their celebration of the birth of her son, for all of which she was then full of praise and gratitude for the Pakistani army) with no contribution to the nine months of the bloody war in 1971 divide the nation in the name of the latter and give all credit only to India and the AL for the liberation of Bangladesh, with no recognition of the other leaders, parties, and people who had made an immense contribution to the creation of Bangladesh and formation of Bangladeshi nationhood before and after? (See Chapter 9).

Hindu India had its own agenda of weakening its age-old arch enemy Muslim Pakistan by breaking it up into pieces behind its support for the armed struggle for an independent Bangladesh, which would have become independent anyway, maybe over a slightly longer time, without any Indian support. The proof of this claim is borne out by three facts: one, India joined the 9-month long war on December 3, 1971, just 12 days before the final victory on 16 December when the Pakistani forces were already facing defeat on different fronts by the freedom fighters of Bangladesh; two, India's enslavement of the still-unborn and newly born Bangladesh by the tight noose of its unequal pacts with Tajuddin and Mujib; and, three, India never helped Bangladesh on any issue—border, business, water—since 1971.

Hegemon India only exploited and imposed (and is still exploiting and imposing) its interest and influence on Bangladesh, which is experiencing a soft-targeted neo-and-near Sikkim syndrome politically, economically, and culturally, in which Indian RAW is playing a big role intelligence-wise. The Sikkim syndrome is clearly palpable in terms of trade imbalance, border killings, lack of water sharing, construction of environmentally destructive coal plant, and various security details, including the clandestine and surreptitious presence of shadowy and সন্ত্রাসী/terrorist commando elements and structures with their snake-like operations here and there.

"It is hundred percent true," Mohiuddin Anwar of the USA argues,

> that India helped Bangladesh's liberation war enormously. The reason is not only for the love of Bangladeshis' aspiration for liberation but also to divide and weaken Pakistan. Pakistanis exploited Bangladesh for a long period of time; similarly, India also is exploiting the Muslim Kashmir even more. We Bangladeshis understand how much painful it is to live under occupation and similarly we can feel the pain of the Kashmiris, Palestinians, Chechens and all other freedom loving people of the World. Although we appreciate the help of India for our liberation, unfortunately, we cannot help the freedom loving Kashmiris […] India occupied Kashmir, Hyderabad, and Sikkim without their peoples' approval, like now Russia occupying some areas near their border, rest of the World can do nothing. (E-mail to the author, July 15, 2017)

Still Bangladesh remains and should remain thankful and grateful to India for its decisive support during the liberation war. But its gratitude and thankfulness must not translate into enslavement. It must not overshadow and overwhelm Bangladesh's freedom, independence, integrity, and sovereignty. Bangladesh's friendship should not be in excess of the events that took place in 1971. It must not be indiscriminate, unqualified, and unconditional—giving all but receiving nothing.

Corruption in Bangladesh under Sheikh Hasina is more widespread than West Pakistan (WP)'s exploitation of the East (1948–1970). The Awami axis's exploitation of its own Bangladesh is more intense and debilitating. Hasina's Bangladesh is in a state of political civil war, which is much worse and dangerous than the Pakistan times. Being an outsider and far apart, WP was an easy target to fight against, but now it is more difficult, the enemy being within, as if it is the case of শর্ষে ভূত and ঘরের শত্রু বিভীষণ, to use Bengali proverbs to drive home the same. Despite WP's exploitation of the East—perhaps not more than slight and mild, if any—there was a real and solid material development in economy, education, and industrialization with much less corruption, better work ethics and environment, and saner, safer, and cleaner office culture during the 20 years of its domination. Despite the WP's (mostly moderate) exploitation of the East, the latter came into being because of the former from which, as Dr Firoz Mahboob Kamal of the UK points out, the Muslim majority East immensely benefited. By contrast, India, where the Muslim minority remains as low and neglected as Dalit untouchables, never wished well to East Bengal and did not want to take East Bengal in its fold in 1930 or 1947.[16]

Communal/ist/ic Hindu chauvinist Rabindranath Tagore, among many other Indian/West Bengal communalists of his time, always remained attached to his Hindu "mother" India. He was discriminatory against East Bengal (East Pakistan/Bangladesh) and its Muslims, for whom he bore an ill will (see Chapter 14). He was never in favor of the University of Dhaka and was never on behalf of the High Court in Dhaka, never ever. Despite his immense and endless contribution to Bengali literature and culture, the Guru of the Tagore devotees and votaries not only wrote several poetical and prose works full of hatred and anathema for Muslims but also campaigned hard against the formation or establishment of those two key institutions in East Bengal. His strong nay to the vital academic and educational interest of the people of East Bengal can only remind a Bangladeshi about Shakespeare's King Lear's nays about his two most treacherous elder daughters. In answer to his youngest and most faithful (but initially misunderstood and banished) daughter Cordelia's question, toward the end of the play (V.3), about those two most ungrateful daughters, "Shall we not see these daughters and these sisters?," fallen father-King Lear replies, "No, no, no, no!" Tagore, however, took the position in the negative out of his communalist and sectarian Hindu chauvinism.

Had there been no lofty, kind, rich, and generous Nawab in Sir Salimullah and his Muslim League and other stalwarts of his family (in the mood, mold, and manner of W B Yeats's aristocratic "big country house" tradition and heritage of the landed estates during the same period of time), there would not have been those landmark installations of East Bengal. From the East Bengal of 1905 to the reunited Bengal of 1912 through the (East and West) Pakistan of 1947 to the Bangladesh of 1971 and, of course, from the Muslim League and Nawab Salimullah of 1905 onward—all are woven with the same thread. One was the origin of another, one led to another, one cannot be thought of without the other. Moulana Bhasani and Sheikh Mujib in the 1950s and 1960s became part of the same thread—two-nation theory of 1947 on the basis of religion (Hindu majority India and Muslim majority Pakistan) leading to the three-nation theory of 1971 on the basis of political and economic disparity alone (please refer to Mujib's 6-point demands and his 7 March speech), never on the basis of secularism and language, both having already been settled in terms of the priority of Islam as the religion of the majority and the 1952 language movement. In other words, religion and language were not to be bargained any more, both remaining in the same status as they were.

All were the major components and catalysts for what happened next and then next. To deny the individual and collective contribution of all is to dismember and mutilate the body and rip off the pages of history. One pays a heavy price for distorting and tampering with large historical truths of national canvas and consequence. So Bangladesh and its institutions, its people, its rulers, its politicians, and its parties continue to suffer incurably and incorrigibly as if there is a poetic justice in reverse—a literary device of punishing the vice and rewarding the virtue, or the logical triumph in the course of events—unfolding and unraveling but without an end in sight though. Mysteriously "lost and found," that is, kidnapped and rescued Farhad Mazhar, an eminent intellectual, poet, writer, and columnist, also used the phrase "poetic justice" in the context of the *Hasina-Hefajote* victory following the Hasina regime-committed bloody and violent suffering of the *Hefajote*.

If WP exploited the East, question may be posed, "To what extent?" It thought Pakistan meant WP. It was in control of the political and religious leadership of the whole Pakistan from the beginning. It was much larger and more imposing in size and politically more dominating. So the exploitation, though definitely detestable and unacceptable, was still understandable. If there was any, it was a socially and politically realistic exploitation of the weaker by the stronger. Qamruddin Chowdhury of the USA thinks about the matter even more strongly:

> After 45+ years of experience with our so called independence, I feel (like many silent others) that we were so much better off being a part of Pakistan, than being an Indian slave Bangladesh. I do not agree to the rhetoric that we were exploited by WP, as it was a pure Indian propaganda, now proven. As a much larger land mass, although with slightly smaller population, it is obvious that WP got larger share of the budget. Yet, with a smaller share, EP citizens were so much at peace and tranquility. EP had turned into a model of development for emerging Asia in the 60s, as even the Koreans and the Singaporeans used to come to see the development of EP in particular. I refer to Newsweek/Time magazines sources of late 60s. We had the best educational establishments that were increasing by the day with momentum. EP people were participating more and more in the governance and on professional levels. Ford Foundation, Asia Foundation, World Bank, IMF, UNESCO and several other international scholarships were available for meritorious students. Educational level was second to none in South Asia (we never looked at India as even an equal). Yes, Pakistanis were sometimes rude, but they were also mostly brotherly. Today's successful educationists, academics, professionals, economists, ex-military officers and business people are all the rewards of being a part of Pakistan. Dhanmondi, Gulshan, Banani, Uttara, Airport, Mirpur, Mohammadpur, Shere Bangla Nagar, Farm Gate, Motijheel, Dilkusha are all the developments done within 10–15 years of post-partition in 1947. Similarly, in all other districts besides Rup-pur Atomic Energy Center, development of universities, colleges, collegiate schools, cadet colleges, medical colleges, BUET/CUET/KUET, civil service, public service commission, etc, and, not the least, other primary and high schools. Instead of being ungrateful, we should be grateful for what we achieved within this short span after partition.

> Now, we have no choice but to enter into a very cordial diplomatic and military relationship with Pakistan and China, as Pakistan has with China, so that Bangladesh can start standing on its own foot, away from Hindu and Indian hegemony. Although the USA had inflicted the most serious human and material losses to Japan and Vietnam during the pre-and-post WW2, yet they have the best diplomatic and security ties with each other! Why not Bangladesh with Pakistan? (E-mail: May 25, 2017)

Thank God WP did not exploit the East more than it did, but it did commit a most heinous crime by committing a genocide in the East in 1971. Even after the massacre, Sheikh Mujib forgave and then forged a new relationship and remained friendly with Pakistan (until he was killed in 1975), just as his daughter Sheikh Hasina remained (and continues to remain) friendly with India even after the internationally conspired 2009 BDR massacre, border killings, unequal treaties, and the withholding of the river water.

Historically, it is clear that Sheikh Mujib never hated the West or the idea of Pakistan remaining united as a single country as much as his daughter Sheikh Hasina does today, and that he never loved India as much his daughter does, out of her pure political intention of staying in power for ever. It is true she also once hated to hate and had in fact very warm feelings about Pakistan as mentioned above. Now she thinks Bangladesh became free of Pakistani control only to be increasingly Indianized under Indian subjugation.

Now Bangladesh (formerly EP) is being exploited by its own dynastic and oligarchical Leagues, its own sharks and vultures, its own crocs and cons. Millions and billions are being systematically sucked and siphoned out and looted and laundered and plundered in and out of the country under the Hasina regime. Hasina's Bangladesh is more terribly exploitative of itself, which is a much deeper and more intolerable shame. While one must be happy that Bangladesh separated from WP in 1971, the country needs to be cleansed of its all-swallowing political and economic injustice, rip-offs, and tearing downs, especially the Awami sort under this Awami regime.

In the context of the full and complete loss of democratic character by the Hasina-AL, there is a denial to the political opposition of its right to assembly, right to demonstration, and right to protest, even the right of its people to stay home. They are abducted, kidnapped, and killed, or forced to disappear for good, in hundreds and thousands, by the mysterious "plain clothes white car" government within the government, again the same as the plot/subplot within the plot. It is as if there is an ongoing reenactment, under this Hasina regime, of the slaughter of the EP/Bangladeshi intellectuals by the Pakistanis and their collaborators on December 14, 1971, just before the final victory two days later.

In the same context, the parliament has been reduced to a cooing, crooning, and crowing pet, nothing more than a toy and teasing rubber stamp. In the same situation the 136th Inter-Parliamentary Union (IPU) meeting in Dhaka (early April 2017) was a flawless farce, as termed by the BNP Secretary General Mirza Fakhrul, like the faultless farce that was the voterless nonelection of 5 January.[17] The IPU meeting was like the glaze and glamour of the private companies' Initial Public Offerings, the showoff of an empty shell with nothing of the substantive democratic core and content inside for the nation. The same is true about the humbug autism awareness talk, mere media hype digital inauguration of bamboo projects that never see successful and quality completion, and countless foreign trips, all diminished in dignity when the home country finds itself landed and left behind in endless cycles of blood and violence, and unending oppression and corruption.

To write the concluding part of this notice, the Hasina regime and its Awami party have brought Bangladesh to the brink of a deadly confrontation. They would have to bear the full responsibility for the consequences in the future when there is a change in the government. There was the murderous Awami লগি বৈঠা তান্ডব (poles and oars and sticks terror) in 2006, which led to the mostly nuisance-creating *Uddinized* interregnum during the following two years. Sheikh Hasina took the credit by claiming that the *Uddins* were able to get to the seat of power by her violent Awami agitation against her powerful opponent Khaleda/BNP and that all their actions, legal or illegal, right or wrong, moral or immoral, would meet with her approval if she was voted to power. Hence the *Uddins*' and the *Uddins*-appointed Huda Commission's sufficiently কোলে তুলে /lifting on the lap promotion of the Hasina-led AL in the late 2008 election, followed by the AL's even more কোলে তুলে/ lifting on the lap self-promotion through the succeeding completely loyalist রকিব-মার্কা/ Rakib-marked Commission and maybe the current Huda Commission too in the future.

Since 2009 Bangladesh has become a one-party system of distortion, detention, discrimination, persecution, prosecution, torture, remand, regimentation, judicial harassment, imprisonment, lawsuits, legal battles, penal punishment, elimination, erasure, occlusion, eclipse, displacement, destruction, annihilation, disaffection, marginalization, coronation, anointing, semi-and-pseudo inauguration; horribly hybrid, controlled, guided, and illiberal democracy; fracture, fragmentation, and commercialization of the spirit of liberation; criminalization of the different branches of the government; police cordons of the opposition party offices, snatching away the opposition rights to its political protests and programs; and the sickening and schizophrenic lack of economic, social, and judicial justice and of democratic and representative character everywhere in the state. All this nihilistic and anarchical negatives, downsides, and shortfalls only serve to ensure the survival not of the fittest and fairest but only of the Awamis, fit or unfit, and to reduce all the rest into an endangered species waiting for the next great dying or mass extinction. All the rest, represented by the opposition BNP, therefore, stands in the dire need of a unified rescue mission that would eventually and ultimately be in the political and democratic interest of all, in fact, for the survival of all in peace and harmony, and, in the long run, for the existence of Bangladesh itself as a whole, as an intact and entire sovereign country, and the Bangladeshis themselves as a democratically vibrant, dynamic, and dignified nation on their own.

Let the crystal clear justice, transparency, objectivity, and impartiality as exercised and executed by the judges of the singing contests, such as Channel I ক্ষুদে গানরাজ and সেরা কণ্ঠ, NTV তোমাকেই খুঁজছে বাংলাদেশ, and Channel 9 Power Voice be the model for Sheikh Hasina to follow, pursue, aspire for, and look forward to, be a great statesman-like politician. Coming from a political family fighting for democracy with an active political background and a broad and wide and open public view, Hasina should not have been shrinking and receding into an oppressive and persecuting Lady Hitler of Bangladesh, taking the country down the path of an authoritarian and totalitarian state controlled by the police. While she has grown to be less than what she could be in terms of the "wave impelling wave, circle without circle" definition of greatness, to borrow the idea from the English writer William Hazlitt, Khaleda has grown in stature more than she thought she would be able to.

Coming from the status of a housewife in the confines of the military barrack, the grieving Khaleda (who had her husband and the greatest president of Bangladesh ever assassinated in 1981) rose through her powerful, grief-turned-into-guts anti-Ershad struggle of the 1980s and then proved to be proudly prime ministerial in a befitting manner. If there were any faults and failures of her and her then very young man, Tarique Rahman, during 2001–2005, those were the defects and drawbacks many of which they mistakenly resorted to by drawing upon the examples of the previous Awami excesses, now far exceeded, again by the Awamis since 2009. The Khaleda–Tarique mother–son duo, as opposed to the Hasina–Joy mother–son duo, must have learnt from their past mistakes (which were nothing compared with the repeatedly committed Awami excesses in moral, political, and economic corruption) and must have evolved today to become highly reliable and reformed personalities.

The BNP secretary general Mirza Fakhrul Islam Alamgir claimed that the AL government was a role model of repression, oppression, suppression, and assassination, which crossed the level of cruelty resorted to Hitler and his Nazi party.[18] It is the fantastically corrupt and fascistic Awami regime that would lead the way for the succeeding others to tread the same path, involuntarily and inadvertently, of course. If Hasina does not change the course of action, full of aberrations, abnormalities, and irregularities as it is and if she does not move, as quickly as possible, toward creating an atmosphere of credibility and legitimacy with respect and tolerance for the opposition BNP, she would go down in history as just another power-hungry dictator of brutal bias, privative and nugatory prejudice and crappy calumny with nothing elevating, ennobling, and exalting for her to be proud of and nothing for the people of Bangladesh to feel good about her. It is all routine, but, far worse and more disastrous, purely partisan, entirely selfish, and severely suppressive and subversive to the point of being neo-and-near dictatorial and neo-and-near fascist!

Q M Jalal Khan/September 14,2017

A *Conch* Preface

Why the Book, Why the Title

"When the fog of fascism seems to come in from the east and west, we as a nation have to determine who we want to be."—Baroness Sayeeda Hussain Warsi of the UK House of Lords, March 15, 2017

Seriously infected with the dire and deadly political Zika, Ebola, and Chikungunya viruses and standing in need of a political pied piper to free it, as completely as possible, from the nuisance of all kinds of political rats and political *aedes* mosquitoes, Bangladesh is now as divided as "our" country and "their" country. It has been brought to this stage by the critically close to authoritarian and exclusionary Awami regime that can also be described as being sluttish, bellicose, belligerent, and baselessly BNP*hobic*.

This book is a detailed account of the divided Bangladesh where there has been a near-total suppression and extermination, since 2009, of the political opposition BNP (Bangladesh Nationalist Party). It is a recount of the ceaseless horror and terror resorted to by the neo-and-near-and-more-than-partially-fascist regime addicted to governing the country through a complete politicization and criminalization of all the branches of the state, including a certain degree of distortion and fragmentation of history. Being a descriptive narrative of the regime's continuing abuses of the state tools, agents, and organs, the volume launches a crusade against the partisan and nearly autocratic and despotic one-party government, which keeps on boastfully bragging about its (denial of) moral, political, and economic corruption, and its obstruction of the democratic rights of the political opposition.

With the instrument of the police, as well as the civil and judicial administration, people of political and religious differences are forced to live a frightened and fragmented life—literally a life of bondage and imprisonment without their freedom of speech and assembly. All the panoply of the state machinery are used to crush and cripple the opposition and push it deeper and deeper into the corner and further and further against the wall. Having lost its moral and political legitimacy and credibility and its democratic character long ago, mainly by the reason of its forced and fearful police suppression and separation of the democratic majority, the regime has been ruling the country for years in a highly humpy, bumpy, quirky, and cliquey manner.

The almost absolutely totalitarian Awami regime of Sheikh Hasina is shielded by the surrounding India in its selfish and hegemonic interest, just as Myanmar and North Korea are sheltered by China; Syria by Iran and Russia; and Israel by America and the West. The stance taken in the book is one of the critical dissection of the popularly perceived puppet regime of Bangladesh overseen by India, with an intentional oversight or direct interference, to "kindle or restrain" as necessary. Similar to the teacherly Nature tutoring and molding William Wordsworth's three-year-old little Lucy to its choice in a morally benign and benevolent influence, India is up to guiding and regimenting Bangladesh to its favor, but in a malicious and malevolent way. If the book sounds polemical at times, it is justified being so against the deeply partisan and polarizing reign of the so-to-speak near-monarchical Awami government, which stubbornly resists and refuses to stay beholden to the democratic ideals of tolerance and accountability.

The situation is going so bad, brutal, and brutish that there is an established pattern of suspicious, misleading, and made-up fabrications and concoctions (সন্দেহজনকভাবে অশেষ নাটক ও নাটকীয়তা এবং গোপনীয়তা) by the regime/government on every single issue, social or political, concerning the opposition BNP, which is falsely and cowardly blamed for everything that one can name and imagine. As the shadowy and সন্ত্রাসী terrorism of targeted assassinations, gory and scary abductions, and the widespread corruption have been going on unabated, Bangladesh has become like a South Asian Chile and Argentina of 1970s and 1980s. With the violence and bloodshed continuing unchecked and the police and political control intolerably tightening, the country has become an unstable South Asian

Egypt, Sudan, Iraq, Yemen, Syria, Lebanon, Venezuela, Zimbabwe, Indochina, and Central Asia.

In addition to the views and findings of the scholars, researchers, and a cross section of highly perceptive, intelligent, and educated watchers and observers of native origin living abroad, the work is mostly dependent on the contemporary Bengali as well as English mass media and online resources, giving it an authentic reader-friendly appeal and freshness, away and different from the hackneyed, the conventional, and the stereotype. It may not be a strictly and rigorously academic text in the conservative sense that, while I make copious literary references, I do not widely reference modern political theory, neither do I follow an orthodox methodology that a political science expert might approach or approve of. This is due to the fact that while this is a political work by a politically conscious English professor, it is not a "political science" book in the traditional sense of the term.

Furthermore, no academic or scientific theory would fit the crafty and cunning police regime of Sheikh Hasina, which is entirely dependent on the power-drunk and corruption-ridden policy of force and politically opportunist expediency, constantly bent upon devising cruel and immoral means to justify its crooked and controversial ends. Critics would like to parody such ends like this on the social media:

> If you're with us, you are a sweet Allama Shafi Huzur; if not, you're a sour *Tetul* (Tamarind) Huzur. If you're with us, you're a freedom fighter; if not, you are a collaborator (*rajakar*). If you're with us, you're our friends and compatriots; if not, you are a terrorist (*jongi*). If you're with us, you're a special ambassador; if not, you're a *shoirachar* Ershad, to be sent to the hospital [or to be visited by Sujata].[19]

The regime does not deserve to be dignified by being explained in terms of an academically political theory. As the Bengali saying goes, সর্ব অংগে ব্যাথা ঔষধ দিবো কোথা (When there is pain all over the body, there cannot be an application of a pain killing ointment for external use). What the South African origin comedian Trevor Noah, host of the American late-night The Daily Show, said of Donald Trump (to Christiane Amanpour on CNN), before the election—that Trump was too shameless, doubling and tripling down on what was just plain wrong and that he was himself too huge a "dent" to be dented—would also be applicable to the Hasina regime. (More about the justification of the nontraditional approach of my work is to follow below.)

In light of the above, I felt I should write a nontraditional dedication consisting of a long roll call of quite a number of people, as long and unconventional as a Bernard Shaw-type preface. Dedication and preface are indeed of crucial importance. English "opium eater" and literary/miscellaneous essayist Thomas De Quincey could not make it to the publication of his economic treatise that he wrote under the influence of the political economists of his time, simply because he could not write a preface and a dedication, which I cite to my students as an example of silly and rare freaks and failures of some geniuses. I'm glad that a small fry like me has been able to do both. De Quincey's two Notices "To the Reader," one at the beginning of Part I and one at the end of Part II of his most famous work, his autobiographical *Confessions of an English Opium-Eater* (1821), whose structure is also marked by as many as three short and long introductions—"Preliminary Confessions" at the beginning of Part I and the other two in Part II—, influenced me to write not only my "Notice" at the outset but also my long Prefatory remarks and my long Introduction, introducing the book more than once in both primary and preliminary overviews of its contents.

Accordingly, I started off my dedication with the memory of the former President Ziaur Rahman, who, as the first proponent and architect of Bangladeshi nationalism, credited with many other landmark achievements and accomplishments during his short administration, must have been the greatest Bangladeshi ever. It also includes his wife, Begum Khaleda Zia, former Prime Minister and the most popular (to be distinguished from the short lasting "populist") and most dignified political leader of Bangladesh. In the 1980s, following her husband President Zia's assassination in Chittagong from where he also had started rising as a heroic soldier and political star in 1971, Khaleda Zia was a valiant fighter against the autocracy of Gen H M Ershad, who succeeded President Zia (not immediately though) and who is alleged to have had a hand in the assassination of his longtime boss both as president and chief of the army. Now Khaleda accurately accuses the present Hasina government of being a "Lady Hitler's repressive regime," trying to establish "monarchy."[20] It is a claim supported by all the political players (except the Hasina-led Awamis and their surrogates and proxies). Noting the absolute power held by Sheikh Hasina, Dr Akbar Ali Khan, an eminent public intellectual and economist, said that "The power of the prime minister of Bangladesh is perhaps more than that of the Russian Tsars and the Mughal emperors."[21]

It is most unfortunate that Khaleda Zia, along with her son Tarique Rahman—who is exiled to the UK and who is also her party BNP's popular Senior Vice Chairman—have long been humiliated and victimized by the Hasina regime, as they also were by the preceding and long-lasting caretaker government of the now forgotten and footnoted trio-or-tetra of the *Uddins*. Begum Zia's other son Arafat Rahman Koko died a premature death abroad (in Malaysia), probably due to his long years of political and physical isolation and psychological trauma.

Repression by the regime has surely contributed to Koko's early death as the same situation of politically cooked punishment, harassment, and loneliness has also taken a toll on the health and mind of his old and ailing mother, the much suffering and much sacrificing, yet very bold BNP Chair Khaleda.

In addition, my present dedicatees include the excruciatingly suffering long prisoner of conscience, Mahmudur Rahman, released after a long time, distinguished for his courage, endurance, and talents; the abducted, exiled, and stranded BNP Standing Committee member Salahuddin Ahmad, who is one of the most suffering and sacrificing golden boys of Bangladesh; another golden boy, Mahmudur Rahman Manna, who even after a long confinement in prison, continues to be a man of milestone political commitment, and, again, the long incarcerated and long forgotten Lutfuzzaman Babar, rotting in jail, in the present hostile Awami environment of fear, control, coercion, destruction, intimidation, and elimination.

However, I abandoned the idea of a longer list of dedicatees in consideration of the fact that the current dedication is already too long and that a longer one may not look quite nice and proper, if not really awkward. Otherwise, my dedicatees would also have included the other golden boys and girls such as the veteran heavyweight Shah Muazzem Hussein; elderly but eminently bold and assertive Asafuddowla; "like father like son" and confidently and courageously intrepid Barrister Mainul Hussein (all these three ever slashing and slamming the authoritarian one party government of Sheikh Hasina); Mahfuzullah; Shafik Rehman; Farhad Mazhar; Maj Akhtaruzzaman; M A Aziz of New Age; Dr Tuhin Malik; Dr Mina Farah; Dr Dilara Chowdhury; Dr Asif Nazrul; Nur-e-Alam Siddiquee and Mubasshyer Hussein (the last two being pro-Awami, yet firmly fair-minded, not fair-weather birds). All these personalities are characterized by their qualities of tireless tenacity and indefatigable enthusiasm. All of their comments and columns, remarkably impressive as they are, remain to be of turnaround effect and impact against the Awami menace, misrule, and mismanagement of the last decade.

My original dedicatees would also have included six other golden girls: *DeshKonnya*/দেশকন্যা[22] Advocate Syeda Ashifa Ashrafi Papia, a woman of mettle and temerity; *DeshKonnya*/দেশকন্যা Barrister Rumin Farhana, a "like father like daughter" woman of cool eloquence and compelling arguments; *DeshKonnya*/ দেশকন্যা Shama Obaid, who left her computer engineering background to be a full-time politician and who is also a "like father like daughter" young woman of indomitable energy; *DeshKonnya*/দেশকন্যা Nilufar Chowdhury Moni, a young woman of winning and assertive style; *DeshKonnya*/দেশকন্যা Afroza Abbas; and *DeshKonnya*/ দেশকন্যা Advocate Fahima Nasrin Munni.

Had I ended up writing a lengthy dedication, as I originally planned, I wouldn't have forgotten to include the living patriots, such as Dr Zafrullah Chowdhury and Professor Badruddin Umar, who are still fighting, even in their present advanced age, for a great cause in the interest of the nation. Nevertheless, I didn't forget to dedicate my book to the nameless dead, who sacrificed their lives, individually and collectively, since 1971, also for the cause of the nation and for the liberation from the despotic Awami terror and tyranny.

In his *Paradise Lost*, Milton describes Satan and his followers—countless in number—kicked out of paradise above into the liquid fire below, as if they were the fallen leaves of autumn along the Italian lake of Vallombrosa. Wordsworth sees a long belt of "ten thousand" (daffodil) flowers at a glance, along the lake in northern England, dancing in the breeze and continuous as the stars in the sky. I see as many victims, in tens of thousands—killed, burnt, maimed, injured, imprisoned, incarcerated, abducted (with mutilated bodies found or missing), and hiding due to the myriads (hundreds of thousands) of ghostly and ghastly lawsuits[23]—continuous as the despoiled leaves, twigs, and branches in a dense woodland ravaged by wild elephants. The staggering numbers of victims were either ordinary people or innocent opposition political leaders and activists, who sacrificed their lives in the "fen" of Bangladesh's "stagnant waters." The last phrase has been borrowed from an 1802 sonnet by Wordsworth describing England as a place of moral decline and degradation, bereft of "inward happiness" and "the heroic wealth of hall and bower."

As Wordsworth invoked the memory of the great moralist Milton as a way out for England from her contemporary moral decadence and as he lamented earlier, in 1798, "What man has made of man," following the bloody violence in the aftermath of the French Revolution, I took the opportunity to invoke the memory of all those who had to leave this world untimely and prematurely, due to the political violence unleashed by the Awami homicidal tyranny, to suggest a way out for Bangladesh from her current state of moral and political decrepitude and dilapidation. If the Bangladesh AL (the two-letter acronym being without the letter "B" of Bangladesh for culturally sensitive reasons) was wrong then, on August 15, 1975, to stay approvingly quiet at the death of their leader Sheikh Mujib, they are again wrong to allow and stay silent at the continuous imprisonments, abductions, and killings of their fellow Bangladeshis, in thousands—indescribably and intolerably miserable and painful.

My original title was *Our Bangladesh, Their Bangladesh: A Divided Bangladesh*, changed to the current title in consultation with the publisher. The first part of the original title may sound similar, to the Bangladeshis at least, to the slogan,

"Amar Desh, Tomar Desh, Bangladesh, Bangladesh" (meaning "My Land/Country Your Land/Country Together A United and Unified Bangladesh"). The patriotically imbued slogan calls for amity and unity, yet implies a long prevailing and preexisting division along the different political interest lines (according to who or which party raises the slogan when and wherever, etc.). All parties raise similar slogans without discrimination and do brag about doing so, some with no basis whatsoever.

The two alternating ruling parties—the AL and the BNP—are locked in a power struggle, pathologically and indignantly intolerant of each other. The BNP, unlike the AL's foreign/alien nomenclature, is, however, happy and proud to have a full Bangla name, *Bangladesh Jatiyotabadi Dal* / বাংলাদেশ জাতীয়তাবাদী দল. Their hatred and distrust of each other run so deep that the ruling AL, from its position of power, has had hundreds of lawsuits (previously filed against its leaders by the preceding military backed government) withdrawn through the political influence over the various sections of the judicial system, while thousands of ill-motivated court cases filed against the members of the suppressed BNP by both the previous military and the present Awami governments have been left active in order to push and pursue and chase and hound the BNP men and women deep into the dark corner of coercion, submission, and subjugation.

"What is more, none of the allegations against Sheikh Hasina and other party members," writes BBC South Asia correspondent Justin Rowlatt, "was ever tested in court because all charges were dropped by executive order when her AL assumed power in 2008. By contrast, similar claims of corruption made against the opposition party BNP were allowed to stand. Many of the main opposition BNP politicians are still technically on bail from the charges."[24] Rowlatt also reports about the "fears over Bangladesh's disappeared" and the Human Rights Watch says the perpetrators of the killed and the abducted go unaccounted for, never brought to justice.[25]

However, those against the BNP leaders, mostly politically motivated (and so, as the observers and analysts describe, concocted, false, and fabricated), have either been retained and revived or newly filed against them. The AL mayors, "elected" through mock and one-sided "elections," boycotted by the opposition, were freed from the criminal charges against them because of "lack of sufficient evidence" and were all allowed to stay in office, whereas the BNP mayors (in city after city, such as Sylhet, Gazipur, Rajshai, Dinajpur, Khulna, Chapai Nawabganj, Tanore, Habiganj, Sonargaon, Comilla, and many other places, as many as 381 mayors), duly elected through contested and participatory polls, have been suspended, arrested, put behind bars for years, and ultimately removed from office.[26]

For all intents and purposes, the AL reverted to the path of suppression and persecution of the opposition BNP. It is out to harass and humiliate its rival and challenger, drain it of its strength, and keep it away from politics, causing its millions of supporters preoccupied with running back and forth between the court and home and preventing them from engaging in their normal and lawful political activities: meetings, processions, and demonstrations. Reflecting on the divisive and despotic political culture of Bangladesh, my title stresses the fact that there exists a deep political division in the nation, born of the AL's desperate hold onto power and that the canyon-and-crater deep crisis has to be admitted first, implying the obvious—the need for the wide rift to narrow down, if not close, and be bridged sooner rather than later.

Apart from suggesting a postcolonial and orientalist "We/Us" and "They" or "Our" and "Their," my original title was also inspired by the following works. William Ernest Henley's patriotic Victorian poem "England, My England" (1900) has the much-quoted title phrase as a refrain:

> What have I done for you,
> England, my England?
> What is there I would not do,
> England, my own?

The poem has since been parodied by others critical of its propagandistic use of jingoist sentiments. D. H. Lawrence has a short story called "England, My England," which is also the title of a collection of stories by him written during the First World War. The Scottish writer A. G. Macdonell has a satirical comic novel called *England, Their England* (1933). In his 1942 essay on Rudyard Kipling, an ardent supporter of imperialist expansionism in India and Africa, the anti-imperialist George Orwell quoted Henley's refrain as an example of the Queen's soldiers' middle class attitude. Kipling's own phrase, "What do they know of England, who only England know?," is just one of the catchy, memorable neologisms suggestive of the imperialist bent he was known for. Orwell's distancing *England, Your England* (1953) is an essay in social criticism of England against the background of the Second World War. Denis Donoghue, who was a Professor of English at New York University (my alma mater), published his commentaries on English language and literature in his 1988 book, called *England, Their England.*

The book grew out of my pain and anguish at the chokehold demise of democratic culture in Bangladesh where press and political freedoms have been seriously threatened, curtailed, and suppressed by the police sandbag-and-garbage trucks, barbaric mass arrests, routine remands, and systematic torture and imprisonments. The popular and dignified opposition leader Khaleda Zia has been repeating the same claim for the last few years.[27] Those freedoms, as precious as life itself in a civilized society, have been evaporating as a result of the poisonous police tear gas and pepper spray.[28] Based on my personal observation and analysis, rather than academically oriented political or philosophical theory, the book is critical of the present autocratic AL government which has been in power since early 2009. Most of the chapters in the book are new, previously unpublished, except a very negligible portion in its earliest rough and unrefined drafts in the weekly *Holiday*, Dhaka.

All materials have been extensively revised, reorganized, and updated as they were prepared and put together to make their way into this collection. All the chapters are in conversation with each other to form a thematic unity and make a statement about the present mid- to high-intensity totalitarian culture of Bangladesh and its elimination and annihilation of the political opposition in the country.

Part of my thoughts and observations in the book coincides with those of Alexandra Stark's, an International Relations researcher at Georgetown University, who puts together her recommendations (not all of which may be agreed upon due to her unfounded Islamophobia) in her recent article, "Bangladesh on the Brink: Between Terrorism and Democracy." Two of them are as follows:

> First, policymakers should put pressure on the leaders of the two political parties to reach a negotiated settlement to hold free and fair elections. Yes, the political arena is deeply polarized, but with a combination of political pressure and incentives in the form of development aid, the parties could reach some form of agreement. The BNP's *recent decision* to end its demands for the Awami League to immediately turn over power to a caretaker government indicates that there may be a fresh window for negotiations to take place. The EU, U.S., and others can also assist by providing elections monitors and support for anti-corruption measures to assure both sides that the vote will be fair.
>
> The international community should also put pressure on Bangladesh's politicians to rein in human rights violations committed by state security forces. *Human Rights Watch reports* that the Rapid Action Battalion (RAB), an elite security force, has engaged in extrajudicial killings, disappearances, and torture, against government opponents. Bringing the RAB to heel will build confidence in the government's anti-corruption efforts and help to tamp down the retaliatory cycle of political violence. The political dysfunction and state-sanctioned human rights violations have eroded support for the democratic process and eaten away at the legitimacy of the state. Peaceful elections and a reined-in RAB will do much to reverse the cynical view that democracy is dead, which in turn drives political violence and radicalization.[29]

The two recommendations above are extremely important in the context of "the rapidly rising tide of political violence" in Bangladesh, to borrow the phrase from

Stark, who goes on to argue that this "violence represents a dispute not just over election results or trial outcomes of the controversial International Crimes Tribunal (ICT) but over the very meaning of Bangladeshi nationalism,"—issues that are the focal points of the chapters that follow.

This publication as a whole is a work of my own thoughts and opinions on the present tyrannical political culture of Bangladesh as I saw it from abroad. It is true that sometimes one can see better, independently and objectively, from a distance. As the proverb says, the bystander sees more of the game than those who watch it from the closest proximity. Full of references and allusions, mostly through web and cyber sources, to local and international political analysts and their views, the volume is essentially a discussion of a number of conflicting and confrontational issues that have been keeping the people of Bangladesh apart and away from each other. It is as much descriptive and reflective as it is informative, deeply critical of the present government and arguing that the ruling AL cannot be given any credit it thinks it deserves for whatever "achievement" it claims it has made in the field of economic development.

First of all, this "development" is not balanced, harmonious, and sustainable. Second, any government does have to carry out its basic and normal share of duties as the state apparatus has to continue to function. Third, the so-called "development" or "achievement" has been heavily weighed down by the festering wounds of corruption. Fourth, it has lost all its "sweetness and light," to borrow the elitist phrase from the English poet and critic Matthew Arnold, due to the Hasina-AL's dictatorial suppression of the other political parties and their rights and voices, leveling them to the ground, notwithstanding whatever political mistakes the latter may have made in the course of being crushed and cornered under the dizzying grinding machine of the regime.

The volume provides an easy and smooth narrative of the violent and vindictive and utterly chilling and cynical political scene in Bangladesh. Consisting of about eighteen chapters, including the Preface, the Notice, and the Afterword, it is a projection of my views and concerns that have long occupied the minds of the people of Bangladesh and that, I believe, generally represent those of the majority of Bangladeshis. Even though it reflects my particular moral and political ethos and my own style of expression, I hope it will prove to be a valuable work, both for the knowledgeable quarters and any interested readers. Being in no way esoteric and bogged down by theoretical jargons and terminologies, the publication is accessible to general readership, from students to nonspecialist readers of all disciplines, while specialist researchers and academics also will immensely benefit from the vast amount of media data it has marshaled. Readers are also likely to walk away with a deep imprint of the imagery and a full plate of humanitarian thoughts on their minds from their reading of the book.

Like the regime's partisan faiths and fallacies and programs and policies, my work too may at times seem to be a partisan and polemical account of the contemporary politics of Bangladesh. Since the country has been rendered into a one-party rule of despotic intent and dictatorial designs, there can be no choice but to profess to be partisan and polemical and that is for the sake of democracy and democratic spirit of tolerance and accommodation. Unbridled partisan reign knowing no bounds of limiting rope and rein calls for a similar patriotic response. Even then, instances of the political faults and weaknesses of the opposition are occasionally mentioned (especially in one of the appendices) and so the work is not purely and completely partisan and polemical.

Being solely partisan and one-sided is the way of the AL governing the country and preventing the patriotic and popular opposition BNP from holding its public meetings and assemblies, including its council, at a (suitable and convenient) venue of its choice. Only the ruling undemocratic AL freely and comfortably makes the venue (e.g., the desired wide and open Suhrawardy Uddyan Dhaka) available to itself for its own council and its all other gatherings. The said venue is also made available to the other smaller, inconsequential, and insignificant parties allied and aligned with it. It is as if all the important public squares belong to the autocratic AL. It behaves in such a way that it seems it owns and has usurped all those places in its favor as a sort of the British-instituted colonial Indian permanent settlement in 1793 in favor of the local Hindu landowners/zamindars, to the utter disadvantage of the local Muslims.

Even if my work is polemical, it is an important polemic of a historical and political content and there are reasons to be so. The AL's highly partisan rule leaves no choice but to be polemical. In Bangladesh nothing is heard unless it is hit hard, asserted with outrage and kept being talked about out loud again and again. The extreme and excessive suffering of the opposition BNP at the hands of the AL since 2009 knows no bounds. So the work cannot but be what it is. The opposition needs the support of the people for the cause of the revival and survival of democracy. Under the harsh and hard and hostile culture established and instituted by the deeply polarizing Hasina regime, there cannot be any conventionally "academic" middle ground in the manner of a detached and objective approach; there cannot be any choice other than being on the side of the opposition; and there cannot be much room for being too "politically correct" or for making too "rational" a discourse in the so-called academic sense. As long as any narrative, academic or descriptive, contains sufficient details to support its views, there should not be any problem that is worthy of criticism, I believe.

To repeat, under the bully that the Hasina government is, one cannot take a saner or more balanced side. In response to a query about how she thought of the current tyrannical political situation in Bangladesh with absolutely no space for the opposition, already crippled and cornered, Harvard-educated Dr Sarmila Bose of Oxford University, who is the author of *Dead Reckoning: Memories of the 1971 Bangladesh War* (Columbia/Hurst) stated, only on the basis of my table of contents, that "Polemical works are perfectly fine as a genre, and in the context of Bangladesh your feelings are understandable." Similarly, Syed Serajul Islam, Chair of Lakehead University Political Science Department, described my work as "a timely reflection of Hasina's authoritarian rule." In the view of S. Mahmud Ali, author of several books on regional and global security issues, including *Understanding Bangladesh* (Oxford/Columbia/Hurst), this volume of mine "reinforces a general belief in the malaise afflicting Bangladesh."

The Hasina regime seems to be guided by the following versified principles or of which the following has proved to be the hallmark:

Democracy our way,
Exclusively one way,
A single-lane freeway.

That's the only way
One super high way
Can't be the other way,
Never to be an inclusive and uniting way.

However, there's going to be
Only a deceiving iota of democratic action
Only this or that bit of free election
Only a jot of freedom of expression
As much as a clotting dot
To camouflage under,
While you may have
A little crumb of action and expression
In exchange for which
We must have all the stuffed-in
Boxes of ballots
By force and pressure, coercion
And the kind help of the loyal administration
Endowed with the spirit of the liberation
Of nineteen seventy one
As a foregone conclusion.

Guided, regimented, controlled,
Illiberally limited to a few talk shows
And a few pieces of the print media
An art of pretention in homeopathic dose
Sampling out in little loosening,
Crushing out in more tightening
"Measured out with coffee spoons."

It's as much at the pleasure of Delhi
As determined in the interest of
The dictate that we stay dug in Dhaka.

You're either with us or against us.

We got our bullets and barrels and batons,
You got nil to nothing,
Except our kindly provided little formalin
To help you with your limping and
Crawling, crouching and crippling
Creeping and cornering
Reeling and writhing
Trembling and tethering,
Left bruised and battered, bashed and blasted,
"Like a patient etherized upon a table."[30]

In the local elections,
Only a necessary but total intervention;
In the national elections,
There was or will be
More than full application.
Level playing field as it only suits us,
Not the others in the popular opposition.

While our right to free speech
Is an exercise in full and proper democracy;
Yours is only a provocation,
Instigation to anarchy
To be swooped down upon
By our rapid action *Gopali*.

While our men free to shoot and shout,
Arrest and beat and kick,
Yours are out there
Only to get the charge sheet.
What's fun to us is death to you,
That's how we care to continue.

Dr Yunus's American hotline isn't hot enough.
Leaders in *Hefajote Huzurs*
Are only good at running and escaping,
Comfortably sitting
In their cozy madrasa (religious institution) compounds
Divided against themselves,
They're safely in their own *hefajotey*.

We do indeed subscribe
All animals are equal,
But we, with our হুন্ডা গুন্ডা (miscreants and motorbikes) are more equal.
True, power corrupts,
Absolute power, no doubt, corrupts absolutely.

So, we hold,
While all the rest are wrongheaded,
Regardless of what the court said,
Louis XIV of France was right to say,
"I'm the State."

As hinted toward the beginning, my version of the recent political narrative of Bangladesh is just one saying; others may have their own versions, "academically neutral and objective," but actually biased, controversial, and polemical in their own way. In the context of Bangladesh, there is absolutely no room for one to be academically neutral and objective, just as there is no space for the BNP-led opposition to act and engage in normal and rightful political programs and activities. I want to be both "academic" by furnishing the details of hard facts and be partisan at the same time to protest against the tyrannical Hasina regime and her AL. Having said that, I take quite a neutral and detached view of her father Sheikh Mujibur Rahman, both praising and criticizing him in Chapter 9, of the trial of the alleged war criminals in Chapter 8, and also of the BNP in the Afterword.

The work is, therefore, as much based on academic research as, actually more, on contemporary media reports. It is also a nonfiction of personal observations and analysis based on real and specific political developments in Bangladesh for the last ten years. It is the record of a country absolutely controlled by its fantastically partisan police, a country of corruption, politicization, and mismanagement—all as macro and massive as the mega and macho development projects the regime is boasting to have undertaken. Like Saddam's Iraq, Gaddafi's Libya, Hafez and Bashar al-Assads' Syria, Zein al-Abedine's Tunisia, Omar al-Bashir's Sudan, Mubarak's and al-Sisi's Egypt, and the Kims' North Korea, Bangladesh has become synonymous with and indistinguishable from the undemocratic Hasina regime, which is involved in the "mega-and-massive" project of suppressing the political opposition by force and ferocity, creating a state of political anarchy and calumny.

However, the work is not a study in history, historiography, or theoretical disquisition of political jargons as such. Most of the existing literature on similar topics is either "conveniently" neutral or pro-government, making for a safely official establishment narrative. They are not without historically debatable and untenable claims and controversies, so that many serious issues, far from being settled, never ceased to exist. This is exactly what Professor Ali Riaz of Illinois State University also argued in his talk at Columbia University on his recently published *Bangladesh: A Political History Since Independence* (I B Tauris, 2016). He said that while writing his book he noticed that there was an attempt on the part of others to follow a government-approved narrative in documenting the political history of Bangladesh and that, in order for the economic development to last and be beneficial, neither the government nor the narrative should lose sight of democratic pluralism and multidimensionality, which he claimed were not mutually exclusive with development.

It is true "there are ample studies in the past years," an anonymous reader of my work says, "which have argued that there has been serious erosion of democracy under the present regime, or that the country is being ruled by an authoritarian regime or that a one-party state is on the making—which seems to be the central argument of this manuscript." Compared with similar other publications, this work gives a detailed facts-based critical account of the present regime that rules by a socially and politically divisive and subversive force. Written largely from the opposition point of view, it provides an academic and nonfictional discussion of the most up-to-date and contemporaneous political scenario of Bangladesh, which no other contemporary works have done or, if at all, done so comprehensively and faithfully.

Apart from making references to scholarly studies, news items, newspaper articles, features, editorials, and research reports, mostly in the Bengali language, the volume also takes note of the first-hand sources, that is, original, spontaneous, and unadulterated, yet representative views and comments made by a number expatriate people of professions in the UK and North America. They are all highly educated, expert in their own professions. At the same time they are also keen political observers. Discerning and discriminating, they are all in perfect command of the political facts and developments with a consuming passion for democratic freedom and fairness as against the democratically nefarious and illegitimate Awami-style fascism. They are all eager and impatient to see an end to the tyrannical Awami regime. These British, American, Canadian, and Australian people of Bangladeshi origin ventilated their views through different channels of both the social and mainstream mass media. Citing them gives an additional authenticity and credibility of a different (innovative) kind to my discussion.

I teach literature that, in the actual sense, has the widest possible scope compared with other disciplines. It includes class, history, philosophy, politics, society, arts, culture, and religion. My research and teaching background lies in politically oriented and socially conscious writings. By nature and definition, literature is interdisciplinary, multicultural, and pluralistic. All writers and poets wrote on/about politics, which is very much a subject of literature in different forms—fiction, nonfiction, poetry, essays, memoirs. Literary academics did and do write political narratives, analyzing and commenting on various country-specific and region-specific political developments. Out of my pursuit of literary studies, I remain interested in the affairs of Bangladesh and beyond. Moreover, people of all professions, without exception—doctors, engineers, professors, architects, journalists, columnists, businessmen, cultural personalities—, especially in Asian or South Asian countries, are deeply embedded in and imbued with political consciousness so that they all talk and write about government and politics all the time as if they were all expert politicians, ready to hold the rein of the government. Ancient Greek philosopher Aristotle of *Poetics* says in his *Politics*:

> Man is by nature a political animal. And he who by nature and not by mere accident is without a state is either above humanity, or below it; he is the "tribeless, lawless, hearthless one," whom Homer denounces—the outcast who is a lover of war; he may be compared to a bird which flies alone.

Well, following Aristotle, one does not have to be a deep-delved political scientist to write about politics.

It is, therefore, not surprising that as a professor of English literature I often refer to Western poets, writers, historians, and philosophers, throughout the book, to draw an analogy for the purpose of illustration and accentuation. Such references deepen the tenor of my themes and arguments. Such blending of literature and politics is particularly unique and intriguing, providing an extra dimension to make the work interesting to the local as well as the foreign readers. My writing style also sometimes smacks of the literary and rhetorical that is intended to leave an impression upon the readers. It is hoped that this rhetorically oriented literary style that my politico-cultural analysis betrays would add a new dynamics to the volume. Most of the chapters begin with a short dramatic political, cultural, or historical anecdote to arrest the attention of the readers and lead them into the panoply of details that follows.

As said above, the book uses literary references while commenting on the current affairs of Bangladesh. This introduction of literary elements is original compared with other political writings or social commentaries on Bangladesh,[31] all or most of which lack the literary slant, a distinguishing feature of this publication, expected to provide a new flavor to the ongoing discussion of the country's society and politics, home and abroad. The correlation of literature and politics is certainly one of the innovative strengths of the book.

Being a contribution toward the fulfillment of the need to give a true picture of what is going on in Bangladesh, the volume is expected to appeal to the educated Bangladeshis home and abroad. It will also be of great interest to students and scholars of Bangladesh studies in particular and of South Asian specialism in general. The target audiences are therefore the Bangladeshis and the people of South Asia/Indian subcontinent living there and in the major cities around the world. The work stands for freedom, democracy, and human rights with, however, some limits in some areas as far as the mandatory religious sanctions and dictates pertaining to any religion are concerned. Press and political freedom, together with social justice, all now being held as a pawn, have lamentably eroded under the Hasina regime. All those values, one is afraid, have been seriously curtailed, controlled, and clipped away, letting the country slide into the completely police-controlled authoritarianism. Hence, the contents of the book are deeply imbued with patriotic zeal and spirit.

Finally, in preparing the book, I relied heavily on website and online materials and the print and social media in Bangladesh and other news portals, both in English and Bengali. We all read newspapers where we come across fresh, up-to-date, insightful, perceptive, discerning, thought-provoking, and even groundbreaking articles, editorials, columns, and news reports. They may not be research articles as we traditionally understand, but without a formidable amount of reading and careful and insightful observations they cannot be written either. They are a key means to disseminating critical thinking and enlightening the readers both academically and professionally. As far as the articulation or organization of critical thoughts are concerned, sometimes the print media and the online posts may even be more challenging than mainstream research papers. They are an interdisciplinary variety of writing across the curriculum often practiced by versatile academics, providing topics for doctoral dissertations.

Supporting the above idea, my Polish-American colleague Dr Mark Tardi argues that traditional genre distinctions are not very useful. With the profusion of information now available electronically, the primacy of "academic" texts over other forms of information has been eroded to the point of near-irrelevance. However, this is not to say, Tardi continues, that some random blog post or media broadcast is equal to a peer-reviewed established and reputable journal, but there are a vast array of print and online media that offer information of value and insight. And it is likely that those venues have much higher readerships than any typical academic publication. In addition, there are newspapers around the world whose regular contributors are well-known academics. All this makes genre attachments or "high" vs. "low" culture attachments fluid and blurry.

Apart from the significance of newspaper reports and articles as a variety of critical thinking and writing by academics, such venues are commonly used and cited as a source for academic research in the bibliographical entries as suggested by the MLA (Modern Language Association) or the Chicago Manual of Style. There are many other links showing how to document such sources, including e-mails.[32] If Hillary Clinton's e-mails were being hauntingly used to hunt her down and if they were among the factors that cost her her presidential ambition, and if Donald Trump's tweets are one of his favorite ways to reach out to the people to get elected, e-mails, Facebook statuses, and Twitter comments can never be dismissed so easily.[33] In fact, their importance and popularity are on the rise by the day. They are indeed very effective modes of modern communication. Many people do not have a chance to come out on the mainstream media and therefore express their views through these very useful alternate mass media.

One last word: I could not directly participate in the liberation war of Bangladesh in 1971 when I was preparing to graduate from my high school. About a year or two before that, I traveled a long distance to attend the public meetings of Sheikh Mujib who used to electrify and galvanize the crowd and the whole nation. I found then Major Zia's declaration of independence in late March over the radio equally gripping and inspiring and arousing. Mujib's words were perfectly matched by Zia's actions, which proved to be an abundant recompense to Mujib's (and Sheikh Hasina's) absence from the liberation front. As one of the liberation war young generation, this book is my contribution to the spirit of that war—freedom, democratic freedom, unity, harmony, morality, tolerance, balance, understanding, compromise, inclusion, peace, dialogue, justice, rule of law, transparency, accountability (all that is desirable and hoped for against the tyranny of all kinds, including the frothy and made-up majority through rigged and tricky stratagem in the garb and gait of pseudo-elections) and then, for sure, prosperity and development as a necessary and required complement.

The upended policy of development and corruption first, without transparency, accountability, and the entire people's electoral participation in the democratic process, is a devil's argument for the devil diet. The trumpet of development cannot be a license or a pretext for the authoritarian oppression and repression on the political opposition, on the one hand, and all-out liberty for the ruling regime to say and do whatever it likes, on the other.

In William Golding's Nobel-winning *Lord of the Flies*, the *conch* shell is both a symbol and a vessel of political legitimacy and democratic power, the erosion of which causes the initially colorful shell to fade. When can the shell return to its original color in Bangladesh with the popularly supported (interim) CTG reinstated? When can there be a Heracles to finish off the serpentine many-headed political Hydra in Bangladesh? Can the disgustingly greenish and loathsome Medusa of snakelike hair ever return to her original maidenly appearance of roseate hue, golden hair, milk white skin, and love-inspiring eyes? Would there soon be a Thomas Hardy's darkling thrush to sing, from among "the bleak twigs overhead," a full-hearted song of unlimited joy and fling its soul "Upon the growing gloom?"

However, like Hardy, one may still be unaware of any ray of hope, as of today, about the people's power in Bangladesh. As the ruthless and relentless Awami regime continues unchecked, one hardly sees any sign, even on the distant horizon, that there is going to be a free and fair, and consensus-and-confidence-building election anytime soon for the sake of a representative government that is likely to solve the crisis the country is facing for too long. Notwithstanding the crucial need for transparency and accountability and the delivery of social justice between the election dates every four or five years, inclusive and participatory elections, the most critical, crucial, and necessary factor in the democratic process, are the best and most important means to establish democracy and gain legitimacy either to stay in power or get to power.

That is why the political parties in Asia, Africa, and the Middle East go to any length, as did Sheikh Hasina and her EC in Bangladesh on January 5, 2014 and after, to twist and trample and tear down all the sanity, decency, and propriety connected with the norms and rules of a national, local, or municipal election, just to "win" on paper by all means and justify their stay in power in the name of having been "elected," regardless of how fake and false and pseudo and semi and sham all those doped elections or electoral games may have been. A government-turned-regime, more corrupt and corrosive, doubly, trebly so, than the previous governments, can have no right to call its predecessors corrupt and bring questionable and controversial charges against them. This preface may therefore be concluded with the antithetical opening sentence of *A Tale of Two Cities* by Charles Dickens, which, only in its negative superlatives, describes the Hasina regime of Bangladesh:

> It was the best of times, it was *the worst* of times, it was the age of wisdom, it was *the age of foolishness*, it was the epoch of belief, it was *the epoch of incredulity*, it was the season of Light, it was *the season of Darkness*, it was the spring of hope, it was *the winter of despair*, we had everything before us, *we had nothing before us*, we were all going direct to Heaven, *we were all going direct the other way*—in short, the period was so far like the present period, that some of *its noisiest authorities* insisted on its being received, for good or *for evil*, in the superlative degree of comparison only.

Finally, in his great book, *Reflections on the Revolution in France* (1790), the famous political theorist Edmund Burke makes his classic conservative argument against the radical reformers, levelers, and revolutionaries in France. Conceiving constitutional continuity and the continuity of national institutions, values, and cultural superstitions over the time as "an inheritance from our forefathers," giving them "the image of a relation in blood," and binding them to "our dearest domestic ties," Burke stresses the importance of home and family as the starting point of patriotic love for the country. According to him, warm domestic bonds and affections are the beginning of love toward the nation that is "locked fast as in a sort of family settlement." I do agree. This book, therefore, acknowledges in its very dedication an appreciation of the role of my parents in my life and that of all other members of my immediate as well as extended family, some of whom figure in a few personal poems I wrote, in addition to the political ones—all yet to be collected and published in a separate volume.

Q M Jalal Khan
September 14,2017

Acknowledgments

In writing this lengthy book and bringing it to a completion, I am thankful to a group of like-minded Bangladeshi expatriates living across the continents. Discerning and discriminating, they all boil and burn and brim with a consuming passion for democratic freedom and fairness as against the democratically illegitimate and neo-and-near-and-more-than-partial and পৈশাচিক (beastly) Awami fascism, considered BAKSAL-II, much worse and more dangerous than BAKSAL-I of the early 1970s (phrases that recur throughout the book).

All of this like-minded circle are eager and impatient to see an end to the tyrannical and authoritarian Awami regime, a reign neither with a limiting rope nor with a controlling rein. They cannot bear any longer with the bullying, boastful, bellicose, and belligerent, yet deeply and darkly BNP*hobic* Sheikh Hasina at the helm (another recurring refrain in the book). She has been ruling the country for years in a highly humpy, bumpy, quirky, and cliquey manner, which has increasingly seen a commodification, compartmentalization, and commercialization of the চেতনা (spirit) of 1971 with a product-and-market value on it (also two more recurring refrains that resonate throughout the work).

Our acquaintance of each other has so far largely remained limited to our "via" electronic means, most of us never getting a chance yet to meet each other personally. We utilize our cyberspace opportunities not only to support and concur but also to critique the views of each other as necessary and appropriate. I am proud of having been a part of such an illustrious company of great minds in diaspora.

Two of this enlightened and outstanding circle were freedom fighters of Bangladesh in 1971. One is Ranu Chowdhury (sometimes writing as A O Chowdhury), an American resident and author of many analytical and informative pieces on the political changes in Bangladesh. His critical comments and perceptive insights have always been welcomed and appreciated by the majority of this politically aware and alert group. The other is Zoglul Husain of the UK, originally a computer consultant but now a full-time political activist, who abandoned his doctoral ambition in order to contribute to the struggle for the independence of Bangladesh from Kolkata. "Dedicated to the patriotic cause of Bangladesh," one of Husain's thoughtful comments is: "Contemporary history is a witness and later history is a judge, and in that judgement, our stand would be vindicated and honored." Husain maintains an incredibly useful archive of references from which he can easily find out, with an amazing ability, any biographical or bibliographical information that one requests him to be provided with. He has been our gifted walking and electronic encyclopedia, not only for the contemporary but also the long lost and long buried research and resource materials.

I am pleased to acknowledge with thanks the help, cooperation, and encouragement that I received from the people I personally know: Dr Syed Serajul Islam of Lakehead University, Canada; Dr Abid Bahar of Dawson College, Montreal, Canada; Dr Nancy K Nanney of West Virginia University; Dr Mohammad Abdul Auwal of California State University Los Angeles; Dr Abdullah Al-Ahsan and Dr Mahmudul Hasan, both of IIU Malaysia; Dr Saidul Islam of Nanyang Technological University Singapore; Dr Sultan Parvez of Louisiana State University Alexandria; and my two direct colleagues for years, Dr Syed Bashir Ahmed of Kashmir and Dr Konstantinos Pitychoutis of Greece, both of whom are teaching in the Middle East. Their readings of the tales of corruption, police repression, political machination and manipulation, vote rigging and vote buying, and the intimidation and violence of all kinds imaginable in Sheikh Hasina's Bangladesh are suggestive of their like-minded deep disappointment and frustration with the Hasina government, which has turned into a dug-in police regime.

I am also indebted to the following, all from the USA, who, besides their own professions, are excellent political commentators of boundless energy possessing a fantastic political acumen and a sharp critical bent of mind. They include: former Bangladesh ambassador to Egypt and Japan, Serajul Islam; and the extremely witty and humorous and satirical mechanical engineer and brilliant conversationalist Mohammad Gani (our Bernard Shaw and our Oscar Wilde), endowed with a remarkable presence of mind, who is also an aspiring short story writer. It is Engineer Gani who provided me with the easy and useful Bengali font link that made it possible to furnish the Bangla words and expressions in translation when and where necessary.

I must go on to mention Engineer Shahadat Hussein Suhrawardy, who is not only into doing excellent political pieces with historical perspectives but who also often dabbles into writing interesting political poems; Dr Rashed Anam, professionally an electrical engineer but otherwise a penetrating political analyst of depth with a solid understanding of the underlying details; health official Rezaul Karim, a committed supporter of anti-Awami court; Shah Deeelder, a man with a flair for caustic attacks on the hooded Awami figures through his visual caricatures and pictorial word pictures; politically well-meaning radiation physicist Dr Muazzam Kazi; Quazi Nuruzzaman, a former UNDP official of international experience; Mohamed Nazir, a retired accounts and audit officer with interest in the real estate investment, but never losing sight of the worm-and-insect breeding political bushes and swamps relative to the Bangladesh of Awami suppression and cynicism; Mohammad Zainal Abedin, former journalist and author of a number of political books on Bangladesh; Dr Zainul Abedin, also a well-read and highly knowledgeable former journalist, who now teaches at a university in the USA (and, besides, who is also a poet of nostalgic pastoral themes); Computer Engineer Mohammad Aleem, who possesses a great insight into the politics of Bangladesh; and the national award-winning Shakera Akhter, a proud daughter of Sylhet, who once had a promising career in singing and dancing till she had left Bangladesh for the USA. Here, I would also like to mention (Ret) Sqn Ldr Mohammed Shoaib, a champion of Muslims and the Muslim cause, who possesses an enormous talent in terms of factual and historical details in support of the growth and development of Islam in the world, especially in the Indian subcontinent.

All of the above were of great help as they posted their opprobrious clips and comments, mutually appreciating and constructively reading through the views of each other that were shared during our frequent e-mail conversations over the years. Business graduate Qamruddin Chowdhury, whose love and support for President Zia, like all the rest in the team, knows no bounds; Syed Margoob Fahim; Javed Helali; Tareque Ahmed, a Benefits Administrator; Mohammed Islam; Syed Haque; and Mohiuddin Anwar, a freelance writer for a news agency—all from the USA, and Capt Farid Hossain of Montreal Canada, all regularly took part in the “soft” discussions, always making valid and vital comments and thereby enhancing the quality of our politically informative and enlightening rapport. All were/are continuously feeding and flooding the forum with their striking views and ideas in support of Islam, Muslims, and the anti-Awami friends and allies.

I am not less thankful to those of the UK, such as Dr Khalifa Malik, a retired professor who has authored a number of books and articles on sciences as well as the history and politics of Bangladesh; medical expert and Islamically grounded prolific writer Dr Firoz Mahboob Kamal; (Ret) Maj Syed Abu Bakar Siddique; (Ret) Maj Faruk Ahmed; and the highly active freelancer Isha Khan, tirelessly touting scholarly materials critical of Awami misrule and malpractices; Capt Razzak Syed and medical expert Dr Fatima Ashrafi, both from Australia and both of deep and daring political and religious convictions; and (Ret) Brig Gen Shamsuddin Ahmed, Barrister MBI Munshi, and (Ret) Prof A I Shams of Bangladesh, all three of Bangladesh, who have displayed an unabashed audacity of hope against the Awami clutches and tentacles.

Many of the above have been noted in the book more than once, some of them more than the others. Their stimulating and perceptive remarks and observations—all expressed in excellent and impeccable English, envy to non-English-speaking educated elite, including English professors in non-English-speaking countries—represented a cross section of the general opinion and common wisdom of the majority of Bangladeshis. As regards their command of and communication in English—superb and inimitable as it is—it must be admitted that some of the above, having authored a number of books and different write-ups in English, stand out, clearly outshining many of their fellow non-native professors and people of different other professions! Their proficiency in English is envy to many members of the educated elite in a non-English-speaking setting, who, no wonder, hardly write in English (except some easy and quick-fix copy–paste so-called research) and who therefore find it safe to refrain from contributing essays, articles, fictions, and nonfictions to English forums and outlets, local or foreign.

Expert in their own fields and professions, their political inputs, though mostly informal, were/are never discursive and disjointed. Their valuable comments and opinions were enormously helpful in providing a great perspective—fresh, charming, original, and authentic—different from the disconnected Awami চেতনা narrative, that is full of twisted distortions and of which—routine and hackneyed as they are—the people of Bangladesh are truly sick and tired. All members of the e-bloc have made and are always making a great contribution to the noble discourse and lofty endeavor of creating an inclusive and unified, yet diverse but not divided and dented political environment with the intention of freeing Bangladesh from the ongoing oppression and prosecution of dissent by the Hasina-led AL.

Finally, I cannot let my immediate family go unacknowledged. The terse retorts and teasing reactions of our young children, though made casually or occasionally, supplied additional instigation and incitement into the narrative of my nonfictional excursions. I knew their innocent remarks came from their mute, passive, and understated frustration at the sad reality that the country of their parents' origin, Bangladesh, has been painfully and forcibly witnessing for some time, especially during the present heavy and weary years of the Awami regime. Although they are not much interested in what is going on in Bangladesh, they come to hear about it once in a rare while from their mixed peers or online media, and sometimes from their socializing parties and picnics at homes, public parks, or community convention centers at a North American location.

Q M Jalal Khan
September 14, 2017

Notes

1. Visit: https://www.youtube.com/watch?v=YM7YeTCIfZM;
   https://mail.google.com/mail/u/0/#trash/152856fd630e80d1?projector=1;
   https://www.youtube.com/watch?v=juJKfsDNQ14;
   https://www.youtube.com/watch?v=MF3bJzmuDW4
2. The two Bengali terms mean "Wake Up!" and "Beware" or "Be Careful!" respectively. See:
   https://www.youtube.com/watch?v=aGx2RSqp2jw;
   https://www.youtube.com/watch?v=31QwD1kmoE8;
   https://www.youtube.com/watch?v=S9SDxr5P8lc;
   https://www.youtube.com/watch?v=tW9s-mscwMM
3. One must never make light of anybody being beaten to the breaking of his backbone. That is extremely inhuman and intolerably pathetic and painful, more than a jail term. Those who broke the young Tarique Rahman's bones must be brought to justice just as those who caused the forced ouster of his mother and former PM Khaleda Zia from her old (Cantonment) home, denying her rights and without giving her a chance for a dignified exit she deserved must be reinvestigated as well, fully and properly. Similarly, those *gopals/gopalis*, speaking in a foreign or deliberately twisted accent to hide their true identity, who blocked Khaleda's way out from her sand-and-cement-truck sieged Gulshan office and most disrespectfully taunted at her must be identified and brought to account. http://datab.us/NQOWA6jq3Z0#Khaleda%20Zia%20Vs%20Gopali%20Girl%20%2829%20December%202013%29; http://datab.us/LEe3PYl-hbs#Gopali%20by%20Khaleda%20Zia

4. Thucydides, a 5th century (BC) Greek historian of the Peloponnesian Wars between Athens and Sparta, was exiled from Athens. Roman epic poet Virgil's Aeneas was a Trojan exile wandering, destined to found a city in Italy. Legend has it that his descendent Brutus, driven out of Italy, was traveling through many lands as an exile and had the fame of founding a new homeland, Britain. English political philosopher Thomas Hobbes wrote his book of statecraft *Leviathan* in 1651 when he was in exile in France. Charles II's father, Charles I, was executed on January 30, 1649, at the climax of the English Civil War. In 1660 he was invited back from exile in France to be the English king under a restored monarchy. French philosopher Voltaire (1694–1778) was imprisoned more than once. He wrote a national epic in prison, *La Henriade* (1724). He spent about four years, 1726–1729, in exile in England. English philosophical historian and author of the *Decline and Fall of the Roman Empire*, Edward Gibbon (1737–1794) was exiled to Switzerland for converting to Roman Catholic faith.
5. http://www.prothom-alo.com/opinion/article/1218106. Translated into English: "The country is outwardly swelling/getting fat with the so-called progress and development—wide roads, long bridges, and the glitter and glare of a big national budget, but inwardly it is all hollow, being eaten into by worms, degenerating and decomposing. A time will come when the question will arise, 'Is that what we wanted our freedom and independence for; is that what lakhs of people sacrificed their lives for?'"
6. http://www.jugantor.com/online/national/2017/02/09/38990;
http://www.natunbd.net/newsdetail/detail/200/281598;
http://rtnbd.net/politic/26444;
http://www.amadershomoy.biz/unicode/2017/02/09/221133.htm
7. https://www.youtube.com/watch?v=yark1N5vC_4
8. https://www.dailyinqilab.com/article/68463; http://jamunanews24.com/jbn/index.php/show/news/12145
9. https://www.dailyinqilab.com/article/72526; http://www.prothombangladesh.net
10. http://www.thedailystar.net/politics/no-search-body-succeeded-last-10yrs-akbar-ali-1359511;
http://www.thedailystar.net/country/huda-led-ec-never-play-neutral-role-bnp-1359496;
http://www.thedailystar.net/frontpage/its-reflection-pms-liking-1357741;
http://www.newagebd.net/article/8877/new-cec-more-loyal-to-al-than-his-predecessor-bnp;
http://www.newagebd.net/article/8820/new-cec-talking-like-ruling-party-spokesman-bnp
11. http://www.bbc.com/bengali/news-38919943
12. http://www.rtnn.net/bangla/newsdetail/detail/1/3/168515
13. http://www.prothom-alo.com/bangladesh/article/1101238
14. http://www.dailynayadiganta.com/detail/news/207758

15. In English translation, the former describes the latter like this: "That clownish man bereft of all human sense by all considerations has recently started going around smilingly but pretentiously selling himself as 'a traveler along the way of enlightenment,' 'an enlightened figure' and as 'one belonging to a world full of light.'"
16. http://www.storyofbangladesh.com/ebooks/historyof71/64-section-5.html
17. http://www.24livenewspaper.com/sinfo/?url=www.prothom-alo.com
18. http://www.newagebd.net/article/20173/al-govt-role-model-of-repression-killing-people-bnp
19. https://www.facebook.com/photo.php?fbid=1819130565073063&set=a.1410694752583315.1073741828.100009284122418&type=3&theater
20. Her and her party's overwhelming popularity is indicated by the large number of people attending her public meetings, one after another, over the years, all across the country, to the worries of the ruling AL. For the last and most recent meeting, see: http://www.dailydhakapost.com/archives/1943;
https://www.facebook.com/engineersaiful/posts/1200103216684680;
http://www.thedailystar.net/frontpage/grievances-now-forgotten-197572;
http://bdnews24.com/politics/2016/01/05/khaleda-calls-for-dialogues-to-discusssnap-elections; http://newagebd.net /190790/khaleda-calls-for-dialogue/; http://thedailynewnation.com/print-a-news/79310/khaleda-seeks-talks-to-restore-democracy.html; http://newagebd.net/199034/al-established-monarchy-alleges-bnp/
21. http://archive.thedailystar.net/beta2/news/pm-enjoying-more-power-than-mughal-emperors/
22. The term or the title means "Daughter of the Land," self-coined, which occurs throughout the book whenever these names come up.
23. Over 74,000 detained in prisons and 31 lakh cases pending: http://epaper.newagebd.net/detail/41841/9723
24. http://www.bbc.com/news/world-asia-35594968
25. http://www.bbc.com/news/world-asia-37618205; http://www.jugantor.com/online/national/2017/01/13/36625
26. http://www.prothom-alo.com/bangladesh/article/740830; http://parstoday.com/bn/news/bangladesh-i35820; http://bangladesh.shafaqna.com/BD/BD/1747640
27. http://www.ittefaq.com.bd/national/2015/09/25/37322.html; http://www.ittefaq.com.bd/politics/2015/09/23/37229.html
28. http://banews24.com/whole-country2/117-whole-country-4/11789-save-democracy-save-bangladesh.html;
http://greenwatchbd.com/save-democracy-save-bangladesh/;
https://www.timesofassam.com/international/save-democracy-save-bangladesh
29. I don't agree with everything Stark says. She seems to be Islamophobic with a tendency to undermine the role of Islam in the Muslim-majority Bangladesh in the name of fundamentalism and secularism. She forgets to mention the type of "democracy" the country began with during 1972–1975, and the same

authoritarian type it now has, since 2009 onward. However, I do strongly agree with her first two recommendations as quoted. Visit http://thediplomat.com/2015/09/bangladesh-on-the-brink-between-terrorism-and-democracy/; http://indopulse.com/2015/09/28/bangladesh-on-the-brink-between-terrorism-and-democracy/

30. This and the other quotation above in the poem are from T. S. Eliot's ironical poem "The Love Song of J. Alfred Prufrock" (1917). This is one of a few other (longer) political poems on Bangladesh by the author.
31. See the list of Selected Works on Bangladesh at the end of the book.
32. London Metropolitan University: https://metranet.londonmet.ac.uk/services/sas/libraryservices/referencing/books.cfm#bookweblearn; Western Kentucky University: https://www.wku.edu/teaching/booklets/newspapers.pdf; University Libraries: http://library.albany.edu/infolit/news/
33. http://www.politico.com/blogs/media/2015/03/ap-sues-state-department-for-hillary-emails-203842

Part A

1

Introduction

Primary, Preliminary, and After

Part A

Continuing with the same or similar themes in the preceding Notice and Preface and previewing the succeeding chapters, here follows a short description of the oppression, persecution, forced disappearance, corruption, denial, distortion, deviation, discrimination, and double standard that have become the hallmark of the political and economic culture of Bangladesh, especially during the last decade.

"That is no country for old men" is the opening line of the Irish/English poet W B Yeats's one of the most famous poems, "Sailing to Byzantium" (1926), indirectly referring to the poet's native Ireland. More than a decade later, in "The Statues," he again described his Irish nation, directly, as:

> We Irish, born into that ancient sect
> But thrown upon this filthy modern tide
> And by its formless spawning fury wrecked,
> Climb to our proper dark, that we may trace
> The lineaments of a plummet-measured face.

This long introductory chapter poses the question if today's Bangladesh too, under PM Sheikh Hasina, is no country for the young and old alike. Being sick and tired of the dire and deadly political Zika, Ebola, and Chikungunya viruses, isn't it desperately seeking a political pied piper to clear away all its nuisance in the form of political rats and *aedes* mosquitoes, if necessary at a terrible cost, as it happens in the old German legend? Are today's Bangladeshis too "thrown upon this filthy modern tide/ And by its formless spawning fury wrecked?"

Isn't the whole country a prison, open or closed, for all the opposition members, from top to bottom, and also the countless ordinary citizens, who find themselves landed in court and jail, nonstop, year after year, month after month, week after week, day after day? Is the whole country, both its lands and the rivers combined, a killing field and an agonizing terror-and-tension filled graveyard (with thousands, not just hundreds, of punishing and punitive lawsuits, gruesome deaths, enforced disappearances, violent rapes, and cruel tortures, with an average of more than a dozen murders daily, for just the last three years alone)?[1]

Mohammad Wasiar Rahman gives the hideous and harrowing numbers, in detail, for 2016 alone.[2] Is Bangladesh like the other violently restless and stressful countries, such as Libya, Somalia, Sudan, Yemen, Afghanistan, Nigeria, Iraq, and Syria? While these countries have their own share of bomb blasts and mass graves in different scales and numbers, Bangladesh continues to suffer under the unbearable burden of state terrorism that conducts not only electoral farce, again and again, but also numerous and nefarious "ill actions," including the mass detentions on a daily basis, as reported on the media, both local and foreign, since early 2014.[3]

Naturally, one can ask, is it a country of moral degradation and decadence? Is it a country of barbaric mass arrests, day in and day out, of patriotic and peace-loving people that may have just a different opinion from the regime's? Is it a country of countless trivial, flimsy, politically cooked and concocted lawsuits against its own people and their enforced disappearances and murders by both known and unknown (secret and shadowy) kidnappers and assassins?[4] Dr Asif Nazrul exposes the beastly inhumanity behind the endless গুম ও খুন (forced disappearances, abominable abductions, and gruesome murders) committed with the direct or indirect knowledge of the Hasina regime, its savagely cruel-hearted and predatory police/ RAB (Rapid Action Battalion; in uniform or plain clothes) and its home minister, who Dr Nazrul said was lacking in commonsense.[5]

Who are these snake-like hidden, horrible, hellish, hideous, hissing, and harrowing terrorists that operate from their underground cells and go by the code name of "Squad 100" in Sheikh Hasina's Bangladesh?[6] Do they appear to be sponsored by the state or not? Are they in the knowledge and knowhow of the regime? If the report by Jessica Fox in the Sri Lanka Guardian is true, the answer is a THAAD-like thumping and thundering "Yes." Fox writes: "The entire project of 'Crusader-100' was originally conceived by Indian Research and Analysis Wing

(RAW) and the project was coordinated directly by the Bangladeshi Prime Minister and her defense advisor Maj Gen (Rtd) Tarique Ahmed Siddiqui."[7]

Is there a government, then, governing the country with the same and one set of rules and laws applied and applicable to all, or, all the terrifying incidents have been happening with the knowledge of the government and, in fact, by the direct or indirect order of the government and its police/RAB? Is it a morally and democratically failed and fallen state with free elections, unfettered political activism, and a complete and comprehensive view of its great national leaders and their glorious role in the liberation struggle forced to disappear into the zone of endangered species and be distorted at will under the heavy weight of the Hasina regime? Hasn't the entire nation been suffering under the regime's absolutely coercive control of all the state tools and organs and its corruption-ridden economic development narratives? Is this government pro-people or anti-people, people-friendly or otherwise, governing in a highly humpy, bumpy, quirky, and cliquey manner?

There is quite a boastful and often a bullying, bellicose, and belligerent prime minister in Sheikh Hasina. She is also known, by contrast, for her deep and dark electoral fear of the opposition BNP (Bangladesh Nationalist Party)—her biased but baseless BNP*hobia*—manifested through her violent and despotic one-party rule and one-party elections that are widely alleged to have been rigged and tipped and tilted and tampered. Such ripped and twisted elections are therefore often boycotted by the popular opposition BNP.

PM Hasina got herself ridden of all the lawsuits and court cases against her through partisan control and influence and, worse, through systemic politicization of the police, civil bureaucracy/civil administration, and judiciary. When Hasina constantly expresses her intolerance and annoyance against ("her majesty's") opposition's valid complaints about the lack of press and political freedoms and about the completely rigged political, constitutional, and administrative systems, it shows the country is already under the groping grip of an autocratic and authoritarian one-party rule.

According to the most recent Qatar-based Al Jazeera and the New York-based Human Rights Watch reports, Bangladesh has been accused of "kneecapping" the opposition party members.[8] Those reports are just a tiny tip of tons and volumes of such national and international reports over the last few years. Even then they pale and fade beside the actual vast reality of pervasive and persistent worries and anxieties over the widespread bloody and life-threatening unrest and uncertainties prevailing in every nook and corner across the country.

When people—men, women, children, known and unknown—are being continuously killed and abducted—abducted to be tortured before being brutally dismembered—and are put behind the bars of bondage en masse, when they cannot cast their votes to elect the candidates of their choice, and when they are not allowed to participate in a free and fair election and find no equal and adequate protection of law, no democratic freedom, no freedom of the media, no civil rights, no individual rights, no political rights, no human rights, and no social justice, they can legitimately raise those questions above (right below the heading) about their country. Given the murderous history of Bangladesh from the very beginning and the history of the country alternately ruled by different parties corrupted as absolutely as possible by absolute power, it is no stranger to terror—be it political, state, or antistate. There is the ruling Awami terror on ("her majesty's") opposition BNP, or the extremist secularist terror, fundamentalist in its own way, on the religious, the pious, and the devout.

All attacks, invasions, intrusions, and infiltrations are by nature terrorist either to this side or that side. What's the difference between the bloody July 1, 2016 terror attack at Holey Artisan Bakery (HAB) in the capital, on the one hand, and, on the other, the Hasina regime's (and the other Grendel-type dark and shadowy creatures') nonstop state terrorism in detaining and abducting and filling the dark dungeons with innocent and patriotic citizens, almost every single day, all across the country, from the capital to the countryside (the number now nearing almost 100,000) and also filing hundreds and thousands of lawsuits against them? Professor Badruddin Umar (a widely known political scientist of leftist orientation, President of Jatiyo Mukti Council/National Liberation Council, and son of the prominent Muslim League Politician, Abul Hashim) does not find any difference. In fact, he finds the current state of state terrorism much more heinous, vicious, and vitriolic as he finds the country under the Hasina regime engulfed by a tossing and devastating wave of anarchy and lawlessness.[9]

What's the difference between the Awami regime and its police owning and occupying and usurping the Suhrawardy Uddyan and the Shahid Minar against the (1971) democratic spirit of unity and equality, on the one hand, and, on the other, the Monem Khan family holding on to its ancestral land in Banani Dhaka (now taken away by the regime in early November 2016)? The nation of the Bangladeshis should not forget that it was during the governorship of Abdul Monem Khan (1962–1969), a lifelong Muslim Leaguer, that as many as twelve, perhaps more, medical colleges and universities were established in what was then East Pakistan. By an irony of fate, the wounded Monem Khan did not receive any treatment at any of the seven medical colleges/hospitals, founded during his time, which, unfortunately, showed no interest in extending medical care to him.

Dozens of Awami Leaguers led by Khandoker Mushtaq Ahmed were behind the plot to kill their top leader Sheikh Mujibur Rahman in August 1975. Does that mean Mushtaq Ahmed's house in Daudkandi Comilla (or, for that matter, any other Bangladeshi's house, regardless of their political affiliation out of their freedom of choice and opinion) has to face the prospect of destruction and demolition, or confiscation in 2017? What kind of political meanness and low mentality is this? Had Monem Khan and Mushtaq Ahmed lived today, they would have perhaps rapproched and reconciled their differences, would have joined the Awami cabinet under Sheikh Hasina, and would have been among her close friends the way Begum Motia Chowdhury, Hasanul Hoque Inu, Rashed Khan Menon, and many others, once bitter foes, have mended their fences only to have become her best and most faithful political associates and compatriots.

In fact, aren't the Awami vendetta and vindictiveness much worse than the other? Doesn't the widespread and relentless Awami torture provide the breeding ground for the formidable contestants in the "other?" Isn't Mark Twain's cunning and crooked gambler Jim Smiley himself responsible for being outwitted by the clever "stranger" in the story of "the celebrated jumping frog?" Similarly, doesn't the blocked and stagnant water cause the mosquito nuisance? After all, all the court cases, in thousands and thousands, made by the Awami police against the common people and the opposition members, are being categorically rejected not only by them in their self-defense but also the popular public perception as unjust and ill-motivated. Also, if all the opposition members, from top to bottom, could be pursued and hounded to the court, why and how all those in power, from high to low, could be freed, extricated, exonerated, absolved, and disentangled from facing the similar harassment in the name of judicial procedure, twisted and manipulated in their favor? Why two rules? Why double standard in the same country under the same government, same police, same judiciary, same bureaucracy, and the same civil administration, when all are from the same nation of bonafide and by-birth Bangladeshis?

What's the difference between the horrible HAB terrorism and the nationally and internationally conspired terrorism of the beastly BDR massacre? Let the people discern into the nature and character of the dubious Awami sound bites and understand the true color of the Awami cohorts and surrogates and their proxies. While they can make those public squares (Suhrawardy and Shahid Minar) freely available to them for their meetings, assemblies, councils, conventions, rallies, festivals, and celebrations, they declare those places forbidden and off-limits to the political opposition BNP in a forced and nearly fascist and utterly partisan and discriminatory manner. Shame on the Awamis and their legion of police. They deserve con and counterfeit "congratulations" for their self-defeating distortions and contravening contortions, contradictions, concoctions, and convolutions.

One would, therefore, like to think of the HAB incident, shrouded in national and international connections and conspiracies,[10] as yet another in the endless series of savageries and mass murders that the country has been witnessing for ages, especially during the term of this Hasina regime, since 2009. HAB was an act of violence added to thousands committed by this or that government that started with the violence, in the scale of carnages and massacres in the 1940s (one of which was the pro-Pakistan Kolkata riots of 1946 with the involvement of Sheikh Mujibur Rahman in them), and the killing of the Language Movement fighters on February 21, 1952 and then of Deputy Speaker Shahed Ali on September 23, 1958.[11] The country was born with indescribable brutalities that occurred in 1971 and that, unfortunately, continued to be committed since. There were unprecedented Pakistani rapes and atrocities, purportedly with direct or indirect collaboration from local agents, to begin with. Similar gruesome acts were committed not only against the innocent non-Bengali minority (Biharis) by the local Bengalis but also against many innocent native Bengalis, out of mere malignity, by members of different Bengali armed groups operating in different rural as well as urban parts of Bangladesh, including those being brutally bayoneted at Dhaka Race Course following the Pakistani surrender.

After the liberation, Bangladeshis continued raping and slaughtering their own folks and fellows, their own kind, their own nation (like Pol Pot and Khieu Samphan's communist Khmer Rouge—Red Khmers—in Cambodia/Kampuchea about the same time—1970s). Bangladeshis continue to do so, on a *daily* basis, as of today. In its horrific brutality and chilling images, HAB is no different than the countless others of the like since the time of the Awami *Rakkhi-Bahini* and JSD *Gano-Bahini* atrocities in the postliberation period, one of which was the extrajudicial killing of Seraj Sikder on January 2, 2005. If the Jamaati elements suspected of criminal activities during the liberation war of 1971 had to be brought to justice by the Awamis, why not the perpetrators of the similarly heinous crimes of Awami collaboration and JSD conspiracy for orchestrating genocidal social engineering in the postliberation period? Weren't the Khmer Rouge leaders somehow held accountable for their crimes against humanity—two million deaths—during the "Killing Fields" of 1975–1979 and made to pay a price in punishment? However, it is to be hastily added that Cambodia's current and long ruling Hun Sen is as dictatorial and authoritarian as Bangladesh's deeply and darkly BNP*hobic* Sheikh Hasina. Both Hun and Hasina are bent upon destroying their political opponents and using violence, intimidation, and partisan corruption to stick to power and maintain their power base.

Forty-five years of independence of Bangladesh, beginning with the very first Awami rule of Rakkhi-Bahini terror, along with their then nemesis JSD Gano-Bahini horror, are crammed with the pictures of deadly violence. Examples of bloody fury and ferocity just during the second half of that period would include the very top Awami leader reportedly inciting the Awami followers that they should take the lives of ten of the opponents for one dead on their side (একটার বদলে দশটা লাশ চাই), which led to 173 days of savage and severe unrest in 1995–1996. It was during that time that Sheikh Hasina promised that the BNP government led by Begum Khaleda Zia would have to be forcibly pushed out and that she would not let the BNP government stay in peace even for a single day. Later, Hasina's home minister Mohammad Nasim led a procession armed with poles and sticks to attack the judicial court judges, for they did not want to be involved in the controversial issues connected with August 15, 1971 in view of what they thought was purely a political matter.

Then there was the deadly June 5, 2004 arson/gun powder attacks on public transport in different locations, especially the one on a double-decker bus in front of Sheraton/Intercontinental Hotel Dhaka, killing many, including a two-year-old girl and injuring more, all those attacks being attributed to today's ruling party AL.

Then came one after another:

- Grenade attack at an AL meeting on August 21, 2004;
- JMB series bombings on August 17, 2005;
- The Awamis' boundlessly brutal and brutish লগি ও বৈঠা (logs, oars, and batons) violence of October 28, 2006[12];
- The beastly (and the nationally and internationally conspired) BDR massacre of February 25/26, 2009, which, it is widely suspected, was possible only with the premeditated complicity of the Hasina government and the government of India and which one may compare to the Nazi extermination of the Jews in the concentration camps in the 1940s[13];
- Poor Felani, the 14-year-old daughter of a Bangladeshi border farmer, shot to death by the cruel Indian BSF on January 7, 2011, who became a symbol of the Bangladeshis being continuously shot to death, in hundreds, at the border by BSF;
- Sagor-Runi murder of February 11, 2012;
- Hefajote Islam massacre of May 5/6, 2013[14];

- Shatkhira massacre of December 23, 2013;
- Narayanganj seven murder incident of April 27, 2014;
- Hasina Government/Gopali terror against the peaceful movement of the opposition BNP in 2013/2014 and 2015;
- Hasina Government's Gopali siege on the most popular political leader of the country, Begum Zia, by sand-and-cement-and-garbage trucks, water cannons, and pepper spray and the Gopali disconnection of all the utility services, including the delivery of food, to Begum Zia's office premises in 2014 and 2015;
- The horrific lynching of Sheikh Mohammad Samiul Alam alias Rajon of Sylhet on July 8, 2015;
- The brutish and barbaric abduction and murder of the BNP student wing leader Nurul Alam Nuru (and hundreds of others before him, since 2009) by the plain clothes Gopali gangs and gongs in Chittagong on March 29, 2017; and
- The barbaric and beastly murder of multitudes of people—such as Tonu, Mitu (Khadija?), Lipu, and Arifa—countless and/or nameless, including the staggering and shivering number of small children, without a single day passing by without blood and violence in the form of Awami গুম ও খুন, হামলা ও মামলা, arrests and warrants, and remands-and-ডান্ডাবেড়ি (chains and shackles), all against the innocent thousands and thousands of members of the nation, the opposition BNP, Jamaat, and other parties.

The HAB-type hellish and horrific atrocities, especially under the Awami regime's police and its other wings' brutalities, have been on and on, so to speak, every single day, without exception, all full of unsettling images—images of myriads of slain men, women, and children.[15] All between, one would find a dismal picture of corpses and dead bodies and dire and deadly chains and shackles. As English Romantic poet Coleridge says in *The Ancient Mariner*:

> The ice was here, the ice was there,
> The ice was all around:
> It crack'd and growl'd, and roar'd and howl'd,
> Like noises in a swound! (Part I)
>
> There passed a weary time. Each throat
> Was parched, and glazed each eye.
> A weary time! a weary time!
> How glazed each weary eye,.... (Part III)

> I looked upon the rotting sea,
> And drew my eyes away;
> I looked upon the rotting deck,
> And there the dead men lay. (Part IV)

No wonder, critics have coined a term called "Bokhate Badrul" or "Bad-Rule" for Awami-affiliated groups, such as Chatro League, whose history in this Hasina regime is one of brutal and violent "*Badrulgiri*," that is, acting like the Bad Badrul of Sylhet.[16] Dr Muhammad Rezaul Karim and Mohammad Abdul Gafour have written about the despotic and dictatorial Awami deviation from democracy and Awami terrorism, starting from the bloody 2006 লগি বৈঠা তান্ডব/massacre at Palton to the murderous 2016 attack on Khadija, all led by Awami cadres of different hues in state or other machineries.[17]

Dr Mina Farah of New York, a powerful columnist, calls the decade of 2006–2016 as soaked and submerged in blood.[18] Bangladesh, especially under the Hasina-led Awami rule, can be "proud" of a steady supply of its own Irish Easter massacre of late April 1916 and the Indian Jallianwala Bagh massacre on April 13, 1919, both committed by the colonizing British government; the Peterloo massacre on August 16, 1819; and the Tiananmen Square massacre of June 4, 1989 in Beijing, China.[19] While Yeats could write his famous "Easter 1916" in poetical protest, Shelley could write his "The Mask of Anarchy" in protest of the Peterloo massacre, and Tagore could relinquish his British-awarded "Sir" title, nothing could unfortunately be done or said in protest of the Hasina-committed massacres in Bangladesh.

Those violent days of bullet shots killing hundreds across the country in December 2013, December 2014, March–April 2016, and those months of petrol bombs and burnt bodies (of about 170) in 2015 could be avoided if there were no autocratic and authoritarian AL and if it did not pursue a policy of exclusion, elimination, extermination, and dismissal of the legitimate opposition demands. It is the draconian Awami despotism that was responsible for all the violence since 2009.

Heartrending images of all brutal and violent incidents are available both on social and mass media archives, including YouTube videos and Facebook reports, all looking equally gory and hellish. All bloody cases have been handled by the Awami government-turned-regime (which people also call BAKSAL-II, much worse and more dangerous than BAKSAL-I) in a way that left in its wake a long trail of questions and speculations related to "h" and "w's"—who, what, where, when, which, and how. Draped in distrust and shrouded in missing links and lack of transparency and reliability, it was a trail as long as the stream of blood left behind the bodies of the slain, mutilated, and dismembered.[20] Many observers such as Dr Zafrullah Chowdhury, Advocate Sultana Kamal, and the Swedish Radio and BBC reports point to the Indian RAW conspiring with the Hasina regime's RAB to commit many of the horrible and horrendous crimes in Bangladesh, including the preplanted terror attacks on its soil, to justify the regime's indiscriminate political repression and legitimize its prolongation and elongation in power.[21] All incidents since 2009, including the BDR and *Hefajote* massacres, are a huge dent into the credibility of the Hasina regime, causing its "credibility catastrophe," as Dr Abid Bahar of Dawson College Montreal Canada terms it.

The nation should mourn the death of all, with moral reckoning, regardless of locals or foreigners on the local soil. It should have seen the army and other special units immediately dispatched and deployed to save lives when and wherever possible (for instance, no army dispatched during the two-day BDR massacre for unknown reasons at the advice of who and from where?). If there was army participation in the case of HAB, questions remain about the mysteriously delayed operation and about who were there during the operation and who conducted the operation.[22] Press briefings deliberately are too short to answer all questions. In any case, the nation should not have seen people in uniform, military or religious or plain, slaughtered like anything in a commando style, either in the recent past or as recently as July 1 and even later.

At the advantage of the wide repression and terrorism going on unabated during the time of the Hasina regime and its politicized police as well as the other branches of the state/government, there are thousands and thousands of innocent victims in arrests, abductions, and targeted assassinations with blood spilling everywhere. Brig Gen Abdullahil Amaan Azmi, Hummam Quader Chowdhury (found after about seven months of abduction allegedly by the regime's secretive plainclothes police), Barrister Mir Ahmad bin Quasem Arman, and writer columnist Farhad Mazhar (also a scary and frightening "lost-and-found" case) are four of the high-profile opposition victims, along with the previously abducted opposition leaders, such as Elias Ali, Chowdhury Alam, and Salahuddin Ahmed (the latter also being a "lost-and-found" case but excruciatingly suffering in exile in India in a state of limbo caused by the shadowy and সন্ত্রাসী/terrorist creatures dangerously active and operating during the current regime).[23]

The country's overcrammed prisons are being fed and filled with more and more prisoners every day, who are suffering from a notoriously flagrant violation of their human rights, even deprived of their basic medical care. They are living a life in death for little or no fault of theirs, all charges being mostly police-and-politically fabricated. Advocate Taimur Alam Khandoker writes about how the overcrowded prisons are also overburdened with prisoners going mentally insane and deranged.[24] Jamuna TV devoted its entire চব্বিশ ঘন্টা (24 hour) program of December 7, 2016 to the inhuman condition of the inmates living the direst and most difficult times of their lives without trial. An eminent journalist and media celebrity, after being released from jail, expressed his pain and frustration like this (in an October 2016 e-mail to the author):

> But the mental trauma is still there, particularly when I remember hundreds of innocent prisoners' life story and how they are rotting. Time has become still for them. Some of them cannot remember when they were arrested and have no interest in the year of their release in future. I read in Time magazine that President Obama has reduced the sentences of almost 800 prisoners—that was a good humanitarian decision. During my captivity, I had the experience of six different kinds of prison cells including the one for solitary confinement. However, I have no plan to write about it. I simply wish, politicians who are imprisoned and then freed should do something about jail reform as did John Stonehouse, who was a UK Labor Minister under Harold Wilson and helped us a lot in 1971 but later on went to prison on a fraud charge and released. He devoted the rest of his life for the improvement of the UK jail situation.

In these circumstances, the string of extremist incidents such as HAB, Sholakia, and Kallyanpur are just three in a long series of bloody events, except that these are being billed as terror attacks in a commando style. In fact, all attacks (including the abduction of Quader Chowdhury and Barrister Arman and the deadly and dreadful abductions of Elias Ali, Chowdhury Alam, and Salahuddin Ahmad), one deliberately or inadvertently deflecting and distracting another, were terror attacks in a commando style, of course, in different settings. Some of them may have directly been committed/sponsored by the Hasina regime and its macabre and monstrous forces in an Egyptian Tahrir Square, Chinese Tiananmen Square, or Anglo-Indian Jallianwala Bagh style. Some were indirectly committed/sponsored and some maybe not, but they are still a part of the larger conspiracy with this or that local or foreign hand behind.[25] Isn't Tony Blair being derided as a terrorist by the parents of the 179 British soldiers killed in the unjust Bush-led Iraq war, leaving the country in a bloody and vicious trail and turmoil till today for which he (Blair) did in fact tearfully express his sorrow and regret?

In Hasina's Bangladesh, facts are hard to get out and get known. There are hundreds of thousands of casualties—some killed, some abducted only to be brutally dismembered, and some arrested and remanded and imprisoned. This has been happening all the time, literally every single day, for years and years, without exception. With a lot of publicity because most of the victims were foreigners,

HAB (and then Sholakia and Kallyanpur) saw a few more murders, added to an endless list of rising crimes and rising death toll in Hasina's Bangladesh, like no other. These were just three other bloody scenes in what is already a death valley, a killing field, a মৃত্যুপুরী.

The regime has divided the country deeply and dangerously. It has caused a deep division and has dug a deep hole in the psyche of the nation by promoting and favoring its own people on purely partisan considerations, fiercely and forcibly suppressing the political opposition, remaining slavishly loyal to India and unequally serving Indian interests. Terrorists took the advantage of the highly charged and polarized political void, vacuum, schism, chasm, or fissure (whatever you call it) created by the Hasina regime and its dastardly control of the nation. Although different countries have different contexts of their own—France, Belgium, Turkey, USA, Bangladesh—all killings are heinous and contemptible, to be condemned in strongest terms, never to be condoned or resorted to.

Under the Hasina regime, Bangladesh fails to fall short of becoming a South Asian version of the Middle Eastern Syria, Iraq, Yemen, Libya, and Lebanon. The only difference in the case of Bangladesh may be that there are more arrests (arrests in fantastically overwhelming numbers) than deaths. That does not mean the number of deaths (also in unbelievably shocking numbers) is to be underestimated. Nothing can exaggerate the number of the dead or of the prisoners. Another difference is that in Bangladesh, the regime police, along with dark underworld forces and natural disasters is constantly in competition with each other to take the lives of people, whereas in the Mid East it is basically the two competing sides, both being of human actions.

What a cross section of the politicians, academics, and labor leaders said—that there was a political crisis facing the country—at the opening session of the 3rd national conference of *Ganasanghati Andolan* (গণসংহতি আন্দোলন) at Dhaka on November 27, 2015 was perfectly representative of the view of the overwhelming majority of the people of Bangladesh, including the whole range of the opposition parties.[26] The same view was shared by Human Rights Watch, Amnesty International, US Congressional Committees, European Parliament, and many other organizations, all rattled and unsettled by the oppressive and repressive Hasina regime. Tom Lantos Human Rights Commission of the US Congress briefed, on December 1, that Bangladesh's human rights situation was deteriorating and that the civil and political rights and religious freedom were being undermined. It expressed its particular concern that "Protests against Prime Minister Sheikh Hasina and her Awami League (AL) have been shut down, critical views censored, and their authors arrested or sometimes disappeared [...] the heightened sensitivity and tension have engendered a hostile environment for civil society operations, and in turn, fostered self-censorship."[27] "Bangladesh is in deep political crisis," said Asian Human Rights Commission on May 5, 2016.[28]

In *The Telegraph* of Calcutta, India, Rama Chandra Guha writes about the looming political crisis of Bangladesh due to all being quiet under force and pressure by the current oppressive one-party government-turned-regime.[29] Since 2009, the Hasina regime continues to double down on its subversive and nefarious commitment to despotism and authoritarianism, turning itself into a modern version of either the Maoist Chinese Cultural Revolution (1966–1976) or Soviet Stalinism (1930s/1940s), both having been "a brutal dictatorship, built upon a cult of personality and enforced by a reign of terror."

In his Financial Times article, "Bangladesh pays for bad politics in blood," Victor Mallet quotes William Milam, a former US ambassador to Islamabad and Dhaka, as saying that:

> He [Milam] fears Bangladesh is now on a "frogmarch towards not only authoritarianism but really one-party dictatorship". Ms Hasina … blamed the "BNP-Jamaat nexus" for the latest killings, calling them "secret and heinous murders to destabilize the country". The truth is that the government faces a challenging task in fighting terrorists, who are usually local radicals impressed by international brands such as Isis, but is making the job still harder by persecuting its legitimate opponents and driving them underground.
>
> The ICG [International Crisis Group] report says the government's heavy-handed measures are damaging its own legitimacy and benefiting extremists. "There is no time to lose," it concludes. "If mainstream dissent remains closed, more and more government opponents may come to view violence and violent groups as their only recourse."[30]

Only the supporters of the ruling AL, who, in no uncertain terms, are in the minority, believe that the country is facing little or no political crisis. This is how the people are completely divided into two parallel lines showing no signs of meeting anywhere. However, one line—the line of the united opposition led by the BNP—is showing the sign of going upward in a columnar movement and the other line—the line of the AL—is horizontal, getting increasingly shorter, making a ninety degree angle possible and drawing its own suicidal demise close. Since it is in power, meaning in control of the entire state paraphernalia in a despotic and dictatorial way, the AL thinks it is the columnar tower while the opposition is the remains of a rubble that it has been reduced to by the uninterrupted police beating and quasi-judicial arrests, imprisonments, remands, and murders.[31] For one side, truly, democracy is as much out as dictatorship is in, and for the other side, falsely and ferociously, it is vice versa. The regime has reinvented the wheel in creating a distorted definition of democracy sans dissent, as Barrister Sara Hussein puts it.[32] Its despotic rule is like that of the dictator pig/boar Napoleon (Joseph Stalin), who redefines socialism or communism in his own cynical way, as opposed to the ideas of democratic socialism put forward by his rival, the pig/boar Snowball (Leon Trotsky) in George Orwell's *Animal Farm* (1945).

Bangladesh became independent from Pakistan in December 1971 with the hopes of peace, unity, equality, harmony, multiparty democracy, and, of course, material and economic prosperity. However, the hope was not just for one-party authoritarian rule and its one-way and one-dimensional economic development, which would be used as a cover to perpetuate a regime of despotic designs on creating division, polarization, revenge, hatred, vindictiveness, repression, and torture.

During its war of independence, Bangladesh was aided by the surrounding "superpower" India and now it is completely controlled by the latter. The fact is well documented in the pieces by Nurul Kabir, Qamrul Islam, Stalin Shorkar, and the speaker on a You Tube video,[33] exposing how Bangladesh is increasingly surrendering its independence and sovereignty to India, not only in the manner of those who betrayed Bengal to the British during the Battle of Plassey in 1757 but also the hypocrite Kazi Lhendup Dorji Khangsarpa (1904–2007), leader of Sikkim National Congress, who let his small Himalayan kingdom of Sikkim (home to Kangchenjunga, the world's third-highest peak) to be annexed by India and who then became its first chief minister (1974–1979). One may also mention what happened to Kashmir, Goa, and Hyderabad in the 1940s and what may be in the offing for Nepal, Bhutan, Maldives, and Bangladesh.[34] According to a more than four decades old document by the CIA, it would take only two weeks for India to take Bangladesh.[35] Who knows how long it would take now?

Critics and commentators opine that Bangladesh also is going through a process of Sikkimization, Kashmirization, or Goaization, so that it has become a joint production of Indian and Bangladeshi intelligence/security together, interested in promoting the Indian agenda of political and cultural hegemony, neocolonization, and economic interests. Unequal and unnecessary pacts with India made Dr Rashed Anam of the USA comment that if the collaborators wanted to politically sell or surrender Bangladesh to West Pakistan in 1971, the Hasina regime has been doing the same now to India, both politically and economically, in a treasonous manner, so that both the "rajakars" of then and the Awami Leaguers of today might be said to be playing the same role and boarding the same boat.[36] Talking about "India-Bangladesh defense pact" as "Honey mixed with poison for a friend" and "Headless democracy heartless neighbor," journalist Minar Rashid describes the Hasina government as "government by India, for India, and of India," and so does the journalist Masud Mazumder and the former army officer Mohammad Ishaq Mian.[37]

Dr Mina Farah gives a vivid word picture of how Bangladesh, being run by pro-Indian elements (in her words, "rajakars" in the Hasina regime), is already undergoing a process of Sikkimization.[38] Journalist and researcher Mohammad Zainal Abedin of New York has written to the same effect—a process of Sikkimization of Bangladesh being underway.[39] There are many who think that politically, culturally, economically, and in terms of the RAW-intelligence making inroads everywhere, Bangladesh is suffering from a sickly Sikkim syndrome and is in fact already a "half Sikkim." The (Late) BNP leader Brig Hannan Shah directly brought the matter to the fore and called for all concerned to thwart the Awami attempt to "Sikkimize" Bangladesh. Robert Boggs and Nicholas Burns have written on Indian hegemony in the smaller bordering countries that takes its lead from the ancient Indian political scientist and economist Chanakya, also known as Indian Machiavelli.[40]

India's neo-and-near Sikkimization of Bangladesh may not yet mean hard physical occupation of Bangladesh by India marching its soldiers into Bangladesh. Modern occupation is soft and silent as high or low blood pressure or diabetes (unlike cancer) is a silent killer. As critics say, if India can milk Bangladesh quietly and for free, why would it take the risk of growing a kicking cow by creating another Kashmir in its eastern border by force?

India has become to Bangladesh what British East India Company became to India during the 18th and 19th centuries. Noting the deep disparity in the pacts and agreements between India and Bangladesh, Dr Farah, in a Facebook status from New York, made the shocking comment that Sheikh Hasina's April (2017) trip to India was like carrying the corpse of Bangladesh along with her to India for several ceremonial funeral prayers with every official meeting led by the Indian leaders and elders.[41] The civil society and the entire political opposition of Bangladesh do not feel any less or different, who are in fact deeply critical as written about by Mohammad Zainal Abedin in his article "Anger in Bangladesh Over Defense MoUs with India."[42]

When there was nothing about the sharing of the much needed Teesta waters, nothing about the joint river commission meetings, nothing about the continuous killings of the poor Bangladeshis by India at the border, nothing about the huge trade imbalance between the two countries, and when there was everything as only the much-befriended India wanted, satisfying 90% of its interest, Hasina's trip was described as an utter failure by the opposition BNP. Referencing the daily

Hindu of India on the Teesta issue, Syed Munir Khasru writes about how Bangladesh became hostage to Indian local and provincial politics.[43]

American poet Robert Frost said, "Good fences make good neighbors." There are no good fences on the either side of the border, so the relationship between India and Bangladesh is one of unequal and so inimical neighbors. This is one of the reasons why, even after forty-five years, Bangladesh is still looking for a true and meaningful sovereignty and independence. It is divided against itself as it manages to survive under a suffocating siege and suppression by the regime. Strangulation and triangulation of all the opposition parties by means of the crafty, crooked, and diabolical Chanakyan, Machiavellian, Mephistophelian, and Lilliputian (low and mean, nasty and nefarious, divisive and despotic) practices, in other words, deadly and dreadful state terrorism, have become its sadistic pleasure since the beginning of 2009. There is absolutely no space and respect for the political dissent in the exclusively exclusionary politics of the regime and its draconian, ball-and-chain policies. It lost its democratic legitimacy and credibility long ago and it had its mandate, if at all, only once upon a time.

There is a one-sided and unequal political "civil war" of purely politically motivated reprisals going on in Bangladesh. In the smear campaign against the opposition, the Hasina regime is aided by the fearful and frightening members of the police, RAB, civil administration, and those of the different wings and operatives of its party apparatus. The democratically illegitimate regime is a neo-and-near-and-more-than-partially fascist and পৈশাচিক way, which may euphemistically called an illiberal, guided, and controlled democracy. It is the style of J R R Tolkien's Dark Lord Sauron, who has created the *Baksalite* "One Ring to rule the other Rings of Power as the ultimate weapon in its campaign to conquer" all of Bangladesh. The regime has been coming down harsh and hard on the opposition on a *daily* basis with scores of charges in the court against all or most of the individual members of the opposition starting from the very top. The widely held opinion is that the state tools are being used in a palpably partisan and politicized way.[44]

The continuous mass arrests and imprisonment drives for month after month, year after year, with thousands and thousands of innocent victims testify to this fact. During the second and third weeks of June 2016 alone, there were around 16,000 illegal, arbitrary, and extrajudicial arrests and more than 50 deaths in a combing operation. It was actually a crackdown and containment of the political opposition in the name of a so-called terrorist clean-up operation, virtually in violation of standing court orders. Critics say any clampdown, minor or major, gives the police a good and golden opportunity for extortion and kickbacks. They also say, in verse: "জংগী জংগী ডাক পারি /জংগী মোদের দাদার বাড়ী /আয় রে জংগী দেশে আয় /জংগী

লগিদের মিডিয়া খায়।” The rhyme may also imply a reference to the deadly Awami কুরুক্ষেত্র (a battlefield in ancient India) and লগি বৈঠা তান্ডব (poles and oars terror) of 2006. It is to be mentioned that there is hardly a day under the Hasina regime without mass arrests, remands, imprisonments, abductions, and disappearances, mostly of the innocent civilians and opposition members.[45]

As it was the fasting month of Ramadan, the widely known columnist and commentator Dr Tuhin Malik of the UK was prompted to say that when there were (holy and festive, cheerful and solemn) mass Iftar gatherings of Muslims over the sundown meal all around the world (with even the non-Muslims such as Mamata Banerjee and Jayalalithaa materially contributing (in charities) to the occasion in their home states in India), there were indiscriminate mass arrests of Muslims in Sheikh Hasina's own Muslim majority Bangladesh.[46] (Ret) Sqn Ldr Mohammed Shoaib of the USA comments (in an e-mail post of June 16, 2016): "You cannot solve a popular uprising reflected in isolated violence simply by arresting people. The fundamental cause of the violence (reaction to dictatorial suppression of peoples' rights) must be addressed. Otherwise, things will get only worse before a wholesale explosion that will take the country to the bottom of hell."

Even in official (government) count, which, in a politically partisan and polarized country like Bangladesh, is generally much less than the actual figure, the number of detainees is over 70,000, as of end of January 2016, crammed into a prison capacity for only a little over 30,000 in the sixty-eight prisons across the country.[47] That number has now gone up to over 80,000 living a critical inhuman/subhuman life of disaster and depravity. Back in 2013, famous Australian-British journalist John Richard Pilger quoted the former prime minister of Bangladesh (then in prison) Maudud Ahmed's wife, the poet Hasna Jasimuddin Maudud, as saying: "The country is a prison, and the world must know."[48]

National and international media have been reporting that the jails in Bangladesh are overburdened with political prisoners. Thousands of others have either been killed or kidnapped or forced to disappear only to be killed soon after.[49] Every time there is an election—local, municipal, city corporation, or national—there is a fresh and renewed round of mass arrests over days and weeks so that the election field goes empty of the opposition supporters and activists and that they are scared into hiding and prevented from electioneering, paving the way for the regime candidates to stuff the boxes with their own ballots as they want and win unopposed. It is the same thing when there is a so-called terrorist murder with hundreds being arrested for no reason except to terrorize and contain the opposition into a corner.

The regime's Prime Minister Sheikh Hasina is gladly inaugurating more and more prisons (which are actually much worse than what are known as correctional facilities in the West), signaling more mass arrests and more repression. Dwindling democracy, in its death throes, is helplessly crying in the face of the detonating dictatorship. Comparison may be drawn to the way many tender and innocent victims must have been heartrendingly crying and lacerating for help as they suffered until they breathed their last from the horrific cruelty of their beastly killers, who beat or burnt or battered or hacked them to death.[50]

In the name of what is in reality a short and fragmented, oblique and angular, partisan and polarized, and dogmatic and palsied view of the spirit of the 1971 liberation war, the regime has embarked on a unilineal and unidimensional economic development, creating more and more gaps and fissures in the society, making the rich more rich and the poor more poor. This defective and self-defeating development is opposed to a democratically lasting and harmonious social, political, and moral development inclusive of the economic prosperity. The regime, far from improving and upgrading democracy and democratic reforms, is letting itself to being engaged in distorting and corrupting history and inflaming and inciting its loyalists, not informing and enlightening the citizens of all shades and opinions as one whole nation.

Fanning the flames of hatred, the regime is completely preoccupied with ruthlessly crushing, crippling, and cornering the entire gamut of dissenting voices. It is not a matter of glory to see that there is a prime minister (Sheikh Hasina) and there is a government under her that came to power through a one-sided, voteless, voterless, ludicrous, and pugnacious "election" with a lamentable reduction and diminishment of the multiparty dynamics into a one-lane freeway allowing only Ms Hasina's party to act and operate, leaving all the opposition parties writhing under its police/RAB repression, dumped, crawling, and crouching, as it were, by the roadside ditches and puddles.[51] A great political figure like Nur-e-Alam Siddiquee thinks that, under the clouts and clutches of one person's autocratic rule (indirectly referring to Hasina), the opposition as represented by the BNP, after having been through political Intensive Care Unit, is already dead with its funeral also either already completed or about to be completed.

Under the pretext of "terrorism," which is, however, common everywhere in the form of stray and isolated instances, more from right-wing Christians than others,[52] the Hasina regime has been subverting, regimenting, and restricting the opposition in every possible way—from the press to political functions and programs. The regime has bottled up all kinds of opposition political activism, falsely, frivolously, and frigidly equating them with the so-called terrorism. This is being done as a way of consolidating its grip on power for an indefinite period of time, to the detriment of what started as a slowly flowering and functioning democracy, surely making an Orwellian and a Koestlerian premature collapse of a budding democratic process happen—a dystopian darkness at noon, a mayhem (animal) farm of inequalities, a 2015 scaled back to 1984 and on to 1948.

Harold Pinter, who received the Nobel Prize in literature in 2005, indicted the collective culture of empire by saying, "Nothing ever happens even as it's happening." So "the victims—the legions of unremembered dead—remain nameless and uncounted."[53] Pinter seems to have echoed W H Auden, who, in 1939, expressed the ironic view that poetry was useless, futile, and ineffective, a "sort of evidence for [its] reductiveness and hermetic inutility." Apparently, Auden lost his belief in poetry as an agent of political change when, on the occasion of the death of Yeats, he wrote:

> For poetry makes nothing happen: it survives
> In the valley of its making where executives
> Would never want to tamper ... it survives,
> A way of happening, a mouth.

Auden's famous phrase "poetry makes nothing happen" may have been uttered out of pain and frustration but it is highly ironic in the sense that it occurs, as a powerful understatement, in a famous poem by a great poet (Auden himself) in praise of another great poet—Yeats—who, as a politically conscious writer—did make things happen at least in the context of modern poetry, Irish literary renaissance, and Irish political independence.[54]

Similarly, this book, being just one telling about the partisan dysfunction in Dhaka, may not make a difference in the capital but it cannot miss to remember all those victims, especially from the AL's 2006 deadly লগি ও বৈঠা (sticks and poles) assault on the people[55] till today, including those who lost their lives during the BDR carnage, the savagery on the *Hefajote* men, and the various sieges and protests called by the opposition in its fight against the AL's increasingly ruthless despotism. Under this regime, every month, full of killings and lootings, is a bloody month, for which it hardly seems to care. The regime seems to be preoccupied with its sticking to power by all means—from verbal abuse to distortion of facts to physical persecution to psychological torture and repression.[56]

Bangladesh is indeed in the midst of a political and human rights crisis. It was never worse than the present. The British lawyer Toby Cadman described the situation as "Bangladesh in Crisis," giving a concise and comprehensive summary in his Congress Blog of May 29, 2015, following the U.S. Congressional

Subcommittee hearing on "Bangladesh's Fracture: Political and Religious Extremism," April 30, 2015.[57] Similarly, many British MPs deliberated that there was no alternative to the transition of power through credible democratic means that was not there in Bangladesh.[58] Although the specter of religious extremism is only a scarecrow suspected to have been created by the Hasina regime itself as a cover or excuse for the purpose of continuing in power, its Islamophobia turns into a love of Islam to secure more and more votes at the time of the national and other major elections in the Muslim-majority Bangladesh.

The sad and pathetic unfolding of events in Bangladesh is all due to the authoritarian AL government's slaughtering of the process of democratization through coarse and comical jokes that are the stories of the biased, unfair, and rigged elections, one after another. The turning point for the worst was of course the one-sided and voterless parliamentary election, mixed with the raw (RAW?) and repugnant Ershad-cum-and-versus-Rawshon and Ershad-and-Rawshon-cum-and-versus-Hasina theatrics, on January 5, 2014 (and another such lame and laughing election may be on the way, as Dr Zafrulla Chowdhury predicts).[59] Thereafter the ball kept rolling downward. It was (and is) the AL's harsh and hardline obstinacy and obduracy in relation to the political rights and freedoms of the opposition BNP that resulted in the bestial and barbaric deaths and disappearances (followed by deeply disturbing and horrific slaughtering) of the innocent people in hundreds and resulting in many a number of such incidents almost daily.

All this senseless irresponsibility occurred in consequence of the Hasina government's "quick rental" cancellation of the previously settled interim measure of the Caretaker Government (CTG),[60] followed by a headstrong rejection of a meaningful, freedom-loving, and freethinking (মুক্তমনা) dialogue with the opposition led by the popular BNP and its leader Khaleda Zia. According to a freelance observer, Dr Muazzam Kazi, who is a radiation physicist in the USA, "When the AL steals our voting rights, they find a lame and laughable excuse to defend their position. To remain in power without rhyme and reason, they abolished the caretaker system, which created a huge hole in the heart of Bangladesh."

As a party, the AL is characteristically, if not congenitally, unyielding, monolithic, and stringent. It proved to be so during its BAKSAL era around the mid-1970s and then again since 2009. Had the Hasina-led AL made a democratic compromise, accommodating and reaching out to the demands of the popular opposition for free and fair and inclusive elections, national as well as local, especially since the beginning of 2014, there would have been no petrol bombs and burnt bodies. It was during the deadly months-long unrest that the misty and mysterious role of certain bus companies (for instance, the Hindu-owned বিহঙ্গ পরিবহন), of certain individuals, such as Sanjoy Saha (a Hindu who adopted fake Muslim identity to attack the Hindu places of worship to malign the Muslim community), and of many Awami-affiliated bomb makers, bomb holders, and machete/ রামদা (sharp, long, and pointed weapons) bearers was also reported, along with the opposition-connected elements too.[61]

BangaBir Kader Siddiquee, despite his once bold, at times brutal bayonet past, went public in putting the burn-blame squarely on Sheikh Hasina.[62] It was the same role that many Awami-affiliated elements played during the sectarian and communal unrest in Ramu Chittagong, Nasirnagar B'Baria, Gobindnagar Gaibandha, and countless other cases and places, including their occupation and appropriation of Hindu lands, more than others.[63] All perpetrators need to be brought to justice with transparency and impartiality, which has unfortunately become as rare as a moon in the dark in Bangladesh politics.

It is suspected that most of the terror acts such as torching men, women, and vehicles committed during the opposition অবরোধ / হরতাল (siege/shutdown) and on various other occasions were done by agents other than the BNP elements. They did so to find it easy to malign and sabotage the BNP-led opposition. It is the same AL and the AL government, obstinate and obdurate as it is by its very nature, along with its Constitutional yet cool and cozy ally in the Election Commission and its partisan players in the police, that were responsible for hundreds of deaths and as many critically injured in the violence during the local polls of March–April 2016 alone around the country.

To prolong its iron rule, the Awami regime has found an easy way to hammer down hard on the opposition by using the state police and other paramilitary forces as its torture tools and by tampering with the democratic institutions, especially the three main independent and coequal branches/pillars of the state—legislature, judiciary, and the executive, not caring to honor, even disregarding the separation of power among them and treating all of them as if they were part of the same—the executive. The late Suranjit Sen Gupta, an AL leader, infamous for his financially scandalous কালো বিড়াল (black cat) associations, cautioned Chief Justice S K Sinha to be careful and controlled in making statements, especially when they were likely to go against the interest of Gupta's party, the ruling AL.[64]

It is the same Justice Sinha who said that the judiciary has been taken hostage by the government and that "law does not rule in Bangladesh, instead it is being ruled by authorities."[65] He has been making neutral and impartial statements since he assumed the office of the CJ, although he does not have the honest courage to accept the overwhelmingly Muslim Bangladesh as having Islam as its state religion and would like to see, illogically, his minority religion to be at par and also an un-Islamic statue in front of the Supreme Court.

The fourth pillar—mass media—also has been made subject to partisan divide and restraining control and scrutiny with many journalists and the major part of the print and electronic media taking the despotic Awami side and submitting to the dictatorial Awami smear campaign against the opposition BNP. Greed for power and money has made them subscribe to the partial and partisan Awami narrative of the spirit of independence, to the extent of its being ruinously fragmented and commodified, as well as to the detriment and destruction of democratic values and institutions.[66]

For years, the noted jurist and politician Dr Kamal Hussein has been speaking about the sick and unhealthy politics that has made all kinds of tricks in corruption, criminalization, and deception possible in every sector of the government, including the election system. "All the institutions, including the judiciary, administration, and police, have been spoiled with politicization," he said.[67] Hussein's words are no different from what the Chief Justice of the country also said. Their words are the voice of the civilized society, in alignment with Montesquieu's *The Spirit of Laws* (1748) and what the English judge and legal writer Sir William Blackstone said in his *Commentaries on the Laws of England* around 1765: that "the regular and practical administration and free course of justice," as "an uniquely inclusive and participatory ideal," was the guarantor of individual rights invested with immense social and human capital.

As the former MP Golam Mowla Roni said, both democracy and the freedom of the press were now in a barren and blocked state. As the former Dhaka North Mayoral candidate Mahi B Chowdhury lamented on the ATN's YoungNite show, "The country is under the control of the corrupt who are plundering the country and tearing it apart."[68] To overcome the unbearable situation of the endless cycles of violence and waves of moral depravity, the root cause of which is the power-drunk and corruption-ridden Awami government alone,[69] the book argues for tolerance, good governance, social justice, rule of law, transparency, accountability, dialogue, compromise, and accommodation, all of which are conspicuous by their absence in Bangladesh under the Hasina regime. In short, it argues for institutionalization of democracy—a word that derives from *demos* (people) and *kratos* (power) in Greek. In theory, democracy may be the best form of political system; in practice, it is not, perhaps even one of the worst; yet no other system has been found to be better than this.

This publication remembers all those artists, public intellectuals, politicians, and civil society members, who, on political, civil and human rights grounds, wished to deliver food and drinks to the popular opposition leader Khaleda Zia during her confinement in her office compound, as the party chair, for months from January 3, 2015. Her party office too (in a different location) was completely shut down many times for an indefinite period over the last few years. Both she and her political offices were made off-limits to her party leaders in a totalitarian suppression by the regime, which kept them barred and blocked, hardly letting anybody or anything in or out with many essential services disconnected, in stark violation of the fundamental rights of a senior citizen, a political leader, and a former prime minister.[70] Both Khaleda and her party leaders shouldering immense and endless odds, impediments, and obstructions in their fight against the Hasina regime are today's heroic political gladiators and unyielding Prometheus-like figures of Bangladesh.

Many of those who wanted to visit the besieged and beleaguered Begum Zia with food and water were either turned away, or all of a sudden bullied and terrorized into being detained. In a barbaric manner, the Hasina regime was implementing on Begum Zia what Ms Hasina's father, Sheikh Mujibur Rahman (who was the immediate founding father of the nation along with a few others, at least three, before him) wished to implement, justly and legitimately, on the Pakistani enemies back then in 1971—তোমরা আমাদের ভাই [...] আমরা তোমাদের ভাতে মারবো পানিতে মারবো (you are our brothers, but if you continue to kill my people, we will cut you off from the supplies/provisions and you will be forced to die of starvation).

The government, again, most unscrupulously, claimed that the former Prime Minister Begum Zia, leader of the largest political party of Bangladesh and wife of the former president and army chief, was not actually confined and that she was free to move. If so, why were her movements restricted? Why the police blockade? Why was it that scarcely anything or anybody was allowed in or out of her office premises? Why was it that Khaleda had to live in fear that once she was out of her office compound she might not be allowed back in to carry out her political activities from there? The fact that hardly anything or anybody was allowed in or out was a clear proof that Khaleda Zia was under pressure, against her will, to get out and not to get back in again. Abnormal and repressive circumstances made it necessary for Khaleda to abnormally continue her stay in her office, not only as a compulsion but also as a protest against the Hasina regime. Additionally, it was absolutely her freedom to go or stay wherever she liked—home or office—for political or personal reasons, as she deemed fit, right, and convenient.

Why is it that almost all BNP men and women have to remain behind bars or continue to be harassed and hounded and detained from anywhere, being safe nowhere—be it home or office? Why was it that Khaleda was violently attacked day after day during her campaign for her party's Dhaka Mayoral candidates, so much so that her convoy, including her own car, were smashed to pieces and dozens of her men were seriously injured with no action taken by the regime police, who merely stood by, cheerfully conniving at the hooligans doing their job? Why was this shameful vandalism by the vain Awami Honda-Goondas allowed to happen? One of Hasina's ministers, once a sworn enemy now a comrade Hasanul Hoque Inu, said that there was enough security provided for Khaleda so that she was able to return home safe, personally unharmed by his and Hasina's rogues and miscreants let loose. Well, then, by the same logic, years ago the Khaleda government must have provided sufficient protection during the grenade attack on Hasina so that she, herself physically unharmed, was able to survive and go home safe.

What the career diplomat and former ambassador to Japan Serajul Islam said in this respect (in a group e-mail of April 2015) is worth quoting:

> The Dhaka and Chittagong City elections are not about the candidates. It is about the level to which the AL can fall. Now it has fallen to its nadir as a party. When people can again speak out freely, anyone who supports the AL would have to hang his and her head in shame for the party's misdeeds during the last six years, in particular in recent times. Khaleda Zia has shown the stuff of which heroes and leaders are made in history, a worthy widow to a great liberator and freedom fighter. We have to see how the people of Dhaka and Chittagong wake up to this responsibility and it is now hardly a matter of the BNP and Khaleda Zia alone. If the people of Dhaka and Chittagong fail in this historic responsibility, then we would have to believe that all things we know of 1971, when people rose against fascism, dictatorship and genocide, were nothing but merely stories. The ball is now in the court of the people of Dhaka and Chittagong.

The questions are, will the hoodlums and hooligans, under the shelter of what the opposition describes as রাষ্ট্রিয় সন্ত্রাস (state terrorism), allow the polls to go ahead peacefully and fairly for the court of the people to decide? Did the Bangladeshis have the ball in their court in the past half a dozen years or so? Or would they have it in their court anytime soon? Has their voice ever mattered or counted? The ground reality of massive and widespread voting irregularities suggests something totally different. If Dr Tuhin Malik's gold statement that there was a *saree*-wearing godmother behind all godfathers, apparently referring to the people at the very top in the Hasina government, the answer to those questions is clearly a thumping "no."[71]

It was Dr Malik again who said (on a Channel I TM program) that it was the same thing to expect democratic fairness and equality from the Hasina-led AL as it was to expect milk from a donkey (not literally but in spirit), metaphorically suggesting that though a donkey does indeed give milk, it is the sense of rarity, strangeness, infrequency, and uncommonness of the availability of that milk that mattered. Another analogy goes like শয়োলরে কাছে মুরগি বাগা দয়ো, that is, to expect democratic freedom from the Awami-Hasina regime is to entrust the fox with chicken in the hope of some return in more eggs and chickens.

Zoglul Husain of the UK, who was a freedom fighter and now a patriotic nationalist political activist, comments (in an e-mail of June 12, 2016 to the author): "মানুষ অপরাধের কবলে পড়লে তারা রাষ্ট্রের দ্বারস্থ হয়। কিন্তু রক্ষকই যদি ভক্ষক হয় তখন মানুষ যাবে কোথায়? এই সরকারের নির্বিচার হত্যা, গুম, সন্ত্রাশ, দখল, সীমাহীন দুর্নীতি, অত্যাচার, অবিচার, বিচারিক হত্যা, নির্যাতন, নিষ্পেষণ, ইত্যাদিতে জনজীবন দুর্বিষহ হয়ে পড়েছে। প্রয়োজন, এ সরকারকে অপসারণ করা।" As rendered in English (by the author), Husain means to say: "Victims of crime seek the help of the state. But when the defender (state) himself becomes the perpetrator of crime, where/to whom would they go? People are intolerably suffering under the yoke of indiscriminate killing, enforced disappearance, state terrorism, occupation, possession, endless corruption, torture, injustice, judicial murder, persecution, and prosecution committed by this government."

Part B: Fragmentation, commercialization, and compartmentalization of the 1971 spirit/ চেতনা of liberation: discussion continues

At the present time that reminds one of Charles Dickens's *Hard Times*, Bangladesh has turned into a one-party rule of ropeless and reinless reign dangerously and despotically crushing the political opposition. The crackdown continues to the extent of eliminating and annihilating the latter with the regime's police/ RAB, who are glued and addicted to detaining innocent opposition supporters and activists in large numbers almost daily. In the present context, one familiar with Yeats would remember:

> Turning and turning in the widening gyre
> The falcon cannot hear the falconer;
> Things fall apart; the center cannot hold;
> Mere anarchy is loosed upon the world,
> The blood-dimmed tide is loosed, and everywhere
> The ceremony of innocence is drowned;
> The best lack all conviction, while the worst
> Are full of passionate intensity. ("The Second Coming")

That is how Yeats lamented in 1919, in the immediate aftermath of the First World War, anticipating the dangers of the Second World War. The appalling picture drawn in the poem applies to Bangladesh's Hasina regime as well—a regime that amply and abundantly examples "Power corrupts; absolute power corrupts absolutely" (an expression variously attributed either to William Pitt the Elder in 1770, Alphonse Lamartine in 1848, or Lord Acton in 1887). The year 2009 on in Bangladesh, it is unlike 1969–1971 and 1975–2005 when the political stage was different and the political alignments and movements could still function, fairly democratically and quite dynamically, though in the way of two steps backward and one step forward. Now there is absolutely no such orchestration and synchronization, no fine intricacies and modulations, no nuances and negotiations whatsoever. It is all a deep polarization due to the ruthless despotism and repressive authoritarianism conducted by the ruling AL's Sheikh Hasina.

Noted and veteran Indian journalist and columnist Kuldip Nayar writes about her authoritarian and dictatorial rule that has resulted in the "Tragedy of Bangladesh" in which, Nayar claims, "She is only busy obliterating the followers of Begum Khaleda Zia, the main opposition leader" and "She behaves as if it were her birth right to rule." "In all of her actions," Nayar continues, "Sheikh Hasina has forgotten the welfare of the country."[72] It is as if there is a race of two runners running along two parallel lines but in opposite directions, never likely to meet and cross and meet again, one runner desperate and determined to keep running and scoring in an empty field with no credit, no competition, and no glory and the other forced to wear out before the finish line and choked out to near death and demise. For the opposition (Khaleda) side, it is all rough and rocky; for the ruling (Hasina) side, it is all childishly and playfully plain and level with the help of its completely partisan police/RAB and other state tools and machineries.

A repetition of the dark days of the Awami 1972–1975, now, after many years, it is again an unprecedented, all of a sudden, Awami reversal of systems and policies, scuttling backward like a crab. Former MP Abu Hena gives a brief (dire and dismal) picture of what is going on in the country and what a mess it has become.[73] It is all an Awami "Social Darwinism" and BAKSALi "Benthamite Utilitarianism," ensuring the survival of not the fittest but only the Awami "Benthamites" and their lobbies, lackeys, and lapdogs, guaranteeing laissez-faire (noninterventionist and noninterfering free trade) only among the hoards and legions of their own, from which many other hidden hoodlums and hooligans also benefit liberally and lavishly. It is all being accomplished in an abnormal manner—bloody and devouring—far from what is normal, civil, civic, social, and civilized. Neither the people nor the opposition parties were/are ready for the unexpected Awami turn of events and change of rules of the game to perpetuate its atrocious and outrageous domination, suppression, repression, control, coercion, coronation, and inauguration.

As in Henrik Ibsen's play *A Doll's House* (in which everything is done and viewed from the male and masculine point of view so that the heroine Nora feels forced, in a bold and controversial decision, to leave her husband and children with the intention of discovering herself freely and independently in her own terms), in Bangladesh too, all things are written and performed according to the myopic and monolithic view of only the Awami party, not only to the exclusion of others but also at the expense of the distortion of facts, reality, and history. Ultimately it may prove that the Awamis have actually lived the life as lived in Tennessee Williams' play *The Glass Menagerie* in which all the characters' dreams and desires are simply crushed and remain unmet.

For now, however, the dire and dangerous survival tactics of Sheikh Hasina caught the people in general and all the opposition parties in particular off guards. As a deep and dark and violent BNP*hobe*, Hasina is also too cowardly to electorally face the popular opposition BNP. Starting with the mysterious BDR massacre of early 2009 and the quashing of all the lawsuits and court cases against her and her party faithful through a completely partisan political control of the state tools, Sheikh Hasina's survival tactics are manifested through controversial judicial processes and outcomes, Gopali police, RAB, politicized bureaucracy, and the other passively pedestrian-type onlooker forces, all aided by the hegemonic and expansionist neighbor India at all fronts, from within and without.

Things are what they were not supposed to be: offtrack, sliding, slipping, serpentine, surreptitious, and supercilious. They are out of control. The center needs to hold, to get back on track, to a normal course of action and evolution, not to continue, as T S Eliot's abnormal and erratic Prufrock does, "through certain half-deserted streets/ The muttering retreats/ Of restless nights [...] Streets that follow like a tedious argument/Of insidious intent." There has to be a miracle, an act of God, or any other mechanism, worldly or divine, to rein in. Otherwise, more bad days ahead are to be braced for!

Apart from the terror, torture, and tyranny that the গুম ও খুন (forced disappearances and abductions and murders),[74] হামলা ও মামলা (persecutions and politically motivated punishing lawsuits), jail and জুলুম (repression and discrimination), and the boots and bullets and batons of the police/RAB are, Bangladesh is being run by the clique-and-coterie-and-intelligence-guided Hasina government-turned-regime (also called by critics as BAKSAL-II, considered far worse and far more dangerous than BAKSAL-I). Nongovernmental human rights organizations in Bangladesh provide a detailed picture of the infernal situation in the country, suggesting the democratically illegitimate regime stands at the threshold of total dysfunction and disconnect with the democratic and legitimate wishes of the people.[75] It is isolated from "we the people," who are divided into the minority "we" and "us," on the one hand, and the majority "other" and "they," on the other. The regime is deeply loyal to the neighboring "big brother" India as it enjoys India's direct backing and blessings, whatever that means—from protection and security to political intervention to cultural invasion and infiltration to unfettered access to the economic market of Bangladesh.

This loyalty to India is so uncritical and unquestioning that it is as if the regime in Bangladesh loves to remain under the Indian sway in an all-giving and all-surrendering love affair, leaving only the immediate selfish desire of hanging on to power fulfilled but the greater patriotic and enduring desire as a sovereign and independent country unfulfilled and unsatisfied. It is an unequal and so impermanent friendship without the reciprocity of interests that has to be there in a mutually satisfying and long-lasting consensual affair. As Dr Asif Nazrul puts it, this dire and deadly inequality has to be seen through the "looking glass" of the Teesta, which makes the difference mostly favoring the all-dominating India crystal clear.[76] Bangladesh's Hasina government's unabashed and uninhibited allegiance to India is so much so that Bangladesh has been termed by critics not only a joint venture, project, or enterprise of the Indian government but also a puppet satellite of Indian hegemony with Bangladesh's integrity and sovereignty as an independent nation being questioned by many.

Attempts—open or submerged, direct or indirect—are being made to fit and push Bangladesh into the Akhand Bharat (Undivided India) visions of Chanakya Kautilya, Dinanath Batra, Jawaharlal Nehru, Rabi Rikhi (a defense specialist), BJP, RSS, HM (Hindu Mahasabha), VHP (Viswa Hindu Parishad), the উপমহাদেশ পুনরুজ্জীবন আন্দোলন (movement for the revival of the subcontinent), HSC (Hindu Struggle Committee), and many West Bengal ministers. Quoting some of those dreamers and proponents of Akhand Bharat, Khodeza Begum writes about how India wants to install a puppet government in what may be called the "crowned" or "anointed" rather than "elected" Sheikh Hasina's Bangladesh and gobble it up the way it did Sikkim, Kashmir, Hyderabad, and Goa (not to speak of its similar and ultimate expansionist and adventurist aims about the other smaller neighboring countries, such as Nepal, Bhutan, and Maldives, already squarely under its powerful sphere of influence).[77] According to a more than forty-year-old document by the CIA, it would take only two weeks for India to take Bangladesh.[78]

Is it going to take longer or shorter for India, now that there is an excessively and exceedingly friendly to puppet government sitting around in Bangladesh?

Not unlike its friend Russia taking Crimea, threatening parts of Ukraine, and eyeing the tiny Baltics, India's ambition to become a superpower and take a seat on the UN Security Council cannot be a deterrent (as some might like to argue) but can actually a propellant in extending its claws and clutches in a show of muscle to justify its demand with respect to the UN body.

Yes, if India wants, it can take Bangladesh in two hours, but it must be wise enough not to do so by way of physically or literally occupying or annexing a neighboring territory and creating another headache like Kashmir, especially when it can easily reap the fruit, politically, economically, and culturally, by way of installing too willing and yielding and too obedient and submissive a government out there ready to cooperate and work together and keep on signing unequal treaties even at the expense of the interest of its own home turf, so long as it is well-protected by India in return. Of the tons of columns and commentaries to the same effect, one is by journalist Kamrul Hasan Darpon, who gives an account of what Bangladesh has received, in small amount, compared with what in abundance it has given to India.[79]

In the meantime, Ms Hasina's coronation continues with her nonstop celebratory participations in national and international forums and platforms in the country and beyond. The result is that Bangladesh is deeply divided—divided between the two camps without any positive differences between them. One is patriotic, democratic, and nationalist, represented by the popular ("her majesty's") opposition in the BNP, the other ruthlessly repressive, represented by the sitting Awami League (AL) government. An Al Jazeera article by journalist Tom Hussain suggests that persecution of the opposition and divisive politics resorted to by the AL set the stage for Dhaka attack on July 1, 2016 and that the AL government has been creating a political vacuum at the same time as ISIS has reached out to struggling jihadi factions across South and Southeast Asia.[80]

According to the Awami policy of who was once ruled a "wrong-headed" woman by the country's High Court, (a) all opposition actions and assemblies are to stop; (b) all opposition leaders and activists, today's heroic Prometheus-like political gladiators, are to be chained and beaten up and remanded and jailed; (c) all free and independent media are to close; (d) all police/RAB officers are to hail from a certain district or districts and minorities of interest; (e) all elections, except the conveniently made rare exceptions, are to be stolen, rigged, and one-sided with a seal of Awami win; (f) all Farakka Dam gates are to be opened by India to let Bangladesh be submerged and go under water; and (g) all the country-wide power lines are to be cut off if protests continue against the construction of the coal-fired Rampal power plant on the bank of the Pasur river near the

Sundarban mangroves, considered environmentally unfriendly for Bangladesh but friendly to India.

Two interesting humorous sayings—one racist and one political—may suffice to illustrate the point. On being asked, a Jewish man spitting on the grave of Hitler said that he was doing so because he (Hitler) killed so many Jews. Then the second man—the questioner—also started spitting on Hitler's grave because he thought Hitler didn't finish the job (of killing all the Jews). While all killings are serious crimes—heinous, contemptible, cowardly, detestable—no amount of killing can actually ever kill or finish anything. Hitler was wrong from the beginning. No extremes should be spared and all extremes are to be spitted upon.

Second, soon after the election of President Barack Obama, an ordinary man stopped by the gate of the White House to ask if he could see President George W Bush and was told by the guard that Bush was no longer the President of the United States. The wandering man returned again and again on the second, third, and fourth day with the same request, only to be turned away with the same answer. The guard asked the man why he would appear again and again to hear the same very answer and leave. The man replied that he was doing so because he liked the answer and would like to hear it again and again, to his great pleasure.

The Hitlers and the George Bushes of the Hasina-Awami regime may take lessons as necessary from these two jokes. They should also rise above hatred and violence by refraining from attacking their political rival BNP for the latter's much fewer faults accrued when it was in power in the past. The story of the sieve/strainer, itself full of pores and holes, telling the needle that it was defective with a hole at one end applies to the AL, itself riddled with faults, but continuously accusing the BNP of its much lighter share.

There are some in Bangladesh who are compatible with the mentally retarded and intellectually impaired Johnny of William Wordsworth's narrative poem, "The Idiot Boy." There are some who are compatible with Feodor Dostoyevsky's honest, sincere, and simple-minded Prince mistakenly referred to as an "idiot" by the greedy and selfish in the novel *The Idiot*. Those who clearly and categorically belong to the first need to make an effort to strive and struggle toward the second, at least as the first step in the right direction. Unfortunately, both kinds of "idiots" find themselves in the circumstances in which there are no opportunities available even to try the initial step, the reason being that the both kinds are under the grinding and oppressive control of the third (Shakespearean) kind of idiots, who keep crowing and parroting the tall tale of life, "full of sound and fury, signifying nothing."

Words fail to describe the horrific repression the nation suffers at the hands of this third kind and the police. In consequence, no party council by the opposition, no reorganization from within the opposition, no new leadership, and no amount of talk-show talking and babbling can, therefore, actually work and produce any result under the regime's all-consuming roller coaster control and coercion. No democratization within the opposition is possible, or necessary, or can be effective so long as there is Awami repression and persecution, leaving the whole country without a shred of freedom and democracy and in a political vacuum and political blackout. The Awami one-person dictatorship is more responsible for everything negative in the country than the lack of democracy within this or that party, which is a small matter in the present circumstances.

The people of the country are fretfully frightened by the all-engulfing Awami flames and fumes, far from being friendly fires, in an early 21st-century version of what is a democratically illegitimate and neo-and-near-and-more-than partial Awami fascism (a phrase that recurs throughout the book), quite brute and brutal in nature and action. Neither the army nor the political parties nor the masses can become united and be on the street like November 7, 1975 when the country emerged from a serious political crisis and found a second life with a sigh of relief. Anything that is fascist and treacherous in nature and action, by any degree or measure, needs to be confronted with the concerted and determined efforts of all together. People must smash and strike through the deceiving semblance of democracy that appears on a few talk shows and select print media and take back the country from the sphere of Indian hegemony with the zeal and spirit of Bangladeshi nationalism.

Patriotic love and fervor, as well as political commitment and dedication need to be expressed in an atmosphere of democratic freedom and fairness, to be ensured and enshrined by any government that claims to be democratic. Unfortunately, that is not the case in Bangladesh. The country is under siege by the AL government, blocking the wind of positive and peaceful change. It does so in a violently exterminating and annihilating manner putting all democratic trust and tolerance not only on hold but in chains. The desirable environment that started budding and blooming years ago (albeit along a bumpy road, on and off, forward and backward) has been completely done away with by this autocratic and authoritarian Awami regime under which the nation finds itself in a bestial and barbaric death valley (মৃত্যুপুরী) or a killing field for all ages and walks of life, causing tears in cusecs, enough to make the drying Padma, Teesta, and Atrai flow in full.[81]

In his Financial Times article, "Bangladesh pays for bad politics in blood," Victor Mallet expresses the same idea linking "human rights disaster" in Bangladesh to its:

> [...] transformation under Sheikh Hasina's Awami League from a rather dysfunctional but manageable democracy into an authoritarian state ... the sustained assault by security forces and the judiciary on government opponents, including editors and liberal and Islamist politicians.
>
> Officials depict the onslaught as a response to the violent campaign of strikes and boycotts waged by the opposition Bangladesh Nationalist party and its Jamaat-e-Islami allies around the last general election two years ago.
>
> But the victimization of the main opposition parties and neutral observers has reached levels extreme even by the standards of the country's traditionally unpleasant politics, with mass arrests, extrajudicial killings and implausible prosecutions.[82]

It is the regime's culture of crimes against humanity—oppression, repression, and discrimination—that has made all kinds of torture (physical, sexual, mental, psychological, judicial) and watching them as they occur in broad daylight a source of sadistic entertainment, to the perpetrators as well as the onlookers. The chilling video images, in thousands, cause a "zero at the bone," to borrow a phrase from Emily Dickinson. Joseph Grieboski, who was nominated for a Nobel in Peace, the UK-based Guardian Editorial, and the US Department of State said it all in excellent articles and press reports/conferences called "Bangladesh Democracy Under Attack" and "Bangladesh history debate: distorted by politics."[83]

The Jewish/Israeli connection: Aslam Chowdhury, Mendi Safadi, and Sajeeb Wajed Joy

Opposition BNP Joint Secretary Aslam Chowdhury was detained on so-called sedition charges for simply having had a six-minute personal meeting with Mendi Safadi of Israel in India where both attended a gathering upon the invitation of the Mayor of Agra and on the sidelines of which both (Safadi and Chowdhury) met, as political or business leaders always do. It is true Israel has been killing Arab Palestinians for ages (just as India has been killing its own Muslims all over the country, especially in Gujarat and Kashmir, who have become the minority "other" in their own country) but Israel has also been able to "divide and rule" and maintain diplomatic, commercial, and even friendly ties with a number of major Muslim countries in the region, such as Egypt, Jordan, Turkey, and Saudi Arabia.

Moreover, Israel and India (the latter having one of the largest Muslim populations in the world, about 172m, many more than Bangladesh) are in the best and warmest of bilateral relationships for ages, taken to a soaring height by Modi during his visit to Israel in early July 2017, all at the expense of Muslim-majority Palestinians. The question is: if the Hasina regime can be all ears to the indignantly anti-Muslim and lovingly pro-Israel Narendra Modi, why can't Aslam Chowdhury simply meet on a personal level for only six minutes with just a private citizen, at best a politically active individual of Israel?

It is worth mentioning that Israel is the most democratic country in the entire Middle East and, unlike Hasina's Bangladesh, one of the most democratically transparent countries in the whole world. In Israel, apart from free and fair elections—the most critical and crucial and necessary part of any democratic process—sitting presidents and prime ministers (Benjamin Netanyahu, Ehud Olmert, and Moshe Katsav) can be questioned and investigated for their financial corruption and sexual misconduct by the law enforcement agents and can be punished, removed from power, and even be jailed, which is unthinkable in the autocratic and authoritarian Hasina's Bangladesh. Her niece British Labor MP Tulip Siddiq is always happy to sign a pledge to support Israel. More significantly, Hasina herself also is happy, as is Nawaz Sharif of Pakistan, to do business with Israel under the table, behind the back of others, especially the Palestinians for whom they seem to be shedding crocodile tears outwardly. According to Padma Rao, on the World Is One News discussion, "Israel has provided the highest export revenue to Bangladesh."[84]

It is the same Mendi Safadi who claims to have met with PM Hasina's son and presumptive heir Sajeeb Wajed Joy for fifteen minutes in the USA, for which there was no charge against Joy. It is the same discriminatory policy according to which BNP Senior Vice Chairman Tarique Rahman has been accused, indicted, and convicted, whereas the allegations of Joy's internationally connected humongous financial scandals have not even been investigated into.[85] That is what has been argued by Dr Tuhin Malik, a rising star in the opposition politics consistently making penetrating comments of phenomenal significance against the Awami authoritarianism. It is the same Mendi Safadi who was unsuccessfully tried to have been bribed into giving up his efforts for the cause of the minorities in Bangladesh by PM Hasina's Youth and Sports State Minister Biren Sikder in cooperation with Joy, whose American wife Kristine Ann Overmire, interestingly, is of Jewish or Judeo-Christian origin.[86]

It is the same Mendi Safadi through whose Center for International Diplomacy and Public Relations the Bangladeshi HSC asked Israeli Prime Minister Benjamin Netanyahu to establish diplomatic relations with Bangladesh in an equation that squared off with India–Israel brotherly relations, but there was no charge against the HSC. It is the same Mendi Safadi who was present with the Bangladeshi American Hindus protesting against the minority problems in Bangladesh in front of the Trump Tower in New York on November 27, 2016. So, when there is nothing against anybody else, why is there everything against Aslam Chowdhury?

While one should have no problem supporting Sheikh Hasina and Nawaz Sharif doing export business with Israel, one can only ask, "Why don't they do so openly and officially, why secretly (and in a hide-and-seek with the Palestinians and others of so-called concern and interest for whom they profess to have a pronounced sympathy)?" More importantly, (a) when Hasina can do business with Israel unofficially; (b) when her foreign-educated son Joy can marry a Jewish woman; (c) when Joy can meet with Mendi Safadi in New York; (d) when her niece Tulip could sign a pledge of support to Israel (though in the context of British politics); (e) when many Muslim countries as mentioned above can have diplomatic and business relationship with Israel; (f) when Israel, Palestine, and Iran can sit down together at the Conference on Interaction and Confidence Building Measures in Asia; and, finally, (g) when Israel offered to recognize Bangladesh soon after the independence, what was wrong with Aslam Chowdhury meeting Safadi in India for only a few minutes? Is it simply because he is a BNP leader? One country, two shockingly different and divergent rules, under the Hasina regime—all stick for the BNP, all carrot for the AL, in a policy of discrimination and double standard? This type of Awami fascistic deception and containment have got to go.

Discussion of the চেতনা / spirit above continues

Before it has had a chance to be on the way to flowering and flourishing, the limping march of democracy in Bangladesh has been made conspicuous by its absence by the uncompromising Awami authoritarianism. During 1973–1975 and since 2009 (especially 2014), the Awami versions of Robespierre's "Reign of Terror," Hitler's "Third Reich," and Pol Pots' Khmer Rouge—all fearful and frightful and terrifying—have been unleashed.[87] Just as Adolf Hitler made no secret of his perverted and exclusionary racism, totalitarianism, ethnic cleansing, Aryanization, social Darwinism, anti-Semitism, and anti-Parliamentary democracy, Prime Minister Sheikh Hasina's AL also is openly implementing its policies of Awamization, systematically exterminating and eliminating the political opposition and cleansing the country of political dissent and differences.

What the American historian and documentary filmmaker Ken Burns said (to Christiane Amanpour on CNN) about Donald Trump—that his playbook was rooted in the Nazis, that he was a proto-fascist, appealing to the dark angels rather than the better ones, that he was a demagogue making enemies of the "other" (Muslims, blacks, Latinos, Hispanics/Mexicans, and the US friends and allies in Europe), and that he was a product of the lowest common denominator—could also be said about the Hasina-led AL, which makes enemies of the entire spectrum of the "other" in terms of its political rivals and opponents and which is a product of the lowest common denomination—একাত্তরের চেতনা (the spirit of '71). The Hasina-led AL's use of একাত্তরের চেতনা in a partial, piecemeal, and fragmentary way has led to the spirit of '71 being described as "so-called" and commodified, labeled, and distributed with a product value on it.

According to the official proclamation of independence by the Mujibnagar Government, dated April 10, 1971, the three main goals of the liberation and creation of Bangladesh would be "equality, human dignity and social justice" for the people of Bangladesh, none of which has ever been achieved in Bangladesh or Bangladesh has ever witnessed, to date.[88] The so-called four, actually five ideals/pillars—peace, secularism, socialism, democracy, and nationalism (in this very same order)—were later introduced at the preamble of the infamous 25-year India–Bangladesh Friendship Treaty signed in Dhaka on March 19, 1972.[89] Later, the first ideal of peace was dropped and "the high ideals of nationalism, socialism, democracy and secularism," with the earlier order changed, were introduced into the Constitution of Bangladesh adopted on November 4, 1972.[90]

To the AL, there is a commodification and compartmentalization of the *চেতনা* /the spirit of independence, which, for them is "no more or better than what is specified" in the mere letter of the phrase with a commercial product value and a price tag on it. In actuality, the *চেতনা*, both literally and figuratively, belongs to all Bangladeshis, not just the AL alone. Nobody holds its sole ownership and nobody can/should monopolize its ownership. It is not a privately owned limited company of this or that party only. All Bangladeshis and all their political parties can and do partake of/in the spirit of the liberation, just as they do in/of the spirit of patriotism.

However, they "need more" and "need better" than the literal wording of একাত্তরের চেতনা, which needs to be decoded and deciphered into for its true and larger meaning that squarely lies in (the implementation and actualization of) social justice, political freedom, and economic emancipation, as the years and ages pass by. Unfortunately, the AL keeps beating about the bush, continuously rehashing the code message—emptied of its real content and shrouded with a shallow and narrow and superficial meaning—and making it "as tedious as a twice-told tale/ Vexing the dull ear of a drowsy man," to quote from Shakespeare's play *King John*.

Like Hitler's National Socialist exploitation of Western democracies as being expansionist and imperialist (but otherwise having a culture of social justice through an effective law and order system of their own), Sheikh Hasina's Awami propaganda is falsely portraying the popular pro-liberation (at the same time, pro-unity and pro-collective harmony) democratic opposition as a force of anti-liberation. Hitler and his National Socialist party came to power in early 1933 through a slim election victory over the other equally strong party. It was the concerns over the rise of the Communists and hence a possible civil war, combined with the support of the other powerful groups such as the Conservatives, Catholics, and center-right Democrats that helped Hitler to secure power. Similarly, Hasina's proto-fascist AL came to power as much through the help of the outgoing army-backed interim government and its administrative and law enforcement apparatus as through the national parliamentary election in late 2008, the credibility of which was open to question.

As at the time of Maximilien Robespierre's extremist and radical "Jacobin" Reign of Terror in France, July 1793–July 1794 when he and his henchmen were responsible for the guillotining of many innocent people, there were tens of thousands (over 30,000) who were either killed or terrorized and traumatized at the time of the Awami *Rakkhi-Bahini* around 1972–1975 in Bangladesh.[91]

Similar atmosphere of terror and tension and turmoil and fear and anxiety prevails today under the frightening Hasina regime. Its ruthlessness can only be compared to certain dictatorial regimes in the Middle East, Africa, and Central Asia. All those who belong to the axis of power are above the law, enjoying an egregious culture of impunity; all the rest, top to bottom, are entirely under the law and subject to the law, sometimes being accused of treason and sedition for simply expressing an opinion—political, religious, personal, or otherwise—with the judicial courts themselves being complained about for judging according to certain political affiliations or being under the political pressure or influence. What rule of law can be established when it is normative that there is a selective dispensation of fear or favor and an indiscriminate interference with the judiciary?

Preceded by a murderous Awami লগি ও বৈঠা (poles and sticks and oars) conflict, there has been an all-out, long-haul, predetermined Awami ball-and-chain confrontation, made possible by the largely politicized and Awamized police and RAB. As in the darkening green (as opposed to the echoing green) marking all political and religious dictatorships (to allude to William Blake's short lyric), there have not just been waves after waves but actually relentless and nonstop horror and terror in the form of thousands and thousands of locally as well as nationally targeted গুম ও খুন, widespread হামলা ও মামলা and jail and জুলুম against the political opposition members, including the massacres of the BDR officers (on February 25/26, 2009) and the Hefajote men (on May 5, 2013).[92]

Then came the blacker than black January 5, 2014 when a farcical melodrama in the name of another national parliamentary election was staged. It was unfair, one-sided, and boycotted—which led to the situation of petrol bombs and burnt bodies (of about 170) early in the following year. Logically and grammatically, it was the Awami oppression and suppression, Awami belligerence and recalcitrance, and the Awami lack of compromise with and accommodation of the popular opposition BNP demands (with PM Hasina still remaining at the top and holding all the reins of power) that were responsible for all the violent situations during the last eight or nine years, since 2009. BangaBir Kader Siddiquee, despite the gruesome extrajudicial instances of his own bayonet past, has precisely meant to say this when he held Sheikh Hasina accountable for all the horror and terror that followed that voterless, manipulative, torn, and twisted election.[93]

The iron rule of the Awami regime, shoddy and sluttish as it is, allows no space and respect for the BNP-led opposition. It is responsible for the deadly deadlock with no end in sight as the insane and unscrupulous repetition of 5 January is on, unchecked and unabated, through the local and municipal elections countrywide, all rigged and bought and stolen. Social harmony and national unity have become a rare commodity of dire need, the lack of which has made all kinds of material and economic development in the country (already weighed down not only by the heavy burden of high interest foreign loans but also the all-devouring corruption and all-swallowing politicization) further lackluster, less dynamic, and less to be proud of.[94]

By the Hasina regime's finance minister Abul Mal Abdul Muhith's own admission, a humongous theft, as huge and humongous as the sea, occurred in the banking and other economic sectors.[95] When Muhith himself said that a theft of 4,000 crore taka was not worth paying attention to, it can only be left to anybody's guess how much he meant by a theft as big as a sea.[96] Joseph Allchin writes about "the routine plunder of Bangladesh's financial system, including by some of its purported guardians."[97] Without a democratic and collective togetherness, informed by values, principles, morality, and transparency, all unilateral development, like the 5 January thing, is "as dry as dust," a phrase that the morally and spiritually oriented Victorian thinker and philosopher Thomas Carlyle used to describe the narrowly specialized historians.

At this time in history, is it enough for anyone—human or animal—to have only a steady supply of food if one finds oneself in a burdensome and cumbersome bondage, with the most precious and priceless of all needs—freedom and security—taken away wholly on partisan grounds? Is it enough to have a good diet in a family where the household members are otherwise locked in a bitter fight with each other? The entire nation has been squeezed into an aquarium constantly under tension, intimidation, surveillance, arrests, and remands.

If the 2006–2008 CTG of the triad or tetrad of *Uddins*, unlike the previous CTGs, was the frying pan, the Awami government that succeeded has been the fire for the political opposition, the BNP in particular, and the democracy in the making in general, the condition of both of which is like the charred and burnt bodies placed in the intensive care unit of a hospital. A similar idea was expressed by PM Hasina herself, who said that, through what continues to be her mid- to high-intensity neo-and-near-and-more-than-partially fascist and পৈশাচিক rule with the help of the police and the RAB, she was letting the opposition survive on a high and heavy dose of the chemical called formalin. One who is supportive of and sympathetic to the Awami reign without any rope and rein may euphemistically describe it as an illiberal, guided, hybrid, and controlled democracy, however fantastically flawed it is, totally unacceptable to the general populace. Kamrul Hasan Darpon gives an excellent picture of the dire circumstances the country has landed in due to the regime's iron-clad and iron-fisted democracy.[98]

Under the Hasina government of Bangladesh, since 2009, politics, political bipartisanship, media, and the civil society have taken an unprecedented downturn, from bad to worse, perhaps reaching the worst stage in the history of Bangladesh. These areas of human interaction have grown to become a breeding ground of "earthworm politicism," "mobocracy," "demo-crazy," "dummy-cracy," "demo-crisis," "structural opposition," "projection politics," and cult-like sacred "totem" entities.[99] The country was not without a democratic culture in the past though the electoral process was often marked by allegations of irregularities. However, the government has become increasingly undemocratic, moving far beyond tampering not only with the electoral system itself but also the various rounds of elections, be they local or national, municipal or parliamentary, intending to perpetuate its power and resorting to ruthless suppression and subversion everywhere—in public as well as the "safe" custody of law enforcement agents. Since the freedom of the media and the activity of the political opposition are largely restricted, guided, and monitored, there is a long-felt need for new and fresh ideas about what has been happening in the country since the time this government, regressed into a dug-in regime, came to power in late 2008/early 2009.

Since then the Hasina government started its steamroller rule, forcing the political opposition to be on a reeling and dizzying roller coaster ride. A probing watcher of the political situation of Bangladesh, Dr Saidul Islam of Nanyang Technological University Singapore, has summed up his observations about the regime's appalling distortions, diversions, and deviations in ten points on his Facebook status.[100] So does *DeshKonnya* (দেশকন্যা)[101] Barrister Rumin Farhana in her cutting-edge catalogue of fourteen points exposing the Hasina regime's ill and evil deeds in violation of the constitution.[102] Journalist Minar Rashid provides his list of the damaging and detrimental consequences of the regime's divisive and destructive policies in an equally succinct manner.[103] To Farhana's and Rashid's list, Ranu Chowdhury of the USA adds:

> সংবিধানে বিরোধী নেত্রীকে মাস কে মাস গৃহবন্ধী রেখে ইটের ট্রাক, বালুর ট্রাক, জলকামান ও গোপালী বাহিনী দিয়ে ঘিরে রাখা, পানি বিদ্যুৎ খাবার বন্ধ রাখা, মরিচগুঁড়া মারার বিধান নাই। সংবিধানে বিরোধী দলকে রাজনৈতিক সমাবেশ না করতে দেয়ার বিধান নাই। সংবিধানে বিনা কারণে প্রধান রাজনৈতিক দলের অফিস তল্লাশির নাম তসনস করা এবং বিনা নোটিসে তালাবন্ধ করার বিধান নাই। তবে তালিকা এখানেই শেষ নয়। সব লিখতে গেলে দু ' চার টন কাগজ লাগবোসর্বোপরি, সংবিধানকে গোত্রীয় পাঠ্যপুস্তক বানানোর ব্যাবস্থাও সংবিধানে নাই।. (E-mail of June 11, 2017)

Translated into English, Chowdhury's words mean: there is nothing in the constitution that allows the opposition leader Khaleda to be kept confined to her house/office for months, barricaded by sand-and-cement-and-brick trucks, water cannons, and the *Gopali* police force; nothing in the constitution to have the basic supplies (water, power, and food) to her premises cut off; and nothing there that allows to pepper spray her and her supporters. There is nothing in the constitution that allows not to let the opposition hold any political meetings. There is nothing in the constitution that allows the ransacking and vandalization of the opposition party office in the name of police search and that allows the police to leave it under lock and key for months without notice. The list of subversive ills and illegalities is endless and will take tons of papers to jot down. However, above all, there is nothing in the constitution that allows it to be turned into a party and partisan textbook.

The AL, in power, is entirely dependent, not on free and fair electoral politics and the people's electoral choices and preferences, but on the protection provided by the strict security and intelligence apparatus at multiple level. Directly or indirectly, these are DGFI (Directorate General of Forces Intelligence), NSI (National Security Intelligence), CTIB (Counter Terrorism and Intelligence Bureau), SSF (Special Security Force), SWAT (Special Weapons and Tactics), Formation Commando Company (FCC), DB (Detective Branch of Police), DMP (Dhaka Metropolitan Police), CID (Criminal Investigation Department of Police), RAB, and BGB (Border Guard Bangladesh). However, given the rampant and indiscriminate rapes, murders, and kidnaps on the streets of Bangladesh, "Safety by police escort [of the privileged few]," as Barrister Mainul Hussein said, is "denial of safety to others."[104] Hussein's assertion is proved by the fact that about 32,000 women have been acid-burnt, abused, raped, and mass raped in the last 5 years alone and that about 500 women raped in only six months.[105]

PM Hasina indirectly admitted her government's disconnect with the people when she met with her security details designed and tailored to become only her own, her party's, her family's, and her government's politicized "messiah" savior.[106] Far from practicing parliamentary democracy and democratic politics and far from sanctioning inclusive and participatory elections, Sheikh Hasina makes loud but empty claims about democracy, which she defines her way, a way of extremely limited and illiberal democracy, at the expense of the rights and freedoms of the people as represented by the opposition BNP and its allies. From the seat of democratically illegitimate power and control, Sheikh Hasina says whatever suits her purely partisan interest and whatever she finds convenient to say, no matter how crude and coarse and ludicrous it is. In reality, her party, the AL, may not even be bagging a quarter of the votes from the eligible voters in any free and fair general election if it were held today.[107]

That is what the former VC of Dhaka University Professor Emajuddin Ahmed correctly claimed.[108] The local and municipal elections, even after having been rigged and bought and stolen, one after another, are an undeniable proof. In a credible and inclusive election at the local or national level, free from coercion, intimidation, torture, and persecution by the police and their accomplices in thugs, Honda-goonda hoodlums and hooligans, and the widely politicized civil administration, the AL would not only lose but lose lamentably and pitiably, to be trashed and trounced and routed. Still the AL petulantly and preposterously claims, জনগণ আমাদের সাথে আছে (the people/masses are with us), going around repeating only its vapid and vacuous political rights while dismissing, dismantling, destroying, and devouring the just ones of the opposition.

The funny thing is that all parties—ruling or not ruling, in or out of power, big or small, mid-size, dime size, penny size, irrespective of size, or with the idea of size not applicable at all—indiscriminately claim that people are with them, even though they themselves know that their assertion is not true and that it is a hypocritical hoax. One may draw the analogy between the truly democratic, Asian economic tiger South Korea, that is, officially, "Republic of Korea," and the poor and fascist North Korea, which, far from truth, baselessly and bombastically calls itself "*Democratic* People's Republic of Korea," ruled by the same family "kingship" for seventy years under the banner of the so-called Workers' Party, which spends all the money on the military bureaucracy and which is far from catering to the needs of the workers living a subhuman life. Until its reunification with the free and capitalist Federal Republic of Germany (West Germany) in 1990, communist and undemocratic East Germany, in a ruse, used to call itself, from 1949, German *Democratic* Republic (GDR), which was a lie.

Although Joseph Stalin claimed to be a socialist or communist, his was "a brutal dictatorship, built upon a cult of personality and enforced by a reign of terror." In the aftermath of the French Revolution in 1789, there were many such as John Reeves who (unlike the moderate to democratic minded Levelers of the English Civil War/Oliver Cromwell time in the 1650s) were the loyalist lackeys of the conservative government against democratic reforms, but, as a sabotage propaganda, they also called for the "Preservation of Liberty and Property against Republicans and Levelers," then the largest political organization in Britain. In Bangladesh also, those who killed and have been killing democracy call for "democracy"—their distorted version of democracy—to be preserved and upheld, at best as a camouflage, just as those who have been fighting for true and real democracy.

Always under the strict three-to-four-tier police protection as a consequence of complete disconnect with the masses (except in a narrowly partisan way), the AL keeps saying that জনগন বিরোধী দলের আন্দোলন সংগ্রামের সাথে নাই তারা এই আন্দোলন সংগ্রাম প্রত্যখ্যান করেছে (people are not with the opposition movement; they have rejected the opposition cause). If the opposition is allowed to hold meetings, assemblies, processions, and demonstrations (from which it is often barred and kept at bay by the AL's messiah police force) and participate in a level-playing field inclusive election, the AL could see, with just one eye, if the overwhelming majority are with them or the opposition BNP.

The true fighters of democracy are calling for democracy to be revived, restored, rescued, and retrieved. They are struggling to save whatever traces of it are left. The killers of democracy also are surreptitiously calling for the same, to deviate, distract, and confuse the people, keeping the entire spectrum of the popular political opposition out of the equation, forcing them to end up either in dark dungeon or being brutally beaten up by the police. If one may use the rustic analogy, the owner of the house is looking for the intruder, trespasser, or the thief, shouting, "Where's the thief? Where's the thief?" To save himself by cleverly tricking the owner, the thief also shouts the same as he finds his way out and runs away. Both the killers of democracy and the upholders of democracy ab/use the analogy of the glass being half full or half empty according to their convenience.

The opposition BNP also claims the same, probably with more justification than any other party. During the last eight to ten years, BNP has been struggling as the voice of popular dissent, only to be crushed and crippled and trampled by the politicized and politically criminalized police boots and bullets and batons. Whatever it does or demands is only a তামাশা (stupid, illogical, and mindless activity) to the dictatorial and disastrous Hasina government. Naturally, the last decade has been a time of consuming tension, anarchy, insecurity, lawlessness, terror, torture, arrests, remands, forced confessions, persecutions, and disappearances for the people in general and the political opposition BNP in particular.

The fact is that the people of Bangladesh are divided more than ever with only a slim and thin portion of them, by clear and common perception, in favor of the royally and monarchically ruling AL, which continues to suffer seriously from aberrations and irregularities, and a chronic lack of credibility and legitimacy. By clear contrast, the overwhelming majority are in favor of the peace-and-freedom loving BNP and its allies, who are all patriotically, democratically, and nationalistically imbued and inspired, looking forward to a return of an effective parliamentary system of government (or even a Presidential form of government in view of the present useless and ineffective parliament), reinstatement of the Hasina regime cancelled (interim stopgap) caretaker system of government, and also the reestablishment of the supreme judicial council to deal with the matters arising concerning the impeachment, if necessary, of the supreme court justices.

Notes

1. According to Odhikar, a great human rights organization, 388 people have been victims of enforced disappearance in the last 8 years and 7 months of the Hasina regime: http://www.dailynayadiganta.com/detail/news/248632. Since 2009, over a thousand oppositionists have been abducted and/or killed:
http://www.dailynayadiganta.com/detail/news/248472. Twenty-four (24) thousand politically repressive lawsuits against the BNP alone: http://mzamin.com/article.php?mzamin=73677;
http://www.mzamin.com/article.php?mzamin=73608;
http://www.dailynayadiganta.com/detail/news/234992;
http://primenewsbd.com/news/110290;

http://www.jugantor.com/first-page/2017/01/07/91153;
http://www.poriborton.com/capital/30557;
https://www.facebook.com/jiblurahman78/?ref=bookmarks;
http://www.dailynayadiganta.com/detail/printcopy/212747

2. http://www.dailysangram.com/post/265755;
http://worldbangla.com/2017/01/08/59456;
http://www.dailysangram.com/post/265907
3. http://www.economist.com/blogs/banyan/2014/01/electoral-farce-bangladesh;
http://viewsweek.com/viewsweek-exclusive/bangladeshs-electoral-farce;
http://viewsweek.com/viewsweek-exclusive/2281
4. A total of 284 people disappeared/were abducted in the last four years, 88 in 2016 alone: http://www.jugantor.com/online/national/2016/12/29/35162/;
https://www.hrw.org/video-photos/photo-essay/2017/07/06/enforced-disappearances-bangladesh;
https://www.hrw.org/news/2017/07/07/no-bangladesh-truth-not-smear-campaign; for more HR information on the secret killings in Bangladesh: https://goo.gl/R8bcdt (or, file:///C:/Users/jkhan/Downloads/HR%20Bulletin%208.pdf);
http://bangladeshpolitico.blogspot.com/2016/10/bangladeshs-enforced-disappearances-2016.html; http://bangladeshpolitico.blogspot.com/2016/10/bangladesh-disappearances-2016-still.html
5. https://www.youtube.com/watch?v=9vwkOcyNrjI;
http://www.dailyinqilab.com/article/65979
6. http://mynewsbd.net/?p=5989; http://mynewsbd.net/?p=5500
7. http://www.srilankaguardian.org/2012/04/bengal-tigers-in-r-cage.html
8. http://www.aljazeera.com/news/2016/09/bangladesh-accused-kneecapping-opposition-members-160929110934409.html; http://www.banglatribune.com/foreign/news/144275
9. https://www.youtube.com/watch?v=7OKT2XkLnBs&feature=youtu.be;
http://www.kolkata24x7.com/special-interview-with-bangladeshi-intellectual-badruddin-umar.html;
http://www.jugantor.com/online/opinion/2017/06/11/49271/
10. See the report about the Indian conspiracy behind at newsbd7.com/main/detail/2737;
https://in.news.yahoo.com/dhaka-cafe-attack-weapons-used-074455331.html;
http://www.kaagoj.com/unknown-facts-behind-gulshan-massacre
11. Hindu nationalist (Medical) Dr Kalidas Baiddya, who was once a trusted adviser to Sheikh Mujib, goes back to Mujib's Tungipara and Kolkata Islamia College (now Moulana Azad College) days during the mid-1940s and provides a damaging picture of Mujib's violent anti-Hindu and pro-Pakistani involvement under the influence/instigation of his political guru/master Suhrawardy. See Kalidas Baiddya, বাঙালীর মুক্তিযুদ্ধে অন্তরালের শেখ মুজিব (Kolkata: Karmakar Book Stall, 2005). For a review of the book and for interesting excerpts from it, click: http://www.muldharabd.com/?p=2039

12 Fifty-four opposition supporters have been killed during that violence for three days. See the daily Amar Desh of October 28, 2015. https://www.youtube.com/watch?v=QqiF5Pky65Q; http://youtube.com/watch?v=jYKch23wj-E; http://youtube.com/watch?v=W9pfPeKONYY&feature=related

13. For the Wikileaks reports and Dr Tuhin Malik's comments that suggest the involvement of the RAW and the Bangladesh government in the BDR massacre, see: http://bdrmutinyexposed.com/?p=353;
http://bdrmutinyexposed.com/?p=407;
https://bangladesh2075.files.wordpress.com/2011/02/bdr4.pdf;
https://www.theguardian.com/world/2009/feb/28/bangladesh-soldiers-rebellion-mutiny; http://www.natun-bd.net/newsdetail/detail/49/286604

14. According to *Odhikar*, a Bangladeshi Human Rights Organization, the number of Hefajote deaths was 61. "Although Hefajat claimed that 2,000 of its leaders and activists were killed in the incident, the government's death figure stood at only 13, including three policemen. Hefajat could not provide names and addresses in support of its claim." http://www.thedailystar.net/Hefajat-e-Islam-Shapla-Chattar-rally-2013-Islamists

15. http://www.dailydinkal.net/2016/12/24/31108.php; http://www.bd-pratidin.com/first-page/2017/02/11/206997

16. Badrul is an Awami Chatro League cadre, who, like the other Chatro League cadres' violent attack on the innocent Viswajit, for example, made a horrific and horrible machete attack on Khadija. For Badrul-type abominable and reprehensible actions, synonymous with the ruling Awami repression and oppression, visit: https://youtu.be/2dEN9T8vAmo

17. http://www.dailysangram.com/post/256820-; http://www.bdface.net/newsdetail/detail/200/253643; http://www.prothom-alo.com/bangladesh/article/1009263/; https://www.dailyinqilab.com/details/45961/

18. www.dailynayadiganta.com/detail/news/164968

19. During the massacre of Irish Easter uprising, about 500 were killed on both sides—English and Irish, but mostly Irish rebels and civilians, and nearly 5,500 were taken prisoners, while many were wounded. During the Jallianwala Bagh massacre, about a thousand of nonviolent Punjabi Sikh protesters were killed. During the Peterloo massacre, the English cavalry put down a protest by killing about fifteen or more protesters from among 60,000 to 80,000 who had gathered at St Peter's Field, Manchester, to demand the reform of parliamentary representation.

20 Dr Rezwan Siddiqui at: http://www.dailynayadiganta.com/detail/news/209640; Dr Mina Farah's column at: http://m.dailynayadiganta.com/detail/news/138685; https://www.youtube.com/watch?v=yaeDePaSXpA&feature=youtu.be; Akhtar Mahmud at https://deshbhabona.com/স্পটলাইট/2017/03/26/16/14

21. http://www.bbc.com/bengali/news-39495128;
http://amar-desh24.com/bangla/index.php/details/nationalnews/7254;

https://m.youtube.com/watch?feature=youtu.be&v=NTpCL35GNGI; http://sverigesradio.se/sida/artikel.aspx?programid=83&artikel=6665807; http://www.prothom-alo.com/bangladesh/article/1134276
22. www.bdface.net/blog/blogdetail/detail/3525/abdur…/78078
23. http://www.bbc.com/bengali/news/2016/08/160830_bangladesh_forced_disappearance; http://rtnbd.net/localpolitics/28721; https://www.youtube.com/watch?v=mc6soyJDKYQ
24. http://www.dailynayadiganta.com/detail/news/175531
25. http://newsorgan24.com/detail/16397; For possible Indian involvement, visit: http://newsbd7.com/main/detail/3067; http://www.bd-desh.net/newsdetail/detail/112/225362; http://newsorgan24.com/detail/16362; https://www.facebook.com/amra.shadinjati?fref=nf
26. http://newagebd.net/179560/country-faces-serious-political-crisis-speakers/
27. http://tlhrc.house.gov/hearing_notice.asp?id=1309
28. http://www.humanrights.asia/news/ahrc-news/AHRC-STM-066-2016; http://newagebd.net/227890/bangladesh-in-deep-political-crisis-ahrc/
29. http://www.telegraphindia.com/1151203/jsp/opinion/story_56299.jsp#
30. http://www.ft.com/cms/s/0/337c285e-0c67-11e6-9456-444ab5211a2f.html#
31. http://www.thedailystar.net/op-ed/politics/homeopaths-guide-police-brutality-bangladesh-205180; http://www.prothom-alo.com/bangladesh/article/740857/; http://thedailynewnation.com/print-a-news/81566/19-juba-dal-jcd-men-sent-to-jail.html
32. www.mzamin.com/details.php?mzamin=MTA0Mjk1&sMQ==#
33 For their views about Indian hegemony and Indian colonization of Bangladesh, see: https://www.dailyinqilab.com/article/76826; http://newsbd7.com/main/detail/2935; http://www.newsbd7.com/main/detail/2936; http://newsbd7.com/main/detail/2928; http://newsbd7.com/main/detail/2929; https://www.youtube.com/watch?v=OmR4Wlhkw3w&feature=youtu.be; https://youtu.be/OmR4Wlhkw3w; https://www.facebook.com/qamrulpage/posts/1126063257417514:0; http://www.dailyinqilab.com/details/48548/
34. See *Sudheer Sharma at* https://blog.com.np/2013/01/31/the-pain-of-losing-a-nation-story-of-lhendup-dorji-and-sikkim/. Also see the article by Mohammad Mustafizur Rahman on how India annexed Sikkim: http://www.bdface.net/newsdetail/detail/49/247898 & the one by Advocate Taimur Alam Khandoker: www.dailynayadiganta.com/detail/news/160745. Also see Shaikh Mahadi's article on the Nehru Doctrine and Hyderabad, Sikkim, and Bangladesh at http://imbdblog.com/?p=1395#comment-853. Also see Khodeza Begum's "United Bengal/United India" article at https://groups.google.com/forum/#!topic/bangladesh-progressives/mgR24VVOQQI

35. http://www.bbc.com/bengali/news-38691282;
http://www.bdnewsmix.com/bn/2017/01/20/25267;
http://www.jugantor.com/online/national/2017/01/21/37330
36. http://www.newsbangla.net/newsdetail/detail/200/298773; E-mail of 8 April 2017 through NABC.
37. http://southasiajournal.net/india-bangladesh-defense-pact-honey-mixed-with-poison-for-a-friend; http://www.dailynayadiganta.com/detail/news/211153; http://southasiajournal.net/headless-democracy-heartless-neighbor; http://newsorgan24.com/detail/25023
38. http://rtnbd.net/opinion/32398
39. http://viewsweek.com/viewsweek-exclusive/india-restaging-sikkim-saga-bangladesh/
40. https://www.foreignaffairs.com/articles/united-states/friends-without-benefits
41. https://www.facebook.com/মিনা-ফারাহ-683177775087205; http://www.primenewsbd.com/index.php?page=details&nc=4&news_id=108821
42. http://www.jugantor.com/online/national/2017/04/10/44366;
https://www.dailyinqilab.com/article/74127; http://www.newsbangla.net/newsdetail/detail/200/299031; http://www.prothom-alo.com/bangladesh/article/1141011; http://viewsweek.com/south-asia/bangladesh/anger-bangladesh-defense-mous-india
43. http://www.mzamin.com/article.php?mzamin=61342
44. http://www.daily-sun.com/post/92596/Opposition-followers-being-denied-justice; http://www.thedailystar.net/police-under-political-control-now-akbar-ali-53740; http://www.sheershanewsbd.com/2015/11/20/104450
45. http://www.voanews.com/a/enforced-disappearances-rise-in-bangladesh/3574161.html; http://www.bdface.net/newsdetail/detail/200/243611; http://www.dailynay-adiganta.com/detail/printcopy/50933
46. https://www.facebook.com/photo.php?fbid=10206582442540613&set=a.4583013854218.56615330.1258120529&type=3&theater
47. http://newagebd.net/236549/jails-overcrowded-3-times-capacity-hm; http://newagebd.net/235491/145-militants-among-11684-people-held-4-days/; http://www.aljazeera.com/news/2016/04/jails-overburdened-political-prisoners-160411071226494.html; http://www.amadershomoys.com/unicode/2016/04/11/97048.htm#; http://www.dai-lysangram.com/news_details.php?news_id=222535;
http://www.bd-pratidin.com/first-page/2015/11/17/110024
48. http://johnpilger.com/articles/the-prison-that-is-bangladesh; http://www.theguard-ian.com/commentisfree/2013/dec/15/prison-bangladesh-moudud-ahmed
49. (A) Over 80% women are victims of physical abuse and persecution: http://www.prothom-alo.com/bangladesh/article/993219; www.ittefaq.com.bd/cap-ital/2016/10/03/86677.html; www.mzamin.com/article.php?mzamin=34144; (B) One hundred and fifty people were killed in crossfire and law enforcement agencies' custody in the last nine months, reports Ain o Salsih Kendra (ASK): http://www.thedailystar.net/backpage/150-killed-crossfire-custody-9-months-1292344;

(C) About the same number of people and children have been killed and raped in September 2016 alone: http://www.amadershomoy.biz/unicode/2016/10/02/179559.htm. About 1,050 women raped in 2016 alone: http://www.thedailystar.net/country/1050-women-raped-2016-1342177; (D) For other estimates of rapes, murder, and extrajudicial crossfire killings during the month of August 2016 alone, click http://www.amadershomoy.biz/unicode/2016/09/01/167174.htm; (E) http://www.shampratikdeshkal.com/special-reports/2016/05/01/23292; (F) http://www.dw.com/bn/১১৫-জনের-কোনো-খোঁজ-নেই-পাওয়া-গেছে-৩২টি-লাশ/a-18895386; (G) http://goo.gl/7CYfba; http://www.dailydinkal.net/2015/11/20/20924.php#; (H) http://newsshomoy.com/bn/2015/11/17/149292.html;(I) http://www.bd-pratidin.com/home/printnews/110024; (J) http://www.dailynayadiganta.com/detail/news/69284; (K) http://www.amardeshonline.com/pages/details/2015/11/10/310373; (L) http://newagebd.net/173677/yet-another-govt-clampdown-on-opposition-before-elections/; (M) http://www.sheershanewsbd.com/2015/11/11/103328; (N) http://www.thedailystar.net/backpage/1500-held-two-days-169606; (O) http://newagebd.net/173905/85-bnp-jamaat-men-among-155-held-in-2-districts/; (P) http://www.sheershanewsbd.com/2015/11/10/103199; (Q) http://newagebd.net/173665/custodial-torture-and-death-must-end/; (R) About 300 died in road accidents in September 2016 alone: http://www.dailynayadiganta.com/detail/news/158828

50. (A) http://www.daily-sun.com/arcprint/details/91890/Trials-of-777-child-murder-cases-make-little-headway/2015-11-18; (B) http://newagebd.net/179319/abducted-minor-girl-found-dead-in-narayanganj/; (C) http://www.daily-sun.com/printversion/details/60653/Brutality-rules-as-2-more-minors-tortured-in-Satkhira
51. http://www.dailynayadiganta.com/detail/news/69286#; and Uri Avnery's article at http://newagebd.net/180607/there-is-no-such-thing-as-international-terrorism/
52. http://www.dailynayadiganta.com/detail/news/73998#
53. http://newagebd.net/166508/where-are-you-when-we-need-you-jean-paul-sartre/#
54. http://www.poetryfoundation.org/harriet/2009/11/poetry-makes-nothing-happen-or-does-it/
55. http://www.amardeshonline.com/pages/details/2015/10/27/308181#
56. http://www.priyo.com/photo/2015/03/08/137576.html
57. http://thehill.com/blogs/congress-blog/foreign-policy/243384-bangladesh-in-crisis. In his blog, Cadman quotes Rep. Matt Salmon of Arizona and Professor Ali Riaz of Illinois State University as saying the current political unrest "may lead to a further breakdown of order that could open space for Islamic militancy or for the military to take power" and "the international community cannot continue to have a 'Business-as-Usual' approach while the country is slowly descending into a situation which has strong potential for engendering a prolonged conflict."
58. http://www.sheershanewsbd.com/2015/06/18/85161
59. http://somoy.net/politics/48660

60. The sitting Chief Justice S. K. Sinha's statement (http://bdnews24.com/bangladesh/2016/01/20/writing-judgments-after-retirement-illegal-chief-justice-sinha) suggests that his predecessor Khairul Hoque's controversial verdict in light of which Sheikh Hasina cancelled the CTG was illegal.
61. Apart from the media archives of those days, visit: http://ekhon.net/politics/53454; http://www.dailydinkal.net/2016/12/26/31134.php; http://www.jugantor.com/online/country-news/2016/12/25/34821; http://newsbd7.com/main/detail/2927; http://newagebd.net/219230/al-leader-held-with-arms-in-tangail/.
62. http://www.jugantor.com/online/politics/2016/12/13/33726; http://www.newser24.com/2016/12/13/25-160/
63. Pease refer to the book edited by Professor Abul Barkat, *An Inquiry into Causes and Consequences of Deprivation of Hindu Minorities in Bangladesh Through the Vested Property Act* (Dhaka, PRIP Trust, 2000): https://groups.yahoo.com/neo/groups/Shetubondhon/conversations/topics/5776
64. http://www.ittefaq.com.bd/politics/2016/01/25/52641.html; http://www.now-bd.com/2016/01/25/478342.htm; http://www.daily-sun.com/post/109852. For Suranjit's 70 crore কালো বিড়াল contexts, visit: http://video.genfb.com/373581419690571; video.genfb.com/1344678918925453; https://www.facebook.com/video/video.php?v=780489652099823; https://www.facebook.com/video/video.php?v=722585861229197
65. http://www.thedailystar.net/country/lower-court-judges-conduct-time-gazette-extended-1375750; http://www.thedailystar.net/frontpage/end-dual-rule-judiciary-1307422
66. http://www.sheershanewsbd.com/2015/11/27/105294; http://www.sheershanewsbd.com/2015/11/28/105499.
67. http://newagebd.net/202528/police-not-any-party-force-kamal-hossain/; http://www.thedailystar.net/city/everyone-not-angels-judiciary-cj-1203172; http://newagebd.net/217043/none-get-justice-in-the-existing-judicial-systemcj/
68. For Roni, see the daily *Amader Shomoy*, June 10, 2015.
69. According to CPD, during the last ten years, the average illicit financial flows stood at $5.588 billion a year, with the highest being in 2013, when a staggering $9.666 billion flew out of the country. The third highest amount, $6.44 billion, slipped out of the country in 2008. http://www.prothom-alo.com/economy/article/897736; astounding money laundering in the amount of Tk 4,423 crore (550.85 million Swiss franc): http://www.thedailystar.net/frontpage/deposits-bangladeshis-tk-4423cr-1248571; http://www.anandabazar.com/bangladesh-news/india-and-america-get-the-benefit-of-smugled-money-from-bangladesh-1.379400; http://www.nytimes.com/2016/04/12/opinion/bangladeshs-other-banking-scam.html?smprod=nytcore-iphone&smid=nytcore-iphone-share&_r=0. For Sajeeb W Joy's alleged involvement in financial scandal, click: http://www.bddesh.net/blog/blogdetail/detail/1659/hassanali/11889#.Vz8Xl1QrK1s Accountability of Public

Officials: $300m in wild goose chase by social media on http://www.weeklyholiday.net/Homepage/Pages/UserHome.aspx. The BNP leader Khaleda Zia raised questions about the US $300 million in the account of the PM Sheikh Hasina's son Sajeeb Wajed Joy: https://www.justice.gov/sites/default/files/usao-sdny/legacy/2015/03/25/Lustyik%20Et%20Al.Indictment.pdf (Section 9).

70. http://www.thedailystar.net/12-ex-armed-forces-officers-barred-from-taking-food-to-khaleda-65957
71. https://www.facebook.com/photo.php?fbid=1735421156680012&set=p.1735421156680012&type=3&theater
72. http://www.thestatesman.com/opinion/tragedy-of-bangladesh-1482361992.html
73. http://www.bd-pratidin.com/editorial/2016/09/19/170734
74. http://www.voanews.com/content/bangladesh-cyber-expert-becomes-symbol-for-forced-disappearances/3266604.html
75. http://www.jugantor.com/online/national/2017/01/05/35793; http://www.banglanews24.com/national/news/bd/545099.details; http://bangladesh.shafaqna.com/BD/BD/1543659
76. https://www.dailyinqilab.com/article/74469
77. Khodeza Begum's "United Bengal/United India" article at https://groups.google.com/forum/#!topic/bangladesh-progressives/mgR24VVOQQI. Also see the article by Mohammad Mustafizur Rahman on how India annexed Sikkim: http://www.bdface.net/newsdetail/detail/49/247898. Also see Shaikh Mahadi's article on the Nehru Doctrine and Hyderabad, Sikkim, and Bangladesh at http://imbdblog.com/?p=1395#comment-853. Also see Khodeza Begum's "United Bengal/United India" article at https://groups.google.com/forum/#!topic/bangladesh-progressives/mgR24VVOQQI
78. http://www.bbc.com/bengali/news-38691282; http://www.bdnewsmix.com/bn/2017/01/20/25267; http://www.jugantor.com/online/national/2017/01/21/37330
79. https://www.dailyinqilab.com/article/75822
80. http://www.aljazeera.com/indepth/opinion/2016/07/divisive-politics-set-stage-dhaka-attack-160704063505698.html
81. Twenty-one people killed in June 2016 alone: https://www.youtube.com/watch?v=sKcispAEl4M; two hundred twenty people kidnapped and killed in the last three and half years: http://www.sheershanewsbd.com/2016/05/18/128112; http://www.amardeshonline.com/pages/details/2016/05/18/336456. In April 2016 alone, eighty people were killed, thirty-four raped, and twenty-two children killed: http://www.jagonews24.com/national/news/96634/. On an average ten people are killed every day: http://www.dhakatribune.com/bangladesh/2016/apr/28/ten-people-being-killed-each-day-bangladesh; about 1,100 children killed and 1,000 children raped in four years: http://www.banglatribune.com/others/news/100873/; 350% increase in child rape in the last sixteen months: http://www.bdsangbad.com/details.php?id=21234. Nearly one thousand and five hundred killed in about three and half months: http://www.kalerkantho.com/

print-edition/first-page/2016/04/23/350498; nearly one thousand killed in the first three months of 2016 alone without the perpetrators apprehended: http://www.prothom-alo.com/bangladesh/article/833293/; Fifteen hundred dead bodies on the streets of Dhaka: http://www.banglatribune.com/national/news/85015/; 321 children killed in thirteen months: http://bangla.samakal.net/2016/02/18/193958/; forty children killed in almost as many days: http://www.amadershomoys.com/unicode/2016/02/20/72358.htm#; ninety children killed in two years by their own parents: http://goo.gl/ZRZGqy; nearly 26,000 killed in only six years, according to the government police source, excluding the staggering number of forced kidnappings or disappearances, still unaccounted for: http://www.amardeshonline.com/pages/details/2016/03/04/326046#. Since the government police estimate in such cases is pushed lower than the actual number, the correct number of the killed will far exceed 26,000. Twenty five killed in one single day: http://www.amardeshonline.com/pages/details/2016/03/05/326136#; http://www.thedailystar.net/backpage/2015-tough-year-minorities-786913; fourteen killed by the police in two months: http://www.amadershomoys.com/unicode/2016/04/06/94650.htm; http://www.shampratikdeshkal.com/special-reports/2016/05/01/23292

82. http://www.ft.com/cms/s/0/337c285e-0c67-11e6-9456-444ab5211a2f.html#
83. http://journal.georgetown.edu/bangladesh-democracy-under-attack/; http://www.thedailystar.net/country/bangladesh-fails-maintain-control-over-security-forces-us-1209154; http://www.bbc.com/bengali/news/2016/04/160414_us_report_on_bd_human_rights; http://www.theguardian.com/commentisfree/2016/apr/08/the-guardian-view-on-the-bangladesh-history-debate-distorted-by-politics
84. https://www.youtube.com/watch?v=LTBa_WHsSX4
85. In April 2016, an exclusive write-up by David Bergman in the Indian website *The Wire* revealed that a "Suspicious Activity Report" (SAR) covering a transaction of US$300 million recorded in a memo of the United States Federal Bureau of Investigation (FBI) was linked to Wazed. But the court documents did not provide any further information about the reference to "US$300 million." For details, see: https://en.wikipedia.org/wiki/Sajeeb_Wazed; http://thewire.in/30447/exclusive-us-court-dismissed-claim-of-plot-to-injure-bangladesh-pm-son/
86. http://www.jerusalemonline.com/news/world-news/the-israeli-connection/bangladeshi-government-attempts-to-bribe-israeli-official-24757
87. The twelve years of Hitler's National Socialist rule, from 1933 to 1945, are referred to as the "Third Reich."
88. http://www.docstrangelove.com/uploads/1971/sbbk/documents/Proclamation%201971_M_Dalil_Vol_03_MMR.pdf
89. http://www.commonlii.org/in/other/treaties/INTSer/1972/6.html
90. http://bdlaws.minlaw.gov.bd/print_sections_all.php?id=367
91. According to Wikipedia, "Jatiyo Rakkhi Bahini turned into a monster within a very short time. Though it was formed as an auxiliary law-enforcement, similar to SWAT [Special Weapons and Tactics teams in the US police], it started misusing its rifles

… The history of Jatiyo Rakkhi Bahini is a history of brutality. The range of the brutality increased day by day. It was a source of fear to individuals. Especially from the last days of 1973, atrocities of Jatiyo Rakkhi Bahini crossed the limit. They were protected by the top level of the government which made them desperate … Professor Ghulam Murshid compared it with Gestapo, while Anthony Mascarenhas said that there were a few differences between Hitler's Nazis and Mujib's Jatiyo Rakkhi Bahini." Mascarenhas, in his book *Bangladesh: A Legacy of Blood* (1986), wrote, "The Jatiyo Rakkhi Bahini, which, roughly translated, means National Security [Defense] Force, was a para-military force whose members had to take oaths of personal loyalty to Mujib. Despite its high-sounding name, it was a sort of private army of bully boys not far removed from Nazi Brown Shirts." Mascarenhas said, "… the nights were made hideous by the wailing of women whose husbands and sons had been dragged away on Home Minister Mansoor Ali's orders. These unfortunate people 'just vanished'." Visit https://en.wikipedia.org/wiki/Jatiya_Rakkhi_Bahini

92. http://chairmanbd.blogspot.com.au/2013/05/mass-killing-on-protesters-in-dhaka-at.html
93. http://www.jugantor.com/online/politics/2016/12/13/33726; http://www.newser24.com/2016/12/13/25-160/
94. http://www.dainikamadershomoy.com/todays-paper/firstpage/57598; http://www.prothom-alo.com/economy/article/708385; http://www.prothom-alo.com/bangladesh/article/399673; http://www.bdnatun.net/newsdetail/detail/200/270779; http://www.prothom-alo.com/bangladesh/article/1018667; http://www.amaderbudhbar.com/2016/07/27/; http://www.jugantor.com/online/national/2016/08/03/21007; http://www.prothom-alo.com/economy/article/897736; http://www.jugantor.com/online/national/2016/11/19/31180; http://www.jugantor.com/online/national/2016/12/26/34862; http://bangla.samakal.net/2017/01/09/261575
95. http://www.jugantor.com/online/economics/2016/06/07/15412; http://newagebd.net/234298/muhith-admits-huge-corruption-banking-financial-sectors/; http://www.prothom-alo.com/bangladesh/article/943927/
96. A bitter parody of Muhith went viral on social media: http://www.amadershomoy.biz/unicode/2017/06/29/260101.htm
97. http://www.nytimes.com/2016/04/12/opinion/bangladeshs-other-banking-scam.html?smprod=nytcore-iphone&smid=nytcore-iphone-share&_r=0. The BNP leader Khaleda Zia raised questions about the US $300 million in the account of the PM Sheikh Hasina's son Sajeeb Wajed Joy: https://www.justice.gov/sites/default/files/usao-sdny/legacy/2015/03/25/Lustyik%20Et%20Al.Indictment.pdf (Section 9).
98. https://www.dailyinqilab.com/article/62100
99. See Syed Serajul Islam, "Bangladesh: Challenges of Democracy and Good Governance," a paper presented at Southwestern Social Sciences Conference at San Antonio, Texas, April 5, 2014. Dr. Islam is Chair and Professor of Political Science at Lakehead University, Canada.

100. https://www.facebook.com/abu.ulfat/posts/10201998632580909
101. The term or the title means "Daughter of the Land," self-coined, which occurs throughout the book whenever the names of Farhana or Papia come up.
102. http://www.mzamin.com/article.php?mzamin=69325
103. http://bangladeshchronicle.net/2017/01/102773/
104. http://www.amardeshonline.com/pages/details/2016/02/06/322330#; http://thedailynewnation.com/print-a-news/82568/safety-by-police-escort-is-denial-of-safety-to-others.html
105. http://www.banglatribune.com/others/news/87579/; http://www.amadershomoy.biz/unicode/2016/06/30/134760.htm
106. http://newagebd.net/140189/pm-says-security-shouldnt-detach-pm-from-people/
107. http://www.thedailystar.net/politics/bnp-win-80-seats-gayeshwar-182293;http://www.thedailystar.net/politics/bnp-win-80-seats-gayeshwar-182293; http://newagebd.net/175279/al-wont-secure-30-seats-in-a-fair-election-bnp/; http://www.dailynayadiganta.com/detail/news/69288#s; http://www.sheershanewsbd.com/2015/10/08/99276
108. http://www.amardeshonline.com/pages/printnews/2015/09/09/301219

2

Democracy and Development

Development With Corruption and Without Democracy

African-American poet Maya Angelou took the title of her autobiographical novel, *I Know Why the Caged Bird Sings* (1969) from the fellow African-American poet Paul Laurence Dunbar's poem "Sympathy." Both works are about the various kinds of sufferings: prejudice, racism, discrimination, injustice, inequality, and physical and sexual harassment. The caged bird sings not out of joy but in hope and prayer for joy, beating the bondage bars with its sore bosom. The Hasina government's dry development drum—the way it is, less than half empty, defective, dented, bereft of common, communal, and collective amity and harmony, much of it being mostly on paper, limited to nefarious propaganda, gaudy showoff, ceremonial opening, and much-hyped photo session inauguration—and, much worse, with the entire opposition choked and chained and shackled—may be likened to a "free," yet mortally stricken and wounded bird. This is exactly what is claimed by the main and popular political opposition of the country, BNP (Bangladesh Nationalist Party).[1]

The BNP's Secretary General Mirza Fakhrul Islam Alamgir gave, in its party council in March 2016, a horrific picture of the Awami torture and persecution of its people, including himself, claiming that 502 of them were killed, 223 abducted, about 4,000 seriously wounded, nearly 75,000 jailed, 430,000 accused of/charged with 24,000 politically motivated "criminal" offences, and 50 given life sentences in false and fake court cases.[2] "Bangladesh opposition [BNP] says 300 men killed, disappeared in a month."[3] According to another report, 440 people killed in 2015 in politically perpetrated crimes; 267 abducted the same year; 337 opposition members seriously wounded or maimed; over 21,000 political lawsuits against over 416,000 people; and about 18,000 imprisoned. Every day, every week, every month it is the same story as that of the "Top Ten Murders by the Awami League."[4]

On the other hand, the fatefully boxed-in democracy in Sheikh Hasina's Bangladesh, severely suffering from deep deficit on legitimacy and credibility, may be likened to a caged bird. If that is so, how long can the "free" bird of her dingy development, dull and drab, enjoy its freedom with mirth and merriment while its complementary and cohabiting companion is still in the cage? Won't its plumes get further "bruised" and "blast-beruffled," only to make it collapse and fall on its face prematurely? Also, isn't it more important to address the current and more contemporary ills and evils, nearer to the time, on the basis of the rule of law and the exigencies of political and national unity and stability before asking for a new hope, which will be there anyway, naturally? However, to challenge the wrongs is more challenging, but to do so is to provide a surer ground and guarantee for the real optimistic spirit to fly with reasons.

Cultivation of democratic culture has become impossible in today's Bangladesh. It is in its last and seventh stage under the quite boastful and often bellicose, bullying, belligerent, and deeply and darkly BNP*hobic* Hasina. According to Shakespeare's philosophical Jacques's "All the world's a stage" speech in *As You Like It*, the mortally weak seventh stage is described as "second childishness and mere oblivion / Sans teeth, sans eyes, sans taste, sans everything." The control and collapse and crisis of democracy and democratic institutions in the country are all in the name of "grab the power glue" and development projects—mostly all-slogan, all-ceremonial, incomplete, half-complete, semi-complete (and, if complete, left seriously faulty and defective). Even then, all is under the heavy burden of high interest debt and all is ridden and riddled with corruption and abuse of power, by which all the freedoms of the people—political freedom, freedom of speech, freedom of press, and freedom of assembly—have been taken away by the Hasina regime with the help of its police and RAB force.

Senior Supreme Court lawyer of Bangladesh Dr Shahdin Malik reflects on the regime's police-controlled "all that glitters is not gold" charade of all-inauguration development projects that he thinks are not only on the reverse gear but also on the wrong track.[5] Another famed lawyer *DeshKonnya* দেশকন্যা[6] Barrister Rumin Farhana exposes the vicious vacuity of the Awami League's (AL's) all-talk development drives of at best mixed intentions, if not completely nefarious and nihilistic.[7] Yet another blogger writes to blast the bragging Awami brand of development for its willful lackings that mischievously blot out "the other."[8] Taken to the threshold of their death-throes, rung with parting and flickering knells, people's freedoms have now become a matter of the nostalgic past, as the regime continues to be long on rhetoric, short on deeds. It is as if opening a restaurant that would prefer not to serve any food and that would have no intention of making any food available, to recall an idea from an old Dhaka English professor (late) Azhar Hussein, who used to teach at Jahangirnagar University later in his life.

Development *sans* democracy is growth without equity and equality—unbalanced, unsustainable, inharmonious, and short-lasting—leaving more and more people behind (in the back) and creating more and more differences among the economic, social, and working classes and professions. This defective and degenerated development, despite making some visible progress, has inevitably created "an intensification of inequalities," as a pro-Awami political science professor, Dr Ahrar Ahmed, of Black Hills University puts it. It is like providing some food to the animals in the confines of a zoo or a farm for mere survival, as it happens in George Orwell's satirical political *Animal Farm*, at the expense of their power and freedom. It is also like the prisoners in a crammed prison being provided with their minimum food, like the slow-moving snail-speed traffic of expensive cars on the congested streets in Hasina's Bangladesh.

Exceptions put aside, this is exactly the kind of faulty and frigid drone development drive that is being claimed to have been done by the Awami government.[9] This development, down and drunken with ill-gotten power and driven by greed for dirty and corrupt money, is like a one-eyed fearsome creature/monster that takes the political opposition as a pawn and leaves thousands of innocent opposition members as inmates in chains and shackles, ill-fed and underfed, under the threatening stare of the prison guards.

Why, then, talk about the people's power and their votes when their democratic rights and opinions are being routinely trashed, trampled, and manipulated, like the folk-and-fairy tale genies confined in a closed bottle? Why, then, pay a lip service to democratic freedoms and privileges when issues, policies, and free speech are being systematically tampered, twisted, and tilted by force and pressure? Had it been otherwise, that is, had there been a consistently incremental practice through an aggressive and steadfast pursuit of democracy, civil rights, human rights, and the rule of law during the last forty-six years, Bangladesh would have been transformed into a great country—kind, compassionate, tolerant, at the same time harmoniously balanced and advanced with sustainable development, to the satisfaction of the entire nation and its whole population.

Is it the right and privilege and prerogative of Sheikh Hasina alone—only Hasina and her top-heavy and top-down regime and none else—to make the development of Bangladesh exclusively her (squint and jaundiced) way without giving others a chance by means of a democratic transition of power? Isn't this one and only way, enforced by her one-party state organs—press, police, civil administration, judiciary, media—comparable to treacherously stealing away one's rights the way the bad people (muggers, looters, thieves, and robbers) snatch away the belongings of others? Hasn't the AL, under the leadership of PM Hasina, hacked and hijacked and backed away from the proper and standard norms and forms of democracy and its rules the way people are regularly kidnapped by the dark macabre and monstrous forces under her watch?

These criminal and clandestine forces are certainly worse and more dangerous than the swampy and marshy mire-living monsters Grendel and Grendel's mother, who nightly drag and kill the great King Hrothgar's sleeping chieftains in the royal premises of Heorot in the Old English epic of *Beowulf.* It is in this kind of Bangladesh that the venomous and vengeful গুম ও খুন (assassinations and forced abductions or disappearances) of men, women, and children, in hundreds and thousands, have become a matter of common occurrence on a *daily*, *weekly* and *monthly* basis—mad, mindless, and senseless, gory and scary, fearful and frightening as they must have been.[10]

Except the ruling party thugs and throngs, common populace and common citizenry find themselves helpless in this brutal oppression. They have none to call their own and no one to turn to except God/Allah the Almighty to Whom they can only pray to send down His swift and severe punishment, with the sound and speed of thunder and lightning, on those beastly perpetrators who keep abducting and killing innocent people most brutally and violently. They also pray for God's curse to come down hard, most incurably and irrevocably, on all those who are responsible for all the killings and abductions and who do not do anything to stop them and bring the criminals to justice. The neutrally minded (Ret) Sqn Ldr Mohammad Shoaib of Los Angeles expresses his frustration this way:

> Our thoughts, feelings, actions are strictly "Bi-Polar"—either Awami or BNP—there is no middle ground, no compromise, no appreciation of each other. In such a partisan environment, there can never be any "Bi-partisan" solution to the country's problems. There is no light at the end of the tunnel—whether BNP or Awami League. The result is a vicious cycle full of vitriol and violence. God never tolerates any intolerable solution for too long. If our leaders are unable to find any solution to our pathetic politics and myriad

> of problems—Almighty Allah will find one. People need to be patient, wait, and hold their breath. (E-mail of January 12, 2017 to the author)

The AL thinks there is no need for democracy, now that they are in power, wishing to prolong and perpetuate their being in power, but they fought for democracy when they sat in opposition in the past. This is their double standard, as commented by Mohiuddin Anwar, a freelance writer for a news agency in Washington DC. They resist and refuse to be ousted by people's votes and voices. That has been decided by Sheikh Hasina and her son and likely successor/heir apparent Sajeeb Wajed Joy, who are of the view that others would have to come to power over their dead body and that there would be no transfer of power while they were alive.

Corruption in countless crores (one crore = 10,000,000)

Unfortunately, the history of the political parties in power is an account of mostly deceiving and defective development projects, mega lootings, massive election riggings, rapes, murders, and abductions.[11] With every successive government—the present AL government topping the list—plunder and corruption become far more fat and frightening than the previous government.[12] Just as A E Housman describes the cherry tree in the spring as "the loveliest of trees […]/ Is hung with" its snow-white flowers (the participle phrase in the passive suggesting the abundance), the Awami regime is "hung" with all-sucking and all-siphoning corruption with the initial budget for every single development project jumping up through an incredulous series of revised budgets over the time and still the project left unfinished with the rods and hollow bamboo sticks dangling or sticking out in or from their allotted place. According to the World Bank, the daily *Ittefaq* reports, the cause of the filthy and horrendously high cost of the projects in Bangladesh is hefty corruption.[13]

Eminent writer and intellectual Professor Badruddin Umar alleges how corrupt and cowardly the present Awami politicians are, including the very top ones, who keep looting, stealing and plundering millions.[14] One consequence of this culture of large-scale economic rape of Bangladesh is the creation of only 50,000 new millionaires in possession of crores in the last eight years alone.[15] Another consequence of financial corruption and irregularities is the capital deficit of over 16,000 crore taka in many commercial and state-controlled banks.[16] The British government is supposed to be investigating into the matter of the humongous amount of

60,000 crore taka, given to the petty and paper-only UK-based DP Rail, which is just one of the countless other financial scandals under the Hasina government and which allegedly involves the members of a top family, not to mention the mystery shrouding and surrounding their luxury home/s in London and Maryland (US).[17]

According to the media sources, 35,000 crore taka vanished from Dhaka stock exchange and share market during the Awami government since 2009 and similar stock exchange corruption took place during the previous Awami government, as if such type of plunder, including the soaring and searing bank scandals and the repression and persecution of the political opposition by the Awami government go shoulder to shoulder, all tied together. Minar Rashid is one of those journalists who wrote about the same and similar Awami black chapters unraveling what is still rolling and unfolding.[18] Critics allege that the Awami government financial adviser and Beximco Group Chairman Salman F Rahman made so much money through share market scams that not less than two Padma bridges could be made with that vast amount (to be counted in crores).[19] Popular Bengali dailies reported about the bottomless and widespread misappropriations and malpractices in the country during the current Hasina regime.[20]

During the last ten years of Fakhruddin-Moinuddin-Masududdin government and a large part of the Hasina government combined (2005–2014), claims the US-based GFI (Global Financial Integrity), 3,57,000 crore taka (4,461 crore 53,000 in American dollar), which is an average of 35,992 crore taka per year, has been looted out of the country.[21] The *Jugantor* report of May 3, 2017 puts the figure at 6,06,868 crore taka for the amount laundered during the same period.[22] In 2013 alone, claimed GFI, more than 77,000 crore taka and, in 2014, about 73,000 crore taka (911 crore in US Dollar) were smuggled out. What a soaring and shameful corruption under the Hasina regime! (See Note #101 below.)

According to another *Jugantor* report of April 5, 2017, the fate of 15,500 crore taka from the top 100 loan defaulters was uncertain, the amount about to be lost in corruption.[23] The Naya Diganta of July 11, 2017 reports that the amount of loan defaulted is 111,000 crore taka. Sanaullah Sakib of the largest Bengali daily, *Prothom Alo*, reports that the four biggest government banks (Sonali, Rupali, Agrani, and Janata) are also on the list of top loan defaulters in the amount of more than 26,000 crore taka.[24] According to the *Ittefaq* report, the amount of default loan stands at 74,000 crore taka, which, being actually stolen, stands no chance to be paid back.[25] All this made Bangladesh's golden boy Dr Tuhin Malik to remark that money/currency/capital has become an easy and cheap, yet most coveted export product of Bangladesh.[26]

Similarly, presumably anti-Islamic and pro-Awami writer Anisul Hoque's prose cartoon এ কী করলেন দুই ব্যাংক-ডাকাত! (What these two bank dacoits have done!), illustrates the widespread culture of corruption in bank looting, negligence, oversight, and overlooking by all the vested interest groups.[27]

Well-known pro-Awami journalist Golam Murtoza writes about how the country is deeply submerged in and devastatingly swallowed by corruption everywhere, including the law enforcement agents.[28] *DeshKonnya* দেশকন্যা Barrister Farhana (who, together with another *DeshKonnya* দেশকন্যা Syeda Ashifa Ashrafi Papia, is one of the finest and most fantastic female politicians of the country), gives a comprehensive list of the black and tainted monies stolen by the people of the Awami axis.[29] One of the recent corruption cases involved the government officials of the Sylhet Haor belt (dams and wetlands vital for farming and fisheries for many in the area) that caused a flood disaster/damage worth crores/millions.[30] There is a large amount of talk surrounding the former Awami Railways minister Suranjit Sen Gupta and his suspicious involvement in the Bangladesh Railways' missing 70 crore taka.[31]

One of the direct consequences of this corrupt culture and financially filthy and disgustingly class-ridden environment is that almost all the parliament members of the Awami regime and their affiliates/associates have swiftly and suddenly metamorphosed into millionaires and multimillionaires, many of them smuggling their black money out of the country, belonging to the wealthy "Begam-Paras" in America, Canada, Australia, UK, Malaysia, Singapore, and elsewhere, and amassing their ill-gotten cash in the Swiss banks amounting to nearly 6,000 crore taka in 2016 and 5,000 crore taka in 2015.[32] The Paras—upscale and exclusive residential colonies of their wives—provide concrete evidence that the Awami politics is a dirty, unclean, booming, thriving, fast track, and quick rental lucrative business of criminal looting and indiscriminate laundering more than worth investigating into.[33] The Awami abuse of power is so gross and abominable that a government minister alone has grabbed 150 plots of land in an expensive residential area.[34]

The mostly "unelected" and handpicked Awami MPs are sanctioned a lot of money in the name of development works in their local districts, just before the elections, so that they can sell the name of the deceiving and eye-washing all-inauguration works, far from being completed, to buy votes at the last moment.[35] The links provided here[36] and throughout this chapter (the longest) and indeed the whole book offer a shocking catalogue of cancerous corruption under the Hasina-led neo-and-near-and-more-than-partially fascist and পৈশাচিক regime (which people also describe as BAKSAL-II, considered to be far worse and more dangerous than BAKSAL-I).

In an exclusive interview with the largest Bengali daily *Prothom Alo* during his recent visit to Bangladesh, Jose Carlos Ugaz, chairman of Transparency International and a Peruvian jurist, said:

> Development is not possible with rampant corruption. The enemy is corruption. The enemy is the corrupt official and the corrupt company that is trying to take money from the people of Bangladesh for the personal gain of a few [...] I've been here only two days. I've heard a lot of stories about corruption. I read the papers, I talked to the people, I talked to journalists, I talked to the authorities, and everyone recognizes there is systemic, structural and widespread corruption around the country. That is reflected in the 25 points Bangladesh has out of 100 in the CPI, or maybe 28 points [...] The Global Financial Integrity reports that about US$9b has been channeled out from Bangladesh, mostly to be deposited in offshore banking and territories. Can you imagine what could have been done in this country with so many billions of dollars, all the people that could have been taken out of poverty, all the infrastructure that could have been built in favour of the children of Bangladesh? That is why we need to identify who are the authors of these crimes [...] It is impossible to achieve economic development with corruption at the same time [...] what is clear from our experience is that it is not possible to achieve development with rampant corruption on the side because corruption increases poverty. Corruption generates inequality. Corruption brings problems of governance.[37]

This stealing of people's money and their democratic as well as human rights is a direct result of the AL coming to power in a general election in late 2008 and then again in a farcical one-sided election on January 5, 2014 boycotted by the opposition. The outcome of the 2008 election was believed to have been prearranged and predetermined with an understanding with then interim and outgoing military-backed caretaker government. That election, therefore, was not free from being questionable and controversial, having been backed by the government in favor of the AL. The AL again returned to power for the consecutive second term through what is described as a fantastically mock and massively fraudulent election of the black January 5, 2014. The snatching of the rights of the people by the Awamis is like stabbing in the back of the nation. It did not have to be that way. The country is not hers (Hasina's) or theirs (her followers') alone, who want to set, according to (Ret) Brig Gen Shamsuddin Ahmed, who was a military secretary to the former President Ershad, a new type of democracy—"demonic," "draconian," perverse, and upended in nature, as one understands.[38]

Democracy and development are the two sides of the coin. One cannot go without the other. They have to be comprehensive, meaning all kinds of development—economic, social, political, human, educational, and environmental—need to be addressed together to make a harmonious and balanced and lasting development possible. Development first and democracy later is the slogan of despotisms and dictatorships. Salauddin Babar argues about how development cannot last long and becomes restricted without democracy.[39] Stressing the fact that development and democracy are complementary processes in which one would not sustain without the other, one of the eminent Bangladeshis of today, Dr Mizanur Rahman Shelley, writes,

> Lack of people's participation in an undemocratic or insufficiently democratic order leads to skewed and inequitable development. Transparency and accountability are absent or present only inadequately. Politicians and public servants find scopes to behave irresponsibly and indulge in corruption. Such system tends to become authoritarian under personal rule and cannot be easily reached by the people. On the contrary, the rich and the privileged often have an easy excess to the rulers. They lobby effectively to secure their class, group or coterie interest by influencing the policy makers, planners and decision makers. When democracy is in exile by dictatorship or disguised autocracy, people at large are deprived of having their say in the processes of public policy formulation and implementation. *Development without democracy remains unable to ensure the common good* (my emphasis).[40]

Dr Shelley's views are shared and supported by the eminent political scientist Dr M Ataur Rahman, who, too, asserts that the ruling regime is determinedly and single-mindedly perpetuating its hold on power by all means possible, including the all-in-name-and-all-on-paper elections, which are in reality nothing more than false and fabricated, morose, morbid, and moribund tricks and tactics.[41]

All parties have their own ideas/ideals and policies, which they think are better than those of others. The AL is utterly wrong to think that only its agendas and leaders are the best. It must accept the fact that all the recognized parties have the right to get to power through a democratic process and build the country by turns by way of smooth, peaceful, and democratic transition. As Gen Ahmed correctly says:

> Democracy is all about change and new blood being brought about in the leadership of political parties and the government. There must be a constant endeavor to further improve and broaden the system of governance. There is no denying that we do not have a functional democratic dispensation in place in Bangladesh now, nor was it ever there before [...] But it is a fact that democracy has not been allowed to strike roots in any sphere of our national life, thanks to our politicians. In fact, the true meaning of democracy is perhaps not known to many of these power-hungry politicians.
>
> Democracy means rule of law, meaning, thereby, that law does not discriminate between the haves and the have-nots, the ruling class and the ruled, the elites and the ordinary people. Democracy means transparency and accountability in the system of governance. Democracy means freedom of expression of the people, the press, and the media.

> Democracy means that there would be an opposition in the parliament to guide and criticize the government objectively.
>
> Democracy means rule by mandate of the people expressed through free, fair, credible, and participatory elections. In a democracy, state institutions—the police, the bureaucracy, the Public Service Commission, the Election Commission, and the judiciary—are allowed to function and play their constitutional role without any interference from the government.
>
> Whenever power is concentrated to one person without sufficient checks and balances, as it often is in authoritarian rule, corruption, nepotism, toadyism, and crime flourish with state connivance, and eat into the vitals of a nation including economy and social equanimity, as it has done in our case [...] If we do not do this, there will always be cracks in our national unity and there will be no end to our political turmoil.[42]

From the above, it is clear that the AL has been doing what it should not be doing and has refrained from doing what it should in fact be doing. The AL's forced suppression of the other parties (by means of sandbag, cement bag and garbage trucks blockades, police barricades, police cordons, tear gas, water cannons, abductions, extortions, shootings, and murders) has led to the situation of nonstop unrest and violence, cocktail and petrol bomb explosions, human chains, strikes, work abstentions, and shutdowns.[43]

The common theme or argument that holds the book together is the fact that the AL government of Bangladesh has been ruling the country and exploiting its political situation and institutions most undemocratically, with ruthless violence. Its tactics and techniques may be compared to those of modern dictators around the world—Omar al-Bashir of Sudan, Zein al-Abedine of Tunisia, Bashar al-Assad of Syria, Muammar Gaddafi of Libya, Saddam Hussein of Iraq, Anwar al-Sadat, Hosni Mubarak, and Abdul Fattah al-Sisi of Egypt (all modern pharos), as well as the totalitarian regimes of Central Asian strongmen. Like Hitler's Germany, which was no doubt very developed but turned, politically, into an aggressive country, without a balanced social and human development, the partisan AL government of Bangladesh is using the pretext of material and scientific development to justify its democratically illegitimate rule sending democratic dissent into banishment or obliterating it to the point of nonexistence. Since 2009, the AL government has been controlling the nation in a Mephistophelian, Machiavellian, Chanakyan, and Lilliputian (low and mean, nasty and nefarious, divisive, and despotic) way—Mephistophelian lure of power (no matter how lowly, ignoble, and densely alloyed it is, far from being ennobled, heightened, cleansed, and purified) and Machiavellian,

Chanakyan, and Lilliputian cruel and crafty mechanism of repression, suppression, persecution and coercion, all summed up in the phrase, deadly and dreadful state terrorism.

The AL government has turned into a regime, intending to forcibly hang on to power by way of bottling up the democratic freedom in the name of so-called, actually one-eyed economic development.[44] It is offering to provide food, jobs, and other provisions, facilities, and opportunities, but in accordance with its own taste and its own choice in its own interest. What is far worse, the regime is doing so on condition that the people should shut up, stay silent, and remain in political confinement, or else! It is behaving as if it is its sole authority, privilege, and prerogative to work on the development of the country, while others are supposed to be merely and obediently working for the "Awami Government and Company" without being any different or having any different opinion, political or otherwise. If economic development alone (albeit stuffed with huge corruption at all levels and in all sectors, including the allegations of financial irregularities and misappropriations against PM Hasina's son Sajeeb Wajed Joy) would have been enough, the entire spectrum of the political opposition—of all shades and opinions—would not have said that this was not the Bangladesh they fought for and dreamed about in 1971.[45]

What the weekly First News editor and an opinion writer/columnist for *The Daily Star*, Mohammad Badrul Ahsan, says about how the growth and flourish of totalitarianism, autocracy, and dictatorship have taken place under a democratic garb in countries like Egypt, Zimbabwe, and Venezuela (all three being in a state of shambles), compared with ancient Athenian democracy, is precisely pertinent in the context of Bangladesh under PM Hasina. Although Ahsan maintains an allegorical and journalistic distance and detachment from directly mentioning Bangladesh, his words do indeed unmistakably apply to Bangladesh where also "Security forces round up and torture hundreds of activists" before and during an/y election. He writes:

> Because elections meant to be the conduit of democracy are being used to confiscate it [...] mischievous rulers have learned to beat democracy at its own game. They are using the political legitimacy of a popular vote to abuse power, enrich allies, and annihilate the opposition as well as the legitimacy itself.
>
> Even worse, these rulers are treating return to power like the refill policy of those stores, which offer unlimited free refills for their drinks. Once in power, the rulers devise ways to perpetuate it. And they do so by staging rigged elections as if one legitimate investment in power entitles them to have many illegitimate returns on it.

> Once these rulers win elections, they uphold electoral democracy in their speeches but utilize its power in their actions to consolidate power and amass vast wealth. They start destroying democratic institutions and emptying the bureaucracy of independent-minded civil servants. In some cases, they try to win the support of their rural populations, promoting economic growth and improved standard of living. Democracy in this masterminded manipulation invariably tends to perpetuate political strife, graft, and muddled economic planning.
>
> What it does is rollback democracy, which first creates stagnancy and then degeneration. Many of the rulers plan to rule for a lifetime and some of them partially succeed until they are either assassinated or toppled. If eternal vigilance is the price of liberty, people are cowered into submission and paralysis by a complex set of maneuverings comparable to card sleight that leaves bettors in a state of perplexity.
>
> Democracy is reduced to a bluff when the packet is intact but the gift is missing.
>
> This type of deceptive democracy is like fruits laced with formalin. It slows down the rot but is downright toxic. And it hollows out a country like termites eating wood.
>
> It's one thing not to have democratic rule in a country. It's another thing when fake democracy is imposed on people. The former whets people's appetite for democracy, while the latter ruins it like junk food hurts metabolism. Frogs blink when they eat because their eyes help them swallow food. Democracy is caught in the false pretense of defenders who are devouring it.[46]

At present, Bangladesh is in the process of moving from a Least Developed Country to a Lower Middle Income country, but this applies only to the upper and upper middle classes, who, as the Communist Party of Bangladesh chief Mujahidul Islam Selim suggests, are riddled with corruption, leaving in their trail an unspeakable difference between them and the lower classes with at least a quarter of the population remaining in terrible, degrading, and dehumanizing poverty.[47] According to the CPD (Center for Policy Dialogue), it would take another decade for Bangladesh to move up to the higher stage of Medium Developed Countries, provided it significantly improved on a number of other sectors.[48] Like China, Hong Kong, Singapore, Malaysia, Kazakhstan, Turkmenistan, Tajikistan, and the Arabian Gulf countries, where free speech, democratic rights, right to assembly, debates, and discussions are either conspicuous by their absence or highly regimented and controlled, to the extent of being absent, the AL tyrannically wants to stick to power under the pretext of business promotion and industrial development, which, they argue, are to take place without or in exchange for press and political freedoms.

Those countries, developed as they are, are at least quite, if not completely, free from corruption. But development in Bangladesh, in popular perception, means as much corruption (and development on paper only) as real development, or as much for the benefit of the general people as for the interest of the corrupt "tenders" and "contract" bidders and their "system loss"—an euphemism for the bribes and black monies that change hands in the process—mostly along the partisan, not patriotic line.[49] As briefly hinted by Ahsan and Ahmed above, bureaucracy in Bangladesh is a victim, forced or voluntary, of the ill-and-evil-intentioned political and financial mismanagement. According to the International Civil Service Effectiveness (InCiSE) Index 2017, prepared by researchers from Oxford University and the Institute for Government, a UK think tank, Bangladesh Civil Service is nowhere to be seen on the list of countries rated high for the effective performance of their government workforces.

With few exceptions, development in Bangladesh means politically motivated and politically converted/reverted camouflage projects, meant more for corruption than commitment and accomplishment, either unplanned and improperly designed or intentionally left incomplete and less than half-done, even long after the gala and gaudy ministerial or prime ministerial inauguration. All this is cooked with the intention of securing a higher budget next time, one more time, yet next fiscal year for more and more corruption as if the initial one-time black amount was not enough for all the people involved in the project, from top to bottom.[50] There is a popular saying that while the village landlord's cows are there only on the list on paper, they are actually not there in his cowsheds, which are empty. Myriad instances such as the far-from-finished metro rail with millions already spent testify to the fact.[51]

One can attack and accuse the all-engulfing institutional as well as individual corruption in Bangladesh the way the 2016 American Democratic Presidential hopefuls Hillary Clinton and Bernard (Bernie) Sanders were critical of the big banks and their shadow banking. Blasting what in his view was his country's oligarchical, not democratic development, the socialist minded Sanders said: "Today, the most serious problem we face is the grotesque and growing level of wealth and income inequality [...]. Let us be clear that the greed and recklessness and illegal behavior of Wall Street, where fraud is a business model, helped to destroy this economy and the lives of millions of people ... I happen to believe that the business model of the Wall Street is fraud and deception."[52]

As the Citizens' Committee for the Good Governance of Bangladesh spokesman Badiul Alam Majumder wrote, "Having been in power for over six years, the AL as a party has gotten lost in the government. The patronage-based politics of the past years has attracted many opportunists to the party, making many committed AL activists inactive. Hence, many observers are concerned that when out of power the ruling party may also be in disarray."[53] Majumder's criticism of the weak and ineffective and also unfortunately long-lived *Rakib-Marka* Election Commission (intolerably and indescribably worse than those under Dr A T M Shamsul Huda and Justice M A Aziz) and the restrictions imposed on the media and the interference with the freedom of the press was a representative criticism by the majority, as reiterated again and again by the opposition BNP chief Begum Khaleda Zia and her secretary general Mirza Fakhrul Islam Alamgir. They constantly accuse the Hasina government of being governed by others in the neighborhood (that is India), of being totalitarian and illegal, allowing no free and fair elections and no differences of opinion, and of being falsely "elected" through a loyalist, "boneless," "worthless," "hopeless," "useless," and "spineless" *Rakib-Marka* Election Commission.[54]

Despite the fact that his commission also was not above shortcomings and controversies, some of them being very serious (such as their attempt to spit on and split the BNP), Dr Huda, however, came to realize the value of strong democracy and fair and equitable social justice, side by side with development, especially in the face of the development of economic inequity.[55] Referring to the unscrupulous and undemocratic Hasina government, Dr Moeen Khan, an opposition (BNP) leader, said that the so-called development drum beaten by it only provided an opportunity for a woman to have her snapshots taken in a photo session with her lipstick on. He made it clear it was not possible to achieve economic and social development with democracy remaining outstanding, hanging in the balance, or sent to exile. Moeen Khan, along with the late ASM Hannah Shah of the same party, also described the development budget as false and fake made by an equally false and fake ("unelected and illegitimate") government, which treated the country as its own property—a sentiment echoed by many other opposition parties, from the CPB to the JSD-Rob to the Chor Monai Pir of *Islami Shashontantro Andolon*, who all said it was a budget of looting by a government out of touch with the masses and unaccountable to them.[56]

Khan's statement is reinforced by the fact that despite the much-hyped Awami branded development, the number of the unemployed, in several millions, is staggeringly high.[57] The number keeps going up with the increasingly high number of foreigners, mostly Indian, as many as 800,000, as of early 2017, being employed by Indian and other foreign or multinational companies, who control a considerable share of the job market in Bangladesh.[58] There are thousands of Bangladeshi unemployed who are risking their lives by small boats to reach the shores of Malaysia and Singapore in search of a better future.[59] Unfortunately, Sheikh Hasina remarked that the impoverished boat people at sea—starving, drifting, destitute, and desperate—were "mentally sick," for which she was widely condemned nationally and internationally, from *The Daily Star* and *Amader Shomoy* of Bangladesh to *The Star* of Malaysia to *The Express Tribune* of Pakistan to *The Sydney Morning Herald* to *Al Jazeera* to CNN iReport.[60] Her comment drew sharp rebukes from critics who recalled the High Court's characterization of her as "a wrong-headed woman" years ago.

Tragically painful migration and/or refugee crisis of Bangladesh is similar to the millions of migrants and refugees, mainly from Syria, Iraq, Afghanistan, Somalia, and Libya via Libyan, Lebanese, and Turkish shores to some of the surrounding Middle Eastern countries and across the Mediterranean to Europe. Finding the regime's development drum empty and deceiving, many Bangladeshis also are risking their lives to migrate to Europe. In fact, as the *Daily Star* claims, they are the highest number of migrant refugees to Europe.[61] Many poor women travel to the Middle East as domestic help only to be tortured and persecuted and to end up selling their body as prostitutes.[62] If there is so much economic development happening, as the Hasina-AL claims, why do so many men and women ruin their lives and families that way?

On his Facebook status, Barrister MBI Munshi, author of *The India Doctrine (1947–2007): A Contemporary Study on Indian Hegemony and Geo-Strategic Perspectives on South Asia*, correctly asserts,

> Multitudes are abandoning Bangladesh despite the claim of economic prosperity breaking out all over the country. Actually only a tiny parasitic, exploitative and corrupt class of people have benefited from the economic acceleration that started in the 80's and spluttered on for the next two decades. In reality only those who are expert in looting the country, cheating their workers and using political influence to obtain business opportunities and contracts have gained while the mass people have only seen slight improvements. The level of inequality in the country is absolutely shocking. Naturally the political parties will not focus on this issue because their leadership has been the primary beneficiary of these developments and the economically well-off do not care. However, such incidents reflect on the whole country and how you are perceived elsewhere is based on these news stories that the rest of the world is viewing.[63]

On another status, a few days later, concerning the ongoing migrant crisis, Barrister Munshi again writes:

> While we know that the Rohingyas are fleeing genocide in Myanmar, why are the Bangladeshis willingly taking to the sea dreaming of a better future and fortune when they can

> do it in "Sonar" (golden) Bangladesh where per capita income has surged to $1,314 and GDP growth hovers at 6%? The obvious answer is huge income inequality, disparity, corruption, nepotism and a parasitic elite class that treats the country as their inherited property making it impossible for the majority of the people to rise up above their *daily* grind. Due to lack of accountability and transparency in all sectors of Bangladesh, there is no redress so the rich continue to get illegally richer and the rest fall behind or murder their way to the top by joining politics or a criminal syndicate. The other option, of course, is to take to the sea. I assume that these issues are as important as the return of democracy to Bangladesh [suffering] from the present dysfunctional economic and political system.[64]

Munshi's observations are in the same vein as those of the former Bangladesh Ambassador to Japan and former Director-General of Bangladesh Ministry of Foreign Affairs, Serajul Islam, who once taught a course on Islam and Globalization at Montgomery College Maryland. He wrote, in his e-mail posting of June 3, 2015, that the two main pillars of Bangladesh economy, Ready Made Garments (RMG) and Manpower Export, were significantly shrinking due to political unrest in the country and its subjugated foreign policy, especially in relation to India. He continues:

> Why else would men, throwing fear of death aside, take to the high seas in thousands with their wives and children if milk and honey were flowing in Bangladesh? [...] It is indeed a very sad commentary where we as a country have fallen [...] Hundreds of graves of Bangladeshis are appearing in Malaysia and the nation of Bangladesh is in denial. What a brilliant testimony to the Spirit of 1971! Both the RMG and the manpower sectors are in fact like the Bangladeshis floating in the seas in search of a dream that is just not there, floating towards disaster. And here we are drumming we would become a middle income country by 2021 and by 2040 join USA/EU/Japan and a developed country!!!![65]

Ambassador Islam's and Barrister Munshi's comments were in line with *The Los Angeles Times*' report on migrant crisis, *The Economist*'s report on the diminishing and dwindling freedom of speech in Bangladesh, Anu Mohammad's "Government is giving wrong information about development," Mahmuda Dolly's "Democracy under the boots, humanity floating on the sea," and Wasim Farook's "Floating humans, sinking humanity."[66] The social, political, and economic situation of Bangladesh is so bleak and discouraging that even the enclave residents do not want to return to Bangladesh and would rather prefer to belong to India.[67] As Prof Azhar Hussein of English (identified above) would have put it, people of Bangladesh are forced to walk with a double constraint: with pebbles in(side) their shoes over a rough and rocky road, not with clean shoes over a smooth road. The road to democratic freedom can only be made meaningful by inclusive and credible elections, public transparency and accountability, and the rule of law to be applied and upheld equally and uniformly, not selectively, in the case of both the ruling and the ruled.

In his work after work such as *Signs of the Times* (1829), the semi-autobiographical *Sartor Resartus* (1831), *Chartism* (1839), and *Past and Present* (1843), the Scottish philosopher Thomas Carlyle exposed the material, mechanical, and dehumanizing tendencies of mere utilitarian and economic progress, which he castigated as a dangerous and inadequate "science of mechanics." His message had to do with the moral and spiritual requirements of human experience, which he called "science of dynamics." He expressed his sympathy for the industrial laborers and argued for the need of the betterment of their lives. He noticed that while economic development brought general welfare, it also caused a degradation in the living conditions of the urban poor. In their social and cultural criticism, John Ruskin and William Morris too developed similar ideas, that work—be it labor or craft—should be collective, synthesized and integrative, not divided and isolated; pleasurable and harmonious, not forced, imposed and tiresome. The end of such work ethics is to develop a morally and materially whole humanity and spiritually balanced society.

Sheikh Hasina's jejune, lifeless, and much-trumpeted development ditties, accompanied by a violent suppression of democratic majority, can be likened to Carlyle's utilitarian "science of mechanics." For a modern 21st century "science of dynamics," both development and democracy need to merge and fuse and move forward together. Despite Carlyle's support for a strong government under a heroic personality, his idea of heroic leadership is completely different from Hasina's dictatorship. Carlyle's idea had a radical and mystical strand about it and would only aim at a progressive and representative view of historical necessity as embodied, he thought, in great men like Prophet Muhammad, the anti-royalist military leader Oliver Cromwell, and Emperor Napoleon (who was a product of the French Revolution with liberty, equality and fraternity as its slogans against the contemporary royal regime's political repression and cruel injustice).

Western and Asian/Western dignitaries such as the Nobel Laureate Amartya Sen and the EU Parliamentary Delegation correctly diagnosed that there could not be any peace and stability in Bangladesh at the expense of human rights and political freedoms and that democratically informed human development needed to take place even if that meant somewhat less or a certain compromise on the side of economic and material development. No one would like to trade their precious and priceless freedoms and collective and individual rights for the so-called peace and prosperity under the yoke of suppression and subversion. To give only a short list:

(1) There are limited job opportunities with the rate of unemployment going up, Bangladesh being the 12th in the 20 countries of the world with the highest unemployment rate, according to United Nations Development Program (UNDP), BBS, and EIU[68];
(2) There is an intolerably dire and dreary lack of drinking water, cooking gas, and electricity everywhere all across the country[69];
(3) There is widespread and rapacious corruption, favoritism, and nepotism, as reported and talked about on all the national media, day in and day out, some of the examples being the whole background and foreground stories of the bank scandals, share market scams, individual and institutional lootings and smugglings[70];
(4) There are widely held and widely perceived serious doubts and suspicions about the administration of equitable justice and the conduct of law enforcement agents;
(5) There is total transport chaos and collapse nearly most of the time of the year, especially during the various festivals and celebrations, causing immense and untold suffering to the millions of commuters;
(6) There is a filthy and ferocious extortion in the amount of 6 crore taka daily in the transportation sector[71];
(7) About 37% of roads and highways are impassable, being full of holes, ditches, puddles, and loose and broken bricks[72];
(8) There are not enough schools for children, who, especially girls, are suffering from the dilapidated condition of their schools, about to fall apart and with inadequate facilities, such as toilets, etc.[73];
(9) There are thousands with fake and false certificates working at educational and other institutions[74];
(10) There are serious issues with the quality of education going lamentably down and the question papers often getting leaked out[75];
(11) There are thousands of "politicized" false freedom fighters enjoying the state benefits under the AL government, many of whom made their way to the list not only through their Awami political connections but also by bribing the Awami politicians and authorities[76];
(12) Colleges and universities often go without classes or are often closed sine die (for an indefinite period) due to political unrest;
(13) Attacks and assaults on the minorities have tripled under the Hasina-Awami rule[77];
(14) Growth or health of children and adults in the millions of poor and low-income families is badly affected. They cannot afford even two full

meals a day and cannot afford, throughout their lives, to have the popular and delicious beef and fish, which remain unaffordable সোনার হরিণ, beyond their capacity due to the exorbitant price of those food items[78];

(15) Millions in the cities and the villages live a slave and slum life[79];

(16) There are countless have-nots who, deprived of all joy and happiness in life, survive by having whatever little and rotting rice they can afford with just onion and green chili, even a simple vegetable curry being a luxury for them[80];

(17) Nearly 530 garments and other industries have been closed down during the last two and half years (2014–July 2016) leaving about 126,000 workers destitute[81];

(18) Jobs are so scarce that there are 40,000 applicants against 178 posts in the fire service (as reported on April 21, 2016)[82];

(19) Most of the millions of digitally produced national ID cards contain wrong information rendering them unreliable[83];

(20) The road to costly megaprojects creates and leaves more and more of the poor behind in terrible poverty (about 100m out of 160m people), also causing higher and higher interest rates for the small businesses and investments[84];

(21) Bangladesh is one of the least business-friendly countries[85];

(22) Bangladesh is #104 on a list of 124 countries on a Geneva-based World Economic Forum conducted global human capital index;

(23) Reports of investigation into crimes, corruption, scams, and scandals are suppressed and hidden in the closet and under the carpet, never allowed to see the light of day;

(24) Opposition political parties, in gagging suppression of free speech, have to seek permission from the regime police to hold a public meeting and the permission is generally withheld or given at the very last minute so that they cannot prepare well and their supporters, who are prevented from coming to the venue anyway, feel discouraged; and, above all,

(25) The entire spectrum of the opposition parties have been brought to their knees by the state tools and machineries (Police/RAB, judiciary, civil administration, and the ruling party wings and thugs and hooligans and hoodlums and operatives).

In the circumstances, all talk of only development remains facile and frivolous, superficial and supercilious, and, in the same circumstances, no development can ever be deemed lasting, enduring, sustainable, meaningful, and worthwhile.

Programs such as Jamuna TV My Report and 360 Degree Investigation, and Shaiykh Seraj's mobile Education budget on Channel I reveal the vapid vacuity and futility of the corruption-ridden big-and-long-and-loud development talk of the Hasina regime.

It is no surprise that of 140 cities around the world, Dhaka has been ranked the second least livable city, just above Damascus, Syria and below Port Moresby, Papua New Guinea, Lagos, Nigeria, and Tripoli, Libya.[86] According to the 2016 Human Development Report launched by UNDP, Bangladesh ranked 139th and the year before 142nd out of 188 countries on the index.[87] According to the 2016 UK-based Legatum Prosperity Index, Bangladesh ranked 114 among the 149 countries on the list. To give yet another partial list of social, political, and economic ills:

(1) There is a massive environmental pollution and ecological disaster of all kinds all over—plains, rivers, canals, dams, wetlands, unplanned business and residential areas, leather industries, brickfields, garment factories, to name only a few;
(2) Cities are infested with mosquitoes and are full of inhuman pauper slums, poisonous drugs, heaps of garbage everywhere, water-logging, water blockages, and clogged sewerage all over;
(3) Cities come to a standstill due to hours-long traffic congestion, with the average traffic speed in the capital city Dhaka, according to a new World Bank analysis, dropped from 21 to 7 km per hour, slightly above the average walking speed, and the traffic congestion in Dhaka consuming 3.2 million working hours per day[88];
(4) The poor die in scores in stampede while collecting occasional charities in clothes and foodstuff;
(5) The regime is utterly inefficient and incapable to manage flood and cyclone and excessive rain affected areas as well as the major annual religious events, such as the Hajj pilgrimages by thousands of ordinary pious and peace-loving people;
(6) Individuals or unnamed people en masse are punished and face legal suits instituted by the police for the offense committed by others, thereby allowing the police to arrest anybody anytime and paving the way for their harassment and humiliation of the innocent people and various kinds of underhand deals with them in bribery[89];
(7) The country is first or second in the world in terms of the number of (detestable and despicable) child marriages and occupies 110th position in terms of standard, peaceful, decent, and dignified living conditions;

(8) There are nearly three and half million child workers in Bangladesh and about 57% child labors are victims of physical torture[90];
(9) There is an increase of 74% in the torture and persecution of women in just one year[91];
(10) Twenty five thousand women and children are smuggled out of the country annually to make them inhumanly suffer from various kinds of cruel, illegal, and unsocial activities[92];
(11) The entire country is inundated with disastrous mobile technology pornography and the physical "red" pockets and corners of blue films irredeemably and irretrievably affecting the young children and their adult family with corrosive and cancerous devastation, without the government blocking such destructive material and closing down such "red" pockets and corners;
(12) An average of thirty-six children are victims of sexual abuse every month[93];
(13) There are innumerable daily road accidents and boat capsizes (with no help in sight for days from the old, small, light, and low-capacity *Rustum*, the only turtle-speed rescue ship), leading to the death of hundreds quite often;
(14) There is a chronic scarcity of clean (running and drinking) supply water causing the people to suffer for days, weeks, and months every now and then[94];
(15) According to the New York-based Human Rights Watch, annually 43,000 people die of arsenic-related diseases in the country[95];
(16) Bamboo sticks are used in place of iron rods in the construction sector and the buildings and bridges are built according to the dangerously wrong or faulty designs, causing wastage of a massive amount of money[96];
(17) The low-priced ration of foodstuff (rice) made recently available, after years of promise, to the destitute and dispossessed is widely looted and stolen by the local Awami gangs and dealers in many a district all over the country[97];
(18) Humans have to become bullock cows to plough the land for agriculture[98];
(19) Poverty-stricken, underfed, and underdressed (especially in cold) children get their basic literacy lessons in the open street under the scanty and insufficient CNG energy light;
(20) There are hundreds of factories making harmful yaba drug in Dhaka alone, in addition to other places around the country[99];

(21) Bangladesh/Dhaka is one of world's worst holiday spots[100];

(22) Filthy and ferocious amounts of money, in millions of dollars, are often being stolen and smuggled out of the country, not only through hundreds of thousands of foreign workers and the *bKash* hijacking and ATM card and booth hacking bandits, but, more importantly, also the frequently occurring bank and share market scams and scandals, the biggest of which, in a thousand years (হাজার বছরের শ্রেষ্ঠ bank dacoity), taking place under the watch of the so-called "promoter" and "propagator" of "digital" Bangladesh, Sheikh Hasina and her son Sajeeb Wajed Joy (who are also the daughter and the grandson, respectively, of the হাজার বছরের শ্রেষ্ঠ বাঙালী/the greatest Bengali of a thousand years, Sheikh Mujib, who is now a proud part of the most mixed, international, interracial, and interfaith family of Bangladesh, far from being a pure and an unmixed Bangladeshi family)[101];

(23) No matter how much dirty money is stolen and smuggled out, it is still very little or hardly any (considerable) amount to the Hasina regime so that the mega lootings (that have been occurring through political and family connections, cronyism, and connivance) are to be ignored and dismissed as nothing worth paying attention to;

(24) Millions and millions of people are panicking due to the digital clone culture, corrupting and pervading the social, communication, and business world, such as the debit card, credit card, ATM booth scheming machine, mobile SIM and number, Facebook and e-mail accounts, virus-affected harmful software, bank server hacking groups, and high-rise lift-making companies[102];

(25) There is as much money embezzled, misappropriated, and laundered as there are many (in thousands) killed and kidnapped and cross-fired and tortured to death on a *daily* basis (again "too few" to be cared and concerned about) and as there are many politically cooked and made-up lawsuits instituted as a repressive measure against the political opposition, as if all these immoral, diabolic, and despotic means are in competition with each other to achieve an equally dirty and draconian end; and, finally,

(26) There are absolutely no safety and certainty of life, no security in the society, and no guarantee of normal and natural death, with the residential houses becoming storage for human bones and skulls.[103]

While any or all of the above exist to eat into the health of the society, no development can have and would have any meaning whatsoever.[104] "Development is futile without freedom," "Progress is meaningless without security," and "It ill behooves the government to speak of the (spirit) of independence when it is ill-motivated and malnourished to be concerned about development only at the expense of democracy," as the former Transparency International Chair Advocate Sultana Kamal and the New Age editor Nurul Kabir asserted.[105]

There have been many more bank dacoities in Bangladesh following the New York Times Contributing Op-Ed writer (and also daughter of Mahfuz Anam, editor of the largest English daily of Bangladesh, *The Daily Star*) Tahmima Anam's almost two-year-old article that documented a series of bank loots in Bangladesh until then.[106] The latest loot, probably the most brazen in the banking history of the world, has been discussed by Michael Corkery, among others.[107] But there is much more to say, below, about this black and brazen loot under the Hasina government.

Banks in Bangladesh and their baneful banalities, suspicion cast as a surreptitious government, and the minority/majority insiders' job

In what is the central bank of Bangladesh—Bangladesh Bank (BB) alone—from where $81 million (800 crore taka) was digitally smuggled out in the banking world's largest heist ever (like the earlier cyber heist of large amounts from the nation's largest commercial banks), there are as many as twenty or more Hindus holding high positions, from Deputy Governor to Director General to Executive Director to General Manager to BB's international IT Consultant, including the one in charge of the mint, not to speak of many other minority officers below them.[108] In an utter mockery of all good faith, Hindu Rakesh Astana of an Indian IT Consulting Firm, called World Informatics, which was found guilty of involvement in the heist, was appointed the IT specialist in the investigation of the very same.[109] If true, as reported in the media, it was like শেয়ালের কাছে মুরগি বাগা দেওয়া (to put the chicken in the "safekeeping" of the fox) by the top government officials, including the PM's Information Technology Advisor and her allegedly high salaried son Joy.[110]

Dr Rezwan Siddiqui comments on the identity of this Astana and provides credible and convincing evidence on how the BB dacoity could very well be an insider job with the government suppressing, like its habitual and horrendous political suppression, the names of those involved and looking for a false cover elsewhere.[111] Daxim Lucas, an investigative reporter of the Philippines

Newspaper Inquirer, suggests the same, that those who committed the huge heist were indeed BB insiders.[112] Some cross-border Indian Hindu criminals are alleged to have stolen money from BB by violating its vault in 2015.[113] The real masterminds of the big theft at BB are based in India, reported the UK-based Daily Mail.[114] Some sources view the minority staff in the BB as being responsible for the heist.[115]

According to the Awami League USA, the minority Hindus are trying to create a রাম রাজত্ব (Reign of the ancient Hindu god Rama) in Bangladesh.[116] American Bengali Hindu Council claims that it were the Hindus who fought for and won the independence of Bangladesh and that the Muslims had hardly any role in the liberation struggle.[117] What an audacity! What an absurdity! What a denial and distortion and perversion and mutilation of history and historical facts? What an amputation and adulteration! What a rape of truth and reality! However, it was found out to be wrong to accuse the Hindus of trying to desecrate and commit blasphemy against the faith of the Muslim majority by placing the statue of the Hindu god Shiva in the holiest and most sacred Ka'bah in a Facebook picture, following which the Awami (fisheries and livestock) minister Sayedul Haque attacked them by using improper and abusive language.[118]

What is equally mysterious is that the then Governor of BB, Dr Atiur Rahman, who had known about the heist months before, quickly flew to India no sooner than the mega looting, reportedly with the help of the insiders, was discovered by others and the news suddenly broke on the media.[119] It is as if everything was being controlled by and from within India. What is also strange is that the Bank's close circuit cameras were off during the theft and all the IT server data were "kindly" erased.[120] The Economist reports that the government failure to publish a report adds fuel to the bank-heist scandal.[121]

Like the shocking, shivering, and shattering scams and scandals connected with most of the major banks—Sonali, Rupali, Agrani, Janata, Basic, Oriental, and Farmers—and companies—Hallmark, Summit Group, Bismillah Group, Titas Gas, GMG Airlines, and Share Market—the hasty heist at BB must have taken place under the conniving eyes of the Awami regime. It must have been a looting of the digital secularist style, with the very top and key figures in the government such as Sheikh Hasina and her outrageously high salaried IT adviser, her own son Sajeeb Wajed Joy, keeping hush and quiet in a digital manner as if it was the case of Emperor Nero playing on his flute while Rome was burning.[122] If the authoritarian and dictatorial Hasina regime could illegally and forcibly take control of the biggest private bank of Bangladesh, it could do anything it wanted with the nation's government-controlled central bank.[123]

Again, mysteriously, trusted local IT and cybercrime experts, such as Tanvir Hasan Zoha, willing to investigate into this nasty and hasty heist, were being abducted by the shadowy and secretive government-within-the-government সন্ত্রাসী/ terrorist elements. They work in a faithful adherence to the socially and politically subversive and destructive tradition of forced disappearances established under the Hasina regime.[124] Again, mysteriously, the normally blind, indifferent, and inanimate fire also became animatingly biased to take side with the criminals in Hasina's Bangladesh where there was a fire on March 23, 2017 as if to protect them and destroy the evidence of corruption in BB's the very foreign exchange section.

To move on to other sectors, the corruption-ridden Bangladesh Airlines (Biman) is ranked the second worst airlines in the world. Why to export rice to Sri Lanka if it is to be imported from India to meet the consumption level? Is it not a dubious and doublespeak development drum that goes in favor of India against the helpless farmers of Bangladesh? When, according to UNFPA Representative in Bangladesh, Argentina Metavel (who appeared on NTV), over 85% women report domestic violence and gender discrimination due to terrible poverty, deadly and repugnant dowry system,[125] and deadly extramarital affairs; when, according to the president of National Women's Forum, women are being subjected to endless violence and persecution; and when, according to the Awami-allied writer Anisul Hoque, nine out of ten husbands, regularly or irregularly, beat up their wives, there is no women empowerment either.[126]

That what the workers make is below the poverty level has been proved by research and survey.[127] When the millions of (mostly female) garments, brickfield, construction, and agricultural workers working for about twelve hours can earn not more than 2.5 dollars a day (much less than what they need to barely survive by living from hand to mouth only), it is a shame to talk about development and women empowerment in Bangladesh.[128] When millions of them are working at the risk of their lives in dirty, unsafe, unprotected, and insecure farm and factory environment or under the hot sun (all for less than the minimum wage with no holidays, no health insurance, and no retirement benefits) and, much worse, when the poor laborers are inhumanly persecuted by the industrial police and other government agents, it is no surprise that Bangladesh is one of the worst countries of the world, along with Colombia, Egypt, Guatemala, Kazakhstan, Philippines, and Cambodia, according to the International Trade Union Confederation's Global Rights Index 2017.[129]

In the circumstances, it is only a melodramatic mockery for Bangladesh to observe the so-called noble (মহান) May Day with empty talks, hollow promises, and useless rallies; for the Awami fan Fakir Alamgir to sing his mass songs in support of the Awami regime; and for the Awami supporters to render the national poet Kazi Nazrul Islam's poem *The Rebel* ("বিদ্রোহী") in mass recitation for actually nothing more than fun.[130]

All this is as fashionable as the rebellious freedom and power mass song, "Beasts of England, beasts of Ireland/ Beasts of every land and clime," sung by the (allegorical/metaphorical) animals (actually suffering workers/humans) against the tyranny of the rich capitalist owner class at the end of the first chapter of Orwell's above-mentioned work. The rebellion of the animals ultimately come to nothing due to the greed, dishonesty, hypocrisy, and the abuse of power by and struggle for power between the two animals leaders at the end (Stalin and Trotsky), so that the last of the seven commandments, "All animals are equal," at the end of the second chapter becomes "All animals are equal, but some animals are more equal than others."

When there are impoverished millions, who cannot eat three meals a day,[131] when there is an excluded caste-based community of over 6.5 million (Dalits or Untouchables) doing the dirtiest and lowest paid menial jobs and suffering from all kinds of the meanest forms of discrimination, intimidation, elimination, and eviction,[132] and when Dhaka International Airport is one of the worst in the world (9th among the 10 worst in Asia), one has to invent a definition of Hasina's digital development in Bangladesh. According to the State Minister Tarana Halim, 75% mobile SIM cards in Bangladesh are fake that criminals take advantage of for committing crimes.[133] Using the pretext of so-called material development, the government wants to confuse and hoodwink the people and throw dust in their eyes, only to prolong and perpetuate its iron-clad sway. The excuse of development over democracy is just a cover for the autocratic and despotic government to continue in power. In the words of Ranu Chowdhury:

> In a virtually regimented situation—like that in communist societies of a few decades ago—where everybody is scared to open his mouth against the state power for fear of arrest, harassment, elimination and torture, what can the political opposition in the popular BNP achieve? All "neutral" or "middle ground" organizations resort to the safe refuge: blame the opposition for the so-called "anti-state" activities but don't dare point finger at Sheikh Hasina's follies and evil games. Nonetheless, they have taken some steps to put pressure, however meek and weak that be, on the ruling class (E-mail of February 15, 2015).

Chowdhury frequently writes on the social and political issues of the original native country he valiantly fought for forty-six years ago. A man of great integrity, patriotic fervor, and personal sacrifice, he believes that the country of his contribution continues to slide backward, especially with respect to the ideals of freedom, democracy, patriotism, justice, social justice, and nationalism, particularly under the present Awami government. He continues saying:

> Hasina kept playing her available cards, the latest being the judiciary one [calling for the opposition-called অবরোধ (siege) to be stopped by all means]—the way she did to quash the CTG—to evade the opposition movement and particularly to prevent her archenemy Khaleda Zia from ever returning to power. I am waiting when all her cards will be played. As the ancient Gauls feared nothing but the "fall of the sky" on their heads, Hasina fears nothing but her own fall, which may be worse than her father's. She may not be blinking yet, but her recent demeanors suggest she is not in good shape.

One could not concur more with the above as one cannot agree more with what Rezaul Karim, a health official in the USA, says, almost proverbially, "Judiciary being the guardian of the constitution is the most powerful branch, only when it is independent of politics, and it is the most dangerous when it is politicized. That is the lesson of history, everywhere. It is about time Bangladesh turns around and faces the injustices in the justice system itself. An independent and transparent judiciary is what we need to see and establish in Bangladesh."

There are positive signs that a few justices spoke out against whatever is/was unfair in the judicial system of Bangladesh. (Ret) Justices Khairul Hoque and Shamsuddin Chowdhury Manik, both unambiguously political/politicized and unequivocally of pronounced Awami inclinations and proclivities, have been severely criticized for being unjust and unfair, to the extent of being unconstitutionally partial and partisan, by Chief Justice S K Sinha and (Ret) Justice Mahmudul Amin Chowdhury.[134] Khairul Hoque has also been accused of being dishonest for going back on his own judicial decision and accepting the (perhaps prearranged) Law Commission position—a government salaried position—after he retired as chief justice.

Out of his out-and-out dislike for the great President Zia and his party of patriotic nationalists, Hoque irreverently found an excuse to connect the ownership of the Mymensingh Moon Cinema with the distantly irrelevant Zia government (like, as the critics say, গরুকে নদীর কাছে নিয়ে গরুর পরিবর্তে নদীর উপর রচনা লিখা অথবা প্রতিবেশীর কাছে প্রতিবেশীর চাল চেয়ে চালের পরিবর্তে চালকুমড়া পাওয়া/ taking the cow to the river and then writing an essay on the river about which the examinee was prepared, instead of the cow which was the actual topic of the test). For this যোজন যোজন দূর/ leagues away connection, Hoque was held to criticism by the BNP leaders, who thought his 5th amendment verdict was as preconceived and premeditated as he and his cohort Manik later thought the Sinha verdict concerning the repeal of the 16th amendment was, both in itself and between itself and its accompanying observations.

Though unanimous, detailed, balanced, and comprehensive it was, both Khairul Hoque and Shamsuddin Manik ran/went amok at the verdict.[135] Both of them have been deeply criticized for being severely contemptuous, in favor of the ruling Awami League, of the Sinha verdict, which was only slightly critical of the AL but more of the opposition. (Ret) Justice Nazrul Islam Chowdhury offered to defend a Jamaat-e-Islami leader, Mir Kashem Ali, against the human rights abuses the latter was accused of by the government before he was hanged to death.[136]

CJ Sinha, who, according to Manik, was behaving like a "rajakar" (which is tantamount to the defamation of court) has had the honest courage to allege that the judiciary was a hostage to the government, that the rule of law could still not be established, and that the government wanted to take control of the higher judiciary after having done so over the lower judiciary.[137] If other justices could do and could get away with their rogue bunch of stuff with the connivance of the Hasina regime, Justice Nazrul Chowdhury's short-term violation, if any, of professional ethics soon after he had retired, could be deemed as nothing serious.[138] As Edmund Burke lamented the disappearance of Chivalric values and virtues in the aftermath of the French Revolution, one can also lament that moralism, idealism, rule of law, and justice for all are gone and banished by the regime for years now in Bangladesh.

Now that it is in power—and only this time around, since 2009—the AL is applying an overdose of the development drug on the people in exchange for their precious and priceless democratic rights. Mephistopheles, Satan's/Lucifer's deputy, applies the magical drug of power and freedom on Dr Faustus in exchange for his immortal soul that is eventually consigned to hell. When the AL was not in power, its role was completely destructive in another way. It was the AL that called 173 days of nationwide হরতাল (strike/blockade) during 1991–1996 and 130 days during 2001–2007 as compared with the BNP's 59 days only during 1996–2001.

Jail and জুলুম cannot be made (halal/permissible), justified, and legitimized in the name of economic development to the advantage of one group only. Under the Awami politics of terror and torture, the only viable challenger to it, the BNP, has been rendered completely incapacitated and disadvantaged. Almost all its members are languishing in jail on politically motivated grounds, alleged and perceived by them to be false, flimsy, fabricated, or microscopic. The democratic minded patriots need to unite and persist in their struggle for freedom, justice, and democratically made balanced and sustainable development. Otherwise, unless something unexpected and miraculous happens in the present dying and dwindling stage of democratic culture and cultivation in Bangladesh, the BNP-led opposition is doomed, if it is not going to be dead yet with still a candle of its political life flickering that is about to be blown out. And that would be a prime-time tragic demise of democracy in Bangladesh!

As all the fair and objective-minded economic and development studies experts of the country, such as Dr Rashed Al Mahmud Titumir, Dr Debopryio Bhattacharya, and Dr Mustafizur Rahman, claim, all indexes of social and human development, human dignity, social and economic justice, rule of law, and good governance are in descending order since 2006 mainly due to the lack of democratic peace, stability, freedom, equality, and harmony. The very first and best and most important step to uphold the spirit of the 1971 independence in its full and complete entirety, not to be torn, twisted, and fragmented, as the AL and its academic and intellectual supporters tend to do, is not to merely keep talking and crowing about it in the so-called sluttish and secularist মুরগি (chicken) style,[139] but to be tolerant and transparent and to avoid being ruthless, repressive, regressive, and retrograde.

Once this desirable situation starts emerging and prevailing, all the rest is sure to fall in place, one welcome step, without fail, leading to another, one free and fair election showing the way to the next. Right to free speech, free assembly, free demonstration, free election, and representative government, along with equal and uniform application of laws—all being greater and more precious, cherished, and treasured, in a peaceful and disciplined way, the nation cannot sacrifice all these for one-sided, half-done, and half-accomplished development alone. It cannot lose one eye for the other. Both are complementary to each other and both are required for lasting and harmonious development, material as well as human, intellectual as well as religious.

Notes

1. http://www.dailynayadiganta.com/detail/news/187034
2. http://www.prothom-alo.com/bangladesh/article/803458/; BNP leader picked up at night, killed and dumped by the river in the morning: https://youtu.be/gci0OiqHVeA
3. http://uk.reuters.com/article/uk-bangladesh-opposition-idUKBREA130YS20140204
4. http://ireport.cnn.com/docs/DOC-1089432; for a picture of fascistic misrule, abduction, murder, looting and laundering under the Hasina dictatorship, see: https://www.facebook.com/hateawami/videos; https://www.facebook.com/video.php?v=896763733701983
5. http://www.prothom-alo.com/bangladesh/article/1178296
6. The term or the title means "Daughter of the Land," self-coined, which occurs throughout the book whenever the names of Farhana or Papia come up.

7. http://www.newsinbd.net/newsdetail/detail/112/318297
8. http://dailyajobbook.blogspot.co.uk/2013/09/blog-post.html (Saturday 14 September 2013).
9. For a sample of fake and false digital development under the Hasina regime, visit: http://www.dailynayadiganta.com/detail/news/234800;
http://www.prothom-alo.com/bangladesh/article/1133771;
http://www.ittefaq.com.bd/wholecountry/2017/04/21/111527.html;
http://www.prothom-alo.com/bangladesh/article/1152756;
http://www.ittefaq.com.bd/wholecountry/2017/04/21/111527.html;
https://www.youtube.com/watch?v=QHJy7ROATgk&feature=youtu.be;
http://www.jugantor.com/online/country-news/2017/04/21/45299;
https://www.dailyinqilab.com/article/69566;
http://www.dailydinkal.net/2017/03/12/33150.php;
http://www.dhakatimes24.com/2017/03/12/23747;
https://www.youtube.com/watch?v=7dzStKR_9K8&feature=youtu.be;
http://epaper.thedailystar.net/contents/2017/2017_03_04/content_zoom/2017_03_04_1_2_b.jpg;
http://www.ntvbd.com/bangladesh/103893;
http://www.jugantor.com/online/country-news/2017/01/02/35556;
http://www.jugantor.com/online/national/2017/03/16/42228;
http://epaper.prothom-alo.com/contents/2016/2016_10_03/content_zoom/x2016_10_03_8_0_b.jpg.pagespeed.ic.IWRSDJDGvN.jpg;
http://epaper.thedailystar.net/contents/2016/2016_10_31/content_zoom/2016_10_31_16_3_b.jpg;
http://epaper.prothom-alo.com/contents/2016/2016_10_30/content_zoom/x2016_10_30_8_4_b.jpg.pagespeed.ic.iNOoQzw5cx.jpg;
http://www.kalerkantho.com/print-edition/last-page/2016/11/01/423541;
http://www.bdface.net/newsdetail/detail/200/254705;
http://www.banglatribune.com/country/news/11303;
http://www.banglatribune.com/national/news/117839;
blob:https%3A//mail.google.com/6b1c6d8e-dbb0-4043-9a24-df4764154639;
http://epaper.thedailystar.net/contents/2016/2016_06_11/content_zoom/2016_06_11_3_6_b.jpg;
https://ruhulrabbi.files.wordpress.com/2014/08/dhaka-streets.jpg;
http://www.amaderbudhbar.com/2016/06/12/;
http://www.banglanews24.com/national/news/bd/496472.details;
https://www.facebook.com/photo.php?fbid=1871003523219100&set=pcb.1871001313219321&type=3&theater;https://mail.google.com/mail/u/0/?tab=wm#drafts/15d279d5cae9ee3f?compose=15d2c6ca75de6064%2C15d2c7fd42fbf5fa;
https://mail.google.com/mail/u/0/?tab=wm#drafts/15d279d5cae9ee3f?compose=15d2c6ca75de6064%2C15d2c79ace8b7c4e;

https://mail.google.com/mail/u/0/?tab=wm#drafts/15d279d5cae9ee3f?compose=15d2c6ca75de6064%2C15d2c752eb72313c
Kacher Bali

10. https://www.facebook.com/jiblurahman78/?ref=bookmarks
11. http://bangla.samakal.net/2016/12/31/259510;
http://www.bd-desh.net/newsdetail/detail/200/222299;
http://www.thedailystar.net/country/bangladesh-ranked-13th-most-corrupted-country-208054
12. http://www.bdnatun.net/newsdetail/detail/200/270779;
http://bangla.bdnews24.com/bangladesh/article1039839.bdnews;
http://www.prothom-alo.com/bangladesh/article/1028303;
http://www.jugantor.com/online/country-news/2016/11/23/31640;
https://www.facebook.com/Zaimarohman/photos/a.131463943693812.1073741828.131398263700380/443405385832998/?type=3&theater
13. http://www.ittefaq.com.bd/national/2017/06/20/118096.html
14. https://www.youtube.com/watch?v=7OKT2XkLnBs&feature=youtu.be;
http://www.kolkata24x7.com/special-interview-with-bangladeshi-intellectual-badruddin-umar.html
15. http://amar-desh24.com/bangla/print.php/nationalnews/10989
16. www.prothom-alo.com/economy/article/1037057/৯-ব্যাংকের-মূলধন-ঘাটতি-সাড়ে-১৬-হাজার-কোটি-টাকা; http://www.dailynayadiganta.com/detail/news/248356
17. http://newsbd7.com/main/detail/3215; https://www.youtube.com/watch?v=JFjSqO_iRUk; https://www.roshikhakim.com/2017/01/01;
http://shirshobindu.com/?p=100340;
https://www.facebook.com/ZahidFSarderSaddi/photos/a.589363327793514.1073741847.459794924083689/1578602068869630/?type=3&theater
18. http://m.dailynayadiganta.com/detail/news/190656
19. http://rtnbd.net/politics/10955
20. http://www.dainikamadershomoy.com/todays-paper/firstpage/57598;
http://www.prothom-alo.com/economy/article/708385;
http://www.prothom-alo.com/bangladesh/article/1018667;
http://www.prothom-alo.com/bangladesh/article/399673;
http://www.prothom-alo.com/economy/article/897736;
http://www.jugantor.com/online/national/2016/11/19/31180;
http://www.jugantor.com/online/national/2016/12/26/34862;
http://bangla.samakal.net/2017/01/09/261575
21. https://www.jagonews24.com/economy/news/262765
22. http://www.jugantor.com/first-page/2017/05/03/121823
23. www.jugantor.com/online/economics/2017/04/05/43938
24. http://www.prothom-alo.com/economy/article/1180861
25. http://www.ittefaq.com.bd/trade/2017/05/18/114224.html

26. http://www.bd-pratidin.com/editorial/2015/12/24/116767;
27. www.prothom-alo.com/opinion/article/1008929/এ-কী-করলেন-দুই-ব্যাংক-ডাকাত
28. http://www.banglatribune.com/columns/opinion/168749/;http://www.poriborton.com/opinion-news/19707/; http://www.ittefaq.com.bd/capital/2016/10/29/89823.html; http://www.banglatribune.com/columns/opinion/166953/
29. http://www.banglatribune.com/columns/opinion/170489;
http://rtnbd.net/politics/20432
30. http://www.jamunatv.net/news_details/4449;
https://www.youtube.com/watch?feature=player_embedded&v=6XkbgYeDP7Y
31. Visit: http://video.genfb.com/373581419690571;
video.genfb.com/1344678918925453;
https://www.facebook.com/video/video.php?v=780489652099823;
https://www.facebook.com/video/video.php?v=722585861229197
32. http://www.newagebd.net/article/18746/bnp-accuses-govt-for-smuggling-looting-money-to-swiss-banks;
http://www.jugantor.com/first-page/2017/05/07/122750;
http://www.thedailystar.net/backpage/al-leaders-wives-have-properties-canada-1401817; http://www.dailynayadiganta.com/detail/news/231814
33. http://www.manobkantha.com/2016/09/24/158101.php;
https://alalodulal.org/2013/06/05/second-home
34. http://www.ittefaq.com.bd/print-edition/first-page/2017/05/08/194107.html
35. http://www.kalerkantho.com/print-edition/first-page/2017/04/11/485389
36. https://www.youtube.com/watch?v=f6luU7SaF9k&feature=youtu.be;
http://www.banglamail24.com/news/153901; http://www.thedailystar.net/country/polls-chased-lawmen-man-hits-wall-dies-1230727;
http://mzamin.com/article.php?mzamin=15885;
http://bangla.samakal.net/2016/05/27/214750;
https://www.facebook.com/photo.php?fbid=1569357540030643&set=pcb.590507781115714&type=3&theater;
http://www.bbc.com/bengali/news/2016/05/160528_bangladesh_union_parishad_election;
http://bangla.samakal.net/2016/05/28/214971;
http://www.amadershomoy.biz/unicode/2016/05/28/117246.htm;
http://www.jugantor.com/online/national/2016/05/28/14383/;http://www.prothom-alo.com/bangladesh/article/871066/;
http://www.banglatribune.com/country/news/108789/;
http://www.amardeshonline.com/pages/home/2016/05/28;
http://www.dhakatribune.com/crime/2016/may/28/child-rapes-see-alarming-rise-bangladesh
37. http://en.prothom-alo.com/opinion/news/126119; http://epaper.prothom-alo.com/view/dhaka/2016-10-23/10

38. http://archive.dhakatribune.com/op-ed/2015/jul/28/setting-new-standard-democracy. However, given the fact that it is debatable whether Sheikh Mujib had great ideals or not, one reserves the right to disagree with Gen Ahmed's views as expressed in his article: http://archive.dhakatribune.com/op-ed/2015/sep/02/best-way-honour-bangabandhu
39. http://www.banglatribune.com/columns/opinion/76995/
40. http://newagebd.net/154180/democracy-and-development-the-contemporary-context/#
41. http://www.amardeshonline.com/pages/details/2015/12/22/316244
42. http://archive.dhakatribune.com/op-ed/2015/jul/08/bring-back-democracy
43. http://www.ittefaq.com/issues/2010/05/24/news0719.htm; http://nation.ittefaq.com/issues/2010/05/24/news0706.htm
44. For a Human Rights Watch report, visit http://www.thedailystar.net/country/freedom-expression-attacked-bangladesh-hrw-208117; https://www.hrw.org/world-report/2016/country-chapters/bangladesh; http://www.daily-sun.com/post/109860
45. For corruption implicating the top officials, see about the US$300 million to be reportedly in the account of the persons of interest: https://www.justice.gov/sites/default/files/usao-sdny/legacy/2015/03/25/Lustyik%20Et%20Al.Indictment.pdf; https://www.facebook.com/photo.php?fbid=10206542162178389&set=p.10206542162178389&type=3&theater. Also, http://www.anandabazar.com/bangladesh-news/india-and-america-get-the-benefit-of-smugled-money-from-bangladesh-1.379400; http://newsbd7.com/main/detail/2346; Accountability of Public Officials: $300m in wild goose chase by social media on http://www.weeklyholiday.net/Homepage/Pages/UserHome.aspx. The BNP leader (who is also the most popular and dignified leader of Bangladesh) DeshNetri Begum Khaleda Zia raised questions about the $300 million in the account of the PM Sheikh Hasina's son Sajeeb Wajed Joy: http://www.amardeshonline.com/pages/details/2016/05/01/334220. So did another BNP leader, Papia: https://www.youtube.com/watch?v=I-xG_qlp9fM; https://www.youtube.com/watch?v=VWYcDlcKWM8; http://www.hungamahub.com/video/52SLsywK7AE/syeda-ashrafi-papia-mp-talks-about-joys-corruption.html. For more details, click: http://www.bloomberg.com/news/articles/2016-03-14/don-t-blame-the-fed-bangladesh-seen-responsible-for-bank-heist?cmpid=yhoo.headline;
    http://www.ittefaq.com.bd/national/2016/03/15/59784.html;
    http://www.sheershanewsbd.com/2016/02/03/115276;
    http://www.worldbank.org/en/news/press-release/2012/06/29/world-bank-statement-padma-bridge;
    http://www.academia.edu/9585699/Arguments_in_favor_of_Corruption_in_Padma_Bridge;
    http://www.arthosuchak.com/archives/266539/;
    http://www.sheershanewsbd.com/2015/12/21/108827;

http://www.sheershanewsbd.com/2015/12/16/108216;
http://www.sheershanewsbd.com/2015/11/16/103912;
http://www.sheershanewsbd.com/2015/11/06/102770;
http://www.sheershanewsbd.com/2015/12/16/108181;
http://www.sheershanewsbd.com/2015/12/16/108181;
http://www.prothom-alo.com/bangladesh/article/1105324

46. http://www.thedailystar.net/op-ed/politics/elected-autocrats-and-the-decline-democracy-213148
47. http://www.ittefaq.com.bd/print-edition/sub-editorial/2016/09/19/144302.html
48. http://www.thedailystar.net/country/bangladeshs-elevation-ldc-status-not-2024-cpd-178444
49. http://www.sheershanewsbd.com/2015/05/26/82011#; http://www.sheershanewsbd.com/2015/06/08/83659#
50. See Note #9. Also, http://bangla.samakal.net/2016/05/27/214750; http://bangla.samakal.net/2016/05/26/214530
51. http://www.banglanews24.com/economics-business/news/491819
52. http://www.washingtonexaminer.com/bernie-sanders-the-business-model-of-wall-street-is-fraud-and-deception/article/2559985/; http://www.newsmax.com/Headline/bernie-sanders-wall-street-democrat-debate/2015/10/13/id/696088/
53. http://www.thedailystar.net/op-ed/politics/bnps-demise-and-possible-consequences-105316
54. http://www.daily-sun.com/post/104593/Illegal-govt-and-boneless-EC-kill-country%E2%80%99s-democracy;
http://www.daily-sun.com/post/105326/Fascism-established-undercover-of-democracy-alleges-BNP;
http://www.thedailystar.net/politics/none-has-right-differ-govt-alleges-fakhrul-198976;
http://newagebd.net/191751/fascism-under-the-cover-of-democracy-bnp/;
http://newagebd.net/190533/incumbent-govt-killed-democracy-says-khaleda/;
https://www.youtube.com/watch?v=Jo69KTcga5c
55. http://m.prothom-alo.com/pachmisheli/article/363505
56. http://www.sheershanewsbd.com/2015/06/02/82885; http://www.sheershanewsbd.com/2015/06/05/83255;
http://www.sheershanewsbd.com/2015/06/04/83203;
http://www.sheershanewsbd.com/2015/06/04/83190;
http://www.sheershanewsbd.com/2015/06/04/83171;
http://www.sheershanewsbd.com/2015/06/12/84234; also daily Amader Shomoy, June 10, 2015.
57. For an estimate of the unemployed, click https://www.dailyinqilab.com/details/35935/; yearly thirty thousand crore taka sent out of the country causing unemployment : http://www.bonikbarta.com/2015-09-15/news/details/49709.html

58. https://www.youtube.com/watch?v=eYEHM322MhM&feature=youtu.be
59. http://www.thedailystar.net/frontpage/1100-died-sea-18-months-133804
60. http://www.thedailystar.net/country/pm-draws-flack-comments-trafficking-victims-87115; also see, "Are these people really mental cases?," Weekly *Holiday*, May 29, 2015.
61. http://www.thedailystar.net/country/bangladesh-single-biggest-country-origin-refugees-europe-1401541
62 http://www.dailynayadiganta.com/detail/news/73203#; https://www.youtube.com/watch?feature=player_embedded&v=_YI7I7jqdyM; http://www.amadershomoy.biz/unicode/2016/05/04/104957.htm#
63. https://www.facebook.com/MBIMunshi/posts/10153312251625645:0 (May 12, 2015).
64. https://www.facebook.com/search/str/Mohammad+Munshi+%241%2C314+and+GDP/keywords_search
65. Serajul Islam, "Will Bangladesh Give India Land Transit?," http://www.thefinancialexpress-bd.com/2015/05/31/94736; ANM Nurul Hoque, "Awaiting Modi's Magic on Teesta," http://www.daily-sun.com/printversion/details/47986/Awaiting-Modirsquos-magic-on-Teesta; M. Shahidul Islam, "Festering wounds beneath a smooth surface," Weekly *Holiday*, May 29, 2015; Shamsuddin Ahmed, "Indian Prime Minister coming to advance transit treaty," Weekly *Holiday*, May 29, 2015.
66 http://www.sheershanewsbd.com/2015/05/22/81460#; http://www.sheershanewsbd.com/2015/05/18/81071#; http://www.sheershanewsbd.com/2015/05/21/81431#;http://www.sheershanewsbd.com/2015/05/21/81420#; http://www.sheershanewsbd.com/2015/06/04/83149#
67. http://projects.aljazeera.com/2015/10/bangladesh-chitmahals/; http://www.bangladeshchronicle.net/index.php/2015/07/600-residents-of-enclaves-within-bangladesh-want-to-migrate-to-india/; http://www.amadershomoys.com/newsite/2015/07/21/353995.htm#
68. http://www.bd-pratidin.com/first-page/2016/12/10/191290
69. Terribly miserable, no power for 12 hrs a day: http://www.prothom-alo.com/bangladesh/article/1189356
70. Common citizenry raise their eyebrows suspecting mega and massive corruption in the under-construction Padma Bridge and its repeatedly revised budget, from initially 4,000 crore to 7,000 crore to the horribly huge and humongous 35,000 crore taka (or from 10,000 crore to 50,000 crore taka), which is many more times the cost of similar projects in other countries. See David Bergman at: https://thewire.in/109388/did-a-canada-court-really-clear-bangladesh-officials-of-corruption. For the media record of the instances of corruption, click: http://rtnbd.net/politics/10955; http://bangla.samakal.net/2016/07/25/226287. Also see the article by Kamrul Hasan Dorpon at https://www.dailyinqilab.com/details/10054/; http://www.amardeshonline.com/pages/details/2016/03/18/327952; Golam Mowla Roni,

http://www.dailynayadiganta.com/detail/news/102604; for an idea about how helpless the masses are in this kind of corruption, see: http://www.dailysangram.com/news_details.php?news_id=228648

71. http://www.jugantor.com/online/national/2017/03/23/42840
72. http://www.jugantor.com/online/national/2017/03/16
73. http://newagebd.net/182239/lack-of-facilities-keep-girls-away-from-schools/
74. http://www.jugantor.com/first-page/2016/10/26/71105
75. http://www.prothom-alo.com/bangladesh/article/1056711; http://rtnbd.net/national/21398; https://www.facebook.com/photo.php?fbid=1161718717205295&set=gm.627207500771455&type=3&theater
76. http://www.prothom-alo.com/bangladesh/article/1043187; http://www.kalerkantho.com/print-edition/first-page/2016/09/25/408994; http://www.dailynayadiganta.com/detail/news/220688; https://www.facebook.com/notes/kaus-kai/228639600906629
77. http://www.mzamin.com/article.php?mzamin=10934 http://www.bbc.com/bengali/news/2016/04/160422_bangladesh_minorities_attacks_on_the_rise_update
78. http://www.daily-sun.com/arcprint/details/94396/Impact-of-food-price-hike-on-nutritional-status-of-children/2015-11-27
79. http://www.thedailystar.net/country/15-lakh-bangladeshis-living-slaves-report-1232239; Child labour and education: a survey of slum settlements in Dhaka
80. http://www.ittefaq.com.bd/wholecountry/2017/06/24/118439.html
81. http://www.banglatelegraph.com/2016/10/
82. http://www.amardeshonline.com/pages/details/2016/04/21/332825
83. http://www.manobkantha.com/2016/10/25/164857.php
84. See the pro-Awami Dr Abul Barakat's research findings at http://www.banglatribune.com/national/news/158305; and the article by Mobaiyedur Rahman: https://www.dailyinqilab.com/details/42496
85. http://www.thedailystar.net/backpage/bangladesh-121st-best-country-business-189184
86. http://www.cnn.com/2015/08/17/travel/most-liveable-city-2015/index.html
87. http://www.thedailystar.net/country/bangladesh-static-human-development-index-190033
88. http://www.newagebd.net/article/20111/dhakas-average-traffic-speed-now-7-kmph
89. http://www.ittefaq.com.bd/wholecountry/2016/02/06/54149.html; http://newagebd.net/218214/banshkhali-killing/
90. http://www.amadershomoys.com/unicode/2016/04/26/102125.htm; http://www.thedailystar.net/country/57-child-labours-victims-physical-torture-study-1207021
91. http://www.prothom-alo.com/we-are/article/814375/
92. http://old.dhakatimes24.com/2015/08/08/77830; http://www.bbc.com/bengali/news-38249811; http://unify24.com/newspaper/search/0/4; https://www.facebook.com/BBCBengaliService/

93. http://www.thedailysangbad.com/first-page/2016/10/27/90979
94. http://www.jugantor.com/online/national/2016/05/03/11664/; http://www.amardeshonline.com/pages/details/2016/04/13/331623
95. http://newagebd.net/218633/govt-rejects-hrw-report-on-arsenic/
96. http://www.thedailystar.net/backpage/bizarre-construction-1206463; http://www.thedailystar.net/editorial/no-supervision-construction-1206664; https://mail.google.com/mail/u/0/#inbox/153fe9f88cd5daf4; https://www.youtube.com/watch?v=NYZVo2Dp1mk; http://bangla.theglobalnews24.com/?p=25342; http://www.thedailystar.net/trending-socially/dohar-bridge-worlds-8th-wonder-1223671
97. While an internet search of media archives would produce many proofs and evidences, just one such is this: http://www.jugantor.com/first-page/2016/12/12/84495
98. http://www.somewhereinblog.net/blog/mostofa_kamal/30042374
99. http://www.bd-pratidin.com/first-page/2017/01/06/197804
100. http://www.thedailystar.net/country/dhaka-one-worlds-worst-holiday-spots-1351234
101.
    - 800 crore taka ($8.10 m stolen from the central bank of Bangladesh in February 2016; for an exclusive image showing the smuggled money trail in 2013 and linking it to the central bank heist, see: http://www.jugantor.com/online/economics/2016/05/26/14144/;
    - 60, 000 crore taka through the DP Rail: http://newsbd7.com/main/detail/3215;
    - 43,000 crore taka remaining unaccounted for/smuggled out each year: http://www.jugantor.com/online/economics/2017/01/16/36824;
    - 30,000 crore taka smuggled out of the country yearly: http://www.bonikbarta.com/2015-09-15/news/details/49709.html;
    - mega looting through bank loan: http://www.prothom-alo.com/bangladesh/article/943927;
    - 4,55,000 crore taka smuggled out in the last ten years: http://www.jugantor.com/online/economics/2016/12/10/33414;
    - 70,000 crore taka looted from different banks: http://www.jugantor.com/online/economics/2016/05/27/14319;
    - 500 crore taka stolen through ATM card scam: http://www.jugantor.com/online/economics/2016/05/24/13904/;
    - another 500 crore taka stolen from the Rupali Bank: http://www.rtnews24.com/economy;
    - another 1300 crore take loan irregularities at the Rupali Bank: http://www.jugantor.com/online/economics/2017/02/27/40663;
    - 300 crore taka looted from the Agrani Bank: http://www.jugantor.com/online/economics/2016/05/25/14012;

- Golam Murtoza (#6 at http://www.shaptahik.com/v2/?DetailsId=11268) writes that 76,000 crore taka got smuggled out of the country in 2014 alone; that the reserves got stolen from the Bangladesh Bank; that the Anandabazar of Kolkata of May 6 reported nearly 50,000 crore dollars smuggled out in the last ten years, which is 39 lakh crore in taka; which means an average of about 4 lakh crore taka every year and which is one fifth of the national GDP.
- Over Taka 400,000 crore skimmed out in crippling corruption during the Awami League regime: http://defence.pk/threads/crippling corruption-by-awami-league regime.171009/page-6;
- For a list of mega bank lootings during the Awami regime, click https://www.facebook.com/hate.infidel/posts/763534027079783:0;
- For Agrani Bank loan irregularities in crores: http://bangla.samakal.net/2016/10/11/242408;
- For 701 crore taka NRBC irregularities: http://www.newagebd.net/article/8140/fake-directors-tk-701cr-shady-loans-scams-galore-in-nrbc;
- Awami MP M K (Mokha) Alamgir's Farmers Bank is one of the most corruption-ridden banks in Bangladesh, involved in scandals and irregularities in the amount of crores and millions of dollars: http://bangla.samakal.net/2017/01/25/265466;
- Out of many, only four government banks lost nearly 930 crore taka in one year (2016) alone: http://www.jugantor.com/online/economics/2017/03/06/41309;
- $250,000 stolen in a cyber heist from the largest commercial bank, Sonali Bank, in 2013: http://newagebd.net/231996/bangladesh-probes-2013-hack-for-links-to-central-bank-heist;
- 27 crore taka worth sea vessel MV Bungalee is useless from the beginning due to corruption: http://www.amadershomoy.biz/unicode/2016/07/01/134973.htm;
- Two crore taka stolen away into Turkey from the largest government-controlled commercial bank, Sonali Bank, in 2013: http://www.jugantor.com/online/economics/2016/05/26/14144/
- For the other countless crores looted and plundered, also visit:
  http://www.real-timenews.com/bangla//newsdetail/detail/1/2/140469;
  http://bangla.irib.ir/2010-04-21-08-29-09/item/83297;
  http://www.prothom-alo.com/economy/article/811354/;
  http://bangla.samakal.net/2016/03/27/202155;
  http://www.amardeshonline.com/pages/details/2016/03/21/328279;
  http://www.bd-pratidin.com/first-page/2016/03/21/133906;
  http://www.jugantor.com/online/economics/2016/05/22/13750/;
  http://www.dailynayadiganta.com/detail/news/103416/;
  http://www.ittefaq.com.bd/national/2016/03/11/59065.html;
  http://www.prothom-alo.com/opinion/article/795580/;
  http://www.jugantor.com/online/national/2016/03/11/6571/;

http://www.dailydinkal.net/2016/03/21/24035.php;
http://www.ittefaq.com.bd/trade/2016/03/22/60628.html;
http://www.bdnow.net/newsdetail/detail/49/207058

102. http://www.bd-pratidin.com/first-page/2016/07/16/157067
103. http://bangla.bdnews24.com/bangladesh/article1238175.bdnews; https://www.youtube.com/watch?v=CSAspkE801Y
104. http://www.ittefaq.com.bd/capital/2015/11/19/43876.html; also see the article by Taj Hashmi: http://www.thedailystar.net/op-ed/%E2%80%9Czakat-deaths%E2%80%9D-bangladesh-old-story-piety-and-power-113527
105. http://www.dhakatribune.com/law-and-rights/2016/apr/24/development-futile-without-freedom-and-security;
http://www.risingbd.com/english/progress-meaningless-without-security-sultana-kamal/33603
106. http://www.nytimes.com/2014/10/11/opinion/tahmima-anam-how-to-rob-a-bank-in-bangladesh.html?_r=1#story-continues-2
107. http://www.nytimes.com/2016/05/01/business/dealbook/hackers-81-million-sneak-attack-on-world-banking.html?ref=todayspaper&_r=0#story-continues-1
108. BBGOVERNORS:https://www.bb.org.bd/aboutus/bbgovernors.php;BBBOARDOF DIRECTORS: https://www.bb.org.bd/aboutus/boardofdirectors.php; BB DEPUTY GOVERNORS AND EXECUTIVES: https://www.bb.org.bd/aboutus/exestaff.php; BB GENERAL MANAGERS https://www.bb.org.bd/aboutus/gm.php. Key Executives For Bangladesh Bank (click on "view more key executives" after going to this link): http://www.bloomberg.com/research/stocks/private/people.asp?privcapId=36769078. Board Members affiliated with Nirmal Chandra Bhakt: http://www.bloomberg.com/research/stocks/private/relationship.asp?personId=107491355&p rivcapId=36769078&previousCapId=36769078&previousTitle=Bangladesh%20Bank; Raghuda writes about the Hinduization of the banks in Bangladesh: https://www.facebook.com/amiraghuda/photos/a.972685896138648.1073741828.972387396168498/1015989675141603/?type=3&thea; concerning the mystery surrounding Rakesh Astana, visit: http://timesofbangla.com/special/19536/
109. http://www.amadershomoy.biz/beta/2016/07/26/651123;
http://deshbhabona.com/uncategorized/2017/03/21/18/34
110. http://banglamail71.info/archives/1251;
dailybdtimes.com/2017/07/25/বাংলাদেশ-ব্যাংকের-রিজার-3/
111. http://www.dailysangram.com/post/263777
112. http://www.bbc.com/bengali/news-39369659
113. http://www.first-bd.net/newsdetail/detail/200/203414;
http://bangla.samakal.net/2015/09/22/163769/print;
http://www.ittefaq.com.bd/national/2016/03/17/59978.html
114. http://newagebd.net/231885/india-based-masterminds-behind-bbs-money-heist-daily-mail/;

http://www.dailymail.co.uk/news/article-3599049/Hackers-81-MILLION-cyber-heist-one-world-s-biggest-Bangladesh-bank-NEVER-caught-untraceable.html#ixzz49kBgPAWu

115. http://newsbd7.com/main/detail/2829
116. http://www.ajkalnewyork.com/newsite/2016/03/11/30617.html
117. http://www.ajkalnewyork.com/newsite/2016/12/23/61668.html
118 মালাউনের বাচ্চারা বিষয়টি নিয়ে বাড়াবাড়ি করছে – প্রাণিসম্পদমন্ত্রী মো. ছায়েদুল হক; http://www.somoyerkonthosor.com/2016/11/04/59199.htm
119. http://www.wsj.com/articles/fbi-suspects-insider-involvement-in-81-million-bangladesh-bank-heist-1462861549;
http://newagebd.net/229061/swift-rejects-bangladeshi-claims-in-cyber-heist-police-stand-firm/
120. http://www.prothom-alo.com/economy/article/794407/;
http://www.jugantor.com/first-page/2016/03/10/17479/;
http://www.ittefaq.com.bd/national/2016/03/11/59197.html;
http://bangladeshchronicle.net/2016/03/bangladesh-bank-it-systems-dangerously-exposed/; http://www.ittefaq.com.bd/national/2016/03/17/59936.html; http://www.thedailystar.net/country/swift-technicians-left-bb-vulnerable-1221019
121. http://www.economist.com/news/finance-economics/21707719-government-claims-publishing-report-would-undermine-efforts-retrieve
122. Dr Zafrullah Chowdhury commented on Joy's allegedly monthly two crore taka ($200,000) salary.
123. "The government initiates a coup at Bangladesh's biggest bank": The Economist (http://www.economist.com/news/asia/21720326-board-members-receive-visit-military-intelligence-government-initiates-coup)
124. http://www.theindependentbd.com/post/37592;
http://www.ittefaq.com.bd/science-&-tech/2016/03/17/59990.html
125. In India, there are dowry murders of 106,000 women burnt to death in 1 year; in the much smaller Bangladesh, the figure is no less. Visit https://genderbytes.wordpress.com/2011/10/02/video-murder-by-fire-100000-women-a-year/
126. http://www.thedailystar.net/city/105-women-children-murdered-last-month-1820;
http://www.prothom-alo.com/opinion/article/740281/;
http://www.amadershomoys.com/unicode/2016/04/16/98812.htm#
127. http://bonikbarta.com/news/2016-12-31/101006; https://www.isealalliance.org/sites/default/files/Dhaka_Living_Wage_Benchmark_Report.pdf
128. http://www.waronwant.org/sweatshops-bangladesh. During the time of the California gold rush in 1849, the workers or the forty-niners as they used to be called made $1.00 a day, which was then considered a good pay.
129. https://www.ituc-csi.org/ituc-global-rights-index-2017
130. http://www.amardeshonline.com/pages/details/2015/12/18/315629; https://www.hrw.org/news/2017/02/15/bangladesh-stop-persecuting-unions-garment-workers;

https://www.hrw.org/news/2016/04/21/bangladesh-garment-workers-union-rights-bleak

131. http://www.banglanews24.com/national/news/480716/%E0%A6%AD%E0%A6%
132. http://www.thedailystar.net/law-our-rights/rights-advocacy/the-dalits-bangladesh-203845;
http://www.independent.co.uk/news/world/asia/oppressed-dalits-of-bangladesh-fight-for-their-future-1205005.html;http://www.upstreamjournal.org/2009/11/the-dalits-of-bangladesh/; http://www.dailynayadiganta.com/detail/news/147175
133. http://www.thedailystar.net/country/75-sim-cards-are-fake-tarana-147112; http://www.dailynayadiganta.com/detail/news/56463#
134. For Shamsuddin Manik's background, see, http://www.analysisbd.com/archives/5202Manik
135. http://www.thedailystar.net/politics/what-chief-justice-surendra-kumar-sinha-said-supreme-court-verdict-16th-amendment-bangladesh-constitution-1447990; http://www.prothom-alo.com/opinion/article/1288451; http://www.newsofbd.net/newsdetail/detail/49/329101; http://www.shomoybarta24.net/?p=99395; http://www.newsofbd.net/newsdetail/detail/200/329031;
136. Khairul Hoque changed some of the key parts of the open court ordering portion in the full verdict that he wrote more than a year and a half after his retirement. This change of the initial/original open court pronounced judgment (ordering portion) in the full verdict written long after his retirement was termed as criminal and unconstitutional by two chief justices, one former (Mahmudul Amin Chowdhury) and one present (S K Sinha). Khairul Hoque's first ordering portion was unequivocal in stating that while the CTG was in conflict with the Constitution, for the greater interest of fair play, another two terms of national/parliamentary elections could however be held under the CTG. Later, in the full verdict, Khairul Hoque inserted the new conditional that those two terms could be held under the CTG "only if the parliament so deemed"—a conditional, already dead or stillborn in view of the "No" tyranny of the questionable Hasina majority parliament, that brought all the chaos and violence to the country. Also visit: http://newagebd.net/201425/judiciary-on-the-verge-of-collapse-says-justice-mahmudul-amin/; http://mzamin.com/article.php?mzamin=806&cat=1; http://www.amardeshonline.com/pages/details/2016/02/10/322860; http://www.sheer-shanewsbd.com/2016/02/10/116186
137. http://www.newagebd.net/article/2284/judiciary-hostage-to-law-ministry-sc; http://www.prothom-alo.com/bangladesh/article/1164141; http://www.dhakatribune.com/bangladesh/2016/feb/18/legal-notice-served-justice-manik; http://www.dailydinkal.net/2017/05/24/35036.php
138. http://www.daily-sun.com/post/115018/ExCJ-Khairul-Haque-to-face-trial-in-future:-Moudud; http://www.sheershanewsbd.com/2016/02/18/117234

139. The reference to মুরগি comes from the rumor that some secularists, who now claim themselves to be infused and imbued with the spirit of the 1971 liberation war, are said to have run a business to supply chicken to the killer Pakistani forces then, thus helping them to eat well and kill more and more Bangladeshis and thereby playing a pro-Pakistani "razakar" role. For the background of মুরগি secularists and Dr Tuhin Malik's courageous comment on them, click: https://www.youtube.com/watch?v=X-0uFoN8NjsY; www.news-bangla.net/blog/blogdetail/detail/5287/Tal2013/34122; http://www.facebd.net/newsdetail/detail/200/263678; http://www.facebd.net/blog/blogdetail/detail/2601/muhon/69119; for Syeda Ashifa Ashrafi Papia's bold comment on the same, see: https://www.youtube.com/watch?v=VwdcbrjcMpc

3

The Role of the Police and the RAB (Rapid Action Battalion) in the "Development *Sans* Democracy" Conversation and the Gopal/Gopali Parrots and Predators in the Police

London and Paris are the two cities riddled with perils in Charles Dickens's *A Tale of Two Cities* set at the time of the French Revolution in the 18th century. On the one hand, there was a severe and heavy-handed application of force against the weak and the politically different, and, on the other, there was a laxity for the criminals let loose without the law enforcement enforcing the law. PM Sheikh Hasina's Bangladesh, a police ridden country, is no exception, chronically suffering from the infection of the police as well as political Zika, Ebola, and Chikungunya viruses. Ruled by a severely subversive (and subservient to India) government, limping with a serious credibility problem, the country is excessively controlled by the police/RAB/RAW, believed to be resorting, widely and opportunistically, to their sweeping arrest authority and fire power.

The innocent Titumir College student Siddiqur Rahman losing his eyes to the barbaric police action on July 20, 2017 is one of the recent victims of the inhuman police excesses and atrocities. The latest UK Foreign and Commonwealth Office reports precisely just that, claiming that there was no improvement of the already lamentable human rights situation in the country due to the unlawful lapses and deviations of the lopsided law enforcement agents. It said that "there were allegations of extrajudicial killings, arbitrary arrests, torture and enforced disappearances involving law enforcement agencies" and that "new laws were introduced that had the potential to restrict freedom of expression."[1]

The New York Times Editorial of July 28, 2017, captioned "The Opposition Disappears in Bangladesh," reports that hundreds of people, as many as 320

> [...] have been unlawfully detained or have disappeared in Bangladesh [...] Plucked from their homes or off the streets by plainclothes members of Bangladesh's rapid action battalion or the detective bureau of the Dhaka police, the victims increasingly include members of the political opposition, as well as suspected criminals and Islamist militants. Among the 90 people who disappeared last year [...] of which 21 were killed and nine remain missing, was Mir Ahmad Bin Quasem, a lawyer for the opposition Jamaat-e-Islami political party [...] Alarmed by these practices, the United Nations called in February for "Bangladesh to act now to halt an increasing number of enforced disappearances in the country." But the pace of disappearances only appears to be quickening.[2]

Not allowing any sort of opposition gathering whatsoever, including even the religious *Eid* and *Iftar* get-togethers, much-needed aid for the suffering Rohingyas, membership drives, and the see-off of the most popular opposition leader দেশনেত্রী /Leader of the Land Begum Khaleda Zia at the airport, on her visit to London, by her party leaders and activists, the police/RAB are the very cause of what has actually become a civilian martial law imposed upon the nation. Their unchecked and unguarded goliath strength makes them engage in widespread corruption and disengage, selectively, out of their self-seeking interest, from where they need to fully exercise their law enforcement ability and capacity as dictated by their professional commitment and obligation for the sake of the people and the nation they are supposed to serve honestly and selflessly without being the playboy plaything of the Awami regime only.

Exceptions of good deeds put aside, the generally sadist and selective inaction and moral misconduct, particularly of the police, in regard to the members of the main political opposition of the country, BNP and its allies; their much delayed action in the case of the Banani RainTree Hotel rape incident; and their strange, bizarre, distrustful, and denial mode statements—partial, partisan, and unconvincing—concerning the abominable abduction of an intellectual and philosophical mind no less than Farhad Mazhar are a few of only the recent umpteen examples of their utter moral and political corruption and degeneration.[3] In many cases their suspicious findings are far from being credible, to the extent of being cooked to cover up in favor of the regime. The state of decadence and degradation the law enforcement agents have retreated and receded into made the senior Supreme Court lawyer, Dr Shahdin Malik, to remark that it has become customary with the regime's reckless and lawless (above-the-law) police to lapse into their unbridled excesses in the parochially police-controlled state of Bangladesh under Sheikh Hasina.[4]

Malik's claim is in unison with the everyday claim made by the opposition BNP—claims amply and abundantly supported by all human rights organizations around the world. In its 82-page report called "'We Don't Have Him': Secret Detentions and Enforced Disappearances in Bangladesh," the New York-based Human Rights Watch (HRW) claimed that "90 people fell victim to enforced disappearance in Bangladesh in 2016 and 21 of them were killed [...] The 90 cases include three sons of prominent opposition politicians who were picked up over several weeks in August 2016; one was released after six months of secret detention, while the other two remain disappeared. In the first five months of 2017, 48 disappearances were reported. There are allegations of severe torture and ill-treatment while in secret custody." Pointing to the law enforcement agencies illegally detaining several hundred people since 2013, including scores of opposition activists, and holding them in secret detention, the HRW found that "Bangladesh security forces appear to have a free hand in detaining people, deciding on their guilt or innocence, and determining their punishment, including whether they have the right to be alive."[5]

The ALRC's (Asian Legal Resource Center's) Working Committee on Enforced and Involuntary Disappearances reported that the number of such victims stood at 212 from 2009 to 2015. International rights groups such as ALRC, FIDH (International Federation for Human Rights) and AFAID (Asian Federation Against Involuntary Disappearances) made a call before the United Nations Human Rights Council in Geneva for UN intervention in enforced disappearances in Bangladesh.[6] The heartrending cries of the loved ones of the disappeared reach out to pierce right into the sky.[7] No doubt, the country is one of countless politically cooked and concocted lawsuits against its own people and their enforced disappearances and murders by both known and unknown (secret and shadowy) kidnappers and assassins?[8] Dr Asif Nazrul exposes the beastly inhumanity behind the endless গুম ও খুন (forced disappearances, abominable abductions, and gruesome murders) committed with the direct or indirect knowledge of the Hasina regime, its cruel-hearted and predatory police/RAB (in uniform or plain clothes), and its home minister, who, Dr Nazrul said, was lacking in commonsense in view of his coarse and cumbersome comments about the abductees and their fate.[9]

Yet another recent example of the legal and moral corruption of the police is that eleven detectives have been found involved in grabbing money and valuables from a club in the capital on April 18, 2017. Punitive actions have been recommended against them, although no action may, however, ever be taken or at best there may be an eyewash measure to show the public that they have been punished and at the same time keep them happy in favor of the regime and motivate them to swoop down upon the opposition with more boots and bullets in a show of more suppression with more aggressive force and power.[10] The BNP, which is completely barred from holding any meetings or assemblies whatsoever by the police/RAB, has correctly accused the Hasina regime of halting, hammering, and nailing down democracy.[11]

Beatrice Janzon, Foreign News Reporter of Swedish Radio, exposes brutal killings by Bangladeshi Elite Police Unit RAB and their involvement in the vile and violent evil, that is, the recurring forced disappearances of the innocent people belonging to the political opposition. In her report Janzon quotes a RAB officer as saying: "If you find him, shoot and kill him, wherever he is. And then plant a weapon beside him […] This can be a way of getting rid of political opponents and there are forces that want to remove a large number of people, according to the RAB officer."[12]

Many watchers and observers such as Dr Zafrullah Chowdhury, Advocate Sultana Kamal, and the Swedish Radio and BBC reports point to the Indian RAW conspiring with the Hasina regime's RAB to commit clandestine crimes in Bangladesh, including the preplanned terror attacks, to justify the regime's political repression and legitimize its prolonged stay in power.[13] The tragic stories of Lt Col Hasinur Rahman Duke and Lt Col Abdullah Ali Zayeed, who, according to reports, were heroically dedicated officers in the Bangladesh army, but made criminals for their anti-Indian and anti-Hasina patriotic fervor, lend support to the critics pointing finger at the law enforcement's brutal cleansing of dissent and difference with the help of the outsider agents in the Indian RAW.[14]

It is mainly with the pernicious help of the police and the RAB that the Hasina regime is practicing its politics of division, diversion, and divergence, instead of unity, convergence, reconciliation, and restoration of political and human rights. Apart from the many, many good things that they certainly do (including detaining LGBTs), which they are supposed to do anyway as part of their paid job without being necessarily thanked for, the police and the RAB also seem to be out there not doing what they are supposed to do impartially without taking the side of the rich and famous and powerful, who are also allied and aligned with the Hasina regime. They also seem to be out there chasing and running after the BNP, snatching away the party's freedoms, but running and jumping up and down with the AL.

To be sure, the police/RAB are supposed to serve the government and work for the government, not to be servile and slavish to it. If they are drunk with power, privileges, and perks, and not motivated by their patriotic ties and ideals to the nation and the country, that is of course a different story. They should not be too friendly, loyal, or loyalist to the government in the sense of being in baneful bondage to it. Service does not mean slavery; it means being objective, truthful, and impartial to the government for the sake of the nation and the country. They must make sure neither they as law enforcement agencies nor the government is above the law. They must keep their eyes and ears open more for the violators of the law, regardless of which party they belong to, than the innocent opposition leaders and activists.

Unfortunately, the police/RAB are blind in their one-sided loyalties. Their eyes are like "those of a vulture—pale blue, with a film over them—as they watch and wait for the BNP to die"—to adapt the idea from Edgar Allan Poe's bizarre murder story "The Tell-Tale Heart." Apart from detaining dozens of BNP leaders and activists every passing day, the Awami police/RAB are in the habit of raiding only into the BNP offices time and again and not into the ruling Awami offices. They do so to torture, persecute, insult, intimidate, harass, and humiliate the BNP. If they raid only into the BNP offices under the search warrant from the court as they claim, why would the court be callous toward the Awami offices? Why would there be a dastardly double standard?

While the police/RAB have an overflow in descending down on the BNP, they suffer from a serious shortfall on the matters of "curb and control" of horrible crimes and horrendous unsocial activities, including the drug dealers and other sorts of hoodlums and hooligans, who have engulfed the society, like a devastating flood, since the Hasina regime took power years ago. Also, it is shocking and shameful that there are so many fake and false policemen in disguise taking advantage of the equally shocking and shameful police laxities in the exercise of morality and honesty and discharge of duty over the years.[15]

Members of the police/RAB have become corrupted by the ills of the society, so much so that the civil society demands either their reform or their dissolution. They liberally allow themselves to get politicized and dogmatically indoctrinated, as if it is their sacred duty to forcibly and ferociously silence the political opponents in the BNP in order to protect, promote, defend, and preserve the Hasina regime and its one-sided agenda. In addition, there is the humongous heap of allegations against their morally and financially scandalous affairs and the enduring public distrust in them due to their dire and deadly follies and failures and their distorted and twisted narratives of the same crimes, criminals, and crime scenes, according to their convenience. Both the local and international media and the Amnesty International have widely covered the police brutalities and their human rights abuses in Bangladesh.[16]

Since 2009 there has been a politics of unprecedented cooperation and collusion between the law enforcement and the regime, compounding the country as a police state of moral and political repression and trepidation. Having consolidated "a plain clothes white micro" government within the government, they are the "boys" having fun in throwing deadly stones at the small frogs of those innocent civilians or opposition members, abducted, dismembered, and killed every passing day. If the Hasina-led Awamis and the people of Bangladesh were wrong to be happy and not to mourn at the death of Sheikh Mujib and his family members on August 15, 1975, they are again mistaken and cruel-hearted in sanctioning, approving, and conniving at the nonstop imprisonments, abductions, and killings of their fellow citizens, in thousands—unspeakably and unbearably miserable and painful. It is an open secret that the police/RAB are out there to champion the Awami cause of autocracy and oligarchy and thereby ruin the goals of the liberation war in terms of justice, social justice, rule of law, good governance, transparency, accountability, democracy, and freedom of speech.

In its lack of democratic practices in relation to the political opposition, Bangladesh is far behind Taiwan, South Korea, Japan, Indonesia, Israel, new Tunisia, Costa Rica, Brazil, Uruguay, Mexico, Colombia, Chile, and many other countries in the world, not to speak of the West. All those countries have become established in their democratic norms and standards, some of them with high democratic performance. The undemocratic countries (such as China, Russia, Hong Kong, Singapore, Malaysia, Myanmar, Zimbabwe, Kazakhstan, Turkmenistan, Tajikistan, Cambodia, Vietnam, Laos, Maduro's Venezuela, Bashir's Sudan, Sisi's Egypt, and the rest of the Arab world) that the Hasina regime is imitating in its savage suppression of democracy have hardly seen any vibrant and vigorous democratic culture and freedom of expression. Those countries lack the democratic tradition of free and open elections—the most critical and crucial of all democratic processes. There is no democratic transition of power with room or space for dissenting political forums and platforms to flourish there. The governments of those countries depend on silence rather than speech and their actions and activities are contingent upon being intellectually and culturally mute, passive, and unruffled on the part of the public.

What those governments do in their democratically dormant (if not dead) countries is being done, obviously in a far worse, more dismal, and more appalling manner, by the Hasina regime in what used to be, until 2009, a democratically fairly active and dynamic country—Bangladesh. Even Ershad's less than absolutely autocratic times in the 1980s were far better than Sheikh Mujib's daughter Hasina's present near-totalitarian times steering the country to full dictatorship.

The other times between 1976–1981 and 1991–2005 were the best in the history of Bangladesh so far. The present morally and politically repressive Hasina regime is in despotic and dictatorial control of Bangladesh through its police and their allied (RAB) forces as well as other coercive tools in the judiciary and civil administration.[17]

The American State Department reported about the human rights abuses in Bangladesh in 2016. The report contains the very word "police" as many as 83 times and the acronym "RAB" as many as 30 times. It sheds light on the "widespread impunity for security force abuses" and "public distrust of police and security services" as it provides details of their involvement in what it calls "Arbitrary Deprivation of Life and other Unlawful or Politically Motivated Killings."[18] Putting aside whatever good works they do and should do as part of their paid job, the police/RAB are mainly used by the regime to indiscriminately detain, arrest, and remand the opposition members, from top to bottom, to deny them their political rights and freedom of speech, and to block and suppress their political programs and activities.

Both local and international press is full of damaging reports about the sour and bitter taste of the police state Bangladesh, which is ranked 84th in the world (according to the British-based Economist's Democracy Index 2016), under the despotic and dictatorial domination of the ruling Awami League and its sole supremo Sheikh Hasina. They cover the country's descent into lawlessness of killings, disappearances, trickeries, and fabrications by which it is ruled with the murderous help and deadly instrument of the partisan and politicized sections of the police, RAB, civil administration, and judiciary.

The commentaries and feature articles give an authentic picture of the authoritarian Hasina regime's repressive, divisive, decadent, and degenerated political culture, thriving and flourishing in a state of denial and suppression of the disappearing political opposition and the blanket detention of the opposition leaders. They are in support of the central argument of this book, which is, basically and virtually, a reaffirmation, confirmation, elaboration, and illustration of the same as delineated in the prestigious New York Times, Wall Street Journal, The Economist, The Diplomat, The Statesman of India, American *Foreign Policy* and *Foreign Affairs* journals, The Hindustan Times, weekly Friday Times of Pakistan, weekly Holiday of Bangladesh, and by Amnesty International, Human Rights Watch, and International Crisis Group.[19]

The combined role of the police, the regime, and the ruling party manifests itself in their ruthless and relentless suppression, subordination, and subjugation of the popular opposition. Every day there are mass police detentions of the BNP leaders, supporters, followers, and workers from wherever they get together for an outdoor or indoor meeting allowing them no activities whatsoever. It is so much so that there is a lawless mayhem every day, like what happened in Ramu Chittagong, Gobindanagar Gaibandha, Nasirnagar B'Baria, Holey Artisan, and many other places all across the country through all these years, especially since 2009. It has become an inevitable and inalienable duty of the regime and its police/RAB not to allow the opposition any political activity in any form and to daily arrest the opposition members from wherever they peacefully gather to discuss the issues facing the country. Mahmudur Rahman, a national hero, was supposed to present a paper on the BSF and Border issues, but the Hasina police broke the meeting at a Dhaka restaurant preventing him from exercising his mere and minimum freedom of speech.[20]

It is also interesting to note that most of the members of the armed tools of suppression and oppression or at least their key members hail from only one or two selected districts (greater Gopalganj/Faridpur) and that people of certain districts of interest (especially, Bogra and Feni) are deliberately excluded from the police.[21] All opposition politicians are in agreement that the regime, out of touch with the people, is pitiably as fragile and ephemeral as not to last even for days without its messiah-saviors in the police and the RAB. In the present situation, the reality on the ground, critics say, is that the government is the police and the police are the government, both being the indistinguishable and conjoined twins of each other, needing especial surgical operation (that is, radically new, positive, and democratic changes in the political and administrative system) to separate them.

Since the police/RAB, like the Rakib-*Marka* and, before, partly Huda-*Marka* Election Commissions (ECs), are by general perception largely unreliable and untrustworthy, gladly and willingly turning themselves into a critically and crucially important savior organ of the Awami government, many of them having come from the Awami wings and backgrounds and harboring the ambition of getting easily promoted and making "quick-rental" black and brown money, in addition to whatever white amount they may have, the opposition BNP always demands the deployment of the more reliable and trustworthy army all across the country, entrusted with the magistracy power, especially during the pre- and postelection period.

To cover for the forced suppression and manipulation of free speech and free elections, the Hasina regime is selling its development dose like a quinine, leaving the whole nation in the chains and shackles of the police and the RAB. (Ret) Major Akhtaruzzaman has vehemently protested against Prime Minister Sheikh Hasina giving unbridled and unlimited power to the police without any accountability.[22]

Possessed with sweeping powers, the police/RAB are in control of everything everywhere, from home to the court premises, from the residential blocks to the public places. Their power to coercively control all spheres of only the opposition life is threateningly and ominously on the increase to extent that they do not care to violate human rights, civil rights, political rights, and legal rights.

When the chief justice of the land complains that young women are detained under #54 and are kept confined illegally and indefinitely for sexual abuse and sexual slavery, the starkly immoral role of the law enforcement agents beggars description.[23] The opposition BNP chief Khaleda Zia has repeatedly alleged that Bangladesh became a police state under the Awami government whereby everything was being run and controlled by the police, who killed whoever they wanted to.[24] Also, the selfish indifference and irresponsibility of the police and their doubtful and dubious role are clear everywhere every day, the last two instances being the communal unrest at NasirNagar B'Baria and the Jamuna TV journalists about to be burnt alive at Shoarighat Dhaka.

One can only watch this video to learn about the police/RAB inhuman tactics or the other dark terrorist creatures committing acts of torture with sticks and using foul and detestable language, all in the name of the RAB.[25] When the civilized countries look for suspects and do not arrest any individual/s unless they are confirmed about one's complicity in a crime, the regime police in Bangladesh conduct a blind, blanket, and barbaric গনগ্রেফতার (mass arrest) in connection with a crime of their interest, on a selective basis (while doing nothing in similar crimes in which they wish not to proceed with the alleged criminals for political or personal reasons and which they wish to cover up in some way or another).

In their continuous mass arrests and repression drives, Bangladesh police not only take sides against the people, thereby losing public trust, but also offer themselves opportunities to make ill-gotten black bucks in bribes, as observed by many such as the senior Supreme Court lawyer Dr Shahdin Malik, senior journalist and political analyst Mahfuz Ullah, Prof Syed Anwar Hussein, and Prof Abul Kashem Fazlul Hoque, along with many international human rights organizations.[26] In addition, the way the police/RAB act in a partisan way, as the massive security arranged during the 20th party council of the Awami League on October 22, 2016 and most of their daily operations obviously suggest, it is as if they have extended into both the government party and the government itself. All three entities leave no doubt that they are more of one another and they have merged into one another at their mutual convenience, duly and properly taking care of and looking after each other with an amiable and expedient understanding among them.

Bengali poet Kamini Rai's message of selfless and egalitarian brotherhood, fraternity and camaraderie—সকলের তরে সকলে আমরা প্রত্যেকে আমরা পরের তরে (we're all for all others, as each of us for the other)—is selfishly applied by the Awamis and their allied forces only among themselves, but not extended toward the members of the rightful and legitimate democratic political opposition BNP. While a public venue like Suhrawardy Uddyan is open for use to the AL and the AL government, it is completely closed and restricted to the opposition BNP. What a dire despotism! It is by virtue of police power, not people's power, that the AL has rendered the BNP a crawling and limping cripple and a drowning man clutching at a straw. By constantly beating and bullying the BNP for years with the help of its police and other totalitarian means, they have successfully taken the BNP into their হেফাজতে (safe custody) the way they have taken the Hat-Hazari based religious group *Hefajote* well indoors, who have shamefully and woefully shut up, following their bloody defeat at their first and only political rally at Shapla Chattar Dhaka a few years back.

In the present neo-and-near-and-more-than partially fascist circumstances, it is not fair to expect the BNP to be able to swim with their hands and feet tied and to be able to fight the crocs from the water and to be able to score goals in an extremely rough and rocky and uneven field. Amid the endless, unlimited, and unprecedented Awami oppression and repression, the BNP is struggling to survive, for which it needs the people's unconditional support and sympathy. Due to the dire lack of space and respect and tolerance for political dissent and political opposition, the BNP has become like a headless chicken or a wounded, stricken deer frantically and desperately running to find a sheltering zone to collect itself from its shattering condition. It is falling apart under the thundering Awami bolts and boots and bullets. In the absence of normal political circumstances when, if the BNP failed, one could legitimately lay criticism on it for its failures, it is the AL that is to be heaped over with all the charges of fascist and ferocious persecution on its challengers, including innumerable innocents.

The Awamis have made the BNP knee broken with the help of their politicized state tools. There is no end to arrests and remands and হামলা ও মামলা, leaving the old and opposition chief Khaleda and the exiled Tarique Rahman and all the rest in the BNP engaged in fighting their court battles on a daily and weekly and monthly basis, having to mark their calendar accordingly, with no time left to engage in political activities and activism.

Khaleda is knee-broken both politically and physically. Her heir and deputy, the second in command, Tarique Rahman, forced to be in exile, is back-broken both politically and physically. The same is true with all the rest of the BNP. The circumstances are extraordinarily abnormal, which should not have been in the first place and to begin with. It is the AL which is entirely responsible to invite and impose such "a darkening green" on the nation, instead of making a delightful green possible. Any conciliatory steps by the opposition are quickly dismissed and interpreted as cowardly and confrontational by the AL, while it is actually the latter that has brought the country to this potentially boiling and explosive point through its (state) police force. Their (AL's) concept of politics is that only they have the right to continue to stay in power ominously setting their Mahathir-style visions for decades and decades hence. Their concept of opposition politics is that the latter has no right to seek power and come to power and should therefore stay away from any political activities that they may undertake to democratically get to power through electoral politics in a peaceful transition, which is the bedrock of a dynamic democracy in motion and function, now at bay and bondage in this regime.

The entire country has virtually become a chokehold subjail where people of different and differing opinions feel frightened, cornered, contained, and subjugated. They find themselves afraid of police arrests and remands and boots and bullets and tear gas and pepper spray, often having to make a deal or a special arrangement with the relevant personnel either to stay out of jail or get out of jail. Under the circumstances, whether they like it or not, people have to abide by the dictates of the regime's তন্ত্র মন্ত্র policy of tightening and squeezing control. Like Mubarak and Sisi of Egypt, Bashar of Syria, Hun Sen of Cambodia, Mugabe of Zimbabwe, and Kim of North Korea, Hasina is presiding over the worst of times in the history of Bangladesh, marked by gross and extreme political, judicial, civil and human rights abuses.

Sections of the Hasina regime's generally distrusted police force and the other plainclothes shadowy and সন্ত্রাসী groups are used as accomplices and perpetrators of the frequently occurring frightening গুম ও খুন (abductions and assassinations). They are as if a hybrid combine or reincarnation of the former fearful and ferocious Awami রক্ষীবাহিনী and JSD গনবাহিনী (brutal paramilitary forces, then opposed to each other). Together, in turn, they seem to be a counterpart of the violent Cambodian Khmer Rouge and Chinese and Indochinese "Cultural Revolution" agents, who were witch-hunting and purging umpteen people in the name of what was a failed movement from the beginning. During the mid-1970s, those two dangerous Awami and JSD বাহিনী slaughtered tens of thousands of innocent civilians. Their criminal activities reminded the citizens of those of the French ultrarevolutionary Maximilien Robespierre's radical Jacobins and their relatively moderate but still extremist rival Gerondins during mid-1793 to mid-1794 when Robespierre and his henchmen were responsible for guillotining many innocent people.

If the mindless mantra of the one-and-single party, that is, AL, governing the nation were true, then the entire Europe, the Americas, Australasia, Japan, Taiwan, South Korea, India, and Israel, it follows, would have done better if they abandoned their long tradition of democratic values and ideals and followed and pursued the path of absolute prime ministerial ends and means, or the royal roads of dynastic kingship and monarchy, oligarchy, dictatorship, or even fascism. Alas! Barack Obama should have been an omnipotent emperor like Haile Selassie, Jean Badel Bokassa, or, following the Baconian fallacy of "power corrupts; absolute power corrupts absolutely," an absolutely corrupt all-powerful prime minister! According to the Hasina regime, then, what a grave and irreversible mistake the Western democracies have made? The Hasina doctrine of full-and-complete authoritarianism should then creep and crawl into the White House, 10 Downing Street, the Hyderabad House, the Diet, the Bundestag, the Storting. and the Knesset just as the al-Qaeda, Taliban, ISIS, Boko Haram, and al-Shabab have crept up, encroaching and intruding into as many places of the world as they could.

The Hasina regime is preaching the gospel of the continuity of the government to continue with its one-sided development program (which as a by-product makes its own partisans fat with corrupt money) as a pretext to hang on to power. If this Hasina gospel could be true, why to change the government every four or five years in the developed democracies of the world? What a funny and preposterous testament!

On the other hand, unlike China, Singapore, Malaysia, and the Gulf and central Asian countries, Bangladesh has a rich and vibrant tradition of free speech and intellectual growth. For ages, it has been enjoying a great freedom of thought. With the exception of brief spells, democratic voices were never stifled there until recently. So, while the economic freedom in lieu of democratic freedom is somehow somewhat working in those countries, which, nevertheless, are struggling for speech over silence in their own ways—however quiet and subdued it may be—, the formula of hardline suppression of dissent, on the one hand, and promotion of corruption-ridden material improvement (affluence mostly along the party line), on the other, is nothing short of being systematically fascist and can never work in Bangladesh.[27] One of the most veteran and neutral politicians of the country, Nur-e-Alam Siddiquee, rightly said (on a *TM* talk show, January 22, 2015) that development had no meaning without democracy and democratically elected representative government, and that it had no value under an unreliable and untrustworthy government intent upon running the show in a choking atmosphere of restraint and regimentation. No comment could be more appropriate than Siddiquee's, with which over a hundred million Bangladeshis would agree without hesitation and reservation.

A lion's share of the credit for whatever development Bangladesh is enjoying goes to the hardworking rural agricultural farmers, overworked garments and construction workers, and the remittance of the sweating laborers toiling hard abroad, not to the government as such. Any government in power—corrupt or not—does something and has to do something anyway for the continuation of the state apparatus; it cannot shut down and has to somehow run the country, however improperly, half-heartedly and sluggishly. What is important to understand is that development does not mean economic development only, just as democracy does not mean an election only, much less so when it is merely a mock, made-up and pre-mapped-out thing like the January 5, 2014 affair with a foregone conclusion.[28] If the Hasina government is a transgressive overreacher (like Mary Shelley's scientist Victor Frankenstein), doggedly and determinedly obsessed with engineering an election, the horrible outcome of that election is its ugly monster in different forms now pushing it to its limit, as the hideously disfigured monster pursues Shelley's Frankenstein to his finish in the Arctic ice.

According to the EIP (Electoral Integrity Project) survey jointly conducted by Harvard and Sydney Universities, it was one of the worst and most failed elections in the world and it remains the main cause of the ongoing political violence in Bangladesh.[29] Progress means clean and corruption-free development and participatory democracy together as best as realistically possible; economic, intellectual, and political freedoms together; rule of law along with trust, tolerance, and transparency together; and general welfare of the masses (health, housing, education, jobs, security) and growth of infrastructure together. All these are supposed to be above the brute biases along the raw and naked party lines. Overall progress means a government of the people—of a clear majority and of accountability with respect for the opposition—not just one and only one party—let alone a power-hungry and bloodthirsty one armed with its own cadres in different forms—with or without uniform—in every sector. The country cannot run on only one wheel, as the former Election Commissioner Brig Sakhawat Hussein remarked.

Snatching away the deeply held democratic and human rights values and privileges can only backfire. The Awamis think they own the country and it is only their monopoly to rule and contribute to the development of Bangladesh and to reap the benefit from, by hook or by crook. Although sticking to power by devious and heavy-handed means with the help of the police, RAB, and BGB, they try to sell themselves as the only patriots of the country, vilifying the democratic and patriotic opposition as terrorists. To hang on to power, they do not want to think about the rest, who also have the equal right to govern and contribute to the development of the country, however, in a different, yet dynamic and democratic way—the way they think best with the mandate of the people. As poet Asad Chowdhury, even though he may be of the Awami court, said more than once (on RTV তারকালাপ) that the quintessential spirit of independence and democracy was to provide equal opportunities for all, which he lamented was far from being present in the country and that the people were still in quest of a true taste of independence, decades after 1971.

The logical conclusion, therefore, is that the Awami government is taking the country backward to a lawless, degenerated, dysfunctional, and dictatorial state. The apex court of the country, in mid-May 2016, called it "an alarming matter that law enforcement personnel in plain clothes still arrest citizens on suspicion and take them into custody for long without producing them in courts in gross violation of the 15 directives issued by the High Court 13 years ago." It is this anarchical prospect that is in the looming, in fact, already materializing for the last few years that made the Hasina regime resort to the evil means of laying siege on the beleaguered BNP leader Khaleda on a number of occasions.

Like the evil witches in *The Wizard of Oz*, who stop at nothing to stop Dorothy Gale, all this was only to weaken the morale of দেশনেত্রী /Leader of the Land Khaleda as the opposition leader. But the evil witches are not aware of the fact that there are also good witches to help Dorothy Gale out of her predicament. The jealousy and vindictiveness of the evil step mothers/queens and step sisters in the stories of *Cinderella*, *Beauty and the Beast*, *Snow White*, and *The Sleeping Beauty* eventually fail to stop the suffering heroines from achieving success and are themselves miserably crushed into pieces at the end!

The main opposition BNP has been trapped since late 2008. When the Hasina regime has everything in its arsenal—all the state machineries, all the firearms, the police, the court, and the civil administration—to apply against the BNP, it can easily trash and thrash and ditch anybody it wants. The AL chief herself said she was letting the BNP survive by the politically suppressive and subversive "formalin." Sheikh Hasina is taking the advantage that the people are now cowed down for fear of police boots and bullets with her party-privileged few having a share of the pie and that there would never be a mass upheaval like 1952, 1971, or 1990. She knows that people are not as hungry as they used to be during her father's time, from 1972 to 1975. She is taking the advantage of the fact that there are about a dozen smaller parties between the AL-led alliance and the BNP-led alliance, regardless of how insignificant and inconsequential they may be, are sitting on the fence indirectly maneuvering to displace the BNP and watching it crushed, cornered, crippled, and squeezed with vicarious pleasure.

PM Hasina is aware that despite being authoritarian and "nonelected" through a farcical "nonelection" with predetermined and preconceived results, she is not under international pressure to give up. International community can only express a diplomatically coated and politically noncommittal concern about the absence of dialogue, to the disadvantage of the cause of democracy. On the contrary, Hasina, in control of the country by force, has the direct or indirect, mute or loud international support, especially when she is under the direct protection and patronage of the surrounding big brother India, which, along with her personal security forces, keeps her insulated from the demands of the opposition at home, however popular, legitimate, and rightful those demands are.

After all, the international community, many members of which are themselves undemocratic, is interested in trade and commerce with whoever they are—dictators, despots, autocrats, kings, monarchs, tyrants. Economic interest being more important than the so-called moral and political visions and ideals, the world pursues a policy of compartmentalization and so hardly cares about the inside or outside view of Bangladesh from the political perspective, no matter how authoritarian its rulers are. Having compartmentalized the ills from the interests, the international "players" are no longer "players" in the internal affairs of a country, even if such affairs are controlled by force and farce by those in power.

All what the outsiders want is to do their business as usual except when unrest and violence go out of control. If Bashar Al Assad, Hosni Mubarak, Abdul Fattah Al-Sisi, Nuri Al-Maliki, Haider Al-Abadi, Omar al-Bashir, and Sheikh Hasina (and her weird, melodramatically handpicked and "unelected" opposition-cum-and-versus-government, like-the-mermaid-tail shareholders in Rawshon Ershad and H M Ershad) are acceptable to foreign governments, what can one expect from them? While visiting Dhaka, their agenda includes, unfortunately, meeting with Rawshon, thereby giving an unjust legitimacy to her.

On the other hand, what they care most is to stop the Islamic parties ("Islamist terrorists" in their language) by all means. Even if the Islamic parties (to be distinguished from ISIS, Al-Qaeda or Boko Haram in no uncertain terms) form democratic majority, they are not acceptable in the eyes of the West. Anything under the banner or umbrella of Islam must go whereas all other religions are welcome and encouraged to rise. Mubarak and Al-Sisi are better to the world than Mohammad Morsi of Brotherhood (who, however, may have had his drawbacks, like any other political leaders or groups). Despite the Indian Prime Minister Narendra Modi's murderous Hindu fundamentalist past, he is a "hero," a darling to the world. However, his strength lies in having been popularly elected by his people in a free and fair election, an opportunity completely denied to the people of Bangladesh by the Hasina regime.

American/Western and Indian moral, political and democratic leadership is lost in the business of economically and militarily driven geopolitical and geostrategic problems and opportunities. These issues in the nuclear charged Indian Subcontinent are as complex as those in the Middle East. They are such that America needs India, not only because India is a growing regional power, big in everything—sheer landmass, population, and the size of its military as well as the economy—but also in view of protecting, or at least balancing the American interest and influence in the region and over the larger Indian Ocean (including the Persian Gulf), together with India, in the face of the increasing Chinese military dominance and economic control. India's other friends and allies, Russia and Iran, must not be left out of the equation, which for sure adds another complex dimension. Had there been no expanding Chinese/Iranian/ Russian belt of influence, would/could America come forward to exercise its moral leadership to help establish democracy in Bangladesh and other smaller Asian countries, whose freedom, independence and integrity are compromised in the friction/conflict between the bigger powers? Lucky Sheikh Hasina's police reign could not have come at a better time. Ranu Chowdhury of the USA, a former freedom fighter of Bangladesh, e-mailed to a group including the author (on January 6, 2017):

> The saddest part is that the US, which calls itself the leader, promoter and protector of democracy, freedom and human rights the world over, could do little to prevent Indian hegemony to its South Asian neighbors. To the contrary, the US-India collaboration seems to be in high gear, especially in military fields, to the growing concern smaller nations in the neighborhood.
>
> The worst example is Bangladesh. Since 1/11/2007, peoples' aspirations have been ruthlessly trampled at the behest of India, which wants to convert its eastern neighbor to a vassal state for its geopolitical necessity, such as to reach and contain its not-so-Delhi-friendly Seven Sisters, who harbor a centrifugal tendency much to Delhi's discomfort. The US and the West did nothing other than condemning the January 5, 2014 farce. And the resulting BAKSAL-II continues its fascism and oppressive activities against the people, the opposition party in particular, pushing them to the margin slowly. India keeps reaping the benefits many times over its investment in Bangladesh, thanks to Dhaka's illegal entity that keep surrendering national interests at the altar of its master in New Delhi.

It is the people who have to ultimately decide. It is the masses that have to play a crucial role in changing their government. But Sheikh Hasina has them trampled and cowed down by force. Like the severe and selective Queen of Hearts in *Alice in Wonderland*, Hasina has the police, judiciary, legislature, civil admin, and the military under her full partisan control and coercion.[30] All nonsensical madness in Alice's Wonderland makes sense to the domineering Queen, while the growing and sensible Alice has to accept all this nonsense in the same strange and peculiar terms as long as she is there and until she gets out of there to return to her real and normal world.

By common perception and calculation, if free and fair elections were held on the blacker than black 5 January, Sheikh Hasina would not possibly have the chance even of an honorable defeat/exit, let alone the support of a simple majority. Her government has increased the number of the police, RAB, BGB, and civil administration members by hundreds of thousands and handed them wholesale promotion over the last few years—mostly along the line of their loyalty to her party and through nepotism and cronyism rather than on the basis of competitive merit-based selection.[31] She may have done so with the intention of using them as tools for the protection of her regime and the systematic persecution and prosecution of the BNP and other opposition leaders and supporters.

The regime is hardly concerned about the everyday safety and security of the people in general. When one shuns and kills democracy to cling to power the way Tennyson's eagle clings to the cliff before it falls deep down into the sea, one is desperate to rely on the forces of suppression and subversion before one falls a really bad fall right into the pit. Without resolving the political issues politically through dialogue, compromise, and accommodation, the regime of the Hasina-led AL has been using the state's law enforcing machineries for partisan intimidation and regimentation and it has been doing so recklessly, indiscriminately, and injudiciously.[32]

As a job creation and employment opportunity, hiring in large numbers is fine, but the police, like the rest of the government sectors, do not enjoy a good reputation in popular perception, their image being low for various reasons such as corruption, lack of high moral standard, being selective in their law enforcement practice, and getting complicit in various criminal activities.[33] It is the prevalent and widespread doubt about the rule of law and the role of the police that makes the people in general and the students and the staff of the educational institutions in particular take to the street at the expense of their classes and academic duties, demanding justice every time there occurs an injustice to them.[34] It is not their responsibility to force the police to catch the criminals (which is the responsibility of only the police themselves), but because the police are suspiciously and surreptitiously lax, lenient, and selective, students and teachers feel morally obliged to get out to create pressure, albeit successfully only at times. It is due to the lack of the rule of law and the transparency of the role of the police that the legitimate demands of the people often go unheeded.

The police of the Hasina regime are busy chasing after the opposition only. That the police and the court services work as a repressive tool of the Hasina regime is proved not only by their nonstop mass arrests of the BNP supporters and candidates, especially before and during any election—local or national—allegedly accompanied by the black money changing hands, but also their demand that no media, especially electronic, be allowed at the voting centers, sending out the message that they are bent upon helping the government with vote rigging and they do not want the media to cover the stuffing of the boxes with pro-government ballots. Also, since the voters do not have any trust in the police, they want deployment of the trustworthy and impartial army soldiers during any election, which the pro-government EC, far from being fair and neutral, never accepts.

The otherwise good performance of the police (which they are obliged and duty-bound to do and are supposed to do without being necessarily thanked for) becomes lackluster owing to the countless instances of their moral lapses. Their carnivorous to omnivorous to predatory criminal misdeeds are thought to far outweigh their otherwise dutiful and responsible behavior automatically incumbent upon them. Sometimes they do not even take the general diary or complaint from the victims, who may have been victimized by those the police want to protect or who are not in a position to buy the police support and influence for money. The late Social Welfare Minister Syed Mohsin Ali accused the police of taking bribes and the National Human Rights Commission Chairman alleged that the police were involved in irresponsible and unethical practices.[35]

While the allegations of scandalous irregularities such as naked biases, extortions, and kickbacks against those who are morally depraved among the police are common, it is such illegal and immoral backdoor lucrative scope and opportunities that hold a lure for landing a position with the police department.[36] More police in Bangladesh means more jobs, no doubt, but it also means more suppression, persecution, corruption, extortion, bribes, kickbacks, side deals and under-the-table deals, all of which actually contribute to the increase of the people's suffering, rather than improving their safety and security (despite whatever good the police may be doing).[37]

According to the US-based World Justice Project, Bangladesh is just a few countries above the lowest among the 102 countries surveyed for corruption in the government and the police and justice departments.[38] Instead of being true friends of good moral character and honesty and integrity for the people to look up to, as they are in developed and democratic Western as well as some Asian countries, the police in Bangladesh are generally looked down upon as immoral and dishonest, far below the people's expectations. They are seen as being not too nice and caring and morally upright. Exceptions are everywhere in God's world. Excluding the exceptions, the police in Bangladesh are widely used as (or have of themselves become out of their Awami loyalty) tools of torture to the extent that they are being viewed as frightening and terrifying to the community, constantly seizing and taking the members of the political opposition to tortuous remands in violation of their human rights.

Then, to hire and promote a large number of the police, RAB, military, and bureaucracy on political considerations in the name of their subscribing to the spirit of the liberation war would mean commodification, compartmentalization, and commercialization of it with a product value/price tag attached to it. It would mean as if the AL holds the company monopoly and sole ownership over such a spirit which no other party can partake of. It would mean men and women in uniform are obliged to act in a partisan and prejudicial way in the vested interest of the tyrannical AL and AL alone and thereby to malign and crush the political dissent opposed to the AL.

What is alarming is that it has been reported, by at least one major TV channel (Jamuna) and the online Real Time News (RTN), that a huge number of foreigners (presumably Indians) are being allowed to enter the police and other job markets of Bangladesh with their foreign identity carefully and cleverly concealed.[39] Rizvi Ahmed, an opposition leader, protested against the frequent visits by Indian ambassadors to the police academies of Bangladesh and questioned the motif of such visits, along with that of other vital issues and inequalities dominated by India.[40] Maj Akhtaruzzaman wanted to know why the son of the Indian President Pranab Mukherjee would visit Bangladesh as frequently as he does. There are reports that Indian intelligence and visa issuing consular service, in a compromise of the integrity and sovereignty of Bangladesh, are working so closely with the Bangladesh police and military that Indian government has opened its offices inside theirs.[41] Also reportedly, Indian BSF is going to train Bangladesh BGB.[42] As in all other sectors, it is apparently only one-way traffic of subservience, subordination and subjection between the two countries.

A few years back, during the same Hasina regime, there were reports that as many as 100 Indian RAW trained secret killers and abductors (Squad 100 or Crusader 100) and many Indian secret operatives were operating from different locations in Bangladesh.[43] Journalist Jessica Fox revealed in the Sri Lankan Guardian that these dark and terrible operatives were operating with the full knowledge and sponsorship of the prime minister and her defense adviser.[44] It is in the similar context that the opposition leader Khaleda posed the question, "Who runs the country—the illegitimate, self-declared Awami government or any other [secretive, clandestine] force behind it?"[45]

There are claims that many of those soldiers and commandoes who took part in the gruesome mindless predawn massacre of (allegedly about 2,000) young sleeping Hefajote students and activists on May 5, 2013 were suspected to be of foreign origin as their very looks and appearance also lent support to the evidence.[46] As mentioned above, according to media reports, foreign special units, jointly with the top members of the Awami government as well as the police/RAB/military of Bangladesh, took part in the cruel and senseless Hefajote operations, as they are also believed to have been involved in the early 2009 BDR massacre and the late 2013 Satkhira devastation.[47]

The chiefs of different law enforcement and paramilitary forces, sounding like they are other political and partisan arms, rather than patriotic state organs or agents, directly follow up on the sound bites of the Awami leaders and waste no time to instruct their officers to use their full force in boots and bullets with immunity and impunity against the democratic political rivals, who are, obviously, the BNP men and women and their allies. Despite the continual increase in the number of the police, most of whom remain occupied to protect the government loyalists only, they have failed to protect the general people, many of whom are getting killed like anything (birds and flies) anywhere (from bedroom to office to open street) every day.[48]

Shockingly, the chiefs of different armed machineries in uniform are also one step ahead in making provocative political statements, both verbally and in their body language, about election, constitution, human rights, social justice and the opposition rights as if they were political leaders themselves or political appointees to act as the mouthpieces or spokespersons of the regime and to solely serve the Hasina government, no matter what the will of the people is.[49] Nurul Kabir was prompted by their words to ask who wagged who: the government was wagging the police/RAB or they were wagging the government?[50] If the police/RAB are used only to serve the political interest of the ruling party, they only contribute to furthering the deterioration of the situation, far from ensuring and establishing peace, justice, and fair play in the society. The Brussels-based International Crisis Group reports about how the police and the ruling government in Bangladesh have joined hands to suppress and persecute the opposition.[51] If the police/RAB cannot free themselves from their irresponsible and unethical actions and activities, what is the point of increasing their number, except creating more of the same—partisan fright, polarized panic, painful apprehension?

Surprisingly, again, as Mujahidul Islam Selim, along with the daily *Anandabazar* of West Bengal put it, while the ruling politicians were talking force with live ammunitions to be used right into the chest of the opponents, the state's "law" enforcement chiefs were talking politics and that also was from only one side.[52] Such an equation mirrors and parallels the common interpretation of today's politics whereby it is said that politicians have become businessmen and businessmen have become politicians. This amalgam—a hotchpotch—according to the British political thinker Edmund Burke, dismantles independent political establishments and destroys the culture of custom, tradition, institutional continuity, historical experience, love, respect, peace and stability. He saw the French Revolution of 1789 as "a volatile mix of new and inexperienced political actors—the 'country attorneys' in the National Assembly and the mob in the streets of Paris." The unwanted mix led him to predict a destruction of those values and principles, making "all politics coercive" and paving the way for "the rise of an unrestrained and possibly military absolutism."

In the context of Bangladesh, the BGB chief asserted that he had the right to make political statements because he thought he also was a tax payer. Echoing Hasina, who said the police did not carry arms to keep them in the pocket, RAB chief Benzir Ahmed claimed his forces carried arms not to kiss "the unruly opposition" or play *ha-du-du* (kabaddi) with or carry flowers at the tip of the barrel. It was a hot-headed, wrong-headed, and provocative statement like the one made by Pakistan's Defense Minister (in late September 2016) saying, in relation to India, that his country's weapons were not for exhibition or decoration but for use if and when necessary. If Pakistan's Nawaz Sharif is facing criminal charges for his Panamagate money laundering accusations and is about to lose his premiership, how is it possible that Benzir Ahmed and many others whose names also appeared on the Panama Papers for their questionable financial dealings are not being investigated and charged? Is Pakistan faring much better in recent years than Bangladesh in terms of the rule of law, independence of judiciary, caretaker government, and free and fair elections?

Following the disorienting "lost and found" ordeal of an excellent opposition politician Salahuddin Ahmed, who was then BNP joint secretary (and a former state minister) and is now a member of the highest decision making body of his party—the largest political party in Bangladesh—, Benzir Ahmed stated that the party made "an abnormal" (অপ্রকৃতস্থ) person responsible for its public relations and press releases, referring to Ahmed.[53] Despite being the chief of a state armed force, Benzir Ahmed continues to make statements that reek of politics and, worse, partisan politics. He said that those who did not believe in the Liberation War may leave the country: "We'll be fine without you. We don't need shameless people." It is only for the politicians, civilians, and intellectuals to say so, not for him, who is supposed to be taking care of law and order situation only, not to be taking sides politically.

In a meeting with the EC, the IGP (Inspector General of Police), Shahidul Hoque, an openly Awami-BAKSAL supporter, dictated that the opposition candidates in the capital city mayoral election in April 2015 would have to be stopped by all means.[54] Later he said that he and his forces would not tolerate anarchy and indiscipline in the name of opposition movement, implying that they would not allow, as they never do, any opposition activities, which they deviously and duplicitously suppress by all means and that they are an organic and integral extension of the Awami regime. DIG Police instructed his forces to shoot straight at who they thought were suspects.[55] Dr Zafrullah Chowdhury, perhaps one of the sanest and most heroic souls of Bangladesh, said it all when he demanded posthumous justice for the extrajudicial killings committed by OC Salahuddin, who was himself killed in a crossfire at Gulshan Holey Artisan Bakery on July 1, 2016, and also when he exposed many other corrupt practices and dangerous immoralities of the police in general.[56]

The Chittagong police chief proclaimed a crusade against the corrupt and their black money when members of the police themselves are known for their doubtful and disreputable acts. Sometimes even the election date are reportedly decided according to the advice of the police as represented by their IGP. During the Eid season of high traffic on the highway, DMP Commissioner threatened the possible thieves and extortionists and rouges and robbers of being shot, although members of the police department were allegedly involved in similar activities in certain areas and were fighting with each other over their black shares. The Commissioner also said, in violation of the civil and information rights, that the details of the cause of death of those killed in police operation could not be divulged to the press, suggesting immunity and endless power for the police.[57] RRF Dhaka Unit chief Mizanur Rahman is exploiting his forces in building his palatial house in Savar Dhaka.[58]

That the police are in the driving seat of how the affairs should be run is determined, as claimed by the daily Dinkal (দিনকাল) editor Dr Rezwan Siddiqui (on a TV Channel on April 10, 2016), by the fact that it is the home minister, their boss, who willingly listens or has to listen to them, rather than they listening to him/her, thereby either showing their superior and superseding authority or their need to be pleased and pampered in order to be at the service of the government. It is insulting, egregious, and neo-and-near fascist that the political parties have to ask for the police permission to hold an assembly at a public square of their choice.

While it is not much for the police just to be informed so that they can remain extra alert on any occasion and extra vigilant for any public event to take place, it is simply too much that people and parties must take the permission of the police to hold a gathering at an open place of their choice. That is utterly repugnant, shameful, and disrespectful. Not only do the police keep cooking and concocting and framing politically motivated (in the opinion of the opposition, fake and false) new charges against the opposition leaders, rearresting them right from the jail gate and putting them behind bars again and again even after they are released on bail, but also keep seizing them from their houses in a mean and undignified (if not deceptive and deceitful) manner.

In Bangladesh, as the saying goes, মাছের রাজা ইলিশ ("king of fish is Ilish/Hilsa"). Under the Hasina regime, দেশের রাজা পুলিশ ("king of country is the police"), as proved by SP Meherpur and DIG Jessore, who did not have any qualms in openly arming the local supporters of the ruling party with bamboo and solid wood sticks, to be weaponized as necessary to kill others at will, obviously of the opposition (in a classic repeat and reminder of the murderous Awami poles and oars and logs terror (লগি বৈঠা তান্ডব)) of 2006.[59] That the police are the king of the country is also proved by the way they brutally beat up the demonstrators against the environmentally destructive Rampal coal fire project near the Sundarbans.[60]

It has become systematic that the police/RAB kill the suspects not only in their "safe" custody but also in the so-called (one-sided) extrajudicial cross-fires—a conveniently used misnomer—with no fires actually coming from the suspects' side (in an unmistakable remembrance of the rigged, stolen, and one-sided Hasina regime elections winning and scoring goals in an empty field).[61] As many as 90 people have been killed in crossfire, most of them by the police, in the first six months of 2017 alone.[62] The BNP Secretary General Mirza Alamgir alleged that "cruel," "brutal," and "indiscriminate" murder of the opposition leaders and activists in the name of so-called "gunfight" has become a "game" for the partisan law enforcers, as he also keeps alleging that the জঙ্গী (terrorist) incidents are actually the Indian-and-Hasina-regime planted shows (নাটক)and conspiracies designed to prolong the Awami rule.[63]

The opposition party (BNP) keeps complaining that the government has turned all the state machineries, including the RAB and police forces, into its tools of terror and torture, using them as menacing mechanisms against it. The opposition protests that the regime is using these mechanisms to conduct state-sponsored terrorism, thereby turning them into the enemy of the people, not their defenders or protectors from the criminals, murders, miscreants, rapists, eve-teasers, thieves, robbers, hoodlums, and hooligans. That is why it is not far to seek why many opposition politicians are languishing in dark dungeon, why nearly 32,000 women have been raped and abused in the last 5 years (prior to 2016), why over a hundred women raped in just three months, and why torture and persecution and sexual harassment of women exceeded all the past records during the time of this regime.[64] In a stark case of the violation of human rights, targeted citizens are picked up and abducted, to the shocking denial of the regime's forces, or their phones are secretly bugged or tapped leaving them without their right to privacy and thus leaving all citizens in panic and insecurity.

All government efforts and attention are directed toward oppressing, maligning, and silencing the BNP and the BNP-led alliance. Abnormal though it is, everything is being done according to the will of only one person—the prime minister—and at a time of her own choosing. Consequently, instead of advancing from good to better, the political situation in Bangladesh has been turning bad to worse, with more and more of the same—tension, unrest, blood and violence. It has been so since its birth four and half decades ago, getting worse from the 2008/9 blueprint election. It got worst since the mockery that was the January 5 theater that engineered a historic "election" farce.

Sheikh Hasina argued, completely on false and perverted grounds, that the nation would not pay the price (in her language, খেসারত, a coarse and rustic word) for the mistake the opposition BNP committed by not participating in that farce. It was actually she, the sole and only center of her party as well as her government, who made the nation pay the price—a heavy price—for her repeatedly broken promises and jugglery of words. While the rhetoric of her assertion made it obvious that it was indeed the January 5 issue that was the crux of the January–March violence, her cronies, armed with the police power, kept crowing and parroting that the opposition movement was not political, having nothing to do with what happened on January 5! What a culture of denial and disowning cultivated in Bangladesh!

There was no question of the BNP participating in what it knew was going to be an unfair and unequal election, solely and exclusively according to the terms of the regime. Those terms, made for and at its own convenience, were to the point of total and absolute rejection of all the just and rightful demands of the opposition. Again, Nur-e-Alam Siddiquee, a veteran AL-turned-neutral politician, was right to say that the BNP must not be made to pay a price for not participating in what was a highly defective, seriously questionable, double standard, hijacked, and predetermined election. After all, there are some voices of reason in Hasina's wonderland just as there are those such as the Cheshire Cat—cool, detached, and clearheaded—in the illogical Wonderland of the Queen of Hearts where Lewis Carroll's little but logical and sensible Alice feels like a stranger.

In the run-up to the so-called January 5 laughable and ridiculous "election," Sheikh Hasina remained at the helm, and the status of her MPs remained active without the parliament being dissolved. This was in violation of all norms of a national democratic election. Even when there were some bait-offers by her (Hasina) such as certain cabinet positions to the BNP to actually make it a mutually agreed manipulation of the election process in Hasina's favor, the BNP leader Khaleda stood firm and did not accept the trap offers. Khaleda understood that Hasina's way of manufacturing the election results from her all-powerful position as prime minister would only make the coveted "big fish" or the তালগাছ (palm tree) go to her (Hasina). Hasina's hasty offer of dialogue, though on short notice, was never rejected by Khaleda, as Hasina would continue to twist it that way.

Khaleda simply wanted to sit down with Hasina any time soon after that evening (when a certain political program by her party was underway), perhaps the very next day. This was totally rejected by the totalitarian Hasina, who, as prime minister, never again made any further gesture or took any other initiative for dialogue, despite Khaleda's repeated calls. In Hasina's inflexible view, dialogue, if at all, had to be held that particular evening only or never.

Hasina also knew that the BNP was not going to take part in what was the pompous, partial, pretentious, and preposterous January 5 election of predetermined results and that the election was not to be made inclusive and participatory so that her (Hasina's) victory as a foregone conclusion could be ensured. At that point, after having previously amended the constitution in her favor and having promised that the parliament would be dissolved before the election, she said that the January 5 thing was going to go ahead for the sake constitutional continuity with the parliament remaining alive and active (in violation of all constitutional norms) and that another election, midterm or otherwise, would be held soon thereafter. As it turned out, PM Hasina never made good on her promise and all the pre-and-post election maneuverings were actually a mischievous politicking resorted to cling to power.

About four years now, one would like to ask Sheikh Hasina, as the veteran politicians Dr Kamal Hussein and Kader Siddiquee did, "Why would the nation have to pay the price for the loss of the innocent lives during the opposition-called countrywide blockade for your dictatorial cancellation of the interim Care Taker Government (CTG) system and then going back on the promise you made about holding an inclusive election at the earliest convenience soon after the dirty

January 5? What did you mean then? What do you mean now? Didn't you say the truth then?"[65]

Similarly, another great politician of the country, Mahmudur Rahman Manna, posed the question that if there had to be a dozen of sand and cement and garbage trucks in the name of "hoax" security purposes (actually to lay a siege on and block the way of Khaleda) at her office premises, why there weren't dozens of such "effective" trucks in front of Sheikh Hasina's gate to provide her better and more permanent "protection." Instead of asking why the BNP had to create a menace during January–March 2015, jeopardizing the public safety, one needed to address the root cause first, as the Miles band vocalist Shafin Ahmed did, and ask why the despotic Hasina government did not keep its word and settle the matter politically through an inclusive and credible election the year before.[66]

William Golding's first and most famous novel *Lord of the Flies* (1954), written in reaction to *The Coral Island: A Tale of the Pacific Ocean* (1858) by R. M. Ballantyne, is an allegorical portrait of a group of young schoolboys' descent into savagery. Based on Golding's experience of anarchy, violence, and brutality during World War II, the novel illustrates the Freudian psychology of good and evil in terms of primordial human impulse, which is, by nature, selfish, immoral, cruel, and Satanic (the title of the novel being a literal translation of the Biblical Beelzebub), not instinctively given to the civilizing rules and regulations of society. Left to themselves in a remote Pacific island of utopian, paradisiacal environment, the children, in their early adolescence, regress into a primitive state as they start governing themselves, only to painfully realize and despair at the loss of their innocence by the end of the novel. Similarly, every time the AL came to power, it proved to be worse and more dangerous than the preceding governments, who had no choice but to run a similar race to catch up as if it were the BNP's or the JP's pedaled bike against the AL's motorbike. It was like the Palestinians fighting with rocks and rockets and mortar shells against the Israeli tanks and bombs and missiles.

On an *Ekushey* TV program (October 21, 2015), *The News Today*'s M A Aziz sounded the majority opinion in saying that prior to August 15, 1975, the country was under the sluttish one-party rule and since 2009 it has been under the sluttish one-person rule. That is the sign of the "progress" of the so-called democracy and development in Bangladesh! Like the *Lord of the Flies* boys led by Jack and Ralph, of whom the latter "wept for the end of innocence" and was horrified at the discovery of "the darkness of man's heart," is not it time for the AL to regret their dark instincts and weep for the loss of their innocence and idealism too? The nation needs a remedy, a cure from the financially corrupt and politically repressive, chaotic and confusing situation it has been suffering from for too long, especially since 2009. It needs peace, stability, democratic equality, development, rule of law, and periodic change of guards through free, fair, credible and participatory elections, not false, rigged, stolen, and biased ones.

If the opposition led by the BNP is peaceful, which it is, and makes peaceful demands and demonstrations, the AL, from the seat of power, does not listen and does not care to adopt accommodating measures and initiatives to properly address the political differences raised by the opposition. The AL does not pay heed because it thinks the BNP is weak and that is why it is peaceful with no show of force, making no demands from the position of strength. When the BNP attempts to be forceful and press home its demands, with some unavoidable and inadvertent violence, the AL says it is acting like lawless miscreants and terrorists and so needs to be beaten up and shot at sight. If the BNP does not participate in the election due to the AL's predetermined mammoth and massive vote rigging, the AL says the party (BNP) does not believe in democracy. If it (BNP) does participate, the AL says it (BNP) is doing so with a hidden agenda, as part of a conspiracy, so that the AL can go ahead stealing the elections anyway.[67]

Which way to go? Isn't the AL playing a devilish dual role, dirtying the water and leaving the opposition in a state of desperation, going nuts and seeing the blues? Isn't it playing Aesop's upstream fox to jump down on the innocent lamb below by any or no excuse whatsoever? Or, in the words of another commentator, "The wolf will make the baby lamb his meal irrespective of the justification of the offence the poor victim can commit."

There are some who argue that both the AL and the BNP have reached a point of no return in their bitter and virulent opposition to each other. One may only partly agree and partly disagree. Having been pushed to the wall, left with no space and reached an existentialist survival of "do or die" situation, it is the point of no return for the BNP only, not the AL. Being in the government, it is the AL that is responsible for creating all the mess the country is going through. The root causes of the political violence and the political stalemate facing the country today are: (1) the authoritarian cancellation of the CTG; (2) establishment of a regime of bad governance—repressive with the entire country turned into a subhuman slum state of 75,000 prisoners, far exceeding the 34,000 capacity of all the prisons across the country (as of May 1, 2015, by now far exceeding those numbers); and (3) not keeping the promise of holding another election—credible, inclusive, participatory—soon after the January 5 "voteless" and "voterless" cheating on the people. It is precisely this situation that the former Prime Minister Kazi Zafar Ahmed, a political luminary in the history of Bangladesh, has so perfectly described as a police and prison state that the country has become.[68] It is therefore the AL that needs to return to its senses to compromise, accommodate, be flexible, and take steps to bring back sanity, normalcy, and decency for all citizens to feel fine and whole and hospitable once again!

Until and unless that happens, even the neutralists and pacifists ought to stop being neutral and pacifist, at least for a while, and should take side with the BNP-led opposition fully, completely and wholeheartedly to bring back democratic freedom on a priority basis for the good of all. In this juncture, to speak for or be critical of the both sides and thereby to remain on the edge is to be with the threat posed by the rulers and strengthen their hands, not the ruled and the oppressed. How can the neutralists and pacifists afford to remain passive and be in the middle when the entire parliament of three hundred members is either unelected or nonelected or semi-elected or pseudo-elected or quasi-elected? How can they afford to walk a middle path when they see that there are many who could never ever be elected through ballot but are still sitting in the parliament, making laws, and holding top ministerial positions deciding for the country?

When the party, the police, the RAB, the government, the parliament, the judiciary, and the EC become synonymous and interchangeable, doing the proxy for each other, as the majority of the opposition parties claim, being on the fence would mean being either in the safe and comfort zone making no difference or passively watching the democratic process trampled down and wither away by the Awami police bolts and boots and bullets for an indefinite and unforeseeable period of time!

Who are these গোপাল/গোপালী parrots and predators in the police?

The unquestioning Awami faithful have now purportedly been joined, as suspected by the BNP leader Khaleda, by their গোপালী friends and unknown cross-border shadowy reinforcements. Khaleda posed the question, "Who runs the country—the illegitimate, self-declared Awami government or any other [secretive, clandestine] force behind it?"[69] As reported, hundreds of thousands of foreigners, mostly from India, are allowed to stay in the country without valid (immigration/legal) status.[70] An alarming number of Indians are allowed to enter the police force with their true national identity concealed.[71] Reportedly, at least 5,00,000 Indians work in Bangladesh and remit about $4 billion to India annually, 5th highest overseas remittance for India. This is only official figure, the unofficial Indians working and sending out their remittance, both legally and illegally, may be much higher.[72]

Khaleda pointed to this during the pre-January 5, 2014 and January 5, 2015 AL-laid sand-and-cement bag siege on her at her party office as well as her residence.[73] Her suspicion was later supported on a *TM* talk show by the prominent Barrister Mainul Hussein, who champions the cause of freedom and independence in an assertive and exemplary way. He also claimed that in today's Bangladesh people were not "independent" despite being independent and that they were not "human" despite being human, referring to widespread corruption and deterioration in every field.[74] Many of those soldiers and commandoes who took part in the brutal and barbaric predawn massacre of nearly 2,000 young Hefajote students and activists on May 5, 2013 are suspected to be of foreign origin from their very looks or appearance.[75] According to media reports, external special units took part in the cruel and senseless Hefajote operations, jointly with the police and other armed units of Bangladesh, as they were also believed to have been involved in the early 2009 BDR massacre and the late 2013 Satkhira devastation.[76]

Former prime minister (late) Kazi Zafar Ahmed and (late) Shafiul Alam Prodhan, both great heroes in the democratic movement against the despotic and autocratic AL, openly described the pro-Indian Awami elements as "Indian *Rajakar*" or "*Bharotiyo Bhajakar*."

Like the polyglot parrot of the fable (as treated by the early 15th-century English poet John Skelton), whose bondage in a cage turns all the knowledge and learning it is stuffed with into a garbled and useless thing, the blind supporters everywhere in every camp, captive in their own mind without moral and spiritual elevation and enlightenment, jump to parroting, cowing, rehashing, and recycling the statements and allegations made by the other (top) members of their own, however baseless and without merit they may be. The closed-eyes-and-ears supporters, especially from the Awami side, hasten to take the opportunity to engage in the bashing of whoever belongs to the opposition BNP, regardless of how sensible the opposition views are. In their respective fealties and buffooneries—foamy and frothy—they can be styled after the characters of Ben Jonson's comedy of humors or Shakespeare's fools, in a way shrewd and entertaining, but actually funny, lowly, and ridiculous.

The long and short of the Awami politics of Bangladesh is that it has become staggeringly one-sided and one-eyed, almost to the extent of being catastrophic and devastating. The Hasina regime has unleashed a hyena-type horror, an Awami-*Baksali* bondage and butchery, and an all-out Awami *RakkhiBahini*-type rapacity, all on the opposition BNP, front and center, right and left.[77]

Khaleda's rule, by and large, was much more democratic, tolerant, and respectful. Despite faults and drawbacks, hers was never despotic and autocratic, incomparably better than what could be expected of the lesser of the two evils. The BNP never came down so low as to vilify Sheikh Mujib and never came down as hard on the AL so as to destroy, dismantle, and destabilize it.

By contrast, the AL is bent upon demonizing Zia and Khaleda and wiping out the BNP with the help of the police boots and bullets and by means of the burden of thousands and thousands of court cases. The regime is virtually nothing short of conducting a state terrorism in which গুম ও খুন (assassination and abduction), remand and ডান্ডাবেড়ি (chains and shackles), হামলা ও মামলা (persecution, prosecution, and politically motivated penal law suits), extortions and imprisonments, rape, murder, corruption, drug addiction, child labor, child marriages, teen pregnancies, and dirty and demeaning dowries have become commonplace.[78]

Democratically and politically, Awami League president Sheikh Hasina as prime minister has utterly failed to live up to the expectations of the people. Her regime is engaged in nonstop and systematic persecution and prosecution of all her political opponents and the entire spectrum of the political opposition, not just one or two. The police, the RAB, and other law enforcement agents, armed with live bullets and unaccountable sweeping powers, have not only been harassing and haranguing the opposition members by their extremely hostile and provocative insults and statements, but also have continuously arresting, remanding, ডান্ডাবেড়ি-ing (chaining) and imprisoning them and sometimes even torturing them to death, even while in the police custody.[79]

The Hasina regime needs to turn and transform itself into a people's government. It needs to both imitate and emulate the Western and Eastern democracies, including Japan, India, and South Korea, where if a ferry accident occurs the transport minister takes the responsibility and resigns, and where if the president or a presidential candidate is alleged to have shared classified information with her/his close friends, by chance or choice, s/he is immediately investigated by the country's free and independent intelligence/prosecution. In Bangladesh, all such entities are as slavish and servile as the regime is despotic and dictatorial. When the cup/glass (of freedom and liberation for all Bangladeshis) is supposed to be full in all respects, there can be no right or reason for the Awamis to be complacent by calling it half-full.

The cup/glass is only questionably half-full under the cover of the biased Awami-*চেতনা* slogan and their axis-and-apex class of material affluence. This all-exploited, all-partial, and all-fragmented *চেতনা*, as used by the Awamis in letters only, not in its whole and entire spirit, doesn't mean much when at least half of the population is either below the poverty line or disenfranchised and self-censored, excluded from political participation out of fear and intimidation, made to stay out of whatever economic boom and benefit are out there, and forced to suffer from ghastly persecution by the Awami police and the feudal and oligarchical Awami policies. Until it is full, let the cup/glass be seen as half-empty, half-empty, half-empty.

While it is a loud "Yea" to economic development, it is a louder "Nay" to crippling, corrosive and cancerous corruption committed by and for and under the Awami administration. It is absolutely a "No" to the jungle rule of the Awami police and their detention, remand, and extortion. Certainly "No" to mutilated and adulterated development without free and peaceful democratic participation of all in the political and electoral process ensured by a level playing field. Forcing the opposition to be like "dumb, driven cattle" by the Hasina regime's persecuting police pissing into the political cisterns must come to an end so that all Bangladeshis can sing with pride the following psalm in unison with Henry Longfellow:

> In the world's broad field of battle,
> In the bivouac of Life,
> Be not like dumb, driven cattle!
> Be a hero in the strife!

It is hoped that neither the Awamis nor the non-Awamis do not have to belong to those who reject the call of the people. Neither the people nor the politicians nor the police ought to belong to the wrong path, like those who reject faith about whom God/Allah the Almighty says early in the holy Qur'aan (as translated by Abdullah Yusuf Ali):

> 002.017 Their similitude is that of a man who kindled a fire; when it lighted all around him, God took away their light and left them in utter darkness. So they could not see.
>
> 002.018 Deaf, dumb, and blind, they will not return (to the path).
>
> 002.019 Or (another similitude) is that of a rain-laden cloud from the sky: In it are zones of darkness, and thunder and lightning: They press their fingers in their ears to keep out the stunning thunder-clap, the while they are in terror of death. But God is ever round the rejecters of Faith!
>
> 002.020 The lightning all but snatches away their sight; every time the light (Helps) them, they walk therein, and when the darkness grows on them, they stand still. And if God willed, He could take away their faculty of hearing and seeing; for God hath power over all things.

Notes

1. http://www.ittefaq.com.bd/national/2017/07/22/121192.html; http://www.newagebd.net/article/20285/uk-to-engage-with-all-bangladesh-parties-to-strengthen-democracy
2. https://www.nytimes.com/2017/07/28/opinion/the-opposition-disappears-in-bangladesh.html
3. While the irreligious and morally immodest boys and girls should take lessons from the incident for being liberal and should refrain from going out freely, for their suffering at the hands of the police, see: http://www.jugantor.com/first-page/2017/05/11/123824; http://www.somoyerkonthosor.com/2017/05/11/129115.htm; https://www.youtube.com/watch?v=h87z5dx4eaE;
4. http://www.prothom-alo.com/bangladesh/article/1178296
5. http://www.newagebd.net/article/19147/90-people-disappeared-in-2016-hrw
6. http://newagebd.net/160585/intl-rights-groups-for-un-intervention-in-enforced-disappearances-in-bangladesh (September 23, 2015); http://www.sheershanewsbd.com/2015/09/23/97658.
7. http://www.thedailystar.net/country/families-disappeared-19-demand-govt-intervention-182302;
   https://www.facebooKcom/533355350042314/videos/796353473742499/
8. 284 people disappeared/were abducted in the last four years, 88 in 2016 alone: http://www.jugantor.com/online/national/2016/12/29/35162/; For more information on secret killings, see:
   https://www.hrw.org/video-photos/photo-essay/2017/07/06/enforced-disappearances-bangladesh;
   https://www.hrw.org/news/2017/07/07/no-bangladesh-truth-not-smear-campaign; for more HR news and reports, on the secret killings, see: https://goo.gl/R8bcdt (or, file:///C:/Users/jkhan/Downloads/HR%20Bulletin%208.pdf);
   http://bangladeshpolitico.blogspot.com/2016/10/bangladeshs-enforced-disappearances-2016.html; http://bangladeshpolitico.blogspot.com/2016/10/bangladesh-disappearances-2016-still.html
9. https://www.youtube.com/watch?v=9vwkOcyNrjI; http://www.dailyinqilab.com/article/65979
10. For more recent instances of gross police corruption and grave demoralization, visit: http://www.dailynayadiganta.com/detail/news/228149; http://www.newsinbd.net/newsdetail/detail/31/315710; http://protissobi.com/?p=6304
11. http://www.daily-sun.com/post/228732/Now-police-regulate-democracy-alleges-BNP
12. http://sverigesradio.se/sida/artikel.aspx?programid=83&artikel=6665807;
    http://www.prothom-alo.com/bangladesh/article/1134276;
    Swedish Radio reveals "RAB" officer's conversation exposing brutalities Video: https://youtu.be/NTpCL35GNGI;
    https://m.youtube.com/watch?feature=youtu.be&v=NTpCL35GNGI;

13. http://www.bbc.com/bengali/news-39495128; http://amar-desh24.com/bangla/index.php/details/nationalnews/7254
14. https://www.facebook.com/photo.php?fbid=637786049754269&set=a.265250320341179.1073741829.100005686397113&type=3; https://www.facebook.com/groups/1715849385302359/
15. http://www.newagebd.net/article/15952/16-fake-db-members-arrested-in-city; http://www.jugantor.com/online/country-news/2017/05/24/47963
16. http://www.prothom-alo.com/bangladesh/article/1132986; http://www.prothom-alo.com/bangladesh/article/1104460; http://www.prothom-alo.com/bangladesh/article/1101238; https://www.hrw.org/news/2014/01/27/bangladesh-end-spate-extrajudicial-killings; http://www.aljazeera.com/news/2017/03/blasts-bangladesh-extra-judicial-killings-170329121314268.html;
"Bangladesh police crackdown on peaceful protesters": https://www.amnesty.org/en/latest/news/2010/11/ofensiva-policial-bangladesh-manifestantes-pacificos; https://www.amnesty.org/en/latest/news/2015/01/bangladesh-must-investigate-deaths-and-release-prisoners-held-opposition-crackdown;
17. http://bangla.samakal.net/2016/11/18/250166
18. http://www.state.gov/j/drl/rls/hrrpt/humanrightsreport/index.htm?year=2016&dlid=265532
19. https://www.nytimes.com/2017/07/28/opinion/the-opposition-disappears-in-bangladesh.html;
http://www.economist.com/news/leaders/21722831-islamists-she-courting-will-never-be-satisfied-bangladeshs-prime-minister-uses-piety;
http://www.nytimes.com/2016/08/23/opinion/disappearances-and-unlawful-detentions-in-bangladesh.html?smprod=nytcore-iphone&smid=nytcore-iphone-share&_r=0;
http://www.nytimes.com/2016/08/23/opinion/disappearances-and-unlawful-detentions-in-bangladesh.html?smprod=nytcore-iphone&smid=nytcore-iphone-share; http://www.nytimes.com/2016/05/20/opinion/the-real-source-of-terror-in-bangladesh.html?emc=eta1&_r=1; http://www.nytimes.com/2016/05/09/opinion/bangladeshs-descent-into-lawlessness.html?_r=0;
https://www.hrw.org/asia/bangladesh?_ga=2.170217696.1178387897.1494175073-548959770.1489372869;
http://www.thestatesman.com/opinion/tragedy-of-bangladesh-1482361992.html; http://foreignpolicy.com/2016/12/16/bangladesh-is-vanishing-the-opposition/?utm_content=bufferecddc&utm_medium=social&utm_source=twitter.com&utm_campaign=buffer%3Cbr%20/%3E%3C/p%3E%3Cp%3E;
http://en.prothom-alo.com/opinion/news/126119/%E2%80%98Development-not-possible-with-rampant-corruption%E2%80%99;
http://epaper.prothom-alo.com/view/dhaka/2016-10-23/10;
http://thediplomat.com/2016/10/bangladesh-just-became-a-vassal-state/;

http://www.weeklyholiday.net/Homepage/Pages/UserHome.aspx; http://thediplomat.com/2016/07/the-downfall-of-democracy-in-bangladesh/; http://www.thefridaytimes.com/tft/blood-dimmed-tide-in-bangladesh/; http://www.economist.com/news/asia/21698677-bangladesh-sliding-one-party-dictatorship-despotic-dhaka; http://www.crisisgroup.org/en/regions/asia/south-asia/bangladesh/277-political-conflict-extremism-and-criminal-justice-in-bangladesh.aspx; https://www.dni.gov/files/documents/SASC_Unclassified_2016_ATA_SFR_FINAL.pdf; https://www.dni.gov/index.php/newsroom/testimonies/217-congressional-testimonies-2016/1313-statement-for-the-record-worldwide-threat-assessment-of-the-u-s-ic-before-the-senate-armed-services-committee-2016\; https://www.foreignaffairs.com/articles/united-states/friends-without-benefits; http://www.wsj.com/articles/SB10001424127887323846504579073510606727756

20. http://www.natunbd.net/blog/blogdetail/detail/2601/muhon/81256
21. http://www.prothom-alo.com/bangladesh/article/57601; http://www.bd-pratidin.com/first-page/2017/01/15/200067
22. https://www.youtube.com/watch?v=xD-sd_8P8lE
23. http://www.notundesh.com/details.php?link=3227&&%20category; www.somewhereinblog.net/mobile/blog/sufiborshan/30043905
24. http://www.rtnews24.com/politics/bangladesh-has-become-a-police-state-bnp-chief-khaleda-says/
25. https://m.facebook.com/mahbub.khan.526/posts/10206490402004981?src=email_notif
26. http://www.bd-desh.net/newsdetail/detail/200/221404
27. http://www.sheershanewsbd.com/2015/06/30/86863#; http://www.bd-pratidin.com/lead-news/2015/07/09/92587
28. See the report of the US Govt. International Religious Freedom at http://www.sheershanewsbd.com/2015/10/15/100117
29. http://www.sheershanews.com/2015/02/20/69759#; http://www.prothom-alo.com/bangladesh/article/457162/
30. See David Hoffman at https://www.timesofassam.com/international/governments-undue-influence-judiciary-bangladesh/; http://www.prothom-alo.com/bangladesh/article/425026; http://newsnine24.com/justice-gobinda-chandra/; https://goo.gl/YFxKgb
31. http://www.daily-sun.com/post/103799/Topheavy-civil-admin
32. http://www.thedailystar.net/city/cops-foil-discussion-where-fakhrul-was-made-chief-guest-1203202
33. For only a few recent examples that are only the tip of the iceberg of widespread police brutality, corruption, abduction, and misconduct, click the links:

http://dainikcoxsbazar.com/2017/04/18;
http://primenewsbd.com/index.php?page=details&nc=3&news_id=106701;
https://www.youtube.com/watch?v=eNYCB1Ti7XM&feature=youtu.be;
http://www.prothom-alo.com/bangladesh/article/1084929;
http://www.banglatribune.com/columns/opinion/177845;
http://www.jugantor.com/online/national/2017/01/22/37384;
http://epaper.prothom-alo.com/contents/2017/2017_01_06/content_zoom/x2017_01_06_5_4_b.jpg.pagespeed.ic.xUTWaCZd33.jpg;
http://www.jugantor.com/online/country-news/2016/12/26/34905;
https://www.facebook.com/mdrakib.rakib.779/videos/1913028622242851/
http://www.banglatribune.com/national/news/164867;
https://www.youtube.com/watch?v=UvtsSAoeUA8&feature=youtu.be;
http://www.prothom-alo.com/bangladesh/article/1031055;
http://www.prothom-alo.com/bangladesh/article/1023211/;
http://www.prothom-alo.com/bangladesh/article/1023389;
http://www.dailynayadiganta.com/detail/news/171489;
http://www.jugantor.com/online/country-news/2016/10/12/27506;
http://www.jugantor.com/online/national/2016/10/09/27220;
http://www.kalerkantho.com/print-edition/first-page/2016/10/07/413675;
http://www.jugantor.com/online/country-news/2016/09/28/26195;
http://www.bdface.net/newsdetail/detail/31/246619;
http://www.bdface.net/newsdetail/detail/200/241458;
https://youtu.be/xNROkyx5l7o; http://www.kalerkantho.com/online/national/2016/07/24/384815;
http://www.jugantor.com/online/country-news/2016/05/23/13849/;
http://www.amardeshonline.com/pages/details/2016/04/04/330370;
http://www.jugantor.com/online/national/2016/03/11/6571;
http://www.amardeshonline.com/pages/details/2016/03/06/326280;
http://newagebd.net/202513/rab-man-held-on-extortion-charge-in-narayanganj;
http://www.ittefaq.com.bd/print-edition/first-page/2016/02/08/100816.html;
http://newagebd.net/199631/4-policemen-suspended-over-tea-vendors-death/;
http://www.dailyinqilab.com/details/2841/;
http://www.amardeshonline.com/pages/details/2016/02/03/321940;
http://newagebd.net/199316/police-si-suspended-in-barisal-for-demanding-bribe;
http://newagebd.net/182296/constable-held-while-robbing-off-tk-9-lakh-in-sylhet;
http://newagebd.net/173033/police-lies-about-arrests-dangerous/;
http://newagebd.net/184778/policemen-sent-to-jail-for-mugging-gold-in-chittagong; https://www.youtube.com/watch?v=NXZNBhhcL08;
http://www.sheershanewsbd.com/2015/07/30/90386#;
http://www.sheershanewsbd.com/2015/07/20/89268;
https://www.youtube.com/watch?v=yMlnLSYISfw;

http://www.sheershanewsbd.com/2015/11/09/103185;
https://youtu.be/jc_LYSz3OqQ;
http://www.amadershomoys.com/unicode/2016/04/20/100483.htm; http://www.sheershanewsbd.com/2015/12/04/106367;
http://www.sheershanewsbd.com/2016/02/07/115781;

34. Under normal circumstances, students and teachers should have no business in the administration of justice and should remain preoccupied studying and attending classes. They have only to lose and nothing to gain by staying away from classes.
35. http://www.sheershanewsbd.com/2015/06/12/84230#;
http://newagebd.net/130632/bring-police-under-accountability-nhrc-chairman/;
http://www.prothom-alo.com/bangladesh/article/573700/;
http://www.sheershanewsbd.com/2015/06/30/86810#;http://www.sheershanewsbd.com/2015/07/07/87869#; http://www.sheershanewsbd.com/2015/07/12/88458#;
36. http://www.amardeshonline.com/pages/details/2016/01/30/321353#
37. http://dailyalochona.blogspot.com/2010/12/alochona-cops-top-corrupt.html
38. http://www.amadershomoys.com/newsite/2015/07/17/351721.htm#; http://www.sheershanewsbd.com/2015/07/16/88848#
39. http://www.noyonchatterjee.com/2016/04/blog-post_43.html;
http://www.noyonchatterjee.com/2016/06/blog-post_7.html;
hhttp://www.rtnews24.com/uncategorized/poloshe-indian/;
ttps://www.youtube.com/watch?feature=player_embedded&v=3o_tZUnvQ6w;
http://www.sheikhnews.com/2016/04/17/bdnews-51/;
http://newsnine24.com/2432-2/; https://www.youtube.com/watch?v=drNrmtaSJJg
https://youtu.be/LVXqHwiVfGI;
http://www.bdnow.net/newsdetail/detail/200/205462; https://youtu.be/3o_tZUn-vQ6w; https://www.youtube.com/watch?v=m1j5KeSFaLY; http://www.bdnow.net/newsdetail/detail/200/205462; বাংলাদেশ পুলিশে পরিচয় গোপন করে গণহারে নিয়োগ দেয়া হচ্ছে ভারতীয়দের;https://www.youtube.com/watch?v=m1j5KeSFaLY&index=4&list=TL5_ff6-BSaoIxODA0MjAxNg;
https://www.facebook.com/sheikh65/posts/1020950946624l596?fref=nf;
http://newsbd7.com/main/detail/2912; https://www.youtube.com/watch?v=2v1JD-2PkJaQ; https://www.youtube.com/watch?v=bl4IPiHMdXI; https://www.youtube.com/watch?v=NtKZKtfmKIc
http://www.amardeshonline.com/pages/details/2016/04/20/332633#;
Faridpur District Awami League President and his family are Indian Hindus: http://www.u71news.com/?page=details&article=21.69370; http://bangla.samakal.net/2016/04/27/208698.
40. http://www.bd-pratidin.com/first-page/2017/02/04/205237
41. http://www.bddesh.net/newsdetail/detail/200/217263;
http://www.natunbd.net/newsdetail/detail/200/285164;
http://worldbangla.com/2017/02/18/62025

42. http://www.natunbd.net/newsdetail/detail/200/285746
43. http://mynewsbd.net/?p=5989; http://mynewsbd.net/?p=5500; http://www.bd-desh.net/videohighlightdetail/detail/6495;
44. http://www.srilankaguardian.org/2012/04/bengal-tigers-in-r-cage.html (23 April 2012)
45. http://newagebd.net/235797/khaleda-asks-force-rules-country; https://www.rbn24.co.uk/?p=7962
46. http://chairmanbd.blogspot.com.au/2013/05/mass-killing-on-protesters-in-dhaka-at.html
47. For Wikileaks and other reports, see http://bdrmutinyexposed.com/?p=353; http://bdrmutinyexposed.com/?p=407; https://www.theguardian.com/world/2009/feb/28/bangladesh-soldiers-rebellion-mutiny; https://bangladesh2075.files.wordpress.com/2011/02/bdr4.pdf; http://www.amardeshonline.com/pages/details/2013/05/07/199017; http://defence.pk/threads/indian-backed-awami-league-massacre-%E2%80%93-satkhira-bangladesh-turned-into-dead-valley.294460/page-4. For Dr Tuhin Malik's views about what he calls a premeditated massacre, see: http://www.natun-bd.net/newsdetail/detail/49/286604; and for Dr KMA Malik's views, see: "The Sugar-coated Poison: India's offer of 'help' to restructure BDR" at: https://ishakhan.wordpress.com/2009/04/06
48. http://newagebd.net/168218/hc-asks-why-inaction-of-police-over-gulshan-accident-wont-be-declared-illegal/; http://newagebd.net/168300/surge-in-al-leaders-relatives-committing-crimes/
49. Taj Hashmi, http://www.thedailystar.net/public-servants-making-political-statements-60869
50. http://www.amadershomoys.com/newsite/2015/08/10/370381.htm; http://www.amadershomoys.com/newsite/2015/08/12/372237.htm; http://www.sheershanewsbd.com/2015/06/17/84985; http://www.sheershanewsbd.com/2015/06/24/86052#
51. http://www.crisisgroup.org/en/regions/asia/south-asia/bangladesh/277-political-conflict-extremism-and-criminal-justice-in-bangladesh.aspx; http://www.anandabazar.com/bangladesh-news/voice-of-politicians-from-police-of-bangladesh-bng-dgtl-1.374912
52. http://www.sheershanewsbd.com/2015/07/19/89167#
53. See Mohammed Zainal Abedin, http://banews24.com/whole-country2/117-whole-country-4/12434
54. http://www.amadershomoys.com/newsite/2015/08/17/375148.htm
55. http://www.dailynayadiganta.com/detail/news/56106
56. http://www.banglamail24.com/news/161932
57. http://www.banglatribune.com/national/news/155405
58. http://www.kalerkantho.com/print-edition/first-page/2016/08/25/397362

59. http://www.thedailystar.net/op-ed/politics/extremism-and-the-bamboo-brigade-1247821
60. https://www.youtube.com/watch?v=w2Zm5roZkkA&feature=youtu.be; http://www.newagebd.net/article/7852/police-thwart-rampal-protests-with-teargas-rubber-bullet; http://www.newagebd.net/article/7865/asi-suspended-for-torturing-journalist-at-shahbagh; http://www.thedailystar.net/city/sundarbans-campaigners-clash-cops-hartal-1351225
61. http://www.prothom-alo.com/opinion/article/1072113
62. http://amar-desh24.com/bangla/print.php/nationalnews/11083
63. http://www.newagebd.net/article/147/so-called-gunfight-now-a-game-for-law-enforcers-bnp; the UK-exiled Amar Desh reporter Oliullah Noman at: https://www.rbn24.co.uk/?p=8273
64. http://www.banglatribune.com/others/news/87579/; http://www.jugantor.com/online/national/2016/04/05/8994/; http://www.banglatribune.com/others/news/93815/
65. http://www.sheershanewsbd.com/2015/03/29/74490
66. https://www.youtube.com/watch?v=oeVrSK0JGcQ
67. http://newagebd.net/188893/vote-rigging-violence-mar-polls/; http://www.prothom-alo.com/bangladesh/article/726181; http://www.sheershanewsbd.com/2015/12/30/110364; https://www.facebook.com/dailymanabzamin/videos/950970008322570/?theater; https://www.youtube.com/watch?v=qdvJ_arC_8w; https://www.facebook.com/photo.php?fbid=10153822904920645&set=a.464006410644.251420.613880644&type=3&theater
68. http://www.amadershomoys.com/newsite/2015/07/25/357335.htm; for a brief sketch of Kazi Zafar's life by Mostafa Jamal Haider, see http://newagebd.net/179988/kazi-zafar-ahmed-a-luminary-lost/
69. http://newagebd.net/235797/khaleda-asks-force-rules-country/
70. http://archive.ittefaq.com.bd/index.php?ref=MjBfMDNfMjFfMTRfMV8xXzFfMTE3Mzg2; http://bangla.samakal.net/2016/03/27/202155
71. https://www.youtube.com/watch?feature=player_embedded&v=3o_tZUnvQ6w; http://www.bdnow.net/newsdetail/detail/200/205462
72. http://www.u71news.com/?page=details&article=21.69370; http://www.u71news.com/?page=details&article=21.69360
73. http://datab.us/NQOWA6jq3Z0#Khaleda%20Zia%20Vs%20Gopali%20Girl%20%2829%20December%202013%29; http://datab.us/LEe3PYl-hbs#Gopali%20by%20Khaleda%20Zia
74. http://www.dailynayadiganta.com/detail/news/38861

75. http://chairmanbd.blogspot.com.au/2013/05/mass-killing-on-protesters-in-dhaka-at.html
76. http://www.amardeshonline.com/pages/details/2013/05/07/199017; http://defence.pk/threads/indian-backed-awami-league-massacre-%E2%80%93-satkhira-bangladesh-turned-into-dead-valley.294460/page-4
77. M H Chowdhury Maya attacked Khaleda saying she was like a witch and a hyena: http://www.sheershanewsbd.com/2014/11/02/56471
78. http://newagebd.net/190238/362-incidents-of-sexual-assault-in-2015/; over a hundred rapes in three months, http://www.banglatribune.com/others/news/93815/; http://www.amardeshonline.com/pages/details/2015/12/08/314118
79. http://newagebd.net/176776/custodial-death-of-jonny-two-policemen-land-in-jail; https://www.hrw.org/video-photos/video/2016/09/28/video-deliberate-kneecapping-detainees-security-forces-bangladesh; https://www.amnesty.org/en/latest/news/2010/12/parlamentario-torturado-fuerzas-seguridad-bangladesh/

4 Politics Bangladesh Style

All Sick and Rotten to the Core

English Romantic poet Coleridge's Ancient Mariner expresses his dire and desperate situation of suffering, isolation, and stagnation thus:

> The very deep did rot: O Christ!
> That ever this should be!
> Yea, slimy things did crawl with legs
> Upon the slimy sea. (Part II)
>
> I looked upon the rotting sea,
> And drew my eyes away;
> I looked upon the rotting deck,
> And there the dead men lay. (Part IV)

The load of sins and crimes getting higher and heavier with the passage of time, politics in Bangladesh has gotten to the stage of being rotten and tainted due to the present Hasina government-turned-regime (which people would like to describe as BAKSAL-II, much worse and more dangerous than BAKSAL-I). Shakespeare's Prince Hamlet sees his Denmark immersed in evil, with cheats, traitors, betrayers, and deceivers all around—his own uncle and the new murderer-usurper king Claudius, the chief adviser Polonius and Polonius's son Laertes, and his friends-turned-enemies Rosencrantz and Guildenstern—all are fraud and crooked playing a nasty and nefarious role against Hamlet. "Something is rotten in the state of Denmark," says Marcellus, one of the guards at the Elsinore Palace, to Hamlet's only trustworthy friend Horatio toward the beginning of the play. And later in the play Hamlet soliloquizes:

> To be, or not to be—that is the question:
> Whether 'tis nobler in the mind to suffer
> The slings and arrows of outrageous fortune
> Or to take arms against a sea of troubles
> And by opposing end them.

Under the grip of the monstrous and atrocious animus-fomenting anomalies and asymmetries in all sectors and areas—be it government or private—with the prime minister's official residence *Ganobhaban* virtually used as a party office, the state of Bangladesh is no better than that of Denmark.[1] Many a man/woman feels obliged and obligated to soliloquize as Hamlet does. They feel choked up amid a reign of gangs and *gopals*, hoodlums and hooligans, looters and plunderers and extortionists, boots and bullets and batons, tanks and teargasses, arrests and remands and imprisonments, and, of course, হামলা ও মামলা (attacks and penal persecutions) and গুম ও খুন (assassinations and abductions)—all in hundreds and thousands.[2] A great majority of the people of Bangladesh, represented by the opposition Bangladesh Nationalist Party (BNP), thinks the nation has gone down to the abyss of a dark and deep narrow sewer pipe, like the little boy Ziad (or Jihad), to be rescued and relieved by any means from any corner—unexpected, strong, courageous, innovative.

On January 4, 2015, a political commentator, columnist, and law professor, Dr Asif Nazrul, made exactly the same analogy to describe the desperate situation the BNP has fallen into. The next day the Awami League (AL) leader Mufazzal H C Maya, charged with corruption and "proud" to have an "ideal" Awami family, made himself a laughing stock not only by denying that the sand-and-cement-and-bricks trucks were actually placed by his Awami government in front of the office of the BNP Chief Khaleda Zia to put her under siege but also by saying that those trucks were brought in by Khaleda herself to renovate her office compound in what Maya claimed was a dramatic stunt and political show-off.[3]

Maya's "home repair" theory বাড়ি মেরামত তত্ত্ব was like his Awami cohorts, then home minister M K Alamgir's "shake" theory ঝাকুনি তত্ত্ব about the collapse of the Rana Plaza and the commerce minister Tofael Ahmed's pre-Ramadan price hike theory that too much media talk was behind the hike পত্রিকায় লেখালেখির কারণেই দ্রব্যমূল্য বৃদ্ধি. It is to be mentioned that all those sand-and-garbage trucks were a paranoid, misogynist, hypochondriac, and schizophrenic deployment by Hasina to block the way of a political leader who was and still is unquestionably and indisputably the most popular (to be distinguished from the short lasting "populist") and dignified politician of the country.

Eighteenth-century English poet and novelist Oliver Goldsmith, a man of moderation as he was, was reluctant to espouse the cause of any political party because he thought political partisanship always degenerated into the extremes for the worst. In the dedication of his poem *The Traveller: or, A Prospect of Society* (1765), he says: "Party entirely distorts the judgment and destroys the taste. When the mind is once affected with this disease, it can only find pleasure in what contributes to increase the distemper." Forty-four years after the independence when Bangladesh is still chronically suffering, to the despicable shame of the successive ruling parties, from corruption, conflicts, contradictions, confrontations, and controversies, Goldsmith's words resoundingly prove to be true. It is almost four decades and a half after the independence, but Bangladesh still remains a deeply divided country, both politically and ideologically, only to have to continue to suffer from the grim and gray partisan friction and internecine factionalism, retreats and regressions, impasses and bypasses, and deadlocks and gridlocks.

As it is, there is absolutely no lack of freedom for the ruling party AL since 2009. It enjoys unlimited freedom, freedom without responsibility and accountability. By contrast, there is hardly any space and respect for the opposition, which is constantly under the AL government-directed police persecution and prosecution. Forcible suppression and subversion of the opposition BNP by the AL government invite similar, though subdued and feeble means of reaction from the opposition, far from being effective and forceful, yet exaggerated by the Hasina government to disproportionate proportions. All what the opposition wants is its legitimate democratic rights, including free and fair elections.

There is a nonstop engagement of the political parties, especially from the side of the ruling AL, in bickering, squabbling, mudslinging, finger-pointing, and making crude and coarse remarks and unfounded and baseless statements. Abuses of rights and freedoms—rampant and reckless—have rendered the body politic of Bangladesh incurably diseased and dysfunctional. Lack of tolerance and widespread abuses of democratic norms and values have led the country to a state of fright, chaos, and uncertainty. It seems the government and governmental privileges, opportunities, and protections are reserved only for the regime and those allied with it—not for the opposition and the rest of the nation. If the opposition or the civil society attempts to exercise their freedom of dissent or expose the corruption of the government even with authentic evidence or documentation, they can expect anything—either getting kidnapped and killed or arrested—like the state terrorism of targeted assassinations and abductions during the dirty war of 1970s and early 1980s in Argentina.

The government, responsible for (the protection of) all individual citizens scarcely takes responsibility for those who disappeared before being tortured and killed or tortured and then released. It hardly cares to apprehend the ghostly and ghastly operatives, with or without (white) uniform. That is really a scary and frightening situation. There are reports that as many as 100 Indian RAW-trained secret killers of hardcore Awami affiliation and many Indian secret operatives are operating in Bangladesh.[4] Do these underground miscreants and criminal parasites act with the knowledge and support of the government? May very likely be. Are they friends or foes of the government? Privy or parallel to the government? According to Jessica Fox who writes about these RAW-trained crusaders in action in Bangladesh with many opposition figures on their hit list, with the full knowledge and sponsorship of the very top of the government.[5]

What happened to the hundreds and thousands of innocent and extrajudicial victims across the country through the machineries of a secret and clandestine government within the conniving public front of the paper government is enough of a reason for the people of Bangladesh to feel terrorized, terrified, scared, and frightened.[6] Most of the vanished have been killed and must have been killed most horribly and gruesomely, like the martyred leaders and intellectuals in 1971 and 1975. The times such as December 2013, December 2014, and January–March 2015 alone saw hundreds and thousands killed, burnt, abducted, remanded, and imprisoned countrywide, mostly due to the authoritarian and uncompromising Awami intransigence about the opposition's legitimate demands.[7] The horrific lynching of a little poor boy, who had as beautiful a name as Sheikh Mohammad Samiul Alam alias Rajon (in the District of Sylhet on July 8, 2015) and the rape and murder of a nineteen-year-old Comilla college girl, Sohagi Jahan Tonu (who was abducted, on March 21, 2016, on her way back from the private tuition she was giving to meet her financial needs) are just two such cases of cruel torture that is going on everywhere in Bangladesh.[8]

Bangladesh is full of the likes of the Syrian Aylan and Omran. In January 2016, every day was a day of child murder.[9] It is a hypocritical show-off to cry for Aylan and Omran on the international platform, while there are no tears shed by the Awami regime for thousands of them at home in Bangladesh. Mohammad Badrul Ahsan, editor of the weekly *First News* and an opinion writer for *The Daily Star*, dwells on the scary phenomenon of beastly brutalities against children in Bangladesh. He says: "Bangladesh Shishu Adhikar Forum found in its study that a total of 968 children were tortured to death in the last three and a half years. The alarming news is that the number of child murders was 61 percent higher in 2014 than the previous year."[10]

Of this kind of beating and battering and hacking to death, or slaughtering with sharp objects, there is no dearth, with several occurring almost on a daily basis. Political and nonpolitical killings—often in a brutal, brutish, barbaric manner—compete to outnumber each other in Bangladesh where members of the public, the police, and the ruling party all have become so cruel and heartless as if they are either devoid of humanity or were born from inhuman to nonhuman. According to CNN, "Local rights organization Odhikar (অধিকার) said in a recent report that at least 903 people were lynched in Bangladesh since January 2009 [during the Hasina regime], and at least 60 people were lynched in the past six months."[11]

Almost the entire opposition team, from top to bottom, were and are being routinely remanded before being put behind bars. Mothers', daughters', wives', and sisters' tears, shed in cusecs every day for their loved ones, are enough to overflow the drying Padma and Teesta and Atrai rivers—getting dry due to the "friendly fire" of Bangladesh's "big-brother-friend" India.[12] Instead of being stirred by the politics of constructive criticism and cooperation, the political scene in Bangladesh has shamefully descended into one of corruption and provocation that irredeemably and irretrievably keeps eating into the vitals of the nation and the society.

The ruling party AL's unbridled and uncontrolled freedom (of action and expression), accompanied by an abusive and autocratic exercise of power, has degenerated into a stifling and suffocating tyranny that has silenced the voice of the majority. The violence, anarchy, and calumny with which the AL rules the country have rendered the majority into a crawling and crouching cripple. It finds itself clawless and faceless under the weight of the AL's politically suspicious judicial hammer and the boots and bullets of its police. The true majority has become like a drowning man helplessly trying to catch at a straw, to the detriment of democratic practices and interests. Repulse and resistance with resilience, therefore, have become necessary for the survival of the completely subdued political parties in the opposition.

Far from the meaningful freedom of speech, the rule of law, and the economic and social progress of the country—all to be achieved and ensured side by side for robust and sustainable growth in all areas—, there have been one-sided restrictions only on the opposition parties.[13] By contrast, there is reckless liberty—licentious and libertine—for those in power and those allied with them. Excess of anything is bad, as power corrupts and absolute power corrupts absolutely. The ruling party has been abusing power for too long without being held accountable and responsible. Instead of consolidating and institutionalizing the democratic process, the Hasina-AL has turned and twisted it into a mechanism for their own promotion, at the expense of democratic dissent.

In a free and democratic polity, it is enough to register one's protest through the (print or electronic) media or any other channels such as peaceful street demonstrations and processions. But the political culture of Bangladesh is such that one got to create unrest, clash with the police, turn violent, and even get killed to get heard and press home one's demands. This sorry state of affairs has become familiar—in fact, too familiar to make one wonder if the country will ever be stranger to such turn of events that keeps dragging it into the dark abyss of chaos and confusion. The deadly and destructive divisions between the two leading parties are glaringly manifested everywhere along the lines of virulent and vitriolic partisan split.

Bipartisan discussion and consensus, even on one single agenda, are banished from the political scene of Bangladesh. Nonpartisan amity and spirit have become an impossible eluding dream, to be hopelessly longed for and endlessly talked about. A critical and constructive debate on matters of national interest is both the elixir and spice of an effective and sustainable democratic system and its dynamic growth and flourish. Under the democratic rules and principles, political parties must have peaceful dialogue to find a bipartisan solution to all issues—however contentious they may be—even if that means a temporary or limited measure for the time being. Unfortunately, in Bangladesh, if the opposition calls for dialogue, the regime dismisses it as its weakness, provocatively terming the opposition as having gone bankrupt and as begging for help in the name of dialogue. What an insane and irrational distortion of reality to the devious and cynical ends, only to be lambasted and lampooned!

But, truth being stranger than fiction, what has become an ugly ubiquitous norm rather than an occasional exception is for the politicians and their intellectual following to eternally differ and clash with each other according to the dictates of their respective party affiliations. All falsely claim their statements to be in the name of mass and majority interest.[14] The rival political parties seem to be parasitically sustaining themselves on differences between them not only over the larger issues of national interest but also the petty follies and frivolous fancies unworthy of being paid attention to. What is sickening is that the people of all walks of life are inimically and acrimoniously divided in their views about different political parties. Their heated, violence-prone, and mischief-ridden allegiances and loyalties would have drastically subsided if the Awami incumbents kept their words and contributed to the building of trust and confidence between them and others. The entire spectrum of democratic voices—political, intellectual, academic, cultural, civil, and business—demands exactly that kind of bridging, patching, and mending.

But, alas! As the radiation physicist Dr Muzzzam Kazi of the USA expressed his disappointment (in an e-mail post of April 22, 2016 through nabdc@googlegroups.com) over the tradition of disgust and distrust, especially concerning the unjust arrest and the repeated ten-day remands of the octogenarian star journalist Shafik Rehman: "Lies, lies, and lies are the basic principles of Bangladesh now. I am praying that my dead body not to be buried in a land of oppression. I am so lucky that I left Bangladesh, the land of prosecution, oppression, injustice, and a ruthless dictator." Yet, in another post, Dr Kazi went on to say that he was so frustrated at the dirty and degenerated politics of the Hasina regime that he was ashamed of identifying himself as an American of Bangladeshi origin.

Quite boastful and often bullying, bellicose, and belligerent, yet terribly BNP*hobic* Prime Minister Hasina, before the farce that was the January 5, 2014 thing, conducted by her in a demolition of democratic tradition, had said that the election boycotted by the entire opposition would have to go ahead for the sake of constitutional continuity. It was a constitution that, prior to the election, was questionably amended by her sole authority through a judicial twist and turn to favor and benefit her government alone. She also implied that, after the January 5 thing, completely controversial and totally unacceptable as it was, arrangements would be made for another interim (participatory, impartial, and credible) election.

Now, after the January 5 mockery, Hasina and her men went back on their promises (the way they went back at the time of 1986 election under HM Ershad) in a national betrayal, insisting that the government would stay in power for the full term. Also, before the 5 January melodrama, she had said that the parliament would be dissolved before the election, later confirmed by one of her advisers, H T Imam, branded as the "Imam" of the AL, both now and then when he conducted the oath-taking ceremony of the AL government under Khandoker Mushtaque Ahmed, who took over after the assassination of their leader Sheikh Mujib on August 15, 1975.[15] Imam said on the ATN News that PM Hasina was going to address the nation to hopefully announce the dissolution of the parliament. Unfortunately, neither did she address the nation nor did she dissolve the parliament. The parliament was dominated by (the tyranny of) her party's absolute majority that was the result of the questionable late 2008 election.

Strangely enough, the weird 5 January theatrical show took place with the same parliament remaining in place. It created a notorious precedent to be found nowhere in the sane and civilized world. The whole thing was therefore a record of broken promises, one after another, not to speak of the tens of thousands of torn and wrecked lives on the opposition side. Right after the 5 January thing, Hasina's own Finance Minister Abul Maal Abdul Muhith dismissed it as "no election at all," saying there would be a full and complete, and valid and legitimate election soon that unfortunately never happened. Stark political betrayals by the Hasina government-turned-regime made Dr Mina Farah of New York comment that she did not see the traitor Mir Jaffar of the Battle of Plassey in 1757 but she did see the "Lady Mir Jaffar" of Bangladesh, apparently referring to Sheikh Hasina.

On a number of occasions, both before and after the blacker than black January 5, 2014, Prime Minister Hasina expressed her intention to continue for an indefinite period of time for the "good" of the people as if it is only she who had the right and who was eligible and capable to do good for the people the way she alone wanted. It is as if it was her sole agency and hereditary prerogative, like a line of royal successors and descendants, to stay in power and enjoy all sorts of privileges and leverages that power brought with it. It is as if she alone was the only upper caste "Brahmin" to perch in the high seat of power in the name of economic development and as if the opposition was no better than the low-caste "Dalit" untouchables or it was only an alien UFO that came from another planet. Time and again, PM Hasina said that nothing, not even the position of Prime Minister, was more important to her than her being the daughter of Sheikh Mujib, who is considered the sole and only father of the nation by her party, although the majority of the Bangladeshis view him as one of the four or five founding fathers together with Suhrawardy, Sher-e-Bangla, Moulana Bhashani, and Sir Salimullah—all four of whom have now descended into scanty respect, if not oblivion.[16]

But in reality Sheikh Hasina's identity as the daughter of Sheikh Mujib has been relegated to a lower position. The PM position has proved to be so overwhelmingly superior to her that she would cling to it at and for any price, no matter what, even if that took destruction of democracy, demolition of electoral politics, daily disappearances and abductions of innocent people by her DB police, and the annihilation and elimination of the political opposition by all sorts of devious and doubtful means available. The PM position has turned out to be so far more outweighing than anything else that she would forget and forgive all those Awami Leaguers who played a compromising or supporting role in and after the assassination of her father. Her regime is preoccupied with enjoying power, ensuring the privileges of its surrogates and supporters, and securing only their safety, rather than delivering on the duties and obligations of a government, including the safety of all others—all citizens and all the political opposition, who are instead put behind bars unceasingly and without a respite.

In addition, the love of the all-important and most-coveted PM position made Hasina "avenge" for her father's death by endearingly drawing close to her the political figures such as Hasanul Hoque Inu, Motia Chowdhury, and Dr Anwar Hussein (brother of Col Taher)—who were once violently and viciously anti-Awami.[17] Top members of her own party such as Syed Ashraful Islam and Sheikh Selim, her ally Kazi Firoz Rashid of JP, and her supporter Prof Mahbub Kamal are highly critical of her stance toward Inu and the such. BNP Senior Joint Secretary Ruhul Kabir Rizvi says to the same effect how Ms Hasina was betraying with her father's blood by befriending those who were once deadly foes of Sheikh Mujib.[18] All of them—Inu, Chowdhury, Hussein (except ASM Abdur Rob)—are like Khaleque Biswas of Neamat Imam's *The Black Coat* (a scathing semi-fictional attack on the AL)—all turned from harsh critics to radical followers of Hasina and her father Mujib. A *kind and forgiving* daughter's historically exemplary political reconciliation and rapprochement with those who were jumping up and down on a tank in joy at the violent death of her father![19]

One may recall that during the BNP-led opposition movement in early 2015, the Hasina regime made a call for the opposition to stop the strike so that the both sides could sit and talk. Nothing has happened since. Now, if the BNP caves in to the Awami demand that the Jamaat be excluded from the opposition alliance, the ruling clique will come up with another pretext, then yet another, then another, with an endless list of preconditions for talk, which may never take place. One line of argument is that the people of Bangladesh need the BNP more than it needs them if they want to topple the regime through a free and fair election, despite whatever the helpless BNP does in the face of the Awami brutalities.

The THAAD-and-thunder-like thumping thud over the thing elephantine

Starting with the Carthaginian general Hannibal's war elephants against the Scipio-led Romans around 215 BC and the Christian king Abraha of Yemen who attacked the Muslim holy place of Makkah around 570 AD with a force that included one or few elephants (হাতি/*Hati*), there are many stories related to the biggest animal on land, however awkward-looking it is (according to the

Wikipedia dictionary). There were tens of individual historical (royal and martial) elephants (similar to Emperor Alexander's horse Bucephalus, meaning an ox head from a branding mark depicting the same). There was ancient elephantry (military units with elephant-mounted troops) all over the world, just as there was cavalry (military units with horse-mounted troops). The world elephant repertoire can boast of a new Indian-Bangladeshi bilateral one added to it. There was a thud of the proportion of thunder and American THAAD (Terminal High Altitude Area Defense) missile over this cross-border elephant.

This elephant that was borne by flood water across the border and got stuck in Bangladesh in August 2016 was very lucky due to her Indian "nationality." Not only was she able to avoid both the police/RAB crossfire and the friendly fire but also to grab all the neighborly Bangladesh's media attention, turned away from the plight of its own tens of thousands of submerged and starving flood-affected victims. Similarly, the BNP has been forced to be lying low under the impact of the itchy and poisonous Awami formalin and has been effectively anesthetized, like the same অচেতন (unconscious) elephant, in consequence of the Awami *chetonized* and politicized state "tranquilizer" police tools of prosecution and persecution.

Again, like the elephant, the BNP may be able to rise up on its feet, if at all, under the relentless Awami police and judicial beating and biting and then stand steady, firm and erect, not to fall down to its pitiful political death, unlike the much hyped waterborne female হাতি. The ordinary হাতি was mock-heroically elevated to the status of an honorable বঙ্গ বাহাদুর/*Banga Bahadur* (like the rape of Belinda's lock in Alexander Pope's poem and rhyming with, even overshadowing the British colonial titles of Khan Bahadur and Rai/Roy Bahadur). The talk-of-the-town Ms বঙ্গ বাহাদুর, however, starved and yielded to her muddy মৃত্যু (death) that was as clumsy as she looked in life. Some say, satirically though, that she died in the month of national mourning for the great leader *BangaBandhu* in solidarity with the flood-hit needy and hungry in the brotherly Bangladesh. The occasion was also an opportunity and a privilege for many to refresh their memory of the nursery rhyme below, which, like the majority of the kind, has a satirical and historical origin and meaning having to do with an English royal as well as a civil war background:

> Humpty Dumpty sat on a wall,
> Humpty Dumpty had a great fall.
> All the king's horses and all the king's men
> Couldn't put Humpty together again.

When so many other wild lives die, get lost, are uncared for, and go unsung and unlamented at home in Bangladesh, in violation of animal rights and of environmental and ecological balance, the trespassing and headline making হাতি, which S Akhter of the USA ironically calls Indian "Felani," became transformed into a বঙ্গ বাহাদুর, alliterating and inviting contrasts and juxtapositions with so many other big and homophonic Bs on the home turf, including West Bengal's civilian awards of বঙ্গবিভূষণ and বঙ্গভূষণ. Having "illegally" crossed the border into Bangladesh, she became the subject of a memorable elegiac narrative as if she was the first of her kind to have met with her tragic end. Well, an আন্ডা (egg) becomes a ডিম and then a poached egg, a scrambled egg, a *mumlet* and an *omelette* as it travels from the rural village to the town and the city, from small restaurants to big hotels, from land to air. Similarly, Banga Bahadur's মৃত্যু বরন (demise) was not an ordinary ইন্তেকাল (death); it was her মহাপ্রয়াণ (grand death) or তিরোধান as it happened in the case of Rabindranath Tagore and Fakir Lalon Shah/Sh'ai.

The epical বঙ্গ বাহাদুর saga shows no sign of coming to an end. It continues through a legal battle against those who are being alleged to have neglected the old and infirm guest of celebrity status to her tragic demise and so are to be fined taka one crore only to be paid to the government treasury. Proposals are underway to retrieve and preserve the Banga Bahadur's skeletal remains, following her state burial, in the national museum of Bangladesh as a sign of love and friendship between the two countries.

Anyway, getting back to the more serious matter, people are concerned not only about the BNP's survival and existence under the Awami police and judicial bulldozer (which has reduced it to a pile of rubble and remains, worse than the death throes of the Banga Bahadur) but also its unity and strength with many leaders threatening to quit after they have been excluded from the new central or executive and other committees. How could Begum Zia, Tarique Rahman, and Mirza Fakhrul (himself a clean and polite man but not so strong and effective as a leader) exclude the able and competent leaders such as Shah Muazzem Hussein, Abdullah Al Noman, Dr Osman Farook, Maj Hafizuddin Ahmed, দেশকন্যা /*DeshKonnya*[20] Syeda Ashifa Ashrafi Papia, and দেশকন্যা Desh-Knonnya Rumin Farhana from high and prominent positions in the party (whatever their past was), to a serious disadvantage to the much needed strength and unity of the party? How come the highly visible Maj Akhtaruzzaman and the well-spoken Sarder Shakhawat Hussein Bokul did not find their way to this or that important committee?

If the BNP falls into pieces and fragments, the weaknesses and inefficiencies of the top trio—Khaleda, Tarique, and Mirza Fakhrul—should be held responsible. In the meantime, the trio must find a way to accommodate all the excluded and deprived as they deserve to unify and strengthen the party. On the other hand, those who are disgruntled and disappointed must not leave the party, considering the fact that their BNP is still the largest political party in the country, much larger than the Hasina-led AL.

Transplantation of the Donald Trump syndrome in Bangladesh

PM Hasina's Bangladesh is as divided as the right-wing nationalist President-elect Trump's America. His ugly and nasty and crazy and contentious campaign has led to an unprecedented nation-wide unrest after the election on November 8. Although now totally suppressed by the Hasina regime's iron rule, similar protests, with every right and reason, are very common in Bangladesh, not just during and after the elections. Isn't Hasina, in her as usual overblown, distorted, and exaggerated claims about the democratic opposition politics, like the reckless and careless Trump and his demagoguery, leaving a wide gap between his rhetoric and the reality? Both Trump and Hasina want to run their respective countries the way they alone want—with authoritarian and dictatorial designs in mind and a peculiar showmanship of their own.

Both of them are inclined to being divisive at the expense of the unity and collective strength of their respective nations. Like Trump's loose and obscene, and deformed and debased comments, far beyond the conventional and the symmetrical, there is a plenty of beyond-the-boundaries bombasts and deceptive stratagems in the political landscape of Bangladesh. Just as Trump is said by Democrats as having no shame or his shame having no limits, in the like manner, it is not far to see there are no limits to the shame the way the ruling politicians of Bangladesh brag about their preposterous claims about (1) the spirit of the liberation war in 1971; (2) the role of the great national leader Ziaur Rahman; (3) those who once hailed the assassination of Sheikh Mujib, but who are now vociferously and ferociously friendly with his daughter Hasina; (4) those who were once friendly with her but are now being hanged by her; (5) absence of democratic freedom; (6) corruption-ridden development; (7) rigged elections; and (8) hanging on to power by force in the name of constitutional authority and continuity, which is exploited to cover the series of untruths and inaccuracies by the government and the host of allegations against the government. New York-based Dr Mina Farah comments, in one of her regular and remarkable columns, that it is actually a continuity of power, Awami style, rather than the continuity of the constitution, which is used as a wrecked and twisted cover.[21]

Members of the Hasina regime and their surrogates would like to grab the media spotlight by making highly controversial comments the way Trump habitually does. Those politicians in Bangladesh and beyond who (a) do not wish to keep their word; (b) who intend to do politics for their personal benefit (and not for the noble, selfless, and exalted public service); (c) who tend to lick their own spit; (d) who seem to lack the patriotic visions of unity, inclusion, freedom, and fairness, and (e) who are disposed to being full of egotistical intolerance for others should learn from the way the erratic, unreliable, and unpredictable Trump has been torn and taken down by his critics and rivals, including many of the higher echelon of his own party. He would accept the election result only when it were in his favor (জিতলে মানি হারলে মানিনা), the way the AL is known to be in Bangladesh, more than its opponent BNP.

Trump has been accused of being a bully, a bigot, and a demagogue. The AL leaders in Bangladesh are no different, talking big and bizarre. Trump, who never held any elected/public office, gained notoriety for narcissistically bragging about himself, his family, his wealth, his business, his buildings, and his billions. Similarly, the Hasina-led AL, full of unelected people, making millions, is also full of boastful pride and praise for the members of the Mujib family and their own half-doings only, in terms of progress and development (which every government does and is duty bound to do and is naturally supposed to do).

Trump has also gained notoriety for making derogatory anti-Muslim and anti-women comments the way the Hasina-led AL shoots anti-Khaleda and anti-BNP hurls and insults in its rhetorical bombasts and rude remarks. Trump has also gained notoriety either for backtracking in the face of criticism or doubling down on his explosive, exploitative and inflammatory rhetoric, sometimes in a somewhat qualified manner. This is similar to the Hasina-led AL's broken promises regarding the total and entire and complete and comprehensive spirit of liberation, free and fair elections, peace and harmony of the nation, and social justice, all being flawed and partial, far from being acceptable. Any commodification, compartmentalization, and commercialization of the spirit of liberation with a product/market value or price tag on it is to be protested and defeated.

Trump is said to have invited Putin's Russia to meddle with American politics in his favor and thus to have become an unwitting puppet agent of Russia, the way the Hasina-led AL would like India to be involved in Bangladeshi politics in her favor. Considered a national embarrassment by many, Trump is targeted for dividing the nation into the postcolonial "we" and the "other." It is the same way that Hasina has done in Bangladesh dividing the nation into "us" and "they." Trump has been derided as a "pathological liar," "huckster," "pied piper," "bully," "hate monger," "showman," "sexist,' "racist," "misogynist," "xenophobic," "megalomaniac," "narcissist," "Islamophobic," "abhorrent," "disturbing," "fact-free, if not fat-free," being no better than "The Apprentice" and the Miss Universe pageant entertainer. In its megalomaniacal and narcissistic demagoguery and in its bullying the popular opposition BNP, the Hasina-led AL is on the same boat as Trump.

All said, the despotic and authoritarian Hasina has still a lot to learn in the positive from Trump as suggested by his completely different, nice, and unifying victory speech (following his shocking and upset win, not by popular votes though but by the complicated yet balancing electoral college majority in American politics). Hasina has a lot of lessons to learn from Trump's rival Hillary Clinton's graceful congratulatory concession speech (though she won by popular votes) the very next day following the election and President Barack Obama's remarks about his commitment to peaceful handover of power to Trump, who was considered only a little earlier, until the election day, temperamentally and experientially and uniquely unfit and unqualified to sit in the Oval Office.

Most importantly, the "unelected" Hasina has got much to learn from the free and fair American election that elected the controversial outsider Trump, who was bitterly opposed to the incumbent administration. That is the bipartisan beauty of American/Western freedom and democracy, which is absolutely lacking in Bangladesh under the current regime. While it is all wild freedom for the ruling Hasina-led AL in Bangladesh, it is all bitter and biting bondage for the Khaleda-led opposition BNP. One country of despotic and dictatorial one-party rule, applying two different criteria to rule—one permitting everything for the ruling party and one nothing at all for the opposition.

Also, while the people of Trump's own party are free to be critical of him and walk away from him in a democratic Republican rift, it is never possible in Hasina's AL for fear of her police and judicial retaliation, reprisal, abduction, assassination, and jail and জুলুম and remand. While there are bits and pieces of mere talking that are allowed in criticism of her and her surrogates, they never fail to make sure they own and control the real thing that matters most: all street activism and all elections to be controlled and counterfeited in their favor through their police and the politicized civil administration, "useless" and "spineless" election commission and, if necessary, certain sections and elements of the allegedly jaundiced judiciary.

The Awami strategy may be summarized in the Bengali saying: বিচার মানি তবে তাল গাছটা আমার; শাক দিয়ে মাছ ঢাকা. In other words, a deceptive and deceiving "yes" only to the outer shell/frame of the empty processes—election, democratic, and judicial, that is, only in name limping as and limited to an eyewash appearance.

The actual end game and the final result have to go in favor of the despotic and dictatorial Awami regime. All means are to be controlled, twisted, and manipulated by the Awami regime, entirely addicted to the promotion of the culture of what is actually a neo-and-near-and-more-than-partially fascist and পৈশাচিক style. This undesirable style is now euphemistically called illiberal, flawed, and guided democracy. Upon fact checking, Trump was found to be the most lying president or presidential candidate in US history. Similarly, upon a reality check, would the Awami regime fall behind Trump in broken promises, going backward along the line of demolition and desecration of democratic tradition and transition?

The shrunk and squeezed media: prominent journalists Mahmudur Rahman, Shaukat Mahmood, Shafik Rehman, Kazi Jesin, Munir Haider, Matiur Rahman Chowdhury, Dr Kanak Sarwar, Oliullah Noman, and Mahfuz Anam—all under mauling and menacing threat, scare, and intimidation

How could PM Hasina and her autocratic and authoritarian AL government talk about democracy and democratic freedoms, including the press freedom, when, similar to the AL-BAKSAL days of 1975, such freedoms have been suppressed to the extent of shutting down tens of mainstream and social media outlets—online, electronic, or print—and preventing people like *DeshKonnya* দেশকন্যা Barrister Rumin Farhana from going abroad (Turkey and Oman) to speak on political issues at home on invitation? Based on the Amnesty International and Article 19 reports on all forms of repression and persecution, BBC South Asia correspondents Justin Rowlatt and Subhajyoti Ghosh separately wrote about the Hasina-AL government's ongoing attempt to completely crush the independent media and the political freedom of the people of Bangladesh, especially during the last few years.[22] Oliullah Noman of the popular but long-suppressed daily *Amar Desh*, imprisoned and then self-exiled to the UK, wrote about how the press freedoms in Bangladesh were limited to the extent of surviving on life support.[23] It is the same story with the ailing Matiur Rahman Chowdhury of the daily ManabZamin, Munir Haider, and Kazi Jesin, among many other journalists, all of whom being either arrested and remanded, or sick, or silenced, or exiled due to their freedom of speech taken away under the threat and intimidation of Clause 57.

In its latest silencing and gagging act, the neo-and-near-and-more-than-partially fascist government-turned-regime (also to be termed BAKSAL-II, no doubt worse than BAKSAL-I) passed a draconian law forbidding any criticism of Sheikh Mujib and the 1971 Liberation War (as the regime alone views it in a fashionable and fragmentary manner in/at its own convenience), from which Mujib was either away by choice or had to be away by force. The violation of the law would be punishable by life imprisonment and a humongous sum in fine.[24]

It is a disgrace to Mujib as well as the Liberation War heroes that their dignity and integrity need to be protected by a partisan and prejudiced promulgation that asks the people to shut up and clog their mind about their national leaders and national occasions, instead of being clean and constructively critical. It is a dishonor to put them above the nation's critical and historical thinking by an official proclamation and not to let them become the subjects of its ongoing objective and intellectual exercise and scrutiny. Should there be no more history, biography, and political science books written in the critical examination of Bangladesh's political leaders and its Liberation War? Does the nation have to come to a static and rusty standstill and not move on with the dynamism of its academically evaluative and comprehensive view, ages and ages hence? It is a shameful disservice to the collective national psyche and the public memory of the great leaders and key momentous events about which the nation should eternally remain vigilant and reserve the right to feel free to unlock and pour out its heart in whatever way it feels comfortable and convenient. That is the only way to impart new life to great people and events and to keep them and their legacies living as times roll by.

The largest English daily, *The Daily Star*, of about 45,000 circulation, made more than one report about the government proposal to drastically limit the freedom of press and tighten the digital noose further. The proposed or approved new diabolical electronic media law would forbid, among other restrictions, (1) any criticism of Mujib; (2) any criticism of the friendly countries (meaning India?); (3) any criticism of ministers and the people considered important by the government; (4) any criticism of the government by the opposition and any announcement of opposition meetings, processions, and হরতাল (blockades/strikes), obviously implying the pro-government programs could go ahead as planned and announced; (5) any untoward news or adverse criticism of armed forces; and (6) any programs, which can be arbitrarily construed by the regime as security risk, etc.[25]

According to the latest US State Department report on freedom of speech and press in Bangladesh, journalists work in an atmosphere of fear, control, coercion and censorship. It says:

> Media outlets that criticized the government experienced negative government pressure. For example, independent journalists alleged that intelligence services influenced media outlets in part by withholding financially important government advertising and pressing private companies to withhold their advertising as well. The government maintains editorial control over the Bangladesh public television station (BTV), and private channels were mandated to air government content at no cost. Civil society said that there was

political interference in the licensing process, as all television channel licenses granted by the government were for stations supporting the ruling party [...] Authorities, including intelligence services on some occasions, subjected journalists to physical attack, harassment, and intimidation.[26]

In addition to the oft-occurring torture and persecution of journalists (Jamuna TV journalists Shakil Hasan and Shaheen Alam being the latest victims),[27] the government has closed down dozens of online news portals and websites (including some of those cited in this book) and many other major outlets, considered neutral, not so sympathetic or not blindly and entirely loyal to the Awami regime. It shut down popular TV channels and print media such as the daily *Amar Desh*, Channel 1 (One), *Diganta* TV, and *Islamic* TV. It shut down popular talk shows, such as Kazi Jesin's "Point of Order" and Matiur Rahman Chowdhury's "Frontline," both used to be aired on Bangla Vision; as well as Dr Kanak Sarwar's "Janotar Kotha" and Munir Haider's show, both on ETV (Ekushey Television). While M Abdullah of BFUJ wrote about the circumstances in which the daily *Amar Desh* was shut down, Dr Naeem Mohaiemen of Columbia University traced the history of censorship in Bangladesh.[28]

Many other existing channels and newspapers, such as *ETV*, *Prothom Alo*, *New Age*, and *Daily Star* were being often threatened and taken to the court for their freedom of expression.[29] Sakhawat Liton writes about how the proposed law on war history is another threat to free speech.[30] Following 1 July terror attack in Gulshan Dhaka when there was a media blackout, Hasina was dictatorially threatening that she might take back the permit she gave to those private channels that attempted to cover live the storming operation at the site in question by the army, the police, and the RAB. (In a similar fashion she threatened to stop the power supply if the people opposed the construction of the Rampal power plant considered by many to be environmentally destructive and more in the interest of India than Bangladesh.)

Mahmudur Rahman, editor of the long suppressed daily *Amar Desh*, who is also regarded as a mega mind, of the proportion of national conscience and national treasure, was languishing in jail for years as a price for his freedom of expression. According to US State Department report referred to above, "The government continued to pursue charges against the editor of Amar Desh, Mahmudur Rahman, whom police arrested in 2013 for publishing Skype conversations between the Chairman of the ICT and a private consultant on ICT cases. Although the High Court granted Rahman bail on September 8, the Appellate Court chamber judge stayed his bail until October 30, further prolonging his detention of nearly four years. Rahman was released on bail on November 23."[31]

Mahmudur Rahman was not allowed to walk out of prison, until very recently, despite his legal rights to do so earlier. So were the other star journalists, such as Shaukat Mahmood and Shafik Rehman, who were released on bail at different times after a long detention in dark confinement. Mahmudur Rahman Manna, a high profile patriotic politician, has been freed after a long time in dark prison. In the context of quality press freedom, these great journalists—Mahmood and Rehman—followed the footsteps of Kangal Harinath, editor of the early 20th-century Weekly Gram Barta, published from Kumarkhali Kushtia, not far from Rabindranath Tagore's Kuthi Bari in Shelidah Kushtia. It is a historical fact that Harinath was critical of the landed and wealthy Tagore family and its discriminatory policies against the poor peasants and farmers for which he (Harinath) had to endure tremendous suffering and intimidation.[32]

In the larger context of the struggle for peace and justice, the suffering journalist community, together with hundreds and thousands of other suffering opposition leaders and activists, are all today's Abu Torab Chowdhury of Sandip (leader of the peasant movement in 1767), Titumir (Hafiz Moulana Syed Mir Nisar Ali, 1782–1831), Indigo Revolt (নীল বিদ্রোহ of 1889) leader Nurul-din of North Bengal, Khudiram Bose (1889–1908), Surjo Sen (1894–1934), Pritilata (Dasgupta/Rani) Waddedar (1911–1932), Kalpana Datta (1913–1995), and many other revolutionaries against the British occupiers.[33] The said journalists were not set free even though they were granted bail on scores of politically engineered and twisted lawsuits filed against them by the Hasina government as part of its continuing repressive measures.[34]

Referring to the political and judicial bondage of the opposition leaders and supporters and the persecution of the finest journalists by the Hasina regime, former US Ambassador to Bangladesh and Pakistan, William B Milam, writes in the weekly Friday Times of Pakistan (July 15, 2016):

> Media organizations—newspaper editors, TV talk show hosts, and the like—who dared to question the government's policies toward the opposition were under dire threat. Sedition charges were filed in court against editors whose articles criticized, or implied criticism, of the government, and were accepted by politicized judges. The editors of the two largest circulation newspapers had over 100 such cases filed against them. Clearly the government's policy was to brook no opposition, and as a one-party government, it was clearly in a position to carry out this policy.[35]

About three and half months before (on April 8, 2016), Ambassador Milam wrote:

> In [Bangladesh] politics, much remains the same. The dog-eat-dog, zero-sum-game nature of politics not only remains the norm, many critics say it is being carried to new

> heights. The BNP is in dire straits, and seemingly has a suicide complex. Its actions have only increased its vulnerability as a viable opposition party. Without a complete overhaul, I believe its future is bleak. The governing party is, of course, primarily to blame for locking up many BNP leaders and for many other repressive actions against it, but the BNP leadership resists every opportunity to recover its standing with the public. The government is also bearing down hard on any other voices of opposition, and trying hard to muzzle some very courageous media voices. A campaign which everybody understands is inspired by the government against two prominent editors, piling up court cases against them, is by now well known in the region and in the West. Theory and history say this kind of government behavior will change with the rise of the middle class, but Bangladesh has resisted both theory and history so far.[36] (my emphasis)

The journalist couple, Shagor and Runi, who were supposed to have had the knowledge of many secrets about government corruption, was killed in their bedroom without the killers ever being caught, to date. More journalists have been killed, imprisoned, and tortured during this government than any other in the past. The former *ETV* executive Abdul Salam and ETV correspondent Dr Kanak Sarwar, both imprisoned, have had to suffer from the grudge of the Hasina government. They have been detained, under the cover of sedition charges and pornography control act, apparently for having their channel broadcast the speech of Number#2 opposition leader, Tarique Rahman, live from London on January 4, 2015.[37] Since the popular channel has now changed hands, with the ownership gone to Awami leaders and supporters with the pro-Awami Manjurul Ahsan Bulbul as its news editor, no objective and independent news service can be expected from it, as already demonstrated by the current anchors inviting mostly Awami supporters on their talk shows.

From the Amnesty International to the European Parliament to the *Daily Star* editor Mahfuz Anam and the *New Age* editor Nurul Kabir—all are critical of the government attitude toward the freedom of the press. All are asking for the restoration of the full independence of the media.[38] The daily *Dinkal*, *Naya Diganta* and *Inqilab* are under watch by the government as it continues unabated in its silencing policies toward the political dissent. The online social media such as Facebook, Viber, Twitter, Skype, Imo, and WhatsApp are on and off, according to what the government wants in its attempt to harden and widen its crackdown on the opposition. While part of the existing media, print and electronic, is working as a bigmouth propaganda in support of the repressive government, part has been forced to feel obligated to shrink into a thin and shrill voice of the regime in order to merely survive.

There is no doubt that journalistic beauty, variety, objectivity, diversity, and excellence are far to seek under the regime's tightening control and containment, even if that means a travesty of the judicial system. This is demonstrated in the above-mentioned cases of Mahmudur Rahman and Shafik Rehman (both having suffered bondage for too long for holding different political opinion and believing in press freedom) and the Shagor-Runi couple, who were mercilessly killed years ago without the perpetrators ever apprehended and brought to justice. Journalist Minar Rashid writes about the farce of the so-called free speech in Bangladesh, poignantly concluding with a reference to Shagor and Runi.[39]

The so-perceived pro-ruling party (AL) Mahfuz Anam's case is different, treated with both discriminating and discriminatory favor. Like thousands and thousands of political opposition leaders and activists and journalists, he has faced more than eighty defamation and sedition lawsuits across the country (what a judicial farce!) for just being honest, forthright and truthful about what he failed to live up to in terms of some disputable and controversial journalistic norms and standards about nine years ago during the infamous, egregious, and ignominious interim (care-taker) government of the *Uddins* (2006–2008).[40] From the BBC to the PEN International to Deutsche Welle (DW) to the pro-opposition to the neutral intellectual community to the citizens' committee (but not the pro-Awami faction or fraction of journalists of Bangladesh, though)—all rushed to raise and register their voices and concerns against the AL/Hasina government's excesses concerning Mahfuz Anam.

In his Financial Times article, "Bangladesh pays for bad politics in blood," Victor Mallet makes the same point regarding the choking control of the media:

> One editor [Mahfuz Anam] is facing 79—evidently co-ordinated—legal actions in courts around the country for sedition and defamation, including demands for the equivalent of $17bn in damages. Two others [Shafik Rehman and Mahmudur Rahman] have been accused of involvement in an improbable plot to kidnap and kill Sajeeb Wajed Joy, Ms Hasina's son, in the US. Legislators are considering the Bangladesh Liberation War (Denial, Distortion, Opposition) Crime Law that would essentially ban free discussion of history by criminalizing views that deviate from those of the Awami League.[41]

According to US State Department,

> In February, members of the ruling party initiated 79 sedition and defamation cases in multiple courts against Mahfuz Anam, editor of The Daily Star, for publishing reports of corruption involving Prime Minister Hasina in 2007 and 2008. Hasina publicly stated Anam's newspaper and its sister media outlet, Prothom Alo, would be punished for publishing the reports.

While many top politicians during the military-backed *Uddins* interim government took a stand, advertently or inadvertently, willingly or under duress, that went against the interest of their respective parties but did not have the honest courage to confess and apologize, Anam should have been appreciated, not attacked, for candidly divulging what he did and honestly admitting that he made wrong editorial judgment in those days. The interim government and certain other quarters caused harm to all the major parties and their leaders, intellectuals and businessmen but in its last days the interim government had a mutually benefiting understanding with the AL, in exchange for which it lent a covert but crucial support to the latter in winning the late 2008 election and forming the government.[42]

It is true, Anam, by his own admission, made mistakes, intentionally or under military pressure, by printing unsubstantiated and unverified news items coming from the military junta that went against both the AL and the BNP. Now he said he was sorry and repentant about what he did or had to do failing to meet journalistic ethics. His honest and courageous confession should be enough to absolve him of the burden of controversies he is implicated in. The big question is, are the press and the media free and fair today under the Hasina regime? Are the journalists free and safe today to conduct their professional responsibility fully? Aren't they divided between the two camps, by choice or by force, and equally biased, clouded and prejudiced? David Bergman says that "Attack on the Daily Star editor is the latest Awami League attempt to restrict criticism."[43]

But, then, not only Mahfuz Anam, but also many top Awami, near-Awami, and BNP leaders (Sheikh Selim, Obaidul Quader, Tofail Ahmed, Amir Hussein Amu, Suranjit Sen Gupta and Anisul Islam Mahmud, among others, not to speak of the late Abdul Jalil) committed anti-Hasina and anti-Khaleda blunders in the *Uddins* era. All this has been pointed out on the media by Sheikh Rehana's husband Dr Shafique Siddiq, two BNP Vice Chairmen—Shah Muazzem Hussein, a great politician on his own strength, and Major (Ret) Hafizuddin Ahmad (who was one of those who then played a strong anti-Khaleda role but now has turned a strong pro-Khaleda figure of articulate and eloquent voice)—and also *DeshKonnya* Papia. So, "Why to chase only Mahfuz Anam when others have been and are being rewarded?," they posed the question.

Mahfuz Anam has been playing quite an independent role for years, both criticizing and supporting the Hasina government, depending on issues, of course. He was vehemently against the farcical January 5, 2014 voteless and voterless election, as much as he was excitedly euphoric about Imran H Shorkar's Shahbug movement at a seminar on Bangladesh at the UC Berkeley in 2013, as Ranu Chowdhury of the USA recalls. As far as his pro-India stance is concerned, that is open to question. Who is not more or less pro-India? Hasina, Ershad, Khaleda—all are and have to be pro-India, in different degrees and shades and guises though.

Having said all this, Anam did not have to face the unjust and painful fate of others. Due to his overall pro-Awami stance, he was not arrested and/or remanded and he got bail in all eighty four cases. Lucky Anam; unlucky Mahmudur Rahman, Shafik Rehman, and Shaukat Mahmood, whose (and tens of thousands of others') jail sentences, sufferings, and incarceration knew or know no bounds.

Anyway, the measures taken by the Awami government remind one of the English gagging acts of the 1790s (especially 1795, in the context of the war between England and France following the French Revolution), lampooned as the Act for General Silence and Repression allowing people to be imprisoned without trial. Does the Hasina government want all media in the country to be biased and one-sided and to act loyally and uncritically as its partisan mouthpiece and propaganda? US Republican Senator and former Republican Presidential Candidate John McCain defended free press, even if it were adversarial, raising the specter of dictatorship from Trump's attacks on the press. Criticizing Trump for calling the media "the enemy," McCain said, "That's how dictators get started," by shutting down the media in order to consolidate their power, to begin with. John Nichols writes that "The real enemy of the people is a President who opposes the free press. No president who takes seriously an oath to 'preserve, protect and defend' the Constitution would say what Trump is saying." The same views apply to the Hasina government.[44]

If one can go through a list of about 43 TV channels, both active and on the way, there are: government-controlled state television *BTV*, staunch Awami supporter Salman F Rahman's *Independent* TV, diehard Awami supporter Mahfuzur Rahman's ATN Bangla and ATN News, Awami MP Kamal Mazumder's *Mohana* TV, Awami minister Advocate Kamrul Islam's *Shomoy* Television, Awami MP Saber Hussain Chowdhury's *Desh* TV, Awami adviser Iqbal Sobhan Chowdhury's Dhaka Bangla Channel (DBC), pro-Awami A K Azad's *Channel 24*, pro-Awami Mozammel Babu's *Ekattor*, Awami leader ABM Mohiuddin Chowdhury's *Bijoy* TV, pro-Awami Omeda Begum's son Nasiruddin Sathi's *My TV*, film-maker Syed Salahuddin Zaki and SA Group's South Asian (SA) TV, Awami minister Syed Ashraful Islam's brother's Channel 9, pro-Awami Tipu Alam/Manjurul Ahsan Bulbul's *Boishakhi* Television, Sayem Sobhan and Naem Nizam's News24, Awami-allied civil aviation and tourism minister Rashed Khan Menon's *Khela* TV, Sheikh Hasina's pet and favorite poet Syed Shamsul Hoq's son's Amar TV, Awami MP Mamunur Rashid Kiron's Global TV, and a few more in the offing, also to be owned by the Awamis. All these channels, with a few exceptions (which profess to be reasonably neutral), tend to be operating with an openly pro-Awami/Indian bias and as such are widely viewed as an extension, if not mimicking copycat, of

Awami and Indian campaigns.[45] The objectivity and neutrality of these media outlets are not beyond doubt. Whether their journalistic ethics and integrity are held to high standards is open to question. The same is true with the majority of the print media, both in English and Bangla.

While the media is asked, even perhaps with a veiled threat, to carry all speeches and statements, including the derogatory and disgraceful ones, made by Hasina and her men and women, against the BNP leaders and activists, it is not allowed, in a suppression of free speech, to carry the views of the politically charismatic and sagacious (like father like son) Tarique Rahman, who is Senior Vice Chairman of the BNP, the largest and by far the most popular party in Bangladesh.[46] Besides, the media was/is also prohibited to carry live the press conferences of BNP leader Khaleda, for instance, the one held in response to Sheikh Hasina's April 2017 visit to India—a failed visit according to the critics and commentators. Moreover, while the government supporters and loyalists do happily and heartily provide testimony on the basis of the pro-government newspapers in favor of their argument, they are reluctant to accept the same from the opposition, in criticism of the government, on the basis of the other national newspapers, which are neutrally and objectively critical of the government. What a bumper promotion of discriminatory, not discriminating, "democratic" freedom and fairness by the Hasina people!

In Bangladesh, freedom of expression and democratic tolerance have been drastically curtailed, in many cases, brought down to zero. As mentioned above, as many as two scores of electronic and print media outlets, considered neutral, have been shut down, obviously for not being blindly and entirely loyal to the Awami regime, while those completely loyal, sympathetic, and biased to it are allowed to flourish. While some selective "bloggers" have unlimited freedom of speech, like freedom of hurting the religious beliefs, traditions and cultures of 90% majority, those critical of the regime are punished and wiped out. On August 21, 2016, Jacob Milton, a Bangladeshi-American owner of a Queens-based cable television show in New York called "We are the people," complained that the Hasina government was trying to silence him. According to the New York Post report:

> Political forces back home are violating his right to free speech—and ruining his business. Hasina's administration has been wracked with scandals in a country controlled by a handful of powerful families [...] Milton believes the intimidation against himself and relatives here and at home are being carried out by Hasina and her son, Sajeeb Wajed Joy, who lives in Virginia. He is suing Wajed in Brooklyn federal court. Milton, 50, claims his business has dropped off because clients are afraid to interact with him due to the attacks, including fires set on his Elmhurst property [...] He wants $500 million in damages and

an injunction against Wajed and the American branch of the Awami League, the current ruling party in Bangladesh.[47]

The free and democratic Western world is daily splashed and overflowed by countless critical and comical TV shows, satirical cartoon pictures, distorted and disfigured nudes and sketches of presidents and prime ministers, and sour and bitter Facebook and Twitter comments, all going viral with the critics, commentators, and comedians mocking their political leaders and even posting racist and hateful visuals about them.[48] Every Western generation produces dozens and scores of comedians who not only make a living but also make millions by mocking and poking fun at others, especially their political leaders. American late-night shows such as NBC's Saturday Night Live (SNL) and The Tonight Show, CBS's Late Show, and The Comedy Central's The Daily Show are a few of the most widely known to make fun of and laugh at the American political leaders, including the Presidents, Senators, Secretaries, and the American rich and famous. The 2009 Eurovision Song from Georgia, "We Don't Wanna Put In," deconstructed and mocked Vladimir Putin as "Put-in" for his de facto control of parts of the small neighboring country. The song created a controversy for its pun on the Russian leader's last name that clearly carried sexual overtones and innuendos.

Carl Paladino is a New York developer and a close friend of Donald Trump. His dirty and nasty Christmas (2016) wishes went viral on the social media. They were to see Barack Obama die of mad cow disease from his mating with cattle and to see his wife Michelle return to Africa, turn into a male, and live with a female gorilla in a cave. The way Trump has attacked others in a mean and indecent manner and the way he has been attacked in turn as being a joke, jerk, fraud, conman, misogynist, sinner, sadist, loud mouth dick, pathological liar, huckster, trickster, pied piper, showman, hypocritical demagogue, "Trash Trump" and "Rape Trump" are good examples (though in a negative way but still freeing creative and intellectual bent) of the freedom of expression and democratic tolerance in the USA.

American film maker Michael Moore, who has a reputation for standing for common causes and concerns, was a staunch opponent of the Bush-led Iraq War and his *Fahrenheit 9/11* won him much acclaim and many awards worldwide. During an Oscar Award ceremony, he felt free to say: "Shame on you, Mr. President [Bush]. Shame on you."

However, in the culture of chokehold suppression in Bangladesh, Jahangirnagar University Professor Ruhul Amin Khandoker was deprived of his minimum right to free speech. He was jailed for three years for a tiny and trivial comment that "Everybody dies but why not Sheikh Hasina?"—a casual and inconsequential comment that cost him dearly, including his job. While everybody is free to be seriously or satirically critical of others in every other country—Trump is being literally accused of lying every day on every American TV channel as he in his turn accuses others of lying against him—, it is impossible in Hasina's police and almost fascistic state.

Another man was detained for a short and simple comment he made about Hasina's father Sheikh Mujib on the Facebook.[49] What was wrong with the Mirakkel comedian Abu Hena Roni's intelligent Facebook status, তিনি পা ভেজালেন আর ইনি গা ভেজালেন (she dipped her feet in open seawater for fun, while the poor man got his body submerged in her government's mismanaged dirty sewage wastewater), for which Roni was about to face a lawsuit? He had to be on the run for what was his minimum freedom of speech expressed in his small, humorous, and oblique comment regarding Hasina's soaking her feet at Cox's Bazar bay beach. Roni's F-status with the picture of a dangerous open manhole in the street served to expose the empty rhetoric of Hasina's highly dented and defective development drum.

There are endless Ronis and Khandokers whose stories illustrate that there is no freedom in Hasina's Bangladesh. People do not feel free to make even the slightest, remotest, mildest, mutest, and most indirect comment, even if that is creatively and constructively critical of her. Like the blocked drainage, people's intellectual vein is clogged to become dull, bleak, and barren. Who is on line to face a charge for making even a gentle comic fun about Hasina's riding a rickshaw in her absolutist and fascistic regime? Is it because of this authoritarian insult and intimidation that other comedians in Bangladesh refrain from being creative and contributing to the moral development of their political leaders? Attacks on the media, free speech, and human rights activists continue nonstop in Hasina's police state.[50]

Many young men and women have thus been unjustly locked up, as it happens in a totalitarian regime, for their fun and freedom of posting creative and expressive comments and pictures of Sheikh Hasina and her father. Is Hasina a royal Sultana or a Queen or an Empress or a Tsarina that she cannot be criticized? Is she the Supreme Ayatollah of Bangladesh, or like the Emperor of Japan, Agong of Malaysia, or the King of Thailand that she cannot be criticized by any means, including artistic sketches and expressions? Only God/Allah the Almighty and His prophets are above criticism. In fact, even an emperor like Napoleon used to be a common and constant target of criticism through satirical drawings and caricatures by the famous artists of the time, such as James Gillray of England. Napoleon said that caricaturist Gillray contributed more to his downfall in 1815 than all the armies of Europe. In his more than 1,000 etchings of caustic humor,

Gillray courageously caricatured monarchs, politicians, and warlords, including the Prince of Wales (later King George IV of the UK) and the young British Prime Minister William Pitt, apart from his most famous subject, which was of course the young French emperor.

By contrast, opposition student leaders in Hasina's fascistic Bangladesh are being beaten up for their free speech.[51] The New York-based Awami supporters had demanded punishment for Shafik Rehman, now released from prison (imprisoned for charges he denies), for merely sharing a small Russian anecdote, which they thought was indirectly hinting at the death of their leader Hasina.

Many politicians in Bangladesh speak in the same language on the media reminding Sheikh Hasina about August 1975. It cannot be wrong to call a spade a spade or every action has its equal and opposite reaction. As a Bangladeshi patriot, Khandoker felt frustrated and made a simple comment, which was just a common verbal expression and/or reaction. Don't we say, "I'll see you" or, in Bangla, "দেখে নিবো" অথবা "খবর আছে," etc? The Awami rulers and their surrogates/supporters overreact to anything critical of them the way Hasina does in relation to her political opponents.

Rehman and Khandoker are just two of many, arrested, imprisoned, threatened, fired, frightened, ousted, reprimanded, or taken to task for exercising their freethinking (*মুক্তমনা মুক্তচিন্তা*) democratic rights in making comments critical of the AL leader Hasina, whose oppressive regime did not even at first allow Rehman to travel overseas, long after his release, to visit his ailing wife in London. Ranu Chowdhury correctly argues that "If one opens print and electronic media, one would find millions expressing various [threatening] warnings daily to leaders that include President Obama and other top world leaders. [Unfortunately] We are talking about a PM who sends people to jail for composing a non-descript parody on her!"

A divided country under the yoke and clutch of state terrorism

There is an alarming deficit of freedom, rule of law, and social justice in all sectors of the society due to (both stated and unstated) state terrorism permeating all over. Under the commercialization and criminalization of politics, and the politicization and criminalization of trade and commerce, sluttish misrule and bad governance have become the order of the day. As the December 2014 Brac University symposium found, lack of good governance has allowed for so much easy profit and manipulation that the government does not feel the need of good governance any more. The rule of law, accountability, transparency, and stability are exiled from Bangladesh's all-engulfing underworld of dirty money ruled by the antistate syndicates and the boots and bullets of the police/RAB. It is the coteries of filthy worm-ridden corrupt criminals that directly or indirectly determine the everyday social and professional life of an average citizen.

From top to bottom, virtually all are affected by a low social and political culture that eats like vultures into the decomposed parts of the society, threatening the whole. The sycophants keep themselves busy flattering and seeking favors from both the local and the higher political as well as administrative leadership. Under the shelter of different dark forces at every level, touts and miscreants gain more and more of muscle and mechanical power and become wilder and wilder, trespassing and transgressing in their conduct and behavior. Gang hooliganism, forced extortion, double dealing, endemic embezzlement and bribery, unbroken unrest, insecurity, murder, violence and bloodshed—all of which are currently the go of the day—occur under the watch, collaboration, and connivance of the politically influential members, including sections of law-enforcement agents, political organizations, and their affiliates. In consequence, what reigns supreme is anarchy, violence, distrust, mistrust and, most importantly, widespread corruption and mismanagement.

All this mess has robbed the country of its potential for huge and harmonious economic growth supposed to be delivered to all classes, not just to create a small wealthy class. While the number of the ripping rich has increased, the number of the poor has gone up with the lower middle class squeezed in between. There is an inhuman discrepancy leading to complete disaster and destruction of the spirit of national unity, democratic equality, tolerance, and transparency. Since its inception, Bangladesh has seen both democratic and despotic experiments, on and off. Far from witnessing a real democratic culture taking root, it is back to despotic drills and diaspora, especially since 2009. While the three elections under the mutually agreed-upon three-month stopgap arrangement of interim caretaker governments since 1990 were more or less fair and credible, the 2008 one under the biased and prejudicial Fakhruddin-Moinuddin-Iajuddin rule was not above dispute. Then the January 5 one, under the full and absolute control of Sheikh Hasina, was simply a joke, a laughable fabrication of all democratic rules and norms with predetermined results.

In violation of all democratic criteria, the center of power has never been the people or the parliament, which or who have simply been used as a scapegoat, a scarecrow, or a rubberstamp to manipulate the system only to suit the purpose of the opportunist politicians and parties to advance their own causes. In the past the country was fairly democratic with the pretty and fairly peaceful change of government by turns but it has recently become an empty shell without the inner democratic substance to be externally manifested in terms of the universally and globally recognized democratic rights and freedoms. There is no reflection of the democratic spirit, to be expressed through the exercise of both freedom and restraint, in the practices of the existing institutions and their operations, which are no more than a cover for the mischievous and nefarious actions and agenda.

The principle of liberty together with its attendant virtues of duty and tolerance makes democracy and democratic freedom take root and grow toward a dynamic and vibrant mechanism of force and strength. Needless to say, these values are conspicuous by their absence in Bangladesh. In the name of what is actually a distorted version of democratic rights and freedoms, there have been sweeping and indiscriminate abuses (and misuses) of the concept of democracy itself, twisted and trampled at will and convenience to suit the ends of the self-seeking opportunist politicians. They allow themselves to be lured away by the "lovely, dark and deep" prospects of material power and corruption but forget that they have "promises to keep" and "miles to go before [they] sleep," to quote from the famous American poet Robert Frost's "Stopping by Woods on a Snowy Evening." In pursuit of their self-centered goals, they prefer to ignore "Good fences make good neighbors," to quote from another poem ("Mending Wall") by Frost. In their "dream of the gift of idle hours, Or easy gold at the hand of fay or elf," they hardly care for "the sweetest dream that labor knows," as Frost says in "Mowing." Consequently, it is the negative side of the system of democracy that has been faithfully followed and consistently pursued over the years.

Great or good poetry and dirty and nasty politics do not go together. If they are both either great or low class, they may do, mutually supporting and keeping company of each other. In the context of the moral, political, and economic corruptions, deteriorations, and degenerations in Bangladesh, it is time for what used to be known in the West as great "conduct books," "advice books," and "courtesy books" for the purpose of the virtues of character and behavior to return. Instead of the newly introduced Hindu and pro-Hindu elements in the school textbooks during the Hasina regime, there is a need for the lessons of the old classic childhood education books, such as বাল্য শিক্ষা to revive and return to the classroom so that the budding, potential, and would-be politicians can grow up reciting and memorizing সকালে উঠিয়া আমি মনে মনে বলি সারা দিন আমি যেন ভালো হয়ে চলি (as I get up every morning let me promise to myself that I would lead a good and honest life during the whole day).

In the absence of such character building and character formation, it is no wonder that Bangladesh is being held hostage to a vicious circle of vested interests under the active patronage of the rich and powerful. The nation has been increasingly engulfed and consumed by an endless cycle of bitter and vitriolic hostilities as manifested by the ruling party's routine attack and accusation of the opposition in a language beneath the dignity of the politicians in a democratic culture. PM Hasina and her top deputies continue to make extremely provocative, even nasty and sinister analogies, to describe the opposition's boycott of the one-sided and deeply flawed January 5 mock show. They continue to make unbecoming and un-prime ministerial statements to attack the opposition's participation in the subsequent local government (উপজেলা) elections. Their punk language proves their malicious intent toward the opposition.

The ruling AL uses every option in its arsenal to push the opposition to the wall provoking it to react and retaliate as much as it can, however little and less forceful and ineffective it may be under the AL's brutal boots and bullets and tanks and tear gas. A ruling party behaving like a Dracula only loses its legitimacy—moral, political, or legal. It thrives by fishing in the troubled waters, throwing dust in the eyes of the people and playing the sly wolf jumping down upon the innocent lamb at the merest and most senseless excuses. To quote Goldsmith again, what he claimed to be true in the case of poetry can also be true in the case of politics: "Every absurdity has now a champion to defend it, and as he is generally much in the wrong, so he has always much to say; for error is ever talkative."

Opposition between the political parties in Bangladesh, far from being positive and constructive, is bitterly and vituperatively confrontational and potentially explosive. It has taken the country, paradoxically, to the point of being static and stagnant, hurling it into the crossfire of virtually two simultaneous and parallel administrations—one government and one opposition—thus creating a country within a country. The two major political parties—BNP and AL—are ideologically different from each other only to some extent. However, they are deeply locked in a simmering animosity over their struggle for power and their mutual mistrust and hatred of their main (and assassinated) founding leaders, the AL being above and ahead of the BNP in this regard. Hence, they are extremely intolerant of and hostile to each other. Their malignant rivalries explode into disputes after disputes over issues ranging from the nationally significant to the nationally slight and unworthy. The unwholesome differences between them due to their quarrelsome step-motherly attitude to each other are so various and numerous that they never ever find any common ground to agree on. This makes the people question their disinterested patriotic feelings, if any. Whatever they do and say is certain to be pre-or-post-determined or highly colored by their merely partisan considerations as well as individual interests, far from being an objective and bipartisan consensus reflecting national unity.

In a democracy, party interests are fine, perhaps even necessary. Parties must have their own agendas to provide viable and credible alternatives and be distinguishable from each other in their ideas about how to serve the nation. They must be prepared and committed to delivering their manifestos to the people. Ultimately their party interests must coincide with the national interest and commensurate with the sure and steady pace of progress and development. Unfortunately, a sizable number of today's politicians and their financially influential cohorts are notorious for their "wealth-amassing," "vote-buying" and "conscience-selling" tactics, acting on the "quick rental" policy of getting rich and buying name in no time, doing politics as a profitable business and making black and tainted money to be made white when there is an opportunity that is expected to present itself quite often anyway.

However, they are not to be confused with the fine, honest, economically advantaged class of businessmen and industrialists contributing to the real development of the country. For the crooked ones, power and parliament provide a means to circumvent the rule of law and subvert the social, moral, and religious values. Politics in the sense of devoted and dedicated public service and dignified and disenchanted noble occupation that aims at building the nation has become a matter of good old days. It has lapsed into mere and meaningless lip-service with the result that there is an ever-widening disparity that keeps dirtying the atmosphere already tainted by intolerance, corruption, conspiracy, violence, and anarchy.

As a consequence of all this, Bangladesh pitifully remains a divided country. It is divided against itself, like no other in the rest of the world. Plunged into a state of deep disarray and dire and dreary doldrums, it remains divided on many issues that date back to the time of its emergence. Its nationhood and national unity are still loose, porous, dilute, diffuse, and disparate. What is even worse, there are no signs in sight about those issues to be settled/resolved once and for all. The paramount concern that the socio-politico-religious-cultural atmosphere is poisoned and paralyzed by ideological confusions about ends and means tends to resist a forward-looking fermentation and crystallization. To achieve that goal, there have to be an understanding and a compromise among the different political parties, which cannot afford to remain mutually exclusive and repulsive to each other and to be dominated by the dogma of the so-called uncompromising ideologues and false prophets.

Generations after the liberation, political stability and tolerance—a must for the solidification of nationhood and steady economic growth with peace and harmony—are still a far cry, a remote possibility, to the nation's frustration, disappointment, and disillusion. In fact, the nation has been waiting too long to stay hopeful about the too familiar pattern of events for which the most responsible is the ruling Bangladesh AL. In addition to its failure to live up to people's civil and democratic expectations and aspirations, the Awami government keeps on making provocative statements about the opposition and resorting to abnormal politicking surrounding what used to be the settled and established interim CTG (Care Taker Government) system and the opposition BNP.

Instead of reforming the CTG, the main sore point between the AL and the BNP, the Hasina-led Awami regime cut it off entirely, citing some irregularities in the past of which they themselves were the only beneficiaries. Like a Saudi or ISIS executioner chopping off the head of a person in an instant, they hastily slashed off the CTG system altogether because they now thought they lost the support of the people and a neutral CTG may not serve their interest or be in their favor any more. The statements Hasina's AL makes are long on revenge, elimination, and annihilation of the opposition BNP but short on sane substance and balance. Empty of dynamically democratic content and vision, they are geared toward the ruthless suppression of people's wishes as represented by the BNP, which is, to repeat, the largest political party in the country.

The result is that the country has been turned into "a fen of stagnant waters," as Wordsworth once described England as he thought it was morally degenerate and decrepit. Or, into the status of "That is no country," as Yeats once implied Ireland to be. No wonder, the Awami government, as a Hindu lady rightly meant speaking from her hospital bed during the time of political unrest, wasted a lot of time contemplating cruel measures to contain and counter the BNP and was therefore a barrier in the way of establishing the rule of law and democratic principles under which the opposition also would function as freely as the Hasina regime itself.

The question of (and the need to document and determine) the number of the martyrs during the 9-month-long liberation war

Not less responsible for the miserable condition of the nation as a diseased body are the হুক্কা হুয়া (uncritical and unassuming) sycophants, lackeys, and zealots, as

Dr Zafrullah Chowdhury of গণস্বাস্থ্য কেন্দ্র (Public Health Center) calls them. They affect the state body as politically poisonous Zika, Ebola, and Chikungunya viruses. They act like indiscriminating remote control robots or the nuisance that is the pied piper of Hamelin's rats, to be destroyed by drowning in the river. George Orwell would like to allegorically describe them as animals of all kinds—pigs, boars, dogs, hens, pigeons, sheep, goats, cows, horses, donkeys, mares, cats, rats, ravens, rabbits, all with different skills and qualities of their own—from being shrewd, evil, and domineering to dull, boorish, and boring.

Himself an eminent freedom fighter, Dr Chowdhury also questioned (as did many others)[52] the veracity of the claim that the liberation war casualties stood at 3 (three) million. The question of the story of 3m goes back to Gen Yahya Khan, President of Pakistan (1969–1971), who is said to have wanted to kill that many, according to Robert Payne, author of *Massacre: The Tragedy of Bangladesh and the Phenomenon of Mass Slaughter* (Macmillan, 1973). It is also a question backed by misinformation and/or misunderstanding (or maybe a slip of the tongue?) during Sheikh Mujib's interview with the then BBC journalist Sir David Frost (January 8, 1972) right after Mujib's arrival in London, following his release from the Pakistani jail—that there may have been an inadvertent mistake or mix up on his part of Bangla 3 lakh with English 3m.[53] The number—3m—does not have to be established without a complete and scientific survey simply because it is now conveniently taken for granted as 3m. If the number is less, let it be; if more, so be that too. Until and unless there is a clear, full, and complete count, politicians, historians, and the future generations would continue to raise questions, preferring not to leave the number unshaken and undisturbed.

Upon his return to the newly independent Bangladesh, Mujib reportedly ordered a 12-member committee, on January 29, 1972, to find out the exact number of the dead. After nearly completing the work two years later, the commission came up with a number in the neighborhood of 58,000 to 65,000. The commission's work, however, did not proceed for reasons unknown, if not mysterious. Some members of that survey team such as (Ret) Secretary Asafuddowla are still alive, who could be asked to provide their testimony, as Dr Zafrullah claimed.[54] Dr Mina Farah, in two of her great and golden columns, addressed the controversy and argued that three million deaths in 1971 meant there had to be at least one death in every twenty five people, which she claimed did not add up to the reality nor did it confirm and corroborate the exaggerated 3m figure.[55] Following the similar argument, Javed Helali of Austin Texas also would like to contend that, even though killing even ONE innocent person was reprehensible, 3m meant 11,000 deaths a day every day for 9 months. Could it be possible, he asked, that somebody made a mistake somewhere in translating 3 lakh as 3m?

The BNP Joint Secretary Ruhul Kabir Rizvi cited different sources giving different estimates. According to the former Awami MP M A Muhaimen in 1990, the number was over 100,000 (1 lakh); according to a Liberation hero, M R Akhtar Mukul, the number was 200,000 (2 lakhs); and Bangladesh's first Prime Minister Tajuddin Ahmad put the number at one million (1,000,000 or 10 lakhs) on January 3, 1972.[56] According to a Wikipedia entry, "In the post-war period, authorities estimated that over a million people had been killed in Bangladesh by Pakistani state forces and collaborating militias." According to an Independence Day (December 16, 1971) Bangladesh Government-released Liberation Supplement, the number was one and a half million (1,500,000 or 10.5 lakhs). According to a BBC report following the execution of Moulana Matiur Rahman Nizami, "Exact number of people killed in 1971 is unclear—Bangladesh says it is three million but independent researchers put the figure at up to 500,000 fatalities."[57]

In her *Dead Reckoning: Memories of the 1971 Bangladesh War* (2011), Dr Sarmila Bose of Oxford University claims the total number of the dead during the war, combatants and civilians combined on both sides, was between 50,000 and 100,000. Prof R J Rummel's estimate in his book *Death by Government* (1997) is 1,247,000. According to Wikipedia:

> The total number of people killed in East Pakistan is not known with any degree of accuracy. Bangladeshi authorities claim that 3 million people were killed, while the Hamoodur Rahman Commission, an official Pakistan Government investigation, put the figure as low as 26,000 civilian casualties [...] A 2008 British Medical Journal study by Ziad Obermeyer, Christopher Murray, and Emmanuela Gakidou estimated that up to 269,000 civilians died as a result of the conflict. The authors note that this is far higher than a previous estimate of 58,000 from Uppsala University and the Peace Research Institute, Oslo. According to Serajur Rahman, the official Bangladeshi estimate of "3 lakhs" (300,000) was wrongly translated into English as 3 million.[58]

Citing evidence from (1) the British journalist William Drummond in *The Guardian*, (2) then BBC Bangla Service journalist Serajur Rahman, and (3) Professor Richard Sisson's and Professor Leo Rose's book, *War and Secession: Pakistan, India and the Creation of Bangladesh*, Dr Firoz Mahboob Kamal, a UK resident, supports the same view.[59] As recently as January 2017, BBC Bangla Service contended why the number of the freedom fighters kept increasing, based on the ever-fluid and varying definition of a freedom fighter.[60] Referring to different narratives in different books, the BNP Chair Khaleda Zia simply said that there was still a controversy about the exact number of people martyred during the Liberation War, adding that different sources in published material suggested different numbers in this regard and implying that there was a need to come up with a clear and final number.[61] Lakehead University Political Science Professor Syed Serajul Islam contends with the same issue:

> Individuals whether they are true freedom fighters or not depend on their belongingness to the party. In this way, being, or not being, in the political party becomes a "yardstick" to identify the individuals who are freedom fighters. This constantly perpetuates division not cohesion. Thus, until now there has been no accurate list of Freedom Fighters in Bangladesh. The BNP, while in power in 1992, prepared a list of the Freedom Fighters that was revised by the AL while it was in power in 1996. Again, the BNP revised that list in 2001 which was further revised by the AL in 2010. How could the list of Freedom Fighters be changed again and again, considering that the liberation war was over in 1971?[62]

Dr Anisur Rahman, a liberal and secular-minded retired nuclear scientist in the UK (who is chronically and catastrophically suffering from a sense of *Islamophobia* to the point of being an atheist!), sounds otherwise perfectly logical and sensible in his view about the number of the war dead:

> Bangladeshis (in fact, the large majority of Bengalis all over the world) are either totally innumerate or totally prone to rumour-mongering [...] Take, for example, 3 million deaths in the liberation war! No more than few thousand dead bodies have actually been accounted for in the whole of the country. But then the official figure had been put out as three million and now it has to be established by force of law, not by statistical or numeric count! In Syria, after 6 years of most vicious and barbaric fights—destroying most of the cities and towns in the country almost completely—the UN figure of death toll so far is around 400,000. But in Bangladesh, in nine months with no clash of armies, no aerial bombings, no tank fights, no suicide bombings etc, three million death figure had been cocked up by illiterate politicians! Now this figure gets into the school text books and so, we are teaching the future generations a total lie about the liberation war! (E-mail of May 11, 2017 to the author)

Like the different estimates of the number of prophets in Islam (varying from 1 lakh 40 thousand to 2 lakhs 40 thousand), the Holocaust dead (the number of Jews killed during World War II), the number of the freedom fighters of Bangladesh, and the number of Myanmar Rohingya refugees entering Bangladesh, the controversy surrounding the number of Bangladesh war casualties during its liberation war is not new. The controversy was there right from the beginning, from the time of the emergence of Bangladesh. It is a pity that there has been no proper and accurate survey of the war dead even after forty-six years of independence, as a result of which many families who lost their near and dear ones may still be unrecognized, suffering from poverty.[63] The fact that there was a need to account for the total number is/was supported by many politicians, political commentators, journalists, academics, and researchers, including the opposition BNP.

That the BNP chief Khaleda Zia used the same controversial, yet the so-called "official" number in her occasional and ceremonial messages in the past as prime minister does not mean it is forbidden for her to raise the issue and take issue with it later. Like many other still unsettled issues facing the nation, this issue also is far from being settled, at least scientifically, unless the present folk-based speculative and hypothetical supposition about the count is taken for granted. Ironically, excepting for nonstop corruption, politicization, criminalization, bribery, intolerance, vindictiveness, গুম ও খুন (abductions and assassinations) and হামলা ও মামলা (persecution and politically motivated low-merit penal lawsuits) and jail o জুলুম (torture, discrimination, and imprisonment), nothing has been settled in Bangladesh. There are still big questions marks (?) about the nationhood that needs to be unified and solidified; the national anthem; status of the two great leaders (Zia and Mujib); state of democracy; free and fair elections; role of the police; election commission; anti-corruption commission; judiciary; quality of education (from primary to tertiary); and the nasty and filthy ever widening discrepancy between the rich and the poor.

Unfortunately, Khaleda, like A K Khandoker, has been singled out to face a purely despotic political harassment, an autocratic sanction on her freedom of expression and an authoritarian government-sponsored sedition trial.[64] Whereas Sheikh Hasina's liberation war minister, AKM Mozammel Haque, was free to say Bangladesh became independent at the bloody sacrifice of Indian soldiers, which undermined that of the millions of Bangladeshi freedom fighters,[65] Khaleda is facing a sedition trial for simply referring to the long-existing difference of opinion, if not a feud, over (the higher or lower) number of liberation war casualties and merely implying the need to determine a correct figure based on a scientific study—a study Sheikh Mujib himself wanted to have conducted.[66] Every measure should be taken to determine an exact or near exact number of the war dead.

In the latest of the hissing, harassing, harrowing, and humiliating bundle of lawsuits against Khaleda, she was sued by the dark Awami fundamentalists undemocratically and intolerably blind to the ruling party for a "defamatory remark" she allegedly made about Sheikh Mujib. She is said to have commented that Mujib did not want the independence of Bangladesh and that he rather wanted to become the Prime Minister of a large and united Pakistan. One wonders where is the "defamation" in the statement, if she said so, because no-nonsense (national and international) historical facts and evidences are out there to affirm, confirm, and corroborate her observation.[67]

As identified above, the most popular and dignified political leader of the country, Khaleda, has now been fighting over twenty five charges against her, all politically cooked and concocted. So is the case with all the (crushed, cornered, and squeezed) leaders of her party, including the second in command, the exiled Tarique Rahman. A young, charismatic, and well-informed politician as he is, Tarique also raised the issue that the number of the war dead could either be higher or lower.

Does Khaleda have to continue to be the lamb, since 2009, for the fox of Hasina, no matter what? As many sane and senior lawyers such as Dr Shahdin Malik said, this must be a flawed and flimsy sedition case against Khaleda, without merit even through a microscope. There can be nothing wrong in trying to find out the truth and reach a consensus about the cost of the nation's historic liberation struggle and how much blood it had to shed without inflating or deflating the number of the war dead, without overestimating or underestimating what actually happened. As much as the nation needs to explore and investigate into the specific role of different players during the war for the sake of its clean and authentic history, it must also need to ascertain the number of people killed and not quarrel over for an endless period of time.[68] As a political leader, it is Khaleda's sacred duty and moral obligation, as much as it is anybody else's, to press for the record to be set straight.

The controversy over the number of the war dead is just one to keep the people of Bangladesh divided. Among the other controversies is the doubt expressed by some politicians about the role of the academics and intellectuals killed on December 14, 1971. Acceptable or not, popular or not, BangaBir Kader Siddiquee and the BNP Standing Committee member Gayeshwar Chandra Roy are among those questioning the role of those martyred, for which Roy was unfortunately about to face a defamation case.[69] Given one's right to freely question anything and critically discern into everything, one must not face any defamation in court, to be silenced and refrained from the exercise of one's freedom of expression, with all due respects, of course, to all those great people who did not have to die so painfully and pathetically.

In the suicidal politics of Bangladesh, parties failed then (that is, after the independence); parties have been more or less failing since. It is to be hoped that they would stop failing and commit themselves to leading the nation to greater heights with both means and goals upheld in an inclusive democratic system of tolerance, respect, and understanding of each other. Sheikh Hasina is not the only patriot of the country; hers must not be the only way (despite her higher and heavier share of misrule). The privilege to serve the nation and the power to govern the nation cannot and does not belong to her alone leaving the others in the desperate situation of Coleridge's Ancient Mariner expressing his plight and predicament in the midst of complete isolation and stagnation thus:

> Alone, alone, all, all alone,
> Alone on a wide, wide sea!
> And never a saint took pity on
> My soul in agony.
>
> I closed my lids, and kept them close,
> And the balls like pulses beat;
> For the sky and the sea, and the sea and the sky
> Lay dead like a load on my weary eye,
> And the dead were at my feet. (both stanzas from Part IV of the poem)
>
> There passed a weary time. Each throat
> Was parched, and glazed each eye.
> A weary time! a weary time!
> How glazed each weary eye. (Part III)
>
> Day after day, day after day,
> We stuck, nor breath nor motion;
> As idle as a painted ship
> Upon a painted ocean.
>
> Water, water, everywhere,
> And all the boards did shrink;
> Water, water, everywhere,
> Nor any drop to drink. (Both stanzas from Part II)

Except Hasina, her family, her dynasty, her Awami League, and their surrogates, cohorts, sycophants, and flatterers, all the rest are in the situation of the Ancient Mariner. There are many in the country who are held in the equal, perhaps even deeper and more representative trust and status than Sheikh Hasina and her AL. There are many who are equally, or even more patriotic and would like to get a chance to serve, govern, and contribute to the country their way too, bringing beauty and variety, and strengthening and consolidating the universally acceptable democratic norm in a credible and confident manner and making the ship of the country move again!. One last word: man is mortal and there is a great opportunity for Hasina to return to her senses and return back the lost and stolen democratic Bangladesh—the Bangladesh that is now completely missing—and thus leave a memorable name and a commendable legacy in history!

Notes

1. The White House, 10 Downing Street, or the Elysee Palace never hosts any party gathering whatsoever.
2. http://www.sheershanewsbd.com/2015/06/26/86244#
3. http://archive.ittefaq.com.bd/index.php?ref=MjBfMDZfMDVfMTRfMF8wXzN-fMTM1OTMz; http://www.theleadnews.com/home/details/1244; http://old.breakingnewsbd24.com/articles/national/breakingnews.12663.details
4. http://mynewsbd.net/?p=5989; http://mynewsbd.net/?p=5500
5. http://www.srilankaguardian.org/2012/04/bengal-tigers-in-r-cage.html
6. Mayor Sanaullah Noor of Natore; Mayor Nazrul Islam, Advocate Chandon Sharkar and several others and the young boy Twoki, all from Narayanganj; Mayor Lokman of Narsingdi; journalist couple Shagor and Runi; BNP leaders Salahuddin Ahmad, Chowdhury Alam, Elias Ali, Riaz Rahman, Anisur Rahman, Majedur Rashid, M. U. Ahmed, and Nuruzzaman Johny—to name only a few of those who were kidnapped and killed or kidnapped and tortured for days and months before being released.
7. http://www.thedailystar.net/online/abducted-boy's-body-found-sylhet-cop's-house-71731
8. There are countless little tender children, in their pre-teens, early teens, and late teens, brutally and mercilessly killed by the savage animals in human form every other day. For some details, visit:
   http://newagebd.net/214403/protests-against-rape-murder-of-tonu/;
   http://www.thedailystar.net/country/tanu-killing-no-arrest-demand-justice-gets-stronger-1198981;
   http://www.ittefaq.com.bd/wholecountry/2016/03/24/61016.html; http://www.ittefaq.com.bd/wholecountry/2016/03/24/61028.html;
   http://www.daily-sun.com/arcprint/details/91890/Trials-of-777-child-murder-cases-make-little-headway/2015-11-18; http://newagebd.net/202261/child-murder-one-of-the-worst-forms-of-savagery/;
   http://www.daily-sun.com/post/113999/Schoolboy-tortured-over-theft-in-Rajshahi-; http://bangladeshchronicle.net/2016/02/2-children-tortured-filmed-in-rajshahi-for-stealing-mobile-phone/;
9. http://www.prothom-alo.com/bangladesh/article/758935/
10. http://www.thedailystar.net/op-ed/politics/the-giants-and-the-pygmies-amongst-us-682420
11. http://edition.cnn.com/2015/07/14/asia/bangladesh-sylhet-boy-lynched/index.html;
    http://newagebd.net/137859/killing-of-rajon-protests-rage-everywhere/#;
    http://newagebd.net/137864/frequent-lynching-poor-justice-delivery-system-blamed/#; http://www.sheershanewsbd.com/2015/07/14/88702#; http://www.sheershanewsbd.com/2015/07/14/88693#

12. The "great neighbor" India is maintaining "friendly relationship" with Bangladesh by having built upstream dams in about 54 rivers flowing into Bangladesh and thus choking and strangulating Bangladesh. Visit: http://bangladeshchronicle.net/2016/02/tista-water/;
    http://www.banglamail24.com/news/148134;
    http://www.amardeshonline.com/pages/details/2016/03/25/328878#;
    http://www.amardeshonline.com/pages/details/2016/03/25/328880#;
    https://www.facebook.com/533355350042314/videos/796353473742499/;
    http://www.thedailystar.net/country/families-disappeared-19-demand-govt-intervention-182302
13. For Transparency International on the deterioration of the rule of law, see http://www.sheershanewsbd.com/2015/06/08/83720#
14. Taj Hashmi, http://www.thedailystar.net/are-terror-and-delusion-new-names-for-politics-62458
15. http://newagebd.net/68092/fakhrul-brands-ht-imam-as-imam-of-al/
16. For an idea about Moulana Bhashani, see http://www.amardeshonline.com/pages/printnews/2013/03/23/193160. See Tennessee State University and Editor Journal of Developing Areas Prof Abu N M Wahid's article on Sir Salimullah (whose death in Kolkata at the age of only forty-four in 1915 is still a great mystery) at http://www.dailynayadiganta.com/detail/news/152928; also Advocate Taimur Alam Khandoker on Sir Salimullah and the Partition of Bengal: www.dailynayadiganta.com/detail/news/160745
17. http://www.amardeshonline.com/pages/details/2013/03/03/190388
18. http://newagebd.net/235678/pm-deceives-fathers-blood-sheltering-inu-bnp/
19. https://www.facebook.com/712675668875586/videos/738691716273981/. Writer columnist Chiroranjan Shorkar wrote: "জাসদ সৃষ্টির আগেই পল্টন ময়দানে আসম রব (তিনি জাসদের প্রথম সাধারণ সম্পাদক হয়েছিলেন) 'বঙ্গবন্ধু' উপাধি প্রত্যাহার করে তিনি তাকে উদ্দেশ্য করে বলেছেন, 'শেখ মুজিব, বাচ্চা দিয়েছিস, দুধ দিবি না? তোর বাণ টেনে ছিঁড়ে দুধ বের করব।" (http://www.poriborton.com/opinion-news/6929), meaning that the then main opposition JSD General Secretary ASM Abdur Rob, in the early 1970s, rejected the title of BangaBandhu for Sheikh Mujib and, comparing him to a cow, demanded that he provide "milk" (food, safety, security, equality, rule of law) for the baby (Bangladesh) he produced and, if necessary, be forced to give "milk" by having his "nipples" squeezed by the people/opposition.
20. The term or the title means "Daughter of the Land," my self-coined, which occurs throughout the book whenever the names of Farhana or Papia come up.
21. www.dailynayadiganta.com/detail/news/169399
22. http://www.bbc.com/news/world-asia-35594968;
    http://www.bbc.com/bengali/39780226;
    http://www.ittefaq.com.bd/national/2017/05/07/113001.html;
    http://www.newagebd.net/article/14727/bangladesh-fails-to-protect-dissenting-voices-ai;

http://www.thedailystar.net/politics/2016-repressive-bangladesh-press-freedom-expression-article19-1399861

23. http://www.natun-bd.net/newsdetail/detail/49/288816; http://www.natun-bd.net/newsdetail/newslist/49
24. http://www.thedailystar.net/country/life-term-jail-dishonouring-liberation-war-bangabandhu-1273756
25. http://www.thedailystar.net/frontpage/digital-noose-be-tightened-further-1226902; http://www.thedailystar.net/news-detail-202118; http://www.thedailystar.net/newDesign/news-details.php?nid=202118; http://www.weeklyblitz.net/1786/bangladesh-enacts-new-broadcast-law
26. http://www.state.gov/j/drl/rls/hrrpt/humanrightsreport/index.htm?year=2016&dlid=265532
27. https://www.facebook.com/amiprtebademay/videos/1745816595682170/
28. http://www.thedailystar.net/news/we-wish-to-inform-you; http://www.dailysangram.com/post/279421
29. http://www.banglatribune.com/national/news/101463/; https://cpj.org/blog/2015/03/mission-journal-bangladeshi-press-reined-in-as-pri.php#more; http://www.daily-sun.com/post/70418; http://www.thedailystar.net/pm-warns-daily-star-65498; http://www.thedailystar.net/free-media-not-the-enemy-65743; http://bdnews24.com/bangladesh/2015/02/25/editors-council-deeply-divided-over-anti-government-statement; http://newagebd.net/98021/freedom-of-expression-restricted-in-bangladesh-amnesty; http://www.thedailystar.net/editors-worried-over-media-freedom-66505; http://www.amadershomoys.com/newsite/2015/02/24/222634.htm; http://www.prothomalo.com/bangladesh/article/651097;
30. http://www.thedailystar.net/frontpage/another-threat-free-speech-1206433
31. For a brief description of the media suppression by what Mahmudur Rahman calls a police fascist government, visit: http://www.newsbangla.net/newsdetail/detail/49/297334
32. See the article by Ebne Golam Samad at http://www.somewhereinblog.net/blog/mahmudh4/29377709 or http://blog.bdnews24.com/Habibb/15918
33. Titumir died of his wounds after his Bamboo fort (Bansher-Kella) was stormed by British soldiers. Khudiram and Surjo Sen, after brutal torture, were hanged to death at the age of 18 and 40, respectively, while Pritilata committed suicide at the age of 20 to avoid being captured by the British forces.
34. For Dr Zafrullah Chowdhury's well-taken comments on both of them, visit: http://www.amardeshonline.com/pages/details/2016/04/13/331582; http://www.primenewsbd.com/index.php?page=details&nc=4&news_id=108821; http://www.dhakatimes24.com/2017/04/11/28000; http://amar-desh24.com/bangla/index.php/details/publishing,focus/7522

35. http://www.thefridaytimes.com/tft/blood-dimmed-tide-in-bangladesh/
36. http://www.thefridaytimes.com/tft/the-more-it-changes/
37. http://www.thedailystar.net/op-ed/politics/ex-etv-reporter-kanak-sarwar-held-4909
38. http://newagebd.net/179268/restore-full-media-freedom-european-parliament-to-bangladesh/
39. https://en-gb.facebook.com/newbasherkella/posts/1284706551617306; http://www.sheershakhobor.com/%E0%A6%8F%E0%A6%95%E0%A7%8D%E0%A6%B8%E0%A6%95%E0%A7%8D%E0%A6%B2%E0%A7%81%E0%A6%B8%E0%A6%BF%E0%A6%AD/2016/12/17/
40. http://www.thedailystar.net/country/35-dignitaries-seek-withdrawal-cases-against-star-editor-574252;
http://www.sheershanewsbd.com/2016/02/18/117252;
http://www.sheershanewsbd.com/2016/02/18/117246;
http://www.sheershanewsbd.com/2016/02/18/117212; http://www.sheershanewsbd.com/2016/02/18/117246; http://www.sheershanewsbd.com/2016/02/18/117193
41. http://www.ft.com/cms/s/0/337c285e-0c67-11e6-9456-444ab5211a2f.html; http://thewire.in/30447/exclusive-us-court-dismissed-claim-of-plot-to-injure-bangladesh-pm-son/
42. http://bangla.irib.ir/2010-04-21-08-29-09/2010-04-21-08-30-45/item/82994; https://www.facebook.com/396694367194602/videos/404801726383866/?fref=nf
43. http://www.amadershomoys.com/unicode/2016/03/20/85558.htm#.Vu9XkDFc0mc
44. https://www.thenation.com/article/the-real-enemy-of-the-people-is-a-president-who-opposes-the-free-press/
45. Ex-BDR Chief Maj Gen A N M Fazlur Rahman sees how ATN News channel covers pro-Hindu stories with a bias against the Muslim majority Bangladesh: www.facebd.net/newsdetail/detail/200/266740
46. For a comparative study of Tarique Rahman and Sajeeb Wajed Joy (including the latter's shoddy behavior and suspicious financial activities, which Joy of course denies) by Shams Mohammad, visit: http://golamami.blogspot.com/2010/02/blog-post.html; http://newsbd7.com/main/detail/2346; https://www.facebook.com/mahmudul.islam.376/posts/1202723246413477; http://www.weeklyholiday.net/Homepage/Pages/UserHome.aspx. For the story of Sajeeb Wajed Joy's life, visit: http://ireport.cnn.com/docs/DOC-1060321;https://www.facebook.com/qamrulpage/photos/a.707572235933287.1073741828.707513919272452/1300199296670575/?type=3&theater; https://www.google.com/webhp?sourceid=chrome-instant&ion=1&espv=2&ie=UTF-8#q=Who+is+Sajeeb+Wajed+Joi%3F+A+criminal%2C+A+terrorist%2C+A+drunken%2C+A+thief%3F
47. http://nypost.com/2016/08/21/bangladesh-pm-is-trying-to-silence-queens-activist-suit/; http://www.news-bd.net/newsdetail/detail/200/237895
48. Barack Obama and his wife Michelle have been likened to gorillas, monkeys, and chimpanzees. For deporting about two million illegal immigrants, Obama, America's

Commander-in-Chief, has been called "Deporter-in-Chief" by a journalist in a face-to-face interview. Also, in this connection, see a reference to the early 19th-century English caricaturist James Gillray versus Napoleon at the end of "The Chiefs and Their *Uddinization*" chapter.

49. http://www.bd-pratidin.com/country/2017/03/18/216073
50. https://www.amnesty.org/en/latest/news/2013/08/bangladesh-arrest-human-rights-defender-sends-chilling-message;
https://www.hrw.org/news/2017/03/29/bangladesh-expands-efforts-stifle-free-speech;
https://www.amnesty.org/en/latest/news/2014/09/bangladesh-disturbing-increase-disappearances-clampdown-press-freedom;
https://www.amnesty.org/en/latest/news/2017/05/bangladesh-dissenting-voices-trapped-between-fear-and-repression;
https://www.amnesty.org/en/latest/news/2016/09/bangladesh-release-facebook-user-who-criticised-prime-minister/
51. http://www.dainikamadershomoy.com/2015/09/14/48306.php
52. Such as the daily New Age editor Nurul Kabir, the New Age special correspondent British journalist David Bergman (http://www.nytimes.com/2016/04/06/opinion/the-politics-of-bangladeshs-genocide-debate.html?_r=0), the New York-based (formerly pro-Awami, now anti-Awami) freelance writer Dr Mina Farah, and the BNP leaders such as Gayeshwar Chandra Roy, Nazrul Islam Khan, Ruhul Kabir Rizvi, Nilufar Chowdhury Moni and Fahima Nasrin Munni, among others.
53. For details, see http://bangladeshchronicle.net/2016/01/name-all-30-lakh-war-martyrs-gayeshwar-to-govt/; http://www.bdzindabad.com/news/post/889; http://imbdblog.com/?p=8000; http://www.bdzindabad.com/news/post/882; http://www.bdzindabad.com/news/post/901; Kai Kaus, MONDAY, 18 JANUARY 2016; https://www.facebook.com/sabina.ahmed.12/posts/10206680087093234; January 18, 2016January 18, 2016 BD ZindabadLeave a comment৩০ লক্ষ শহীদ নিয়ে বিতর্ক, মুক্তিযুদ্ধ ও বাংলাদেশের স্বাধীনতা, মুজিব কাকু; http://www.storyofbangladesh.com/ebooks/myth-of-3-million/author/60-firozmahboobkamal.html
54. http://www.amardeshonline.com/pages/details/2016/01/28/321116#
55. Mina Farah writes: "অনেকেই বলেন, জামায়েতকে চেনেন না? আমি বলি, যারা আওয়ামী লীগ আর এরশাদ লীগ চেনে, অন্য দলকে চেনার প্রয়োজন আছে কী? দীর্ঘদিন ধরে ভারতীয়দের বানোয়াট গল্প শুনেছি। যখন নিজের মতো করে ভাবছি, দেখলাম, ৭১ নামের মহাষড়যন্ত্র। আসল কথা, পাকিস্তানকে দুইখণ্ড করার যুদ্ধ ৭১। ৪৫ বছর পরে হলেও ভারতীয়দের নগ্ন আগ্রাসনে ৭১এর কাপড় খুলে যাচ্ছে।দেশ স্বাধীন হওয়ার অনেক পরে জানলাম ৩০ লক্ষ শহীদ। অর্থাৎ প্রতি ২৫ জনে একজন। অথচ দেশে ফিরে দেখলাম, আমার শহরে পাকিস্তানীদের হাতে ৩০ থেকে ৪০ জন মারা গেছে। শহরের কোথাও রক্তপাত বা লাশ দেখিনি। দখল করা সম্পত্তি গুলো অক্ষত ফেরত পেলো হিন্দুরা।৭১এর পর যুদ্ধবিরোধীরা পালিয়ে গেলে লুটপাটের অভয় আশ্রম শুরু করলো আওয়ামী লীগ, যা আজব্দি অব্যাহত। আওয়ামী লীগের অবস্থা দ্বিতীয় বিশ্বযুদ্ধে নাৎসীদের মতো।বদরদের দখলে থাকা হিন্দু সম্পতিগুলো ফেরত পেলেও ৭১ পরবর্তী আওয়ামী আগ্রাসনে লক্ষ লক্ষ হিন্দু সম্পত্তি দখল অব্যাহত। আমার কথা, আওয়ামী লীগকে চিনলে আর কাউকেই চেনার প্রয়োজন নেই": www.bd2day.net/newsdetail/detail/112/211855; "শহীদের রক্তের দাম

শোধ করার ক্ষমতা কারোরই নেই। ইন্টারনেটে ভৌতিক তালিকার মধ্যে এই সংখ্যা ২০ হাজার থেকে ৩০ লক্ষাধিক। এরপর খালেদা নয়, বরং মামলা হওয়া উচিত ছিল রাষ্ট্রের বিরুদ্ধে।" http://www.dailynayadiganta.com/detail/news/163267

56. For details, see Tarique Rahman's highly informative speech at https://www.facebook.com/engineersaiful/posts/1260339540661047?fref=nf; http://newsbd7.com/main/detail/2861
57. http://www.bbc.com/news/world-asia-36261197
58. https://en.wikipedia.org/wiki/Yahya_Khan
59. See *Behind the Myth of Three Million* (1996) by Abdul Mumin Chowdhury; http://www.drfirozmahboobkamal.com/2011-01-23-21-55-47/1065-chapter-3-story-of-3-million-deaths.html
60. http://www.bbc.com/bengali/news-38758647
61. http://www.thedailystar.net/politics/khaleda-kicks-controversy-over-1971-war-death-toll-190486; http://www.prothom-alo.com/bangladesh/article/734743/
62. Syed Serajul Islam, "Bangladesh: Challenges of Democracy and Good Governance," a paper presented at Southwestern Social Sciences Conference at San Antonio, Texas, April 5, 2014.
63. https://www.youtube.com/watch?v=zn5F4dKpBWc&feature=youtu.be
64. http://www.dailyinqilab.com/details/2694/
65. http://www.bdmorning.com/desh/149492
66. Although there are many records and writings to show that Mujib ended his 7 March speech with "Long Live Pakistan," A K Khandoker was singled out for bitter and brutal Awami criticism for saying so in his 2014 book. For the controversy surrounding the number of the war dead, see http://www.prothom-alo.com/bangladesh/article/402211/, 20 December 2014; http://minafarah.com/?p=1529. Also see http://www.dailynayadiganta.com/detail/news/29311#; http://www.thedailystar.net/top-news/hundreds-protest-khaledas-statement-martyrs-193936; http://www.amadershomoys.com/newsite/2015/12/28/475810.htm#
67. http://www.thedailystar.net/politics/khaleda-sued-defamatory-remarks-bangabandhu-1350706
68. http://www.dailynayadiganta.com/detail/news/87503
69. http://m.bdnews24.com/bn/detail/politics/1077772; https://www.youtube.com/watch?v=uAx70bWuf5w; http://www.prothom-alo.com/bangladesh/article/723243; http://www.prothom-alo.com/bangladesh/article/746482/

5

Bangladesh

A Trial Separation or a Complete Divorce in a Broken or Near-Broken Family?

In his 2004 incomplete draft of an article, "Towards an understanding of Bangladeshi political culture," Professor A E Ruud of South Asia Studies at the University of Oslo wrote about the intense and paralyzing rivalry between Sheikh Hasina and her Awami League (AL), on the one hand, and Begum Khaleda Zia and her Bangladesh Nationalist Party (BNP), on the other. By quoting a number of negative factors from other scholars and researchers, Ruud attempted to explain the "politics of intransigence," "absence of a responsible opposition," "imperilled democracy," "destructive politics," "spiralling lawlessness," and "confrontational political culture" in Bangladesh.[1] It has been more than a decade since Ruud drafted his article and since then all the negative characteristics he mentioned turned for the worse by the day. It is Sheikh Hasina and her AL that may be held mainly responsible for the turn from bad to worse.

The AL and the BNP, in terms of their fight for their own ideas of "power," "democracy," and "ideology," are diametrically opposite to each other. Blaming each other for everything that goes bad either inadvertently or according to a preplanned and preengineered design in an endless and ever-unfolding political drama (in which the AL is a past master compared with the BNP), the two parties present two wildly different visions. The oft-boastful, oft-bullying, oft-bellicose, and oft-belligerent, yet, electorally, deeply and darkly BNP*hobic* Sheikh Hasina, presiding over a ruthlessly repressive regime, keeps saying that the country needed to be safe from what she termed as "hyenas," again apparently referring to her rival BNP chief Khakeda Zia and the members of the BNP. On the other hand, Khaleda Zia, struggling to return the country to a democratic rule, says PM Hasina and her AL sent democracy, democratic tolerance, and bipartisan consensus into exile. Both women and their parties are locked in bitter hostilities aggravated by the relentless Awami judicial and police torture of the BNP out of venomous and vitriolic vendetta. The leading English dailies of the country reported as follows:

> The ruling quarter is hindering our democratic growth and national progress by indulging in politics of vengeance [. . .] An evil force established one-party rule by destroying the country's hard-earned democracy. Now again, the country's democracy is at stake. The evil force has exiled democracy today. It is weakening our hard-earned sovereignty and quashing people's democratic rights.[2]

This is how Bangladesh has become a split nation, the split being as deep and dangerous as a crater or a canyon. The split along the lines of "we" and "other" and "us" and "they" is so wide and steep that if one of the two parties, especially the AL, comes to power, not only does it rout the other party with the help of the tools of the state—police, civil admin, and judiciary—but also erases the names of the leaders of the other party from the places previously and politically named after them. In America, Democrats and Republicans come to power by turns, but nobody would ever think of changing the name of the federal capital Washington, D C (District of Columbia), named after the country's first President George Washington and the continent's discoverer Christopher Columbus. No one would ever imagine changing the names of John F Kennedy International Airport in New York, John F Kennedy Center for the Performing Arts in Washington, D C, John F Kennedy School of Government at Harvard University; and Abraham Lincoln Memorial, Thomas Jefferson Memorial, George Washington Monument, and George Washington University—all four located in Washington, D C.

Apart from the pernicious divisions along the lines of north and south (that is, rich and poor, high and low, educated and uneducated, employed and unemployed), Bangladesh is painfully down in disarray, fraught and fragmented by an overwhelming amount of contaminated, discordant and disharmonious partisan politics. It has been reduced to a two-faced Janus-nation: one face is the so-called মহান জাতীয় সংসদ (great/noble parliament, though only in words) as the center of all political activities and the other is the dull, lifeless, ineffective, and stagnant parliament (alleged by TIB to be no more than a doll dance show/puppet theater)[3] with the actual center lying in the wills and wishes of Sheikh Hasina. It is a joke to see that there is a prime minister and there is a government under her that came to power through a one-sided voteless and voterless "non-election" with a shameful reduction of the multi-party political dynamics into a one-lane freeway available only for their party AL to act and operate. That has left all the opposition parties under the police/RAB suppression and repression, which has brought them to their knees, to the point of mass extinction and annihilation, not unlike the endangered species.

Again, this one face is her currently ruling and despotic AL and its constant beating of a development drum accompanied by its brutal suppression of democratization and democratizing process, to the forced police/RAB exclusion of the popular opposition. The other face is the opposition, previously ruling BNP-led alliance, now under the heavy yoke and clinching fists and clutches of the AL. The situation is similar to the Myanmar military repression of the popular dissent by Aung San Suu Kyi and her party for decades until the end of 2015. Another similarity may be found in the international step-brotherly opposition between the communist China (red) and the democratic and nationalist Taiwan (blue), South Korea and North Korea, Pakistan/Kashmir and India, Ukraine and Russia, Cuba and America (until recently), Israel and Palestine, (Shiite) Iran and the (Sunni) Muslim world, and the Kurds and the Arabs/Turks.

In any case, the AL carries with it:

- The burdensome baggage of the 1975 single and sole party called BAKSAL, formed of a gagging policy that changed the character of the country's constitution in minutes—the BAKSALIite policy continuing in the form of the ruthless and repressive Awami regime even today and its sudden and swift cancellation of the caretaker form of government[4];
- The background of its brutal and brutish paramilitary *Rakkhi-Bahini* (National Security/Defense Force, headed by Tofael Ahmed), enjoying the parliament-approved indemnity, in the roughly mid-1970s (similar to then challenger and counterpart JSD *Gano-Bahini*, whose leaders are now closely and cozily allied with the AL), both *Bahinis* having been a sort of reincarnation of the French "Jacobin" Reign of Terror (July 1793–July 1794) under Maximilien Robespierre and Cambodian Khmer Rouge under Pol Pot in mid-1970s, both having been responsible for the deaths of tens of thousands[5];
- The heart-rending memories of the 1974 famine (a man-made famine, according to the Nobel laureate, Amartya Sen) under the Awami rule that left hundreds of thousands dead, destitute, and displaced, harking back to the man-made Bengal famines of 1943 and 1769–1773[6];

- The bloody August 15 military coup the following year;
- The symbolic sleeveless "Mujib" (waist) coat, which gives the title of Neamat Imam's widely reviewed dystopian political fiction, *The Black Coat* (2013), depicting Mujib "as a totalitarian ruler who distorted truth and suppressed political opposition to strengthen his tyranny" and calling him a "monster" and a "disgrace" (Wikipedia);
- The Awami brand of religion-neutral (in reality, Islam-demoting and Islam-bashing) secularism;
- The "*Joy* Bangla" slogan (not "Joy Bangladesh");
- The identity of the Sheikh family being the most international, interracial, and interfaith family in the world, rather than being the most *Bungalee* or Bangladeshi family;
- The choice of the song "*Amar Sonar* Bangla" as the controversial and disuniting national anthem;
- The heavy-handed and excessive politicization of bureaucracy, civil administration, judiciary, and bureaucratization of politics;
- The dozens of party-and-family related দিবস (days/anniversaries) for nationwide celebration, commemoration, and observation;
- The naming of innumerable institutions and organizations after *Bangabandhu,* a title given to Sheikh Mujib by the AL;
- Portraying, alienating, and maligning the majority of the patriotic people who differ from the AL on political matters as anti-Liberation, pro-Pakistan, pro-Jamaat, and pro-Rajakar;
- The February 25, 2009 *Pilkhana* BDR mutiny, still shrouded in mystery with many questions about the interparty and intraparty involvement, including the hidden role of the Hasina government, that resulted in the barbaric massacre of (only 57!) great army officers and about 20 others with the plotters still unidentified (a massacre that may be compared to the Nazi extermination of the Jews in the concentration camps in the 1940s)[7];
- The May 5, 2013 heart-breaking late night/predawn massacre of about 2,000 innocent sleeping Hefajote students and activists in Dhaka in one of the worst mass killings in the history of the country[8];
- The controversial January 5, 2014 when the AL held the most awful, farcical and shameful thing of an election ever in the history of Bangladesh, observed as the day of the demise of democracy (democracy killing day) by the BNP-led opposition (as opposed to the AL, which observes the day as democracy saving day) that resulted in the dire and dreadful crisis of a high density of ills and troubles in which the country has lamentably landed today;

- The rampant and widespread "digital" looting, in dirty and filthy and ferocious and crazy amounts, by allegedly in-house/inside thieves, bandits, robbers, crooks, criminals, traitors, scoundrels, and swindlers, from the banks and share markets, about which top and key government leaders maintain a mystical and mysterious "digital" silence and which kind of scams and scandals and snake-like hissing heists and heinous crimes, having occurred again and again since 1974–1975, have traditionally become associated with the AL regime, prompting the people to ask not only সোনার বাংলা শশান / শোষণ কেন? (Why is the golden Bengal burnt and barren like the Hindu cremation field?) but also why the Bank dacoity and share market plunder occur again and again under the rule of the Sheikh family[9]; and
- The thousands and thousands of গুম ও খুন, হামলা ও মামলা (corporeally punishing, insulting, and harassing) remands and ডান্ডাবেড়ি, forced confessions, and jail o জুলুম during the AL's despotic and autocratic rule, especially since 2009, all under the cover of upholding the partisan and politicized একাত্তরের চেতনা (the spirit of 1971), the way millions were killed in China and Indochina in the name of the violent (failed) cultural revolution of the 1960s and 1970s.[10]

On the other hand, the BNP bears with it:

- The memories of the eventful November 7 (which it celebrates as the National Revolution and Solidarity Day);
- The credit of introducing multiparty system that took democracy and development forward together;
- The tragic memories of the assassination of its leader President Ziaur Rahman in a military coup on May 30, 1981;
- The ideal of a robust, patriotic, and uniting nationalism;
- The Long Live Bangladesh/Bangladesh *Zindabad* slogan;
- The strength and identity of the Zia family being the most Bangladeshi political family;
- The song "*Prothom* Bangladesh *Amar Shesh* Bangladesh," along with "*Amar Sonar* Bangla," which is the official, yet controversial national anthem of Bangladesh; and
- The controversy over the celebration of Begum Khaleda Zia's (questionable) birthday on 15 August (instead of 5 September, reportedly, according to some documents)—15 August being a day of mourning for the AL. (For more on this issue, see "The chiefs and their *uddinization*" chapter, through the halfway).

On a lighter note, like the comic scenes that at the same time intensify and accentuate the serious themes in a tragedy, the two parties (BAL and BNP) are as divided as their present leaders. One is only Sheikh Hasina of the AL, with her late husband's name hardly used at the end of her name. Even when he was alive, his wife Hasina hardly wanted to be known by him. (Critics have their own versions about the couple's relationship.) The other is Khaleda Zia of the BNP, with her late husband's name always fondly attached to her beautiful name. Khaleda is older but, even after the age has taken its toll on her, more beautiful, graceful, stylish, glamorous, ladylike, fashionable, fair complexioned, reserved and serious-looking, speaking both Bangla and English with an impressive accent and nice pronunciation.[11] One starts her day early and the other late. They also differ in their traditional wear to make a personal statement about Bangladesh. While one wears printed cotton saree, the other prefers lace and chiffon saree with matching satin veil.

These may seem to be small details but no less significant, like the small plants and flowers and ferns and creepers that add to the beauty of the vegetation under the trees of a forest. Women's outfit, more than men, especially the first ladies', is always a news item, a source of their charm, attraction, and gracefulness, all over the world. Hasina wears what goes well with her. Khaleda does the same. Their clothing style and body wear make a statement about their demeanor and conduct. Apart from major political and ideological differences, those in style and personality also come into play everywhere.

Could there also be, then, a psychological warfare of personal jealousy and personality clash between Hasina and Khaleda? One came to power as the daughter of one of the great political leaders of the country; the other as the wife of a military general, who was also a great liberation hero after having declared the independence of Bangladesh (albeit in the name of Sheikh Mujib) and who later became a great war hero and a great president of the country. Both women are grooming their sons to take charge of their respective parties and eventually the country. Could this family orientation further contribute to their rivalries?

The two parties are so bitterly opposed to and resentful of each other that if someone belonging to one of them dies, no matter how big a leader s/he was, the other party would not even care to send a message of condolence, let alone attending the funeral and saying a kind word about his/her public service or political contribution, which, if any, is hardly anything in the eyes of the other party. The personal as well as political antagonism between the two either as individuals or as parties, especially the present AL's relationship with the BNP, since 2008, has been like the vitriolic relationship between the American North and South during the civil war in the 1860s; or between the whites and the blacks as depicted in the American classics such as *Uncle Tom's Cabin*, *Adventures of Huckleberry Finn*, *Gone with the Wind*, and *To Kill a Mocking Bird*; or between the Jewish (non-Arab) state of Israel and the Arab state of Palestine.

In the most recent case of the death of Arafat Rahman Koko, the younger son of Begum Zia, everyone expected that the event had the potential to be a turning point in creating a thaw in the divisive and intolerant relationship between the two parties as well as the two ladies, with PM Hasina seizing the opportunity to pay a visit to Khaleda Zia, a widow, to offer her condolences, the way the latter visited Hasina, also a widow, following the death of her husband Dr Wajed years ago (although the circumstances were different then). At the same time, everyone had a ray of hope that Hasina, who is holding the office of the prime minister through a sham, hypocritical election, would also offer an olive branch in the form of a proposal for political dialogue that might open a new window for the withdrawal of the BNP-led (by then) month-long January (2015) siege and the possible next steps, including the immediate release of thousands of political prisoners. Hasina did indeed pay the hoped-for visit but fortunately or unfortunately she was not successful in entering the premises of Khaleda's office compound that was then under siege by the Hasina regime.

There were a few who made wrong-headed comments over the prime minister being turned away like that. True, it was unwanted, unexpected, and undesirable. There was a confusion and mismanagement in the handling of the whole incident by the both sides—the BNP and the AL. However, the episode should be viewed in the broader context of the culture and history of hostile, vindictive, and venomous politics between the two female leaders and the two parties. Considering the facts that (1) Khaleda could not see her two sons and her three grandchildren for about eight years now, living a lonely life (due to the Moinuddin–Fakhruddin times army torture and Sheikh Hasina's politically motivated double standards) and that (2) there was an indescribably harsh treatment and unprecedented humiliation of Khaleda and her party members for as many years, one got to see things in a different light, not just black and white.

Democratic norms, niceties, and courtesies have been generally lacking in the political culture of Bangladesh for decades. Especially during the Awami regime, since 2009, they are as rare as the full moon in the lunar dark. When the BNP calls a meeting in the capital, the regime practically closes down the city hotels and restaurants, all other common places of room and board, and all the means of mass transportation (trains, buses, steamers, launches) from different locations across the country. It calls a meeting at the same place at the same time where the

BNP has already called a meeting. The Hasina-Awami regime, thus, unlawfully foils and forces the opposition to stay away from holding any political gathering. This is a democratically illegitimate suppression in a neo-and-near-and-more-than-partially totalitarian manner.

In tightening the noose around the neck of the opposition, the despotic AL government not only cut off the opposition leader Khaleda Zia, confined to her office in Gulshan, from public contact and free movement more than once but also closed down her party office in Naya Paltan, preventing her supporters and activists from gathering to conduct normal political activities. In an exercise of what is no less than authoritarian usurpation, the office started being occupied by the Hasina police for some of their activities. Consequently, there are many, including the BNP leader Sadek Hussein Khoka (in New York) and Khaleda herself, who held the Hasina regime responsible for hastening the premature (heart-attack) death in the Khaleda family.

In a moment of deep personal bereavement, an oppressor like Sheikh Hasina could not be the last word nor her position as "questionable" prime minister the only consideration. She did not show any human, motherly, or womanly consideration for Khaleda for the last eight years. She kept Khaleda under confinement many times over the years, as recently as the blockade of January 2015. Immediately following Koko's death (on January 24) when his mother was mourning for him and the prime minister made a (more political than social, consolatory, and sympathetic) attempt to see her, there was a number of politically motivated lawsuits and arrest warrants against Khaleda, to add fuel to the fire, and to add to dozens of lawsuits already filed against her.

What is even worse, all fifteen corruption charges against the top AL leader/s—related to NAIKO, MIG 29, Korean Frigate, construction of Novo Theater, Tungipara Bangabandhu Monument (Memorial/Mausoleum), and Meghna Ghat Power Plant, among others, were one-sidedly dropped in a partial and prejudicial abuse and influence of power years ago. Considering the years of persecution and suffering of Khaleda, even after the death of her son Koko, it does not take long to claim that what happened that day was only right. Naturally, on a *TM* talk show on January 25, Major (Ret) Akhtaruzzaman had the honest courage to defend the fiasco concerning Hasina's attempted and aborted visit to Khaleda.

Yet it is not difficult to agree with those who argue that the matter should have been treated more sensitively and wisely, regardless of how relative is the meaning of these adverbs are. On the BNP side, Khaleda's office staff should take all the responsibility for their irresponsible behavior. But again even if they opened the gate and welcomed the Prime Minister only to inform her that the former Prime Minister Khaleda, being irreparably shocked at the sudden death of her 45-year-old son (who was away from the mother for seven long years) and sedated by her doctor, was not in a position to receive the sitting Prime Minister, there would have been other objections raised by the critics. They would have said Khaleda slighted the incumbent (Hasina) by rebuffing (and not meeting with) her. On the other hand, the staff of the office of the |Prime Minister Hasina also should share the responsibility for some communication gaps on their part.

However, many people thought all opportunities were not lost. They thought the situation could still turn around when the body of the young man would arrive from Kuala Lumpur with both Khaleda and Hasina meeting over the same during the funeral, if that sort of reconciling or narrowing-the-gap gesture was ever to happen. A reader of ancient Greek/Homeric epic poetry remembers the way the Trojan King Priam met the killer of his son—the Greek hero Achilles—, both the old king and the young hero softening and weeping over the dead body of Hector, the greatest Trojan hero. In the case of Khaleda and Hasina, that never happened, dashing the hopes of millions, despite the fact that Koko's funeral, drawing millions, was one of the largest in the history of Bangladesh, that of his father, the assassinated President Zia, in 1981, being the largest. Moreover, in a classic example of meanness and lowness, even Koko's burial rights in terms of the selection of the grave site were denied and the politics of revenge and vindictiveness continued.

To make her cup of misery full, Khaleda, facing for years the Hasina politics of destruction of Khaleda-led opposition, continued in a sort of "house arrest" or semi confinement in her office premises amid her fresh personal grief about the death of her son. All the basic utility services were cut off for a while that forced her to live in darkness and isolation along with her two small recently orphaned granddaughters and her widow daughter-in-law. To leave the besieged Khaleda without water, electricity, gas, phone connection, and internet services even for a short time was to deny her fundamental rights as a citizen.

In addition, the AL government was pointlessly criticizing that if Koko's children could go back to Malaysia for their schooling, why it was that the SSC examinees in Bangladesh had to face the countrywide blockade during their exams. The fact was that it was the AL-government created stalemate over its unelected status that was responsible for the predicament of the SSC examinees and that the government did not want to refer to the fact that the Koko children were already suffering for the last seven years with their young father beaten up like anything in 2007 and then the AL-government filing a number of politically motivated lawsuits against him, forcing him and his immediate family to be away from home in Bangladesh.

Instead of agreeing to disagree in the positive sense of that quintessential democratic principle for the greater cause of unity and prosperity of the nation, the two faces represented by the two parties are intolerably averse, inimical, confrontational, and cantankerous to each other. To be fair, it is the AL which is many times more so than the BNP. Each party claims the spirit of the struggle for independence in 1971 as its own—a struggle in which the founder of the BNP, Ziaur Rahman, fought most heroically from the very beginning (in the absence of the AL leader Sheikh Mujibur Rahman, who and whose family had to be away from the battlefield and remained under Pakistani care and custody for political reasons, but not without leaving a great influence and deep inspiration behind).

The BNP claims it has more of the living freedom fighters among its frontline members than the AL, which, starting with BAKSAL, has repeatedly failed to establish democracy and democratic tolerance, compromise and understanding in accordance with the spirit of the liberation struggle, which has unfortunately been commodified, compartmentalized, and commercialized with a product/market/face value on it. The deadly distrust and intolerance between the two parties have left the nation torn and drifting. It is as fatefully and frontally divided as are its hundreds of other political parties, secular or religious, rightist or leftist (some too small to be known and reckoned with, yet managing to survive under the shadow of this or that alliance led by either of the two major parties and changing from one alliance to another according to their either material or ideological convenience).

That the nation is regressively segregated into two main mutually exclusive camps is reflected by the differences within the members of some of the politically well-known families. Take, for example, the antagonism between the honest and illustrious Mainul Hussein and his Awami-allied brother Anwar Hussein Manju; between the BNP vice chairman Selima Rahman and her great anti-Awami brothers—wonderful (late) Sadek Khan and Shahidullah Khan Badol of the *New Age*—, on the one hand, and their differently oriented pro-Awami brother Rashed Khan Menon, on the other; the Islamic-minded and somewhat anti-Awami Kader Siddiquee and his (recently disgraced) Islam-bashing and fully Awami elder brother Latif Siddiquee. While some of the above exemplify the ideal brotherhood of Prof Mahbub Ullah and the journalist columnist Mahfuz Ullah, others are far from it, differing on everything related to politics, policies, and principles.

Other examples of similar divide and distance would include the leftist and heroically honest Prof Badruddin Umar and his famous Islamic-minded father Abul Hashim, who was a great Muslim League leader in Bengal during the pre-and-post partition in the 1940s and 50s and who wrote about the role and importance of Islam in the reconstruction of society. Another example is the young rising and patriotic BNP leader Shama Obaid and her BNP-rebuffed mother Prof Shaheda. Out of power struggle and differences of opinion, the mother, Shaheda, would grudgingly want only her daughter's BNP to wage a mortal fight against the ruthless AL, while she herself would not join the fight. She has taken the quarrel one step further by preferring to go by her first name only, detached from the name of her late husband, K M Obaidur Rahman, who was once a top AL, then a top BNP leader. The ruling AL chief Sheikh Hasina also prefers, for personal reasons, to be known by her first name only, without her late husband's name Wajed attached to hers.

All that glitters is not gold. Neither are the golden crests given as gifts to the friends and allies of Bangladesh nor are its golden (SSC and HSC) GPAs.[12] Nor is its golden fiber (jute) any longer. Nor is its golden (Sonali/Rupali) Banks nor is the golden *Amar Sonar* Bangla, both weighed down by pure and corrupt partisan politics. All this gold has become as rare and elusive as সোনার হরিণ/golden gazelle. The atmosphere of mostly Awami-generated animosity prevailing in the country is challenged not only by the BNP-led political opposition but also virtually all the fair-minded and forward-looking political and social thinkers with their vitally and vigorously neutral, constructive, moral, ideological and often sensibly and understandably political (not necessarily partisan) stance (see "who's who" section toward the end of the Conclusion chapter).

Another glaring example of the gaping divide is how the only Nobel Laureate (in peace) of the country, Dr Mohammed Yunus, has been treated by the ruling AL. It is as if Dr Yunus is a stepson of Bangladesh and not a son of the soil. It is as if he was a non-*Bhumiputra*, a term used in Malaysia to describe the ethnic Chinese and Indians to separate them from the ruling native *Bhumiputras*, that is, Malays.

The dire and deep division among the leading members of the public, as different from constructive and agreeable differences, reminds one of the post-independence unhappy relationship between the once close comrades/associates, Tajuddin Ahmad and Sheikh Mujibur Rahman, both key figures in the history of Bangladesh (the former playing a direct and definite role during the independence struggle when the latter was away in the safe custody of the Pakistanis, thereby missing out on the glorious independence struggle and failing to lead his people at the time of the crisis when they needed him most). Tajuddin had his dark spots too in the context of his infamous 7-point agreement with India, which did not have absolute trust in his new government in exile and, therefore, created a rival/parallel force in the Bengal Liberation Front (BLF), also called Mujib Bahini.[13]

In any case, the two leaders fell out with each other with the consequence that Tajuddin is being accorded little or no respect by today's Awami regime—a fact recently brought into sharp focus by many, notably his own daughter Sharmin Ahmad and a high-ranking independence figure, A K Khandoker. The latter supported the post-Mujib rebel government of Khandoker Mushtaque Ahmed and also managed to become a cabinet minister later both in the Ershad government and, ironically, in the government of Mujib's own daughter Hasina too.[14] After he left the Hasina government (2009–2013), A K Khandoker, a senior citizen, again became a subject of criticism by the Hasina-led Awami circle for registering in his book, *1971: Bhetore O Baire* (2014), that Mujib ended his March 7, 1971 speech with "Long Live Pakistan" and for casting doubt on the Hasina-AL's claim that Mujib wrote/sent a telegram to the effect of the declaration of independence to an Awami leader in Chittagong a short while before he was taken into custody by the Pakistani authorities in Dhaka on the night of 25 March.

Although Khandoker's claim is supported by many other writers, politicians, and researchers (such as Justice Habibur Rahman, journalist Nirmal Sen, Maidul Hassan, Shamsur Rahman, journalist Ataus Samad, and Col (Ret) Nuruzzaman), the Hasina-AL could not tolerate it because it not only came from one of their own but also contradicted its version of the narrative relative to the history of liberation, sometimes twisted and distorted at convenience to suit their political agenda.[15] Khandoker's claim lent support to the opposition argument that Mujib's 7 March speech, full of ifs and buts and flips and flops, fell short of full and clear and decisive declaration of the independence of Bangladesh, which it claims was made by then Major Zia over the Radio from Chittagong on March 26.

It was the similar division within the ruling AL that led to the fateful August 15, when Mujib's other close associates, led by Khandoker Mushtaque, replaced him in a bloody coup, making statements of their own in justification of their successful rebellion. However, going back in history, the present political environment of bloody, violent and anarchical acrimony between the two major parties in the country and its corrupt class-ridden society takes us back to similar tribal and treacherous, and modern and mythological hostilities between the kings, emperors, heirs, princes, dukes and lords, sometimes fratricidal. For example, the divisions and rivalries between:

- Cain and Abel; 8th century BC Amulius and Nomitor; their grandchildren, legendary she-wolf suckled founders of ancient Rome, Romulus and Remus; Pompey the Great and Julius Caesar during 49 BC-45 BC;

succeeding tyrants of the Roman empire (and across the world); the noble, wealthy and aristocratic ruling class of the patricians and the poor, ordinary plebeians; and the feudal lords and their vassals;

- (Netaji?) Subhas Chandra Bose and then Indian Congress High Command, including Mahatma Gandhi in the context of WWII and the independence of India from the British rule with or without the help of Hitler's Germany and its ally Japan in the 1940s;
- Joseph Stalin (Orwell's pig/boar Napoleon) and Leon Trotsky (Orwell's pig/boar Snowball);
- The tragic 1857 Indian Mutiny;
- Edmund Burke, on the one hand, and, on the other, Rousseau, Thomas Spence, Richard Price, Tom Paine, Mary Wollstonecraft, William Godwin, William Cobbett, Joseph Priestly, John Horne Tooke, John Thelwall, and many others during the French Revolution in the 1790s;
- The (17th-century) sixth Mughal emperor Mohiuddin Muhammad Aurang-zeb (also known by his imperial title *Alamgir*, meaning "world-seizer")—the wealthiest and most expansionist of the Mughal emperors, yet simple, pious, and conservative—and his father and predecessor, the fifth Mughal emperor Shahabuddin Abu Muzaffar Shah Jahan and his (Aurang-zeb's) three siblings—Dara Shikoh, Murad Bakhsh, and Shah Shuja;
- The 15th-century Muslim Spain Sultan of Granada Hassan and his traitor son Abu Abdullah, whose betrayal of his father in 1492 paved the way for the final fall of the Muslims to the Spanish Christians under Ferdinand and Isabella, whose horrible treachery in turn led to the tragic death of hundreds of thousands of Andalusian Muslims; and so on.

The difference is that in those times the nations as a whole were not as deeply split against themselves (as it was a matter of palace coups and power struggles confined only to the ruling cliques and families) as it is today in Bangladesh where the entire public, from top to bottom, are divided by the body politic that is completely poisoned by the clashing opinions of its own members.

Had the opposition between the two major and alternately ruling parties in Bangladesh been as civilized, tolerant, respectful and understanding as in the developed and established democracies of the world, including the surrounding India, let alone the USA, the UK, and the rest of the Western world, it would have been a welcome, longed-for and sought-after political culture materializing. Instead, there are countless issues—divisive, explosive, and divergent—along the ethically, morally, democratically, and politically incorrect lines. One of them has to do with the proper recognition of the past two leaders of the country—Sheikh Mujibur Rahman and Ziaur Rahman (both brutally and mercilessly assassinated by members of the army in 1975 and 1981, respectively, under different circumstances).

Unfortunately, the dispute over their status and their historic contribution both before and after the creation of Bangladesh could not yet be solved to the satisfaction of all with an open, objective and dispassionate mind by the parliament and the political leaders of the country.[16] Perhaps it would never be until and unless there are, in the best and highest interest of the nation, (1) an all-winning forgiving attitude of each side, noting the fact that both leaders, now resting in peace but still representing the two major parties in an iconic manner, had exactly the same greatest attribute of Almighty *Allah*/God—that is, *Rahman*—meaning "the most kind, merciful and compassionate"—as their last name; (2) an overriding and outweighing honest political will; and (3) an all-inclusive political correctness to overcome the existing obstacles and irreconcilables.

These would include:

- Whether the people of Bangladesh (according to the post-independence constitution) should be known as "*Bungalee*/Bengalese," hence extending the idea to wall in the Indian province of the Hindu-majority West Bengal bordering with the Muslim-majority Bangladesh, both sides speaking the same language and sharing a number of cultural aspects and both being fairly secular and moderate in their religious and political leanings, or "Bangladeshi" (according to the fifth amendment to the constitution) thus in effect walling out the neighboring Indian West Bengal and priding itself on the geographical area within the physical land borders of the independent Bangladesh);
- Whether the Bangladeshis should all raise and chant the slogan of *Joy Bangla* (meaning "victory to Bangla"), again practically invoking the idea of both Bengals as one and single geopolitical entity), or "Bangladesh *Zindabad*" (Long Live Bangladesh) that confirms the hard-earned territorial boundary that is the sovereign Bangladesh of today and its integrity together with the people of various ethnic, tribal and religious origins living there)[17]; and
- More importantly, whether Bangladesh should continue to have the existing national anthem as its national anthem—highly lyrical and emotionally charged as it is, but, considered calmly, dispassionately, and rationally, seems to be a wrong choice, illogical, untenable, and disuniting.

There are a host of other controversies that dim and diminish the image and status of the nation without fail. To enumerate some of them:

- There are questions over the autocratic and authoritarian Hasina administration (termed as democratically illegitimate, neo-fascist, and neo-Hitler by the opposition BNP),[18] which would neither allow for inclusive and participatory democracy to take hold and be institutionalized nor would let the opposition (under sand-and-cement truck confinement and the whirlpool and thunderstorm of boots and bullets and batons and bludgeons and teargases and arrests and remands and imprisonments) carry out its political and peaceful activities freely[19];
- The sudden and expedient and convenient cancellation of the four-term fairly neutral interim Caretaker Government (CTG) system (except perhaps in 2006–2008), for which the AL-Hasina had earlier fought a bloody fight against the BNP for nearly six months in 1995–1996, to the purely partisan advantage of the AL, so that it (AL) could now cynically manipulate the electoral machine/process to achieve its desired dark and dangerous one-party goals without an iota of neutrality that was previously represented by CTG;
- The dull, ineffective, lifeless, listless, spiritless, rubber stamp parliament of auto-elected and self-elected members that blindly and uncritically goes along and complies with the wishes of the one-person show of the party leader and prime minister at the expense of the national consensus and to the detriment of the interest of the national affairs that ought to require the involvement and participation of the majority;
- The January 5, 2014 blueprint of an obese, obscene, botched, bungled, bowdlerized, adulterated, duplicitous, rigged, ludicrous, pugnacious, morbid, and mutilated "election," mocked and belittled by the opposition as a 420 মার্কা Circus মার্কা কুত্তা মার্কা ছাগল মার্কা নির্বাচন (a dogged, dodged, duped, and dog-and-goat marked election, the idea coming from dogs and goats found sleeping in the deserted "voter-less" booths).[20] The most staged "non-election" in the name of election was billed as a parody, travesty, distortion, and perversion of all democratic rules and norms, being nowhere near the sample and semblance of an inclusive and credible election. It was an election further hideously disfigured by the creation of a loyal, conjoined, handpicked, handicapped, and domestic opposition (termed by critics as গৃহপালিত ঘরজামাই লেংরা লুলা লুজা বিরোধী দল in a strange and rare species of democracy (বিরল প্রজাতির কিম্ভূত কিমাকার জগাখিচুরি গণতন্ত্র). One can draw an analogy with

Hawthorne's dark, faith-shaking, witch-hunt characters in the story of Young Goodman Brown; the ugly monster created by Mary Shelley's Promethean scientist Frankenstein with the monster pursuing its creator Frankenstein to death in the Arctic ice, or the horrible miscreant stranger of Indian origin who appears at the Faustian (transgressive) overreacher Vathek's Gothic tower in William Beckford.

- The stifled, trampled, triangulated, strangulated, and stumbling democracy "of my way or no way," to the exclusion of the dissident, differing, and democratic voices and to the extent of crushing everything that falls outside the narrow, myopic, and monolithic Awami way;
- The highly partisan, politicized, and polarized rule of "you're either with us or against us";
- The retrograde and repressive Awami politics whereby there are unrelenting and ruthless suppression, oppression, persecution, and humiliation of the political opposition led by the BNP, constantly made subject to indiscriminate sieges, blockades, lawsuits, arrests, captures, remands, imprisonments, abductions, and assassinations as if the nation was governed by the jungle or medieval feudal lord-vassal laws;
- The "grand festival" or "festive carnival" of corruption, right and left, top to bottom, so that critics say they only see thousands of all-swallowing omnipresent Awami খাওয়া ভবন all around, as opposed to the BNP's old and single হাওয়া ভবন (inactive since 2005 and may have been active for only a couple of years before), which was nothing compared with the current all-consuming Awami Hall of Devouring (খাওয়া ভবন)[21];
- The cruel and controversial role of the politicized police and the RAB (Rapid Action Battalion) with many an abhorrent act committed by them, who are used as the ruling AL's torture tools turning the whole country into a prison-near-prison-semi-prison house;
- The complete deterioration of the law and order situation and a total lack of security in the face of the unprecedented and unaccounted-for gruesome slaughters, assassinations, and abductions, of which men, women, children, civilians, politicians, businessmen, professionals, and the young and adult alike—all have been poor, pathetic, and helpless victims;
- The allegedly opaque, disputable, disreputable, and politicized judiciary, far from enjoying wide and permanent public trust, almost on the verge of collapse[22];
- The weak, ineffective, incapable, and unassertive EC (Election Commission)—as alleged to be by the opposition as well as the civil

society—working only at the pleasure of the government and not "we the people," who assume that the EC—আজ্ঞাবহ (blindly and uncritically loyal) and মেরুদণ্ডহীন (spineless)—is just an HMV (his master's voice/her majesty's voice), okaying the pugnacious and egregious January 5 farce and playing the role of an Awami organ in all rounds of local elections year after year, thus proving that the present *Rakib-Marka* Commission is far worse than those before (just as the present Awami government is perceived to be way to the bottom below compared with all the previous governments)[23];

- The public perception of bias against and the lack of fairness and firmness about the ACC (Anti-Corruption Commission), which the opposition keeps accusing of being a দায়মুক্তি commission (release from reckoning/accountability) rather than an anti-corruption (দুর্নীতি দমন) commission for being selective in clearing some while holding others accountable under charges of corruption;
- The often soft but at times conveniently loud HRC (Human Rights Commission)[24];
- The charges of partisan bias against the PSC (Public Service Commission); and
- The debate over the inclusion of the controversial Islamic political party *Jamat-e-Islami* in the national governments, parliamentary elections, and the nationally proposed political dialogues, although it was at one time with the AL against the BNP and now with the BNP against the AL, while at the same time it is rumored that the AL is again trying to secretly woo the Jamat away from the BNP, which in turn would like to draw the on-again-off-again player Ershad on its side, away from the AL, all out of politically convenient election strategy.

These dividing issues in the power and ideological struggle of the two major rival parties are yet to be worked out with a view to injecting and fostering the spirit of tolerance and understanding in the political culture of Bangladesh, long dominated by intolerance, cynical distrust, and cyclical conflict. As a consequence, the whole nation—students, politicians, professionals (teachers, professors, lawyers, doctors, engineers, journalists, commentators, analysts, economists, artists, actors, intellectuals, media personalities, business community, religious (*Ulema*) community, civil servants, admin staff, factory workers, farmers, labor unions)—and its institutions—be they secular or religious, private or government, entertainment or educational—, print and electronic media, TV channels, and the entire range of the general masses—remain sharply divided, literally locked up in a chronic, corrosive, and cancerous state of sluttish polarization that has been dangerously and disastrously eating into the national and patriotic vitals for years and years now.

Since the journalists may be considered the most vital and highly knowledgeable and intellectual in a dynamic democratic environment, it is most painful to see that they are divided into "us" and "they" or "our journalists, their journalists." Had the Awami journalists[25] been less staunchly Awami and had they maintained more patriotic neutrality and impartiality, the media community would have been more united and respected and would have enjoyed more popularity and public trust without being denigrated and accused of being "fake news" as Donald Trump keeps describing the American media, except perhaps the Fox. While all have the right to differ and disagree and all are entitled to their political leanings and likings, journalists are supposed to be more objective than partisan for the sake of their very profession and professional integrity, which is the case in the open and established democracies both in the East and the West.

Such a situation—popularly described as one of abysmal and unbridled politicization, criminalization and commercialization of all areas in the government and beyond—makes one recall the English revolutionary of the time of the French Revolution, John Thelwall (who was a friend of Wordsworth, Coleridge, and Godwin) and who was imprisoned and charged with treason, about to be hanged and finally freed. During a sleepless night in 1797, he described what he called the English "hypocrisy and intrigue," "the detestable system of persecuting opinions" and "the suppression of peaceable associations," thus:

> The dire pangs …
> Of deep corroding wrong
> Visions …
> That show this world a wilderness of wrongs,
> A waste of troubled waters, whelming floods
> Of tyrannous injustice … the tired foot
> Of persecuted virtue cannot find
> One spray on which to rest, or scarce one leaf
> To cheer with promise of subsiding woe.

Yet in another poem, Thelwall describes the sordid world of hatred, disappointed hopes, regrets, and miseries as "a world most scorpion-like/That stings what warms it, and the ardent glow/Of blessed benevolence too oft transmutes/To sullen gloom and sour misanthropy." Such poetical, political, and philosophical comments are precisely appropriate to what is happening in Bangladesh for years now—a split and divided nation, where dynasty, democracy, and development are conspiring against, not cooperating with, each other, to the point of turning the country into a failed and dysfunctional state.

Yet the people's hope and trust reside neither with the dangerously authoritarian AL and its continuing BAKSALite gagging acts nor the so-called third force consisting of some otherwise well-known but fence-sitting zero-sum fringe figures and public intellectuals. They include H M Ershad, Badrudduza Chowdhury, Kamal Hussein, ASM Rob, Kader Siddiquee, Nur-e-Alam Siddiquee, Mahmudur Rahman Manna, Khalequzzaman, Saiful Hoque, Nazmul Huda, and maybe a few others, all equally inconsequential. Those *discrete* political lone wolves are at the moment too myopic, shortsighted, and monolithic to be *discreet*, discerning, and discriminating to be able to join the BNP-led alliance for the greater interest of the country. Since no one is without a controversial past, all of them can get united and should get united, at least for the short term, for the common and higher goal of ousting the Awami regime. They should all put up a united front to launch an effective and coordinated movement, on a priority basis, to topple the autocratic Awami axis and its coteries as the first order of business for the benefit of the nation and the masses.

If Rudyard Kipling's impossibly idealistic poem "If" (full of first conditional "ifs") is their bible, those isolated zero-sum politicians would never be able to achieve anything: zero multiplied by anything being zero; zero plus zero plus zero also being zero, nothing more, nothing less. Hope and trust lies with the BNP-led alliance, which, in the current circumstances, represents the forces of good—patriotic, democratic, nationalist, and reformed—or, at the worst, the lesser of the two evils. It has reclaimed much of the traditional popular association between patriotism and political opposition. It has done so the way many (of both the secular and religious and both the aristocratic and working class backgrounds) did, for example, in the British culture of the age of wars, revolutions, and industrialization during 1776–1832.[26]

Throughout history, all parties, all systems, all societies have gone through their evolutionary or revolutionary reforms. Unfortunately, only Bangladesh is lagging behind, retreating backward into the chokehold plight and predicament, for which the AL and only the AL may be held responsible. All the BNP-led opposition leaders are either under arrest or the heavy weight of thousands of politically harassing lawsuits or are forced to stay in hiding. Unless the realistic and practically possible miracle of all the opposition parties united happens (like the survival stories of the Nobel Malala, Rana Plaza Reshma, and Sylheti Khadija), getting together and exploding in the streets, the BNP is likely to break up.

Others in the BNP-led opposition may opt to switch over to the government, as Barrister Nazmul Huda and some other elements have already done in stark betrayal. Translation and prediction: if all the opposition forces do not join hands, election in 2019 or at a time of Hasina's choosing may result in the foregone conclusion that the AL is going to return to power again and again and then forever or at least for the foreseeable future. As I have said in a poem of mine, "Beauty of that land: the reverse" (yet to be published in full):

> The greatest beauty of that land lies, however,
> Not in the too idealistic souls'
> Too simple neutrality
> And their third option advocacy
> But in the new and reformed, yet trusted views
> Of many a leader out of power
> United under one common banner
> (Reform being better than radical leveler),
> And their enlightened strategy, as necessary,
> On which has missed out, miserably,
> The ruling party, drowned in mayhem
> Drenched in partisan divide
> Drunk in power
> Corruption-ridden, openly,
> Paving the way for
> The opposition's winning popularity. (From a poem by the author)

Let me conclude with the assertive and hopeful words of the computer consultant Zoglul Husain, who participated in organizing the liberation struggle of Bangladesh from Kolkata in 1971 and who still remains a fervent and patriotic political activist in the UK. In an e-mail correspondence of February 13, 2015, he wrote:

> In spite of the present dark and dreary state of general demoralization, brought upon the nation in the main by the Awami-BAKSALi fascists and other obsequious minions of Indian hegemonists [...] the great hope is that [...] there are millions of patriots throughout Bangladesh. We need to unite, organize and mobilize them to defeat the heinous machinations of the Awami-BAKSALi fascists and their mentors, home and abroad. We are determined to defeat our adversaries, and achieve our goals in the end, come what may. The choice for us today is either becoming a foreign puppet colony, or valiantly carrying out the struggle for freedom, democracy, justice, human rights and harmonious development. We must all do our bits in this struggle, as permitted by our circumstances.

None can disagree with the above for the sake of social justice and human rights, which are being continuously violated and trampled down in Bangladesh, reaching the worst stage in the last few years under the Awami regime. When Saddam was still out there, ruling with iron hand, many Iraqis used to say, out of frustration, that no one, not even the Americans would ever be able to topple him; only God/*Allah* the Almighty could do so if He wanted to. The same (painful) opinion used to be held about Gaddafi, Hosni Mubarak, Zein al-Abedine, Sheikh Mujib, Duvalier, Idi Amin, Adolf Hitler, Benito Mussolini, Erich Honecker, Nicolai Ceausescu, and many other dictators. Their fate is now known to the world. Some of them like Zein al-Abedine, Duvalier, Idi Amin, and the Shah of Iran (who was being joked about as saying "I run from I-raan") had to run away for life. Bashar Al-Assad, Kim Jong Un, and Abdul Fattah Al-Sisi are awaiting their fate too. History, taking its own course, does fully or partially repeat itself from time to time. May the history of Bangladesh come full circle and start unraveling as it is hoped that the country would find a way out of the maiming maze and mutilating morass it has descended into, sooner rather than later, through a peaceful, if not violent means.

Again, the remote possibility of the Hasina government giving midterm polls is being heard about for more than two years now as the story of the BNP reorganizing itself and setting its own house in order is being heard about for as long. Whether midterm elections are held sooner or later or not at all, it does not really matter if the AL's police/RAB policy of repression and persecution continues unabated. Every single day the BNP and its wings and alliance leaders are being arrested. The Hasina-AL will announce elections, if at all, in its own terms and according to its own convenience. There may not be any free, fair, and universal suffrage. The AL government and its party leaders will make sure they can stage and repeat another January 5 or another April Fool city corporation election. They are doing everything they can to split the BNP, as Major (Ret) Akhtaruzzaman alleged by referring to some tall-talking sycophants or কালো বিড়াল (black cats) of the AL-alliance, or they are conspiring to predetermine the election outcome by giving the BNP a few সাদাকাহ (charity) seats—25–35.[27] A Kansas-based banker, college professor, and researcher-writer in social sciences and international affairs, Esam Sohail, wrote in Dhaka Tribune: "I am one of those many who consider the so-called election of January 5 to be an utter farce, and the government legitimated by it to be little more than an autocracy whose absolutist tendencies get stronger by the passing day." Later he predicted that the results of any future elections under this government would not be in doubt.

The issue of political/family dynasty

Battling the dynastically entrenched Hasina regime's courts of law, Khaleda's and Tarique's future is very uncertain. Here it is worth arguing that in the context of Bangladesh/South Asia, the tradition of dynastic politics, however nasty, may be dyed differently (like the same drink in the bottles of different shapes and colors) but will never die away in the foreseeable future. Perhaps it should not die away too soon either. While the Kennedys, the Bushes, the Clintons, the Trudeaus, the Gandhis, the Bhuttos, the Bandaranayakes, the Kims, and the Assads are only a similar, yet a much different story (in terms of building leadership through stages, democratically), dynasty in South Asia provides an easy compromise and an easy formula to keep a party together and win in the election. So it is not too bad. While practicing democracy within the party is difficult, it is not impossible.

However, the problem is, if a major party takes steps to democratize from within and thereby runs into the risk of disunity, the other party has only to gain if it does not do so, remaining as it is—undemocratic, yet strong. In electoral politics, tradition needs to be broken simultaneously by the major parties competing for power, as a matter of policy from within or without, so that no one stands to lose. For the time being, therefore, whether one likes it or not, there cannot be any AL (which, at every level, from national to local, is hundred times more family dynasty based than the BNP) without a Sheikh at the top; there can be no BNP without someone from the Zia family.[28] Dr Zubaidah Rahman is likely to enter politics soon to keep the BNP whole and intact in the absence of Khaleda and Tarique. Koko's wife Sharmila too should enter the fray. Hence my verses to them at the start of the book.

Ershad, Rawshon, and G M Quader have already made their party a family romance. While India and Pakistan are still within the fold of family circle, Sri Lanka has probably managed to come out of the ring after the Bandaranayakes. While monarchy may be bad, enlightened monarchy and benevolent dictatorship may not always be so. A reformed dynasty may not be either, at least for the time being. If Sheikh Hasina would have been a democratic minded and democratically elected leader with respect and tolerance for the opposition BNP, accommodating and compromising with the popular demands of the latter, there would not have been a problem. It is the circumstances and the style of government that would determine the future development of how the political parties are going to be structured and democratized from within.

Bangladesh needs special treatment, which lies, under the present circumstances, in a mix of political dynasty and democracy. As we all agree and understand, political dynasty cannot be an ideal situation or solution in the long run, but the ground reality in Bangladesh is such that political dynasty has proven to be the cure of many political ills. So it cannot be dismissed and written off right away. Time hasn't come yet to do so. One has to take a pragmatic/realistic approach in view of the fact that democracy in Bangladesh is not so well-developed that the necessity of political and family dynasty stands to be denied and discarded. Indeed, in the present context of Bangladesh and many other countries in the region, political dynasty is still a big factor, in fact, a crucial factor to keep the parties united, moving, and functioning. There can be nothing wrong if the dynasty is devoted and dedicated, popular with the people and delivering on the promises it projects. While the increasingly authoritarian AL has utterly failed, the by-now reformed/maybe already reformed BNP still remains a great hope and a great possibility for the people to further explore and experiment with.

As the political pundits say, dictatorship is the best form of government, provided it is benevolent, which is rarely the case, unfortunately. They also say, democracy is the worst form of government, but to date no other system, fortunately or unfortunately, has been found to be better. Therefore, in the political reality of Bangladesh, democracy and dynasty have to get along and go together for the foreseeable future. We do not have to be too idealistic and impractical to run after illusions and be impatient about dynastic politics so prematurely and so hastily. For now it is working fine in Bangladesh. The only thing is that it needs to be reformed and improved for the greater interest of the nation, which the BNP has been trying to do, while the AL has chosen the path of despotism and authoritarianism.

Ranu Chowdhury makes a good point when he says that "Dynastic and dictatorial rules may have been necessary evils at certain juncture of history for a nation, yet it cannot be preferred over pure democracy despite various inherent weaknesses in the system. A dictator or dynastic ruler can be benevolent when he/she follows democratic means to rule [...] It is the individual ruler, dynastic or dictator, that matters" (E-mail, December 4, 2016). In a message on the same day, Khoniker Othithee of the USA argues that there are bigger and more burning issues than dynasty in party politics, saying, "I know of no country that banned dynasty in party leadership. In democracy, people should have the choice to reject dynasty at polling booths through free and fair elections; that is the only retribution I can think of. There is no such thing yet on term limits on family members."

If the BNP is now an irrelevant "dying cow," which some say it is, it is because of the Awami brutality. If the BNP was not so until 2006, why is it or should it be now? It is primarily because of the Awami-BAKSALi neo-despotism and neo-fascism and its terror and torture, the sole cause for the BNP to be in doldrums. The Awami persecution of the BNP has known no bounds, far exceeding the suppression of the 2006–2008 Moinuddin Fakhruddin era. If both the AL and the BNP were in bad shape then, completely cowed down, why to expect the BNP to be in good shape now? When all the BNP leaders and supporters, top to bottom, are facing the egregious harassment of scores of court cases each, hiding or running between home and court and prison, how to talk about the collective leadership of the opposition party?

Democratization from the dire and stark situation of the Awami sand and cement blockades and barricades is next to impossible, if not nipped in the bud. When the AL does not even give the BNP the slightest space, how to start the process of democratization both in particular and in general? When there is no democracy at the state level, there cannot be any democratization at the party or local level. That would be like expecting, unrealistically, sweet mangoes from a sour tamarind tree. Already concerned about the ailing health of its party leader, her health further worsening due to the political repression both she and her number two (her own son Tarique) and all her party leaders are going through, Begum Zia's retiring or relinquishing her apex position now would only hasten the early demise of her party. Peaceful means are possible only under peaceful circumstances.

However, the only good news is that the BNP is hopefully trying to bring back the old stalwarts and maybe a few others in the like-minded opposition spectrum into the party or the alliance soon. Unless the Awami neo-and-near-and-more-than-partially fascist style changes into a clean and clear democratic style and unless the polls, midterm or otherwise, local or national, are made to be inclusive, participatory, and credible, it is going to be all the same—*jei lau shei kodu* (it is the same gourd whether one calls it "lau" or "kodu" in Bangla), *alu-gosh* or *gosh-alu* (it is the same curry whether it is beef and potato or potato and beef), or *jahai ekanno tahai bahanno* (what is fifty-one is at best fifty-two making little or no difference), to use local expressions in idioms and proverbs.

Until then, no amount of reorganization within the already knee-broken BNP (but still the largest political party in a nation of 160 million) will ever work—since its leaders and activists would continue to be detained, remanded, and put behind bars. "In the face of the existing neo-fascism by the AL," Ranu Chowdhury of the USA asserts, "the so-called inter-party democratization will be of little consequence. Rather, the fascist nemesis is likely to intensify its maligning tactics to score points to its advantage, the reality being that the opposition is not likely to see the light of the day anytime soon."

Recep Tayyip Erdogan versus Sheikh Hasina

The failed coup in Turkey on July 15, 2016 may have been both an irate irritation and a welcome relief to Sheikh Hasina—relief because the coup failed, sending a warning message to Hasina's military against such adventurism, and an irritation because the Islamically minded and extremely popular Erdogan managed to put down the coup and remain in power. There is no love lost between them, who differ on a number of political issues, including Hasina's controversial hanging of those Islamic leaders who she thinks were war criminals long ago, even though they were once her bosom friends against both Ershad and Khaleda (as Fethullah Gulen was once to Erdogan). Hasina is the head of an "unelected," "non-elected," "semi-elected" and "pseudo-elected" and, therefore, "illegitimate" government, whereas Erdogan is the head of a duly elected, legitimate, popular government. There is a promotion of Indian Hindu-influenced sectarianism, communalism, and hegemonic colonialism rather than "secularism" (India being a highly sectarian and communal country under the cover of secularism) at the expense of democratic freedom and free and fair elections in Hasina's police country of Bangladesh, but there is a promotion of Sunni Islamic and nationalistically compatible democracy in Erdogan's model Turkey.

Erdogan survived the coup because he and the cause of Islamism he champions and espouses had the support of his people, in masses and millions. His popularity can only be a dream or an envy for the terrifying, tyrannical, and terrorizing Hasina. Would she and her pro-Hindu and pro-Indian "sectarian" rather than "secularist" stance survive if she were to face such a plot, however imaginary and hypothetical that may be, although her once deputy Syed Ashraful Islam keeps alerting the nation about such a possibility, which he says could not be easily dismissed? Does Hasina have the support of the masses and millions, except the police/RAB and other special unit (RAW-cooked and RAW-made) messiahs from India?[29] Hasina should better return to a democratic rule and declare a national election soon—to be free and fair, inclusive and participatory, of course—a rule in which the police/RAB would not be a *thola* (an enemy of the people) but, like the Turkish forces under the great and glorious Erdogan, friends and comrades to the people (that is, *Arkadas*, in Turkish).

What the hugely popular Erdogan has done (and done rightly) after the failed coup, that is, rounding up the plotters and conspirators, is being done by the extremely unpopular Hasina every day without an end. She has been detaining tens of thousands of innocent democratic opposition leaders and activists, taking them to court on countless lawsuits of political cooking and concoction, leaving the field empty of opposition activists and leaving the opposition leaders breathtakingly busy running back and forth between the court and the home, so that she thinks she could avoid any untoward incident threatening her position due to the fact that there is a lack of mandate and legitimacy on her part and for her government. If and when Hasina returns to a responsible, reliable, and transparent rule, including a true, real, and actual (not fake) election, no new government would have to undertake any Turkish-style purge.

The situations in Turkey and Bangladesh are not the same. The actions of the democratically elected Erdogan, enjoying a popular mandate, have been warranted and called for, whereas those of the "unelected" and "illegitimate" Hasina with no military attempt ever to overthrow her and therefore to justify her unwarranted and uncalled-for actions against the opposition are nothing short of being proto-fascist. If Hasina and her cohorts and compatriots can have more of Indian-and-Hindu-tinged "secularism" and less Islamism and less democracy, why can't one prioritize Islamism and downgrade (Indian-and-Hindu-informed) secularism and democracy too? Erdogan is walking a fine line between all these three and has had a mighty triumph. Let Islamism take an upper hand through him at the expense of a bit of the other two, whatever that means in the modern world of 2017.

If Hasina and the like-minded can be friends with the anti-Muslim and anti-Kashmir India, which keeps killing Muslims and Bangladeshis every day, why can't others be in rapport with Israel, though (sadly) Palestinian-killing, but friends with the entire West as well as Saudi Arabia, Egypt, Jordan, and Turkey? Although one does not have to buy into the formulaic solutions like A = B, B = C, so A = C, one cannot deny their logic either. Politics makes strange bedfellows, there being no permanent friends but only permanent interests. All Sunni Arabs, all Iranians, all Shiites, and all the West up to Vladimir Putin's Russia abandoned the Syrian plight letting the butcher Bashar kill and displace millions over the last several years. Erdogan tried to help but he alone could not do much except sheltering a majority of those displaced in his own country. He has to fight the separatist Kurds at home, who are supported by all the rest to destabilize his Turkey. Now he has to fight against certain sections of his own military, who are supported by some international players, again to dislodge him.

Let the great Islamic-minded Erdogan do as necessary to give Islam and Islamic culture a footing as a legacy of the great Ottoman Empire amid the hostile Islamophobia of all the neighboring and international foes. What would have happened if he didn't survive the coup? That would have been a disaster for the Muslim world and the Muslims' feelings of pride and dignity. They are looking up to him to provide an Islamically oriented political leadership in the modern world in the face of Islam-bashing secularism. If the Hasina-led Bangladesh of police rule and reign can promote the secularism of anti-Islamic and pro-Hindu bias in a highly controlled, guided, and regimented environment, a rise of Islam and Islamic culture is always welcome in a Muslim majority country, even if that means somewhat limited or illiberal democracy.

In view of Ranu Chowdhury,

> Hasina is no Erdogan. Erdogan is a nationalist; his country's interests are supreme in all his actions and considerations—be that Islamic values, Turkish pride, public sentiments, democracy, or national security. Erdogan may be a little dictatorial when it comes to protecting national interests, but there were no credible evidences that he rigged election process to be in power. Nor did he carry out large scale oppression to his political opponents, other than those needed for national integrity and security. Hasina's dictatorial records and political oppression will put most other such records to shame [...] Besides, Hasina's popularity is marginal to very low; that is the reason she is afraid to face a fair and participatory national election. (E-mail post of July 25, 2016)

An action has an equal and opposite reaction. Instead of being moderate and balanced, the Shah took the Shiite Iran too far in the direction of the Wild West, hence the Shiite revolution under Ayatollah Ruhullah Khomeni in 1979. Sunni Islamic-minded Erdogan has been elected leader of Turkey through free and fair elections, not like Hasina's theatrical farce jointly staged by her enemy turned close crony Ershad and Rawshon, let alone the actors of the earlier farce, Fakhruddin, Moinuddin, and Masududdin. However, Erdogan's foes in the form of Western secularist liberals wanted to stab him in the back, so they got to pay a price. Erdogan's Sunni Islamic Turkey, still moderate and balanced, needs the peace loving people's uncritical support, both in Turkey and beyond. Since no democracy is perfect, Eastern or Western, and all democracies are made with some local color, Turkish democracy, under Erdogan, like Trump's, Netanyahu's, Mahathir's, Modi's, and Putin's, needs a chance to survive and succeed by overcoming the concerted foreign conspiracies to disturb and destabilize it.

Erdogan's wholesale purging, if true, is for the great cause of the democratic majority of the Turkish people and the greater cause of Sunni Islam in the face of the rising Iranian, Syrian, Lebanese, and Iraqi Shiite Islam and also the liberal/Western God-less secularism all around. One needs to stand for Sunni Islam or Shiite Islam? Rise or demise of Sunni Islam? While one condemns Putin's and Bashar's wholesale killing of Syrian civilians in the strongest terms, one also knows politics unfortunately makes strange bedfellows, from Hasina and Inu and Motia and Ershad to Erdogan and Putin. In the case of Erdogan, he thinks he has no choice but to stand up to America and the West by standing with Putin's Russia, which, by the way, has traditionally demonstrated a soft corner for the Palestinians against the Israelis.

Case by case. Which makes one support Putin's annexation of Crimea. Crimea mostly speaks Russian and feels brotherly with Russia. It never belonged to any country forever. Sometimes it was independent, sometimes it was with Ukraine, sometimes with Turkey, and sometimes with Russia. It changed hands many times, back and forth. I would support Putin taking the Russian speaking eastern parts of Ukraine too. The majority there want to be with mother Russia. So why not, language, culture, and religion all being the same and the rejoining being the popular demand and desire of the eastern Ukrainians, like the Koreans in the South and the North?

Individuals are separate from institutions. In the case of Erdogan, he is trying to increase the power of the institution of Turkish presidency through a democratic mandate for the sake of the stability of his Sunni Muslim country in the face of both Eastern and Western efforts to destabilize it. But in the case of Hasina, it is a power drunk Awami individual who wants to stay in power not by a democratic mandate but by playing an Indian puppet. Trump in his own way and Erdogan in his own way got elected through free and fair elections, which have become a far cry in Hasina's police state.

Conclusion

Owing to Hasina's harsh measures, opposition leader Khaleda Zia and her son and deputy Tarique Rahman (who is in exile in London for a long time) have been effectively deactivated and incapacitated. The Hasina government-turned-regime poses a grim and grave prospect for democratic freedom and politics. Strangulated as they are, there are hardly any chances for fair freedom and dazzling democracy to be revived and reactivated. The obvious reasons are tyranny, torture, threat, and tell-tale treason.

Also, today's situation in Bangladesh is different from the 1980s when the entire people led by Khaleda and Hasina were together against the minority military rule of Ershad. Now the popular and democratic Khaleda and Tarique are alone facing the authoritarian Hasina and the autocratic Ershad together and their politicized court and the more politicized police. There are the Hasina-Ershad-Rawshon joint masque-cum-pantomime theater and the Hasina-and-the-other small and inconsequential splinter elements forming a common front in a political marriage of power-and-profit-sharing convenience, opportunism, and coterie and personal interests, popularly known as predatory লুটেরা ভাগ বাটোয়ারা হালুয়া রুটি politics, phrases aptly coined by the seemingly ideological leftist outfits.[30]

What dirty and dubious, maligning and malicious, and vilifying and villainous propaganda the popular and democratically committed Khaleda and Tarique are facing today should not have been faced by them at all in a polity of minimum sanity, balance, and civility. Had there been a politically level playing field, they could keep on fighting, in a sane and civilized way, against the prevalent and prejudiced Awami menace, misrule and mismanagement. There is a serious lack of democratic space as well as of individual and associational freedoms, which have been completely clipped and cropped and curtailed by the Hasina regime.

As the leaders of not only their own party BNP but also the entire range of opposition that counts cool and matters most in the whole country, Khaleda and Tarique have been rendered totally isolated and incapable/incapacitated by the regime's judicial and police strangulation with an active support from the neighboring India. Therefore, there cannot be any change in the government of Bangladesh unless there heralds, on the horizon, a magical miracle or an act of Almighty God, including a change of heart in Hasina for the better, to be immaculately welcomed by the masses in and millions.

So, let there be a political pied piper (or many and multitude of the same indeed) to free the country from its political rats and worms and insects and drain it of its dire and deadly political Zika, Ebola, and Chikungunya viruses, if necessary, even at the expense of a terrible loss to make things work as it happens in the old German legend originating in the town of Hamelin!

Notes

1. www.uio.no/studier/emner/hf/ikos/SAS1503/v05/Bangladesh.doc
2. http://newagebd.net/184102/keep-country-safe-from-bnp-jamaat-hyenas-pm/; http://www.thedailystar.net/politics/democracy-exiled-khaleda-186622
3. http://newsorgan24.com/detail/13136; http://www.sheershanewsbd.com/2015/10/25/101328; http://newagebd.net/174271/calling-a-spade-a-spade-cannot-be-a-crime/
4. General Ataul Gani Osmani, Commander-in-Chief of the Liberation Forces of Bangladesh in 1971, and Barrister Mainul Hossein, Editor-in-Chief of the Daily Ittefaq, were the rare and bold instances of resignation from the Parliament in protest of the formation of the gagging BAKSAL. Nur-e-Alam Siddiquee, another courageous voice, made long and loud speeches in the Parliament criticizing the BAKSAL.

All three were of Mujib's own party, the AL. Two opposition members, Abdullah Shorkar and Moinuddin Manik, had to lose their Parliamentary seats due to their unwillingness to join the BAKSAL. For a bitter criticism of the highly undemocratic and unpopular BAKSAL, see today's AL minister, Abul Mal Abdul Muhith's *বাংলাদেশ:পুনর্গঠন ও জাতীয় ঐকমত্য* Bangladesh: Reconstruction and National Consensus), UPL, 1991, pp. 6–10.

5. For the AL's Capt. Mansour Ali and Tofail Ahmed-led *Rakkhi-Bahini*'s India connection and its killing of about 30,000 Bangladeshis, see http://en.wikipedia.org/wiki/Jatiya_Rakkhi_Bahini. Also see the famous Bangladeshi writer Humayun Ahmed's edited and posthumously published last novel, *Deyal* (Wall), *Annyo Prokash*, February 2013, pp. 85–96.
6. The rapacious profiteering practices of the British East India Company during the early 1770s caused a famine during which three million Bengalis died, reducing the population of Bengal by a third. While then British PM Robert Walpole did not condone the famine, British PM Winston Churchill during World War II not only supported but in fact caused the 1943 Bengal famine mainly because of the Bengali nationalist Subhas Chandra Bose's ill-conceived plans for the independence of India with the armed help of Japan, Italy, and Germany, the story of this famine being the basis/background of the disturbing film *Ashoni Sanket* by Satyajit Ray. Subhas Chandra Bose, now Netaji, was partly responsible for the 1943 Bengal famine. Without being adequately prepared, he broke away from and alienated the other Indian leaders and went for an armed struggle for the independence of India with the help of the Japanese (indirectly, Hitler and Mussolini). Cruel Churchill accordingly took revenge by taking away all the foodstuff from Bengal to feed his army and having the people of Bengal starve to death. Like the cruel and heartless Aung San Suu Kyi, Churchill's 1953 Nobel Prize for Literature should be posthumously taken away, if possible. In connection with the famine, please read:
   (1) http://www.genocidebangladesh.org/1974-famine-an-unfashionable-tragedy-by-john-pilger/;
   (2) http://xa.yimg.com/kq/groups/16006544/1575541575/name/PROFESSOR+AMARTYA+SEN+AND+THE+1974+BANGLADESH+FAMINE.pdf; (3) https://www.amarblog.com/ehhamida/posts/93256; (4) https://www.facebook.com/notes/hidden-truth/196539497043836/; Also, Ahmad Safa's writings at: https://www.facebook.com/kay.kavus/posts/458498014332088; http://www.bbc.com/bengali/multimedia/2011/12/111228_sg_bd40_famine.shtml
7. For the Wikileaks information and other details about the national and international (Indian RAW) conspiracy, including the role or involvement of the Hasina government and her AL behind how and why the BDR officers were killed, see (1) http://bdrmutinyexposed.com/?p=353;
   (2) http://bdrmutinyexposed.com/?p=407;
   (3) http://probasebangladesh.com/2015.02.25.25633.html;

(4) https://groups.yahoo.com/neo/groups/mukto-mona/conversations/topics/64384;
(5) http://www.labanglatimes.com/news/details/National/1133?fb_comment_id=900361303318564_900712296616798;
(6) http://www.telegraph.co.uk/news/worldnews/asia/bangladesh/4982518/Bangladeshi-army-officers-blame-prime-minister-for-mutiny.html;
(7) https://bangladesh2075.files.wordpress.com/2011/02/bdr4.pdf; (8) https://bangladesh2075.wordpress.com/2011/02/23/bdr/;
(9) http://newagebd.net/205703/bdr-mutiny-victims-families-demand-tracing-plotters/; (10) http://ziacyberforce.com BDR; (11) http://www.first-bd.net/newsdetail/detail/49/192388; (12) http://www.bdzindabad.com/news/post/798; http://www.bdzindabad.com/news/post/795; (13) Major (Ret) Ashfaque's comments at https://www.youtube.com/watch?v=fesZF4MYT2E; (14) for Dr Tuhin Malik's views about what he calls a premeditated massacre, see: http://www.natun-bd.net/newsdetail/detail/49/286604; (15) https://www.theguardian.com/world/2009/feb/28/bangladesh-soldiers-rebellion-mutiny; (16) for the Indian journalist and columnist Sunita Paul's views, see: http://blackfebruary25.blogspot.com/2009/04/another-article-of-sunita-paul.html; (17) https://www.facebook.com/ibrahim.bnpnews?fref=nf; https://www.facebook.com/photo.php?fbid=1569825790003543&set=a.1410694752583315.1073741828.100009284122418&type=3; and (18) Mohammad Zainal Abedin, *BDR Massacre: Target Bangladesh* (2009) and a review of the book by M T Hussain (https://uglyduckblog.wordpress.com/2013/02/25/a-book-review-bdr-massacre-target-bangladesh/). For the secret video of the BDR mutiny, watch https://www.youtube.com/watch?v=-5Oh4TIAN8o; https://www.facebook.com/photo.php?fbid=10153887542482158&set=gm.587699231378418&type=3&theater; https://www.facebook.com/photo.php?fbid=10153887542482158&set=gm.587699231378418&type=3; https://www.facebook.com/btpnews247/videos/804609452972874/. For the BDR questioning Sheikh Hasina and Moin U Ahmed, watch https://www.youtube.com/watch?v=cuyIJrLfRy0. For a list of the officers killed and other related information, see Shafik Rehman's book, মৃত্যুদন্ড/ Death Sentence or Capital Punishment (http://www.dailynayadiganta.com/detail/news/52741). For an investigative report about the RAW/Indian involvement in the BDR massacre, see http://www.shomoyershathe.com/. For the bloody violence inside the BDR officers' quarters and the related business of Moin Uddin Ahmed's Indian horses, watch http://www.youtube.com/watch?v=uFlqZhc1IQk; http://www.youtube.com/watch?v=cb-er6F9DqE

8. For the graphic images of the brutal massacre, visit: http://chairmanbd.blogspot.com.au/2013/05/mass-killing-on-protesters-in-dhaka-at.html;
http://www.amardeshonline.com/pages/details/2013/05/07/199017;
http://defence.pk/threads/indian-backed-awami-league-massacre-%E2%80%93-satkhira-bangladesh-turned-into-dead-valley.294460/page-4

9 Shuvo Sikder, son of Comrade Seraj Sikder, associates bank loot with the Sheikh family: http://www.prothombangladesh.net/news/15904. Joseph Allchin writes about "The high-flying cyberscam … the routine plunder of Bangladesh's financial system, including by some of its purported guardians." Visit: http://www.nytimes.com/2016/04/12/opinion/bangladeshs-other-banking-scam.html?smprod=nytcore-iphone&smid=nytcore-iphone-share. For the statement by Shuvro Sikder, son of Seraj Sikder, see: http://www.prothombangladesh.net/article/15904; for Sajjad Husain Khan's details on the corruption, see: http://www.dailysangram.com/news_details.php?news_id=228209; for other incriminating reports, see:

- http://mzamin.com/article.php?mzamin=4783;
- http://www.reuters.com/article/us-bangladesh-bank-idUSKCN0W91RY;
- http://www.first-bd.net/newsdetail/detail/200/196105;
- http://www.ittefaq.com.bd/national/2016/03/17/59978.html;
- http://onlinebangla.com.bd/post/16012;
- http://www.amadershomoys.com/unicode/2016/03/13/81919.htm;
- http://www.prothom-alo.com/economy/article/796810/l;
- http://www.prothombangladesh.net/article/15850; and
- www.nbcnews.com/tech/tech-news/how-hacker-s-typo-helped-stop-billion-dollar-bank-heist-n536526

10. For a short list of the Awami League's evil and atrocious misdeeds during a period of five years only, see http://www.first-bd.net/blog/blogdetail/detail/1919/malamgir/35314#.VvEN1jFDT74
11. https://www.youtube.com/watch?v=hFQttBV3yNQ
12. https://www.youtube.com/watch?feature=player_embedded&v=MSSt_AWm-IY
13. See the "Bangladeshi Nationalism" Chapter for the details of the agreement. Journalist Oliullah Noman of the now suppressed popular Amar Desh, now living in exile in the UK, wrote about this 7-point agreement and Kalidas Baiddya: https://www.rbn24.co.uk/?p=6353. Also, Rifat-ul-Ahsan, *India-Bangladesh Relations : after 1971* at http://defenceforumindia.com/forum/threads/india-bangladesh-relations.4411/

14 For the liberation war time enmity and distrust between Tajuddin Ahmad and BLF/Mujib-Bahini led by Sheikh Moni, Tofael Ahmad, Abdur Razzak and Serajul Alam Khan, see http://tajuddinahmad.com/banga-babdhu-tajuddin-and-bangladesh-by-major-general-amin-ahmed-chowdhury-bir-protik; and Nurul Kabir's *Politics of history and history of politics: On partisan narratives of Bangladesh's liberation war*—XI, http://newagebd.net/80236/politics-of-history-and-history-of-politics-10/. In this respect see the article by Mahmudur Rahman Manna: http://www.dainikamadershomoy.com/2014/10/19/172754.html

15. Watch Dr Asif Nazrul on this at https://youtu.be/7zfyU8nVEpI
16. Sheikh Mujib was killed by some members of the army with the help of many top-ranking members of his own party, who took over after him and who memorably

made extremely damaging, derogatory, and disgraceful comments about him justifying his assassination the way Brutus and Cassius justified the assassination of Julius Caesar. According to *Wikipedia, the Free Encyclopedia* (http://en.wikipedia.org/wiki/Father _of_the_Nation), "The title 'Father of the Nation' is sometimes politically contested. The 1972 Constitution of Bangladesh declared Sheikh Mujibur Rahman to be 'father of the nation.' The BNP government removed this in 2004, to the protest of the then opposition AL, led by Rahman's daughter Sheikh Hasina," who in turn does hardly recognize, to the chagrin of the BNP, the exceptionally bright and glorious role of Gen. Ziaur Rahman. As a result, both sides are deadlocked in their long simmering rivalries and continue to question, challenge, undermine, and even vilify the life and career of the two leaders.

17. Barrister Mainul Hussein, a prominent lawyer and a bold, neutral, and impartial political analyst who courageously championing the cause of true freedom and democracy, has recently gone on record arguing for the slogan of "Joy Bangladesh" as opposed to "Joy Bangla," in confirmation of the geographically demarcated territory that defines and determines the entity and existence of the sovereign and independent Bangladesh. Hussein is a son of the even more prominent journalism personality—Tofazzal Hussein alias Manik Mia—who fought for democratic freedom and independence all his life and as such was a lifelong associate of Sheikh Mujibur Rahman.
18. In a press club meeting on March 15, 2015, former President B. Chawdhury said that Hasina exceeded even Hitler and Mussolini in her despotism. Former Prime Minister Kazi Zafar Ahmad leveled a similar charge: http://www.sheershanewsbd.com/2015/07/10/88221#
19. http://newagebd.net/83246/24-trucks-parked-as-khaledas-confinement-continues/
20. http://www.thedailystar.net/politics/pm-slams-khaleda-calling-election-officials-people-%E2%80%98dogs%E2%80%99-199474;
    http://www.sheershanewsbd.com/2016/07/18/135321;
    "The Electoral farce in Banglades the minus-one solution: The government prepares for a charade."—The Economist, http://www.economist.com/blogs/banyan/2014/01/electoral-farce-bangladesh;
    http://www.eastasiaforum.org/2014/02/09/democracys-no-show-at-bangladeshs-elections;
    http://www.economist.com/news/asia/21593476-sheikh-hasina-plans-hang-office-after-electoral-farce-another-beating
21. http://www.thedailystar.net/bangladesh-14th-most-corrupt-country-53165; www.news-bangla.net/newsdetail/detail/41/306588; www.news-bangla.net/videohighlightdetail/detail/6940; http://www.banglanews24.com/fullnews/bn/471976.html; http://www.bbc.com/bengali/news/2016/03/160307_bangladesh_bank_hacking; http://www.ittefaq.com.bd/national/2016/03/07/58620.html; http://banglamail24.com/news/137962

22. http://newagebd.net/201425/judiciary-on-the-verge-of-collapse-says-justice-mahmudul-amin/; http://www.daily-sun.com/post/112432/Govt-controlling-judiciary http://www.amardeshonline.com/pages/details/2016/02/06/322373#; https://www.google.com/search?q=War+crime+imbroglio%3A+Road+to+Islamabad+runs+through+Delhi+Shahid+Islam; http://www.amadershomoys.com/newsite/2015/07/10/345324.htm#; http://www.sheershanewsbd.com/2015/07/16/88848#
23. http://www.sheershanewsbd.com/2015/11/10/103303
24. Dr K M A Malik details some stark human rights violations in Bangladesh at http://southasiajournal.net/state-of-human-rights-in-bangladesh-k-m-a-malik/; for the mass killing at the Hefajote Islam gathering, see http://chairmanbd.blogspot.com.au/2013/05/mass-killing-on-protesters-in-dhaka-at.html; https://www.youtube.com/watch?v=dOKaHc5VbUA&oref=http%3A%2F%2Fwww.youtube.com%2Fwatch%3Fv%3DIBwshK6xQO4&has_verified=1
25. Iqbal Sobhan Chowdhury, Subhas Singh Roy, Golam Sarwar, Abed Khan, (late) Abidur Rahman, Z. E. Mamun, Manjurul Ahsan Bulbul, Mozammel Babu, Manzurul Islam Manju, Pranab Saha Apu, Mozammel Hussein Manju, Manzurul Alam Panna, (late) Altaf Mahmud, Naimul Islam Khan, Munni Shaha, Noim Nizam, Pir Habib, Shamol Dutt, Shaban Mahmud, Shafiqur Rahman, and Anjan Roy, among others. For some details on Mamun, click: http://dailybdtimes.com/2017/06/18/রাজাকার-পুত্র-জ-ই-মামুন-টে/; www.sheershakhobor.com/2017/07/04/খালেদা-জিয়ার-বাসায়-মদ-আর-ফ/; https://www.facebook.com/mimhasansp/?hc_ref=PAGES
26. For instance, Richard Price, Tom Paine, William Blake, Lord Byron, Sir Francis Burdett, Percy Shelley, Charles James Fox, Mary Anne Clarke, Lord Holland, Henry Brougham, William Hazlitt, Leigh Hunt, Thomas Clarkson, Joseph Johnson, William Wilberforce, and many others. Discounting the radicalism of some of the working class leaders such as William Cobbett, Horne Tooke, Thomas Spence and William Benbow, it is the profound liberal and humanitarian reform elements in most of them that need to be taken into account in our context.
27. http://www.amadershomoys.com/newsite/2015/07/22/354748.htm#
28. In this respect, see a nice article at https://www.facebook.com/minar.rashid/posts/492238867643216
29. Mohammad Zainal Abedin of New York has written extensively on the matter. See, for example, http://banews24.com/national2/13553-india-let-loose-terror-to-bag-benefits-from-unstable-bangladesh.html; http://banews24.com/whole-country2/13552
30. For the details of Justice Enayetur Rahim, who passed on a verdict against Tarique, visit http://www.desh-bd.net/newsdetail/detail/200/229176

6

The Chiefs and Their *Uddinization* of the 2006–2008 Caretaker Government

Once upon a time there were four *Uddins*. They came and left the political scene of Bangladesh as the plot of a folk or fairy tale unfolds. They came all of a sudden, though not so unexpected, and when they left the scene after a couple of years, they started "living happily ever after," as they of course lived before. They have been rewarded, directly or indirectly, by their beneficiaries, the Awami regime, who came to power with their help.[1] Except the old and infirm one, who must be living happily in the hereafter, all the *Uddins* are living pretty "happily ever after." Their fate is luckily unlike what pitifully happened to the historical hypocrites and notorious betrayers: the 1757 traitor Mir Jaffar (Ali Khan Bahadur) of Bengal and his other traitor followers; the last Mughal emperor (Mirza Abu Zafar Sirajuddin Muhammad) Bahadur Shah Zafar, though of neutral to pro-Hindu and pro-British sympathies in Delhi in 1857; and Lhendup Dorji of Sikkim National Congress in the 1970s, all having lived an ignominious life and died an ignoble and pitiful death after their infamous betrayals and stark violations of trust.

The *Uddins* are fortunate that they as yet did not have to face the tragic fate of the jealous and treacherous Meherunnesa (Ghaseti) Begum in the palace coup of the time (1757), nor of the one called Netra Sen, who betrayed the heroic Surjo Sen to the British soldiers in 1933. However, as a retired army officer living in the USA commented, when the true history of Bangladesh will be written, the *Uddins* will be consigned to historic garbage with disdain, the way Mir Jaffar and his other followers in (Muslim, Hindu, and Sikh) traitor kings, courtiers, generals, wealthy merchants, and rival cousins are known today (see Note #7). All those traitors are now nowhere compared with the heroic and patriotic Nawab Mirza Muhammad Sirajuddowla, Haider Ali, Tipu Sultan, arguably the Nizams, certainly Surjo Sen of Chittagong, Nurul Din of Rangpur, and many others.

To start with the main plot, since the early days of 1/11, following the Awami League (AL)'s murderous লগি ও বৈঠা (sticks and poles and oars) battle,[2] both the former army chief General Moin U Ahmed (Uddin#1)[3] and the former chief adviser Fakhruddin Ahmed (Uddin#2) seemed to have taken sides in the majority of their actions and statements.[4] They had with them the senile and imbecile and second-childhood former President Iajuddin Ahmed (Uddin#3) and the behind-the-scene player former army officer Masududdin Ahmed (Uddin#4). Had the pro-AL and highly controversial Justice Shamsuddin Chowdhury been there (like the even more controversial Justice Khairul Hoque, both criticized for their biased or preferential judicial role), Shamsuddin would have probably been Uddin#5.

However, apart from being an administration of torture and corruption,[5] the two-year rule of the four infamous *Uddins* has been termed a rule of brute law by Justice Sharif Uddin Chaklader (finally, a great Uddin!), who also suggested that the succeeding Awami government was indeed the most undemocratic government, cut off and isolated from the people, out of touch with the masses.[6] The CTG *Uddins*' preferential treatment of a certain political side did not fail to invite trouble for the nation as a whole as it did not fail to do so for themselves as well. While collectively the group of the *Uddins* were hailed for taking a few steps with the intention of containing corruption and cleaning up the old mess and should have, therefore, gone on bringing the country back on track and making arrangements for holding a national election at their earliest convenience, some of their actions and opinions, especially with respect to Sheikh Mujibur Rahman and the AL, were not regarded as neutral and impartial.

As an army-backed interim CTG, there was no need for them to open the old political debates by touching on something that should have been better left untouched. The prescription by the two chiefs (Uddin#1 & Uddin#2) about the recognition of Sheikh Mujib as the father of the nation was not taken to be a right measure toward forging a national unity, at least not then under those circumstances. It did not cure the abysmal corrosive national disease of corruption and intolerance they thought it would excepting the fact that the *uddinized* CTG-recognition of Sheikh Mujib was very welcome to the AL, only one of the two major parties. Like the 2013 mini *shorkar* (government) of the *Shahbug* youths and their "Joy Bangla" slogan, the *Uddins* obviously wanted to please the party of Sheikh Mujib's often bragging, boastful, bellicose, and belligerent daughter Sheikh Hasina, electorally (if not characteristically and temperamentally) a deep and dark and violent BNP*hobe*. They wanted to do so by their politically motivated actions and keep their transitional government going as long as they could. The *Uddins* were supposed to be impartial and neutral; they should not have alienated other parties and should not have risked losing the balanced and unbiased character a care-taker government always had and was expected to maintain by all means.

If the *Uddins* were personally enthusiastic about Sheikh Mujib's father-of-the-nation status—a status that had to be granted him by a law passed by the AL, a historically unprecedented and controversial way of proclaiming one as the father of the nation—, they as CTG members should not have made their personal enthusiasm public. Ironically, all four *Uddins* rose to the height of their career on the most direct and open blessings bestowed upon them in the pre-1/11 days by the BNP, the other major party. Once they were there at the helm, they turned their back to and on the BNP, who, for political as well as ideological reasons, were (and are still) opposed to granting such (singular) status to Sheikh Mujib. Their betrayal was as sour and bitter as Shakespeare implies in a song in *As You Like It*: "Blow, blow, thou winter wind,/ Thou are not so unkind/ As man's ingratitude:/ Thy tooth is not so keen,/ Because thou art not seen ..." Or, as Sir Samuel Garth said, "Ingratitude's a weed of every clime,/ It thrives too fast at first, but fades in time."

Starting with (1) Nawab Sirajuddowla, the last independent ruler of Bengal, succeeded by his traitor army chief Mir Jaffar (who was Sirajuddowla's immediate predecessor and his grandfather Nawab Alivardi Khan's sister's husband) in a historic betrayal in favor of his (Mir Jaffar's) atrocious benefactor Major General Robert Clive of the East India Company, causing the loss of the independence of Bengal to the British in 1757 (Jaffar himself being later ill-treated by his beneficiary British)[7]; (2) Bahadur Shah Jaffar, the last Mughal emperor, who betrayed his fellow Muslims to favor the British and the Hindus, who in turn betrayed him; (3) Surjo Sen, who was betrayed by Netra Sen (who was in turn beheaded by a fellow revolutionary of Surya Sen's) and was to be brutally tortured before being hanged by British soldiers in Chittagong (now Bangladesh) in 1933; and then (4) the small Himalayan kingdom of Sikkim (now an Indian state and home to Kangchenjunga, the world's third-highest peak) being betrayed by its own son Kazi Lhendup Dorji Khangsarpa (1904–2007), who became its first chief minister (1974–1979) as he let his motherland to be annexed by India—treasonous betrayals and harsh-and-hyper hypocrisies are not uncommon in the history of the region, including Bangladesh, not to speak of what happened to Kashmir, Goa, and Hyderabad in the 1940s and what may be in the offing for Nepal, Bhutan, Maldives, and Bangladesh.

Sheikh Mujib was betrayed by members of his own party, including his army chief K M Shafiullah, who is now a close ally, ironically, of Mujib's own daughter and the current Prime Minister Sheikh Hasina. The Supreme Court of Bangladesh called Shafiullah a "liar and coward general" for his failure to order his forces into action to save the life of Sheikh Mujibur Rahman.[8] One may argue that Shafiullah did not actually betray. By his own admission, he was helpless when he found that the whole army was supportive of the August 15 coup with the result that the people came out in the streets rejoicing or feeling a sigh of relief at the fall of Mujib at a time when they thought Mujib's rule completely deteriorated into the repressive and dictatorial one-party BAKSAL.

Interestingly, it is the same "coward" Shafiullah, under criticism for his August 15 controversial role from some Awami leaders (particularly Sheikh Fazlul Karim Selim), who has recently found a low cover for his earlier cowardly role. In his convenient and crafty style to remain close to the Supreme Hasina, Shafiullah called his senior peer and cohort and much decorated freedom fighter, much older, A. K. Khandoker, as somebody less than a freedom fighter for writing a book every detail of which did not necessarily conform to the partisan line of the pro-Hasina narrative.[9]

Both Shafiullah and Khandoker played quite a similar role during the turn of events around August 15, especially in siding with the forces of the rebellion for which, from time to time, they came under fire—friendly fire through. Over the years they changed, like winds, and closed ranks with the AL. Although Khandoker's book is pretty neutral and nonpartisan, Shafiullah, in tune with Sheikh Selim, in an effort to save and shield himself from Selim's wrath and cozy up to the supreme Awami leader Hasina, was now attacking him (Khandoker) for not being blindly loyal to what PM Hasina would love to see and was trying to revoke the liberation forces' second-in-command Khandoker's freedom fighter status.

President Zia was betrayed by his fellow freedom fighters serving in the army, including his army chief H M Ershad (who, however, was not a freedom fighter). Zia appointed him in that position and promoted him to the rank of lieutenant general in 1978. It is widely believed that Indian Intelligence RAW and Ershad had a hand in the assassination of Zia in 1981.[10] That RAW and Ershad were involved in the deadly coup against Zia is claimed by Maj Gen (Ret) Amin Ahmed Chowdhury (in his book, *1971 and My Military Life*) as well as Nazma Mustafa.[11] However, in contrast with the hush and quiet and peace and silence that attended the death of Sheikh Mujib, more than two million people gathered to mourn the death of Zia. The AL betrayed the BNP by joining hands with Ershad in 1995–1996, although they both fought together against Ershad in 1990s. The AL alleges that it was betrayed, "subtly," if not openly, by those two CTG chiefs during whose terms it lost the national parliamentary elections, just as the BNP alleges the same, though more mildly and in a more subdued manner, when it lost under the other CTGs.

Now it was the turn again for the BNP to be betrayed by all four top *Uddins*, who, ironically, received their top career favors and honors from this party. Theirs was like a stab in the back of the BNP. The old and infirm Uddin#3's behavior was very heinous and hurtful. Like the other *Uddins*, this octogenarian *Uddin* was a wrong choice by the BNP. All of them violated the trust the BNP placed on them. This "Yes" *Uddin* was not only spineless but also weak and imbecile, like Mrs Packletide's tiger in Saki's story. He was as uncritical a "yes" man, as and after the other *Uddins* took over, as he was fully loyal to his benefactors before the *Uddins*' takeover. It was a pity to see how unceremoniously he left from the scene of the worldly life.

After all, loyalty, gratefulness, and thankfulness to one's benefactor pay off in the end, some way or another. The former BNP leader Abdul Mannan Bhuiyan was another similar case, deprived of the last farewell or funeral ceremony even by his own party, which he had left earlier in a betrayal, before he died. Sheikh Shawkot Hussein Nilu is another example having faced the same fate. Barrister Nazmul Huda and Prof Shaheda (plus minus Obaid) are among the other betrayers against the BNP. It was the BNP which made them known in the country by giving them high positions but today they are against their benefactors. Who would have known them if the BNP didn't benefit them in a big way? President Zia allowed Sheikh Hasina to return to Bangladesh in 1981 to lead her father's party AL, whereas she is now busy bullying, butchering, bulldozing, and bifurcating Zia's BNP, led by his wife and former prime minister Khaleda Zia.

It was especially, however, the short-looking Uddin#1, described by some critics as today's Mir Jaffar, who played a key and crucial role in a most deceptive and hypocritical manner, to the utter disadvantage of his benefactors, the BNP and Khaleda Zia.[12] Did Khaleda pay a heavy price for violating the seniority line to make him the army chief? How could Uddin#1 be so unthankful and ungrateful to her? One day (on Channel I *Trityo Matra*), Uddin#1, while still the army chief, defended his declaration of Sheikh Mujib as the father of the nation as his right as a citizen of Bangladesh, claiming he was just exercising his right to self-expression and his personal views as a Bangladesh citizen while he was still a top member in the government. His various political statements, mostly partisan to suit a certain party, were wrong, misplaced, if not punishable under the military law (which is to be determined by experts). If all public servants and state officials took sides in the name of their (private) citizen rights just as he did, one can imagine what pandemonium, what hullabaloo, and what Pandora's Box the People's Republic of Bangladesh would be.

It is a general rule (or regulation) that while in active service, government officials are not supposed to take any political sides, not openly at least. If they do, the extent of factional and partisan politics that would jeopardize the government would be too chaotic to control, too deep to fathom. As the sitting army chief and the mainstay behind the caretaker government, Uddin#1 (with his Generalship conferred upon him by Uddin#2 at this time of their *duo* supreme authority) should have held his politically sensitive views in check. Instead of uniting the nation on balanced and neutral grounds, the pro-Sheikh Mujib stance of both (or all) top *Uddins*, at the expense of the other parties' views and opinions, had the potential of plunging the nation into further trouble—more violent, more militant, more confrontational. Thanks to the state of emergency, though in some cases it was used questionably in favor of the *Uddins*' self-promotion!

Moreover, one need not prove one's neutrality just by ceremonially and symbolically visiting the graves of both Mujib and Zia on their death anniversaries. One can do so by exactly the other way—firmly and quietly staying away from both sites. However, in the present context of Bangladesh, until the differences are bridged and the both leaders are duly recognized and respected by the both sides of the aisle, there is no way to demonstrate that kind of neutrality (by refraining from going to the both) and the president of the country must physically pay a visit to either this or that grave to pay his/her respects, out of loyalty, gratitude and thankfulness, to the original (founding) leader of the party by virtue of which s/he became president and of which s/he was one of the greatest beneficiaries. Merely sending a formal message on the occasion of the anniversary could not be deemed enough.

Dr Badrudduza Chowdhury's intention to visit both cost him his presidency. He was a veteran BNP leader, who was a close associate of the BNP founder Zia. He was made president by his party, none else. But he wished to be too idealistic, too neutral and too presidential, unnecessarily and unrealistically ahead of his time in the political culture and climate of Bangladesh. The Awami-made presidents never ever rose above their party line and never ever wished to pay a visit to the grave of Ziaur Rahman. They never missed going to Mujib's Tungipara grave only. So, why would Dr Chowdhury try to rise above his party? He should have cared to offer *Fateha* at the burial internment of Zia only.[13]

Even the *Uddins* did it precisely the Awami way. Since they were unelected with no accountability to this or that party, they could easily abstain from visiting any of the two grave sites. They were supposed to be neutral and impartial; instead they started leaning toward a certain party (which claimed they were in power because of its movement against Zia's BNP). Of course, doing *ziarah* the Muslim way would no doubt enhance one's Islamic piety and humility, but in the case of the *Uddins*, it was more a politically motivated than an Islamic *ziarah*. One did not have to prove one's piety and humility by being involved in such a politically charged matter when one's motives could easily be gauged and understood by the vigilant and discerning public. There must have been and there would have been plenty of opportunities for one to visit the graves of the past leaders, if one wanted to, before one came to a top position and after one would have left the same position to become a private citizen for the rest of one's life. When one had hardly done so before coming to power and might never do so again after leaving office, one's *ziarah* could mean nothing more than scoring political mileage.

Since there are no easy solutions to certain problems, it is perhaps wise and sensible not to suddenly prescribe or impose one. A complicated problem should be left on its own to find a slow and gradual remedy over the course of time. To reiterate, sometimes it is better to leave something to itself and its natural course of evolution, not to be tampered or interfered with, especially by those who ought to be perceived as nonpartisan and as neutral as possible. Let such matters be rather prudently resolved politically through a credibly elected, active, and trustworthy parliament on the basis of bipartisan consensus.

Out of their so-called neutrality, born of their *minus two formula*, the temporary government of the *Uddins* chose it wise to imprison the two female leaders of the country until finally they had to give up. As they did so, they ended up by (unofficially) throwing their support to one of them and manipulating the way for her to win the 2008 election. According to her power-hungry pre-election political promise of convenience, Sheikh Hasina easily forgot her imprisonment woes as she approved all the doings and misdoings that the *Uddins* committed during their controversial two-year rule. The six expensive Indian horses gifted to Uddin#1 probably symbolized the romance behind the tripartite India-*Uddins*-Awami alignment, including the would-be coming BDR tragedy, as expected.[14] The Indian army made a free gift of expensive horses to cement its one sided friendship with Uddin#1 in its own interest, just as India helped Bangladesh more in its interest of breaking up Pakistan than helping Bangladesh (which, very true, the latter needed very badly). To this effect, Obaid Chowdhury of the USA (aka

Ranu Chowdhury) provides an incontrovertible and irrefutable argument about the Uddin#1's stark and shocking betrayal:

> He (the Uddin#1) did not make any secret of his love for Sheikh Mujibur Rahman and his Awami League while detesting the BNP, which installed him as army chief in the first place superseding a few seniors on the recommendation of his old pal Major Sayeed Eskandar, brother of Khaleda Zia. Royal-style treatment and a cavalry gift to Moin in India point to an underhand horse-trade. It was widely believed that the Moin backed Caretaker administration worked to see Hasina's AL win the election they masterminded on December 29, 2008, a fact later publicly admitted by Hasina's newfound "brother" and Jote partner Ershad.[15]

Ironically, while the AL chief Sheikh Hasina would enjoy the fruits of the *Uddins*-made election for years, since 2009, she would use the unelected *Uddins*' two-year stay in power (more than normal) as one of the excuses or pretexts to axe the CTG system that she herself had fought for about two decades ago to ensure a fair and participatory election. She then thought election under her rival Khaleda Zia in power would not be fair. Now, she, in power, facing massive electoral defeat, thought that election would have to be under her, not the CTG, so that she could conveniently choose the terms to suit her and ensure her victory and that the previously established interim, stopgap, neutral system would not work in her favor. So, it had to be scrapped and dispensed with, however one-sidedly, to facilitate her way to hang on to power.

All arguments, all protests, all rational sense, all sane and sound logic, unfortunately, fell on deaf and blind ears. The AL is full of ears only for themselves. The consequence is that it has created a country within a country, a government within a government, letting the country slide into chaos, confusion, anarchy, lawlessness, torture and persecution of all her opponents. No wonder, the country is divided more than ever, getting worse by the day. It seems the AL came to power only to crush and cripple the opposition in the BNP, wipe out all the memories of one of the greatest sons of the soil, Ziaur Rahman, and harass and humiliate his wife and former prime minister Khaleda Zia and his son Tarique Rahman, two of the most popular leaders with the widest support base in today's Bangladesh. Justice system, civil service, civil society, legal profession, media, academia, intelligentsia, journalism—all are suffering from internecine factional fighting. What a sorry state of affairs!

In all the major and model democratic countries, both serious criticism and comic jokes, publicly as well as privately, about the political leaders are perfectly acceptable. That is the beauty and strength of democracy and that leads to creativity, intellect, and critical thinking. In the case of Bangladesh even the slightest criticism of the AL or a trivial, frivolous taunt of its leaders meets with punishing lawsuits countrywide. What a mockery of democratic values and freedom of expression! Journalists feeling free either to remain seated or stand up and ask the prime minister any (tough, tricky, or critical) questions they like, and the members of the government feeling free to stay in their offices and run the affairs of the state as usual, instead of all of them rushing to the airport to see off or receive the prime minister coming back home from a foreign trip—that is democracy in action.

When the former Dhaka University Vice-Chancellor Prof Emajuddin Ahmed said that the country was robbed of democracy by the AL, he was actually reading the people's mind and expressing the majority view.[16] Many a political leader is thought to be correct in claiming that even the Ershad government in the 1980s was way—way—better than the present democratically illegitimate and neo-and-near-and-more-than-partially totalitarian AL government.[17] It is so ruthless, brutal, and monstrous that it did not have any scruple to put thousands and thousands—nearly thirty thousand or more—behind bars and turn the whole country into a prison and police state.[18] There is not a single sector of the country that has not been politicized and politically criminalized by the present Awami regime.

Bangladesh has become a country of police persecution and deception. Like India, in Bangladesh, too, "The problem is complicated because of the 'symbiotic relationship' between ruling politicians and policemen."[19] Its government has achieved a notoriety for not keeping its words. There have been extrajudicial killings at an alarming rate, to the denial or disowning by the police and the ruling politicians. In response to Dominique Mosbergen's at times one-sided report in *The Huffington Post*, Ranu Chowdhury, who was a valiant freedom fighter, correctly asserts that if one takes a hard look at January 15, 2014 election,

> One would see in no time how the opposition was treated during those days, how their offices were locked up and cordoned by the police and RAB, how the opposition leader was confined at her office and surrounded by five battalions of Gopali police and RAB plus water guns, sand trucks. If one saw the victims in hospitals' burn unit a year later, one need not fail to note who was responsible for that, or the brutalities of the Gopali agencies on the opposition members. It was a stage-managed election by the ruling Awami administration that earlier scrapped the constitutional provision of elections under a neutral authority with a view to orchestrating its victory in the face of complete loss of public support. The whole world, including the US, the UK, the EU and the UN, was against it. Only India supported the one-sided election so that its protégé Sheikh Hasina stayed in power. All other political parties, including the country's largest party, the BNP, boycotted the elections knowing it to be a তামাশা (farce). Indeed, majority

> members, 154 out of 300, were unelected, meaning more than half of the country's electorates did not have a chance to vote. In the remaining 146 seats, only 5–10% cast votes. The entire international community, saving India, rejected that election. Yet, Prime Minister Hasina continues to run a fascist regime with the overt and covert support of her only sponsor and her loyal Gopali forces.[20]

On the occasion of the April 28, 2015 Dhaka and Chittagong Mayoral elections, the EC (Election Commission) said it would get the army deployed on the ground, in response to the opposition demand, to ensure free and fair and peaceful polls, without any fear on the part of the voters. However, the hoodlums and hooligans were out there to create pre-election terror and violence on behalf of the ruling party. Soon after, the EC sided with them and reversed its position and said that the army would stay where they always were—inside the barracks in the cantonment—to be available on call only, if and when necessary. Was that a deployment or it was just a dust-throwing deception? If the EC was honest about its intention to stop the violence that took the lives of hundreds in different elections, why not the army be placed at every poll station to patrol the streets around with magistracy power? Would the *Awamized* civil administration ever feel it necessary to call the army when the open rigging would only take place in favor of the ruling AL?

Even if the army were to be deployed, but without any judicial power of magistracy, what good would that deployment be, except helplessly conniving at and turning a blind eye and a deaf ear to a situation deliberately created for cheating and rigging? That is why while the opposition candidates asked for an effective and meaningful army deployment on the ground with magistracy power, the government candidates and the EC were either silent or opposed to the idea so that they could bag an easy win anyway.

Before the ominous January 5, 2014, PM Hasina said she would dissolve the parliament before the election; she didn't. She obviously implied she would arrange another free and fair election after what was going to be a one-sided election on 5 January that had to be held, in her own words. to merely maintain constitutional continuity; but she didn't. Former President B. Chowdhury repeatedly reminded her of the promise she had made and broke.[21] It was that faulty and fraudulent farce, in the name of an election, that is the main cause of the present ongoing violence, in addition to the scrapping of the popular stopgap interim CTG system. One cannot but agree with the New Age editorial that:

> Regrettably, however, words and deeds of the prime minister and her government cannot be any farther from the spirit. In fact, by refusing to recognize the current crisis as

> political and also resorting to tightened and heightened security and law enforcement as its solution, the incumbents seem to have well and truly spurred it to spiral out of control. It does not seem that the government has been able to either stem the widespread violence or coerce the opposition into submission. In such circumstances, its insistence on denial and persistence with a counterproductive approach could only be explained as its desperation to cling to power at any cost. After all, except maybe its diehard supporters and crony intellectuals, no one in a sane state of mind would buy the government's claim for political legitimacy of its stay in power through an election which, according to a report published in a Bangla daily on Friday, was branded as failed in the electoral integrity perception by the Electoral Integrity Project of the Harvard University of the United States and Sydney University of Australia, which took into account 127 elections in 107 countries in 2014. If the prime minister truly wants non-interference by outsiders in resolution of the ongoing crisis, her government needs to recognize the crisis as what it is, political that is, and immediately initiate a constructive and comprehensive dialogue with the opposition for its resolution.[22]

All along, until 2008, Hasina said she would uphold democracy and democratic norms and standards by all means; however, from 2009 onward, she, at the helm of the government, let democracy go down the drains through corrupt oligarchical intrigue and get rusted through high intensity suppression of political dissent. It was during her government that democracy was sent to political burn unit or ICU (intensive care unit), letting it survive, in her own words, with the help of a dose of political formalin.

PM Hasina's situation may be likened to that of the mayor of the old German town of Hamelin, who went back on his promise of payment to the magical pied piper for ridding his town of rats. The Hamelin mayor, as described by Robert Browning in his poem, ended up paying a heavy price by losing all the children of the town to the piper into the mountain cave through the piper's retaliatory flute music. Hasina's situation is also like that of the Sultan, who broke his promise of giving his daughter in marriage to Aladdin, only to pay a price before he agrees to the marriage as Aladdin's magical ring and lamp worked wonders. Hers is a "bunch of stuff," to use the interesting phrase that Joe Biden used to discredit everything (as fabrication) as told by his rival Paul Ryan during their Vice Presidential debate in 2012. One can only hope that the AL will stop deceiving the BNP and start a culture of democratic tolerance and understanding the way the deceiving fox finally starts a friendly and faithful relationship with the dumb and unwitting crocodile in the folktale of Bangladeshi origin.

Retired career diplomat Serajul Islam wrote a lot about the amount of lying, untruths and falsehoods of the Hasina government.[23] In an e-mail posting of February 22, 2015, he said how the State Minister of Foreign Affairs was established as a liar by the EU Human Rights delegation and the President's office lied about the President's meeting with the UNSG, to be nailed by the UNSG's office. Ambassador Islam went further saying that the Foreign Minister was nailed for lying about the Prime Minister's meeting with the British Prime Minister. She and her ministers in a chorus lied to the country and the international community about Khaleda Zia. When everyone saw Khaleda was indeed interned, they all ashamedly and unabashedly lied that she was free to move anywhere she liked, which was again a distortion of fact.

Time and again, Hasina, in power, put the beleaguered Khaleda, the most popular political and dignified leader of the country for decades, under long siege, both at her home and her office, though the usual (comical Donald) Trump-like culture of denial made her and her men claim they did not. Again and again the basic utility services to Khaleda's office compound as well as her residence got cut off; but Hasina's men under her nose said they didn't know anything about it. Hitler gassed his people; the Hasina regime was "killing" Khaleda by having her gas, water, food, and power supplies snapped, including her telephone line, satellite TV channels, mobile phone and internet access disconnected. In 1971 her great father Sheikh Mujib said—rightly—he would kill the Pakistani (enemy) army by denying them access to food and water (তোমরা আমাদের ভাই [...] আমরা তোমাদের ভাতে মারবো পানিতে মারবো you are our brothers, but if you continue to kill my people, we will cut you off from the supplies/provisions and you will be forced to die of starvation).

In 2015 the regime of his undemocratic daughter Hasina was trying to "kill" the opposition leader (who is her fellow countrywoman, her political rival, a former prime minister, and the wife of the greatest president of Bangladesh Ziaur Rahman) by doing the same. The forced eviction of Khaleda from her old (near Cantonment) home, in violation of all common courtesy and decency, needs to be treated like a national shame deserving of total accountability and full investigation (visit the links in Note #15). Similarly, those who have been in the business of kidnapping and killing political leaders and civilians must be brought to justice and those who made cruel, repugnant, reprehensible, disgusting, and demeaning remarks about the tragic fate of those abducted or gone missing should be brought under custody for questioning.

Like the host of other hoaxes, the AL said if the BNP stopped agitation and violence, there would be a possibility for negotiation. When the BNP stopped, the AL forgot their carrot and followed the path of stick. The AL said if the BNP dropped its demand for the interim Care Taker Government (CTG), it would start talking about political compromise. When the BNP did drop, the

AL reneged and started making new demands on the BNP including asking it to unconditionally accept the 15th amendment nullifying the CTG. The upstream fox of the AL must get at the downstream lamb of the BNP at any cost, by all excuses and subterfuges, with the AL's kaleidoscopic goalpost keeping shifting, proving the party to be unreliable and untrustworthy.

Like the great majority in South Asia and Africa, who do not know their exact date of birth and who are not automatically issued a birth certificate upon birth but still would have one ready for official purposes with a convenient date on it making them either older or younger as necessary, Khaleda also, about to be seventy, has a date of birth probably not so well recorded when she was born. There is a controversy, therefore, over the celebration of her (unfortunately questionable) birthday on 15 August, a day of mourning for the AL. Even if there may not be any confirmed and conclusive proof about the date, she thinks it is the date and so be it—an issue Khaleda strongly defended during the famous telephone conversation between her and Hasina, saying there must have been many children born on 15 August, implying she being one of them. The AL should therefore first accept it as it is (as true, not fake), admit that Khaleda has every right to celebrate her birthday as she wishes, and then only can make a request to Khaleda to celebrate her birthday either before or after 15 August out of respect for Mujib, leaving it solely and completely to her discretion. Last year (2016) Khaleda chose not to celebrate her birthday on 15 August, to the satisfaction of some sensible AL leaders, while the dull dullards saw deception and hidden agenda behind this. Compromise or no compromise, concession or no concession on the part of the BNP, the vindictive and vengeful AL would never find a way to appreciate the democratic opposition, repair the rift, mend fences, and establish a democratically healthy rapport with Khaleda and her BNP.

The AL is now sending indirect messages, through Suranjit Sen Gupta (associated with the Railways কালো বিড়াল/black cat financial scandal causing him to lose his cabinet position) that if Khaleda stopped celebrating her birthday on 15 August, it could open a prospect for some kind of dialogue with the BNP—something, he made clear, the BNP was begging and dying for as a mercy from the AL so that it could overcome the legal and political hurdles it has been put into by his despotic and authoritarian AL. Is this another trap thrown at the BNP?

The moment Khaleda stops doing so, the AL would immediately be on the offensive saying, "Look, how false she is, which we have always been saying, and now we have proved to be true in our claim and she should therefore apologize to the nation for her false celebration for years," as the AL publicity secretary Hasan Mahmud said. Next time they would ask Khaleda to retire from politics, go into exile, or disown her son Tarique Rahman, who is next in line. The AL would never make peace with the BNP without a fight. The BNP men and women are being locked up by the police every day and put behind bars without bail. They are being long humiliated and long victimized by the AL with the possibility that even Khaleda, back and forth between home and court, let alone other hundreds of opposition leaders, may be put in prison soon.

The nation cannot wait to start a united movement with all the opposition parties together, big or small, under one banner, standing side by side, shoulder to shoulder, hand in hand. The nation needs a remedy to its mounting political problems. It needs a savior like Ziaur Rahman for a change for the better. Alternatively, the nation needs an enlightened, benevolent dictator, with no clear political affiliation, for a brief period of time, of course, to pave the way for free and fair elections sooner rather than later. It needs a judiciary and a police force above bias and controversy. It needs a host of cures, for sure, "antibiotic" cures. Stricken with a dire pestilence and sinking under the weight of endless ills, the country needs an immediate fix, followed by a hard fix, probably through a strong and patriotic people's force. Metaphorically embodied in and represented by a people's pied piper, such force would cleanse the country of its diseased, dying and dysfunctional condition (due to political rats and political Zika, Ebola, and Chikungunya viruses), first leading to a quite tolerant and inclusive democratic culture, and then on to a healthy, robust, and vibrant one, of course.

There is a debate (though not in great favor in modern democratic era) about whether it is history that is shaped and impacted by the actions of the great heroes or able men (according to Thomas Carlyle, Soren Kierkegaard, Friedrich Nietzsche, and Oswald Spengler)[24] or it is the heroes that are produced by society, social conditions, and sociological circumstances (as Herbert Spencer thought), or the two—the hero and the environment—are reciprocal, influencing each other (as William James, Sidney Hook, and Leonid Grinin discussed), or the hero is an agent of the World-Spirit, providentially assigned to play a great role (as Friedrich Hegel and Leo Tolstoy believed). Leaving aside the debate, Bangladesh, given the mountain of mistrust and misunderstandings and conflicts and confrontations between the parties, needs *a bit of vision and idealism* blended with elements of a historical superman, as properly and positively understood, in who would primarily be a practical minded civilian or a military leader with a good grasp of ground realities.

Schiller and Carlyle (as in the latter's essay on Cromwell and Napoleon) would say that while ideals could not be perfectly embodied in practice, it is very important that they are realized and approximated in good measure to avoid complete wreck and ruin, just as a bricklayer, in building a wall, has to lay his bricks upon bricks in as much an erect and straight manner as to avoid complete chaos and collapse, total toppling and tumbling down, due to the law of gravitation, although it is not possible for him to achieve a perfect perpendicularity. Carlyle used those metaphors in relation to the fall of the false Pope-centered Catholic Christian Church with the Reformation of Martin Luther and the failure of the French Revolution with its slogan of liberty and equality that, however universal a cry that may have been, went into creating "a level immensity of foolish small men" in what he called the "machine," "steam engine," "skeptical," "unbelieving" and "effete" age. In Carlyle's view, only spiritually and morally dynamic and superior heroes or great men could master the competing forces of political, economic, and practical nature and direct these energies effectively, replacing ideologies or ideological "formulas" or "isms," as he called them, by heroic human action.

Professor Abdullah Abu Sayeed of বিশ্ব সাহিত্য কেন্দ্র (World Literature Center) in Dhaka, out of frustration with the continuous bad governance of the alternately "elected" parties, stated that whatever good governance there was in Bangladesh was during the period of the British rule and then at the time of the military rule.[25] In a similar vein, well-known journalist Golam Murtoza argues that even the time-to-time military rulers of Bangladesh did not cause as much havoc to the politics of the country as the Hasina-led AL has done over the last years, since 2009, or were not involved in corruption as much as the Hasina-led AL is, all in the name of development.[26]

Opposition BNP chief Khaleda Zia spoke about the internal military indiscipline, if there was any, during a public meeting in Chittagong a few years ago (2012?). She again spoke, during her Bogra meeting later, about the role that the half a million-strong military should play if and when the occasion demanded, apparently referring to its passive onlooker role that showed the least concern about the future of the country, especially the BDR massacre that took the lives of its own officers. While she was lauded by many patriotic minds, such as DU Prof Shahiduzzaman, on television talk shows, she was, however, criticized by the Hasina loyalists. As a former prime minister, opposition leader, and the most popular political leader of the country, Khaleda should not have faced any criticism for what were her patriotically imbued, leader-like, and statesman-like statements. If somebody no less than her cannot say what she said, who else can?

Dr Abdul Moeen Khan of the BNP said that following the example of the legendary Zia in 1975, leadership should/might come out of the military cantonment/establishment to save the nation from the horror and terror it has been witnessing for years.[27] It is precisely the same point that Ranu Chowdhury of the USA makes when he says, "I am no fan of Martial Law or Emergency. But if Martial Law brings peace and good governance, I will go for it 100 times than groaning under civilian fascism that we saw in 1972–75 and are experiencing from 2009 to date" (E-mail of April 11, 2016). However, witnessing frustratingly the passivity of the military in the face of "civilian fascism" in the police-controlled Bangladesh and the unequal military treaties between India and Bangladesh, Computer Engineer Mohammad Aleem of the USA comments: "Bangladesh Army—Is it something alive or dead? I do not see any difference of taking or not taking a dead entity under India" (group e-mail of March 20, 2017). For all practical purposes, it is unfortunately the same whether the army in question is on its own or made subject and subordinate to others out of excessive friendship with the master India.

All countries, big or small, Eastern or Western, are proud of their patriotic military. Their gaudy and golden hope lies with their military as it (the military) is expected to accomplish a swift and effective turnaround in rescuing them in times of crisis, political or natural, internal or external. A friend in need is a friend indeed. While it does not and should not get involved in the routine civilian politics, as generally and traditionally understood, the military, however, cannot turn its back and remain complacent about being awarded financially lucrative government offers it enjoys in the construction of roads and bridges across the country. That would be at the expense of its national obligations it is supposed to perform when the nation finds itself battered and bruised, and bashed and blasted due to civil and political unrest and instability. "The price of freedom is eternal vigilance," said Thomas Jefferson, one of America's founding fathers, principal author of its Declaration of Independence and its third President, from 1801 to 1809. "To stand in silence when they should be protesting makes cowards out of men," said Abraham Lincoln, America's 16th President, from 1861 to 1865 when he was assassinated.

Since 2009 this kind of situation has primarily been precipitated in Bangladesh by the Awami-led partisan and factional suppression and oppression. All militaries are highly patriotic, proud to play a great and glorious role in the critical and chaotic circumstances of their nations. Bangladesh's military is no exception. They are proud to have a track record of keeping and maintaining peace in other countries, no doubt. However, is there peace in their own country, especially since the early 2009 brutal massacre of nearly sixty of their own BDR officers? Do they have to be "color blind" to stay peaceful and patriotic? Do they belong to the state or the government or both, irrespective of all political developments? Aren't they citizens of Bangladesh, to collectively discharge their duties as they always have been doing, as the situation demanded? Doubt can never be good; in fact, it is detrimental to the cause of democracy and democratic ideals and aspirations, especially in a developing country struggling and stumbling in its fight to achieve transparency and accountability.

The US House of Representatives Member Matt Salmon of Arizona expressed his concern (on April 30, 2015) that the current political unrest in Bangladesh "may lead to a further breakdown of order that could open space for Islamic militancy or for the military to take power."[28] As Chairman Foreign Affairs Subcommittee on Asia and the Pacific, Salmon said:

> The political crisis in Bangladesh is worsening. There is an increased risk of military intervention as political battle lines become ever more entrenched. The situation after the general election in Bangladesh is deeply worrying and casts a long shadow over the future of the country. After holding 2014 general elections, Bangladesh is facing a political deadlock. A military intervention seems possible, but it would deal a heavy blow to democracy in the South Asian nation.[29]

Although critics and commentators would like to ask the questions as above, perhaps what is best and most preferred is for Sheikh Hasina not to succumb to her baseless boastfulness and, yet ironically, to her cowardly BNP*hobia* but to succeed in collecting courage to give up those negative and regressive impulses and start the political and democratic process of healing and uniting the country together with the most popular and dignified political leader of the country, Begum Khaleda Zia. The bragging yet frightful to face the BNP, Hasina as prime minister cannot follow the double standard of two rules with a mischievous, malicious, and manipulative intent: one rule to drop/withdraw all the hundreds of judicial trials against her and her surrogates and another rule to pursue all the hundreds and thousands—all categorically rejected as laughable and ridiculous—against the opposition leader Khaleda and her surrogates to harass and harangue them, to stifle their voices and restrict their political as well as civilian movements. What a cowardly and dastardly means to achieve a cruel and wicked end!

At the same time, one must not make light of anybody being beaten up to the point of having the backbone broken. That is a notorious violation of one's most fundamental human rights. That is extremely inhuman, totally unacceptable, and intolerably pathetic and painful, more so than a jail term with or without labor or years of community service. So, those who broke young Tarique Rahman's bones must be held accountable, brought to justice, indicted, and convicted, however hard and tough that may be.

By the same token, those who caused the forced and shameful ouster of the weeping and helpless Khaleda from her old (Cantonment) home, denying her citizen rights and without giving her a civic chance for a civilized and dignified exit through negotiation befitting a three-time former prime minister, who was at the time and is still the de facto opposition leader, must be reinvestigated, fully and properly.[30] The way she was ousted from her home was completely unacceptable. It was atrocious, outrageous, and terribly insulting. Instead of serving a legal notice on her and forcing her to vacate the premises, Khaleda, who was no less than what she was (former prime minister, opposition leader, and wife of a former president and a heroic freedom fighter, who declared the independence of Bangladesh), should have been consulted and discussed with first, to give the political way of talking her into relinquishing the house a chance. Was Begum Zia less deserving than Sheikh Rehana to be sanctioned a house from the government? Rehana has been donated a house in Gulshan by the government of her sister PM Hasina, for which an amount of Taka 10 crore only was sanctioned in 2016 for necessary repair and renovation.

Similarly, those *gopalis*, speaking in a foreign or deliberately twisted accent to hide their true identity, who blocked Khaleda Zia's way out from her Hasina-laid sand-and-cement-truck-sieged Gulshan office and most disrespectfully taunted at her must be identified and brought to account.[31] Those government-sponsored hoodlums and hooligans who beat her people and smashed and vandalized her convoy, including her own car, during her Dhaka Mayoral campaigns, in a complete violation of the democratic rights of a political leader, must be brought to book. Those thug policemen who attempted to block her way to the Shaheed Minar (Language Martyrs' Memorial) in the early hours of the 21st February (2016) must be apprehended and punished.

The BNP, the largest political party in the country, has been reduced to a desperate and decrepit situation—the miserable situation of a drowning man catching at a straw or of the long-beaked stork tempted by the tiger into helping it out with the bone that got stuck in its throat. This is not because the party is weak in numbers (of which it has many more than the AL) but it finds itself helpless and hapless in the face of the despotism of the governing autocratic AL and its might and muscle, boots and bullets, batons and barrels, and remands and repressions from which the BNP has no break and no respite at all. The BNP cannot be said to be as power-hungry as the AL is power-drunk. It is only fighting for the stagnant, strangled, and strangulated democratic process to be freed, revived, resumed, reactivated, and reestablished. There is nothing wrong for a political party to get to power, but to get power-drunk for those who are already in power is as dangerous for democracy as the chicken in the care of the fox.

The reality is that the forces of good and the forces of evil alternate by turns. Good, regardless of how good, cannot and does stay too long. Bad, irrespective of how bad, still manages to hang on for a long time. In his poem, "The New Year," the 17th-century English poet Charles Cotton says:

> For the worst ills (we daily see)
> Have no more perpetuity,
> Than the best fortunes that do fall;
> Which ["best fortunes"] also bring us wherewithal [ways or means][32]
> Longer their being to support,
> Than those do of the other sort: ...

One can, therefore, only hope the bad has run out of its time after more than seven or nine years. But the way the Hasina regime is talking tough and ruthlessly rounding up the opposition members and activists every day, thousands of them by now, one's concern is that it seems it still has the upper hand in trying to stay on, like Bashar Al-Assad. The regime's vicious and barbaric cycle of হামলা ও মামলা (assault, attack, lawsuit under the notorious penal codes) and its capture and cruel remands of the opposition members are continuing with no end in sight. Its armed police, acting like party operatives, seems to have been able to slice and size up the opposition faithful, at least for the time being.

In this critical juncture, if those in the middle shifted unequivocally and unhesitatingly to the side of the opposition for the sake of democracy (that is, to save democracy) and were out on the street together, instead of posing like lone wolves, the balance would have tipped long ago and there would have been a different January 5, 2014. Their unity and solidarity with the opposition (BNP)-led democratic alliance would have an altogether different impact nationwide, helping the anti-Awami movement gather more steam and forcing Hasina to accommodate the opposition demands for a credible, inclusive and participatory election on January 5. She seemed to be more flexible then than later. Unfortunately, the parties in the middle are hysterically neutral, long on talk (at the press club and on TV talk shows only) but short on plan and action, some even sleeping on the street with no tangible political effect.[33]

Bangladesh is far from the state of the stable, transparent and democratic India. No one can achieve anything in the police state Bangladesh has slid and slipped into as Anna Hazare did in the more civic and civil India. Those sitting on the fence think that they would move into the second position from the distant third if the BNP is displaced into nowhere. That is their cynical, myopic, and monolithic view. That may not be easy, with them facing the possibility of losing all—আমও যাবে ছালাও যাবে (both the mangoes and the sacks containing them to be lost); অতি চালাকের গলায় দড়ি (too much courtesy, full of craft); অতি লোভে তাঁতি নষ্ট (Grasp all, lose all). Their position (with the courtesy of Dr Rashed Anam of the USA) is not unlike the one described in the famous quotation by the prominent German Protestant pastor Martin Niemöller, who spent seven years in a concentration camp for being an outspoken critic of Adolf Hitler:

> First they came for the Socialists, and I did not speak out—
> Because I was not a Socialist.
> Then they came for the Trade Unionists, and I did not speak out—
> Because I was not a Trade Unionist.
> Then they came for the Jews, and I did not speak out—
> Because I was not a Jew.
> Then they came for me—and there was no one left to speak for me.

The AL demands that the BNP dissociates itself from the ideologically strong, organizationally well-disciplined, and financially relatively clean Jamaat, but it demands so only to weaken the BNP. One must keep in mind that even if the BNP disowns and distances itself from the Jamaat, the AL will still spare no pains to find other faults and excuses to corner the BNP. If the AL is allied with the Ershad-JP, the BNP can be allied with the Jamaat too. So the BNP should think twice before it leaves a potentially potent and powerful ally only to step into the AL-laid trap. If the great freedom fighters such as President Zia, Col. Oli Ahmad, and Maj. Gen. Syed Mohammad Ibrahim, along with the JAGPA chief Shafiul Alam Prodhan, JP chief Barrister Andalib Rahman Partho, and NAP chief Jebel Rahman Ghani could have an alliance with the BNP-Jamaat for political reasons, others such as the former President Dr Badrudduza Chowdhury (who worked together with the former Prime Minister Shah Azizur Rahman in the late 1970s), ASM Rob, Mahmudur Rahman Manna, and Kader Siddiquee should have no problem joining the BNP-Jamaat alliance in a common cause against the AL's dictatorship and despotism about which they are all loudly vocal.[34]

People's hopes started dimming from 2008/2009. Since then they have been receding, eroding, fading, and flickering. They never had a chance, even a remote one, to fly and flutter, shine and dazzle. Today they are all dead, totally blown out. People can only ruminate remembering the famous Indian (non-Bengali) Tagore critic Abu Sayyid Ayub's এই পথের শেষ কোথায় (Where and how would be the end of this path). However, they would hold mainly those in the middle responsible for not having come forward to the end of the tunnel. If they would have joined hands with the BNP from as early as 2012/2013, today's situation could have perhaps been avoided. But they preferred to stay in isolation as if Khaleda was to them as she was to Hasina—someone not to talk to, not to deal with, not to be sided with, but to be kept at bay. They were asking Hasina to talk to Khaleda; why didn't they talk to Khaleda themselves to be united with her, under her leadership, at least for the sake of democracy and political expediency, if not ideology and ideological interests? What good their ideologies and interests could be when they must have been useless in a dictatorship?

If it were the BNP-AL combine fighting against Ershad, as they did in the past, the fence-sitters would not have been needed. Now that it is a major party against the other which is ruthlessly using all the money and muscle power on earth, the barefooted BNP alone cannot do much and so may have been in need of their help to be on the street together for the good of all. Though a major party, the BNP has been rendered a faceless and clawless cripple long ago, crawling and crouching since 2008/2009, from the time of the Moinuddin-Fakhruddin-Masududdin trio. Since then it has been trodden and trampled down by the relentless remands, boots and bullets, jail and জুলুম (torture and discrimination) and হামলা ও মামলা.

Also to be held responsible are the Nobel Laureates, Knighthood achievers, and other prominent sons and daughters of the soil, who, despite their weight and stature, have done nothing and have made no effort to break or at least bend the divisive stalemate created by the Hasina regime. As the American Gold Star parent Khizr Khan, who lost his 25-year-old son Captain Khan in the Iraq War, said of Donald Trump, "You have sacrificed nothing and nobody," won't the suffering nation of Bangladesh cry out soon saying the same to its famed children? The nation expected that its illustrious sons and daughters, not necessarily aligned with any party, would be coming forward to help it tide over the crisis it has been going through. Along with the fence-sitting middle ground politicians (such as Kader Siddiquee, ASM Rob, Kamal Hussein, Badrudduza Chowdhury, Mujahidul Islam Selim, and the hopelessly hibernating Hefajote Huzurs) as well as the neutral or near neutral artists, actors, singers, intellectuals, journalists, professionals, businessmen and the civil society representatives—all of whom are neither here nor there—, the nation's great sons and daughters could easily be forthcoming, actively and forcefully, in doing something together to break the deadlock.

Those otherwise admirable men and women have unfortunately preferred to remain "dreadfully dull," to borrow a phrase from Thomas Carlyle, who used it to describe a "similar" group of famous but ultimately useless English public figures. In their having been glued to the genre of neuter gender, the eminent

Bangladeshis have been like the copycats of ancient Sybarites and golden grasshoppers, settled into their luxurious ways of life.[35] If they could not forget the small differences over the Jamaat issue (Sheikh Hasina forgot her differences with JSD and its terrorist and terrifying GanoBahini and, until a few years ago, with the very Jamaat too, which she is now harrowingly hounding) and could not forge a unity with the opposition for the sake of the greater interest of the country, they would prove to be as hopeless as the political parties under the relentless Awami beating. They should have taken the road to engaging themselves, like the Nobel winning Tunisian National Dialogue Quartet, in working out a formula to help the nation pursue the active and dynamic path of pluralistic political reforms with a sense of mission and vision accompanied by care and commitment.

The Bangladeshi notables' completely cold and anodyne passivity in remaining noncommittal and immune to the national plight and predicament would take away from, rather than add to their prestige and dignity. That is how they are likely to be seen in historical hindsight in the future! It is true that some of them may already have a low point in their attempt to form a party during the interim 2006–2008 *Uddins* era; that they may have been much maligned by the Hasina regime; that some may have a big stake in their non-governmental bumper business wanting no disturbance to their safe and comfortable life. But nothing can excuse them from and relieve them of their high moral duty to come forward to save and salvage the nation. They are supposed to play a role of courage and fortitude out of their patriotic and nationalistic spirit, befitting their station in life. Lack of well-coordinated response from the eminently noted and neutral people, especially in times of a polarized national impasse, can encourage the dictators to cause even more harm than otherwise and that is what the Hasina regime is doing without having to face any challenge or pressure from any corner whatsoever.

When the well-known Indian journalist and diplomat Kuldip Nayar can say what follows, the nation of the Bangladeshis can expect something firm, bold and decisive from its own great sons and daughters. Here is what Nayar writes:

> I do not know why and for how long we have to support the authoritarian rule by Prime Minister Hasina in Bangladesh. True, she is the daughter of Sheikh Mujibur Rahman, who liberated East Pakistan from distant and oppressive West Pakistan. But that does not give her the right to flout the Constitution and accepted norms. Take for example, the recent municipal polls at Dhaka and Chittagong. Ballot papers in favor of candidates of the ruling AL were shoved into the ballot boxes to the horror of voters and others. Sheikh Mujib must be turning in his grave. He had restored the people's right to express themselves against the military junta ruling from Rawalpindi [...] In fact, the cavalier manner in which Hasina has suppressed dissent arouses doubts about her credentials. Did she ever have conviction about a free state and the democratic way of governance?[36]

Anyway, an antibiotic boost by and from the young patriotic men and women is the need of the moment, many believe, to help keep the ship of the nation afloat, navigate well, and sail ashore and offshore as necessary with the winds of democratic freedom blowing favorably. A united and powerful movement of all the anti-Awami forces is necessary to establish truth, balance, and sanity, thereby to destroy the increasingly intense, insane and systematic Awami-sponsored fascism and authoritarianism. A swift, forceful and overwhelming intervention is needed from all concerned—neutrals, civil society, international community, and patriotic political forces—but in a shapely, disciplined, well-organized and well-directed manner as symbolized by William Blake's 1794 lyric poem "The Tiger":

> TIGER, tiger, burning bright
> In the forests of the night,
> What immortal hand or eye
> Could frame thy fearful symmetry?

One may recall Picasso's *Guernica* (1937), against the Spanish Civil War background, became a universal symbol against the sufferings and devastations in unjust wars. It speaks volumes, which many volumes of text in words cannot. Abraham Lincoln's Gettysburg speech (1863) fired the imaginations of the whole world, as the words *government of the people, by the people, for the people, shall not perish from the earth* reverberated throughout the nations and the peoples. Maxim Gorky's *Mother* (1906) inspired millions. One could also add John F. Kennedy's arousing, uplifting and patriotic inaugural address of 1961:

> And so, my fellow Americans, ask not what your country can do for you; ask what you can do for your country. My fellow citizens of the world, ask not what America will do for you, but what together we can do for the freedom of man.

Here one may also remember Bob Dylan's 1960s antiwar song, "Blowin' in the Wind," containing the question, "How many times must the cannon balls fly before they're forever banned?," in reference to the Vietnam War and the civil rights in the USA. Similarly, one may ask, "How many people need to be hurt, beaten, burnt, remanded, killed, abducted, chained, imprisoned, and incarcerated by the Hasina regime before the ongoing suffocation in Bangladesh comes to an end?" Emperor Napoleon said that English caricaturist James Gillray, a masterly satirical draughtsman, contributed more to his downfall in 1815 than all the armies of Europe. In his more than 1,000 etchings of caustic humor, Gillray boldly caricatured monarchs, politicians, and warlords, including the young

French emperor, Prince of Wales (King George IV of the UK), and the young British Prime Minister William Pitt.

All alternatives are not and cannot be equally desirable. While alternative medicine and alternative diet and eating habits are fine, alternative (and perverse) lifestyle (different from mainstream, civilized, normal, natural heterosexual family life) is not. And so is the alternative provided by the AL, which has turned into an equivalent of the ancient Athenian oligarchy of the time of Socrates that consisted of thirty tyrants—a group of rich and powerful men—who destroyed the democracy their city-state Athens was enjoying during the 5th century BC.

It is not far to seek why the AL was described as অভিশপ্ত/cursed by Fazlur Rahman, formerly one of its own men, a top *Chatro* League leader, now a BNP leader of Tangail District, known for his excellent powerful speeches. Fazlur Rahman said so in view of the fact that since its creation, especially since the creation of Bangladesh, many leaders left the AL for its extremely antidemocratic and notoriously infamous role—a role also justly criticized by the once great Awami Leaguers such Nur-e-Alam Siddiquee, Mahmudur Rahman Manna, and Kader Siddiquee,[37] or some of the still fine, fair, and sensible Awami Leaguers such as (the late) ABM Musa, Prof Abu Sayeed, architect Mubasshyer Hussein, and Sultan Mansur. It is therefore only fit to conclude by saying that the change from the interim (care taker) government of the *Uddins* to the Awami government that followed was like jumping from the frying pan into the fire, especially for the democratic opposition in the BNP-led alliance and then the nation in general.

Notes

1. For "The Truth Behind Twelve Twenty-Nine (12/29/2008)," click: http://newsbd71.blogspot.com/2011/02/truth-behind-twelve-twenty-nine.html; http://opinion.bdnews24.com/2011/02/02/from-wikileaks-to-hillaryleak/
2. http://www.amardeshonline.com/pages/details/2015/10/27/308181#
3. http://www.prothombangladesh.net/article/14691
4. See David Hoffman at https://www.timesofassam.com/international/governments-undue-influence-judiciary-bangladesh/
5. Reportedly, the 1/11 men did not return the money (more than 123 million dollar) they forcibly took from the businessmen. See Ortho-Banijjyo at http://www.purboposhchimbd.news/2016/03/10/
6. http://www.amardeshonline.com/pages/details/2016/01/20/320049#
7. In the palace conspiracy and the battle against the British, Sirajuddowla, elder son of Nawab Alivardi Khan's daughter Amina Begum (one of three daughters), had only

Mir Ma(r)dan Khan (new army chief but soon to be killed in the war) and Mohon Lal on his side. The betrayers included: his army chief Mir Jaffar, several other officers in the army, his wealthy aunt (Amina's elder sister) Meherunnesa (Ghaseti Begum), his cousin Shaukat Jung, Bengali trader Jagat Seth, Raja Krishna Chandra, Raja Mahendra Rai (Rai Durlabh), Raja Rai Ballov, Raja RamNarayan, Yar Lutuf Khan, Sikh merchants Omichund (Amir Chand), Mahtab Chand, Manik Chand, and Khadem Hussein. Sirajuddowla was executed, at the age of 24, after only a year on the throne, on July 2, 1757 by Mohammad Ali Beg at the orders from Mir Jaffar's son Mir Miran at the Namak Haram Deorhi (The Traitor's Gate) to Mir Jaffar's residence in Murshidabad, West Bengal, now in ruins, as fittingly called by the posterity. The conspiracy in Bengal continued, even after Sirajuddowla, through the reigns of Mir Jaffar and his son-in-law Mir Qasim Ali Khan Bahadur with the machinations of the British and the Dutch East India Companies To know how all the traitors died a pathetic death, click: http://archive.prothom-alo.com/detail/date/2012-06-22/news/267615; http://www.dailynayadiganta.com/detail/news/232374; and the other links on the net.

8. http://newsfrombangladesh.net/view.php?hidRecord=291014
9. http://www.prothom-alo.com/bangladesh/article/353677/
10. http://www.countercurrents.org/khan131007.htm;
    http://www.mzamin.com/details.php?mzamin=MTEzOTI4&sMQ==;
    "Mr. Subramaniam Swamy, Janata Dal MP, a close associate of Morarji Desai said that Rameswar Nath Kao, former Chief of RAW, and Shankaran Nair upset about Sheikh Mujib's assassination chalked a plot to kill General Ziaur Rahman. However, when Morarji Desai came into power in 1977 he was indignant at RAW's role in Bangladesh and ordered operations in Bangladesh to be called off; but by then RAW had already gone too far. General Zia continued to be in power for quite some time but he was assassinated after Indira Gandhi returned to power, though she denied her involvement in his assassination" (Weekly Sunday, Calcutta,18 September, 1988).
11. http://www.mzamin.com/details.php?mzamin=MTEzOTI4&s=MQ==;
    http://www.amardeshonline.com/pages/details/2016/02/04/322039#;
    https://nazmamustafa.wordpress.com/2015/12/12/;
    http://www.mzamin.com/details.php?mzamin=MTE0NDYx&s=MQ==
12. http://bangladeshchronicle.net/2015/11/where-is-infamous-villain-gen-moin/; for more details, see Ranu Chowdhury, "General Moin's Story—Some Comments," http://newsfrombangladesh.net/view.php?hidRecord=248824*; or* https://groups.yahoo.com/neo/groups/dhakamails/conversations/messages/2828*; or http://daily-alochona.blogspot.com/2009/02/alochona-general-moins-storysome.html*
13. If the BNP disgraced B. Chowdhury by removing him from the Bangabhaban, it was of his own doing. Then he got even with the BNP by siding with Sheikh Hasina in late 2008, during the *Uddinized* elections. It is nice to see that he realized his mistake and is now back by the side of the BNP.

14. Please see the Indian media report: Indian hopes for a season of friendship: https://asianwindow.wordpress.com/tag/maitree-express/.
15. http://www.weeklyholiday.net/homepage/pages/UserHome.aspx?ID=20&date=12/21/2012; "Hasina's Ziaphobia" and "Unforgettable Zia that I knew: A flashback," also by Ranu Chowdhury: http://dailyalochona.blogspot.com/2010/12/alochona-eviction-of-khaleda-zia-latest.html; and http://www.weeklyholiday.net/homepage/pages/UserHome.aspx?ID=20&date=12/21/2012
16. http://newagebd.net/106476/country-robbed-of-democracy-emajuddin/#
17. http://www.amadershomoys.com/newsite/2015/07/19/352841.htm#
18. http://newsshomoy.com/bn/2015/11/17/149292.html#
19. http://newagebd.net/173627/police-brutality-and-impunity-in-south-asia/#
20. Ranu Chowdhury's e-mail of July 2, 2015, in reaction to the report at: http://www.huffingtonpost.com/2015/06/30/bangladesh-politics_n_7642602.html
21. http://www.sheershanewsbd.com/2015/07/10/88227#
22. http://newagebd.net/97307/lofty-rhetoric-not-enough-to-resolve-ongoing-crisis/#sthash.bVQqAdGK.dpbs; http://newagebd.net/97307/lofty-rhetoric-not-enough-to-resolve-ongoing-crisis/#sthash.bVQqAdGK.dpuf
23. http://ambassadorseraj.blogspot.com/
24. Carlyle stated that "The history of the world is but the biography of great men," suggesting that heroes shape history through their personal attributes as well as divine inspiration. His heroes included Old Norse/Scandinavian/Germanic mythological god Odin, Islam's prophet Muhammad, Dante, Shakespeare, Martin Luther, John Knox, Samuel Johnson, Rousseau, Cromwell, Napoleon (questionably), and Frederick the Great.
25. http://www.amadershomoys.com/newsite/2015/06/10/314542.htm#.VZ_v51_vMdV
26. http://www.banglatribune.com/columns/opinion/168749/
27. http://www.sheershanewsbd.com/2015/06/02/82885#
28. http://thehill.com/blogs/congress-blog/foreign-policy/243384-bangladesh-in-crisis; http://docs.house.gov/meetings/FA/FA05/20150430/103406/HHRG-114-FA05-Transcript-20150430.pdf
29. https://www.youtube.com/watch?v=q2AoWa9L_2I&sns=em
30. https://www.youtube.com/watch?v=4o4IMXnlkIs
31. http://datab.us/NQOWA6jq3Z0#Khaleda%20Zia%20Vs%20Gopali%20Girl%20%2829%20December%202013%29;
http://datab.us/LEe3PYl-hbs#Gopali%20by%20Khaleda%20Zia; http://newagebd.net/83246/24-trucks-parked-as-khaledas-confinement-continues/
32. Bracketed material/meaning in this line is my insertion.
33. Yet, thanks to *BangaBir* Kader Siddiquee for his strong moral stance.
34. http://www.sheershanewsbd.com/2015/07/07/87839#
35. The people of the ancient Greek city of Sybaris in southern Italy were known for their effeminacy and luxury. Going back to *Aesop's Fables*, grasshoppers are symbolic of

luxury, happiness, and cheerfulness. According to the ancient historian Thucydides, the golden grasshoppers are symptomatic of the Athenian degeneration from the Spartan to the Ionic qualities, as they lay aside their arms and became weak and idle. Richard Lovelace, John Keats, Leigh Hunt, all wrote poems about the grasshopper. Tennyson's Tithonus is changed into a golden grasshopper.

36. http://www.thestatesman.com/news/opinion/a-shot-in-the-arm-for-hasina/68705.html
37. http://www.sheershanewsbd.com/2015/05/26/82011#

7

From the Opposition's চুদুর বুদুর (Wishy-Washy Dalliance) to the Position's নিষিদ্ধ পল্লী (Red Light District)

In Defense of the Three (Former) Female Opposition Parliament Members, the PAR (দেশকন্যা / DeshKonnya[1] Ashrafi Papia, Shammi Akhter, and Rehana Ranu)

Indirectly referring to Begum Khaleda Zia, the most popular political leader of Bangladesh, and her tortured and exiled but young, dynamic, charismatic, and highly popular son Tarique Rahman, who is the second in command of her party, the frequently bragging, bullying, boastful, bellicose, and belligerent Prime Minister Sheikh Hasina decries, dismisses, and disparages all those who are different from her as কুলাঙ্গার (black sheep). Consistently and chronically coming down hard and dirty on Khaleda and Tarique and their party BNP, Hasina may also be characterized, electorally speaking, by her irrational aberrations related to her darkly and deeply rooted BNP*hobia*. The abusive slang of কুলাঙ্গার (black sheep) is just one instance of the kind of inflammatory and provocative language—other examples to follow—that is used by Prime Minister Hasina. According to the late senior academic Dr Ahmad Sharif in 1996:

> হাসিনার মধ্যেই কেবল মৌরুসী সম্পত্তির মতো বাংলাদেশ দখলে রাখার এমনি আস্ফালন ও মায়াকান্না দেখা যাচ্ছে। তার মধ্যে শিক্ষার সুরুচির বিবেচনা-শক্তির কোন পরিচয় মেলে না। তার স্বপ্ন ও সাধ অনেক কিন্তু যোগ্যতা নেই। প্রতিহিংসাপরায়ণতার রাক্ষুসে হিংস্রতা এবং ক্ষমতার গদী স্থায়ী ভাবে ধরে রাখার লিপ্সাই পরিবারকে মানে, যশে, খ্যাতিতে, ক্ষমতায়, বিত্তে, বেসাতে, অর্থ-সম্পদে চিরপ্রতিষ্ঠ রাখার মোহ তাকে পেয়ে বসেছে। এ পথেই তার ঘটবে আশু পতন॥ (Hasina is ineligible and incompetent, does not show any evidence of class, taste, and good education, and wishes to keep Bangladesh under her sole and sheer control as if the country was a piece of her family inheritance. She is vengeful, vindictive, greedy, power-hungry, cruel and ruthless like a ferocious female demon. She is likely to fall soon along this evil way).[2]

Hasina came to power through a detestable, disputable, boycotted, and uncontested national election in 2014 (not to speak of the controversial previous election of late 2008). She is a prime minister who is hanging on to power not only through shamefully divisive naming and shaming names but also the questionable means and methods, teaching others, after her, to follow the same route of denial, dismissal, destruction, and devastation, both by words and actions.

Under the Hasina regime, Bangladesh has been reduced to a culture and community of গুম ও খুন (abductions and assassinations), হামলা ও মামলা (physical and penal persecutions), jail and জুলুম (imprisonment, torture and discrimination), boots and bullets, লগি ও বৈঠা (sticks and poles), machetes and pointed iron rods. There are also rampant rapes, widespread corruption, repugnant violence, and dreadful drug addiction. For long (and recently even more), Bangladesh has decayed into a society of deadly and disgusting premarital and extramarital affairs, inhuman child labor, abhorrent child marriages, repulsive teen pregnancies, and dirty, despicable, and disgraceful dowries—an unjust, unbearable, and anti-religious burden to be borne by the poor girl's helpless and miserable parents.[3]

The ruling party AL's despotic grip on power compels and compounds all these into a series of ongoing problems—of immense proportions, making its power-drunk and vainglorious leaders, thriving in a corruption-ridden economic culture, establish a tradition of indecent and abusive rhetoric. Naturally, no opposition movement can be launched in the repressive police state that Bangladesh has become; there cannot be any flow of full tide in the "dead river" of the opposition Bangladesh Nationalist Party (BNP)—as dead and dry as many a real river across the country due to environmental and industrial pollution—as Communications Minister Obaidul Quader is known to be repeatedly hurling a satirical attack at the BNP, using the same imagery.

Often the Awami leaders use the Donald Trump-like slings and arrows in low-brow and low-class language (if not as vulgar as the diatribes of the foul-mouthed Rodrigo Duterte of the Philippines and Robert Mugabe of Zimbabwe, but still distasteful to the extent of being vicious and malicious) against the popular BNP and its patriotic leaders and founders. In their explosive, inflammatory, and unhinged rhetoric, often smacking of scorched-earth gutter and slander, against their political challenger BNP, the Awami leaders have descended to the level of the crude and coarse language of vilification. They have termed the BNP "a poisonous snake" and have called the three-time former prime minister Begum Khaleda Zia "Lady Laden," "Lady Emir" (in counter, Sheikh Hasina was called "Lady Hitler" and "Lady Mir Zaffar"), "Hyena" (fox) and শকুনি (female vulture), doing all the তামাশা (something laughable without sense or logic) and making the "hiccups of relish and contentment." Well, the situation is like, "When they go low, we the opposition led by Khaleda go high," to echo the powerfully resonating words of the US First Lady Michelle Obama.

PM Hasina, from the power and position of prime minister, did not mind going low in referring to Khaleda and/or her son Tarique as অশিক্ষিত (illiterate), although the mother's and the son's style of speech, both in Bangla and English, in terms of their choice and pronunciation of words, are far better and more standard and accurate than not only Hasina but also many other top Awami leaders. People of Bangladesh know how many of their presidents and prime ministers passed their school/college exams and got their degrees with the help of grace marks, compartment opportunities, and proxies. They know the educational background of Sheikh Mujibur Rahman, Sheikh Hasina, and Abdul Hamid, as they also know that of Albert Einstein, American astronaut and senator John Glen, Bill Gates, Steve Jobs, Mark Zuckerberg, Mark Twain, Jonathan Swift, Oliver Goldsmith, Edward Gibbon, Lord Byron, A E Housman, William Shakespeare, Winston Churchill, Edward Heath, John Major, Ben Jonson, George Chapman, Alexander Pope, William Blake, Robert Burns, John Keats, Thomas Love Peacock, John Clare, Charles Dickens, Robert Browning, Walt Whitman, Mughal Emperor Akbar, and the National Poet Kazi Nazrul Islam.

All of the above either did not distinguish themselves academically or had little or no formal education and who were mostly self-taught. Caedmon, an Old English poet, was an illiterate cowherd, who miraculously received the gift of singing, entered the monastery of Whitby, and became the founder of a school of Christian poetry. In this way, many writers, poets, thinkers, and politicians were not highly educated in terms of formal education.

This is the fall of 2017. Tried and tested and exiled and much suffering Tarique has already demonstrated his youthful vision and maturity, along with dynamic ability, agility, and adroitness, capable of commanding the nation of Bangladesh and being their commander-in-chief straight away. In an August 2017 post online, Engineer Rashed Anam of the USA points to Tarique's other admirable and enviable qualities:

> Despite Tarique having some considerable shortcomings, such as lack of judgment in choosing his surrounding advisors, there is ONE UNIQUE and most important quality he possesses. That is his patriotism!! He will not sell out Bangladesh!! His uncompromising stand still has the resonance of his father President Ziaur Rahman!! That's why India [...] is scared of him and DOES NOT WANT HIM IN POWER!! They know he will clean up the Dalals and Corporate Robbers, etc. Only Tarique has the guts to build a party, politics, country that is based on sovereign Bangladesh, empowered Bangladesh. Till now there is no other viable leader in the horizon, from any party who can meet such criteria! We have to judge him as whole and what he brings to the table. And we should advise, pressure and promote good policies and processes so that he and his leadership improves and mitigates the known shortcomings! Only Tarique can generate euphoria and energy and enthusiasm needed to build a new Bangladesh. The son has the father's flavors and politics. The BAKSALI Awami League has finished itself off to be included in the imagination of the nation for the next leader.

In his Facebook status, Sheikh Hasina's son Sajeeb Wajed Joy, in violation of all civic and political courtesy, called Khaleda a thief and a liar and described the two of the notable Bangladeshis, Mahmudur Rahman and Shafik Rehman, as Khaleda's pet servants.[4] An Awami cabinet minister, Shahjahan Khan, in the style of a gangster muscleman, wanted to pluck out the eyes of a senior political opponent Barrister Rafiqul Islam Mia during a televised talk show. If Trump has normalized the American public's "worst racial impulses," the AL has done the same with respect to the bitter and vitriolic anti-BNP rhetoric.

The Awami leaders mock at the BNP supporters and sympathizers as আঁতেল/antels (a corrupt and satirical version of "intellectuals" when they are attacked as being false, frivolous, petty, peevish, petulant, pretentious, and preposterous). Speaking for the need of the control of press freedom, an Awami alliance minister in charge of information would make a travesty of himself by referring to such unnecessary things, in his view, as lovemaking চুমাচুমি (kissing) between husband and wife to be avoided on the media. These are only some of the examples in point, reminding the readers of Trump's pattern of odd and odious, and derogatory and offensive comments about women he did not like. Trump called women "fat pigs, dogs, slobs and disgusting animals … eating machine, eating like a pig

[...] having a fat ass." If he would not like the questions of an interviewing woman journalist (Megyn Kelly on Fox News), he would attack her by calling her a "bimbo" and referring to her menstrual period ("blood coming out from everywhere").

Trump would not mind being bizarre and obscene in rating women by their looks and referring to his own and their private parts in response to Florida Senator Marco Rubio's barb that he was as small minded as his own small hands. He would not have qualms calling other presidential candidates buffoons and bullshit; Hillary Clinton "nasty" and "crooked" and "a world class liar" and "a devil;" and the reporters, on his suspicion that the "crooked" media was up against him, "the lowest forms of life" and special interest groups. He himself was being attacked by others as a bully, loud mouth dick, conman, hypocrite, huckster, sociopath, sinner, sadist, racist, sexist, xenophobic, misogynist, narcissistic, megalomaniac, Islamophobic, abhorrent, disturbing, temperamentally unfit and completely unqualified to be President of the United States of America.

Despite the countless A–Z problems in which the country is immersed, the AL is excessively concerned with the armed protection of its own people while completely "disarming" and dismantling the opposition, the BNP, which is by far the largest political party with the widest possible mass support in a country of 160 million. As the following catalogue of personal and political raw invectives (not to be confused with more civilized and sophisticated jabs and jokes and pokes and prods) demonstrate, it is the AL and its Sheikh Hasina that are way ahead of the BNP in dirtying the political waters with abusive and offensive language.[5] The BNP protested thousand times, in vain though, against Sheikh Hasina and her party using distasteful and disgraceful language and making baseless and preposterous accusations such as the most recent ones: holding the BNP leader Begum Khaleda Zia, on a personal family visit to the UK, responsible for the murder of the two foreigners (one Italian and one Japanese national), the two LGBT activists in Dhaka and one SP's wife Mitu in Chittagong.

The moment anything bad happens in the country, PM Hasina points her finger at the BNP-Jamaat. By virtue of her strange and incantatory power, she seems to possess a foreknowledge of who the killers are, whereas the police are still looking for a clue to guide them into apprehending them. Is Ms. Hasina a (sibyl) priestess descended from the ancient Greek Oracle of Delphi? After the murders, she issued a false and insinuating fatwa, the virtual edict/verdict, that the BNP-Jamaat were involved in those killings as if the killers were hiding somewhere, to her occult and miraculous foreknowledge. She claimed she, as head of the government, had all the information about all the secret killings. Would she then reveal who killed or kidnapped Chowdhury Alam, Elias Ali, Shagor-Runi, and thousands of others, including the February 2009 BDR massacre?

For the crimes committed, for example, in the UK or the USA, it is anybody's guess what kind of pandemonium, commotion, or hullabaloo the whole country would be if the president or the prime minister even indirectly or remotely hinted that the rival opposition was behind those crimes. The Hasina style thundering before there is lightning demonstrates that she is not only in the habit (as the second nature) of making herself light and silly by comments and statements that did not become her station but also that she and her men are incorrigibly, constitutionally, and congenitally allergic, jealous, and vindictive toward their political rivals, Khaleda and Tarique. Under Hasina, Bangladesh has become an example of how absolute power corrupts absolutely, allowing her (Hasina) to say anything she likes (without restraint or responsibility) to keep the BNP-led opposition out of her way.

As the people of Bangladesh are sick and tired of being aware, not a single demand by the BNP is any good in the eyes of the authoritarian and autocratic AL. As expected, the wrongheaded AL talks down and tramples down anything and everything the BNP says, regardless of how sound and sensible it is. The headstrong and hypochondriac AL dismisses, meanly and misanthropically, all the BNP's democratic agendas and activities as mere তামাশা and অন্তঃসারশূন্য (illogical and mindless, without any substance). Even the BNP leader Khaleda Zia's floral respects offered to the language martyrs is a তামাশা to the intolerant, vindictive, and paranoid Sheikh Hasina. She and the other leaders of her party attack Khaleda as a "queen of terror," "witch," and "hyena."[6] To them (that is, at least to Shahjahan Khan), "Khaleda is as inefficient as a bus driver." Anything Khaleda does or says, such as her political meetings, statements, and campaigns, is a mere নাটক (theatrical show) to the AL leaders.

The endless Awami comical analogies remind one of Macbeth's famous soliloquy, in of course a different (tragic) context:

> Life's but a walking shadow, a poor player
> That struts and frets his hour upon the stage
> And then is heard no more. It is a tale
> Told by an idiot, full of sound and fury,
> Signifying nothing.

The question is: if the political activities of the opposition are simply a নাটক (drama), why then so much police brutality and persecution, গুম ও খুন, হামলা ও মামলা, arrests and remands of the opposition members? Why then the AL would have to go on justifying the relentless neo-and-near fascist and totalitarian repression and implying even more of the same to follow, saying the opposition needed "higher antibiotic?"

The opposition also claims that it is Sheikh Hasina who has been playing a সন্ত্রাসী (terrorist) role since the day when, years ago, she allegedly said she wanted ten of the other side dead for one of her side (একটার বদলে দশটা লাশ চাই) and the June 5, 2004 series of arson/gun powder attacks on public transport in Dhaka, especially the one on a double-decker bus in front of Sheraton Hotel, killing nine passengers, including a two-year-old girl and injuring fifteen, to mention only a few among the countless other instances of the like. In his review of *BDR Massacre: Target Bangladesh* by Mohammad Zainal Abedin of New York, Dr M T Hussain comments on Ms Hasina's "politics of reprisal":

> The other amazing point was that the two days of killings and massacres went on almost uninterrupted not only in full knowledge of the PM of Bangladesh and her Army Chief but also of their curious inaction and a sort of playing with the lives of nearly five dozen senior and brilliant army officers.
>
> One may recall here a verbatim quote of Hasina made public by the [late] London based Octogenarian BBC Bengali Service journalist Serajur Rahman: "AMI RAJNITI GHRINA KORI KINTU PITRIHOTTYAR PROTISHODHER JONNYO RAJNITITE ESHECHI' (I hate politics but just only to take revenge of my father's killing I have taken on to politics)". That she is after the blood of the 15th August 1975 coup heroes is no secret … as all evidences are clear to anybody keeping track of facts surfacing. Soon after she took the Chair of the PM in 2009 she has already cleaned off the general administration, law enforcing agencies, education, etc from all her "undesirable" lots and replaced them with the party men and women. She has then put her ugly hand on the army as well. Many brilliant senior officers have already been sacked and removed at her free will for she is the Defense Minister. Should not the skeptics doubt that she enjoyed playing with the valuable lives of the five dozens army officers in the mayhem for her sadist pleasure? Even though some of the facts about Hasina's abnormal behavior as mentioned in [Motiur Rahman] Rentu's autobiography AMAR FANSHI CHAI may be questioned, the fact has been proved beyond doubt from many other sources that she is really a psychic case, and so possibly had her sadist pleasure in the BDR massacre.[7]

On March 14, 2015, Ms Hasina disgracefully and distastefully suggested that the BNP leader Salahuddin Ahmad, who was a victim in an ongoing series of alarming and terrifying abductions (of hundreds and hundreds) during her regime, could actually be smuggled out of the beleaguered Khaleda's office compound into the underground by Khaleda herself in a trash bag, along with the other bags of rubbish taken out of her office premises after months.[8] What a low and pitiful travesty the Hasina politics has degenerated into! When the facts are that (1) those bags were checked by the police, (2) that Salahuddin was abducted from a relative's home by dozens of mysterious (state-sponsored?) agents for his anti-Hasina political activism, (3) that these elements were armed and identified themselves as belonging to the detective branch, (4) that his whereabouts have remained unknown since 10 March, and (5) that his abduction followed some of the other members of his household picked up from his home by the regime's forces, how could a prime minister and her men make such a rude, inhuman, indecent, cruel, and sadistic remark?

The AL is of course habitually prone to attacking the BNP like anything at every step along the way, saying that the BNP must not play with fire: আগুন নিয়ে খেলা করবেননা, as Sheikh Hasina frequently warns the BNP leader Khaleda. One must not forget that Hasina became prime minister out of a farcical, duplicitous, and deceptive election held on what *BangoBir* Kader Siddiquee termed as one of the ugliest days in the history of Bangladesh—January 5, 2014. It was an election not unlike those held (actually "not held" or "un-held") in the most suppressive and authoritarian (to be distinguished from the most isolated and secretive) countries of the world, starting from Egypt, Zimbabwe, and Venezuela. Hitler also was an "elected" leader, to say the least.

As discussed below, the language used by Sheikh Hasina and her party men in attacking those who are opposed to them is rural and rustic, raw and repulsive, vulgar and vituperative, and low-class and substandard (if not absolutely dirty, filthy and nasty).[9] While inaugurating the intelligence and secret services headquarters in Dhaka, a top Awami leader sarcastically addressed the public intellectuals, critical of her government, as আঁতেল—a corrupt and distorted version of the word "intellectuals," just as another top Awami leader called those in favor of dialogue with the opposition to find a way out of the present political unrest as পাগল (mad, irrational, crazy). Such a dismissal, in a mocking manner, as many of their opposition-targeted comments normally are, was beneath their dignity.

If the past is an indication, the AL seems to be temperamentally unsuitable to govern and play a constructive role in bringing the nation together. It is characteristically and congenitally inclined to politicking, politicizing, plotting, and polarizing, with the intention of pushing the BNP to the wall and punishing it by sand and cement trucks, among various other torture tools and terror tactics. The AL's main intention is to crush, corner, and cripple the opposition by force, which in turn is forced to incline toward adopting similar, though ineffective and low-key tactics for survival in what is an extremely hostile and horrendous atmosphere of distractions and obstructions. Dependent on the politicized police-and-court-and-civil administration, as constantly alleged by the popular opposition, rather than on the wishes of the people, the overpowering AL is responsible for the sick and cynical political environment—social and political—prevailing in Bangladesh today.

Sheikh Hasina and her party members are known for slurs and insults against others. Many of the abusive expressions came and are coming directly from her and thrown at the top public figures of the nation. Despite holding the highest executive office, by force or farce, she does not mind going below her position in violation of all civilized norms, etiquettes, and standards. Twisting the name of the former president of the country, Dr A Q M Badrudduza Chowdhury, who was once briefly allied with her but is not with her any longer, she remarked that he was only a বদু কাকা, a low form of address for an uncle in an ordinary, rural Bangladeshi family. Dr Chowdhury, a highly respected political veteran on his own, was only a poor and pitiful বদু কাকু, accused by Sheikh Hasina of hobnobbing with Khaleda Zia.

Dr Chowdhury, however, politely protested against such ridicule thrown at him by the prime minister, pointing out the nice meaning of his good name. Similarly, she (Hasina) also twisted the name of another former president, Dr. Iazuddin Ahmed, as "Yes-Uddin". She and her son Joy (next in line) described the BNP, the largest and most popular political party of the country, as a party of চোর বাটপার জুয়াচোর (thieves and cheats and swindlers and gamblers) whereas their own party AL, in popular perception, is traditionally more so, forcing the BNP to follow similar tactics and call a spade a spade. As reported by RTN (rtnews24.com), Dr Asif Nazrul commented that Joy's remarks were of so low quality that he did not seem to be educated enough.

By all accounts as well as by common consent, Khaleda is the most popular and dignified politician in the country. She has been so for decades. She never lost any electoral seats or constituencies she contested from. When she visited the strife-torn Ramu, Chittagong, after the sectarian violence there (in her capacity as head of the largest political party in the country), her visit was described by Sheikh Hasina as সর্প হইয়া দংশন করে ওঝা হইয়া ঝাড়ে (biting as a snake and then treating the wound as a village quack for the snakebite).

As usual, Hasina jumped to the accusation that Khaleda was behind the Ramu vandalism and that her visit was like a false attempt to mend the rift caused by the religious strife in the Buddhist Ramu locality. Hasina described the BNP-led blockade of January 2015 as a last resort, following her all-out crackdown on the BNP-led opposition for years, as the bite of a poisonous snake. It has become an obsession for the authoritarian AL to immediately blame the BNP for anything that goes wrong in the country, although the Pandora's Box of ills and wrongs was opened by the AL in its nonstop persecution of the political opposition led by the BNP.

In the manifestations of the step-motherly, step-sisterly, and step-brotherly animosities and grudges that the AL harbors, as the characters in the folktales of *Cinderella*, *Beauty and the Beast*, and *Snow White* do, toward the opposition BNP, the সর্প (snake) politics was going on for a while both inside and outside the parliament. Among others, such Awami stalwarts as Mahbubul Alam Hanif, Hasan Mahmud, Motia Chowdhury, Suranjit Sen Gupta, Apu Ukil, Kamrul Islam, and the closely Awami-allied (in fact, more Awami than the Awamis) Hasanul Hoque Inu, Dilip Barua, and Rashed Khan Menon entered the fray by describing the relationship between the BNP and one of its alliance members, the Islamic party Jamaat, in similar terms. They said, provocatively, that the BNP, being in alliance with the Jamaat, was kissing the expanded hood of the snake only to be mortally bitten one day.

Sheikh Hasina sneeringly declared that she would not accept any opposition demands and would not give the opposition any space. She said there was no question of moving even by a hairbreadth from the (one-sidedly reconstituted) constitution, thus effectively telling the opposition of her resolve to hold the farcical and melodramatic "non-elections" on January 5, 2014 at any cost and warning the opposition not to play with the snake. Keeping in tune, her "yes" folks and ডুগডুগি men continued to say that they would treat the BNP like a *neri kutta* with গণধোলাই (meaning they would let loose mob violence to beat up the BNP like a stray female bitch).

The AL, like the BNP, has formed an alliance with several other small entities of little or no significance. The Inus, the Baruas, and the Menons, all as unelected as unelectable or questionably "elected" in sham and mock elections, have been rewarded with cabinet posts for getting onto the Awami boat. The coveted posts were like a dream come true for them. The Awamis and the Awami-sheltered elements said, incitingly, that Khaleda, in her political alliance with the Jamat, was the lady emir (chief) of the Jamat, that she was like a ডাইনি বুড়ি (old witch), and that she should take a political exit taking লোটা কম্বল (an earthen pot for water and a blanket used by poor village wanderers) with her as her last belongings.

It is this Inu (who, by the way, must be living up with a hearty laugh to the meaning of his name in Japanese, nicely exemplified by Russian President Vladimir Putin's loyal and faithful dog),[10] who was once equally sarcastically referred to as ইন্দুর/rat by the BNP Vice Chairman Shah Muazzem Hussein for organizing the terrorist *Ganobahini* that destabilized Sheikh Mujib's government in the 1970s and that attempted on his life too—a claim lent support to by many politicians, including the AL's Sheikh Fazlul Karim Selim and Syed Ashraful Islam and then BangaBir Kader Siddiquee and others. It is the same very Inu who indecently remarked that everything was possible in a prison except the supply of men and women for the detainees for the purpose of intimate physical relationship.[11]

As the LDP chief Col (Ret) Oli Ahmad and the fiery and fluent Papia (in her parliament speech) recalled, Inu's slogan, during the first half of the 1970s, was মুজিবের চামড়া তুলে নিবো আমরা ("Mujib is to be stripped/extracted off his skin ... We will take off Mujib's skin") and also জাতীয় বেঈমান *Sheikh Mujibur Rahman.*[12] It is this despotic, dictatorial, and power-drunk Inu who now most preposterously vilifies the most democratic and most popular leader of Bangladesh, BNP Chair Khaleda, as falsely crying for democracy like the mother fishes crying for the baby fishes they themselves ate up.

Ironically, Mujib's daughter Hasina, as Prime Minister, would still award the color changing Inu a cabinet position and Inu's once anti-Awami comrade Dr Anwar Hussein (brother of Col Taher) a vice chancellor position.[13] As if to faithfully and profusely return her favor, Inu has allowed himself to be transformed into an all "Awamite" or "Awamized" being than the original Awamis themselves are so that the hardly ever elected Inu would never stop handing out his ridiculous "extrajudicial" verdicts on Khaleda, the most popular and polished leader of the country, saying she was not a "medieval queen" to be above the law, she would be detained at Kashimpur jail and continually hurling taunts and insults at her.[14] True, no one should be above the law (except perhaps those in power like him) but to say so one does not have to resort to using mean analogies out of vengeful sadism. Secondly, unfortunately, the law has only been selectively (as opposed to equally and uniformly) applied against those out of power, leaving many criminals above the law while framing others on very light and small to completely unfounded evidence, inflated, magnified, distorted, and exaggerated out of pure political vendetta.

(There are no last words in politics. Finality is not the language of politics. This makes strange bed fellows there.) It is the same auto-elected হুক্কাহুয়া Inu, like the rest of the auto-elected majority in the Awami alliance he belongs to, who, in a baneful banishment of democracy and bipartisanship, said that Khaleda, chief of the largest political party BNP, should be banished from the country to save his "Awami" kind of "democracy" that would keep him in power for many more years! What a sham and shameless "champion" of democracy that slavishly serves to perpetuate dictatorship in a completely reverse gear! Hannan Shah, a late BNP leader, shot back saying Inu was licking the foot of those who once wanted to kick him out of the country.

Khaleda's protest against the autocratic Awami cancellation of the settled and popular Care Taker Government (CTG) and her demand for its reinstatement was mockingly described and dismissed by Hasina in the psychosexual terms of কোলে তুলে (lifting one on your lap).[15] The prime minister's low and mean hypothesis was that the former prime minister was wishfully longing to be put back in power by the interim CTG as if they (CTG) would let her ride on their arms or lap, which carried the hints of warm and cozy psychosexual innuendos. When Hasina returned to power several times during similar CTG administrations, one can then ask, as did দেশকন্যা Papia, "Did she also return to power with Ershad and Ghulam Azam doing the same favor to her?" One more example of her unpleasant and unbecoming language is when she said Khaleda did not have the strength in her waist কোমরে জোর নাই to topple the government.

It is true, Khaleda, being older, absolutely lonely for many years and completely subdued not only by the persecution and harassment of the Hasina police but also numerous politically motivated spurious court cases, may be said to have not as much physical strength as Hasina does. The latter has been in the best of her health, surrounded by her family members and enjoying the height of power in her political career to date. However, such a language of psychosexual flavor as above is not expected from someone of her position. If she could publicly enjoy, most rudely and discourteously, referring to the elder Khaleda's personal and private relationships (if there were any), one only needs to know what দেশকন্যা /*Desh-Konnya* Papia said on the parliament floor about her[16] and one only needs to read with relish the freedom fighter Motiur Rahman Rentu's 1999 book আমার ফাঁসি চাই (I Wish/Want/Long To Be Hanged) to find out the details of her young age affairs.[17] There is a Hadith by Prophet Muhammad that if anyone refrained from (unnecessarily) disclosing another Muslim's secrets (for mischievous purposes), God/*Allah* the Almighty would also conceal her/his faults in this world and the next. One, therefore, should not engage in the low-level smear politics of personal destruction.

Nonetheless, attacks by the AL—silly and obnoxious—continued, with Khaleda not to be allowed to fulfill her long-standing খায়েশ (a word meaning as much political and material as bodily desires). Directly or indirectly referring to Khaleda, the top AL leader described Khaleda as a শকুনি (female vulture), to be stopped by all means. On another occasion, the AL leader rebuffed Khaleda's democratic demands and protestations by saying, শকুনের দোয়ায় গরু মরেনা (cows or cattle do not die just because the low-flying vultures looking for food wish them to die so that they can live on the carcasses). Well, on a lighter note, if not for the sake of a serious argument, neither Hasina nor Khaleda will perhaps mind playing the role of a শকুনি so long as they can work as an agent to gather intelligence about each other the way Israel is said to have used vultures of long wings/tails equipped with GPS tracking devices as intelligence agents in Lebanon and Saudi Arabia, probably to bluff or scare its neighbors about its all-enveloping tentacles.

Anyway, to continue with the AL's low-quality attacks on Khaleda, her visit to India was described as তেল মারতে (oiling, worshipping, flattering and appeasing) the Indian leadership as if she was a willing sycophant of India. In popular perception it is exactly the opposite, that it is the AL who/which stand/s in the allegedly servile and slavish (নতজানু *mew-mew/coo-coo*) relationship with India and manages to remain in power with active and direct help from India.

When the veteran Barrister Rafiqul Hoque offered to head the CTG if it was to be reinstated for the cause of peace and democracy, which he thought was the only way to remedy the national tension and unrest, Hasina hurled an insulting taunt at him, saying, in local dialect, মুই কার খালুরে? (Whose uncle am I?), and making the senior Supreme Court lawyer the butt of a joke. Barrister Hoque was neglected as being nobody's uncle, meaning neither the CTG would be reinstated nor Hoque would be accepted as anybody on the CTG. Yet another former respectable CTG member, Dr Akbar Ali Khan, became an anathema to Hasina and earned the title of ব্যর্থ হোমরা চোমরা উপদেষ্টা (failed tall-talking adviser), following his suggestions to tide over the long persisting national crisis, turning from bad to worse, especially during the Hasina regime. There is a chronic tendency on her part to discard anything as trash and devalue everybody to an ordinary invisible anonymity. Only she and her cohorts are as indispensable as invincible!

It is a constant for Hasina to claim that Khaleda would not be allowed to come to power through the opportunist পেছনের চোরাগলি (dark and narrow back-door lanes and by-lanes). The question is, did Khaleda ever do so? Did the people of Bangladesh ever vote for her through dark back doors? Never. On the contrary, was not it Hasina who did so through an unholy backdoor blueprint understanding with the Iazuddin-Fakhruddin-Moinuddin-Masududdin (I-F-M-M) men in 2008 and then an immoral, vote-less, voter-less "elections" on January 5? By her own admission, the 2006–2008 CTG, claimed to be illegal by all opposition politicians, was the fruit of her anti-BNP movement, her আন্দোলনের ফসল. She therefore promised to award immunity and legitimacy to all the actions of that particular CTG if she were to be voted in, thus indirectly seeking the help of the I-F-M-M government to get to power. Obviously, as mapped and arranged, she got their help in procuring the necessary electoral votes and collecting the desired results in her basket. She faithfully kept her promise to F-M and their associates.

Hasina is happy that she was anxiously and agonizingly successful in keeping the BNP out of the pre-chalked-out voter-less January 5 "election" with the pre-determined results. She was able to do so by autocratically having the CTG system scraped and politicizing all government apparatus in her favor. She was satirical in saying that Khaleda missed the election train and that she should now take a train to her পেয়ারে (dear) Pakistan. Hasina should remember with gratitude that during the liberation war her family was on regular monthly financial assistance from the Pakistani government.[18] Following August 15, 1975, Hasina's love for the Pakistani army and her dislike of the Bangladesh army are on record.[19] Even if one puts aside Hasina's remark about Khaleda, one could say, she also may like to take a shuttle train to her beloved (পেয়ারে) India.

Having been able to keep the BNP out, Hasina is now happy that she does not have to listen to the opposition demands and deliberations in the present "unelected" (and so illegitimate) parliament, which, prior to the unacceptable January 5 "election," used to be, in her words, a bunch of খিস্তিখেউরি (nonsensical bull and cock narratives) by the BNP. The BNP was forced to stay out of the national parliamentary election, the only means by which governments change hands in a country all over the world. The BNP had issues with the Hasina government over the national election because it thought the harsh Hasina government would rig and manipulate the election—and would do so massively—to its favor. The BNP was right in its calculations and apprehensions. The rest is now history.

Since it had no serious quarrels with the government about the other elections, the BNP with its wide support base at all levels participated in the local municipal and city corporation elections after the national parliamentary election. Like the national parliamentary election, Hasina did not like the BNP taking part in the local elections because she rightly thought she would lose if the BNP participated. However, she could not stop the BNP from participating in the local elections. So she grudgingly accused Khaleda of licking her own spit (যেই থুথু একবার ফেলে দিয়েছে সেই থুথু আবার চেটে খাচ্ছে), referring to the BNP's boycott of the parliamentary election that, as mentioned above, was held under Hasina's own terms, not on the basis of national consensus or level playing field as demanded by the BNP.

Obviously, the whole world knows, Sheikh Hasina won the national election of January5, 2014 in the most farcical, phenomenally fantastic, and preposterous way. Now she attacked Khaleda, most distastefully and disgracefully, that she (Khaleda) was licking her own spit by taking part in the local elections while having previously boycotted what was actually a sick, stolen, and one-sided parliamentary election.

Sheikh Hasina and her lieutenants keep attacking Khaleda meanly and recklessly, saying she has to apologize (for what they view as her political wrong doings) by making নাকে খত (drawing a line on the ground by her nose, considered a very low form of humiliating punishment for the poor pickpockets or small thieves, চিকাচোর. They argue, with utter indignity, that Khaleda should recant, repent, and seek unconditional forgiveness for doing what they did not like and that she should promise not to do the same again by running her nose against the ground—নাকে খত দিয়ে তওবা করতে হবে.

Hasina's deputies and assistants, protected by double to triple security tier, keep on throwing insults at the former prime minister Khaleda, who is by far the most popular and polished leader of the country. They are asking her to do মুখে লাগাম (meaning, to stop talking by putting a bridle on her mouth like a horse). They keep rejecting the opposition leader's demands as stray মামা বাড়ির আম দুধ / দুধ ভাত আবদার (entreaties that children affectionately make to their aunts or uncles over the traditional delicious rice dishes of milk and mango).

The ruling regime routinely rejects everything from the opposition—all proposals, propositions, offers of dialogue—, as one of its ministers—Abul Ma'al Abdul Muhith—always does, as *rubbish* and ফটকাবাজি (fun fire-cracking). It views everything that is different from its own খায়েশ as simply trash. In their fulsome flattery and sycophancy of their leader Hasina, the Awami leaders blindly support all sorts of her government's oppression of the opposition, proudly proclaiming, as both Suranjit Sen Gupta and Muhammad Nasim did, that: বাঘে ধরলে ছাড়ে হাসিনা ধরলে ছাড়েনা (while even the tiger sometimes lets its victim go, Hasina never does).[20] Nasim and Suranjit, knowingly or unwittingly, out of their cult-like worship of Hasina, implied that, like Shakespeare's King Lear's eldest daughters—Goneril and Reagan—their Hasina was like a tigress in human form. Some critics have described this as a kind of oiling that turns a woman into a man and brings huge favors to the oiler.[21]

By the way, Suranjit was a Railways minister for a short while and then was made a minister without a portfolio, also for a short while, following his alleged involvement in the bribery scandal of midnight sacks of Railway money and many other financial scandals, especially in his later years, that completely negated and discredited his once bright political past. His deep deviations suggested he compromised the moral and political principles he was once known to have upheld.[22] He compromised whatever integrity he had in his political career, including his walking back on the CTG issue, and went out of his way to show and shower his excessive and overflowing praise on Sheikh Hasina (as all her supporters, cronies and sycophants normally do, with no limit to their democratically detrimental panegyric, eulogy, encomium of their two leaders—Mujib and Hasina). All this was perhaps done by Suranjit in an effort to get away with the financial slips and pitfalls he was alleged to have succumbed to and for which he should have been fully and properly investigated then and should still be thoroughly investigated now that he is dead, posthumously, with no exception, of course, to other miscreants, regardless of their color.

Sheikh Hasina, however, let Suranjit go half-way, instead of kicking him out all the way. To prove his moral courage, he should have left both the party and the government on his own, but he didn't, proving himself to be a downright coward (like many others in the political history of Bangladesh). Bold and courageous BNP Vice Chairman Shah Muazzem Hussein, who is of a great and glorious political career, described Suranjit's dubious and doubtful political journey as one from "a black cat" to "Alhaj Sufi Darvish Khaja Islamic thinker."[23] It is this Suranjit who initially did not support the killing or quashing of the CTG system but then caved in to Hasina's wishes and desires, as many others also did (and always do in the political culture of Bangladesh). It is this less than morally upright, in fact, more than morally bankrupt Suranjit, who, as an uncritical follower of Hasina, kept asserting, in a politically incorrect way, that Khaleda, the most popular political leader of Bangladesh, had to be uprooted from politics.

Midnight talk shows of democratic views and differing voices are টক (sour) to Ms Hasina. To her, political analysts and commentators appearing on those late night shows are no better than সিঁদকাটা গলাকাটা rogues and miscreants (midnight thieves and murderous robbers). Using the undemocratic language of force, she makes repeated calls that nobody would be allowed to play foul ছিনিমিনি with the people's right to vote. Unfortunately, if elections after elections—local or national, city or parliamentary—were an indication, it was exactly she who played ছিনিমিনি to steal the people's right to vote through her party and government machinations and manipulations.

The AL is there to bully the BNP out of their unelected brute majority and follow the formula of the East India Company monopoly. Except the AL, all the rest are subject to force and made vulnerable. Except theirs, patriotism of others is nothing but a seditious subterfuge. Patriotism is theirs only to have the ownership of and keep control over. They think the love of the country is a sole agency of theirs alone. The former home minister, M. K. Alamgir, asserted that the BNP did not have the মুরোদ (slang for manly strength and courage) to do any আন্দোলন (movement). In the AL's view, American Assistant Secretary of State Nisha Desai Biswal was only দুই আনার মন্ত্রী, চার আনাও না (a minister worth at best a dime, not even a quarter) and she was only a বালিকা মন্ত্রী (a teenage immature girl minister); and then American ambassador to Bangladesh, Dan Mozena, was no better than a domestic maid.

Like the Jews (Israelites), who think they are the only chosen people of God, Hasina thinks she and her party and her police/RAB are the only chosen people of Bangladesh, the only nexus, and the only righteous standard bearers all the way. She and her police/RAB think theirs is the only way and theirs to find a convenient way, of their own choosing, to do away with the political opposition. They put their men everywhere to secure the state apparatus in their possession for their singularly partisan and parochial use.

Hasina and her men leave no doubt that they are there to forcibly hold on to power and to crush and cripple and corner and silence and squeeze and eliminate and annihilate and eradicate the opposition BNP by all means possible and available. Time has come when the people of Bangladesh are about to agree to the lesson of Aesop's fable "The frogs desiring a king" that no rule is better than cruel rule, in other words, cruel rule is worse than no rule.

Slighting with neglect the 50-year old BNP Senior Vice Chairman Tarique Rahman as the তুই of a little boy with runny nose, as if he also was of the level of a housemaid, an AL leader, Tofael Ahmed, claimed, most impolitely, that his father, President Ziaur Rahman, was busy, during 1972–1975, greeting the AL leaders with *salams* and polishing their shoes as his (Zia's) seniors and superiors. There being nothing wrong with respecting the higher-ups, which is a standard practice in human society, the first part of Tofael's comment was fine except that it was made with the intention of belittling a heroic freedom fighter, who was also a former army chief and a former president of the country.

The second part of Tofael's comment is of course totally unacceptable and disagreeable. Weren't the many likes of Tofael busy polishing General Zia's shoes when he was President? Ms Hasina threw verbal assaults at Tarique as Khaleda's কুপুত্র কুলাঙ্গার (evil son black sheep), and অশিক্ষিত জানোয়ার (an uneducated beast), who was admonished to hold his tongue in check.[24] She retorted that Tarique needed to be treated in a "befitting" manner and be given lessons like an animal in order to make him hold back—all in response to Tarique's political attacks on Mujib.

All these are part of an ongoing political rhetoric and personal attack, sometimes really foul and filthy, hurled at each other between the two major rival parties. People know what Motia Chowdhury said about Mujib decades ago—the ডুগডুগি thing (small *tabla*-like drums for musical fun), to be made of Mujib's raw skin. Ironically, she is now a close friend and literally a cult-like worshipper of Mujib's daughter and prime minister Sheikh Hasina, describing the latter's two quite average children, Joy and Putul (like anybody else's, minus the government privileges they now enjoy) as being made of diamond, while castigating the BNP leader Khaleda Zia and her children as nothing but thieves.[25]

The reality is, when one is in power, especially the near-fascist power, one's misdeeds, no matter how mountain-high they are, can get a blanket cover and draw a total blank. While the great freedom fighter Shamsher Mobin Chowdhury was called a বেঈমান (betrayer/traitor) by Hasina for siding with the BNP, there are countless, such as Motia and Inu (who once wanted to see Mujib with his skin off) and Abdul Gaffar Chowdhury, who have become trustworthy to her by turning their back and bonding with her in an unctuous and flattering political fealty.[26]

When the journalist couple Shagor and Runi were murdered in their own home, ATN Bangla Chairman, Mahfuzur Rahman, claimed in London that Hasina sometimes talked like a *bachal* (one who is senselessly talkative and garrulous) or an *orbachin* (one who is foolish and childish). Again, simply because Mahfuzur Rahman and his TV channel were and continue to be uncritically loyalist and supportive of the Hasina government in a fulsome manner, Mahfuzur's "family feud" words were taken equally uncritically and no action against him ever followed. Similarly, he, along with Mozammel Babu of Channel Ekattor, attacked Channel I Chairman Faridur Reza Shagor as a "neo-cultural rajakar," who they said was involved in the conspiracy of Bangladeshi ads being aired on Indian channels.[27] Since it is a pro-Awami friendly fire, nothing is expected to happen.

By contrast, political or nonpartisan critics (like the JU teacher) who do not support the prime minister or her government are thrashed into the tortuous police remand and thrown behind bars for their slight and modest criticism of her, although they are simply exercising their democratic freedom of expression within limits. One knows how President Barack Obama, his wife, and their family were depicted as monkeys, gorillas, and chimpanzees in a culture of free expression with no strings of penalty.[28] There are so many TV shows in Europe and America bitterly and pungently satirical of the world leaders.

One remembers what Abdul Malek Ukil said about Mujib in London in 1975 and what Humayun Rasheed Chowdhury said in Sylhet, justifying Mujib's assassination.[29] One recalls how Shah Muazzem Hussein, then an Ershad cabinet minister and now a BNP leader of great courage and charisma, once undermined the status of the two ladies—Khaleda and Hasina—and their joined movement against H M Ershad during the 1980s. People did not forget how Salahuddin Quader Chowdhury (SQC) once belittled his party leader Khaleda, who, he thought, was acting under the influence of her young son Tarique Rahman. Chowdhury drew an unpalatable analogy of whether it was the dog that wagged its tail or it was the tail that wagged the dog.

Unlike Hasina, Khaleda is known for her dignity and decency. Her nice choice of words in beautiful Bangla is always commendable. Her lapses and blemishes are too few to count, too few to matter. Since, however, she is known for courtesy, politeness, and her laconic but powerful understatements, hardly using any odd or awkward language, her rare and uncharacteristic লেংড়া ও লুলা (lame and limping), directed at the AL years ago, did not go down well with the public. That was perhaps the only instance of the kind in her long political career—an instance dwarfed and drowned beside the countless many and more from her political opponents, including Sheikh Hasina herself.

On the other hand, compared with the frequently used rough and reckless verbal and body language of Hasina and her cronies (such as Motia Chowdhury, Amir Hussein Amu, Sheikh Selim, Hasanul Inu, Kamrul Islam, Mahbubul Hanif, and Hasan Mahmud, among others), that of an interesting personality no less than SQC was more well-intentioned. He was after all a senior leader, of the highest echelon of his party, and his offensive was later ignored, especially there being no last/final word in politics. Hasina forgot Motia's most abusive and attacking ডুগডুগি thing and Inu's most vilifying চামড়া stuff, because both of them, like Khaleque Biswas of Neamat Imam's realistic political fiction *The Black Coat*, turned from being harsh critics to radical followers of the AL.

Khaleda also forgot about SQC's *wag* thing, although he (SQC), unlike Motia and Inu, never became a full and complete Khaleque Biswas due to his distinct, distinguishing, and discriminating personality. After all, SQC was never like Inu, who, far below the former as he is in terms of national stature and ideological standing, is, according to the BNP leader Gayeswar Chandra Roy, a জাতীয় বেয়াদব/national thug, a Gano-Bahini জঙ্গী/terrorist, and a paid agent of a foreign intelligence (RAW?).[30] Inu's and Motia's most recent verbal abuses, anarchically and nihilistically nasty, including those by Sheikh Selim, hurled on the parliament floor, over the abolition/abrogation of the 16th amendment by the Supreme Court, against Chief Justice S K Sinha and the senior lawyers like Dr Kamal Hussein and Barrister Amirul Islam, turned the so-called "noble," actually what is in practice a rubber stamp parliament into a true শুয়রের খোয়াড়/pig farm, a notorious nomenclature originally coined by Chairman Mao Zedong in China and imported into Bangladesh by ASM Abdur Rob in early 1970s.

In any case, it is the AL that started the ignoble tradition of war of words. It started attacking Zia, Zia's family, and the BNP in the most unacceptable manner. Only once in a while the BNP strikes back. It is simply following the footsteps of the AL in this offensive and indecorous tug of war, just as it was taking on the lead of the AL in other areas—corruption, politicization, criminalization, so on. Its stock defensive reply to the ever offensive AL, that ইট মারলে পাটকেল খেতে হয় (tit for tat, or every action has its equal and opposite reaction) sums it all. These things would not have happened if the AL established good governance and good political conduct, to begin with. This kind of verbal abuse will continue until there is a real change in the political culture of Bangladesh.

It is in the heels of this acrimonious background that the PAR trio came into the picture. In the context of the unwelcome and unwholesome contribution mainly by the AL, they had one's cheers for their performance in the parliament. They had one's applause—many rounds indeed, especially when there was already a full plate of un-parliamentary things taking place in the parliament. Let the red turn green for them—honest, courageous, spontaneous, outspoken, eloquent as they were, committed to the pressing national causes of the moment. They stood up to challenge the evils committed by the AL government the way they thought was effective, appropriate and point blank. They simply exercised their right to freedom of speech in protesting against what was in their view a violation and miscarriage of justice in many fields of national concern.

Rhetorical skills, including comic and satirical twits and taunts, cartoons and caricatures, portraits, shows and sketches (within limits, of course), are considered an important component of not just political oratory, public speeches, and persuasive writing since the ancient times but also free speech in general. The PAR's rhetorical style, however low it sounded, was in fact articulate, timely and to the point. Far from being rude and obscene, they merely seemed to have been edging toward the rough and tumble with the flavor of colloquial dialect. The PAR trio must have done so to only forcefully speak their mind—what they passionately believed in for the sake of the political and democratic freedom of expression.

When the parliament was seen as being nonfunctional, dysfunctional, malfunctional, funny, stagnant, one-sided, short-sighted, merely routine and rubber stamp, and also abusive to the dead as well as the alive, the PAR trio breathed a life into it and gave it a motion and "a local habitation". The way they made their protest through a reverse gear was supposed to pave the way for constructive dialogue and food for thought. Their bold contribution can therefore be regarded as something more meaningful and far better than that of the nefarious and mischievous 1/11 terracotta tetra—Moinuddin, Fakhruddin, Masududdin, and Iajuddin—all combined.

Some may argue that freedom does not mean license, that it means responsibility and that it has its limits. True. But, instead of howling ("full of sound and fury signifying nothing") and hurling baseless attacks on the person of anybody, dead or alive (which some government members were recklessly free to do, sometimes even invoking the red district culture, as Dipu Moni did), the PAR trio were actually critical of the Awami system as a whole. They were perfectly within limits in ventilating their repressed emotions that accumulated over the years of what they (and the majority of the electorate) must have thought as the sluttish Awami misrule and mismanagement.

By the way, part of the Awami extravagance and inefficiency is not only Hasina's expensive tours of the USA with large delegations but also her ex-উড়াল (flying) foreign minister Dipu Moni's excessively frequent flights. As the American Presidential aspirant Carly Fiorina took a jab at the ex-American foreign secretary Hilary Clinton, who is now a likely Democratic Party nominee for President, one can also say to Moni that her nonstop flying was "an activity, not an accomplishment," which makes one recall the kids learning Toys "R" Us V-tech laptop that starts with "Choose an activity."[31]

English writer Saki (pseudonym of Hector Hugh Munro) wrote, in the ironically humorous, yet human context of his famous story "Mrs. Packletide's Tiger," that "there are limits beyond which repressed emotions become dangerous." Thanks to the PAR trio, who by no means took it to any dangerous length, not even by the Awami standard illustrated above, and who, like Saki, wisely gave expression to their emotions with a good amount of salty humor. Humor—sad or sweet, light or wry—is a universally winning element in all political and public rapport. It is a civilized and advanced linguistic and rhetorical means to persuade others to a certain point of view. This means that it does not always have to be achieved or carried out in an elevated, exalted and dignified epic style. Those who are creative, capable and courageous can always find room to manipulate and maneuver the mode of humor in their own way. That is what the PAR trio did, following the standard already set by the AL.

Bangladesh needs the PAR in the public interest and the interest of the great majority. Bangladesh needs them to protest against the unjust. The country needs them as the voice of the oppressed, persecuted, and bedeviled. Their vocal and verbal attacks were like wake-up calls against the rampant rapacity resorted to by the Awami regime. That is why Muazzem Hussein Alal of the BNP defined the AL government, with rhetorical humor, as a government "*off* the people, *far* the people, *bye* the people." In other words, it is a one party government of the AL, for the AL, by the AL. It is also a one-party government of the police, by the police, for the police. Talking about how "India-Bangladesh defense pact" was "Honey mixed with poison for a friend," journalist Minar Rashid describes the Hasina government as "government by India, for India and of India."[32]

Had Abe Lincoln known the lamentable state into which democracy in Bangladesh degenerated, ridden and riddled with a strong dose of neo-and-near-and-more-than-partial despotism, personality cult, and foreign intervention, he would have probably agreed with Alal, Rashid, and all the political opposition with a light-hearted laugh, not unmixed with a sour note of despair and disappointment and discontentment.

Both Shammi Akhter of Sylhet and Rehana Ranu of Noakhali deserve public support for their honest courage and bold free speech. The decaying and decadent Awamis who are full of foul and filthy language for the country's Chief Justice S K Sinha, both inside and outside the parliament, have no right to criticize the great patriotic women's sarcastic slangs in the parliament out of their sincere protest and frustration about the relentless Awami horror and terror, suppression and repression. Akhter's well-intentioned চুতমারানি was hurled on the parliament floor at the endless Awami abuses in the form of গুম খুন হামলা মামলা, including the forced disappearances of hundreds of BNP leaders for whom their wives and children are still crying to the point of being left with no tears any more.

It is ironically surprising that the nonstop গুম খুন হামলা মামলা, police detention of dozens a day, and the bloody political and physical butchery of the opposition under the Hasina regime make every day a doomsday, a black day of mourning, while August 15, August 21, November 3, December 14, and May 31 also were very painful.

Ranu's spicy and spontaneous তত্ত্বাবধায়ক সরকার লইয়া চুদুর বুদুর চৈলতোন (no hanky-panky, no kidding, with the CTG) was directed at the authoritarian and tyrannical Awami machinery of control and manipulation, not any person in particular. When the country has been reeling and whirling and wriggling, like T. S. Eliot's image of the earthworm fixed on a wall for dissection, for many years of Awami horror and terror, and injustice and intolerance, Ranu's street slang চুদুর বুদুর was just a mild ventilation of anger and frustration. Even the West Bengal press reported that it was a common rural expression, neither vulgar nor obscene.[33] Look at how many an AL and their alliance leader, from top to bottom, has been constantly (ab)using and indulging their freedom of expression in undesirable and unacceptable language against the BNP. The language used by Rehana Ranu, Shammi Akhtar, and Papia was no more than point by point rebuttal and frontal attack on what was consistently perceived to be an unyielding Awami trend of obstinacy and obduracy.

The debacle over the parliamentary versus un-parliamentary language was tantamount to making a mountain out of a molehill. Those pro-AL elements crying foul over the "just fine" PAR recipe did so as if the Awami dull and dry invectives were more acceptable to them while blowing the trumpet to make a clarion call to only the BNP to avoid its style of attack on the AL. It was too simplistic of them to consider the vigorous and vehement PAR expression more dangerous than the other truly destructive ills and evils of the society. In being excessively critical of the PAR, they thought they were either launching a crusade against the countless ills and evils of the country or turning a blind eye to them. They were like the strainer or the sieve, itself full of pores and holes, but blaming the needle for its one single hole.

The pro-Awami overreaction to the sour and salty PAR style in the parliament was made as if it was an attempt by them to save the country from what were far more critical, corrosive, and cancerous: poverty, illiteracy, subhuman slums, dehumanizing drug abuse, Indian-made Indian-exported *yaba* and phensedyl plague,[34] low working conditions in garment factories, prostitution, child abuse, child marriage, child labor, inhuman dowry system, teenage pregnancy, alarming mobile and internet porn, physical and sexual violence against women,[35] open immoral and unsocial nudity, mosquito nuisance, formalin food, and traffic jam, let alone the abysmal wholesale corruption and oppression and blanket politicization and commercialization of politics and public service the country has descended into from the beginning but more deeply and irretrievably under the present government.

When the ship of the country is sinking, just as a boat sinks when it sinks, under the weight of widespread repression, suppression, oppression, and persecution the list of which is as endless as the flies and vultures and crows constantly buzzing and whirling and hovering over the rotten Municipality rubbish with hundreds and hundreds of horrendous and harassing হামলা ও মামলা (physical and penal suffering) against the opposition members, getting loud against the PAR is nothing more than shedding crocodile's tears or putting the cart before the horse.

Let us not be a one-eyed onlooker, jaundiced and prejudiced against the so-called offensive un-parliamentary language used by some opposition members. The extent of offensiveness one can read in their language is nothing compared with what has been detailed above by the "position" members in power. Attacking the unfair and unjust in somewhat offensive language by the opposition is one thing; making vindictive, venomous, and vituperative personal attacks by the ruling party members is quite another. While the latter is totally unacceptable, the former is different in the context that it could be taken as an outburst of frustration and helplessness in the face of the deeply entrenched Awami autocratic power, regardless of whether that explosion of frustration took place in the parliament or elsewhere, on the TV talk-shows or beyond.

Unlike the West, in Bangladesh, as the saying goes, সোজা আঙুলে ঘি উঠেনা (you cannot help yourself with *ghee*, an oily butter-like thick delicious substance, made from the cream of milk, by a straight finger, which metaphorically means nothing can be done by being naïve, simple and innocent). In the Indian subcontinent, those wishing to avoid duty, responsibility and accountability traditionally suffer from the obvious mania of জেগে ঘুমানো (pretending to be asleep while actually awake). In many countries, including Bangladesh, everything needs a push, a hard push, a forceful push, a violent thrust, even to the scale of bloody agitation and violence. There, everything needs to be fought for and fought out to the last, sometimes with the power of language to the extent of using it in an untraditional, even prejudicial way.

Bangladesh is a country of immense and endless possibilities, on all fronts—good or bad, except patriotic politics and clean elections. Such possibilities are symbolized by countless political instances such as the senior citizens Rawshon-cum-versus-Ershad as the surreal parliamentary opposition leader (handpicked by Hasina even before the rigged and stolen election with its predetermined outcome). The awkward mermaid-like tail has its flippers in equally weird and absurd arrangements about some cabinet positions from the Hasina government-manufactured "opposition" party made into part of the government at the same time. The same instance extends into the old melodramatic Ershad, who is the head of the (same government-made) "bait" domestic opposition and who is also a part of the bizarre hotchpotch/ হ য ব র ল Hasina government.

Similar possibilities include: (1) the miraculous survival of the young Reshma of Rana Plaza; (2) thousands of poor workers dead in the fire of the garment factories; (3) little Ziad (or Jihad) and little Nirob of the deadly WASA manhole; (4) young Felani and countless killings on the border with India; (5) "only" one or two children murdered a day[36]; (6) young men and women such as Sagor and Runi, Faisal Arefin Dipon, Ovijit Roy, Viswajit Roy, and cook Jamal all killed; (7) daily about a dozen women raped, murdered, burnt, and sexually harassed[37]; (8) nearly 32,000 women raped, mass raped, acid burnt and abused in last 5 years[38]; (9) nonworking close circuit cameras here and there or everywhere (if working, they go "nonworking" at the time of crime on the crime scene; (10) smart and intelligent young mechanical engineers outwitting the experienced professionals and lifting the dead little Ziad out of the dark hole; (11) the frequently occurring গুম ও খুন (of thousands and thousands, forcibly abducted only to be killed and, if it is a girl, mass raped and then killed by the forces of a shadowy "government" within a government); and (12) hundreds of thousands, mostly from India, allowed to stay in Bangladesh without valid legal status, confirming the suspicion about the dark elements engaged in a variety of subversive and anti-social activities.[39]

To refer to Saki's story once again, under the Hasina regime, all in its axis are bound to each other in a bait or dowry or bribery system: some play the hypocritical Mrs. Packletide, seemingly winning but actually paying a heavy price for their name and greed; some play the role of the exploiting Miss Mebbin, her hired companion, taking advantage of her vulnerabilities; some are like the poor Indian villagers hungry for whatever tiny peanut pieces of the pie they receive; some are the quiet and passive tool like the bait goat of the story, chained and shackled and tied and tethered to a post; some are happy to be in the position of the old and weak tiger helplessly looking for its hunts to somehow survive and yet inevitably stepping into the trap only to die of heart attack at the merest attempts by others.

Anything and everything is possible in Bangladesh, except free and fair elections. Shakespeare's witches can easily find a fertile ground there, as they do in the land of Macbeth and Duncan, to sing or chant the morally reversed "fair is foul, foul is fair." When there is too much on the negative side, there is inevitably chaos and confusion. So, why to be so critical and perturbed about what may at best have been a language thrust toward the foul by certain well-intentioned MPs?

Unlike the witches, the PAR must not have intended to compromise with the fair. Their style of expression must have been in an effort to address a host of crippling wrongs, all of national magnitude. When the mild, polite, pure, standard, and straightforward language of democratic opposition goes unheard and, unfortunately, falls on deaf ears (which are otherwise all ears for their own vested interests), some roughness or uncouthness is occasionally needed as a sort of jolting awakening and therapeutic shock. It is not unusual that the voice of right and legitimate protest sometimes takes an oblique, slanted, and unexpected turn.

Let us not stifle the voice of democratic challenge and just and positive and constructive criticism in the name of cleansing the parliament by imposing restrictions on the so-called un-parliamentary language. Let us not take away from the freedom of speech—even if that means freedom of expression with an element of coarse and unrefined humor. That would be myopic and monolithic. Let us not unnecessarily censor the free and forceful utterance of democratic dissent unless it descends and degenerates into the humorless, utterly raw, and most unrefined. In his classic *Areopagitica*, Milton eloquently and convincingly argues that people would automatically reject the unspeakable and unreadable; there is no need to subject such stuff to censorship, which is likely to create a problem for the free flow of the good. If nudity and pornography can be an art (sometimes for private pleasure, sometimes for public display in world-famous museums, sometimes for recognized businesses), if bad words and nasty phrases find way into first-class poetry, and if overtly sexual and graphically pictorial scenes can be there in classic novels and films, why to overreact to the otherwise interesting choice of local vocabulary by the PAR and SQC? (By the way, I am against all kinds of nudity and pornography).

People know and would agree that the root of all this lies in the injustices of all kinds perpetrated all the time in Bangladesh. As it has been detailed from the beginning, the culture of not so pleasant a language, almost to the extent of being coarse and vulgar, was first introduced from the very prime ministerial level. It is this initial introduction, to be in practice without a break, that provoked and prompted the spontaneous reaction from some of the patriotic quarters in perfectly legitimate rebuttal only. All might not be expected to employ the similar language. Some would prefer plain and simple Bangla; some, more standard Bangla; some might choose to spice it up a bit, according to their well-intentioned style and rhetoric.

In the case of the PAR, it was a follow-up only of the precedents set earlier by other leading politicians from the AL, with a slangy touch, which, naturally, started trickling down as an inherited tradition. The bottom line is that no one, let alone the personalities of national prominence, is a mean Shylock to be spitted upon, out of hate, by an abusive Antonio, under the shelter of this or that undue despotic and autocratic privilege. The only exception here is Ershad, president of Bangladesh from 1982 to 1990, who came down to be vilified as a থুথু বাবা (a low class "father" to be spitted upon), a বিশ্ব বেহায়া (a world class person of no shame) and a CMLA (cancel my last announcement) for constantly changing his mind and being chronically unreliable and fickle-minded.[40]

One may bring up here the instance of SQC. He had a distinctively funny and witty style of his own—a body language that might have been born of his personal pride, upbringing, and convictions.[41] Some may or may not have liked that, but it was his natural body language—irreverent yet colorful. It was what and who he was, influenced or affected by his rich political and family background of long standing. Why to be so critical about his saucy demeanor, which was not without humor? It was far better than many testy and irritating Awami leaders. Don't Hasina and her men and women have their body language with objectionable expressions against Zia, Khaleda, and others?

One reserves the right to strongly protest the awkward statements made by those in reference to SQC's colorful body language and his charming and entertaining verbal assaults at others, adding a variety necessary to complete the diversity of the political class of the country. They thought he was a psychopath, as it were. He simply was not. He knew himself well. On a Channel I *TM* program, he wittily made light of the negative media reports against him as if they were waters spilt (or sprayed) over a duck, which characteristically keeps itself clean and dry of such things. Similarly, he denied his involvement in any goods illegally coming through his shipping lines just as Biman Bangladesh Airlines MD might not be responsible for tons of gold smuggled aboard through the Biman flights. Now that SQC, along with others, met with a tragic end for crimes they denied, doubted, and disputed at a judicial or quasi-judicial court they considered partial and unfair, may they all be forgiven of their sins and given the award-winning permanent resident status in a divinely endowed floral and riverine hillside abode of endless undisturbed peace and repose!

Once the culture of democracy and democratic trust and tolerance is established and institutionalized, all kinds of dirty and filthy vilifications would fade and filter away. It is then that all kinds of outrageously unscrupulous words of mouth—all taken from the Awami playbook—are likely to wither away, of and by themselves. Until that happens and in order to lead to that goal, let the PAR feel free to air their grievances and champion their causes the way they like—from magisterial and stately to the vernacular of local and street slangs—with only one condition attached though. And that is, so long as it does not lapse into mere character assassination of the national heroes or, for that matter, anybody—dead or alive—let the freedom of expression fly up and up.

Notes

1. The term or the title means "Daughter of the Land," self-coined, which occurs throughout the book whenever the names of Farhana or Papia come up.
2. As posted on https://sathkahonbd.blogspot.com/2017/04/blog-post_38.html (আহমদ শরীফের ডায়েরি থেকে/From the diary of Ahmad Sharif).
3. http://www.ittefaq.com.bd/capital/2015/11/19/43876.html
4. https://www.dailyinqilab.com/details/16589/
5. http://www.sheershanewsbd.com/2015/11/13/103639; http://www.prothom-alo.com/bangladesh/article/646222/. Since Sheikh Hasina refers to Khaleda's personal relationships, one needs to look at Hasina's private relationships in this book banned by her: http://amarfashichai.blogspot.com/2013/07/amar-fashi-chai-by-motiur-rahman-rentu.html; http://amarfashichai.blogspot.co.uk (in English translation).
6. http://www.daily-sun.com/post/98623/Be-aware-of-BNPJamaat-hyenas:-PM; M. H. Chowdhury Maya attacked Khaleda by saying she was like a witch and a hyena: http://www.sheershanewsbd.com/2014/11/02/56471#

7. https://uglyduckblog.wordpress.com/2013/02/25/a-book-review-bdr-massacre-target-bangladesh/
8. See Mohammed Zainal Abedin, http://banews24.com/whole-country2/117-whole-country-4/12434
9. The BNP has always criticized Sheikh Hasina for her offensive style: http://www.sheershanewsbd.com/2015/10/04/98778
10. http://www.thedailystar.net/offbeat/putins-barking-dog-takes-center-stage-media-interview-1330318
11. http://www.amardeshonline.com/pages/details/2016/01/13/319159; http://www.dainikamadershomoy.com/2016/01/13/68014.php#
12. https://www.youtube.com/watch?v=Re_6xt3qZWY; https://www.youtube.com/watch?v=gkFWqmBaCnY
13. http://www.amadershomoys.com/content/2014/04/26/middle0830.htm; http://www.amardeshonline.com/pages/details/2013/03/03/190388
14. http://www.sheershanewsbd.com/2015/06/26/86280#
15. https://www.youtube.com/watch?v=baAX_B7GGj0; https://www.youtube.com/watch?v=BCb9it7AiOQ
16. http://www.rtnews24.com/video/6767656/
17 The book of gripping details about the personal and political life of Sheikh Hasina was banned by her but is available online: http://amarfashichai.blogspot.com/2013/07/amar-fashi-chai-by-motiur-rahman-rentu.html; https://www.youtube.com/watch?v=3rpAXMm7y9U; http://bdnews24.com/politics/2007/11/10/controversial-author-of-amar-fashi-chai-dies-in-paris; for the English version of the book: http://www.angelfire.com/planet/amarfashichai/Amar_Fashi_Chai.pdf; http://amarfashichai.blogspot.co.uk.
18. In 1971 Begum Mujib received Pakistan govt.allowance:
http://www.amadershomoys.com/newsite/2014/12/22/171698.htm. The writer of the report has quoted from Oli Ahad's book to confirm that Mrs. Mujib was on monthly government allowance in 1971. The amount was 1,500 taka per month, which was a lot of money then, in addition to all other expenses borne by the Pakistani government, which treated Mujib's family, including Hasina, as special guests while genocide was raging throughout the country. Mujib' safety was assured by the US ambassador Joseph Farland beforehand.
19. http://priyoboi.blogspot.co.uk/2012/09/blog-post_16.html. Hasina's outlook about the armies of Bangladesh and Pakistan is narrated in the book, আমার ফাঁসি চাই (I Wish/Want To Be Hanged) by Motiur Rahman Rentu: http://amarfashichai.blogspot.co.uk The narration (in the English translation of the book, http://www.eboi.ml/2017/02/amar-fasi-cai.html), is as follows:
"UNCIVILIZED UNPATRIOTIC FORCE On May 3, 1984, in the late afternoon, Sheikh Hasina was chatting with a few people at Bangabandhu Bhaban. In the course of discussions the topic of liberation war and Pakistan Army came up. Also came up

for discussion the subject of Bangladesh Army, which emerged through the war of liberation. The leader Sheikh Hasina commented about Bangladesh Army, "Is it an Army? It is a barbaric Force composed of ill-disciplined, greedy, unruly and blood-thirsty men. This Army has no sense of loyalty, no discipline, no patriotism. They are disobedient and benefit of any humane attitude. Talk about the Pakistan Army. You will not find such a gentle, civil, polite, courteous and loyal Army in the whole world. They really are so decent and modest [...] They came in the night of March 25 and saluted my father, (Sheikh Mujib) my mother and even me. Then they said to my father, Sir, we have come only to provide security to you. You can go wherever you want, wherever you please. Anyone can come and meet you. We will only ensure your security. If you go out we will accompany you to provide security. We will search an incoming guest properly before we let him in." Really, whatever the Pakistani Army did was meant for our security. On the twenty-sixth of March when Abba (Sheikh Mujib) was taken away by the Pakistan Army, General Tikka Khan himself came, saluted my father and my mother. He kept standing and courteously told my father (Sheikh Mujib)—Sir, Yahya Khan has asked us to take you for consultations. I have come here to take you. A special flight is ready for you. Please get ready, and if you so wish you can take anyone, including the Madam (Begum Mujib). Abba consulted my mother and went away alone. As long as the Pakistan Army performed their duty, they came and saluted us first. "Not only that. When my paternal grandmother had some fever, the Pakistanis got her transported by a helicopter from Tungipara to Dhaka for treatment at the PG. Hospital. When I was expecting Joy (Hasina's son), I was taken every week to the Combined Military Hospital (CMH) for medical checkup. I was admitted to the CMH a month before Joy was born. When he was born in 1971, the Pakistan Army personnel distributed sweets. All the cost associated with the birth of Joy was borne by the Pakistan Army. We went wherever we wanted to go. The Pakistanis accompanied us in two jeeps. They guarded us to provide security. And the Bangladesh Army! These animals, these inhuman brutes killed my father, my mother and all my brothers. I wish their destruction." http://www.eboi.ml/2017/02/amar-fasi-cai.html

20. http://www.sheershanewsbd.com/2015/07/11/88324#
21. http://www.bdfirst.net/newsdetail/detail/49/148951
22. http://archive.samakal.net/print_edition/details.php?news=17&action=main&menu_type=&option=single&news_id=251880&pub_no=1023&type=&view=archiev&y=2012&m=04&d=14; https://nazmamustafa.wordpress.com/2017/02/06
23. http://www.amardeshonline.com/pages/details/2016/05/07/335049
24. http://www.ittefaq.com.bd/archive/2014/12/17; http://www.ittefaq.com.bd/national/2014/12/17/9146.html
25. http://www.sheershanewsbd.com/2015/10/24/101271
26. By the way, my corollary in this respect is that if the AL men and women do not question and do happily gloat and glide and swing and surf and dance and undulate

in the dark tunnel and twilight of Hasina's and her party's decadent and despotic rule, why is it that Shamsher M Chowdhury, Moeen Khan, Mahbubur Rahman, and Maudud Ahmed should suddenly be so unrealistic and idealistic as to question the BNP policies, especially when, at this critical juncture, the party needs unity and solidarity in its rank and file more than ever?

27. http://www.dailynayadiganta.com/detail/news/174911
28. http://www.huffingtonpost.com/news/obama-monkey/; http://www.salon.com/2015/07/17/gorilla_face_michelle_obama_only_attractive_to_monkey_man_barack_wa_mayor_refuses_to_resign_after_racist_facebook_rant/; http://www.cbs19.tv/story/14461089/email-depicts-president-obama-as-monkey;
29. They and many other AL leaders breathed a sigh of relief making comments too negative to be forgotten. Apart from the print media of the time, including the later Matiur Rahman Chowdhury's *Kutnitir Andar Mahol*, please see *Weekly Sugandha* (November 1, 1996) and "August 15, 1975 Coup and the Executions" by A O Chowdhury (February 7, 2010) at https://beta.groups.yahoo.com/neo/groups/khabor/conversations/messages/27448
   Also see Appendix A, "August 15: Know the Facts, Not Fiction" by A O Chowdhury.
30. http://tazakhobor.net/bd/politics/92582-2017-04-01-06-00-59; http://bangla.bdnews24.com/politics/article1312481.bdnews; http://rtnbd.net/politics/37181; http://rtnbd.net/politics/36918
31. This site, http://www.shomoyershathe.com/, contains some very damaging and disturbing reports about some top AL regime leaders, who should check if they are true or mere lies and propaganda.
32. http://southasiajournal.net/india-bangladesh-defense-pact-honey-mixed-with-poison-for-a-friend/
33. https://www.youtube.com/watch?v=gkFWqmBaCnY
34. http://www.dhakatribune.com/bangladesh/2016/mar/25/made-india-yaba-hits-market
35. http://www.thedailystar.net/city/105-women-children-murdered-last-month-1820; http://www.ittefaq.com.bd/wholecountry/2015/12/05/45729.html
36. Only a few examples are: little Rajon, little Champa, little Nazim, little Rakib, little Rupa, little Farhad, little Shourov, little Abu Sayeed, little Porosh, little Pulok, little Mustasim, little Yasir Arafat, little Raihan and Rois, little Shakil, little Abdullah, little Rahat, little Rahimul Islam Ronok, little Solaiman, little Zakaria, little Tajul, little Monir, little Ismail Hussein, little Pronob Basu, little Ananda alias Bishal Chandra, little Purnima, little Hazrat Ali, little Tipu Sultan, little Mahatir, little Aroni and little Alvi, little (dumb) Momo, little Sadia, two brothers (little Zahid Hasan and little Iman Ali), two brothers (little Obaidulla Khan and little Nazmul Hasan), little Shamim, little Ismail, little Imran, little Ibrahim Hussein, little Ibrahim Khalil, little Attahi Al Rashid, little Fardin Ahmed, little Ashikur Rahman, little Romanur Rahman, little Habibur Rahman Sani, little Alifa, little Shagor, little

Rubel, two young teen brothers (Jibon and Nasir), early teen Bhoje, young pregnant school girl Putul Bala, young Risha, young Khadija, and the young Comilla Victoria College student Sohagi Jahan Tonu. For more details, click: http://newagebd.net/214403/protests-against-rape-murder-of-tonu/; http://www.thedailystar.net/country/tanu-killing-no-arrest-demand-justice-gets-stronger-1198981; http://www.ittefaq.com.bd/wholecountry/2016/03/24/61016.html; http://www.ittefaq.com.bd/wholecountry/2016/03/24/61028.html; http://www.prothom-alo.com/bangladesh/article/758935.

Mohammad Badrul Ahsan, editor of the weekly *First News* and an opinion writer for *The Daily Star*, dwells on the recent alarming phenomenon of beastly brutalities against children in Bangladesh society: http://www.thedailystar.net/op-ed/politics/the-giants-and-the-pygmies-amongst-us-682420

37. http://www.amar-sangbad.com/jatio/articles/13094/
38. http://www.banglatribune.com/others/news/87579/
39. http://archive.ittefaq.com.bd/index.php?ref=MjBfMDNfMjFfMTRfMV8xXzFfMTE3Mzg2
40. http://www.sheershanewsbd.com/2015/09/11/96072#
41. http://www.bdfirst.net/newsdetail/detail/200/171406

8

Let's Follow the Example of Mujib's Clemency and Compassion and Not Set One of Cruel *Otherization*

In his Wall Street Journal review of Princeton Professor Gary J Bass's *The Blood Telegram: The Blood Telegram: Nixon, Kissinger, and a Forgotten Genocide* (2013), Peter R Kann, who won a Pulitzer Prize for his reporting of the India–Pakistan War for The *Wall Street Journal* (WSJ) and who used to be Chairman/CEO of Dow Jones and its publication, WSJ, writes:

> As for Bangladesh, it stumbles along, making halting economic progress but plagued by poverty, overpopulation, corruption and periodic calamities both natural and self-inflicted. These days Bangladesh barely registers on the radar screen of any great power and receives fleeting public attention only when a river ferry sinks or textile factory goes up in flames. For the Bangladeshis, that "liberation" struggle of 1971 remains, as Mr. Bass writes, their "defining national trauma," and still today they are convening tribunals to punish old enemies of the people who allegedly collaborated in war crimes. As one who lived through many of these events, I can only wish them to deal with their many present problems rather than wallow in their painful past. (my emphasis)[1]

When hundreds of thousands and millions of Bangladeshis are being subjected to political profiling by Sheikh Hasina's authoritarian government for their different political opinion and their legitimate political activism and are being discriminated against either in government service or when applying for government jobs, isn't the prime minister taking their fundamental citizen rights away? Is she uniting or dividing the nation? Is she a prime minister of all Bangladeshis or only those who belong to her party, in a way far worse than her father's BAKSAL days in 1975? How fair and ethical is it to be solely partisan and exclusionary in a fanatical and fundamentalist way? Isn't she quite boastful, often bellicose and belligerent and frequently bullying, yet (when it comes to the electoral map) darkly and deeply, in fact, violently BNP*hobic*? On the other hand, why would Sheikh Hasina shun her father's attitude of kindness, clemency and compassion by continually establishing a legacy of cruel *otherization*?

Determination of right and wrong by humans has never been easy. It has ever been relative and contextual. It is a universal problem full of gray areas and rife with moral complexities. In addition to universal human experience, all history, philosophy, and literature testify to this human dilemma. One certainly feels sorry and has a great empathy for all those innocent people killed on both sides in the hard and sad reality that was unfolding in Bangladesh at war in 1971. But there are many exceptions in which it is not difficult to make a moral choice. Bangladesh under the Hasina regime is a crystal clear example. While all killings are to be denounced and accounted for as heinous crimes, killings then and killings thereafter, almost on a daily basis, till today, are totally different. It is left for the readers to figure out for themselves on the moral and political differences and implications between the two situations. While one has the right to differ even on what may be the most just and legitimate, the disagreement does not dispel or cancel out what may ultimately be so.

During the French Revolution of the mid-1789 that saw the storming of the state prison Bastille (to release all the political prisoners) and the royal palace of the Versailles and the execution of King Louis XVI and Queen Marie Antoinette within two and half years, followed by Maximilian Robespierre's extremist "Jacobin" purge or the Reign of Terror (July 1793–July 1794 when thousands of many innocent moderates in the form of almost equally leftist Girondists/Girondins in their rival faction were guillotined) and the Napoleonic aftermath until 1815, there was a pamphlet war of revolutionary and counter revolutionary views now referred to as the Revolution Controversy. It was over the issues of human rights, rights of man and woman, feminism, patriotism, antislavery, representative government, and separation of church and state. Poets, writers, thinkers, commentators, and philosophers of the time were engaged in a mode of response and counter response arguing for or against the revolutionary changes, tradition, status-quo, or slow reforms, either from the conservative or radical point of view. Thomas Spence, Richard Price, Edmund Burke, Mary Wollstonecraft, William Godwin, Tom Paine, Horne Tooke, James Mackintosh, Helen Maria Williams,

Mary Robinson, William Wordsworth, S T Coleridge, Sir Walter Scott, Robert Southey, Lord Byron, P B Shelley, William Hazlitt, Leigh Hunt, Thomas Carlyle and many more—all, in England alone, took part in the contemporary conversation and contributed to the unfolding history.

Since its birth in 1971 Bangladesh has been going through a war of its own, full of political controversies over numerous issues—one party rule or multiparty rule, development with or without democratic freedom, creation of ruthless paramilitary forces parallel to the army, debate over the national status and military assassination of the two top political leaders, the choice of the national anthem, and the each subsequent government's increasingly relentless politicization and interference with the law enforcement agencies, especially the police, and the other entities such as judiciary, civil administration, human rights commission, anti-corruption commission, and, most importantly, election commission. One of the bones of contention among the parties is what to do with the collaborators with Pakistan during the liberation war. The following essay deals with this divisive topic from my personal analytical observation and argues that the German Nazi analogy is not applicable to the war criminals in Bangladesh, that the country has lost its moral standing to try them, and that they should be set free with some strong conditions attached, of course.

There is no denying that the Jamaat and the Muslim League had every political right to support the united Pakistan in 1971, just as the Indian National Congress, along with even many from the then Indian Muslim League, supported the united India (sometimes out of emotional attachment) during the 1947 Partition of the Subcontinent into India and Pakistan. Jamaat opposed the creation of Bangladesh just as the Congress and many Muslim Leaguers opposed the creation of Pakistan in the past. However, the Jamaat made a serious mistake by not only sticking to and continuing with their support for Pakistan over the months until the very end when the defeat of Pakistan was looming large and became inevitable and the creation of Bangladesh was becoming a certainty. Jamaat also made a grave and grievous mistake by allegedly getting involved in some horrible human rights violations to further their end. It seems there were some collaborators who may have committed heinous and horrendous crimes during the liberation war of Bangladesh (just as some *Mukti-Bahini*, *Rakkhi-Bahini,* and *Gano-Bahini* elements did during and after the liberation), for which they must face a reckoning.

Personally, I never got involved in the Jamaat-Shibir politics and I am not one of those who would like to share their ideological vision and institutional aspiration to get to the level of controlling or governing the country. Jamaat and all other religious parties should always remain contained and be kept under the control of fair and honest democratic governments. However, Jamaat can be proud of the honesty and sincerity of its people and their organizational discipline and integrity, for which they can of course be a good partner in any electoral alliance (except in 1995 when they made the mistake of joining hands with the wrong party—Awami League). Their presence lends a necessary dimension of balance, representation, and objectivity in the political landscape of Bangladesh. They can play the vital role of a pressure group/power broker, but not the key principal player (which they may never be in a position to be anyway).

Kind of akin, in terms of rigidity and inflexibility, to the ideologically "committed" Communists and Socialists, there may be an element of "obstinacy," "eccentricity," and "defiance" about all these parties, who are "only idolatrous to their own political philosophy; and thus are more idealistic than pragmatic," as observed by a fine and fabulous political commentator from the USA, senior mechanical engineer Mohammad Gani.

However, all political entities/parties are rigid in one way or another, in varying degrees, as observed by Ranu Chowdhury and Dr Rashed Anam (both from the USA). So the Jamaat has/had every right to be free to determine its policies and its own course of action, instead of being coerced into something else for however unpopular their political decisions may be or may have been. Neither an individual nor a party should be demonized by being pushed to or beyond the limit, they point out, and denied the right or at least the benefit of doubt to belong to the mainstream politics. To do so would mean the violation of the principle of free speech itself. Jamaat should be allowed to do politics on its own terms just like any other party and let the people decide through a free, fair, and credible election, not a rigged and stolen and pre-stuffed ballot box one.

This brings me to say that, like many philosophers, including the 18th-century French Enlightenment philosopher Voltaire (pen name of François-Marie Arouet), I would like to believe in what they said: "I disapprove of what you say [or I do not agree with what you have to say], but I will defend to the death your right to say it"—a statement attributed to a number of writers, not just Voltaire alone. Similarly, about an age after Voltaire, during the French Revolution, English lawyer and rebel Thomas Erskine defended in the court, though unsuccessfully, Thomas (Tom) Paine, the famous author of *Common Sense* and *The Rights of Man*, for his right to free speech. Paine was accused of sedition and Erskine did not quite agree with all of his radical and revolutionary ideas/ideals. Championing the cause of the freedom of expression that, argued Erskine, brought glory and radiance to England, he also defended the radical John Horne Took, this time successfully though. Accused of treason, Horne Tooke was acquitted after six months in jail.

Now the question is, didn't Bangladesh forfeit its *moral* right to try the alleged war criminals of 1971 when the situation itself was very complex not only for the Jamaat but also the great leader Sheikh Mujib, which is why he had to play an uneasy, confusing, controversial, and dilly-dally role at the time? Not only was his March 7, 1971 speech somewhat vague and unclear (taken in its entirety), full of ifs and buts, and flips and flops, but also his meeting with General Yahya Khan and Zulfikar Ali Bhutto during March 15–24 (probably to leave a window for compromise or decide on Pakistan's future constitution) and then his surrender to Pakistan the very next day, and then, after nine months of war, Pakistan surrendering to India on 16 December (as if it was a war between Pakistan and India only), not to the *Mukti Bahini* (Liberation Forces of Bangladesh)—these are/were all shrouded in mystery with more questions than answers.[2]

The Awami League (AL) supporters use some of the key words such as এবারের সংগ্রাম মুক্তির সংগ্রাম এবারের সংগ্রাম স্বাধীনতার সংগ্রাম (the struggle of this time is the struggle for liberation, this struggle is for freedom and independence) by taking them out of the context of the whole March 7 speech in which Mujib made four other key demands to Pakistan: withdrawal of Martial Law, return of the troops to barracks, investigation into the killing of the Bangladeshis by the Pakistani military and transfer of power to the elected representatives. His 17-minute speech ended with জয় বাংলা (Victory to Bengal), *Pakistan Zindabad* (Long Live Pakistan, this last part having been deleted from the original version). Under no circumstances, this could be termed as a clear-cut declaration of independence, his sitting with Yahya and Bhutto later providing the definitive proof that Mujib did not declare independence on March 7. All this was in keeping with his lifelong demand for the full autonomy of the eastern wing of Pakistan and his commitment that the unity and integrity of Pakistan should be preserved. Mujib chose to surrender to Pakistan instead of leading his people in the war thereby missing the glorious liberation war that saw millions dead and wounded.

Anyway, those who opposed the independence of Bangladesh were later magnanimously forgiven by the Bay of Bengal-like broad-minded Sheikh Mujib, who offered a "general amnesty" with a view to forging unity and harmony among the people.[3] It was the true Islamic spirit in him that prompted him to say to Indira Gandhi, upon landing in New Delhi on January 10, 1972, on his way from London to Dhaka, that he was first a Muslim and only then a *Bungalee*/Bengali. Following his participation in the OIC summit meeting in Lahore on February 23, 1974, the tripartite agreement between India, Pakistan, and Bangladesh (signed in New Delhi, 9 April) contained the statement in Clause#14:

> The Prime Minister of Bangladesh had declared with regard to the atrocities and destruction committed in Bangladesh in 1971, that he wanted the people to forget the past and to make a fresh start, stating that the people of Bangladesh knew how to forgive.[4]

According to Clause#15 of the same agreement, all 195 Pakistani war criminals were forgiven and freed: "[…] having regard to the appeal of the Prime Minister of Pakistan to the people of Bangladesh to forgive and forget the mistakes of the past, the Foreign Minister of Bangladesh stated that the Government of Bangladesh had decided not to proceed with the trials as an act of clemency. It was agreed that the 195 prisoners of war may be repatriated to Pakistan along with the other prisoners of war now in the process of repatriation under the Delhi Agreement."

To repeat, all the identified Pakistani criminals were let off the hook by India with Mujib's consent. All the Bangladeshi war criminals also were granted forgiveness by Sheikh Mujib in 1973 when he failed or chose not to proceed with the conviction of any of the nearly 7200 accused.[5] They were subsequently politically reinstated and reconciled to by all the successive ruling parties, including Mujib's AL, currently led by his daughter PM Hasina. From time to time, Sheikh Hasina sought their support in her movement against H M Ershad and Khaleda Zia with the intention of going to power at any cost. The AL Presidential candidate Justice Badrul Haider Chowdhury visited the late Jamaat leader (and former DUCSU GS and one of the 1952 Language Movement heroes) Prof Ghulam Azam for "Do'a" (blessings) in 1991.

Earlier, Hasina's today's information advisor Iqbal Sobhan Chowdhury was among the other pro-Awami journalists to sign the petition for the restoration of Prof Azam's Bangladeshi citizenship. It is widely known how Hasina worked together with the Jamaat leaders such as Matiur Rahman Nizami and others, especially in 1996 when the Jamaat was instrumental in returning the AL to power and when the AL offered cabinet positions to the Jamaat, who instead chose to take only two female parliamentary seats. Reportedly, Hasina then not only visited Prof Azam twice seeking his party's support to form the government but also touched his feet in reverence. At that time she got close to the Jamaat the way she has been befriending Ershad since 2009. Now that she has been autocratically exercising power in a democratically illegitimate and neo-and-near-and-more-than-partially fascist style, she, out of political reprisal, wants to put Khaleda on trial for being in alliance with the Jamaat.[6]

PM Hasina made a controversial and contradictory U-turn—from being friendly to Pakistan in 1971 and having expressed a great liking for the Pakistani army during the liberation war to a Pakistan hater later, from being allied with the Jamaat to being inimical to it, from being once and occasionally democratic-minded to increasingly and permanently dictatorial-minded. Her financially and democratically corrupt and commercialized Zilla Parishad (District Council) elections, as all elections under her being deeply doubtful and questionable (with few exceptions), are considered to be nothing short of imitating the one party "Basic Democracy" ideology of General/Field Marshal Mohammad Ayub Khan of Pakistan (which, in terms of fishy financial bribing, was of course far better than Hasina's elections today).[7] Her way of political U-turn was also the way of her favourite poet and writer Syed Shamsul Haq, who turned from being a fervent Pakistani to anti-Pakistani, from anti-Indian to pro-Indian, from pro-Islamic to offensively anti-Islamic, from pro-Zia (it is said that it was Zia who gave him a house in Gulshan) to pro-Hasina, from being "fatherly" (to the thirty years younger Taslima Nasreen) to having a (both fictionally and biographically suggested) intimate relationship with her and others, and from being pro-Nasreen to anti-Nasreen (though however the elements of loose and lewd obscenities remain common to both writers).[8]

Neither Hasina nor Haq took part in the liberation war of Bangladesh, the former having been in the care and custody of Pakistan during those nine months and the latter, having once been proud of Pakistan as a holy, sacred land and having purportedly played a pro-Pakistani role during the liberation war, until November when he left for the UK to work for BBC.[9] Dr Abdus Sattar of DU Fine Arts Institute provides evidence of how poet Haq, poet Shamsur Rahman, Prof Kabir Chowdhury and Prof Mustafa Nurul Islam (like M K Alamgir and Dr Kamal Hussein, according to other sources[10]) played a pro-Pakistani role during the liberation war, only to sell themselves as secularist pro-liberation elements after the independence and how Prof Syed Ali Ahsan, Begum Mustari Shafi and poet Al Mahmud actually played a pro-liberation and anti-Pakistani role in 1971, only to be vilified as anti-liberation later for simply being Islamic minded.[11]

What an unprincipled and politically expedient (if not outright hypocritical) turn around by Haq and others! What a political trick and trap! On her part, despite being a decade-long enemy of Ershad and despite Ershad's once brief anti-Bangladesh role in 1971, PM Hasina is now one of his closest allies. First, Jamaat was in, Ershad out; now, Jamaat out, Ershad in, although he is being ridiculed by critics as a বিশ্ব বেহায়া (shameless person of world class), a জাতীয় বেঈমান (nationally unreliable/untrustworthy person), a থুথু বাবা (a fake priest to be spitted upon), or a CMLA (cancel my last announcement, as people mockingly say about him) for his fickle-mindedness and untrustworthiness that made him constantly switch sides and change his decisions between today and yesterday. Ershad was once chairman of a tribunal that was formed by Pakistan to try the Bengali army officers leaving the Pakistani army for Bangladesh liberation forces during the emergence of the country.[12]

Where is the spirit of the liberation struggle when Hasina and Ershad forge a close and cozy alliance? What is the point of observing the Asad, Milon, and Nur Hussein days and the other mass uprising/upheaval days or these or those days, when all of them involved sacrifice and martyrdom for the cause of patriotism, democracy, and nationalism? What is the significance of oath taking for office when, after taking office, all those nice and idealistic words are crossed out and sent into banishment, far from being translated into action.

Didn't Bangladesh forfeit its *moral* right even further if the trial of the war criminals was to be conducted out of pure political revenge and reprisals, now that those once befriended by the AL in its electoral politics are now allied with the opposition BNP (and not beside the AL as it would love to see)? Hasn't Bangladesh's *moral* standing diminished when it did not bring to justice all those who committed crimes (in the style of French 1793–1794 Reign of Terror) during the *Rakkhi-Bahini* and *Gano-Bahini* days in the first half of 1970s after the independence[13] and when murders, assassinations, and abductions are being committed every day, with or without the direct support, sponsor, and knowledge of the Awami regime, many of which go without being accounted for?

How about the February 25, 2009 *Pilkhana* massacre of about eighty BDR men, most of whom were high ranking officers? Doesn't the mystery and conspiracy behind the savagery, along with the complicity of both the Indian government and the Awami regime, if any, need to be investigated and revealed? How about the Awami regime's massacre of the sleeping Hefajote men in the dead of night on May 5, 2015? How can Bangladesh cleanse its soul and pray for the victims of abduction to rest in peace when the tears of mothers, sisters, daughters, and wives, shed daily in cusecs, are enough to make the drying Padma and Teesta and Atrai flow again?[14] Hasn't Bangladesh's *moral* authority deeply eroded when it failed to ensure the rule of law for everybody, both in and out of power—a failure which is causing serious social rift with scores of lawsuits against every single opposition leader and activist, from top to bottom, numbering in scores of thousands?

While the wrong-doers and human rights violators of 1971 were the AL's fine and fast friends when they were once with them, lending them their kind and vital support the Hasina-AL then needed from them, they are now their mortal foes (since 2009). They are to be exterminated and wiped out just because they were not with the Hasina-AL (during 1991–1995) and they have not been with them (since 2001). Instead, they became a political partner of their former ally AL's bitter and powerful rival, the BNP. The question of trying them as war criminals did not arise when the AL was in power in the past (from 1972 to 1975; then 1996 to 2000) because they were then with them.

As soon as the BNP distanced itself from the Jamaat in 1996, the AL grabbed the opportunity to take the Jamaat with them immediately. In fact, Jamaat helped the AL to come to power in 1996. The question of trying the Jamaat leaders did not arise during 1981–1990 when Sheikh Hasina welcomed the military dictator Ershad as he took over, saying she was not unhappy at the move by him. Now that the Jamaat belongs to the BNP-led opposition alliance (1991–1995; 2001–), it is the AL's bounden duty, out of pure and unmixed political animosity and jealousy, to chase after the Jamaat leaders, put them in jail for years before hanging them, and thereby break the alliance opposed to its authoritarian rule.

The AL's policy toward the Jamaat is, সাথে থাকলে সঙ্গী না থাকলে জঙ্গি (If you are with us, you are our friends and comrades; if not, you are terrorists). Pir Habibur Rahman, a well-known journalist, puts it in a pithy and witty way, that if the BNP has an openly politically permissible (honeymoon) affair with the Jamaat (though in a sort of unequal and unadjustable "marriage" of convenience and expediency), the Hasina-Awami party is involved in a politically cheating cat-and-mouse-and-hide-and-seek (illicit, immoral, adulterous, duplicitous, and deceitful) extramarital union (পরকীয়া) with the Jamaat.[15] In the translation by Dr Zainul Abedin of the USA, "The BNP made a bed with the Jamaat, while the AL did paramour."

The same is true with regard to the JP of Ershad—one major party openly sleeps with it and another would like to sneak into a relationship when it can. It has all become a politics of convenience and expediency, a matter of fantastical skill and proficiency in pragmatism and ground realities as tied and tagged with strategic alliance, economic interest, and electoral politics of vote getting and winning. Idealism and morality have been banished long ago not just from Bangladesh but everywhere in the world. Any party is doing everything it can to oust the other and return to power. So, to expect idealism and morality and ethical standards from this or that party only is, unfortunately, nothing short of being myopic and monolithic and unrealistic.

Still, if the war criminals are to be tried (Tony Blair also has been derided as a war criminal for going into the bloody war with Iraq for which he recently apologized and took full responsibility during and after his interview with CNN's Fareed Zakaria), why not all the perpetrators of the capital offence from 1971 until now? Many local Bengalis were brutally bayonetted during the liberation and immediately after the liberation—extrajudicial executions on suspicion of collaboration with the Pakistani forces. Also, why not those of the *Baksalite Rakhkhi-Bahini* and *Gano-Bahini* for their brutal excesses during 1973–1975 when over thirty thousand people were reportedly killed? Before them, during the nine months of the liberation war, members of certain armed groups allied with this or that *Bahini* killed many innocent people in different parts of the country, local or otherwise, including many innocent Urdu-speaking *Biharis* in different parts of the country, out of their personal vendetta or motiveless malignity.[16] In just one instance, Advocate Balaram Guhathukarata testifies to the killing of such non-Bengalis and the looting of their money by the political elements of the time.[17]

Doesn't Bangladesh need to bring to justice those who committed such brutalities as well? Why doesn't Sheikh Hasina bring to book those of her party, at least the high ranking ones, including those of her relatives, who are claimed to have had a role in the collaboration with the Pakistanis? Why only the Jamaat leaders?

In her *Dead Reckoning: Memories of the 1971 Bangladesh War* (2011), Dr Sarmila Bose, affiliated with Oxford and Harvard Universities, wrote of the war crimes and crimes against humanity by both sides. It is to the same effect that Maidul Hasan, in his *Mooldhara 1971* (1986), quotes Tajuddin Ahmad, one of the greatest heroes/architects of the independence of Bangladesh. In this connection, MBI Munshi's *The India Doctrine (1947–2007): A Contemporary Study on Indian Hegemony and Geo-Strategic Perspectives on South Asia* (2007) is also worth-mentioning. As Bangladesh's first prime minister in exile, Tajuddin was not, however, without a blemish and had his murky and maligning role in entering a highly adverse and controversial agreement with India.[18]

How about (Hasanul Hoque) Inu-led post-independence terrorist organization *Ganobahini-cum-JSD* and their slogans of মুজিবের চামড়া তুলে নিবো আমরা (Mujib needed to be peeled off his skin) and national traitor/জাতীয় বেঈমান *Sheikh Mujibur Rahman*?[19] How about Shahriar Kabir, who, on the testimony of the eminent essayist and columnist Professor Badruddin Umar, used to attack Sheikh Mujib in filthy and foul language and is suspected by many political leaders to have played a rajakar-type dubious role during the independence struggle?[20] It is a shame that instead of addressing the following issues of nuisance and nonsense, that:

(1) millions of people across the country live a financially destitute life without any real taste of freedom, especially in the sense of financial solvency, equality and social justice;
(2) millions of children need help with their education and their old dilapidated schools;
(3) sex offenders remain at large, as free and loose as the foul and stinky rubbish everywhere;

(4) thousands and thousands of people are being systematically killed, abducted, and imprisoned on a regular basis—every day, every other day, every few days;
(5) it has become routine for the miscreants to leak out the exams at school and college levels;
(6) rape, drug, pornography, and (both domestic and public) violence against women are of alarming and epidemic proportion[21]; and
(7) there are inhuman child labor, child marriages, teen pregnancies, demeaning and disgusting dowries, and dirty and deadly pre-and-extramarital (*porokiya*) affairs all around, leading to countless unnatural deaths and domestic violence;

The AL government is preoccupied with hanging, lambasting, and haranguing the once-lionized (by the AL) and now vilified (also by the AL) war criminals as it is also completely engaged in persecuting and prosecuting the entire team of the main opposition BNP leaders, right and left, out of political mischief and politically motivated animosity and antagonism. The AL government is also often allegedly involved in abducting, arresting, harassing and humiliating the Jamaat/BNP leaders' sons and lawyers.[22]

It is this double, dubious, and deadly standard (heartily acceptable if "you" are with "us," but intolerably unacceptable when "you" are against "us") in the policy of the AL's brazenly opportunist politics of expediency that ultimately led the Jamaat-Shibir to recently claim that they also took part in the liberation war of 1971 and to bring out colorful rallies on the independence and victory day (March 26, 2016), all across the country.[23] It is the same lack of consistency in terms of moral principle and political integrity on the part of the AL, or its off-and-on flexibility and compromise on a selective basis as they find suitable and convenient that made one (S Akhter of the USA) seek the legitimacy and justification for the Jamaat-Shibir claim and express it all in rhyme.[24]

Does the Jamaat-Shibir claim of contribution to the liberation of Bangladesh suggest an attempt to: (1) distance their younger generation from the old predecessors and thereby signal a slow but sure break with their politically controversial past; and (2) transition toward a course of moderation from the position of an Islamic ideology-oriented political party (like the Communist, Socialist, Ultra-Nationalist, or even Fascist parties with radically different yet peculiarly similar ideologies) and be more aligned with the mainstream politics of Bangladesh? Through a process of evolution, Jamaat-Shibir, similar to any other political party, may be undergoing a change for the better.

After forty five years of independence and after having been, unlike the Nazis in Germany, politically rehabilitated and legitimized by all the successive governments since 1972, including the Hasina-led AL, those war criminals now find themselves demonized in a highly trumpeted trap of the so-called চেতনা of একাত্তরের স্বাধীনতা সংগ্রাম (spirit of the struggle for independence in 1971). Even the members of the pro-AL Sector Commanders' Forum that had surfaced later and that had consisted of only a selected few of the commanders did not demand the war criminals' trial until recently. They did not do so probably because of the marriage of political convenience that changed with the change of time and that did not fall short of commodifying, compartmentalizing and commercializing the চেতনা/spirit of independence with a market value on it. Ironically, it is the same AL that has been hounding the war criminals and their party members since 2009 and that at the same time continues to enter into political and marital relationships with many of them and continues to accept and rehabilitate many more into its fold, without any qualms of conscience.[25]

And how about the International Crime Tribunal (ICT) without international representation at any level (judges' panel, prosecution, investigation, and defense counsel)? If it is an ICT, does it live up to international standards in terms of justice and transparency as many international organizations questioned?[26] Shahid Islam, a Canada-based practitioner of international law, wrote about his doubt concerning ICT.[27] The New York-based (previously vehemently pro-Awami, now strongly anti-Awami) Dr Mina Farah, a rich mine exploding in her writings to debunk and demolish the myths, untruths, and falsehoods of the Hasina regime, quotes International Jurists Union questioning the Bangladesh ICT for its deep and serious flaws.[28] In one of her best argumentative articles, Dr Farah finds faults with everything the Awamis under Hasina have been doing, including the defective ICT trials and the Awami Sikkimization process of Bangladesh at the orders from New Delhi.[29]

Salahuddin Quader Chowdhury, one of those tried at the ICT, was a memorably interesting political figure of his own kind, of well-known political background, once a great candidate for the OIC Secretary General post. Despite his having been a controversial character (who is not in Bangladesh?), he had an entertaining charm of his own and his humorous but somewhat offensive comments were far better than the lousy, vulgar, coarse, fatuous, notorious, inane, obnoxious, dry and dull comments of many others belonging to the Awami court and *Baksali* camp. Why is it that he was inhumanly tortured by the police to the extent that his toenails and finger nails got removed causing him suffer in not being able even to stand on his feet, blood dripping from his years, as charged by his weeping daughter Farjeet Quader Chowdhury, full of moving tears, as any daughter would be?

Why is it that the international witnesses in S Q Chowdhury's ICT case were barred from entering the country and providing testimony in what was described as an unfair and questionable trial not only by his family but also Amnesty International, Human Rights Watch, the US Congress, and many other international organizations and global war crime experts of repute?[30] Why is it that only four witnesses were allowed for the accused (S Q Chowdhury) whereas as many as forty four witnesses allowed for the government prosecution? How is it possible that a prosecution witness who was born in 1977 could provide eye-witness account of crimes claimed to have been committed by Mir Kashem Ali in 1971?[31]

According to the Tom Lantos Human Rights Commission report of December 1, 2015, "Two political opposition leaders were executed in recent days, following death sentences by a controversial war crimes tribunal criticized for lack of due process."[32] It is precisely the same argument that Joseph Grieboski, once a nominee for the Nobel in Peace, and the UK-based Guardian Editorial make in articles called "Bangladesh Democracy Under Attack" and "Bangladesh history debate: distorted by politics" respectively, both containing blistering criticisms of the ICT.[33] It is the same contention about the "trial standards" of the ICT being objected to at least as procedurally unfair and the weaknesses and controversies in the trial process concerning the capital punishment of many accused, including Matiur Rahman Nizami, and the authenticity of the statements made by the prosecution witnesses against the accused that David Bergman so cogently and convincingly raises.[34] These are fair concerns about the trumpeted "fair trials" just as there are fair concerns about the rigged and stolen elections.

If the AL, in power, could bring in international witnesses (American FBI agent Debra LaPrevotte and American journalist Lawrence Lifschultz) to support its politically motivated allegations against some of the BNP leaders, why is it that there was a double and different standard against Chowdhury? Is it that, like the increasingly international coalition against the ISIS, which it prevents from being internationalized and from getting international help, the AL's approach to getting internationalized and using international help is only selective and one-sided, on the consideration of when it favors them only, not others, as proved by LaPrevotte and Lifschultz?

If there was any international participation in the ICT-related business, it was the damaging "international" Skype dialogue between an ICT judge (Nizamul Huq) and his overseas lawyer-friend Ziauddin Ahmed, following which the judge had to remove himself from the ICT panel to sit on a regular High Court bench.

If there was any other international presence on the ICT, it was the embarrassing "international" (Indian)-influenced determination of the outcome of the cases against the accused for their role in 1971.[35] If it is in reality no more than a domestic court, the ICT should have been called Bangladesh Crime Tribunal (BCT), after the Bangladesh Supreme Court (BSC).

The nomenclature of the ICT as a tribunal does not have to give one the excuse of drawing an analogy with the names of cities and countries, whatever their origins may have been. Los Angeles is not necessarily a city of angels; Las Vegas not necessarily a city of meadows; Pakistan not necessarily a land of the pure; and Islamabad not necessarily a place that thrives on the fervent practice of Islam. The same could be said about Hyderabad, Allahabad, and Ahmedabad in India, where Muslims are no longer a dominant force to help inspire the cultivation of Islam and Islamic culture and architecture.

The poor and fascist North Korea calls itself, baselessly and bombastically, "Democratic People's Republic of Korea," ruled by the same god-like and kingly Kim dynasty for seventy years under the banner of the so-called Workers' Party, which is far from serving the poor living a slum life. The vast island of Greenland is probably without any green, all being cold and icy there, except that it is green in the sense that this (Northern/Nordic) polar region is all pure and pristine all around.

There are no royal Bhawal elephants any more to bathe in the wetlands of *Hatirjheel* Dhaka. The District of *Mymensingh* means neither "my men sing" nor "my men are lions" nor are there any lions to sing about; there is the District of *Rajshahi*, where there are no traces or trappings of royal regalia, except in the form of today's cricket team Rajshahi Kings; *Comilla* Victorians are not those under Queen Victoria; *Sonargaon* is not as golden anymore as it once used to be during the time of the Bengal Sultans; *Rangpur* is without the festive or cheery *rong* or colors; and *Roopganj*, being one of the most backward and neglected places on the outskirts of Dhaka (in Narayanganj), is without any *roop* (beauty) whatsoever, far from the magical beauty of *Roopnagar* of the princess (*Rajkonnya*), as expressed in the famous Bangla song "Ami Roopnagorer Rajkonnya Rooper Jadu Enechi." In this way there are many place names which are at odds with the places themselves, there being hardly anything in common between the places and their names.

A "pick and choose" method (as Barrister Sarwar Hussein keeps alleging on the television talk shows), citing the evidence of a newspaper statement, allowing only a few selected witnesses (some of whom were too young to know or remember the details of what happened forty-five years ago), producing controversial witnesses to try a war crime suspect, and causing some witnesses in favor of the defendant (Moulana Delwar Hussein Saidee) disappear mysteriously and then reappear in the cross-border territory, only served to let the accused question the whole procedure. According to Ranu Chowdhury, who was a great freedom fighter, "Sometimes the role of the Jamaat leaders in 1971 was flimsy and the credibility of the prosecution witnesses was questionable."[36]

On top of all this, the judges are not nonhuman objects or beings to remain above and insulated from human biases, prejudices, and instincts. They are very much human either to wrestle with or exercise their emotions depending on how much they are able to rise above their অনুরাগ বিরাগ (passions, impulses, and inclinations). Given some recent precedents, especially in the context of the present politically partisan and polarized environment, one hardly rises above and does indeed act according to the political mindset and preconceived notions s/he brings along, no matter what it may otherwise be. This leads the watchers and observers to arrive at a conclusion that the outcome of the process on hand, be it legal, judicial, administrative, academic—is predetermined. There is a Bengali saying: one cannot be awakened from sleep if he is actually awake pretending to be sleeping.

Regardless, after all that said, one may still assert, out of respect for the rule of law, that a thing is actually what it is. "What matters is what something is, not what it is called." As the American imagist poet Gertrude Stein says in her poem, "Sacred Emily" (1913): "Rose is a rose is a rose is a rose." Her famous poetic utterance, hard and bare, is similar to Shakespeare's Juliet saying to Romeo: "a rose by any other name would smell as sweet." Similarly, a tribunal is a tribunal, an ICT is an ICT, of its own legal framework and legal jurisdiction, status and apparatus, to be respected by all means. The ICT, *in its view*, must have had its compelling and convincing reasons and hard evidences, laid out in hundreds of pages, to convict a suspect, again *in its view*, beyond any reasonable doubt. That is, however, not to undermine the equally strong arguments made by the defendant. Like a team wins in a match, debate, or parliament, here the prosecution won with the tribunal giving its verdict in its favor. The crux of my argument, however, lies elsewhere.

All wartime killers, regardless of their political shades, need to be tried without discrimination and, if found guilty, punished or pardoned as necessary in the higher interest of the country. This interest lies in taking the country forward on the road to unity, peace and prosperity. After all:

- the President of the country, who is also an AL leader, has set a tradition of forgiving many Awami-connected convicted criminals, as many as thirty, out of political considerations or political recommendations (not from within legal framework, questionable judicial procedures, or humanitarian grounds);

- the AL government, through an authoritarian ab/use of power, had thousands of lawsuits, political or criminal, against its own people withdrawn with the connivance of a friendly and obliging judiciary and an anti-corruption commission (while hardly any, from thousands of lawsuits against the opposition BNP leaders, has been quashed, in a naked display and demonstration of political repression harassing and keeping the opposition men and women, from top to bottom, busy running between home and court and sending them into jail);
- the so-perceived and so-alleged controversies over the judicial or quasi-judicial dispensations in favor of the ruling AL leaders and supporters[37]; and
- the AL government, in a wide display of its neo-and-near-and-more-than-partially fascist character, has been using its torture tools of the state machinery to unleash atrocities against the opposition BNP and has adopted the most undemocratic tactics to crush, corner, and cripple it to the extent of elimination and annihilation from the political scene.

The opposition BNP is sometimes even prevented from holding public meetings, processions and human chains to exercise its political rights and press home its demands. Under the tyranny of the majority and the authoritarian and dictatorial power amassed and concentrated in the hands of the prime minister, mostly directed toward the oppression of the opposition, an atmosphere of suffocating unrest and sluttish misrule reigns supreme. When peace, stability, accountability, and transparency are stranger than myth and fiction and are therefore conspicuous by their absence, there grows a fertile ground for the underground evils to creep up. It is then that corruptions are committed, scandals crop through, and indiscriminate murders and forced disappearances and kidnappings take place.[38] The result is, many such cases go uninvestigated and unpunished and are covered up and suppressed.

National unity and national reconciliation are much more important than the existing low and lawless politics dictated and determined by the policy of the abuse of power and fishing in dirty waters. The Awami parliamentary majority, already fraught with the defective system of "winner takes all," has turned into a *Baksali* dictatorship that ignores the proportional democratic representation. In its authoritarianism, the AL cannot be more callous and careless and unheeding about the wide mass support the BNP has been enjoying over the years. The latter's popularity was demonstrated, again and again, by the amazing success of its series of road marches, street processions, and public meetings, despite the Awami barriers and blockades and its spectacular wins in the earliest round municipal elections when such elections were somewhat free and fair before the all-out wholesale Awami riggings started.

Let Bangladesh think again as it keeps chasing a group of alleged war criminals and see if it can find any alternative way to deal with the divisive issues facing the nation. Let Bangladesh think about if it can drop the decades-old matter altogether (of course, with strings attached) and move forward on the path of democracy, economic development, peace and unity. Old wounds, whether of Jamaati or *Baksali/Rakhkhibahini/Ganobahini* origin, are sometimes best left as they are, with the intention of letting them heal and recover on their own by a natural process through the course of time, the best healer. "Better late than never," as some would like to argue regarding the trial of the alleged war criminals, may not always be a wise and widely applicable panacea. It is not always the best proposition and probably should not be used in such a politically incorrect and in fact potentially explosive issue. It is neither necessary nor appropriate to open the old wounds especially when it is too late and when the AL itself nursed the wounds at times.

The nation is already beset with too many miseries and problems that need the government's immediate and continued attention. It is already sinking under the weight of:

- chronic and rampant corruption;
- top-heavy, politicized bureaucracy;
- terrible poverty;
- killing illiteracy;
- overpopulation;
- environmental pollution;
- drug addiction;
- acrimonious and intolerant political partisanship;
- wide disparity between the rich and the poor;
- alarming deterioration of the law and order situation;
- gross gender discrimination;
- violation of women's rights;
- dangerous teen age marriage and deadly dowry system;
- child abuse and child labor;
- widespread nudity and obscenity on the screens and stages, films and commercial advertisements, giving rise to sexual violence;

- deadly extramarital affairs[39];
- excessive lapses in the cultivation of religion and morality;
- low quality education; and educational unrest and session blocks; and,
- the constant pain in the neck, that is, the intolerably heavy traffic jams.

The nation should be working together to see the light at the end of the tunnel—long and dark and deep as it seems to be. It must not stop by the attractive excuses of the war crimes woods and the one party alone hanging on to power. It should be working together with the larger and nobler ideals of unity and progress, reconciliation and development, peace and prosperity in mind. It must not allow itself to be overpowered and overwhelmed by the cheap shots called by the foreign-influenced liberal and libertine elements and their self-conceited, jack-of-all-trades and semi-and-pseudo-and-quasi intellectual coolies.

It is true that the German Nazis of World War II are still being pursued and hunted down and brought to justice, but their case is completely different. Let the ঘাদানি (acronymed from ঘাতক দালাল নির্মূল/uproot the killers and collaborators) members know that the Nazi instance cannot be used as an argument for the trial of the war criminals of 1971, simply because the Nazis, unlike the Jamaat leaders, have always been shunned and boycotted by all quarters across the political spectrum without exception, both in Germany and the rest of the world. They have never been recognized anywhere—neither in their own country nor anywhere else.

On the contrary, the Jamaat, under the leadership of the same very leaders who have been hanged by the AL during the last few years or who are still under trial, was always rehabilitated, legitimized, befriended, and reconciled to the political process of the country so much so that the Jamaat was allowed to take part in all the elections, has always had parliamentary representation, and until recently was one of the duly registered political parties in the country. So those who rush to eagerly and excitingly draw an analogy between the Nazis and the Jamaatis, gloating over the success of being finally able to hook and noose the Jamaat leaders to the gallows of what they call "justice," are morally and historically wrong. Their argument is politically misplaced, mistaken, untenable, and incorrect. The *Ghadani*[40] gong need to try the Awami leaders first for hobnobbing and rubbing shoulders with the Jamaat in the past before they (*Ghadani*) ask for the Jamaat to be put on trial. The *Ghadani* group, along with their new-found Awami cohorts, is now bringing the Jamaat leaders to trial out of their solely political jealousy and vindictiveness. They are doing so only to vicariously scratch the old sore and settle the old score with their step-motherly opposition BNP-Jamaat alliance in the game and gamut of electoral politics.

More than four decades after the liberation, the AL is still bickering over an anachronism—over what should not have been an issue at all at this stage in the history of the country. It is the issue of the participation of the Jamaat in the political process of the country. They are determined to complete the trial of the Jamaat elements thought to have committed crimes during the liberation war. The lack of compromise and accommodation on the part of the Awami government has created a tension in the already polarized and divided country causing it to slip and plunge further and deeper into a rough and rocky terrain. Politically motivated as its steps are, the Awami government is not leading the country forward, in the true sense of the word, but dragging it back into the violent conflict of the past.

Without solving the millions of problems that require immediate attention, without stopping or caring for and even causing the bloody political unrest that at times reaches to the extent of carnage (of the scale of the 2009 BDR massacre and then [1989 Chinese Tiananmen Square massacre type] 2013 *Shapla Chattor* Hefajote Islam genocide),[41] and without establishing the rule of law for everybody equally (not selectively), both in letter and spirit, the Awamis are busy hanging the alleged 1971 killers and criminals, through what many alleges to be questionable trials, without letting the due course of justice to be fully completed and exploited beyond the doubt of all parties concerned, especially the defendant, who has more right than the government prosecution to ask for so. While they all (Hefajote-Military-BNP) failed to avenge the BDR and Hefajote massacres and the anti-BNP repression by the Awami regime, the Awamis are running after who set the house on fire first, about forty-five years ago, instead of extinguishing the still rising, burning, and engulfing social and political flames first. They may be doing so to score the myopic political mileage of an immediate gain but they cannot achieve the lasting democratic vision or ideal of unity, reconciliation and statesmanship.

It is a fact that the Jamaat's current standing is that it is a recognized and lawful political party with its not-to-be-overlooked public support and parliamentary representation. It was legitimized and rehabilitated by the successive ruling parties, including the AL, from the beginning. When the AL formed the first government following the independence, its leader Sheikh Mujib, big-heartedly and broad-mindedly, offered amnesty to anti-liberation elements in a gesture of reconciliation. "It was Mujib," as Shahed Anam of the USA claims, "who had freed all Pakistani war criminals. It was Mujib who had pardoned 50,000 collaborators. It was Mujib who freed a collaborator like Shah Aziz. Mujib's daughter Hasina herself championed Nuru Rajakar and married her daughter to a well-known Rajakar family of Faridpur" (E-mail of February 18, 2016).

In the view of Ranu Chowdhury, "In Mujib's time, over 7000 Rajakars and alleged war criminals were arrested (that included Kader Mollah) and after nearly two years of investigation, none of them could be implicated, even though the evidences should have been fresh [then, in the first part of the 1970s]. A concerned Mujib quickly granted amnesty to them in 1973. The question is: how all those incriminating evidences surfaced overnight after over four-and-half decades? As a humble Freedom Fighter of 1971, I would like to see the war criminals hanged a hundred times each. But making cheap politics over the issue is highly detestable" (E-mail post of February 18, 2016). Whatever it was, it is certain that it was a wise decision by a bold and courageous leader like Mujib to do what he did in the form of amnesty in order to bring the country together and take it forward.

Later, the BNP, the AL, and the Jamaat fought together to topple the Ershad government during the 1980s. When the AL was in the opposition in the early 1990s, it was glad to form an alliance with the Jamaat, became politically reconciled with the Jamaat, and sealed a marriage of political convenience against the second (first Khaleda-led) BNP government (1991–1995). The AL knew that the Jamaat as a political party with a considerable number of firm and committed and forceful following had a strength to be reckoned with and that it needed the Jamaat to win the election and broker a balance of power.

When Ziaur Rahman, one of the greatest and most illustrious sons of the soil, came to power in mid-1970s, he took steps to rise above bitter partisanship (as Mujib did before him by pardoning anti-liberation elements) by inducting some pro-Jamaat figures in the government. Later, his party, the BNP, continued the precedent—forming a political alliance with the Jamaat when necessary and even including them in the second Khaleda-led BNP government (2001–2005).

All this had greatly contributed to the legitimacy and establishment of the Jamaat as a significant political force, far from being neutralized or marginalized. It cannot, therefore, be viewed as fair to oppose the participation of the Jamaat in the political process of the country and, for that matter, in any national dialogues with the end of fostering democratic unity and equality and thereby bringing and building the country together. Walling the Jamaat out would be part of the problem; walling them in, part of the solution. Walling them out would be detrimental to the cause and interest of a unified and reconciled nation and, in all likelihood, may lead to unnecessary debacle and disintegration.

Jamaat made a mistake in 1971 by supporting the then united Pakistan (which it had every political right to do since it was after all one country then), just as the Hindu-dominated West Bengal supported the united Bengal under the domination of the Hindu *Zemindars* and not the separation of Bengal in 1905. However, it was purely a political mistake. It was a time when a quarter of the then East Pakistan's population was opposed to the idea of separation from Pakistan and the creation of an independent Bangladesh for various reasons.[42] As Dr Anam made a comment in his e-mail post of November 16, 2015 to the author:

> There was nothing criminal about those who did not want Pakistan to be divided. Taking unpopular political stand is part of democracy. Try to respect it. The majority do not have to agree with or support something, but trying to demonize them in a criminal way is totally anti-democratic. In the USA, the North did not criminalize the South for its civil war differences in the 1860s. [Capitalist West Germany did not criminalize the Communist East after their reunification.] Similarly, Mandela's ANC did not criminalize the white Botha government party. There is a HUGE difference between unpopular political stand and war crimes. One is part of democracy and the other is criminal.

Any party under similar circumstances was likely to do that kind of mistake, as the Jamaat did, out of ideological principles or strategies. Didn't the AL make a similar suicidal mistake in 1975 by creating BAKSAL and torturing many people through the vicious paramilitary *Rakhkhi-Bahini*, for which the AL is yet to apologize to the nation? BAKSAL was a "leap in the dark"—to borrow a phrase from a journalist who used it to describe Adolf Hitler's rise to power. Fascist leaders like Hitler were also elected, but as soon as they were elected, they began to implement irrational laws. That is how Dr Abid Bahar of Dawson College Montreal puts it when discussing that what was interesting about law in a democracy was the question of irrational law.

Like the Baathists, the *Baksalite Rakhkhi-Bahini* forces used violence to silence opponents and resorted to coercion to force them into political conformity. It was a time of shocking and shivering moral trauma as it was at the time of the Nazis and the Chinese Cultural Revolution. Like the latter in the Indochina (Vietnam, Laos, and Cambodia) of the 1960s and 1970s, the period of 1972–1975 in Bangladesh still haunts the people and seizes them with a shock of fear and panic. If the Jamaat was responsible for many senseless deaths in 1971—sad and cruel as they must have been—just as those unnecessarily committed by some *Mukti-Bahini* elements in some localities/communities, wasn't the AL equally responsible for many horrendous, blood-chilling activities in the post-independence Bangladesh as well?

While no one condones what the Jamaat did in 1971, one may like to argue, if the Jamaat was wrong (certainly it was), at least one understands why it was wrong. In the history of the world, every country's struggle for cessation and independence was bloody and violent. No country's road to liberation was ever rosy.

No government did or would ever let go part of the country it was/is governing so easily, without putting up a challenge. Remember all the wars of the past, including the Anglo-American and the Anglo-French wars and the wars in India since the Mughal and British times. Look at today's Indian Kashmir and Assam, Ukraine, Tibet under China, Palestine under Israel, the Basque and Catalan regions in Spain, Scotland in the UK, and Quebec in Canada, for example. The difference is that in modern developed Western democracies, the matter is faced politically while in most of the Asian and African countries, it is handled militarily.

Post-independence failures and betrayals of the leading pro-independence parties such as the AL were more harmful and destructive than those of the anti-independence elements before the independence. The AL as the major political party under whose banner the country was able to successfully fight the liberation war and which, therefore, formed the first government of Bangladesh, should have lived up to the expectations of the war-torn, starving people. Unfortunately, it miserably failed to provide leadership and deliver on security, rule of law, democracy, and economic stability. Instead, there were chaos, corruption, and misrule, for which the country is still suffering and paying a heavy price. Had there been no anarchy in which banks were looted and the relief blankets were stolen, Mujib did not have to express his frustration about not having his own blanket and did not have to sigh about his country being full of thieves, not mines of gold.

Had the AL been able to lead, in the true sense of the term, and not turned the country into "a bottomless basket," today's Bangladesh, after more than four decades, would not have been full of domestic maids and slums and child labors and rickshaw-pullers and human haulers and low wage expat workers and mosquitoes and filthy drains and rotten rubbish lying all over. Had the rule of law been established, today's Bangladesh would have been an Asian tiger—both democratic and developed, peaceful and stable, with no dire and deep disparity between the rich and the poor. It could then have been compared with South Korea, Japan, Taiwan, Thailand, Malaysia, Singapore, Philippines, Vietnam, Iran, Turkey, and Tunisia (though some of them being run by a single unitary national government, based on consensus, consisting of many parties on mutual understanding and being highly democratic with hardly any party left out/behind).

Being "happy" or "peaceful" or "quiet" is different from "stable"—all "peaceful" is "stable" but all "stable" is not "peaceful." Western democracies, as well as the Eastern ones are all currently both stable and peaceful. Even in their industrial preoccupations, it is not far to seek a life tinged with the roseate glow of the rural countryside symbolizing peace and happiness. They possess a sense of what W. B. Yeats says in his pastoral "The Lake Isle of Innisfree:"

> And I shall have some peace there, for peace comes dropping slow,
> Dropping from the veils of the morning to where the cricket sings;
> There midnight's all a-glimmer, and noon a purple glow,
> And evening full of the linnet's wings.

A country under dictatorship may be stable by force but not happy and peaceful by freedom of choice. There is always a strong current of tension and unhappiness running underneath the seemingly quiet surface. In Thomas Carlyle's view, there is an everlasting truth of Nature whereby

> Nature is preternatural [exceptional, uncommon, extraordinary]; if not divine, then diabolic; that Semblance is not Reality; that it has to become Reality, or the world will take fire under it,—burn it into what it is, namely Nothing! Plausibility has ended; empty Routine has ended; much has ended. They are the wisest who will learn it soonest. Long confused generations before it be learned; peace impossible till it be! (Lecture VI: The Hero as King: Cromwell and Napoleon)

As the Nobel laureate Amartya Sen and the EU Human Rights Parliamentary Delegation recently visiting Bangladesh stated, stability and development must not be at the expense of human rights and political freedoms. Democratization and human development needed to be upheld even if that meant settling for less on the side of economic or material development. Sen said that dialogue was needed for peaceful transition and that liberty did not need to be curtailed for upholding democracy: "I don't believe that liberty has to be cut down for the sake of democracy."[43]

Similarly, the members of the EU delegation noticed the deterioration and diminishment of civil and political rights against the backdrop of violence that resulted from the current political confrontation and impasse. "Peace and stability should not be restored at the expense of civil and political rights," said a press release issued by the delegation. It said freedom of expression was a fundamental pillar of a pluralistic and vibrant democracy. Members of the delegation underlined the need for consolidating democratic institutions and stressed their expectations that there be adequate space for civil society organizations to continue working for the betterment of the situation of vulnerable populations. "This is also critical for the smooth implementation of EU funded development projects," the release said.[44]

Since Bangladesh, both before and after its emergence, has had a rich and robust long tradition of free speech and free thinking, and of being intellectually stimulating for decades and centuries, it cannot be compared with the basically undemocratic and intellectually and culturally passive (not so vibrant, creative, and dynamic) Malaysia, Singapore, China, the Arabian Gulf and some Central Asian countries. These countries are outwardly stable but internally suppressed with so-called peace coming down over them as an imposition. After all, they are historically devoid of any democratic tradition to long for or build upon. They suppress democratic freedom and hide their iron hand under the guise of outward material development alloyed with only an iota of free speech.

If the Jamaat men are to be tried at the court and barred from political activities and declared ineligible to stand in the election, all other criminals and murderers and looters from different political parties, beginning with the AL, should be identified and tried for their equally reprehensible and devastating black misdeeds. Let the setting of the house in order begin from those who are in power first.

The AL-led hue and cry over the issue of the religion-based parties and war criminals after years of hobnobbing with them will only create further rift and tension. The AL is prone to mischief with a hidden agenda of "divide-and-rule." When they thought, in the past, they could exploit the Jamaat, cynically though, as a political tool, to their advantage, they did not hesitate to do so. However, they at the same time legitimized the political existence of the Jamaat. Now that the AL sees that the Jamaat has turned away from them and that they would not get the Jamaati votes any more, they are crying foul against the Jamaat and trying to break the BNP-led alliance. When it came to their political advantage, they did not have any scruple to be allied with any religion-based parties, the Jamaat or any other, just as they did not have any scruple to make Ershad-cum-versus-Rawshon their close and cozy ally, their "poodle" as Tony Blair is said to have been George Bush's. But when the same Islamic parties side with the BNP, the AL starts having the blues and calling for a ban on them. Bangladesh would like to see an end to this hypocritical double standard! It is also the AL who are exploiting the people's religious sentiments by raising the slogan "*La Ilaha illallah* নৌকার মালিক তুই আল্লাহ" (that the boat, her party symbol, belongs to God/Allah) and by putting out a picture of the party leader Sheikh Hasina with a rosary (prayer beads) in her hand on election posters. Yet her personal or political Islamophobia is well-known.[45]

The AL demands that the BNP dissociates itself from the Jamaat, an ideologically strong, perhaps even radical and extremist to some extent, but organizationally well-disciplined party, financially relatively clean from corruption with its own business and industrial network. It is not difficult to understand the AL does so only to weaken the BNP. One must keep in mind that even if the BNP disowns and distances itself from the Jamaat, the AL will still spare no pains to find other "scarecrow" faults and excuses to crush and cripple and challenge and push the

BNP to a corner. So the BNP should think twice before it leaves a potentially potent and powerful ally only to step into the AL-laid trap. If the great freedom fighters such as President Zia, Col (Ret) Oli Ahmad of LDP, and Maj Gen (Ret) Syed Mohammad Ibrahim of BKP, JAGPA chief Shafiul Alam Prodhan, JP chief Barrister Andalib Rahman Partho, NAP chief Jebel Rahman Ghani and many other secular and religious parties could have an alliance with the Jamaat under the leadership of the BNP for political reasons, other smaller opposition parties can do the same.

Despite doubts and misgivings about the final outcome or consequences, former President Badrudduza Chowdhury (who once worked together with the former Prime Minister Shah Azizur Rahman in the late 1970s), ASM Rob, Mahmudur Rahman Manna, Kader Siddiquee, and Junaid Saki should have no problem joining the BNP-Jamaat alliance in a common cause against the dictatorship and despotism of the AL. If the Hasina-AL has no problem working together with the weird Ershad-cum-and-versus-Rawshon, why should those leaders have problem working together with the BNP-Jamaat alliance in what is actually going to be an electoral rather than an ideological struggle? Who doesn't have a controversial past and present in Bangladesh to put behind and move forward?

Finally, the nation will surely be better off and would have much to gain if it extends an olive branch of peace and forgiveness on behalf of those who lost their loved ones and sees the whole episode with an eye to bridging the widening gap and mending the old sore. To complete the process of moral mending and national healing, the ruling Awami government should first apologize to the nation for its past marriage of convenience with the Jamaat, followed by the BNP doing the same, and then demand from the Jamaat an unconditional public apology both to the nation as well as the families of their 1971 victims. Let it be left to the conscience of the perpetrators to repent and ask for forgiveness from Almighty Allah, the most just and gracious and compassionate and merciful and forgiving. It is not asking too much when bloody violence and tragic loss of innocent lives and tender loves, both at home and on the street, have become an everyday phenomenon without the perpetrators apprehended and often without the rule of law upheld and enforced.

Far from endorsing, supporting, or promoting the Jamaat, Mohammad Gani of the USA too believes that "any approach of the nature of saying sorry to the nation for its past mistakes would be a very smart move and wise political strategy for Jamaat to rise again. Chances are, this politically correct move could make the nation's pain much lighter and its heart kinder!" (E-mail of June 22, 2017). It is true the wartime alignments and allegiances in 1971, as it is in the case of many violent conflicts in the world, were very complicated, made further complex by Sheikh Mujib's forgiving the collaborators, following the various bipartite or tripartite agreements that were quite in their favor. Thus the post-liberation scenario emboldened the Jamaat and made it stubborn and unapologetic and resistant to the idea of offering an apology. Regardless, Jamaat should have made a public apology to the nation having witnessed a change in the political developments in the 1990s. It was in their interest and for their existence. Bangladesh is their country too where they have been seeking to get politically reestablished and rehabilitated. A politically correct apology would have helped them to go a long way and gain a big political mileage toward their reestablishment, rehabilitation, and successful survival.

Another way to go about the matter was the South African style of Truth and Reconciliation through a process of confession, apology, and financial compensation. "To avoid violence, stabilize and unite the nation, and attract investment in the economy," writes the Harvard Business School Professor Rosabeth Moss Kanter, "Mandela appointed a racially integrated cabinet, visited the widow of one of the top apartheid leaders, and created the Truth and Reconciliation Commission that would clear the air and permit moving forward."[46] Journalist and Human Rights Activist William Nicholas Gomes also wrote about the need to search for Truth and Reconciliation in Bangladesh in reference to the "judicial murder" of Abdul Quader Mollah on December 12, 2013 and the others that followed.[47]

In conclusion, one may argue that Sheikh Hasina could also have pardoned the army officers who killed her family members, including her parents. She could be kind, merciful, magnanimous, bountiful, and forgiving to grant amnesty and commute their death sentences. After all, many other convicted criminals have been released by her government. Mercy is a divine quality—perhaps the highest and greatest quality supremely appropriate and befitting in the context of a powerful giver like her as a prime minister, in possession of that opportunity to dispense mercy. She could rise to a heroic level in consideration of the following:

- She was not going to get her family members back anyway; and somehow she may have come to terms with her painful loss over the long years.
- The perpetrators committed a crime at the direct instigation of the inside as well as outside elements (without which they would not have dared to do what they did). The other key players, both from within the AL and without, including the foreign hands, were able to get away with their complicity in the crime without being brought to justice or having to pay any price.

- Prior to August 15, those men had a clean record and not a criminal background. They were not terrorists or serial killers. They may have been partly motivated to resort to their act of cruel assassination by the state of tremendous political unrest existing in Bangladesh at that time. It seems the overall political, social, and economic situation, instead of being a deterring discouragement, acted like a catalyst to drive them to that fateful night with the result that there was no protest from any corner, not even from within the AL, either out of (loud or tacit) approval or cowardice.
- The perpetrators suffered long in the dark lonely cells for years and paid the price that way. Languishing in jail for so many years was no less than the capital punishment hanging over their head so long.
- Ms Hasina saw that justice was done, more than once, with the death sentences upheld by the highest court of the land again and again; and,
- Not only did she get the fullest amount of judicial justice in the court of law but also she got to the helm of power herself.

That the assassins were handed down capital punishment did not mean it had to be carried out on the gallows. The verdict itself must have brought some closure, however uneasy, and some consolation, as much as possible in this life. Hanging those men may have brought some more closure but it did not necessarily bring the full and complete closure to the whole saga, anyway. That is impossible on earth. So why not spare them the remaining years they would have lived and allow them a quiet exit, like Khandoker Mushtaque Ahmed had his, from the turbulent scene they themselves once created?

The officers were already old and weak and sick and frail and dying. I'm sure they were chastened and subdued and exhausted with an unbearable bundle of sad reflections on Bangladesh's past long before they walked the gallows to die a violent death. Sheikh Hasina could give them a chance to retire into a remorseful private life to ruefully and dolefully reflect on the eventful past the way Shakespeare's old and imbecile King Lear contemplates to do before he breathes his last with the dead body of his daughter Cordelia in her hands.

Finally, humans always like, long, and aspire to do an act of mercy, charity, and kindness in the hope that the icy hand of death ever ready to touch them in their last moment would be less icy and that it would let their souls rest in more heavenly peace than they would otherwise deserve! In the fine article of a somewhat but not entirely different note, "Great Leaders Know When to Forgive," which is quoted from above, Professor Kanter correlates between business and politics and refers to how Nelson Mandela and General Douglas MacArthur were wise to forgive their opponents and oppressors, and shun the idea of revenge, which they found to be neither justice nor strategy. Echoing Sir Francis Bacon on "Revenge" (quoted toward the end of the Conclusion chapter), Kanter writes:

> Leaders must be firm and foster accountability, but they also must know when to forgive past wrongs in the service of building a brighter future. One of the most courageous acts of leadership is to forgo the temptation to take revenge on those on the other side of an issue or those who opposed the leader's rise to power.
>
> Instead of settling scores, great leaders make gestures of reconciliation that heal wounds and get on with business. This is essential for turnarounds or to prevent mergers from turning into rebellions against acquirers who act like conquering armies. … Anger and blame are unproductive emotions that tie up energy in destroying rather than creating.
>
> Those whose main motivation is to settle scores and get payback—to obstruct rather than construct—are on the wrong side of history. Their legacy is not rebuilding, but rubble. From (ahem) members of Congress to leaders in any turnaround situation, it's a lesson worth remembering: Taking revenge can destroy countries, companies, and relationships. Forgiveness can rebuild them.[48] (my emphasis)

As pain, loss, and suffering not only alternate with but are also, however humanly bitter and undesirable they may be, truer, more lasting, and more purifying than pleasure, profit, gain, and happiness, what is higher, more ennobling, more glorious, and more triumphant than revenge and "eye for an eye" tactic is reconciliation, forgiveness, peace, and unity.

Notes

1. http://www.wsj.com/articles/SB10001424127887323846504579073510606727756
2. No one from the freedom fighters *(Mukitijoddah*), not even M A G Osmani, nor a representative from the "Mujibnagor Government" was allowed to attend the surrender ceremony. *The text of the Instrument of Surrender document is as follows*:
   "The PAKISTAN Eastern Command agree to surrender all PAKISTAN Armed Forces in BANGLA DESH to Lieutenant-General JAGJIT SINGH AURORA, General Officer Commanding in Chief of the Indian and BANGLA DESH forces in the Eastern Theatre. This surrender includes all PAKISTAN land, air and naval forces as also all para-military forces and civil armed forces. These forces will lay down their arms and surrender at the places where they are currently located to the nearest regular troops under the command of Lieutenant- General JAGJIT SINGH AURORA.

The PAKISTAN Eastern Command shall come under the orders of Lieutenant-General JAGJIT SINGH AURORA as soon as this instrument has been signed. Disobedience of orders will be regarded as a breach of the surrender terms and will be dealt with in accordance with the accepted laws and usages of war. The decision of Lieutenant-General JAGJIT SINGH AURORA will be final, should any doubt arise as to the meaning or interpretation of the surrender terms.

Lieutenant-General JAGJIT SINGH AURORA gives a solemn assurance that personnel who surrender will be treated with dignity and respect that soldiers are entitled to in accordance with the provisions of the GENEVA Convention and guarantees the safety and well-being of all PAKISTAN military and para-military forces who surrender. Protection will be provided to foreign nationals, ethnic minorities and personnel of WEST PAKISTAN origin by the forces under the command of Lieutenant-General JAGJIT SINGH AURORA.

Signed: (JAGJIT SINGH AURORA) Lieutenant-General General Officer Commanding in Chief Indian and BANGLA DESH Forces in the Eastern Theatre

(AMIR ABDULLAH KHAN NIAZI) Lieutenant-General Martial Law Administrator Zone B and Commander Eastern Command (PAKISTAN)

December 16, 1971"

3. "A general amnesty for the collaborators was declared by the then prime minister, Sheikh Mujibur Rahman, on November 30, 1973." See Shahiduzzaman, "Cases Buried, Laws Revoked," *New Age,* December 15, 2005.
4. http://www.genocidebangladesh.org/text-of-the-tri-patriate-agreement-of-bangladesh-pakistan-india/;
   https://casebook.icrc.org/casebook/doc/case-study/bangladesh-india-pakistan-1974-agreement-case-study.htm;
   http://www.desh-bd.net/blog/blogdetail/detail/2601/muhon/78522;
   https://www.thenews.com.pk/print/75103-hasina-violates-her-fathers-commitment-to-forget-forgive
5. According to Ranu Chowdhury, who was a soldier and a freedom fighter, "It was Mujib who exonerated the war criminals, including the 195 known and charged Pakistani military officials, said to be in exchange of 300,000 Bangladeshis stranded in Pakistan. I recall, Bangladesh Army had already prepared a temporary camp in Dhaka cantonment just opposite to the CMH, to receive those 195 war criminals. One fine morning, we were told those criminals were not coming. No explanation given. The camps were dismantled soon. Bhutto played a dirty game in the process. He threatened to try some 400 Bangladeshis, out of those stranded Bengalis, on 'specific charges.' There was also pressure from the OIC and many other Muslim countries for Mujib to compromise. Bhutto played another trick assuring that Pakistan itself would try those 195, which never took place. Former Secretary Asafuddowla was an eye witness to those developments.

[...] Mujib could not even convict any of the 72,000 Rajakars he arrested. To save the situation, he quickly declared an amnesty in 1973. All the local Rajakars were released that included Kader Mollah and Mir Kashem Ali. When the memories were fresh, no evidence could be collected against those alleged criminals. Yet, strangely, after more than four decades, scores of evidences cropped up like mushrooms overnight, and deposed by some who were toddlers or below the age of puberty in 1971. A dozen have already been sent to the gallows. It is no secret that the RAW-devised plan is to score political points for Hasina, who otherwise has no ground to stand on." E-mail: December 21, 2016.

6. http://www.daily-sun.com/post/100103/Khaleda%E2%80%99s-trial-must-for-honouring-war-criminals
7. http://www.ittefaq.com.bd/politics/2016/12/27/97388.html
8. Refer to Haq's jointly authored *Ranangon* (Warfront) of 1966, his *Khelaram Kheley Ja* and *Mora Moyur*, and Nasreen's *Ka*. For Nasreen's views and comments in this regard, visit: http://www.bd-pratidin.com/facebook/2016/09/29/173274; her interview with Karan Thapar on itv.in/?page=9&&option=com_video&view=list&Itemid=8&v=1; itv.in/index.php?option=com_video&view=detail&v_id=406&Itemid=8. For more on Haq's anti-Islamic controversies and sexual obscenities, http://banglamail71.com/others/news=1112; http://newsbd7.com/main/detail/3147; http://newsbd7.com/main/detail/3150; https://sathkahonbd.blogspot.com/2015/12/blog-post_29.html; http://islambangla24.gq/forum2_theme_112241447.xhtml?tema=16&n=0&-vdo=%2B&vch=d553fad11b8e262c5c92d945984d4750&vmsg=7011090661; http://islambangla24.gq/forum2_theme_112241447.xhtml?tema=17
9. For the controversial past of Syed Shamsul Haq, see: http://www.bdface.net/news-detail/detail/41/246799; http://newsbd7.com/main/detail/3147; http://newsbd7.com/main/detail/3150; http://www.roshikhakim.com/2016/09/27; http://www.roshikhakim.com/2016/09/28/; http://www.roshikhakim.com/2016/09/29/; http://www.bdface.net/blog/blogdetail/detail/10854/Ahmed_Firoj/79497
10. To this effect, Kai Kaus quotes Sheikh Abdul Aziz, Dr Sadat Hussein, Kamruddin Ahmed, and Roisuddin Arif, among others: https://www.facebook.com/kai.kaus.7/posts/242701966167059
11. http://www.dailynayadiganta.com/detail/news/184521
12. http://youtube-music-videos.info/video/NkCJGGJZSCk/dec-19-2013.html; for the story/history of Ershad's unceasing on-again, off-again flip-flops, see Kai Kaus's Ershadnama at Kai Kaus February 15, 2016; and Kai Kaus February 16, 2016
13. http://www.bdfirst.net/newsdetail/detail/49/150122
14. http://bangladeshchronicle.net/2016/02/tista-water/; http://www.amardeshonline.com/pages/details/2016/03/25/328878#; http://www.amardeshonline.com/pages/details/2016/03/25/328880#; https://www.facebook.com/533355350042314/videos/796353473742499/

15 http://www.amadershomoy.biz/unicode/2016/05/11/108863.htm#; https://wadud-bhuiyan.wordpress.com/2015/10/30/dissection-of-bnp-new-trouble-begins/; https://www.youtube.com/watch?v=HY_U40kTWww

16. http://www.drfirozmahboobkamal.com/2011-01-23-21-55-47/1084-some-horrific-accounts-of-1971.html; https://www.youtube.com/watch?v=Ep8fNT4-A9g; https://www.youtube.com/watch?v=HXarbPJF9Pc. Also: "In the last eight months there was no semblance of any law and order in the whole of Bangladesh, people expected that after liberation there will be peace and the common people will enjoy the fruit of freedom with complete sense of honor and security which they were deprived of for hundreds of years. Unfortunately things are happening otherwise. In the liberated areas people have taken law in their own hands. Worst of all are allegations against Niamito Bahini and Gono Bahini whose atrocities can be compared with those of the Pakistan army and in most cases these allegations are painfully true ... About 95% of the Rajakars are victims of circumstances. Same is the case of those people who had been in political parties other than Awami League. What is happening today is that innocent people are being killed by the members of Niamito as well as Gono Bahini on the plea these people are Rajakars, Muslim Leaguers and so on. Actually in most cases revenge or personal enmity is being taken. Even if a man has been helping Pak Army—no one knows the tragic circumstances which forced him to work for them. I know one incident in which a young girl of 16 was raped and then sent to India to collect information keeping her younger sisters and parents as hostages ... These are the hard realities of life in the occupied areas of Bangladesh and incidents of this nature are too many to be mentioned. Can we then afford to kill a Bengalee whatever he might have done—without proper trial? Can we deny the fact that the whole nation stood united for independence! If not then, we—as a new nation must be able to search our heart and find out the causes and circumstances which compelled many of our people to work against us. It is a fact that there are some real culprits but then it is not too many. If we want to establish law and order, peace and if we want to honor our freedom, imperative we take the following actions. Otherwise Bangladesh will be an Independent nation only for geographical identity where primitive savagery will domain." Major M. Rafiqul Islam (Commander—Sector 1), তথ্যসূত্র : বাংলাদেশের স্বাধীনতা যুদ্ধ : দলিলপত্র (একাদশ খন্ড)/সম্পাদক : হাসান হাফিজুর রহমান ॥ [তথ্য মন্ত্রণালয়—নভেম্বর, ১৯৮২ । পৃ: ৫৪৭-৫৪৮]

17. তথ্যসূত্র: দিনাজপুরে মুক্তিযুদ্ধ [সুবর্ণ, মার্চ, ২০১১।পৃ: ১৮২]: https://www.facebook.com/kai.kaus.7/posts/224376421332947

18. See the "Bangladeshi Nationalism" chapter for the details of the agreement. Also, Rifat-ul-Ahsan, *India-Bangladesh Relations : after 1971* at http://defenceforumindia.com/forum/threads/india-bangladesh-relations.4411/

19. http://www.amadershomoys.com/content/2014/04/26/middle0830.htm; http://www.sheershanewsbd.com/2015/10/10/99527

20. http://www.facebd.net/newsdetail/detail/200/263678

21. http://newagebd.net/190238/362-incidents-of-sexual-assault-in-2015/; http://www.amardeshonline.com/pages/details/2015/12/08/314118
22. For example, Matiur Rahman Nizami's lawyer AssadUddin and Ali Ahsan Mohammad Mujahid's lawyer Shishir Monir.
23. http://www.banglatribune.com/national/news/90447
24. Shakera Akhter is a graduate in Bengali language and literature from the National University of Bangladesh. She was done with নতুন কুড়ি (a singing and dancing school for children) in 1978 when she won the National Children Award (জাতীয় শিশু পুরস্কার). She won the same award again in 1986. She received the President's Award for Dancing during the National Education Week (জাতীয় শিক্ষা সপ্তাহ) in 1988. Her aunt was a member of parliament from Sunamganj Sylhet. She writes or quotes from another from Boston: "এখন তো দেশের সবাই মুক্তি যোদ্ধা / কেউ শাহবাগি মুক্তি যোদ্ধা / কেউ চেতনাবাদী মুক্তি যোদ্ধা / কেউ বা আবার কলকাতায় বসে / মুক্তি যুদ্ধ করেছেন / আবার কেউ জেলে বসে মুক্তি যুদ্ধ করেছেন / কেউ ধানমন্ডি ৩২ নম্বরে পাকিস্তানি / ভাতা খেয়ে মুক্তি যুদ্ধ করেছেন / তবে "ছাএ শিবির" আর "জামাত "এই / মুক্তি যুদ্ধ থেকে বাদ যাবে কেন / তারাও এখন জোর গলায় বলুক / আমরাও দেশের জন্য প্রান দিয়েছি / যুদধ করেছি I" (E-mail post of 13 July 2014 to the author).
25. http://www.newsbangla.net/newsdetail/detail/31/293788. In addition, there are allegations/controversies surrounding many Awami leaders such as Mowlana Nurul Islam, A K Faizul Haq, Engr Khandoker Musharraf Hussein, Kazi Zafarullah, Ashikur Rahman, Mokha Alamgir, and Farid, brother of Ivy Rahman, among others.
26. http://www.thedailystar.net/country/un-calls-dhaka-abolish-death-penalty-177331
27. https://www.google.com/search?q=War+crime+imbroglio%3A+Road+to+Islamabad+runs+through+Delhi+Shahid+Islam
28. Read Mina Farah's amazing columns in the Bangladeshi print media, especially the daily *Naya Diganta*. Here is one in the daily *Amader Shomoy*: http://www.amadershomoys.com/newsite/2015/11/26/450268.htm#. There was an international outcry against the execution verdict:
    https://www.washingtonpost.com/world/national-security/us-criticism-grows-over-bangladesh-war-crimes-tribunal/2015/11/20/f6805c6a-8feb-11e5-934c-a369c80822c2_story.html?postshare= 5 851448112108574&tid=ss_tw;
    http://www.dailynayadiganta.com/detail/news/68749#; http://www.mzamin.com/details.php?mzamin=MTAyNDM4&sOA==;
    http://www.dailysangram.com/print.php?news_id=209213; http://www.sheershanewsbd.com/2015/11/21/104550
29. http://rtnbd.net/opinion/32398
30. http://www.clickittefaq.com/editorial-oped/justice-not-served-in-bangladesh/;
    http://www.sheershanewsbd.com/2015/11/21/104591;
    http://www.prothom-alo.com/international/article/690031/;
    http://www.dailynayadiganta.com/detail/news/71350#;
    http://www.dw.com/en/bangladeshi-government-has-vengeful-thirst-for-execution/a-18858285;

http://www.huffingtonpost.co.uk/lord-carlile/bangladesh_b_8592828.html; http://www.thedailystar.net/country/halt-execution-mojaheed-sq-chy-hrw-175390; http://www.dailydinkal.net/2015/11/20/20917.php#; http://www.sheershanewsbd.com/2015/11/19/104382; http://www.thedailystar.net/country/apologise-bangladesh-tells-amnesty-170362; http://newagebd.net/174231/govt-asks-amnesty-to-apologise/; http://www.dailynayadiganta.com/detail/news/64208#; http://www.sheershanewsbd.com/2015/10/24/101250; http://newagebd.net/171812/wife-challenges-sq-chys-conviction-for-war-crimes/; http://www.thedailystar.net/country/war-crimes-sq-chy%E2%80%99s-wife-challenges-trial-individuals-166183
31. https://www.facebook.com/newbasherkella/?fref=nf; বাঁশেরকেল্লা—Basherkella
32. http://tlhrc.house.gov/hearing_notice.asp?id=1309
33. http://journal.georgetown.edu/bangladesh-democracy-under-attack/; http://www.theguardian.com/commentisfree/2016/apr/08/the-guardian-view-on-the-bangladesh-history-debate-distorted-by-politics
34. http://bangladeshwarcrimes.blogspot.com/2014/10/initial-thoughts-on-nizami-conviction.html; https://www.facebook.com/golam.nabiul.10/posts/997060067056557; https://www.youtube.com/watch?v=mbB8QazT8jw
35. http://www.thehindu.com/news/national/bangladesh-minister-mahmood-arrives-tomorrow/article8292963.ece; http://www.first-bd.net/newsdetail/detail/200/194146
36. http://www.dailynayadiganta.com/detail/news/61435; http://www.dailydinkal.net/2015/10/15/20085.php
37. Why is the top terrorist Tofael Ahmed Josef enjoying the luxury hospital bed for 20 months?: http://www.prothom-alo.com/bangladesh/article/1166576
38. http://www.amardeshonline.com/pages/details/2016/02/06/322330#
39. http://www.ittefaq.com.bd/wholecountry/2015/12/05/45729.html; http://www.thedailystar.net/city/105-women-children-murdered-last-month-1820
40. Ghadani/ঘাদানি is an acronym that derives from Ghatok Dalal Nirmul (uprooting or elimination of the 1971 killers and collaborators) Committee.
41. https://www.youtube.com/watch?v=DW6ap5DxnwM; https://www.youtube.com/watch?v=HbhDhqik664; https://www.youtube.com/watch?v=a6Ig_PmhPVI; https://www.youtube.com/watch?v=Jb1DPi1y36k; https://vimeo.com/77047183; http://www.stsoftindia.com/?q=5+may+hefajote+islam; http://www.stsoftindia.com/?q=hefajote+islam+dead+body; http://ireport.cnn.com/docs/DOC-968893

42. Craig Baxter, "Bangladesh," in Y K Malik, et.al. *Government and Politics in South Asia* (Boulder, Colorado: Westview Press, 1987), p. 251, 268. See also Baxter, *Bangladesh: A New Nation in the Old Setting* (Boulder, Colorado: Westview Press, 1984).
43. http://www.thedailystar.net/democracy-not-at-cost-of-liberty-66329
44. http://newagebd.net/96849/ep-delegation-for-immediate-end-to-violence/#sthash. k5ELOTty.dpuf; http://newagebd.net/96849/ep-delegation-for-immediate-end-to-violence/#sthash.k5ELOTty.dpbs
45. "২০০২ সালের ২৪শে ডিসেম্বরে ঢাকার "The Independent" পত্রিকায় শেখ হাসিনাকে উদ্ধৃত করে লেখা হয় হাসিনা বলেন যে "বঙ্গবন্ধু সীরাত মিশন প্রতিষ্ঠা করেন, মাদ্রাসা বোর্ড স্থাপন করেন, টঙ্গীতে তবলীগ জামাতের জন্য জমি বরাদ্দ করেন, কাকরাইল মসজিদ ও তার সংলগ্ন জমি তবলীগ জামাতের কাছে হস্তান্তর করেন আর বায়তুল মোকাররম মসজিদের জন্য তিন একর জমি নিবন্ধন করে দেন।"(মুক্তমনা) "১৯৯৬ নির্বাচনের প্রাক্কালে শেখ হাসিনা হিজাব পরা ও ঘন ঘন উমরাহ করা শুরু করেন, আওয়ামী লীগ তাদের ম্যানিফেস্টোতে আল্লাহু আকবর ও "লা ইলাহা ইল্লাল্লাহ, নৌকার মালিক তুই আল্লাহ" শ্লোগান যোগ করে।"(মুক্তমনা) http://www.theguardian.com/world/2015/sep/16/british-jihadis-bangladesh-extremism-uk-isis-sheikh-hasina
46. https://hbr.org/2013/02/great-leaders-know-when-to/
47. http://www.counterpunch.org/2013/12/27/searching-for-truth-and-reconciliation-in-bangladesh/
48. https://hbr.org/2013/02/great-leaders-know-when-to/

9

The Quagmire of Partisan Politics Over the Dead

Controversies Over the Image and Status of Mujib and Zia

Donald Trump's America, both before and after the election of November 8, 2016, was divided and still remains divided, so much so that many Americans, perhaps for the first time in American history, do not consider or regard him as their president often protesting against him from the very next day of the election. No wonder, CNN's Kate Bolduan hosts a show called "The Donald Trump Presidency and A Nation Divided." Similarly, in the far more polarized and bifurcated Bangladesh, the disaffected majority under the sluttish Hasina regime cannot consider or regard her as their prime minister. It is therefore no wonder that the most popular and main opposition leader of the country, Begum Khaleda Zia, calls Sheikh Hasina simply by "Hasina" out of dislike, disapproval, and denigration, rather than affection and admiration, not even affected or pretended affection.

When can all Bangladeshis, wholeheartedly, with no hesitation whatsoever, regardless of their party affiliation, consider their prime minister or president, whoever and whenever it is, *their* prime minister and *their* president, who, by virtue of their bipartisan consideration, impartiality, neutrality, and objectivity, can earn the status of being loved, not loathed, by all or at least the absolute majority of their people? When can the people regard and admire *their* prime minister and *their* president without impatiently having to change the TV channels or turn off the set altogether, or quickly turn over the pages of a newspaper, or walk away from the drawing room to wherever, out of their deep dislike and distrust, even total antipathy and animosity, no sooner than they see such top figures and their হুক্কা হুয়া (uncritical and unassuming) sycophants, lackeys and zealots on the screen or the paper?

The appearance of a prime minister or a president on TV is not supposed to be a commercial break, unless they are the president or the prime minister of their own party only, ever looking after their myopic and monolithic partisan interest without exception and receiving a choric/choral bandwagon *Mabrook ya Habibi* ("Congratulations, my beautiful sweetheart") from their HMV (His/Her Master's Voice) "yes" men and women sitting right in front of them.

To switch to another channel or flip through the pages of a daily paper in the case of advertisements or those who are very unimpressive to look at with scary and strange-looking eyes (for instance, some among the media faces on a Bangla channel) or those in the public service with depressing and deplorable accent/pronunciation, deeply colored with the flavor of their local dialects (such as that of George Bernard Shaw's Eliza, at least in the beginning, in *Pygmalion*) is of course an entirely different matter. Eliza, however, is trained to improve to the level of perfection, but there are no signs that some public figures would ever improve, confirming that they would prefer to remain as they are—incorrigible and intolerable!).

Getting back to the focus of this chapter, once, in Malaysia, there was a talk on international politics by an American professor on Fulbright exchange program. It was the time of President George W Bush, an Ivy League (Yale) graduate and Governor of Texas before becoming the US President. Yet he was perhaps the most criticized and least well-liked President ever for having been perceived as a politician of average IQ (with which, however, many might differ). Some members of the audience, not surprisingly, posed questions related to what they thought were Bush's political mistakes that they believed were attributed to his low level of intelligence quotient (IQ). The professor politely dodged the questions, reminding the audience that he (Bush) was still their President/American President—elected twice. One of the reasons of his electability, as the American media sometimes brought up, being that he was indeed a man of humor and, in fact, of average qualities, not outstanding intellect, but effectively harping on and confining himself to a limited number of issues only, with which the average citizens could connect well.

Once Bush himself humorously dodged a question from a journalist about the Obama candidacy for president, saying, "You're the pundit. I'm just a simple president," or brushed off the information about the side sources of his finances that John Kerry said he (Bush) had, during a presidential debate, by saying, "That's news to me." (Compared with all the American presidents, Donald Trump may however be an exception being negatively down and different on many things, from personal to political, sometimes in a coarse and cumbersome, if not completely crooked and clownish manner.)

Unlike the Americans/Westerners, the Bangladeshis keep on fighting over the image and integrity of their presidents and prime ministers. This lack of acceptability by all citizens due to the partisan and authoritarian politics of their leaders—who are sometimes nonelected, unelected, pseudo-elected or quasi-elected through a mock and mean election like the one on January 5, 2014—is by far much worse than the somewhat questionable and less than excellent quality of a top politician. Is it a long way to go before the Western type of political culture and maturity develops in Bangladesh, where hard suppression is the order of the political show under what many analysts and commentators describe as the present BAKSAL-2 regime, much worse and more dangerous than BAKSAL-I?

This chapter deals with the dispute over the status of Sheikh Mujibur Rahman and President Ziaur Rahman and their historic contribution both before and after the creation of Bangladesh. It also expresses concerns over the past-centered, past-oriented, all-title, and all-ceremony style of Bangladesh politics.

Bangladeshis are deeply divided over a great number of political issues that stand on their way to getting united as one country and one nation. One of the issues is who the two leaders—Sheikh Mujibur Rahman and Ziaur Rahman—are or were in terms of their political status, identity, position, or contribution. Both of them were brutally and mercilessly assassinated while they were still in office. Mujib lost his life in his own home together with most of the members of his family in 1975, except his two daughters (who were then away in Germany), including the would-be prime minister Sheikh Hasina. Zia lost his, away from home, on a trip to another part of the country, in 1981, leaving behind the rest of his family, including his would-be prime minister wife, Khaleda Zia.

Until today the people of Bangladesh are struggling over what the two leaders' respective historic roles were, how their identities could be unanimously and comprehensively defined and determined, and, in recognition of their exemplary contribution, what their fitting and popular titles should be. The people cannot arrive at a clear and concrete decision because they think some aspects of their two leaders' total vision and philosophy may have been controversial with their leadership or statesmanship, having fallen short of the widest possible national appeal both before and after the independence—short of the long way toward forging a national unity in the war-torn country.[1]

All the people of Bangladesh, as one single nation, are not wholeheartedly united in accepting the two leaders without question and according them the national status they deserve equally unequivocally. "The title 'Father of the Nation' is sometimes politically contested. The 1972 Constitution of Bangladesh declared Sheikh Mujibur Rahman the 'father of the nation.' The BNP government removed this in 2004, to the protest of then opposition Awami League (AL), led by Mujib's daughter Sheikh Hasina."[2] Now that the AL is in power, the title has been reinstated.

(Late) Kazi Zafar Ahmed, himself a former prime minister and a highly respected veteran politician (flanked by another great man of Bangladesh, Dr Zafrullah Chowdhury), citing the examples of India and the USA, raised objection to making Mujib alone "the father of the nation," saying it was bewildering to call only and singly him so.[3] Depending on who they like, people are happy that they have this or that leader to be proud of as if they are all set on the basis of the traditional adage that something was better than nothing or, as the English poet Tennyson put it in a different context, in *In Memoriam* (1850), that "'Tis better to have loved and lost/Than never to have loved at all." In addition, those who want to accord especial status to anybody may do so if they so wish, on their own, but they cannot force or impose their view upon others who may have a different opinion out of their democratic freedom of choice.

The issue is also related to who first declared the independence of Bangladesh—Zia or Mujib—and in what form and style. There are many post-colonial nation-states (or those countries which became unified and independent after a violent struggle), which regard their leaders as their founding fathers, bestowing the title of the "father of the nation" on no one alone or in particular. It is true one of them is indeed singled out to be accorded an extra and special but not a singularly unique status so that the sacrifices and the contributions of others are not undermined.

Some nations, such as the USA, have in fact a number of leaders rather than just one as their father figure. The democratic-minded Americans, with a belief in individualism, do not have to necessarily express their veneration for their founding fathers by constantly attaching an epical epithet or a long honorific before their names, no matter how whole, intact, and uncontroversial the image of those "fathers" was. Yes, there are also those with a title almost permanently prefixed to their names, but all such are indeed blessed with a clean and consistently uniform record from the beginning to the end. Should Bangladesh also have an ideal combination of "founding fathers" or, alternatively, no father at all, instead of a controversial one, who, with a broken record of both mega and milestone achievements (until March 1971) and monstrous, gaping, and glaring failures during 1972–1975), in view of the majority of the nation, was/had to be in the safe custody of Pakistan, away from the battlefield for the entire duration of the nine months of the battle (March-December 1971), apparently through a negotiation with the Pakistani and American government, instead of staying back and providing an active and frontal leadership on the ground?

No doubt, Mujib was a great, bold, noble, inspiring, arousing, and charismatic pre-and-pro-independence leader. Along with the three other founding fathers of Bangladesh—Hussein Shaheed Suhrawardy, Sher-e-Bangla A K Fazlul Hoque and Moulana Abdul Hameed Khan Bhashani, all three of whom are now unfortunately neglected, being not remembered as much as they deserve—,[4] Mujib was a legend, a monumental figure, a towering personality, a Himalayan hero, and an Oceanic phenomenon during the 1960s that ultimately led up to the independence of Bangladesh. Both in soul and stature and mind and body, Mujib was as big and broad as the Bay of Bengal.

Leaving aside the debate on which "great man" or "able man" theory he fitted in—Carlylean, Spencerian, Hegelian, Kierkegaardian, Nietzschean, Spenglerian, Tolstoyan, (William) Jamesian, or the related discussions by Frederick Adams Woods, Sidney Hook, and Leonid Grinin—it can safely be said that Mujib made history and influenced history as much as he was a product of history or he was an agent of the World Spirit to play the role providentially assigned to him. In view of Ranu Chowdhury, a decorated freedom fighter and also a regular in the army, who risked his life to escape from West Pakistan to fight for Bangladesh, "Mujib was great before 1971. He generated hope among the Bengalis to redeem their political and economic rights. His Six Points concerning সোনার বাংলা শশান কেন [Why Is The Golden Bengal Barren Like A Graveyard/Cremation Ground] did wonders in uniting the Bengalis and speaking in one voice against the West Pakistani leadership, and those finally led him to absolute victory in December 1970 elections."[5]

Unfortunately, Mujib had to be away from the liberation war for reasons still being debated, some claiming that he arranged his surrender to Pakistan through the mediation of then US Ambassador Joseph Farland. He remained confined to his safe detention in West Pakistan during the entire period of the 9-month long liberation war of Bangladesh (still East Pakistan). It was also with Farland's help that Mujib arranged full safety for his family, to be provided by the same junta that would kill millions of Bangladeshis, starting right from the night of March 25. According to various reports, for instance, Oli Ahad's জাতীয় রাজনীতি (*National Politics: 1945–1975*), the Mujib family was on a monthly Pakistan government allowance of 1,500 taka, in addition to all other expenses being borne by the same, which treated its members, including today's Hasina, as special guests while genocide was raging throughout the country, outside their safe haven under the protection of the Pak army.[6]

It is said that the Pakistanis even celebrated the birth of Hasina's son Joy in the Dhaka cantonment over sweets when they were killing the people of Bangladesh in the capital and beyond.[7] No wonder, PM Sheikh Hasina, according to the freedom fighter Motiur Rahman Rentu's 1999 book, আমার ফাঁসি চাই (I Want/Long To Be Hanged/I Wish My Own Hanging), developed a great liking for the Pak army, while she had a dislike for the Bangladesh army, especially after the assassination of her father Sheikh Mujib in 1975.[8] Rentu's book is one of the best and most authentic records of the pre- and post-1975 Awami Baksali horrific brutalities and their grave and grievous ill-and-evil deeds.[9]

Mujib's assassination followed his three-and-a-half years of uneasy and unstable rule (misrule?), badly tarnished by some malicious malpractices, intentional or otherwise.[10] These included, among others, (1) his undemocratic and unpopular *Rakhkhi-Bahini* (similar to then challenger-now-turned-ally JSD wing *Gano-Bahini*)[11]; (2) his cracking down and unleashing terror and torture on several fronts[12]; (3) his creation of only one-party political system—the authoritarian BAKSAL[13]—; (4) his unequal 12-point agreement with India (March 19, 1972), to stand good for 25 years, very much like Tajuddin Ahmad's unequal 7-point agreement the previous year (and Nawab Mir Jaffar Ali Khan Bahadur's unequal 12-point agreement with Maj Gen Robert Clive (June 3, 1757)[14]; and (5) the 1974 famine when tens of thousands died of hunger as they were searching for rotten foodstuff in the city's garbage and when, by harsh and discordant contrast, the weddings of the members of the Mujib family were still going ahead in a gaudy and grandiose manner (like in today's Zimbabwe and North Korea where, despite poverty and malnourishment, lavish rewards are being reserved for the loyalists of the fascist dictators Robert Mugabe and Kim Jong-Un and lavish birthday celebrations for themselves).[15]

In his autobiographical book, *From Third World to First: The Singapore Story, 1965–2000*, Lee Kuan Yew provides an eyewitness account of the spendthrift Mujib's luxury and extravagance as he saw it at work during the Commonwealth Summit in Ottawa in 1973, just before the famine the following year.[16] Dr Abid Bahar of Dawson College Montreal Canada gives a detailed sketch of Mujib's record, both good and bad, positive and negative, as he (Mujib) spectacularly rose and miserably fell and failed with a sudden and abrupt fall.[17] Dr Jamshed Chowdhury's doctoral dissertation at Heidelberg University, later published as a book, was entirely devoted to Mujib's governing years as a failure marked by the characteristics of a "bottomless basket" and a soup kitchen—favoritism, nepotism and corruption leading to an unprecedented famine.[18] Similarly, the UK-based Dr Firoz Mahboob Kamal's entire series called *Ekattorer Itihas* (History of 1971) is devoted to the listing of the helpless and hapless Mujib-era tragic pitfalls.[19]

Professor Syed Serajul Islam, who teaches Political Science at Lakehead University Canada, writes that Mujib,

> had a record as an abhorrent failure as a statesman. He was a man with extraordinary charisma and incredible oratory capacity more powerful than a bulldozer, but he failed to rebuild the war-wrecked country and to combat corruption of his own people. Mujib's move towards a tyrannical rule by creating the draconian paramilitary *Rakhkhi-Bahini* and the only one party, BAKSAL, putting a ban on all the rest of the political parties, killing thousands of political opponents, and by closing down the media houses, along with the death of millions during his three and half years of office due to famine and the lack of good governance led to the fading and evaporation of his own once-upon-a time dream for democracy in Bangladesh.[20]

According to the former American ambassador to Bangladesh and Pakistan, William B. Milam, "By 1974, the country was a mess, the veritable 'basket case' that Henry Kissinger is alleged to have called it."[21] Indian writer-journalist Kuswant Singh wrote in the *Illustrated Weekly of India*:

> Within a couple of years, [Sheikh Mujib] had lost much of his charisma and lived in a cocoon of self-spun esteem. He came to regard honest critics as traitors and sycophants as loyal friends. It was a classic case of folio de grandeur. He was blissfully unaware that the very people who called him *Bangabandhu* to his face were behind his back called him *Banga-Shatru*.[22]

Writer-Scholar-Professor (late) Dr Ahmad Sharif claims exactly the same blasting Mujib for what he thought were his and his party's ill and evil nature of conduct, behavior, and actions.[23]

Mujib's assassination was committed by some army officers with the covert/overt support from the large majority of all sections of people in the nation, including the armed forces and Mujib's close associates of his own party. It had the support of many international players as well. In all international politics and world history, heroes are terrorists and terrorists are heroes, depending on who one asked. Similarly, the August 15 coup leaders are saviors of the nation, aka সূর্য সন্তান (great sons of the soil, as great as the sun) to some, who would like to celebrate it as the "Bangladesh Day of Deliverance" (BDD), as the veteran politician Ataur Rahman Khan termed it soon after the coup. On the other hand, others view the coup plotters as unforgivable murderers.[24] (Similarly, today, the police and the RAB are heroes to the ruling AL while they are dangerous partisan tools of persecution and rogue villains to the opposition).

Unfortunately, the killing of Mujib went unlamented and was in fact welcomed by the rejoicing majority over the sweets distribution, including the mass media of the time and many frontline members of his own party, who were glad to take over after him without any regret or remorse whatsoever.[25] Even in the words of Lawrence Lifschultz, who is otherwise quite well-disposed to the Awami politics,

> The reaction in Bangladesh, although one of extraordinary shock, was not one of a vast popular fury against the coup makers. To a certain degree there prevailed *a general mood of deliverance from a regime which had become nepotistic, corrupt, and oppressive.* Further on more will be noted about *the reasons and forces behind Mujib's political decline*, but it may simply be said that Mujibur Rahman, who had returned from imprisonment in Pakistan in 1972 as an unparalleled national hero to his people, would within three years die *almost without a whimper of support.*[26] (my emphasis)

Almost all of the nearly forty cabinet members under President Khandoker Mushtaq Ahmed, soon after the assassination of Mujib, were from Mujib's own party, who thereby made no secret of their support for the coup, their greed for power, and their solidarity with the violent takeover.[27] The whole world, including India, recognized the new government in no time. ASM Abdur Rob, a liberation hero, reiterated this historical fact and made a claim to the same effect.[28] Those who would have wished to lament, if there were any, the murder of Mujib probably did not dare to come out on the street for fear of reprisal from the popular army as well as the overwhelmingly large majority of the public in support of the coup). Eminent Barrister Mainul Hussein repeatedly says he was shocked and surprised to see that it was quiet all around, there being none on the street to protest against, when he went out on that fateful Friday morning to have a feel of what it was like, implying that people were relieved at the bloody turn of events. "অনেক মানুষ এই হত্যাকান্ডে উল্লাস প্রকাশ করেছে। হত্যাকান্ডকে সমর্থন করে কেউ কেউ স্লোগানও দিচ্ছে। [...] পঁচাত্তরে মুজিব কাকুর জনপ্রিয়তা ছিল শূন্যের কোঠায়। তার নেতৃত্ব সম্পর্কে হতাশাগ্রস্ত জনগণ তার স্বৈরশাসনের অবসান কামনা করছিল।," writes Tajuddin Ahmad's daughter Sharmin Ahmad in her book *Tajuddin Ahmad: Neta O Pita* (2014).

Barrister Hussein and many others are of the opinion that many of those Awami leaders who were then silent, preferring to stay home and not to be seen on the street that day, are now crying crocodile tears for Mujib.[29] The old timer Awami-Baksalis who are shedding crocodile tears today on August 15 may be asked: "পঁচাত্তরের পনোরই আগস্ট কোথায় ছিলেন?," the way Jibanananda Das's Banalata Sen asks the speaker/poetic persona of the poem, তেমনই দেখেছি তারে অন্ধকারে; বলেছে সে, 'এতোদিন কোথায় ছিলেন?' Did those Awamis also পাখির নীড়ের মতো নিরাপদ স্থানে আশ্রয় নিয়েছিলেন?

Kai Kaus, one of the eminent bloggers of Bangladesh, provides documentary details of the times immediately before and after the assassination of Sheikh Mujib.[30] For the (highly negative) international press coverage of the political developments in Bangladesh during 1974–1975 in, for example, the New Statesman, Daily Mail, Daily Telegraph, Far Eastern Economic Review and the Los Angeles Times, one only needs to check the archives.[31] Hindu nationalist (Medical) Dr Kalidas Baiddya, who was once a trusted adviser to Sheikh Mujib, goes back to Mujib's Tungipara past and Kolkata Islamia College (now Moulana Azad College) past during the mid-1940s and paints an authentic picture of Mujib's anti-Hindu and pro-Pakistani violence ridden days under the influence of his political guru/master Suhrawardy.[32]

Similarly, today's otherwise very popular BNP-led opposition, an "irritating" and "obnoxious" anathema to the Awami rulers of neo-and-near-and-more-than-partially fascist and পৈশাচিক characteristics, cannot come out on the streets for fear of the police beating under the dictate of the ruling AL (with most of the opposition leaders and supporters, in scores of thousands, being thrown into jail, only to push the limit of the prison capacity to worse than slum-like subhuman level).[33]

All's Well That Ends Well—that is the name of a comedy by Shakespeare, which contrasts with the tragedy of Mujib's life. In the case of Mujib, whose saga spanned decades of his political career, all was not well since it did not end well. Many renowned sub-continental politicians—Mujib, Zulfiker Ali Bhutto, Benazir Bhutto, Ziaul Hoque, Mahatma Gandhi, Indira Gandhi, Rajiv Gandhi, and Ghulam Azam—all ended unhappily, though all of them began happily and promisingly (with Azam, for instance, having played a great role in the language movement in the late 1940s and early 1950s as a prominent student leader, especially as the twice elected General Secretary of DUCSU—1947–1949).

There was a time when Mujib had the profound trust of the people, which he lost in no time. Even though he was away for the entire duration of the liberation war, the people of Bangladesh showered all their love and affection on him upon his return from Pakistan on January 10, 1972. He, however, failed, as Ranu Chowdhury observes, to deliver on good governance, establish the rule of law, and maintain a balance in the military as far as the officers who took part in the liberation war and those who returned from Pakistan after the liberation were concerned, and also those who secretly formed the JSD-linked *Biplobi Sena*

Bahini (BSB), led by Col Taher. Within three years, Mujib's fortunes turned from "the most loved" to "the most hated and disliked." Consequently, Mujib paid the ultimate price with no tears shed on August 15, 1975 when the people did in fact celebrate his downfall.[34] Nevertheless, it was a tragic end for Mujib and the majority of his family members, who were also killed with him.

In the view of the retired Bangladesh Air Force Officer Mohammed Shoaib, who claims he was once a freedom fighter: "Sheikh Mujib was a brilliant leader only till the 16th December, 1971. His ultimate treachery was to create BAKSAL to perpetuate his one-man dictatorship."[35] In his dystopian political fiction, *The Black Coat* (2013), referring to the sleeveless Mujib coat, Bangladeshi-Canadian author Neamat Imam depicts Mujib "as a totalitarian ruler who distorted truth and suppressed political opposition to strengthen his tyranny," calling him a "monster" and a "disgrace" (Wikipedia).

Mujib's rise and fall were like the rise and fall of Julius Caesar of Rome, who was once a hugely popular republican and then turned a dictator, to be killed by his own close associates, Brutus and Cassius. Mujib's tragic fate was similar to the initially rosy and promising French Revolution of 1789, which, with the massacre of thousands and the execution of King Louis XVI and Queen Marie Antoinette in 1793, turned violent in no time, leading to Maximilian Robespierre's year-long extremely radical "Jacobin" Reign of Terror until July 28, 1794, the day Robespierre himself was guillotined. Mujib's painful end is comparable to the end of Napoleon, child of the French Revolution, who was one of the greatest and also one of the meanest, as the poet Lord Byron described him, with his spectacular rise and pathetic downfall, directly suggested by Byron's contemporary, poet P. B. Shelley, in his sonnet on Ozymandias (ancient Egyptian Pharaoh Ramses II, who ruled probably at the time of Prophet Musa/Moses).[36]

The cruel reversal of Mujib's fortune was like the rise and fall of Shakespeare's ambitious and tragic character Macbeth, and those of Browning's Patriot ("It was roses, roses, all the way,/ With myrtle mixed in my path like mad [...] For they fling, whoever has a mind/ Stones at me for my year's misdeeds") and Tennyson's politically and symbolically suggestive Eagle ("Ring'd with the azure world, he stands [...] And like a thunderbolt he falls"). The tide and ebb of Mujib's unfortunate career and most of the members of his family were similar to Saddam Hussein of Iraq, Muammar al-Gaddafi of Libya, Zein al-Abedine (Ben Ali) of Tunisia, and Ferdinand Marcos of the Philippines. Mujib's fate was like that of Czar Nicholas II of Russia and his Romanov family, all unfortunately executed by the Bolshevik revolutionaries in 1918. Bearing the official title of "Emperor and Autocrat of All the Russias" (including Finland and Poland) during his rule as the last emperor of Russia, Nicholas II was also nicknamed by his political opponents as "Nicholas the Bloody" because of his violent political crackdowns and persecutions.[37]

When Saddam was still out there, ruling with iron hand, many Iraqis used to say, out of frustration, that no one, not even the Americans would ever be able to topple him; only God/*Allah* the Almighty could do so if He wanted to. The same (painful) opinion used to be held about Gaddafi, Hosni Mubarak, Zein al-Abedine, Sheikh Mujib, Jean-Claude Duvalier, Idi Amin, Adolf Hitler, Benito Mussolini, Erich Honecker, Nicolai Ceausescu, Ferdinand Marcos, and many other dictators. Their fate is now known to the world. Some of them like Zein al-Abedine, Duvalier, Idi Amin, and the Shah of Iran (who was being joked about as saying "I run from I-ran") had to flee away for life. Bashar Al-Assad, Kim Jong Un, and Abdul Fattah Al-Sisi are probably awaiting their fate too.

The truth of the matter related to the assassination of Mujib was borne out not only by the subsequent political development in Bangladesh but also the media in the immediate aftermath of the assassination and even long afterward. Gen K M Shafiullah, then army chief, understood the heartbeat of the people and the writing on the wall, so he welcomed the bloody change. He and the chiefs of the navy and the air force pledged their allegiance to the new government one after another.[38] Although they were tried and executed after long confinement in prison, the army officers, who had carried out the coup operation, were hailed and are still being hailed as heroes or vilified as being misled, according to the individual perspective and viewpoint. Ranu Chowdhury (sometimes as Abu Obaid Chowdhury) recounts the tragic story in his "August 15: Know the Facts, Not Fiction."[39]

Dr Taj Hashmi, who teaches at Austin Peay State University, Tennessee, contends that while today's Awami leaders/supporters are making confusing and convoluted statements describing the whole thing as a "sporadic criminal act by a handful of misguided soldiers," it was actually a popular mutiny supported by all the stakeholders, including the general public.[40] Dr Hashmi also claims that while Mujib was no doubt a great charismatic leader,

> [...] due to the situation beyond his control and understanding, his charisma was fast evaporating like camphor soon after his return from Pakistan in January 1972. By 1974 he was out and out an alienated, discredited and anything but a failed leader among his millions of erstwhile supporters and die-hard admirers. Since nothing succeeds like success; and I may add "nothing fails like failure," with the failure of the Mujib government to deliver the promised goods in his utopian Golden Bengal within less than two years of his ascendancy as the Prime Minister, it was only a matter of time that his oft-touted package of Nationalism-Democracy-Socialism-Secularism, also sold as Mujibism [like a still born child], would die a natural death.[41]

On the contrary, the nearly four-year rule of the enlightened army general-turned-politician President Ziaur Rahman was generally perceived to be positive, benevolent, and clean from corruption, as Moulana Bhashani also admitted.[42] Zia's honesty and austerity were widely known. Unlike the cars of the Awami digital leaders who are in the seat of power without the people's mandate, Zia introduced no more than Toyota Corolla as the official car for all. He himself used a Corolla for routine travels within the cities with only a small police escort in a jeep in front of him.[43]

That Zia was an incorruptible President of fair attributes is proved (as Dr Zainul Abedin, a former journalist in Bangladesh, who has worked on American racial issues and the NYT coverage of the liberation war of Bangladesh in 1971, recounts), by the fact that when Zia's brother Ahmed Kamal (an officer in the local government) was posted in Chittagong Hill Tracts, people were wondering how come a President's brother was not in the capital city! That Zia was above favoritism and nepotism is also proved by the fact that a first cousin of him, an Executive Editor of the (daily) Dainik Bangla, got only a small plot (দুই কাঠা) allotted for the journalists, for which no তদবির (effort of favoritism and nepotism) was allowed through connections. Ranu Chowdhury wrote a long piece in the weekly *Holiday* about how incorruptible Zia was and yet another piece giving the details concerning Mujib's and Zia's rise and fall.[44]

President Zia's popularity rating was so high that the whole nation poured onto the streets of Dhaka to join together in mourning the tragic loss of its beloved president as if they felt irreparably orphaned. More than two million people attended Zia's funeral. Zia's body brought from Chittagong to Dhaka to be received by millions took one back to Walt Whitman's elegies, "O Captain! My Captain!" and "When Lilacs Last in the Dooryard Bloom'd," on the assassination of the popular US President Abraham Lincoln. Zia's funeral was also comparable to that of great Irish Home Rule leader Charles Stewart Parnell, "the uncrowned king of Ireland," in 1891, which drew the biggest crowd ever in the history of Ireland.

On the other hand, Mujib's was a poor show with only a handful of people (probably less than twenty) present during his funeral at his Tungipara birthplace. It was like the poorly attended Sholakia Eidul Adha prayer behind the pro-Awami Maulana Fariduddin Masud in September 2016. Mujib's Tungipara house, according to (the late) popular writer Humayun Ahmed and the veteran journalist Anthony Mascarenhas of *Bangladesh: A Legacy of Blood*, was looted upon the news of his death.[45] There is a huge amount of documentary evidence and media archives, including You Tube videos, showing Zia's enviable and unprecedented popularity both during his life and at his death as well as afterward.[46]

Again, Zia was assassinated by some deviant and devious army officers, ironically in the same city from where he had begun his heroic rise—the port city of Chittagong in the south. Zia took the risk of his life, most heroically, to make the most crucial and most direct announcement of independence from the Chittagong *Kalur Ghat*-based radio station in the most timely fashion on the evening of March 26/27, 1971.[47] He made so first in his own name, then, in a short while, on behalf of the indisputable leader of the time, Mujib, who was already in the Pakistani custody.

Mujib's 7 March speech was indeed a great, unique, historic, and electrifying speech, but, having always been a fighter for the autonomy of East Pakistan, he avoided declaring its independence outright, or at least was wishy-washy about it. There being a sense of ifs and buts, if not flips and flops in it, the speech fell short of a decisive declaration of independence. Whatever may have been the reason—that he may not have wanted to be branded as an illegitimate separatist so hastily by unilaterally declaring independence without exhausting the avenues of negotiation, or he may have wanted, until the last moment, to end up being prime minister of an all and united Pakistan, the fact remains that there was an element of hesitation and hide-and-seek in Mujib that was confirmed not only by his conversation with Tajuddin and Ambassador Farland, but also his not attending the all-party united students front meeting on 23 March to receive the new flag designed by then student leaders for a new independent country—a flag that was later handed in to him at his home.

The full and clear declaration of independence was certainly left for Zia to make in unequivocal terms. According to Prof Srinath Raghavan of King's College London, "Even as late as March 1971, the Awami League was not stating it wanted outright independence. They were asking for a loose confederation with devolution of political and economic autonomy to East Pakistan."[48] Zia's declaration, in no uncertain terms, reads as follows (according to Wikipedia entry on him):

> Major Ziaur Rahman's opening words in Bengali, "Ami Major Zia Bolchi," that is, "I am Major Zia speaking," were picked up by news agencies, and were given wide publicity across the globe. "Ami Major Zia Bolchi" was followed by declaration of a sovereign and independent Bangladesh on 26 March 1971 evening, in these words:
>
> This is Swadhin Bangla Betar Kendra. I, Major Ziaur Rahman, do hereby declare that Independent People's Republic of Bangladesh has been established. On the circumstances, I have taken the command as the temporary Head of the Republic. I call upon all Bengalees to rise against the attack by the West Pakistani Army. We shall fight to the last to free our motherland. Victory is, by the Grace of Allah, ours.

> On 27 March 1971, a second broadcast that included the name of BangaBandhu Sheikh Mujibur Rahman was read: This is Swadhin Bangla Betar Kendra. I, Major Ziaur Rahman, Provincial Head of the government, do hereby declare the Independence of the People's Republic of Bangladesh on behalf of our leader Bangabandhu Sheikh Mujibur Rahman.

In this regard, Tajuddin Ahmad's words also (as recorded in Bangladesh Document Vol-I, Indian Government, p. 284) are worth-quoting:

> ১৯৭১ এর এপ্রিলে প্রবাসী সরকার গঠনের প্রাক্কালে বাংলাদেশের স্বাধীনতা যুদ্ধ কিভাবে চলছে সে সম্পর্কে স্বাধীন বাংলা বেতারে প্রচারিত এক ভাষণে তাজউদ্দিন আহমদ জাতিকে অবহিত করেন, "The brilliant success of our fighting forces and the daily additions to their strength in manpower and captured weapons has enabled the Government of the People's Republic of Bangla Desh, first announced through Major Ziaur Rahman, to set up a full-fledged operational base from which it is administering the liberated areas."

In an article in the Daily *Prothom Alo*, November 2, 2015, Commander H Gaffar of then 22 East Bengal Regiment asserted that it was Zia who declared the independence of Bangladesh and as such was highly popular in the post-independence army rank and file. Another report in the Daily Dinkal, December 16, 2016, makes the same claim calling Zia as Provisional President and Liberation Army Chief.[49] Similar claims have been made/suggested by both Sharmin Ahmad and A K Khandoker (in the latter's ১৯৭১: ভেতরে ও বাইরে/ *1971: Inside and Out*, 2014, pp. 57–58). Khandoker claims that Mujib, who wanted to become prime minister of Pakistan, ended his 7 March speech with "Jiye Pakistan" (Long Live Pakistan). Khandoker also cast doubt on the Hasina-AL's claim that Mujib wrote/sent a telegram to the effect that a declaration of independence be made to an Awami leader in Chittagong a short while before he was taken into custody by the Pakistani authorities in Dhaka on the night of March 25. Khandoker's and Sharmin's claims about Mujib's less than clear, certain and declarative statements about the independence of Bangladesh are supported by many others, such as Justice Habibur Rahman, Nirmal Sen, Maidul Hassan, poet Shamsur Rahman (in his memoirs, কালের ধুলো/Dust of Time), Ataus Samad, Col (Ret) Nuruzzaman, senior academic and columnist Ebne Golam Samad, and the young academic researcher Dr M Mujibur Rahman in their writings.[50] In this respect, two of the most definitive and analytical writings were perhaps done by Abdullah Al Amin and Tuhin Reza, both claiming it wasn't Mujib who could be credited as the declarer of the independence of Bangladesh.[51]

"You might have had a loose confederation which, in some ways, is what the Awami League and Sheikh Mujibur Rahman wanted—even as late as March 1971, the Awami League was not stating it wanted outright independence. They were asking for a loose confederation with devolution of political and economic autonomy to East Pakistan"—this is from the December 2013 Times of India interview by Dr Srinath Raghavan, a senior fellow at the Centre for Policy Research and senior research fellow at King's College, London.[52] According to Dr Raghavan's book, *1971: A Global History of the Creation of Bangladesh*, "Bangladesh's creation wasn't inevitable and if the Pakistani response wasn't so heavy-handed, there would not have been an independent Bangladesh."

To get back to the role played by Zia, considering the fact that he was the senior most military officer available—then a Major—with an exceptional tonal quality, endowed with a penetrating and far-reaching look of his eyes, his announcement of independence worked magic in arousing and inspiring the whole nation and putting it in a real fighting gear. That it was no less than Zia in his military profession, possessed with an especially firm and gripping voice, gave a whole new dimension to the scene and transformed it into one of quality, strength, credibility, authenticity, and popularity. The words of Bangladesh's first Prime Minister Tajuddin Ahmad and Bangladesh's most popular writer Humayun Ahmed bear testimony to this.[53] Even an Awami affiliate and sympathizer, Syed Badrul Ahsan, says that Zia's announcement of Bangladesh's independence on March 27 was:

> [...] a turning point in those early stages of the War of Liberation against Pakistan. It was Zia's finest hour, one which heralded the beginning of a long twilight struggle for national liberty. There is little question about the single-minded dedication Zia brought to his efforts for the liberation of Bangladesh. As commander of the Z Force, he acquitted himself well on the battlefield despite all the obstacles that came his way. He was not the finest soldier in that war, in terms of intellectual abilities or strategic skills. But he was as patriotic as all his fellow officers were in those nine months of blood-drenched struggle. He was stern, with that no-nonsense approach to discipline. He came home from the war, like all other freedom fighters, with his sense of politics and statecraft sharpened in ways that are characteristic of a revolution … His voice inspired a fearful nation in late March 1971. His quashing of Abu Taher's adventurism put a check to disaster and perhaps even prevented a civil war. He brought about a semblance of discipline in the army.[54]

To briefly expand on the Taher issue mentioned by Ahsan, the left-oriented Col Taher and his deputy (today's Awami-Hasina favorite) Hasanul Hoque Inu initiated a dangerous movement in the military with their JSD-backed BSB, alleged to have killed many innocent officers after the pro-Awami Brig Gen Khaled Mosharraf's conspiratorial counter coup on November 3. According to Brig Gen Syed Ashrafuzzaman,

> On November 07, ordinary soldiers, who mutinied against the newly appointed army chief Brig Gen Khaled Mosharraf, rather forced Gen Zia to become the army chief. There being no government in existence in those tumultuous days, Gen Zia had no choice

> but to proclaim himself as the CMLA too. Later he had to become the president under circumstances beyond his control [...] If Gen Zia had refused to be the army chief on that day only God knew what would have been the fate of the army and the country.[55]

The revolutionary Col Taher wanted to capture power by a Bolshevic-type uprising within the army with the help of the soldiers loyal to him with a view to establish a socialist classless society. To him Khaled Mosharraf was a traitor, who stole and executed his (Taher's plan). Maj Gen (Ret) Syed Mohammad Ibrahim, a liberation hero, portrays Gen Zia as one who did not succumb to the pressure or influence of Taher and did not allow himself to step into the latter's plan.[56] It is clear from the valiant freedom fighter Maj Gen Amin Ahmed Chowdhury's description of those dark November days that it was Gen Zia who was the only rallying force then with the majority of the army insisting that Taher be put on trial.[57] Two and a half months earlier, it was Taher who demanded that Mujib's dead body be thrown into the Bay of Bengal and not buried anywhere in Bangladesh.[58]

It is ironic how politicians sacrifice their ideals/ideologies to be part of the state power and how the once leftists such as Rashed Khan Menon, Hasanul Hoque Inu, Motia Chowdhury, Dilip Barua, and Abdul Gaffar Chowdhury are now lost in the cozy capitalist corner of the Awami court. This is the age of power and power sharing, not ideals/ideologies, which are a matter of bygone days. A pity it is that this craze for power made the AL approve of all the measures taken by the military backed *Uddins*' (Moinuddin Fakhruddin Masududdin Iazuddin) 2006–2008 interim Care Taker Government (CTG). Although declared "a rule of brute law" by Justice Sharifuddin Chaklader, the *Uddinized* CTG did faithfully return the favor to the AL. It all reminds one of the day when, despite her provocative decades-long anti-Catholic activities, American pop star Madonna was allowed to perform in skimpy dress before the Pope, even to make fun of the Pope in front of the audience as recently as September 2015—Madonna and the Pope/Pontiff/Holy See/Holy Father! Like the ballet dance performance at the Islamic Foundation of Bangladesh in 2010!

Going back to Zia and the time of independence in 1971, Zia organized the historic armed struggle for the liberation of the country, effectively rising to the need of the hour.[59] That as a Sector Commander he was one of the most brilliant and outstanding stars in the battlefield makes Ahsan's questioning of Zia's "intellectual abilities or strategic skills" questionable. He directly took part in the war of independence and did so most courageously and successfully. According to Ranu Chowdhury, who was one of Zia's unit commanders during the war, he (Zia), whose Z Force won the maximum number of gallantry awards in 1971, never bragged about his achievements.

In addition, Zia provided the much-needed statesmanlike leadership in tiding over the political crisis in which the country was plunged in the post-Mujib period. It is to be mentioned that Khandoker Mushtaq Ahmed, who was the leader of the whole show behind the fall of Mujib and so to become President thereafter, was one of Mujib's closest comrades and, as ill luck would have it, his main nemesis too. Zia, one of the most heroic sons of the soil, saved Bangladesh twice: once by making the historic game changer declaration of independence (not just merely reading out an announcement) in March 1971 (without which the story would have ended right there or would have taken ninety years, not nine months to finish) and then, by taking over in November 1975 at the popular demand of the masses and the military combined. By saving Bangladesh twice—first in 1971 and then in 1975—and by introducing the concept of Bangladeshi Nationalism, and the annual একুশে পদক /21st February Medal (1976) and the স্বাধীনতা পদক /Independence Medal (1977), both in recognition of the contribution of all the (past, present, and future) great sons of the soil and in reversal of the earlier Awami policy,[60] Zia consolidated the integrity and independence of the political and geographical entity and territory called Bangladesh.

The UK-based managerial policy analyst Dr Mahdi Amin writes, in reference to his video documentary entitled "The Legend of Shaheed Zia and the Independence of Bangladesh" under the auspices of Bangladesh Policy Forum Cambridge, that the historic documentary is about:

> A charismatic young man's journey from being Major Zia to being Shaheed President Ziaur Rahman. It encompasses the journey of us—all the Bangladeshis spread across the world. It is the journey from our great liberation war through the declaration of independence against all odds, to the global recognition of our sovereignty and the formation of our Bangladeshi nationalism. It is the journey from our intimidated stance against the Western oppression as a handicapped community, to our turning into an economic tiger, social role model, and regional power out of an international "basket case." Hence, it is no surprise why Shaheed Zia—more than just two words—is the symbol of patriotism that amounts to sovereignty, statesmanship that amounts to prosperity, and inclusiveness that amounts to national unity.[61]

At any rate, হাজার বছরের শ্রেষ্ঠ বাংলাদেশী (the greatest Bangladeshi ever, of a thousand years indeed), as he may deserve to be called, Zia's nation-building measures and the unifying multiparty system he introduced were unprecedented. Democratic rule was restored in Bangladesh, as if it was the second birth of the nation, in place of the earlier Mujib-era one-and-single party rule. Zia had to fight extremist forces from within and without for being a moderate democratic leader and unifier. According to Milam, "Zia was tremendously popular throughout his tenure. He not only restored stability (while overcoming at least 23 mutinies by radicalized factions of the military); he also restored faith by practicing the politics of hope."[62]

That was why the people of Bangladesh loved to raise the popular slogan, টেকনাফ থেকে তেঁতুলিয়া সবাই বলে জিয়া জিয়া (from the very southern tip of Bangladesh to the country's northernmost point, all were chanting "Zia," "Zia," out of love and admiration). Another wonderful chant raised in tribute to him was, সারা বাংলার ধানের শীষে, তুমি জিয়া আছ মিশে), meaning "Zia, you are everywhere, blended with the rice (paddy) stalks/sheaves all over Bangladesh," such stalks being the symbol of the party, BNP, that he founded. It is not interesting that Rihat Hossain considers Zia a greater, nobler, and more effective Head of State than Mujib.[63]

What Mark Twain proverbially said as "Truth is stranger than fiction" was said by Virginia Woolf as "Fiction is likely to contain more truth than fact." By "truth" Twain meant hard and bare truth, sometimes strange and unexpected. What is "truth" in Twain is probably "fact" in Woolf, who distinguishes between truth and fact, the former being broad, wide, complete, complex, comprehensive, neutral, objective, "incandescent" and "androgynous," compared with the narrow, partial, and isolated latter (fact). Woolf's idea of truth is closer to the unbiased, equal-minded and entire picture of life, including its "blind" and invisible spot, portrayed and projected in fiction, by which both writers meant the world of realistic possibilities in the positive spirit.

In the context of Bangladesh, fiction has lost its positive connotations and has been diminished to the level of something merely fictitious, made-up, concocted, having no sense of causal plausibility or likelihood. That being so, fiction has been propagandized, through a series of unwanted and undesirable turn of events and nefarious machinations, only to be made more familiar than the truth that has been grossly and grievously distorted and compromised over the years. The true context and the reasons for killing the national leaders such as Mujib and Zia have been deliberately occluded, elided, devalued, and evaded by the biased, selfish and evil-intentioned sections in and out of power. Nobody is asking why Mujib and Zia were killed and what were the reasons that led to their being killed. All are consciously groping in the dark of the blind spot without ever letting it come to light.

Independence and Victory days come and go without the slightest mention of Zia by the Awami regime and its media, in fact all the media being under its threatening stare and squeezing control. The regime shows it is shaken by and afraid of Zia's popularity even after his death in 1981. In its mean and "wrong-headed" actions and the culture of despotic denial and division it has established, the Hasina regime is determined to deprive and discredit Zia of his glorious moments and patriotic achievements before and during his only few years of memorable Presidential rule, declared illegal by it in a political vendetta.

Among the epochal and historic deeds that are being denied to Zia by the Awami regime's perverse distortion of history are: (1) his key declaration of independence; (2) his fantastic record as a frontline war commander; (3) his twice liberation of the nation (first in 1971 and then in 1975); (4) his introduction of multiparty democracy displacing and deflecting the previously pursued one party system called BAKSAL by the Awamis; (5) his introduction of the great ideal of Bangladeshi nationalism; (6) the innovative economic and agricultural modernization he undertook; and (7) his historic international (SAARC, OIC, and the Iran-Iraq War) initiatives. Further examples of the regime's intolerance and animosity toward Zia include: (1) his name being taken off from the only national institution named after him (Zia International Airport Dhaka); (2) his murals at the lounge of Shah Amanat International Airport Chittagong destroyed; (3) he being stripped or hijacked of the independence award, Shwadhinota Padak, that he posthumously earned in 2003 and that has been removed from the national museum in September 2016 (while, in a low contradiction, keeping the one awarded to Mujib the same year); and (4) his remains (Mazar) to be shifted away from where they are now in Dhaka. All these steps and actions have been taken by the Awami government only to multiply and set more examples of its mean and destructive politics and out of a low form of political revenge.

To let the name and memory of Zia go without recognition and remembrance and to name only one or two names—Mujib and Hasina—are to be as sluttish and divisive as those women who "In the room … come and go/ Talking of Michelangelo" and are therefore merely and myopically fashionable in showing off their gutter glitter.[64] To belittle Zia is to slight the independence of Bangladesh and downgrade the country itself, as Shah Muazzem Hussein said, as he also pointed out the glorious role of Begum Zia and the inglorious role of Sheikh Hasina during the independence.[65]

The nation can never forget that it was Zia who proclaimed the independence of Bangladesh in a short eight-line text, first in his own name, calling himself to be the interim Head of State (hence arguably the first president of Bangladesh, or the first directly elected president of the country in 1978, as some would like to claim) and, shortly thereafter, magnanimously, in the name of "our great national leader Bangabandhu Sheikh Mujibur Rahman," reportedly at the plea and pressure of then local Awami leaders present.[66]

Zia did the historic declaration (to be distinguished from mere reading out an announcement) over the radio from a remote location in Chittagong, not only in the most heroic manner but also in the unprecedented God-gifted magnetic and thundering voice he was endowed with.[67] Millions of people heard Zia's fascinating tone of voice, the memory of which must still be fresh and living to those who are still alive, just as they would also remember his far-reaching and penetrating eagle-eyed looks and his unique smile and confidence-exuding and courage-building individual style. The smart Zia was multilingual and could speak several languages fluently: Bengali, English, Urdu, so on. He was truly a modern man of versatile skills and innovations—linguistic, military, political, patriotic, and statecraft. He was Bangladesh's Renaissance man and hence its Sir Philip Sidney (1554–1586), Sir Lucius Cary (1610–1643) and his noble friend Sir Henry Morison (as celebrated in English/Elizabethan poetry, especially Ben Jonson's Cary-Morison Ode) and Major Robert Gregory (who lived from 1881 to 1918 and was commemorated in W B Yeats's trio of poems), all having lived a short life of heroic fighting and other multitude of high qualities, all dying in action.

Zia's role in the battlefield (from which Mujib was away, by chance or choice, living in the safe or uncertain custody of Pakistan)[68] and his political leadership during 1976–1981 were and remain as bright and exemplary as the most visible and conspicuous star in the sky. He was able to overcome the irrational and primordial element that, according to German sociologist Max Weber, lies in the quality of charisma and used his positive charisma, rationally and intelligently, to build foundations and institutions, not to destroy them. Zia was the Gluck (good luck) of John Ruskin's famous "long" short story "The King of the Golden River," who becomes synonymous with the title character at the end of the story after having quietly, patiently, and persistently confronted the mean and greedy in his own elder brothers.

Mujib also had his great voice and style and stature. The voices of both Mujib and Zia still keep ringing into the ears of millions. Both of them "shine like a polestar through smoke-clouds, dust-clouds, and all manner of down-rushing and conflagration," as Carlyle said a hero was to be, in his *On Heroes, Hero-Worship, and the Heroic in History* (1840). He said that great men were a profitable company as Mujib and Zia were (and are) to us. Carlyle went on:

> We cannot look upon a great man without gaining something by him. He is the living light-fountain, which it is good and pleasant to be near. The light which enlightens, which has enlightened the darkness of the world; and this not as a kindled lamp only, but rather as a natural luminary shining by the gift of Heaven; a flowing light-fountain, as I say, of native original insight, of manhood and heroic nobleness;—in whose radiance all souls feel that it is well with them. On any terms whatsoever, you will not grudge to wander in such neighborhood for a while.[69]

Mujib and Zia were great men. May God/*Allah* the Almighty forgive their sins and grant them a special corner in the gardens of *Jannah* (paradise).

Coming back to history, if Mujib's contribution was to make the iron red-hot at the advent of the liberation war—a glorious achievement as it was—, Zia rose to strike the iron at the right moment. In this respect, the eminent Dr Zafrullah Chowdhury's claims about the crucial contribution of both Mujib and Zia bear historical significance.[70] Zia mobilized and led the nation, along with other military heroes, to a splendid and spectacular success in December 1971. Without his key and crucial role, which worked miracles in arousing the entire nation through his thundering voice and eagle-eyed vision, the freedom struggle, at least at the beginning, would have floundered in doubt and disarray. His announcement or declaration of independence, followed by his action on the war front, reminds one of what Thomas Carlyle said about the French Revolution in his essay on Oliver Cromwell and Napoleon Bonaparte: "Truly, without the French Revolution, one would not know what to make of an age like this at all. We will hail the French Revolution, as shipwrecked mariners might the sternest rock, in a world otherwise all of baseless sea and waves." Zia's formation of the BNP provided the much-needed political balance, nationalist dimension, and a viable, liberating alternative to the militant totalitarianism of the post-independence *Baksalite* AL.

One cannot think of the emergence of Bangladesh and its victory in 1971 without Zia, who, to repeat, had declared the independence of Bangladesh in March and then valiantly fought to turn the dream into reality. When Mujib and his family, in the safe custody of the Pakistani authorities, were away from the battlefield, Zia was there fighting at the front line. One cannot think of multiparty democracy in Bangladesh without Zia. He revived democracy and brought it back to life after it was earlier hacked and battered to death through the formation of BAKSAL by Mujib. Today's Hasina-led AL owes its existence to Zia, who gave it a second life as he allowed it to resurface after its pitiful demise in 1975. Zia was as great a politician and a statesman as he was a soldier of flying colors in the field. It is a glory of the Cantonment that it had produced a super son like Zia.

Zia was the maker of modern Bangladesh, as the former president B. Chowdhury and political analysts such as Minar Rashid always asserted.[71] Among a host of other things that he achieved in a short period of time, it was Zia who started the modern industrial and agricultural revolution in Bangladesh. Militarily and innovative policy-and-management-wise, he was the Oliver Cromwell, George Washington, and Dwight Eisenhower of Bangladesh. His actions and achievements were like those of Charles XII of Sweden, Pericles of Athens, Leonidas of Sparta, Lucius Cincinnatus of Rome, Nebuchadnezzar of

Babylon, and the tragically short-lived and short-lasting Nawab Sirajuddowla of Bengal. He can be compared to Cyrus the Great (of ancient Persia, 550–330 BC), whom even the Greeks, his enemies, acknowledged as an exceptional leader.

The fourth century (BC) Greek historian Xenophon's prose romance, the *Cyropaedia* (Education of Cyrus), portrayed Cyrus as an exemplary hero and an ideal prince for his progressive and humanitarian statecraft. More than a military general, Cyrus showed great tolerance of other peoples' views and faiths so that the Cyrus Cylinder is sometimes referred to as the first declaration of human rights. President Zia had the same traits and characteristics. Just as Cyrus allowed the Jews in exile in Babylon to return to Jerusalem and rebuild their temple, Zia did the same in relation to the AL and many other parties to regroup and be born again. He allowed Mujib's daughter Sheikh Hasina to return from abroad in 1981 to lead his (Mujib's) party AL.

Both Zia and Mujib were Bangladesh's Nelson Mandela, though in different ways. Like the long imprisoned Mandela, the imprisoned Mujib was an inspiration to his people; like the free Mandela in power, Zia took steps to unite the country by taking people of different political orientations and ideologies in the governance of the country. One of them was his brave and brilliant Prime Minister Shah Azizur Rahman (apart from another minister Abdul Alim), who was once an Awami League leader, from 1962 to 1970, and then turned a supporter of Pakistan during the liberation war, for which he was arrested after the liberation, to be released by Mujib a year later. It was for the same purpose of peace and unity that Mujib forgave thousands of anti-liberation men (over 7,000), including Shah Azizur Rahman, who he thought had a political right to support an undivided Pakistan during the war. (American Presidents also pardoned hundreds of thousands of Confederate soldiers of the American South, who were responsible for more than a million casualties during the Civil War).[72] Now that the country became independent, all belonged to one and the same Bangladesh and all were Bangladeshis. As Dr Rashed Anam of the USA said in his e-comment:

> There was nothing criminal about those who did not want Pakistan to be divided. Taking unpopular political stand is part of democracy. Try to respect it. The majority do not have to agree with or support something, but trying to demonize them in a criminal way is totally anti-democratic. In the USA, the North did not criminalize the South for its civil war differences in the 1860s. [Capitalist West Germany did not criminalize the Communist East after their reunification.] Similarly, Mandela ANC party did not criminalize the white Botha government party. There is a HUGE difference between unpopular political stand and war crimes. One is part of democracy and the other is criminal.

Following Mujib's footsteps, Zia went one step forward in uniting the nation and taking into his government some of those who had previously differed with him politically.[73] If Hoque, Bhashani, and Suhrawardy were the three not-so-distant direction-giving stars in the northern sky of Bangladesh and Sheikh Mujib was a lofty beacon (like the ancient lighthouse of Alexandria, essential to the long-tossed sailors in the open sea), Zia was the sunshine to provide the immediate life-giving and life-sustaining heat and light to the nation both during and after the liberation, especially during his few years of rule in the mid nineteen seventies. While Mujib and Zia were the two massive superstars in Bangladesh's political playground, all the five national leaders mentioned here (as well as Nawab Sir Khwaja Salimullah Bahadur and Syed Nawab Ali Chowdhury) deserve a "High 5" and ought to be paid equal tribute the way (Faruq Mahfuz Anam) James does pay homage to them in his patriotic motherland song, "Amar Sonar Bangla."

Both Mujib and Zia had a Promethean spark in them. Both died a tragic death; both sacrificed a lot for the country; both shone out and stood out in their own best ways. Both depended on their political means—good or bad, right or wrong—to achieve their otherwise noble ends, not necessarily through the dire straits of state terrorism or the crooked and crafty Machiavellian, Chanakyan, and Lilliputian (low and mean, nasty and nefarious, divisive and despotic) way. However, like the dark shadow at the bottom of the lamp or the spots in the moon or the thorns of the rose, both are thought to have had their negative side too. One remembers William Blake's:

> O Rose, thou art sick.
> The invisible worm,
> That flies in the night
> In the howling storm:
> Has found out thy bed
> Of crimson joy:
> And his dark secret love
> Does thy life destroy.

In the newly created Bangladesh, Mujib sidelined Zia, who was superseded by his junior K M Shafiullah as the army chief. Sensing resentment from the top freedom fighter officers, Mujib made Zia the deputy chief, a post especially created for the purpose. Mujib did not like the fact that Zia stole the show by declaring the independence on March 26/27, 1971, which should have been done by him but which he did not or could not for whatever reasons. The credit of the declaration put Zia in a historical limelight forever. If the fate of Tajuddin is another indication, Mujib, like many other leaders in developing democracies or newly independent third world countries, never tolerated anyone outshining him.[74] Tajuddin was the wartime leader who presided over the victory of the *MuktiBahini* (the armed forces fighting for independence) in gaining an independent Bangladesh. Upon his return from his 9-month custody in Pakistan, Mujib reportedly ignored Tajuddin, even scolded him "for breaking Pakistan," according to Professor Aftab Ahmed of Dhaka University (who was killed at his own home in 2006 without the perpetrators ever being caught). However, Tajuddin had his own faults especially when he made an inglorious and humiliating agreement with India, which Mujib did not seem to like at all.[75]

The AL alleges that Zia had a hand in the assassination of Mujib. In the circumstances that led to Mujib's assassination, the allegation can neither be dismissed nor established and will always be under a question mark. However, Zia made it possible for the AL to reenter and rehabilitate itself in politics as part of his policy of multiparty democracy following the assassination of Mujib. Zia made it possible for Mujib's daughter Hasina, a would-be boastful, bullying, bellicose, and belligerent prime minister, to return to Bangladesh on May 17, 1981 to be at the helm of her father's party. This is a fact for which Hasina ought to have remained ever thankful to Zia, instead of being, ironically, a deep and dark Zia-*phobe* and thereby a violent and vindictive BNP*hobe*. She should not have given a chance to her critics such as Mechanical Engineer Mohammad Gani of the USA to satirically say in hindsight that Zia had brought crocodiles by digging his agricultural farming canals (খাল কেটে কুমির আনা).

Hasina should not have been as ungrateful to Zia and his BNP as Duke Frederick is to his elder brother, the rightful Duke Senior, in Shakespeare's *As You Like It*. It is this betrayal of one brother of another brother that makes the loyal Lord Amiens to sing the following sing to Duke Senior in the pastoral and peaceful Forest of Arden:

> Blow, blow, thou winter wind,
> Thou art not so unkind
> As man's ingratitude;
> Thy tooth is not so keen,
> Because thou art not seen,
> Although thy breath be rude. …
> Most friendship is feigning, most loving mere folly …
> Freeze, freeze, thou bitter sky,
> That does not bite so nigh
> As benefits forgot:
> Though thou the waters warp,
> Thy sting is not so sharp
> As friend remembered not. (Act II Scene VII)

Fortunately, the usurping younger brother realizes his mistake and becomes reconciled to his elder brother who regains and returns to his dukedom by the end of the play, as a comedy it is.

It was Zia who made H M Ershad, then attending an officers' course in Dehradun, India, his deputy. Zia then promoted him to Lieutenant General in quick succession to take over as army chief after he (Zia) relinquished the command of the army to devote himself full-time to politics. The BNP has always been suspecting, even claiming that Ershad not only connived at but in fact was a complicit in the RAW orchestrated assassination of Zia in 1981.[76] According to some sources, during his stay in India in 1976/77, Ershad managed to establish a good political rapport with India through different channels, especially RAW—a connection that has been playing well in his favor since and that remains alive through his frequent visits and his total and complete obedience and loyalty to India.[77]

Far from adopting an anti-Indian foreign and defense policy, as India may have seen it that way from its own perspective, Zia tried to make Bangladesh strong. He tried to do so not to fight against India, but to keep his small country independent and sovereign as best as he could. In foreign policy, Zia took an independent and a pro-Islamic stance. As a true nationalist, he wanted to take Bangladesh out of the Indian sphere of influence. His initiative of SAARC (South Asian Association of Regional Cooperation) and its summit meetings were a milestone in this regard. That the SAARC failed to rise to the expectations of the people of the region—thanks to Indian lack of seriousness, if not opposition—is another matter. "Zia was popular," according to Dr Hashmi,

> as he could read the public mind much better than Mujib did. Moreover, he had an advantage as he experienced in the wake of the bloody August 15th military takeover (outcome of a joint civil-military conspiracy) how various Islam-oriented and even "secular" leaders successfully manipulated the Islamic sentiments of the people to legitimize the putsch. Clever Zia also felt the pulse of the people, who for all the negative reasons by 1975 had turned into avidly anti-Indian, anti-Awami BAKSALi one-party government under President Mujibur Rahman, and pro-Islamic, if not pro-Pakistani […] There is no doubt that Zia played the Islamic card to get support from the Islamists as well as from the average Bangladeshi Muslim who finds no contradictions between his religiosity and support for Bangladesh. It is worth mentioning here that, in 1971, not only Islam-oriented and Islam-loving Bengalis […] but many secular, and even pro-Chinese leftists … apprehended that [the new Bangladesh] would either merge with India or would be under Indian tutelage. As the "India factor" was an important catalyst, Zia and others took full advantage of this factor (see the article cited above).

To sum up, President Zia was one of the brightest stars in the political sky of Bangladesh. He was the maker of modern Bangladesh. Unlike Mujib, Zia made the key declaration of the independence of Bangladesh; unlike Mujib (who was sort of "missing in action" and whose family was under the proper care and protection of the Pakistani military), Zia fought in the frontline of the war of independence for nine long months while his wife Khaleda was hiding from place to place in Dhaka only to be betrayed by a petty spy and arrested by the Pakistani army. Kai Kaus gives a detailed documentary evidence, collected from contemporary authentic and authoritative sources in the military generals, political leaders, and academic scholars, of how Zia revolted against the Pakistani army and started in full gear the war of liberation for Bangladesh.[78] Ranu Chowdhury, in his article "I, Zia, Speaking," provides more details about Zia's phenomenal role from the beginning to the end of the war. He writes:

> Upon learning of the Pakistani attacks on the Bengalis from Capt Chowdhury Khaliquzzaman, Major Ziaur Rahman declared on the night of March 25, "In that case we revolt" and started the independence war with his 8 Bengal Regiment at Sholoshahar Chittagong. While regrouping at Kalurghat on March 27, he made the historic declaration of independence. The original declaration went in his name. Then the local AL leaders MA Hannan and others, whom Zia knew from before, rushed in and begged him to make it on Mujib's name, otherwise they would lose face badly. Zia obliged. Colonel Oli, Brigadier Khaliquzzaman, Major Shamsher, Maj Gen Subid Ali Bhuiyan, Maj Rafiq and a few others who were witness to the events are still alive to corroborate the story.[79]

After he saved the country from the critical conflict following the 15 August coup and rescued the nation from the Awami BAKSALi brutality and the reckless Awami Rakkhi-Bahini rapacity (granted indemnity by Mujib in 1974),[80] Zia became the head of its army. Soon after, he became President of the Republic and introduced multiparty democracy, free market economy, agricultural innovation, and freedom of the press, all of which had earlier been severed and snapped and tattered. Zia also introduced the concept of the politically, practically, and philosophically correct Bangladeshi nationalism, among the many other achievements he is historically credited with. In the words of Dr Rashed Anam of the USA, "Zia epitomized the essence and meaning of Bangladesh, Bangladeshi nationalism, and the self-identity and self-dependence of Bangladesh."

Zia's manifold and multifarious contribution was too large to make the people of Bangladesh stay home and not to make them lament hard and loud with shock and surprise at his assassination. They came out in millions to mourn. The mourning by masses was borne out even by the testimony of Zia's opponents, such as then গণতন্ত্রী (Democratic) Party's (later Awami) Suranjit Sen Gupta and the completely Awamized Rashed Khan Menon, on June 3, 1981.[81] Unlike Mujib, Zia never failed and always pushed the country forward progressively and incrementally in a democratic amity and harmony with the people. He was and remains a beacon of hope, success, and achievement. During those critical, chaotic, and crucial November days in 1975, the nation was reborn for the second time under his smart and wise leadership as he had provided equally great war-front leadership when the nation was first born in 1971.

The record needs to be set straight about one of the greatest sons of the soil, President Gen Zia, whose most heroic and patriotic role in 1971 as well as 1975–1981 was as luminous and illustrious as the sun that shines in the skies of Bangladesh every day. The glory that was Zia was the glory that was Bangladesh itself, both being inseparable and synonymous with each other. His name and memory are there to dazzle, radiate, and suffuse over everything Bangladeshi and to dwarf everything contrary down. He was born to win, outshine, and outsmart the negative forces of all kinds and leave a legacy not to be forgotten but to be carved in stone and marked in indelible ink on the pages of history about Bangladesh.

It is only fitting that Zia is being paid powerful poetical homages on the occasion of his each and every martyrdom anniversary. One example: নও তুমি কোন জাতির পিতা /নও তুমি কোন বংগের বন্ধু/তুমি এই বাংলার সাধারন মানুষের প্রান/তুমি ছিলে সদা মহান/তুমি রেখেছো বাংলাদেশের মান/শহীদ প্রেসিডেনট জিয়াউর রহমান। (as collected from S Akhter's e-mail post of September 8, 2016). Yet another example is the following poem taken from Selim Anwar's blog post:

রাখাল রাজা জিয়াউর রহমান স্মরণে
হে অধিনায়ক, হে বিজয়ী বীর
দারুণ এক আহবানে ৭ কোটি বাঙালীরে শক্তি দিয়েছো
সাহস দিয়েছো প্রেরণা দিয়েছো,
করেছো উন্নত শির।
জীবন বাজি রেখে লড়েছো লড়াই
অসম এক যুদ্ধে
তাই তোমারে কুর্নিশ করে
সকল আবাল-বনিতা-বৃদ্ধে।
বাঙলা মায়ের সাহসী সন্তান বাংলাকে ভালবেসে
হানাদার বধ কাব্য তুমি লিখেছো কেমনে
ভাবি আজও বসে বসে।
দেশ যখন অরাজকতায় ,কান্ডারীহীন,
বঙ্গবন্ধু খুনে
আবারও তুমি দাঁড়িয়েছিলে সমুখপানে,
রাষ্ট্রমাতার চরম ক্রান্তি ক্ষনে।
গনতন্ত্র ফেরত এলো তোমার দুহাত ধরে
দেশের অর্থনীতি সচল হলো তোমারই যাদুর করে।
হে বিজয়ী বীর, লও সালাম ,লও ভালবাসা ,লও বিজয়মালা
তোমার সততা দেশপ্রেম আর কীর্তি স্মরি

শ্রদ্ধা লয়ে দিবানিশি সারাবেলা।
দুঃখে পরাণ যায় বুকটা ফেটে যায়
কেমন করে দানিল আঘাত তোমার সারা গায়
তপ্ত বুলেটে তোমার পিঞ্জরায়
এ সবুজে গায়ের লালি ঢেলে দিলে
তুমি এই বাংলায়।
দেশের মানুষেরে তুমি পথ দেখিয়েছো স্বপ্ন দিয়েছো
মাথা তুলে দাঁড়াবা
তোমার মরণে লাখ লাখ বাঙালী
তাই কেঁদে হলো জারে জার।
হৃদয়ে তোমার বাংলাদেশ ছিল, ছিল কমল প্রাণ
কাস্তে-কোদাল হাতে করেছো কাজ,
গেঞ্জি গায়ে সেজেছো শ্রমিকের সাজ
আর কেহ তা পারে নাই
সারা বাঙলার অগণিত লোক তাই স্মরে তোমারে,
তোমারে ভুলে নাই।
বাংলাদেশী জাতীয়তাবাদ শ্রেষ্ঠ সৃষ্টি তোমার
যার মন্তরে এক হতে পারে সকল নরনারী বাংলার।
দেশ রত্ন শহীদ প্রেসিডেন্ট জিয়া -উর- রহমান
আজও তাই স্মরি তোমারে দিয়ে মম মন প্রাণ
কীর্তি তোমার থাকবে অমলিন হে দেশপ্রেমী সন্তান,
যতদিন রবে পদ্মা- মেঘনা-যমুনা বহমান। [82]

Great men are never dead. They never die. They can never be finished and dismissed and done away with, simply because they are physically dead, leaving seemingly divergent legacies to live on behind them. Their lives and memories are always a guide and an inspiration to posterity and future generations, who ought to spare no pains to find a common ground and a common platform on which the views may actually converge with positive differences narrowing the gap rather than diverge with irreconcilable contradictions widening the divide.

American poet Robert Frost wrote his short poem "The Road Not Taken" in England for his English poet-friend Edward Thomas, who sometimes might have shown a problem of indecision. The poem is about the dilemma in making even a small choice without reservation that many like Thomas face in life. It is regarded as one of the trickiest (so most misread and misunderstood), yet one of the simplest and most popular poems ever. It is about the difficulty of decision-making, however inconsequential or insignificant that decision may be. In the poem, Frost (or the speaker/poetic persona) takes the road "less traveled by."

Frost does so just to make a difference—"all the difference," as he says. After all, he has to make a decision because he "could not travel both/ And be one traveler." The road he takes has a "better claim" at the moment because it is "grassy and wanted wear." However, Frost does not do so without a doubt or qualm. It is not really a happy and exciting, or conclusive and decisive moment for him. He knows that both roads, which "diverged in a yellow wood," are equally attractive ("just as fair") and both "that morning equally lay/In leaves no step had trodden black." As he takes the one, he wishes to take the other the next time he thinks he might come around and so he now casts a longing look at it as it "bent in the undergrowth."

It is the same bridging argument made by Abu Rushd in his article on the same occasion (of Zia's 35th death anniversary); Shah Mohammad Saifuddin Maruf of Bangladesh Strategic and Development Forum in "Why did India help in 1971?"; Isha Khan in "RAW: An Instrument of Indian Imperialism;" and the Calcutta-based Weekly Sunday report about the RAW engineered assassination of Zia with complicities from various other persons and parties (thanks to the freedom fighter, UK-based Zoglul Husain, for providing the sources).[83]

Notes

1. "The title 'Father of the Nation' is sometimes politically contested. The 1972 Constitution of Bangladesh declared Sheikh Mujibur Rahman the 'father of the nation.' The BNP government removed this in 2004, to the protest of then opposition AL, led by Mujib's daughter Sheikh Hasina" http://en. wikipedia.org /wiki/Father_of_the_Nation. Now that the AL is in power, the title has been reinstated.
2. http://en. wikipedia.org /wiki/Father_of_the_Nation.
3. http://www.amadershomoys.com/content/2014/04/27. Indians are exposing contradictions of Mahatma Gandhi's views and raising objections to him being their father of the nation: https://www.facebook.com/justicekatju/posts/1508250539215487; https://www.facebook.com/justicekatju/posts/1508269525880255
4. http://www.amardeshonline.com/pages/printnews/2013/03/23/193160. মাওলানা ভাষানীর একটি দূর্লভ এক্সক্লুসিভ ভিডিও। স্বাধীনতার স্বপ্নদ্রষ্টা যখন বাঙ্গালীদের স্বাধীনতার স্বপ্ন দেখাচ্ছিলেন, তখন জনতা স্লোগান দিচ্ছিলো "আমাদের জাতীর পিতা- মাওলানা ভাষানী। বাঙ্গালীর জাতীর পিতা- মাওলানা ভাষানী"। https://www.facebook.com/palash88/videos/10205389138287310/
5. http://www.bangladeshchronicle.net/index.php/2013/01/august-15-know-the-facts-not-fiction;
   http://newsfrombangladesh.net/new/index.php?option=com_wrapper&view=wrapper&Itemid=542;
   http://defence.pk/threads/august-15-1975-and-august-15-2011-the-contrast.125607.
6. Oli Ahad suggests that Mujib's surrender in March 1971 conformed or fitted to a pattern. Oli Ahad says: "[…] শেখ মুজিবুর রহমান ১৯৫২ সালের ২৬শে ফেব্রুয়ারী কারামুক্তি পেলেন, কিন্তু

ঢাকা-নারায়ণগঞ্জ আন্দোলনের অগ্নিঝরা দিনগুলোতে ঢাকায় এলেন না নেতৃত্ব দিতে। বিদ্রোহের অনলেও ঝাপ দিলেন না। এমন কি খুনি শাসক নুরুল আমিনের বিরুদ্ধে ৫ই মার্চ দেশব্যাপী যে হরতালের ডাক দেওয়া হয় শেখ মুজিব তাতে অংশগ্রহণ করে মারমুখো জনতাকে নেতৃত্ব দিতে ঢাকায় আসেন নাই। তারপরও মুখপোড়া আওয়ামী লীগ ও ভারতীয় দালাল চামচারা বলে ১৯৫২ সালে শেখ মুজিবর নাকি ভাষা আন্দোলনে নেতৃত্ব দিয়েছে। ধিক তাদেরকে ॥"- অলি আহাদ / জাতীয় রাজনীতি : ১৯৪৫ থেকে '৭৫ [বাংলাদেশ কো-অপারেটিভ বুক সোসাইটি—অক্টোবর, ২০১২ (পঞ্চম সংস্করণ) । পৃ: ১৪৭] In English translation: On 21 February 1952, he was in jail and upon his release on the 26th he didn't turn up to lead the people's movement during those violent days in Dhaka and Narayanganj neither did he show up in the revolt against the killer-ruler Nurul Amin on 5 March. Even then, the AL and their Indian lackeys say Mujib led the movement in 1952. That's a shame.

7. http://www.newsbd7.com/main/detail/2759
8. For Hasina's admiration of the Pakistan army and hatred of the Bangladesh army, visit: http://www.prothom-news.com/selected-columns/2015/05/14/27364/; http://www.somewhereinblog.net/blog/chondonblog/28792938. For an English version of the same, see Notes #17 and #19 in "From the Opposition's *Chudur Budur*" Chapter. Rentu's banned book of gripping details about the personal and political life of Sheikh Hasina is available online in (English): http://www.angelfire.com/planet/amarfashichai/Amar_Fashi_Chai.pdf; http://bdnews24.com/politics/2007/11/10/controversial-author-of-amar-fashi-chai-dies-in-paris; https://mail.google.com/mail/u/0/#inbox/1547a0e26f61483a?projector=1; http://amar-fashichai.blogspot.com/2013/07/amar-fashi-chai-by-motiur-rahman-rentu.html; https://www.youtube.com/watch?v=3rpAXMm7y9U;
9. http://priyoboi.blogspot.co.uk/2012/09/blog-post_16.html; https://www.facebook.com/zoglul.husain/posts/1948059475450798
10. For some details by Col (Ret) Sharful Hoque Dalim, one of the August 15 coup leaders, click: https://www.facebook.com/photo.php?fbid=302718716782587&set=gm.1856491537913478&type=3; http://www.majordalimbubangla.com/71.html. For more details about the life and times of Sheikh Mujib and his family as covered in the local and foreign media, click: http://mynewsbd.com/?p=7044; https://groups.google.com/forum/?hl=el#!topic/islamconcept/vloy6eLvmWU; https://www.facebook.com/note.php?note_id=179957442035375; http://chudurbudurbd.blogspot.co.uk/2012/02/blog-post_08.html; https://www.bnpbd.org/page/details/392
11. The second amendment of the constitution was made on September 22, 1973 making provisions for proclamation of a state of emergency and giving *Rakki-Bahini* indemnity for political prosecution.
12. It is said that there were thousands killed by the dangerously fearsome Awami paramilitary force of *Rakkhi-Bahini* during the Mujib regime. In a way they were an incarnation of Maximilien Robespierre's extremely radical suppression against the equally extremist left but slightly more moderate rival political faction "Girondins" or "Girondists," from September 6, 1793 to July 28, 1794 when he and his henchmen were responsible for the guillotining of thousands of innocent people. See http://

en.wikipedia.org/wiki/Jatiyo_Rakkhi_Bahini; also Ahmed Safa's narration of the evils during the Mujib era: http://www. somewhereinblog.net/blog/anwar-shakil10/29814744. One recalls, in the early 1970s, the JSD's slogan was একটা দুইটা রক্ষী ধর সকাল বিকাল নাশতা কর (get one or two members of the Awami *RakkhiBahini* forces for the cannibal breakfast in the morning or snack refreshments in the evening).

13. The fourth amendment of the constitution, made on January 25, 1975, was regarded as one of the most controversial changes in the country's constitutional history as it marked the country's switch-over to one-party (BAKSAL) rule and the presidential form of government. It is to be mentioned that Mujib's longtime associates such as Gen M A G Osmani and Barrister Mainul Hussein had the courage and honesty to resign from the Parliament in protest while Nur-e-Alam Siddiquee, though he did not resign, had the integrity to be sharply critical of the country's descent into the gagging one party rule.
14. For details, see http://newsbd7.com/main/detail/2765. See the "Bangladeshi Nationalism" chapter for the details of the Tajuddin agreement. Also, Rifat-ul-Ahsan, *India-Bangladesh Relations : after 1971* at http://defenceforumindia.com/forum/threads/india-bangladesh-relations.4411/
15. For the details of the contrast, visit http://akramsbd.blogspot.co.uk/2013/08/blog-post_1134.html
16. Lee Kuan Yew wrote, on p. 363 of his book: "Another person I remember from the Ottawa meeting was Prime Minister Sheikh Mujibur Rahman, the hero who had opposed Pakistan and led East Pakistan to independence as Bangladesh. He arrived in style at Ottawa in his own aircraft. When I landed, I saw a parked Boeing 707 with 'Bangladesh' emblazoned on it. When I left it was still standing on the same spot, idle for eight days, getting obsolescent without earning anything. As I left the hotel for the airport, two huge vans were being loaded with packages for the Bangladeshi aircraft. At the conference, Mujibur Rahman had made a pitch for aid to his country. Any public relations firm would have advised him not to leave his special aircraft standing for eight whole days on the parking apron." https://www.facebook.com/notes/139244142936111/?pnref=story
17. See Abid Bahar, *The Life and Death of Bangabandhu Sheikh Mujibur Rahman: An Illustrated History of Bangabandhu and Bangladesh* at http://documents.mx/documents/the-life-and-death-of-bangabandhu-sheikh-mujiburrahman.html; and http://dailyalochona.blogspot.com/2010/05/alochona-sheikh-mujib.html
18. Jamshed S A Chowdhury, *Bangladesh: Failure of a Parliamentary Government 1973–75* (2004). Details are available at (http://rubibook.com/books/index.php?route=product/author&author_id=173; and
http://www.amazon.com/Bangladesh-Failure-Parlimentary-Government-1973-75/dp/9848120548.
Reviewed under the title *Bangladesh Failed Years–1972–75* at https://jamalsyed.wordpress.com/2008/04/12/bangladesh-failed-years-1972-75/

19. Firoz Mahboob Kamal's *Ekattorer Itihas* (History of 1971), yet to be published, is available on his personal website: http://www.drfirozmahboobkamal.com/2011-01-23-21-55-47.html. Also visit: http://www.drfirozmahboobkamal.com/2011-01-23-21-55-47/1149-chapter-31-mujib-and-his-rule-in-bangladesh-media.html; http://www.drfirozmahboobkamal.com/2011-01-23-21-55-47/1152-chapter-28-the-catalogue-of-crimes-of-shaikh-mujib.html
20. Syed Serajul Islam, "Bangladesh: Challenges of Democracy and Good Governance," a paper presented at Southwestern Social Sciences Conference at San Antonio, Texas, April 5, 2014.
21. William B. Milam, "Bangladesh and Burdens of History," *Current History* (April, 2007), p. 156
22. Quoted by Ranu Chowdhury. See Notes #5 and 37.
23. https://sathkahonbd.blogspot.ca/2017/04/blog-post_38.html (আহমদ শরীফের ডায়েরি থেকে/From the diary of Ahmad Sharif)
24. Refer to the media archives of the time, such as http://www.thedailystar.net/who-said-what-after-august-15-37449.
25. http://www.amadershomoys.com/newsite/2015/08/20/377522.htm. Some AL leaders (such as Abdul Malek Ukil and Humayun Rasheed Chowdhury) breathed a sigh of relief making disgraceful and derogatory comments, including those by Motia Chowdhury, Col Taher, and Hasanul Hoque Inu, all of whom welcomed the assassination of Mujib. Their remarks were too negative to be forgotten. Following Mujib's assassination, Malek Ukil of his own party remarked in London that Bangladesh was saved from the tyranny of a Feraun (pharaoh). H R Chowdhury said in a public meeting in Sylhet in the late eighties that even if Mujib was to be hanged hundred times, he would not be cleansed of his sins (*Weekly Sugandha* November 1, 1996). Apart from the print media of the time, including the later Matiur Rahman Chowdhury's *Kutnitir Andar Mahol*, and "August 15, 1975 Coup and the Executions" by A O Chowdhury, https://beta.groups.yahoo.com/neo/groups/khabor/conversations/messages/27448. Also see "August 15: Know the Facts, Not Fiction" by Ranu Chowdhury, Note #37.
26. See his *Bangladesh: The Unfinished Revolution* at http://www.nirmanblog.com/wp-content/uploads/2009/03/unfinished-revolution.pdf
27. For a list, click: http://www.somewhereinblog.net/blog/durontoislam/29223601; http://www.timenewsbd.com/news/detail/58826; http://www.londoni.co/index.php/history-of-bangladesh?id=199
28. http://www.ourtimebd.com/2015/09/awami-league-created-the-circumstances-for-bangabandhus-death-rab.html;
http://www.ittefaq.com.bd/politics/2015/09/09/35445.html; http://www.amadershomoys.com/newsite/2015/09/11/394786.htm#
29. Barrister Hussein's daily *Ittefaq* wrote an editorial welcoming the coup, the fall of Mujib and the change of government the very next day of the coup (August 16,

1975). He had since remained more or less consistent on his stand about August 15. But his brother Anwar Hussein Manju, who was said to have written the editorial later changed his color.

30. http://kaikaus.blogspot.com/2016/06/blog-post_80.html
31. http://www.majordalimbubangla.com/87.html
32. Kalidas Baiddya, বাঙালীর মুক্তিযুদ্ধে অন্তরালের শেখ মুজিব (Kolkata: Karmakar Book Stall, 2005). For a review of the book and for interesting excerpts from it, click: http://www.muldharabd.com/?p=2039
33. Asif Nazrul, http://www.sheershanews.com/2015/02/19/69654
34. mzamin.com/article.php?mzamin=70283. In Ranu Chowdhury's words, "Nobody killed Mujib; he invited it on himself. No wonder people celebrated his fall as another Victory Day." E-mail: 10/11-14/15.
35. (Ret) Sqn Ldr Shoaib is as full of praise for Zia and Mujib as he is critical of both of them. That is what he said in his e-mail post of February 16 and April 17, 2016.
36. http://www.drfirozmahboobkamal.com/2011-01-23-21-55-47/1148-chapter-32-shaikh-mujib-and-his-rule-in-foreign-media.html
37. However, he was later made a saint—"Saint Nicholas the Passion-Bearer"—by the Russian Orthodox Church and has since been referred to as "Saint Nicholas the Martyr."
38. See the very last part on this link based on Oriana Fallaci's interview with Sheikh Mujib in 1974: https://www.youtube.com/watch?v=gt9l8Vm8W9U&feature=youtu.be
39. http://www.bangladesh-web.com/new/readers-opinion/5681-august-15-know-the-facts-not-fiction;
    https://groups.google.com/forum/#!topic/bangladesh-progressives/eghV30IHei8;
    http://bangladesh-web.com/new/index.php?option=com_content&view=article&id=5681:august-15-know-the-facts-not-fiction&catid=28:readers-opinion&Itemid=11(December28,2012); https://beta.groups.yahoo.com/neo/groups/khabor/conversations/messages/27448;
    https://groups.yahoo.com/neo/groups/notun_bangladesh/conversations/messages/33986 (December 24, 2012).
40. http://opinion.bdnews24.com/2009/11/25/1975-the-crime-and-verdict-in-retrospection/
41. Taj Hashmi, "Ziaur Rahman, Islam and Bangladeshi Nationalism," https://groups.yahoo.com/neo/groups/ saldwr/conversations/messages/710
42. http://www.bdfirst.net/newsdetail/detail/49/169179
43. Only a few Mercedes in Bangabhaban were used for the visiting foreign VVIPs.
44. http://www.weeklyholiday.net/homepage/pages/UserHome.aspx?ID=20&date=12/21/2012; "Hasina's Ziaphobia" and "Unforgettable Zia that I knew: A flashback," also by Ranu Chowdhury: http://dailyalochona.blogspot.com/2010/12/alochona-eviction-of-khaleda-zia-latest.html; and http://www.weeklyholiday.net/homepage/pages/UserHome.aspx?ID=20&date=12/21/2012

45. "Mujib's body alone was flown by Air Force helicopter to Tungipara and buried in the village graveyard. It was there that Bangabandhu's final humiliation took place. According to Brigadier Manzoor, when the news of the coup and assassination became known some villagers broke in and looted Mujib's ancestral home." See Anthony Mascarenhas, *Bangladesh: Legacy of Blood*, pp. 82–83. When Humayun Ahmed's last novel দেয়াল (The Wall) was first published (after his death), there was a huge outcry among the Awami-BAKSALees because the writer failed to give the respect they wanted for their leader Sheikh Mujib. Humayun Ahmed quoted Anthony Mascarenhas to the effect that Mujib's Tungipara house was looted immediately after August 15 coup. The Hasina administration orchestrated a court order against *Deyal*'s publication in the existing form, even though it was a novel, not a history book. Subsequently, *Deyal* was published after being heavily edited by the Awami intellectual Professor Anisuzzaman. One can easily find the "gaps" in the flow of the story. For *Deyal*-related controversies, readers may wish to google for more information. See the report of the New York-based poet and journalist Fakir Elias about the incomplete and fragmentary novel *Deyal:*
http://www.jagonews24.com/opinion/news/112091/; http://bn.sherpurtimes.com/2016/07/19/page/2/
46. https://www.youtube.com/watch?v=YM7YeTCIfZM;
https://mail.google.com/mail/u/0/#trash/152856fd630e80d1?projector=1;
https://www.youtube.com/watch?v=juJKfsDNQ14;
https://www.youtube.com/watch?v=MF3bJzmuDW4
47. To know about Zia's role in his own words, visit http://www.prothombangladesh.net/article/15971. According to Gen K M Shafiullah, Zia was the heroic declarer of the revolt against Pakistan (who killed his Pakistani commanding officer Lt Col Rashid Janjua and others in Chittagong on the 25th of March), as he was also the great declarer/proclaimer of the independence of Bangladesh from Kalurghat Chittagong on the 26th. For details, see Major K M Shafiullah, *Bangladesh at War* (Dhaka: Dhaka Academy Publishers, 1989), pp. 43–45.
48. Srinath Raghavan, *1971: A Global History of the Creation of Bangladesh* (Harvard UP, 2013); http://timesofindia.indiatimes.com/interviews/Even-in-1971-Awami-League-wasnt-stating-it-wanted-independence-Srinath-Raghavan/articleshow/28114458.cms
49. http://www.dailydinkal.net/2016/12/16/30964.php
50. Watch Dr Asif Nazrul on this at https://youtu.be/7zfyU8nVEpI; http://www.dailynayadiganta.com/detail/news/134470;
http://www.bdnatun.net/newsdetail/detail/49/271693
51. https://groups.google.com/forum/#%21topic/soc.culture.bangladesh/J1HiOos-R1Zw; http://dailyalochona.blogspot.co.uk/2010/03/alochona-7-march-71-speech.html
52. http://timesofindia.indiatimes.com/interviews/Even-in-1971-Awami-League-wasnt-stating-it-wanted-independence-Srinath-Raghavan/articleshow/28114458.cms

53. https://www.facebook.com/photo.php?fbid=1162510510450592&set=a.503164543051862.119174.100000749625200&type=3&theater
54. http://opinion.bdnews24.com/2015/05/30/the-legacy-of-general-ziaur-rahman. For more details about the three military coups of 1975, see Dr Nadir Junaid of DU at http://opinion.bdnews24.com/bangla/archives/20388; and Shawkot Masum at https://www.amrabondhu.com/masum/2963
55. Among the tons of critical literature on the subject, Maj Gen (Ret) Syed Mohammad Ibrahim, former DU VC Prof Emajuddin Ahmed, Prof Abdul Latif Masum, and Mujtaba Khandoker are among those who recently wrote about the events of August and November 1975 and their significance. See Gen Ibrahim's book, মিশ্র কথন/Mixed Talk/Discrete Discourse (Anonnya Publications, 1911); Prof Ahmed's column at www.dailynayadiganta.com/detail/news/167889; or http://khobor52.com/2016/11/07; Prof Masum's article at http://www.dailynayadiganta.com/detail/news/168192; and Khandoker at http://www.poriborton.com/opinion-news/23176. See Ibrahim's article "Tinti Shabda: Bangladesh Zia and November" at www.dailynayadiganta.com/detail/news/166413. Also, on this subject, visit: www.dailysangram.com/news_details.php?news_id=42085; http://www.mzamin.com/article.php?mzamin=39094;
https://bnpbd.org/page/details/72;
http://srzaman.blogspot.com/2010/03/col-taher-sheikh-mujib-gen-zia-and.html;
http://rumiahmed.wordpress.com/2011/03/22/the-crimes-of-col-taher-and-pilkhana-trial/; http://zias19points.blogspot.com/p/blog-page_22.html
56. http://www.bdhotnews.com/detail.php?id=44171
57. http://currentnewsbd24.blogspot.com/2016/02/blog-post_671.html;
https://wakeupbd.wordpress.com/2011/04/06/death-sentence-and-final-statement-of-taher-and-ziaur-rahman/;
http://tajuddinahmad.com/banga-babdhu-tajuddin-and-bangladesh-by-major-general-amin-ahmed-chowdhury-bir-protik;
http://www.mzamin.com/details.php?mzamin=MTE0NDYx&s=MQ==
58. Media was abuzz in August 2015 with Col Taher's demand that Mujib's body should have been dumped in the Bay of Bengal. "They've made a big mistake. They shouldn't have allowed Sheikh Mujib's burial. Now a shrine will be built there. His body should have been thrown into the Bay of Bengal" (https://en.wikipedia.org/wiki/Abu_Taher). Taher, then field commander of the Revolutionary *Gano Bahini* of JSD, said this on August 17 when Naim Jahangir, a Dhaka University student who had fought in the Liberation War alongside Taher, visited him at his residence—according to Mohiuddin Ahmed's জাসদের উত্থান পতন: অস্থির সময়ের রাজনীতি (The Rise and Fall of JSD: Politics of a Restless Time). Taher was reportedly present at Khandoker Moshtaque's oath-taking ceremony. Visit: http://www.thedailystar.net/who-said-what-after-august-15-37449. Ranu Chowdhury also claims that when Brig Khaled Mosharraf staged his drama on November 3–6, 1975 to undo the August 15 Revolution, there was a protest against Mujib's death (see The Bangladesh Observer, November 5, 1975). The procession was led by then Awami MP Rashed Mosharraf, Khaled's

brother, and their mother. Khaled, a great freedom fighter, was reportedly unhappy about this telling his mother, "You dug my grave, mother." He was right. The people soon rejected his move and foiled his India-inspired conspiracy through the Sepoy-Janota Revolution on November 7, 1975. Unfortunately, Khaled and many others had to lose their lives because of this foul adventurism.

59. https://www.youtube.com/watch?v=zDnAfMkF7gM&feature=player_embedded
60. The first award (EP) is on the occasion of the February 21, 1952 language movement and the second award (SP), on the occasion of the December 16, 1971 Independence Day.
61. https://www.facebook.com/mahdi.amin.37/videos/10153935406085591/; https://www.dropbox.com/s/e89jr7sxg7dbf6m/26%20-%20Final.wmv
62. Milam, "Bangladesh and Burdens of History," *Current History* (April, 2007), p. 156. Also visit http://www.presidentzia.com and http://www.storyofbangladesh.com/ebooks.html
63. http://www.digantabarta.com/archives/1287
64. Lines from T S Eliot's ironical poem, "The Love Song of J. Alfred Prufrock."
65. http://www.dailydinkal.net/2015/11/21/20945.php; http://rtnbd.net/video/19156
66. See the Awami MP Maj Gen (Ret) Shubid Ali Bhuiyan's testimony in his book, *Nine Months at the Liberation War/front*. He fought closely alongside Zia from the very beginning and saw him rise heroically. For his recent conflicting comments and denials, under the Awami pressure, see: http://www.banglatribune.com/columns/opinion/133123/; http://www.news-bd.net/newsdetail/detail/200/236309; http://www.bd-pratidin.com/first-page/2016/08/19/164234; http://www.prothom-alo.com/bangladesh/article/950287/. Regarding Zia as the first president who was the first to declare the independence of Bangladesh in 1971 and then as the first directly elected president in 1978, see former DU VC Professor Emajuddin Ahmed at http://www.sheershakhobor.com/2017/03/26; http://www.bd-pratidin.com/news/2016/11/09/183396; http://english.thereport24.com/article/7705
67. I was then an SSC candidate, one of the millions to directly hear, from quite far, the heroic declaration of independence by the immortal Zia over the Radio. I also saw the huge crowds at the equally immortal Sheikh Mujib's mammoth meetings in 1970, one or two of which I traveled from far to attend.
68. Mizanur Rahman Chowdhury, a senior AL leader, commented in 1978 that whenever there was a risk or fear of life, Sheikh Mujib chose to get arrested. This is also borne out by Siddiq Salek's book, *Witness to Surrender*, in which he mentions that Mujib sent two aides to General Khadem Hossain Raja in Dhaka Cantonment on the night of March 6/7 asking to be arrested. When General Yahya was supposed to make an official declaration on March 25 to hand over power to Mujib as the elected representative of the majority, Mujib was waiting the whole day for his coveted position of the PM of Pakistan without any "good news." Little did he know that Yahya already ordered the Operation Searchlight aimed at annihilating the Bengalis as he had secretly left Dhaka.

69. The Selected Works of Thomas Carlyle, p. 91: https://books.google.ca/books?isbn=1312254319
70. http://www.amardeshonline.com/pages/details/2016/01/28/321116#
71. For an estimate of Zia's historic contribution, see: http://www.dailynayadiganta.com/detail/news/26275#; http://www.sheershanewsbd.com/2015/05/30/82497; https://www.facebook.com/minar.rashid/posts/492238867643216
72. https://en.wikipedia.org/wiki/List_of_people_pardoned_or_granted_clemency_by_the_President_of_the_United_States#
73. Journalist Shafik Rehman and UK resident (Ret) Maj Syed Abu Bakar Siddique wrote to this effect: https://www.facebook.com/ShafikRehmanPresents?_rdr; www.somewhereinblog.net/blog/abushethi/29411669; amader-kotha.com/page/234164; http://www.sheershakhobor.com of 2016/11/05
74. Mujib never visited Meherpur, Kushtia—renamed Mujibnagar—where the government of Bangladesh in exile was formed on April 17, 1971. Poor Tajuddin, arguably the most competent Awami leader, had to quit Mujib's cabinet and finally met with a tragic end.
75. Ebne Golam Samad writes: "শেখ মুজিবের সাথে তাজউদ্দীনের বিরোধের বাস্তব কারণ ছিল। শেখ মুজিব মানতে রাজি হননি প্রবাসী বাংলাদেশ সরকারের এই চুক্তিকে।"—www.dailynayadiganta.com/detail/news/167300. Also see the "Bangladeshi Nationalism" chapter for the details of the agreement. Also, Rifat-ul-Ahsan, *India-Bangladesh Relations : after 1971* at http://defenceforumindia.com/forum/threads/india-bangladesh-relations.4411/; http://www.bdnow.net/blog/blogdetail/detail/2472/arafathasan/75391#
76. http://www.mzamin.com/details.php?mzamin=MTEzOTI4&s=MQ==; http://www.thedailysangbad.com/open-discussion/2016/05/24/66815
77. http://www.prothom-alo.com/bangladesh/article/425026
78. https://www.facebook.com/kai.kaus.7/posts/176903616080228
79. http://zias19points.blogspot.com/p/blog-page_22.html
80. https://www.facebook.com/permalink.php?id=1575479672706059&story_fbid=1580516578869035
81. https://www.youtube.com/watch?v=4l3u02ZScc8; https://www.facebook.com/officialbnpnews/videos/999687003442907/
82. http://www.somewhereinblog.net/blog/selimanwar007/29836234 (30 May 2013)
83. http://www.dailynayadiganta.com/detail/news/124034;http://bangladesh-web.com/view.php?hidRecord=173793; and http://www.countercurrents.org/khan131007.htm. According to the Weekly Sunday report, "Mr. Subramaniam Swamy, Janata Dal MP, a close associate of Morarji Desai, said that Rameswar Nath Kao, former Chief of RAW, and Shankaran Nair, upset about Sheikh Mujib's assassination, chalked a plot to kill General Ziaur Rahman. However, when Morarji Desai came into power in 1977 he was indignant at RAW's role in Bangladesh and ordered operations in Bangladesh to be called off; but by then RAW had already gone too far. General Zia continued to be in power for quite some time but he was assassinated after Indira Gandhi returned to power, though she denied her involvement in his assassination" (Weekly Sunday, Calcutta, September 18, 1988).

10

The Politics of the Past and the Honorifics of Titles

Bangladesh has become a land of honorifics, epic epithets, endless adjectives, adjectival nouns, and noun phrases superfluously and superciliously coming out of the mouth of the politicians and political and entertainment talk show hosts in introducing their guests. Examples: বিশিষ্ট কবি কালজয়ী সাহিত্যিক সব্যসাচী লেখক প্রাবন্ধিক গবেষক বিশ্লেষক বুদ্ধিজীবি ভাষাচার্য অধ্যাপক সমাজচিন্তক অভিনেতা নির্মাতা নাট্যজন নাট্যশিল্পী নাট্যাচার্য নাট্যব্যাক্তিত্ত্ব সংস্কৃতিজন প্রজোযক পরিচালক নির্দেশক সংঘটক সুরকার রূপকার কণ্ঠশিল্পী কণ্ঠযোদ্ধা সংগীতশিল্পী শব্দসৈনিক কলমসৈনিক গুরুজন গুনীজন গুনী শিল্পী নৃত্যশিল্পী আবৃত্তিকার ছড়াকার সবার প্রিয় অতি সুপরিচিত বিশ্ব নন্দিত জাতীয় পদক প্রাপ্ত বিভিন্ন পদকে ভূষিত বিদগ্ধ বিখ্যাত প্রখ্যাত অভিজ্ঞ বিশেষজ্ঞ দেশবরেণ্য মান্যবর সাবেক অমুক তমুক আজকের অতিথি আমাদের প্রানপ্রিয় জনাব Sir so and so.[1] It goes on and on and on. Starting with আলহাজ হাজী মাস্টার মৌলভী, here are a few more examples: তুখোড় ছাত্রনেতা (brilliant/outstanding student leader), অনলবর্ষী বক্তা or বক্তৃতা (fiery speech/speaker), অভিজাত (upscale) shopping center, চৌকষ সেনাবাহিনী (smart and well-trained army), নিশ্ছিদ্র নিরাপত্তা (total and complete tight security), চিরুনি অভিযান (combing operation), লাল গালিচা সংবর্ধনা (red carpet reception), গুণী কিংবদন্তি শিল্পী (great/legendary artist), and আন্তর্জাতিক খ্যাতিসম্পন্ন (internationally famed and famous) nuclear scientist, political scientist, digital software scientist so and so. (More to follow below).

What an *oilish, pamperish, admirish*, infantile and imbecile overdo on the part of the fantastically cheap presenter in introducing just an ordinary person of a normal common profession! What a much ado about nothing! What a hubbub culture of endless epical, encomiastic, and panegyrical extravaganza of flattering apostrophes and addresses! More introductory titles than the content or the main talk! অতি মাত্রায় অতি কথন Long on words, short on substance! In the West, no one is introduced, regardless of how expert and experienced they are in their respective professions, with an unnecessary and superfluous adjective except her/his professional or academic title. That's all. And the presenter hardly talks except asking the bare and precise questions, letting the invited guests talk. In Bangladesh it seems it is more for the shameless presenter to talk like a showboat or grandstander than the guests who are invited to talk on the show.

There is an anecdote of Bangladeshi origin, probably true, that goes like this. A man had two degrees—academic or professional, earned or honorary. He called on a senior experienced scholar, more accomplished than him, to share how glad and proud he was about his two new titles or achievements. The wiser older person responded: "So what? A cow also has two horns." A simple introduction of one degree, one title, or one adjective should be more than enough in a modern civilized context!

In Bangladesh, incongruously and discordantly, there are as many titles for individuals as there are floral days (ফুলেল দিবস), in dozens: homecoming days (দেশে প্রত্যাবর্তন দিবস), release from jail days (কারামুক্তি দিবস), jail killing (জেল হত্যা) and other killing days, these or those demands days (দফা দিবস), birth and death anniversary days, victory and independence days, democracy preservation or destruction days (গণতন্ত্র হত্যা বা রক্ষা দিবস), and different movement and establishment/formation days (আন্দোলন বা প্রতিষ্ঠা বার্ষিকী). All such days are observed with great fervor and fascination that attend and accompany the floral meetings and gatherings to mark the occasions concerned. One's calendar is full of as many work days and holidays and weekends as the days to be celebrated and remembered with fanfare and formalities, away from being productive and fruitful.

By contrast, the assassination days of the world leaders, such as the American presidents Abraham Lincoln, James Garfield, William McKinley, and John F Kennedy; American civil rights leaders Martin Luther King Jr. and Malcolm X; British Prime Minister Spencer Perceval; India's Mahatma Gandhi, Indira Gandhi, and Rajiv Gandhi; and Islam's Caliphs Umar, Othman, and Ali—all come and go without being observed in any noticeable manner whatsoever (except of course the quiet and imperceptible federal holidays on the birthdays of George Washington and Martin Luther King).

Moreover, sometimes a title is utterly misplaced. While one who is a great upholder of a great cause such as the democracy of bipartisan consensus against the fascist or communist dictatorship may be described as a লৌহ মানব (iron man), one who is considered by the great majority a killer of democracy and user of brute force and beastly suppression cannot be called so. The quite boastful and often bullying, bellicose and belligerent, yet staunchly and stringently BNP*hobic* Sheikh Hasina rules by a democratically illegitimate and neo-and-near-and-more-than-partially fascist and পৈশাচিক policy. It is therefore completely wrong to call her a লৌহ মানবী (iron lady), as some Awami leaders would like to do so to elevate and upgrade her status out of blind and uncritical loyalty without realizing that their leader Hasina, in the role of a despot or an autocrat, is not deserving of this. In fact, she is far from being so.

Why to be guilty of applying a misnomer to somebody who does not deserve it? The term or rather the nickname of "the iron lady" was first used to describe the former Conservative British Prime Minister Margaret Thatcher for firmly standing up against Soviet authoritarianism even before she came to power in 1979. It "was invented by Captain Yuri Gavrilov in a January 24, 1976 article in the Soviet newspaper *Red Star* about Thatcher's 'Britain Awake' speech where she expressed her staunch opposition to the Soviet Union and to socialism" (from the Wikipedia, the free encyclopedia).

Apart from the dispute over the status of Mujib and Zia and their historic contribution both before and after the creation of Bangladesh, the matter of the titles and epithets before the names of Bangladesh's political leaders seems to be another disuniting factor—more disuniting than otherwise. The semantic issues surrounding the honorifics cannot, however, be a problem in (and by) themselves and would not have been a problem had they not openly reflected the disrupting political partisanship fragmenting the nation. If the people of all shades of opinion across the political spectrum loved to show their allegiance and admiration for both Mujib and Zia and both Khaleda and Hasina and their legacy without reservation, the titles they're addressed with—dead or alive—would not only have promoted tolerance, understanding and acceptance of responsibility but also have helped solve many problems facing the country and paved the way for political dialogue between the feuding parties.

Unfortunately, the real or symbolic honorifics are limited to the supporters of the respective parties only. With few exceptions, generally, if one is a member, follower or supporter of the Awami League (AL), one does admiringly use "জাতির পিতা *Bangabandhu*" before the name of Mujib; if one is a supporter of the BNP, one does the same with regards to "শহীদ President" Zia, clearly associating the terms with one's party affiliations and thus widening the differences between the two. The same is true about "দেশনেত্রী" (Leader of the Country) Khaleda and "জননেত্রী" (Leader of the People) Hasina, although, unfortunately, the latter is far from facing the people through inclusive and credible elections in what can be described as a classic example of difference between appearance and reality, between chant and slogan and actual situation. It is difficult to understand how a জননেত্রী becomes afraid of free and fair elections and suppresses the popular political opposition, which, finding no space, feels forced to call countrywide shutdown accompanied by sporadic violence.

The two female leaders, vehemently opposed to each other, are distinguished by their separate yet similar and synonymous appellations—one meaning "leader of the land or country" and the other, "leader of the people." One is "Chairperson" of her party; the other is "President" or "সভানেত্রী" of hers. As the titles of the latter ("*Bangabandhu* কন্যা") keep on piling up, her latest ones could be "দেশরত্ন" (Jem or Jewel of the land) and "ধরিত্রীকন্যা" (Daughter of Earth) as proposed by the pro-Awami citizens committee and the aviation minister Rashed Khan Menon respectively. That is, Hasina is being proposed to be deified as Gaia or Gaea and also Theia, who, as daughters of the mother earth, are two of the primordial deities in ancient Greek mythology. Despite the city of Dhaka being one of the dirtiest on earth and its river Buriganga one of the filthiest, there are some who would still like to worship her as their cult figure as they are out to mythologize both her and her father Sheikh Mujib, whose picture is making its way even into Muslim prayer halls.[2]

However, the true fact is that the mountainous collection of titles—light or heavy—and the differences in the designations of the top ranks keep coloring, widening, defining, and determining the divide not only between the parties but also among the people of the country. Khaleda at least mentions and remembers Sheikh Mujib with respect (thanks to her magnanimity and nobility of mind), while Hasina, in her scant respect for Zia, is always busy hurling insults at him and vilifying him for no reason and thereby maligning the real and main opposition without being noble, responsible, leader-like and statesmanlike. Ideally, both sides should call the national leaders the same way, without hesitation, doubt or discrimination. This certainly would have contributed to creating an atmosphere of harmony and appreciation auguring well for the country as a whole.

Since it all continues to be divisive and disruptive, widening the gap and breeding contempt among the opponents of each other, why not reduce the use of all those merely ceremonial and ornamental titles to a minimum in the everyday public discourse (meetings, talk shows, seminars, print and electronic media) and instead make appropriate and elaborate note of them in the textbooks and history books? These great decorative and, in some cases, deserving honorifics would never fall into disuse, for sure, but an overuse of them may sound jejune, hackneyed and charmless, if not abusive. Such obsession is hardly known in modern Western democracies. Setting aside the old style of Ramses the Great (that is, pharaoh Ramses II, known as Ozymandias in Greek, who called himself "king of kings"), the Venerable Bede, Cyrus the Great, Darius the Great, Alexander the Great, Constantine the Great (Constantine II), Pope Gregory the Great (Gregory I), Richard the Lionhearted (Richard I), Pedro the Cruel (Pedro I), Ivan the Terrible, Catherine the Great, Peter the Great, Frederick the Great, Nicholas II Emperor and Autocrat of All the Russias (also known as Nicholas the Bloody, Saint Nicholas the *Passion-Bearer* and Saint Nicholas the Martyr), and Suleyman I of the Ottoman empire, also known as Suleyman the Magnificent or Suleyman the *Kanuni* (lawgiver), leaders in modern times hardly make it a fashionable and constant practice to use the earned or honorary titles before the names of their national leaders in the various fields of human endeavor.

Jawaharlal Nehru, Indira Gandhi, George Washington, Abraham Lincoln, Franklin D Roosevelt, John F. Kennedy, Martin Luther, Martin Luther King, Karl Marx, John A Macdonald, Winston Churchill, Vladimir Lenin, Mao Tsetung, De Gaulle, Margaret Thatcher, Francois Mitterand, Fidel Castro, Simon Bolivar, Garibaldi, Mazzini, Gustav I, Sukarno, Lee Kuan Yew, Jomo Kenyatta, Nelson Mandela, Bill Clinton, Tony Blair, Barack Obama, William Shakespeare, John Milton, W B Yeats, Johann Goethe, Isaac Newton, Galileo Galilee, Michelangelo, Leonardo da Vinci, Albert Einstein,—all were and are still being known by their simple proper names, notwithstanding whatever common titles, earned or honorary, some of them may have had, such as *Sir*, *Dr.*, *Lord*, *Rt. Honorable, Chairman*, or *Comrade*. Not only that, there were many who refused to be awarded any titles. The 16th-century Italian Renaissance sculptor, painter, architect, poet, and engineer—one of the most influential artists of all time—Michelangelo rejected all offers of noble titles. Thomas Gray, Sir Walter Scott, Samuel Rogers, and Rudyard Kipling declined the royal offer of England's Poet Laureate position. One of the greatest modern writers, Jean-Paul Sartre refused the Nobel Prize for Literature in 1964. A great person/leader remains great with or without a title. A title may also sometimes serve as a catalyst to make the recipients more open to ridicule and critical dissection. Except once in a blue moon or on rare occasions, nobody feels obliged to address a great leader by his/her title and everybody feels free to call him/her by the last or first name only.

Similarly, unlike Bangladesh's মহান জাতীয় সংসদ (Noble/Great Parliament, though in reality—in its partisan, undemocratic, uncritical, and ineffective status—it is far from being noble or great), Americans simply call it "The Senate," "House of Representatives," and "Congress;" the British call it "Parliament;"

Japan "Diet;" Germany "Bundestag;" Israel "Knesset;" and Spain "Cortes," using no adjectives before the names of those national institutions, formally or informally, though all are active, effective and dynamic in a model, exemplary way. However, the Norwegian supreme legislature is called "The Storting," meaning "The Great Council," which, being one of the greatest democratic institutions, lives up to its name in all respects.

By contrast, it is a common phenomenon in some countries, especially South and Southeast Asia, to quickly and indiscriminately award long descriptive adjectives before as well as after the names. It is the same phenomenon that is evident in the attribution of titles that are meant to be, as it were, an integral part of the proper names of the personalities in question. For example: Africa's *king of kings* (as Muammar Gaddafi called himself, like the pharaoh Ramses II/Ozymandias); Turkey's *Ataturk* (Father of the Turks); Pakistan's *Kaed-e-Azam*; India's *Mahatma* and *Netaji*; and Malaysia's monarch and head of state, the Yang di-Pertuan Agong (literally "He Who Was Made Lord") and the lesser titles there such as *Tan Seri, Dato Seri, Dato W*ira.

In addition to the above, Bangladesh has its store of titles, endless, and inexhaustible: শের-ই-বাংলা or বাংলার বাঘ (a Bengal Tiger), বিদ্যাসাগর (a sea of knowledge), গণতন্ত্রের মানস কন্যা (a daughter of democracy even if one is widely regarded as a killer of democracy), অগ্নিকন্যা (a fiery daughter), রত্নগর্ভা (a mother who made babies who grew up to be as great as priceless jewels), শহীদ জননী (a mother of martyrs), জননী সাহসিকা (a mother courage), পপ সম্রাট পপ সম্রাজ্ঞী (an emperor/empress of pop), বাউল সম্রাট (an emperor of spiritually meditative but highly secular Baul music), সাহিত্য সম্রাট (a literary monarch), সাহিত্য বিশারদ (a vast literary expert/especialist), সাহিত্য রত্ন (a rare literary jewel), শিল্পাচার্য (a supreme master of art), জ্ঞানতাপস (a committed and sacrificing cultivatot/inculcator of kniwledge). লৌহ মানব (an iron man/iron lady), নায়ক রাজ্ (a king of actors), দেশ নায়ক (a hero of the nation), পল্লীবন্ধু (a friend of rural Bengal), পল্লীমাতা (a mother of rural Bengal), পল্লীকবি (a great pastoral poet); বিদ্রোহী কবি (a rebel poet), বিশ্বকবি (a world poet), চারণকবি কবিগুরু বঙ্গভূষণ বঙ্গবিভূষণ and the last but not the least মহান মে দিবস (despite the fact that the domestic housemaids, workers and laborers of all kinds in all sectors—factory, construction, industry, agriculture—continue to live a worse than slavish and subhuman life).

Such titles can remain and can be recorded, documented, and footnoted on the pages of introductory history books or text books and do not always have to be uttered, pronounced, appended, and rehearsed before the respective proper names in public forums, speeches, talk-shows, and academic discussions. Moreover, assigning big and humongous laudatory titles to a few only may be daunting, discouraging and intimidating to others. It may hinder them from trying their best and striving for the higher. They may feel more free to put out their best efforts if they know that they do not have to confront the unsurpassable so that, as they might think, they could have the motivation to become the first to hit the highest and target the most and best from their respective levels.[3]

In the case of Sheikh Mujib, he has been idolized and eulogized by his party so much so that it has reached the level of fanatical hero worship without limit and reservation. As Sharmin Ahmad, daughter of Bangladesh's first prime minister Tajuddin Ahmad, has pointed out in her book, Mujib not only chose (or had) to be away from the battle field but also declined to declare the independence of Bangladesh and wanted to become the prime minister of the undivided Pakistan.[4] It is not only foolish but also imbecile and infantile to say that Sharmin Ahmad was only a child in 1971 to become a pundit about Mujib's thoughts and strategies back then.

Well, how old were the Imran H Shorkar-led *Shahbugees* then to now demand the trial and capital punishment of those who are alleged to have been involved and implicated in the human rights violations in 1971? Why are the leaders calling on the youngsters of today as if they were pundits about 1971? Does one have to live in a past era to know about that the days of বাকশালী সন্ত্রাস/*Baksali* terror and torture and the Awami বাকশালী famine of 1974 to know what they were like? One may like to go without food for days and mix poison with কচুর লতি (a kind of common South Asian semi-underground vegetable called taro or eddoe and its stems/stalks) to eat and die and see how it feels.

Yet, under the present despotic, autocratic and authoritarian rule of Mujib's daughter Hasina, it is Mujib's picture and only his picture and nobody else's but solely his, argues Sharmin, that has found its way to the full range of the monetary paper bills of all denominations in Bangladesh. It is as if Mujib alone, despite being away (and despite his undeniably enormous influence during his absence), was the only person to contribute to the liberation war.[5] Moreover, ironically, even though she lost most of her immediate family members in the 1975 bloody military coup, it seems Sheikh Hasina did not learn from the pain of losing near and dear ones. If she did, she would have unlearned and stopped the violence and refrained from creating any excuse or environment, either as prime minister or opposition leader, that caused hundreds, even thousands of deaths, during her several terms of office and otherwise.

If Sheikh Hasina claims she is the daughter of জাতির পিতা (father of the nation) *Bangabandhu* Sheikh Mujibur Rahman, how could it be that there have been so much hoodlum hooliganism, rampant corruption, appalling criminalization, bloodshed, violence, horror, terror, and torture all around her on a daily basis?

How could it be that there have been so many arrests, remands, and imprisonments under her nose? How could it be that there have been so many dark and sinister forces creeping up their ugly heads under her watch? The renowned Indian journalist and diplomat Kuldip Nayar writes:

> Unfortunately Bangladesh, a product of the people's right to a say in governance, has lost the vigor of expression which the nation once had. This is a sad development by itself. But it becomes all the more poignant when the person changing it is from the family which liberated the people from the clutches of West Pakistan. No one else is to blame except Hasina. She is herself extinguishing the flame of democracy. That it should be done by the daughter of Sheikh Mujib is not only disappointing but also disconcerting. That she can shackle the nation still further is a harrowing thought. But it can happen since she has effaced the lines between right and wrong, moral and immoral. In this atmosphere of Hasina representing a dictatorial figure, Modi's visit was all the more unfortunate.[6]

Like her father, Hasina should have been as nice and kind and broad as Bangladesh itself, if not bigger, and democratically correct and legitimate by taking all Bangladeshis together, especially the political opposition (which for a fact represents the majority), through dialogue and discussion. The trial of 1971 war criminals and collaborators would have been more meaningful if social justice, rule of law, and democratic rights of all across the spectrum were established with neutrality and impartiality, with no bias, culture of denial, and eye-wash politics. The trial has therefore lost a great degree of its beauty and strength when (1) murders, abductions, and mothers' lacerating tears have become an everyday affair in an apparently lawless state of unequal application of laws, twisted at will, and (2) unbridled criminalization of all sectors has been going on with no state control or restriction.

When a house is on fire, it is the fire itself that needs to be extinguished first before chasing after who or what caused the fire. A farmer needs to evenly and smoothly clear up the field of its weeds first as he ploughs and prepares it for sowing and eventually reaping a good harvest, turning disadvantages into advantages as best as possible. To be full, complete, and effective, one needs to cover all, both front and back, with a totality of the needful, not just with loose patchworks here or there, which is in fact much worse if there is a political ill will or evil intention behind it.

English dramatist Christopher Marlowe's Doctor Faustus, seeing the shadowy phantom of the most beautiful woman Helen (raised by the evil Mephistopheles at the end of the expiry of Faustus's twenty-four-year contract with the devil), pays eloquent tribute to her, saying, "All is dross that is not Helena." Similarly, to the AL, all is dross and gross and hopeless and useless, of no value at all, that is not Mujib. This is demonstrated by its naming everything, in a very cheap and sickening manner, after the name of *Bangabandhu* Sheikh Mujib:

1. *Bangabandhu* Avenue,
2. *Bangabandhu* Parishad,
3. *Bangabandhu Motshyajibi* Parishod,
4. *Bangabandhu* International Convention Center,
5. *Bangabandhu* National Stadium,
6. *Bangabandhu* Gold Cup Football,
7. *Bangabandhu* International Volleyball Championship,
8. *Bangabandhu* Tungipara Monument,
9. *Bangabandhu* Medical University,
10. *Bangabandhu* Agricultural University,
11. *Bangabandhu* Maritime University,
12. *Bangabandhu* Science and Technology University,
13. *Bangabandhu* Communication Satellite,
14. *Bangabandhu* National Agriculture Award,
15. *Bangabandhu* Memorial Museum,
16. *Bangabandhu* Jamuna Setu (Bridge),
17. *Bangabandhu* Cultural Alliance,
18. *Bangabandhu* (Julio Curie) fortnightly Magazine,
19. *Bangabandhu* Fellowship,
20. *Bangabandhu* Textile Engineer's Association,
21. *Bangabandhu* EcoPark,
22. *Bangabandhu* Safari Park,
23. *Bangabandhu* Graphic Novel,
24. *Bangabandhu* Foundation,
25. *Bangabandhu* Government College, Gopalganj,
26. *Bangabandhu* Hall Debating Club,
27. *Bangabandhu* Fishermen Association,
28. *Bangabandhu Media Complex* (31-storey National Press Club under planning/construction);
29. *Bangabandhu* Awami Poribar (Family) League; and,
30. *Bangabandhu* High-Tech Park,
31. *Bangabandhu* Kurmitola Airbase,
32. *Bangabandhu* Shahittyo Parishad.

There are over 250 organizations and entities, big and small, light and large, funny and formidable, trivial and jovial, coolie and কাউয়া, that are all named after *Banganandhu* Mujib and his extended family members—his parents and his children—and his Awami/Baksal party.[7]

Like the excessive inflation of "golden" marks, GPAs, and balloons—toy balloons, Boishakhi balloons, birthday balloons, wedding balloons, and anniversary balloons—, excessive corruption, looting, and plunder under and during the Awami regime, and the excessive suppression of the opposition BNP by the (B) AL, there is an excessive inflation of naming names after only one name and one family and one party. It is as if Mujib and the AL alone were the only history to be obsessively celebrated and worshipped like a cult hero and a cult totem in a communal culture.[8] One Haider Ali Chowdhury has even published a book calling *Bangabandhu* Mujib a (new) Caliph of Muslims and the book was launched at a ceremony attended by some of the top Awami figures.[9]

Moreover, there are over a hundred parasitical organizations that make a lot of money just by using Mujib's name or Awami League's name, thereby belittling him and his party. A great national leader should not be belittled like this, AL leader Obaidul Quader said.[10] Mujib's younger daughter Sheikh Rehana also did not seem to like the bandwagon of using her father's name so indiscriminately and suggested that the great name of either Sheikh Mujib or Awami League be used more selectively and judiciously. Professor Afsan Chowdhury suggested that, in addition to the hundreds of institutions and organizations named after Mujib, his family and the AL, there also be a "Jatri League" and a "Rogi League" (bus passenger league and hospital patient league) to reap some benefit and protection from the AL government in the face of transport workers' or medical doctors' strikes causing endless suffering to the ordinary commuters and patients.

It seems the AL and Sheikh Hasina are still happy and proud to see that there are hundreds of things named and many more still to be named after them and their near and dear ones. They must be as excited as the people of the old German town of Hamelin were to see that the flute music of the colorfully dressed pied piper brought out the "army" of all the rats of different colors, freeing the townsfolk from the rat nuisance:

> You heard as if an army muttered;
> And the muttering grew to a grumbling;
> And the grumbling grew to a mighty rumbling;
> And out of the houses the rats came tumbling:
> Great rats, small rats, lean rats, brawny rats,
> Brown rats, black rats, grey rats, tawny rats,
> Grave old plodders, gay young friskers,
> Fathers, mothers, uncles, cousins,
> Cocking tails and pricking whiskers,
> Families by tens and dozens,
> Brothers, sisters, husbands, wives—
> Followed the Piper for their lives.

Had Hasina felt embarrassed, she would have stopped this low trend of naming names after her family members and herself (such as "Hasina Awami League," "Awami Shavanetri League," "Awami Hybrid League") long ago. Some small and almost unknown parties from within the AL-led alliance, to please Hasina and her AL, are raising the demand that the capital Dhaka be renamed after her father as Mujibnagar.[11] Dr Tuhin Malik said that, in its fascination to name everything after Mujib, the AL, if possible, would even like to rename the Facebook as *Bangabandhu* book.[12] One would not be surprised if the country is renamed as *Bangabandhu's* (*Bangabandhur*) Bangladesh, like the Saudis named their country as Saudi Arabia, the only country in the world to be named after a family (Saud family)—family of the founding monarch. After all, the opposition BNP is alleging that the Hasina government is bent upon establishing monarchy in Bangladesh.[13]

Erection of Mujib's name everywhere is nothing short of the fruition and fulfillment of the once Awami slogan of এক নেতা এক দেশ বঙ্গবন্ধু বাংলাদেশ (One Leader One Country *Bangabandhu* Bangladesh). But the strategy also seems to be in compensation, in a negative way though, for whatever deficit there is in the actual historical record of Mujib's failures, besides his successes. Despite deficiency, Mujib is what he was—a great continental point or rather the eighth summit, to be aspired after, so to speak, by the already seven summiteer Wasifa Nazreen. To name a host of things before and after the name of Mujib—one after another—is to put on him more and more waxen wings of Icarus, to melt down in the heat of the sun or to fall off with the passage of time, rather than letting Mujib stay on the solid rock on a peak.

On the other hand, whatever little—a tiny, less than a tiny, tiny fraction of Mujib's—was named after the great Ziaur Rahman was anathema to the AL and so was repealed and replaced by other names, so that all his traces and memories can completely be erased from the public and national front. One Nurul Haque writes that "Both Bangabandhu and Ziaur Rahman are well placed in our history as national leaders. Their positions in history cannot be changed by renaming and de-naming the existing institutions and installations. Bangabandhu named the finest part of the capital as Sherebangla Nagar, the historic park of the country as Suhrawardi Uddyan and the largest avenue of the capital as Manik Mia Avenue."[14]

Similarly, all national figures should have their due and fair share, instead of the colonial East India Company type monopoly of one name only. Even then, the AL supporters, far away from Bangladesh, could not accept the Chicago City Council's decision to name a local road as "Ziaur Rahman Way" about a couple of years ago. They were of course finally defeated in a US court there. Fortunately, they also did not have a chance to stop the Moroccan government's naming an avenue in French after Ziaur Rahman long ago.

There are page-long titles before the names of many religious saints, royal members (Kings and Sultans) and political figures in some parts of the world like Central Asia, South Asia, South East Asia, and Africa for no good reason other than that there has been a long-standing tendency—from noble to notorious, benevolent to malevolent—to develop a personality cult by some rulers and their fanatical devotees. Cambodia's long-ruling Hun Sen (born Hun Bunal), who, like Sheikh Hasina, brooks no political dissent, has a lengthy honorific, perhaps longer than his physical size: "Samdech Akka Moha Sena Padei Techo Prime Minister Hun Sen," loosely translated as "Lord prime minister and supreme, glorious, powerful military commander Hun Sen." The long honorary title of Tsar Nicholas II in the early 20th century has been mentioned above.

The ancient Assyrian King Esarhaddon, father of the more famous King Ashurbanipal of the 17th century (BC), who lived at the time of the later Egyptian pharaohs, had this message carved in stone, after conquering Egypt: "I am a hero, I am gigantic, I am colossal, I am magnificent." The great 14th century Central Asian empire builder Tamerlaine (or Tamburlaine, as Christopher Marlowe called him) was also known as Amir Timur or "Sahib-i-Qirani," meaning "Lord of the Fortunate Conjunction of the Planets."

The 16th century founder of the Crimean Tatar Khanate dynasty, Menli I Giray, took the imperial title "Sovereign of Two Continents and Khan of Khans of Two Seas." The "Nizams" of Hyderabad, that is, the Asaf Jah family/dynasty, who adopted the title of "Nizam-ul-Mulk," since 1724, meaning "Administrator/ Governor of the Realm," were conferred with another two titles—"His Exalted Highness" and "Faithful Ally of the British Government"—by the colonial British government for their collaboration in the wars against their neighboring fellow Muslim rulers Hyder Ali and Tipu Sultan of Mysore in the mid-19th century, thus becoming the only Indian prince/s to be given both these statuses. The Nawab Nazims of Bengal, Bihar and Orissa also enjoyed a bundle of titles at the same time. Mirza Mohammad Sirajuddowla (1733–1757), who was Nawab of Bengal and Nazim of Bihar and Orissa, had the titles of Mansur-ul-Mulk (Victory of the Country), Siraj-ud-Daulah (Light of the State), and Hybut Jang (Horror in War). His successor Mir Mohammad Jaffar Ali Khan Bahadur was also Shuja ul-Mulk (Hero of the country), Hashim ud-Daulah (Sword of the state), and Mahabat Jang (Horror in War).

In their excessively boastful pride, the above mentioned went too far, to the extent of claiming to be as powerful as God/*Allah* the Almighty, who says, in the holy Qur'an (verse 79:24), "I am your Lord, Most High." In not so dissimilar a context the English poet Tennyson was satirically critical of the "pompous epithets the Oriental writers [were] accustomed to bestow on their monarchs," because he saw the futility of their pride when they were actually too weak to defend their own countries.[15]

This love of and for titles—deep or superficial—with the attendant slavish, sycophant, feudal and colonial mentality and the lurking hero-worship syndrome has seriously affected the area of everyday journalism too. For example, in Bangladesh, no talk shows, public meetings, or formal gathering introductions are ever complete without mentioning at least a few (redundant) titles of embellishment or other forms of elaborate epic-epithet style address connected with the family stock before every name every time it is uttered—from "Sir," "Madam," "মাননীয়" (Honorable), "মহামান্য" (Highly Honorable) to "Your Excellency" and "My Lord." It is as if nobody would know those personalities, well-known and prominent though they are, by their simple proper names if they were addressed with just one common standard title of "Mr," "Miss," or "Dr" only.[16] It is an unpardonable offence, as it were, not to use a number of honorary or earned designations and descriptive epithets related to the family dynasty every time their names are mentioned. It is as if there was a shameful intention for everyone to somehow become a permanent "Former" ("*সাবেক*") rather than a selfless and illustrious "current/present" somebody, however short-lived that may be.

Since one cannot be a "সাবেক" (Former) before becoming an incumbent, one has no choice but to aspire to become a "Current" first, by hook or by crook, regardless of how short or long that incumbency would last. Hundreds of politicians and other high positions, young or old, have found it an easy way to establish themselves in the permanent position of "সাবেক" ("Former") and thereby bring themselves a certain amount of undying social aura and prestige so that their sons and daughters and grandchildren also could everlastingly feel proud to have belonged to and have descended from the family of a "সাবেক." As a result, the children and grandchildren of a "সাবেক" so and so feel as much pride as those for whom it is now their turn to enjoy the limelight of having come from the family of a current so and so.

In some "Royal" or authoritarian countries in Asia and Africa, the royalties and the public officials enjoy page-long titles before and after their names. While it looks funny in the free and democratic countries, it is their (royal/authoritarian) way of meaning business and getting anointed and gaining prominence, however old, epical, tribal, medieval, or colonial style it may seem to be. The government dignitaries in those royally or autocratically run countries are happy to receive such titles and, in return, remain loyal, quiet and silent, ensuring so-called "sheepish" stability and continuity. Another equivalent of this heavily alloyed governance style is the wholesale promotion of public administration officials in the government bureaucracy, as in Bangladesh, so that they remain happy and keep their mouth shut.[17]

The country-specific royalty and the same long lasting ruling coalition, in conjunction with each other, take the opportunity to create a privileged and foregrounded titled class that effectively helps them to hang on. The postcolonial critics favoring democratic equality and unity may find this as a legacy of colonial master-slave mentality, decadent pomp and splendor syndrome, inferiority complex, and outlandish royal trappings. Both the Western and the Eastern standard bearers of democracy, democratic openness, human rights and human dignity in the 21st century would view such practices as laughable and unacceptable, as suggested by Barack Obama's recent comment that he was not the king or emperor of the United States to do things as freely and singly as a king or an emperor could easily do, unaccountable as the position is to the people, by the stroke of his pen.

Another thing in point is that if the very election/s, claimed by the majority to have been fake and false, bogus and botched, boycotted and bowdlerized, a deceiving ruse or a devilish stratagem, totally unacceptable, why to prefix "মাননীয়" before the names of the persons in question? As a corollary, why to invite the corrupt and convicted, and the shameless and harmful nonsense-and-foul-talking loose talkers on TV and in meetings, in front of young students and civil society members, giving them social and political recognition and legitimacy? Isn't it a strong antidote for them to be shunned and not to be invited in public to be in the limelight of the media?

Today's political parties in Bangladesh should not remain mired in the backward-looking "remembrance of the things past" in their meditative stream of consciousness. As it is, they are deeply engulfed in the politics of the past with no agenda for the future and for the real harmonious development of the country—economic, social, moral, and democratic, all together. They must function in an environment of democratic freedom, peace, tolerance, and equality. When in power, this or that party must establish the rule of law as opposed to any particular party such as the AL that, more than any other parties, nakedly politicizes and commercializes all sectors of the government with the intention of brutally suppressing, crushing, crippling, cornering, eradicating, and annihilating the opposition.

There is a clear tendency on the part of the AL to openly criminalize, in an unalloyed abuse of power, the state machineries and their boots and batons and bullets and barrels, which must belong to the state as a whole, to be used for the general welfare of the masses and the nation building. By all index, it seems the AL is the biggest abuser of democracy in its ruthless tactics to cling to power and stifle and silence the opposition views and voices. Every time it came to power, since 1972, it is believed to have far exceeded its immediate past predecessors in corruption, politicization, repression, suppression, suffocation, eradication and annihilation.

As some would like to argue, the later BNP drifted from the first Zia-led BNP and consequently it committed mistakes and suffered for its failures. True. But the drift was perhaps necessitated by the Awami League's foul political tricks and misdeeds from the beginning, since the independence. That does not mean an attempt to support and justify the malpractices committed by the BNP. But the reality is that one has to ride at least a simple bike to run a race with one on a motorbike. The BNP, though ever enjoying a large popularity, was always weak, lacking in true guts. And now the AL has again been resorting to evil hundred times more than before. So how can the BNP politics, or, for that matter, any Bangladeshi politics be expected to be clean and healthy? It is not too much to say that the AL has taken the country hundred years back in terms of its (the country's) moral stamina and mental robustness from within. The AL is not giving the party politics and political culture in Bangladesh a chance to change for the better.

All the patriotic people and parties have the equal and legitimate democratic right to contribute and take part in the comprehensive and harmonious development and future welfare of the country. It is not the sole monopoly of the AL only to do so in its own way, excluding the others representing the majority, and remain in power by force in the name of a face-saving but corruption-ridden and discrepancy-riddled development. Even the arguably pro-AL Imran H Shorkar, finally coming to his senses (since a majority may have and do indeed have many disagreements with him, who was born after the liberation), is critical of the pretension and false cover into which the spirit of liberation has degenerated, to the lucrative materialism of and the lack of judicial remedy under this Awami government.[18] In other words, the spirit/চেতনা of liberation has increasingly been commodified, compartmentalized, and commercialized with a market (product) value or face value on it.

The AL has turned Bangladesh into a country of no democracy, "mobocracy," "dummy-cracy," "demo-crisis" and oligarchy, no better than a roadside public সরাইখানা (place of rest and refuge) filled with bugs and brutes. It is only right and fair and sane and natural that all the major parties and alliances take their turns democratically and be given an opportunity through democratic means to serve and work for the homeland they all love so deeply from the vantage point of their respective programs, initiatives and agendas—new, diverse, different, innovative and creative.

People of Bangladesh must not be obsessed with the memory of their founding fathers; they need not invoke them every time every day everywhere. The Americans, the Canadians, the British, or the French, for example, hardly invoke the names and actions of their great political predecessors or founding fathers. In their forward-looking politics, they remember them only occasionally and when they do they do so meaningfully. Great American presidents such as Lincoln and Kennedy and great Indian Prime Ministers such as Indira and her son Rajiv Gandhi and their father of the nation *Mahatma* ("Great Soul") Gandhi were assassinated but their death anniversaries come and go without notice by the American or Indian public. They met their tragic fate but their nations and their people, united together in patriotic fervor, have since been paying their best tribute to them by remaining true to their legacies, moving forward, and taking their countries to newer and newer heights, peacefully and democratically, without regressively falling back or solely banking upon the memory of their long-lost leaders. Too much praise or attention to a dead leader, in the worldly or political sense, is surely a hindrance and an obstruction to the creation of a new leadership endowed with a new vision and a statesmanship. Successful Eastern and Western democracies know that the best way to honor the dead is to serve the country well and they are therefore glad talking about their current and future programs, to be objectively debated, honestly reviewed and finally implemented with all sincerity and patriotic ardor and fervor.

In conclusion, the AL's '66–'69–'71–'75-centric politics is counterproductive. While it is a civilized virtue to cultivate a sense of history, it is absolutely dull to remain stagnant and stay bogged down in history. Politics is a continuing, an ever evolving living process. Political parties must therefore map out and follow a future-oriented, realistic yet dynamic, patriotic yet tough, popular yet determined, flexible yet principled course of action. Like the organic growth and evolutionary development of a plant or a human being, parties too must not just survive but renew, replenish and succeed with a firm belief, hope, and conviction in better tomorrows. Finally, as suggested above, to resolve the preeminent issue of the status of the national leaders, let it be done by consensus through an absolutely impartial and elected parliament or a grand all-party assembly—all parties, big and small, secular and Islamic, leftist and rightist—in a spirit of mutual tolerance, understanding, compromise and sacrifice. No care-taker (interim) government, let alone an army chief or a chief adviser, both positions to remain above the political fray, should impose any forced solution on any matter of far-reaching national significance and deep-seated national symbolism.

Notes

1. Well-known poet famous writer popular poet famed poet formidable philosopher timeless litterateur ambidextrous writer essayist columnist researcher analyst intellectual thinker supreme linguist great professor social thinker actor builder maker dramatic artist drama/tic personality theatrical master cultural figure cultural worker producer director organizer composer musician singer vocal artist vocal fighter sound soldier speech soldier pen soldier respectable person a person of qualities quality artist dancer dance artist recitation artist versifier highly praiseworthy world famous world-wide well-received receiver of national awards/medals experienced specialist passionate committed reputed reputable respectable nationally famed honorable former so and so our dear our beloved so and so is our today's guest and s/he is so and so.
2. http://banglamail71.com/others/news=7054
3. Periodic, highly selective, and judiciously selected especial one-time achievement titles and medals such as Nobel laureate, British knighthood (Sir/Dame), Indian *Bharot Ratno* and *Padma Bhushon,* Bangladeshi *Bir Sreshthya, Bir Bikram, Bir Uttam,* and American Congressional awards of freedom are altogether a different matter and should remain in practice. The awardees are all selected through a lengthy discriminating vetting process and become the role models for others.
4. http://www.amadershomoys.com/newsite/2015/07/12/346562.htm; http://www.sheershanews.com/2014/04/30/34923; http://www.amadershomoys.com/content/2014/04/24/middle0413.htm; https://bnin.facebook.com/Baserkella2013/photos/a.493315934050012.1073741826.493311867383752/674796072568663/?type=1&relevant_count=1; https://www.facebook.com/photo.php?v=10202033917555117&set=vb.1401707249&type=2&theater&notif_t=like; http://dailynayadiganta.com/details.php?nayadiganta=MzYwMTU=&s=Nw==
5. http://tajuddinahmad.com/banga-babdhu-tajuddin-and-banglaby-major-general-amin-ahmed-chowdhury-bir-protik
6. http://www.thestatesman.com/news/opinion/a-shot-in-the-arm-for-hasina/68705.html
7. http://www.bd-pratidin.com/first-page/2017/03/24/217395
8. For more things named after Mujb and the AL and his family members, to their happiness, visit: http://www.bd-pratidin.com/first-page/2016/03/27/134978; http://www.bd-pratidin.com/first-page/2017/02/15/207991; http://www.amadershomoy.biz/beta/2017/02/25/818616

9. https://www.facebook.com/photo.php?fbid=10155212333839796&set=a.40346289795.48054.632289795&type=3&theater; http://www.roshikhakim.com/2016/12/20
10. http://www.thedailystar.net/parasites-feast-on-ruling-al-49542; http://dailyasianage.com/news/3383/opportunists-belittling-mujib-floating-organizations-quader
11. http://m.banglanews24.com/national/news/bd/560916.details
12. https://www.youtube.com/watch?v=09sGUwjdwkA
13. http://www.thedailystar.net/frontpage/grievances-now-forgotten-197572; http://newagebd.net/199034/al-established-monarchy-alleges-bnp/
14. See A N M Nurul Haque, "Politics of Renaming," http://archive.thedailystar.net/newDesign/print_news.php?nid=119375
15. See the note to his poem "The Expedition of Nadir Shah into Hindostan," based on William Jones's translation of the *History of Nadir Shah*. The poem is a bitter indictment of Nadir Shah of Persia, the last great Muslim conqueror of India, who ravaged Delhi in 1739, leveling thousands to "the dust of the plain" and laying waste—"a wilderness dreary and bare"—what was the "Eden" of Hindustan.
16. It is to be noted that an American President or a British Prime Minister is simply addressed as "Mr. President" or "Mr. Prime Minister." Only rarely or in very formal circumstances, such a position is addressed as "Honorable Prime Minister," "Madam Prime Minister," "Dear Mr. President," or "President of the United States," with absolutely no other terms added before or after. Thanks to Asafuddowla, a former secretary to the government of Bangladesh, founding editor of *The Bangladesh Today* and a Nazrul-song artist (brother of the late Nazrul *Geeti* icon Firoza Begum), who has always expressed his objection and resentment against such agonizingly "colonial" forms of flattery, appeasement and patronization on a number of occasions on various TV channels.
17. http://www.daily-sun.com/post/103799/Topheavy-civil-admin
18. http://www.ittefaq.com.bd/capital/2016/02/06/54264.html. Imran Shorkar talked sense when he said that Abul Mal Abdul Muhit could not absolve himself from the complicity of Bangladesh Bank robbery and launched a praiseworthy role in protesting against the abduction, rape and murder of a young college girl, Shohagi Jahan Tonu, in or around the Comilla Cantonment compound. However, popular disagreements with Imran Shorkar would include his "Joy Bangla" slogan and his blind, direct and uncritical demand for the hanging of the 1971 human rights violators. In the evolving circumstances, he could have at least changed to "Joy Bangladesh" and/or added "Bangladesh Zindabad." It is to be pointed out that Shorkar was not even born when the liberation war took place and when Sheikh Hasina, under Pakistani safety and away from the war field, was receiving financial benefits from Pakistan.

Part B

11

Bangladeshi Nationalism

A Cause and Concept Right and Just

This chapter argues that the freedom, independence, and sovereignty of Bangladesh are to be upheld on the basis of its geographical territory and nationalist ideology, which must not be compromised in its deeds and dealings, especially with the neighboring India in the name of its friendly ties with the latter, no matter how large it is. Bangladesh cannot be rendered into *The Tragedy of Hamlet, Prince of Denmark*, which T S Eliot considers to be an artistic failure because he finds Hamlet's emotions, being in excess of the external actions happening to him in the play, to be lacking in "objective correlative." This chapter also argues that Bangladesh's Islamic identity as a Muslim majority country should be maintained by adhering to the religious fundamentals, without ever being extremist or fundamentalist. It claims that Bangladesh, like Malaysia, can very well ensure social and economic justice for all, including the minorities, and still be officially and practically a Muslim country of peace, harmony, and equality. After all, one of the core principles of Islam is to guarantee the safety and security of the minorities belonging to any race, sect, caste, and creed.

The South East Asian country of Malaysia, a mixed population country, has a strong Islamic identity. It has only 60% Muslims (25% Chinese and 15% Indians). Yet, according to its constitutional provision, the Prime Minister and the Deputy Prime Minister shall have to be Muslim. The King (Agong) is always a Muslim, rotated among the Sultans of its constituent states.

There is nothing to be afraid of or worried about when Islam is sanctioned an active promotion and predominance in what is already an overwhelmingly Muslim majority country. It needs to be made clear that there is nothing in this world that is not differently interpreted by different people and different groups throughout the ages. All "isms," "ships," "ideologies," "tantras" and "mantras," starting from Kingship, Feudalism, Chivalry, Oligarchies, Democracy, Capitalism, Communism, Feminism, Religion, Nationalism, Wealth of Nations, Laissez Faire (leaving the people alone about their economic activities and thereby separating between the state and its economy)—all have thousands of hues and hallows.

Secondly, a minority member would see the presence of the majority religion in the social and public life in a different way. That should not cost the majority religion its right to healthy and strong, and vigorous exposure in the life of the nation. A majority member would like to see Islam remain and promoted as the state religion of the Muslim majority Bangladesh without the minority religions threatened and their followers frightened by any means. When all other religions of the world are united against the fast-growing Islam, Muslims should remain united in supporting, defending, protecting, and propagating their religion. No internal divisions and differences should be allowed to be taken advantage of by the followers of other religions. No infighting should be allowed to invite the non-Muslim others like S K Sinha to meddle with, dictating about the state religion of an overwhelmingly Muslim country. When it comes to the interfering charade and parade of the third party, Muslims should close their differences and act together.

Unfortunately, secularism is grossly abused in Bangladesh by promoting all other religions while demoting Islamic culture and values. Like the Hindu India, Christian West, Jewish Israel, and the Muslim Arabian and Persian Gulf, Bangladesh can basically remain an Islamic/Muslim country in its ethos, spirit, and orientation without diluting its Islamic tradition and culture and at the same time with the minority interests being fully and properly taken care of. There is no reason that the wrong notion of secularism and its widespread abuses (in the context of Bangladesh) should erase and efface the climate of Islamic feelings and rituals, and occlude and displace the fervor and environment of Islamic practices in the overwhelmingly and predominantly Muslim majority country, religion being the deepest bond and impulse in the human mind, more than language and solely the language-based culture.

It is the respective religion, more than one's own country and one's own language, that unites the Muslims, Hindus, Jews, and Christians in their own religious ways in the free, multicultural, and multilingual world, including the

Middle East, which is full of expat workers and professionals. In terms of priority, therefore, religious faith is the topmost bonding between the humans, followed by the country and then the language of speech. In the world of cultural and linguistic pluralism, one is at first a Jew, a Christian, a Hindu, or a Muslim and only then one is American, British, Canadian, or Indian, and then one is English-speaking, French-speaking, German-speaking, Bangla-speaking, Urdu or Hindi-speaking, and so on.

One is born with a religion and one dies and is buried/burnt (cremated) with a religion, one's religion being thus the first and the last, countries and languages, however, being never a barrier but never coming before the faith. A practicing Jew and a practicing Muslim can live together, though they may be speaking different languages and may belong to different countries, in the middle of nowhere in the desert wilderness, but they would hardly be able to live together with a pork-eating individual/community, even if they belong to the same country and the same language, unless it is a question of life and death.

As Muslims, the people of Bangladesh must support a Muslim Bangladesh, which must maintain an Islamic identity—precious as it is—alongside its territorial integrity and independence and its language. Religion coming first, the people must cling and remain committed to their religion, as best as they can, never withdrawing, distancing, disengaging from, and desegregating from it. If the world is going far right, including Narendra Modi's India, which has slid into the sectarian and communal Hindu nationalism that suppresses the Muslim and other minorities, Bangladesh should feel safe and proud to stay Islamic and to stand in the way of the rise of the narrative of Western and Indian populism.[1]

It is only fitting that further discussion below may begin with a quotation from Ahmed Safa, a Bangladeshi writer and public intellectual, who wrote the following:

> তবুও আমি মনে করি, একটা স্বনির্ভর [দেশ] নির্মাণ করতে হলে আমাদের কিছু কিছু ক্ষেত্রে অবশ্যই ভারতের বিরোধিতা করতে হবে। এখানে অনেকে ভারত বিরোধিতা মানে হিন্দু বিরোধিতা বুঝে থাকে। কিন্তু আমি কথাটা বলছি সম্পূর্ণ অর্থনৈতিক দৃষ্টিকোণ থেকে। ছোটদেশকে তার নিজস্ব অস্তিত্ব টিকিয়ে রাখার প্রয়োজনেই বিশেষ বিশেষ ক্ষেত্রে বড়দেশের বিরোধিতা করতে হয়। এর মধ্যে সংকীর্ণতা কিংবা হীনমন্যতা খোঁজার কোন অবকাশ নেই। ছোটদেশকে তার নিছক ইচ্ছাশক্তি প্রয়োগ করে বৃহত্তর প্রতিবেশির প্রতিবন্ধকতার জাল ছিন্ন করতে হয়। যে জাতি ইচ্ছাশক্তি প্রয়োগ করা শেখেনি তাকে বড় দেশের লেজুড় হিসেবে অস্তিত্ব রক্ষা করতে হয়। [2]

What Safa wants to say, translated into English, is that he thinks that Bangladesh has got to oppose its bigger neighbor India on certain issues if it wants to establish itself as a free, sovereign and independent country. This opposition to India is not an opposition to Hindus, as some people mistakenly think so. This opposition is purely from economic point of view. A small country needs to oppose a big country on certain issues for the sake of its own existence. There is no scope for narrow-mindedness or inferiority complex in this stand. A small country has to overcome and tear down the web of the obstacles created by the neighboring bigger country by exerting its sheer will power. If a nation did not learn how to apply and exercise its will power it has to live on by being servile and subservient to the bigger one.

Safa's idea of independence and sovereignty of Bangladesh is not discordant or contradictory to the idea or ideology of Bangladeshi nationalism. In fact, one informs and reinforces the other. Although the name of the former President Ziaur Rahman, maker of modern Bangladesh is gladly and gloriously associated with the concept of Bangladeshi nationalism, it is said to have been first framed and floated by Khandoker Abdul Hamid in his Daily Ittefaq article (February 21, 1976), which was earlier (15 February) presented at a Bangla Academy seminar.[3] In his excellent piece, Khandoker Hamid stresses the validity of the idea of Bangladeshi nationalism, while cogently and convincingly pointing out how the idea of *Bungalee* (Bengali) nationalism is politically and historically a misnomer, as faulty and incorrect as it is, having taken into account the different contexts and questions related to both Bangladesh and the Indian state of West Bengal.

There are those who would like to argue that if the Hindu majority West Bengal separates from India and joins under the flag of the Muslim majority Bangladesh to form a greater Bangla/Bengal, it is unlikely that any Bangladeshi would ever have any reason to object and in that case the both ideas of *Bungalee* (Bengali) nationalism and Bangladeshi nationalism could be bridged and broached together into each other to mean the same and become identical.

That this argument is plain wrong is proved by the former BDR chief Maj Gen ALM Fazlur Rahman, who, citing the negative examples of the unstable India (from Kashmir in the north to the states in the north east), Kurds in Turkey and Iraq, Rohingyas in Myanmar, Hill Tracts unrest in Bangladesh, Shiite-Sunni fights in Yemen, Iraq, and Bahrain, and the Muslim-Christian fights in the Sudan and Indonesia before the creation of South Sudan and East Timor, shows how disastrous it would be or it would have been if the idea of *Akhand* Bharat (United, Undivided, Larger, & Greater India) were to materialize.[4] Mohammad Jasim Uddin of Charuta Foundation, Areefur Rahman, and Sufi Borshan argue exactly the same, that the idea of a united India or united Bengal would be suicidal.[5]

Although the both subjects—nationalism and secularism—are deep and complex, discussed in many different forums, with plenty of resources available and endless debates conducted, I would like to keep my comments and observations as easy and simple as possible, free from being a discursive disquisition of scholarly bombast. The intention is to enable the general readership to comfortably connect and engage with the views and findings herein. No attempt would therefore be made to bring up Jean-François Lyotard's notion of the negation of the "metanarrative" or "grand narrative" about the whole of the universal human family, which he thought was not possible in the postmodern age. As Zoglul Husain, a Bangladeshi-British social and political activist and commentator, who was also a great freedom fighter in 1971, points out in his "Nation-states, Narratives, and Bangladesh" article,

> We can see that there are narratives of religions, for example, the Islamic narrative, the Christian narrative, the Jewish narrative, the Buddhist narrative, the Hindu narrative, etc. There are political and economic narratives, such as the narratives of socialism, capitalism, developmental economic theory, etc. There are ethnic narratives, linguistic narratives, cultural narratives, etc. Similarly, there are narratives of Freudian theory, feminist theory, periodization of history theory, etc., among others.

One of the controversies in the political history of Bangladesh is whether the people of Bangladesh are "Bangladeshi" or "Bengali" (*Bungalee*) and whether theirs is a Bangladeshi nationalism or *Bungalee* nationalism. The matter deserves cool and critical attention in view of the fact that India's ruling BJP warmly embraces the idea/ideal of *Akhand Bharat* as envisioned by the ancient Indian emperor Chandragupta Maurya's political and economic advisor Chanakya Kautilya (aka Vishnu Gupta) in the 3rd century (BC), followed, in modern times, by Pundit Jawaharlal Nehru's "Nehru Doctrine" as sketched in his *Discovery of India*. "India will inevitably exercise an important influence," Nehru says. "India will also develop as the center of economic and political activity in the Indian Ocean area. The small national state is doomed. It may survive as a culturally autonomous area but not as an independent political unit."[6] Now it is clear why and how Hyderabad, Kashmir, Goa, and Sikkim were made part of India at the cost of a sea of blood and why there has been a deep Indian RAW involvement in Sri Lanka, Maldives, Nepal, and Bangladesh.[7]

The same idea/ideal has been expounded by Dinanath Batra in his as many as six books, made a "must read" by Gujarat Education Ministry for students of 42,000 primary and secondary schools in the home state of India's Hindu Nationalist Prime Minister and BJP leader Narendra Modi.[8] "Students, how would you go about drawing a map of India? Do you know that countries like Pakistan, Afghanistan, Nepal, Bhutan, Tibet, Bangladesh, [Kashmir, Sikkim], Sri Lanka and Burma are part of undivided India? These countries are part of *Akhand*

Bharat," writes Batra in his *Tejomay Bharat* (Shining India). In his narrow and fragmentary view of Indian nationalism. Batra would like to see the thoughts of and references to Tagore, Mirza Ghalib, Fida Husain, and the Mughals taken out of Indian school textbooks.[9]

India, Pakistan, and Bangladesh will reunite to form *Akhand* Bharat, said BJP General Secretary Ram Madhav in an interview with Al Jazeera. Referring to the fundamentalist Rashtriya Swayamsevak Sangh (RSS), Ram Madhav said,

> The RSS still believes that one day these parts, which have for historical reasons separated only 60 years ago, will again, through popular goodwill, come together and Akhand Bharat will be created. As an RSS member I also hold onto that view.

However, Madhav added that it "does not mean we wage war on any country, [or that] we annex any country. Without war, through popular consent, it can happen."[10] Madhav's views have been corroborated by the Governor (Rajjyapal) of the Indian state of Tripura, Tathagata Roy, who, first in early 2015 and then on March 26, 2016, said that there was no need for passport-visa between Bangladesh and India.[11] Later, Roy also made highly provocative tweets about what he thought was a need for Hindu-Muslim riots and conflicts to solve the problems between the two religious communities.[12] Press Council of India chairperson Justice (Ret) Markandey Katju also expressed his dream of *Akhand* Bharat when he said that "Pakistan is a fake country and one day India, Pakistan and Bangladesh will reunite. It may take 15–20 years."[13]

There is an active armed movement called স্বাধীন বঙ্গভূমি আন্দোলন (Independent Bengal Movement) operating from within West Bengal, which wants to capture and occupy Bangladesh.[14] "Bangladesh (or East Bengal) would soon be ours," said the BJP Indian West Bengal President Dilip Ghosh.[15] Former Indian Defense Minister, currently Chief Minister of Goa, Manohar Parrikar, said India would never give up the dream of *Akhand* Bharat and would continue to work to achieve the goal of *Mahabharat* that would include all the neighboring states together.[16] He went on to say India conquered and gave back Bangladesh the way Lord Sri Rama (or Ramachandra), the seventh avatar of the Hindu God Vishnu, conquered Lanka and gave it back to Vibhishana, younger brother of the Rakshasa Raj (demon king) Ravana of Lanka. During the February 19–21, 2015 visit of West Bengal Chief Minister Mamata Banerjee to Dhaka, one of her delegation members, film actor and director Dev (Deepak Adhikari) had the audacity to call for the Muslim majority Bangladesh and the Hindu majority West Bengal to unite. He made the outrageous call in the midst of a radical secularist pro-Indian audience (who are ironically, perhaps deceptively, claiming to be the bearers of the spirit of the 1971 Bangladesh liberation war), so that there was no protest against. There was absolutely no protest from the Hasina government either.

Soon after the nationalist Bangladeshi film maker and director Mostafa Sarwar Farooki registered his criticism of Indian political and cultural aggression on his Facebook status, saying that West Bengal should first launch a movement to detach itself from India to qualify to call for a reunification with Bangladesh. Farooki, himself not without controversy over the content of his own films, went on to say that while Bangladeshi culture and cultural programs were closed or off limits to India, Bangladesh, by contrast, was as open as Sunny Leone to Indian culture and entertainment.[17]

Farooki did so to the cheers and applause of many other patriotic nationalists, such as the vocal artist Asif Iqbal. Because of his pro-opposition political stance, Asif has been totally sidelined under this Awami regime and has even been denied a visa by Indian High Commission in Dhaka twice, despite his having been invited by Indian artists to perform there in India. In any case, the Indian Dev forgot that it took a bloodbath for the sovereign and independent Bangladesh to have been born in 1971 and that his West Bengal played an anti-Muslim role in the 1911 annulment of the 1905 Partition of Bengal that had created, for only about six years, a Hindu majority Western Bengal together with Bihar and Orissa and a Muslim majority East Bengal together with Assam.[18]

In 2012 Indian Gen Ashok Kumar Mehta said India needed another Hasina government to fulfill its strategic aims.[19] On the occasion of the native and international mother tongue day on 21st February 2016, West Bengal Food Minister Jyotipriyo Mallik has called for the abolition of the passport requirements between the two Bengals.[20] But the fact is that the people of Bangladesh do require those "requirements" to stay in place because they are a Muslim majority independent country for which they fought with their lives. They do not want to be one with the Hindu majority West Bengal. It is for sure the people of Bangladesh would not subscribe to the economically, culturally, and religiously homogeneous EU formula. If the current debate over the issue of Brexit (exit of Britain from the EU) is taken into consideration, even the EU is not free from or immune to disintegrating and falling apart!

Mallik's illogical and inappropriate proposition is similar to the (eastern) Ukrainian Russians asking for a similar abolition of border control between Ukraine and Russia. Although they have more reason to ask for so, they all being of the same race, religion, and language, still the government of Ukraine finds it impossible in the face of the larger and more powerful Russia's tendency to grab and absorb more and more of the sovereign and independent Ukrainian territory.

Then, again, the question is, as the freedom fighter Ranu Chowdhury of the USA posits: "Is Jyotipriya Mallik's Bangla (Indian state of West Bengal) an independent state? If a Bangladeshi visits his Bangla without passport and visa, can he also visit other parts of India? If not, how a person of ministerial rank say such a weird thing? Once [his Bangla] becomes an independent country, Bangladesh may think of free travel between the two countries."

Another freedom fighter, a former student leader and a former journalist, Mohammad Zainal Abedin of the USA, author of a number of books on Bangladesh such as *RAW and Bangladesh* (1995) and *BDR Massacre: Target Bangladesh* (2009), also makes a compelling argument against the Indian (and Indian West Bengal's) political ambitions to slowly but surely swallow the sovereign and independent Bangladesh, similar to what India did to Sikkim and Nagaland. By dwelling on the essential differences between the two Bengals, Abedin effectively dismisses Mallik's suggestion of the abrogation of border control between the two Bengals.[21] Historically, Abedin points out, West Bengal Hindus always remained a pro-All India and pro-Hindi people with flip-flops on the issue of a united Bengal, which, in contrast with the 1905 Partition, they did not want in 1947, although that was what the majority of Bengali Muslims wanted then.

Although the Muslim League leader Muhammad Ali Jinnah did not have any objection to a united Bengal (as proposed in the Suhrawardy-Abul Hashem-Satyen Bose plan, which envisioned to revive an independent Nawabi Bengal combining Bengal, Assam, Bihar, and Orissa), the WB Hindus and Congress leader Jawaharlal Nehru opposed it probably in view of the fact that such a Bengal would/might have a Muslim majority. This uncertainty led the Bengali Muslims away from the idea of a united and greater Bengal and pushed them to gradually and ultimately side with the prospect of a separate homeland for them that materialized in the form of Pakistan.

In addition, when there is so much violence and bloodshed between the Sunnis and the Shiites in Iraq, Syria, Lebanon, Yemen, Bahrain and even Saudi Arabia and between the Jews and the Muslim Arab Palestinians, the question of the two Bengals uniting with two different religions dominating is simply out of the question/equation. Moreover, it is the Hindus who rejected the idea of a united, greater Bengal in 1947 as they earlier supported the same, again in an anti-Muslim role, in 1905, at the time of the Partition of Bengal.[22]

As also mentioned in the chapter on the National Anthem of Bangladesh, the great Bengali/Indian poet Rabindranath Tagore wrote two songs, আমার সোনার বাংলা/My Golden Bengal and বাংলার মাটি বাংলার জল as a campaign for the abolition of the 1905 Partition of Bengal.[23] He meant one and undivided Bengal and that is why he used the word "Bangla," rather than East Bengal (which was to become East Pakistan in 1947 and later Bangladesh in 1971). Tagore's "Bangla" is similar to the Awami League (AL)'s "Joy Bangla" but dissimilar to the BNP's "Bangladesh Zindabad," which is specific about the Bangladesh as we have it today as an independent country.

Bangladeshi nationalism is absolutely necessary to uphold the Bangladeshi nationhood and establish the integrity and sovereignty of the geopolitical entity and territory called Bangladesh. The story of Bangladesh under the Hasina regime does not have to be the story of the poor Felani killed by the Indian BSF at the border or the other border/partition story of the sick and dying Rupsha in Goutam Ghosh's India/Hindu dominated and sectarian tension-building 2016 film "Shonkhochil," at least in the eyes of the former BDR chief Maj Gen Fazlur Rahman.[24]

According to Kamal Ahmed and Sudha Ramachandran, the more than 2,500-mile long India-Bangladesh border dotted with jungles, mountains, and rivers is the bloodiest and most dangerous border in the world, more than the Israel-Palestine, India-Pakistan, and the USA-Mexico borders.[25] According to Kiriti Roy, Bangladesh subserviently accepts all the political and cultural wrongs and injustices done by India at and along the border just as it accepted the Indian looting of Bangladesh during the pre-and-post independence days.[26] Mahmudur Rahman, a national hero, was supposed to present a paper on the BSF and Border issues, but the Hasina regime's police broke the gathering preventing him from exercising his mere and minimum freedom of speech.[27]

As Rezaul Karim, a politically minded health official in the USA, comments: if the Kashmiris and the Kurds are shedding their blood daily for independence, Bangladesh must never give up its own, for which it shed blood in 1971.[28] The issue demands a serious attention in view of the fact that there are many Indian and Bangladeshi pro-Indian politicians who would like to see the two Bengals—(Hindu majority West Bengal of India and the independent Muslim majority Bangladesh)—merge into one and be part of India. This unification into a larger and greater India is at least according to the visions of Chanakya, Batra, Nehru, Rabi Rikhi, and the "Upamahadesh Punorujjibon Andolon" (movement for revival of the sub-continent). Quoting Nehru, Rikhi, UPA, and others, Khodeza Begum writes about how India wants to install a puppet government in Bangladesh, Nepal, Bhutan, and Maldives and gobble them up the way it did Sikkim, Kashmir, Hyderabad, and Goa.[29] Nazma Mustafa provides a detailed list of why there is a reason for the Bangladeshis to be afraid that they may one day lose their independence.[30]

Verbally, that is, by way of the word of mouth, Bangladesh's (more "crowned," "coronated," and "anointed" than democratically "elected") Prime Minister Sheikh Hasina, manifestly boastful, bullying, bellicose, and belligerent, yet violently BNP*hobic*, is a strong advocate of the country's independence and sovereignty. But she never protested against the cacophonous clamors of the Indian politicians as mentioned above. Moreover, she has a problem of trustworthiness with the patriotic nationalists who find it difficult to believe what she says. Her actions and activities seem to be leaning more toward the "United Bengal/United India" visions than otherwise, for which she has been facing overwhelming criticism. Print and social media have been rife with sour and bitter remarks about Sheikh Hasina when she was/is being seen as:

(1) going without protest against the outrageous and preposterous Indian claims as mentioned above;
(2) having a great love for and trust and faith in Hindus, as claimed by her former APS Matiur Rahman Rentu towards the middle of his book "আমার ফাঁসি চাই" যেখানে শেখ হাসিনা বলেন : "মুসলমানরা বেঈমান ও অকৃতজ্ঞর হিন্দুরা ঈমানদার ও কৃতজ্ঞর আমি (শেখ হাসিনা) হিন্দুদের উপর ভরসা করতে পারি, বিশ্বাস রাখতে পারিে কিন্তু মুসলমানদের বিশ্বাস করা যায় নায় ভরসা করা যায় না"—a claim confirmed and corroborated by her appointment of a disproportionately huge number of Hindus everywhere in every sector of Bangladesh, especially since 2009[31];
(3) signing off widely unequal (economic, military, and overland communication) treaties with India according to the unlimited, unbridled, and unbounded Indian hegemonic wishes and demands and paving the way for a 21st century master-slave (and the slave revolt under Spartacus vs. the Roman oligarchical legions under Crassus and Pompey in the 1st century BC) relationship between India and Bangladesh[32];
(4) allowing as many as 66 Bangladeshi products to be patented by India under the Geographical Index policy that benefits the latter[33];
(5) going without protest against the continuous Indian killing of poor Bangladeshis at the border and the persecution and discrimination of Indian Muslims in India (whereas the Indian government takes no time to protest if there is anything against the Hindus in Bangladesh);
(6) letting questions arise about the Indians entering Bangladesh in the name of quelling terrorist attacks; secretly operating in Bangladesh in promotion of her groping grip and control of power; and demanding open sky access to Bangladesh[34;]

(7) wearing the tricolor Indian flag *saree* on Bangladesh's national occasions and thereby encouraging others such as the actress and presenter Deepa Khandoker of pro-Awami A K Azad's Channel 24 to follow suit as part of the increasing Indianization of Bangladesh even in the month of liberation and victory December[35];
(8) purchasing the same tricolor trains from India with Indian employees on duty in the compartments that carried the sign of Indian Railway along with the other signs in the Indian national language of Hindi;
(9) staying away from the India-Bangladesh cricket match (so that she could avoid the embarrassing situation of cheering for this or that team to the chagrin of the either);
(10) expressing full-hearted solidarity and sympathy and sending heartfelt condolences whenever there is a natural or technical disaster in India killing Indians but not doing anything and staying most cruelly aloof from the alleviation of the inhuman plight of the bordering (Burmese) Rakhine Muslim Rohingyas, who are subject to systematic ethnic elimination, torture, and cleansing in the most barbaric and horrendous manner;
(11) keeping quiet and proving weak and submissive about the continuous and countless "Felani" border killings by India (while Nepal could be strong enough to register a loud protest against the killing of even one single Nepalese national by India)[36];
(12) allowing Indian cultural aggression to continue in Bangladesh and Indian channels air Bangladeshi advertisements (the latter has now apparently stopped) as if both India and Bangladesh were one and the same country[37];
(13) not doing enough about the Hill Tracts unrest over the conflicting claims of land ownership between the mountain tribes and the inhabitants of the mainland moving there to settle that may lead to the area to be slipping away from the control of Bangladesh[38]; and,
(14) allowing the BGB youth saluting the Indian BSF Chief that led to the question if the sovereignty of Bangladesh was compromised and if those BGB men and women were actually of Bangladeshi origin or Indian origin.[39]

There continues to be a criticism of Sheikh Hasina for: (1) appointing excessively high number of Hindus in the overwhelmingly Muslim majority country's government positions; (2) conniving at the Bangladeshi Hindu Struggle Committee asking Benjamin Netanyahu, through Mendi Safadi's Center for International Diplomacy and Public Relations, to establish diplomatic relation with Bangladesh in an equation that squares off with India-Israel brotherly relations; (3) allegedly letting (or ignoring) both Indian and Bangladeshi flags fly at the same time at the Taj Hotel in London on May 15, 2016 when she was staying there on her way to Sofia Bulgaria; (4) sometimes being addressed as a মুখ্য মন্ত্রী/ chief minister (of an Indian state) with no protest from her; (5) entertaining Avijit Mukherjee, an Indian MP and son of Indian President Pranab Mukherjee, with 81 different items on the menu when millions are underfed in her own Bangladesh[40]; and (5) allowing Bangladeshi TV channels such as Mozammel Babu's একাত্তর/71, which is apparently an extension of Awami and Indian campaigns, to broadcast live Indian PM Modi's speeches, while disallowing those by popular and prominent politicians of Bangladesh such as Tarique Rahman from being aired.

Ms Hasina's power minister Nasrul Hamid stated that India and Bangladesh were going to be one country with the differences between the two nations about to be withering away while referring to the contracts and agreements between the two (privileging and favoring India, of course).[41] Her another minister, AKM Mozammel Haque, said that Bangladesh became independent at the bloody sacrifice of Indian soldiers, which undermined the sacrifice of the millions of Bangladeshi freedom fighters.[42] Bangladeshi Hindu-Buddhist-Christian Organization, in an attempt to further divide the already dented and divided Bangladesh, are asking for sixty reserved seats for them in the Bangladesh parliament, a demand not only democratically illegitimate and immoral but also disproportionately high in number, given the fact that they are only 8% of a population of 165 m.[43] Even if they were more, why to demand for undemocratic reserved seats? Why not get elected by Hindu Muslim popular votes and serve and represent the people of a constituency irrespective of their religious denominations?

There was an announcement of Bangladesh army recruitment through the Indian government job portal. Some are reportedly said to have expressed their preference for recruits in the Bangladesh army to be as tall as Indian Punjabis (let alone, presumably/understandably, as tall as Hasina's son and likely successor Sajeeb Wajed Joy and his maternal grandfather Mujib), although many world renowned military commanders and generals were short in size, including the locally made Awami ally Moin U Ahmed.[44] Some are said to have defended the job announcement in the interest of raising a modern army regardless of national borders. Bangladesh fire service and civil defense department advertised its job vacancies against which there was an opportunity for Indian origin applicants also to apply.[45]

Together with the above, the reports:

(1) that extremist Hindu leaders of Bangladesh, such as Gobinda Chandra Pramanik, Rana Dasgupta, and Pijush Bandopaddhaya were making provocative and baseless sectarian statements and calling for Indian intervention in Bangladesh;
(2) that India is increasingly enjoying open and unfettered access to Bangladesh markets and consolidating its hold on Bangladesh through vast business interests[46] the way the East India Company did through trade and commerce in Bengal and the rest of India back then, ultimately to take control of the whole Indian subcontinent;
(3) that a great number of Indian Hindus thought to be entering Bangladesh with false and fake papers so that there was an increase, in as many as 15 lakhs, in just one year and claiming lands in Bangladesh as their own;
(4) that India is going to start a Radio channel targeting the audience only in Bangladesh; and,
(5) that Indian especial security units with or without uniform may have a presence in Bangladesh to help the Hasina government with various terror threats and other matters of partisan political concern—bear deeply ominous and troubling signs that remind one of those Hindu, Muslim, and Sikh traitors during the 1757 Battle of Plassey; traitors of the 1857 Indian Sepoy Mutiny against the British; and Lhendup Dorji of Sikkim in the 1970s, all of whom were later ignored by their masters and died in utter ignominy and obscurity.

There have been similar claims, made again and again, for a long time by so many Indian as well as Bangladeshi politicians, but to no protest from the AL. It seems they are glad to be gobbled up by India and therefore at the prospect of Bangladesh giving away its independence and the two Bengals getting united and becoming part of India. Where is Awami Fakir Alamgir singing দাম দিয়ে কিনেছি বাংলা কারো দানে পাওয়া নয়/"Dam Diye Kinechi Bangla Karo Daney Pao-a Noi?" Where are the artistes of স্বাধীন বাংলা বেতার কেন্দ্র/ Shwadhin Bangla Betar Kendra to protest against—Abdul Jabbar (now no more), Shahin Samad, Apel Mahmud, Sujeo Sen, beautiful Bulbul Mahalanabish, Rupa Farhad, Mala Khurram, Rafiqul Alam, outstanding Kaderi Kibria, Rathindra Nath Roy, and many others still alive today? Don't they have a moral and political obligation to speak up and refute and reverse the idea as expressed in Abul Mansour Ahmad's 1982 book, বেশি দামে কেনা কম দামে বেচা আমাদের স্বাধীনতা/ Our Freedom: Purchased at High Price and Sold Cheap?

It is precisely for the reason of the hard-earned Bangladesh that the country's former President Ziaur Rahman prudently and farsightedly introduced the concept of Bangladeshi nationalism. His name is inextricably and indispensably associated with the nationhood of the Bangladeshis. His intention was to give permanence to the idea of the territorial and geographical sovereignty of Bangladesh. The move was made with a sense of pride and dignity in the religious, tribal, and cultural diversity of Bangladesh. This view is supported by Lakehead University Professor Syed Serajul Islam, who says: "Ziaur Rahman created a vision of national identity and defined the nation by territory and religion, as opposed to the primordial definition of Mujib, which is based on language and culture."[47] The same view is shared by Professor Harun Rashid of Environment and Earth Science of the same University, who argues that:

> Many leaders in Bangladesh do not have a broader vision about the justification for an independent nation. This is the reason for which I am not a big fan of so-called Bengali nationalism, which has been unfortunately transformed into an anti-Muslim nationalism. In reality, these two philosophies are not mutually exclusive of each other. A truly independent and secular Bangladesh could still be a pro-Muslim Bengali nation. Indian hegemonic philosophy will not allow that. You know that today India is the only neocolonial power in the world. Look at what they have done to Sikkim. Now they are after Nepal, trying to deprive them of their natural right to exist as an independent nation-state. In the case of Bangladesh, they have screwed us up in a big way! So depressing! Even if we cry our heart out, nothing will happen.[48]

The point made by Professor Rashid in stating that "A truly independent and secular Bangladesh could still be a pro-Muslim Bengali nation" is absolutely well-placed and well-taken. Although Islam is the official religion of Bangladesh, supported by all the parties, including the currently ruling AL, it is only on paper and its status as the declared state religion does not affect the non-Muslim Bangladeshis at all in their day-to-day existence and their perception of national identity as Bangladeshi.

Only race-and-language-and-culture based *cross-border* Bengali or *Bungalee* nationalism is just a loose and idle idea—as useless, impractical, and nonworking as the wider Pan Arab and Pan African nationalisms, which, given the separate and distinct nationalism of each independent postcolonial nation-state, are in tatters and which no longer hold together. Ideologically oriented Arab nationalism—that there would be one united Arabia, from Aleppo to Aden, as originally promised by the allied Anglo-French forces at the time of the Arab Revolt (led by T E Lawrence, among others) against the Ottoman rule during WWI—collapsed when England and France went back on their promise and carved the region into several large and small nation-states now feeling superior to each other and even fighting with and against each other.

Tracing through the political development in the Indian subcontinent, Afsan Chowdhury argues that a common and inter-communal Bengali nationalism that united East Bengal and West Bengal and the Hindus and the Muslims together never existed.[49] With the rolling back of imperialism and imperialist hegemony, the cross-border or the overseas British, French, Portuguese, and Spanish nationalisms, as opposed to within-the-border nationalism, have completely subsided. Hitler's militant and racist Pan German nationalism was defeated, if it did not completely die, in WWII. This was also the fate of the cross-border Slav/Balkan nationalism of Slobodan Milosevic, Radovan Karadzic, and Ratko Meladic in the 1990s.

Although there is an emergence of a general European nationalism (like the slow and feeble undercurrents of Arab or African nationalism) based on common culture and currency, individual EU members, especially the UK, France, Germany, Austria, and the Netherlands are strongly nationalistic about their language, culture, and heritage within their respective boundaries, so much so that many of them have their own nationalist parties that resulted in Brexit and may also result in Frexit soon. Similarly, there is a robust Russian nationalism in Russia. Although many peoples in Eastern Europe (Russians, Poles, Czechs, Serbs, Ukrainians, Belarusians, Bulgarians, Slovaks, Croats, and Bosnians) speak different Slav/Slavic/Slavonic languages, they are proud of their own nationalisms with respect to their own borders, just as the Indians, Iranians, and the Zionists are proud of their Indian, Iranian, and Israeli nationalisms.

In modern times, the politically and nationally determined nationality and the ideological concept of nationalism have become indistinguishable from each other. Roughly transformed into one and the same through the process of political evolution/revolution, they have in fact merged and coalesced into each other. In other words, modern nationalisms are more nationality-based (or vice versa), there being hardly any difference between a people's allegiance to a nation-state and their fealty to a pan-nation concept of identity. In the early 20th century, the Irish fought for their independence based on Irish nationalism, separate from England, just as in the present decades Kurds (who are all or mostly Sunni) are fighting for their own homeland, separate from Arabs or Turks, be they Sunni or Shiite. Similarly, Catalans are asking for their independence from Spain; Scots and Northern Irish from the English; Brits from the UK (Brexit); Kashmiris from India; and many Quebeckers in French Canada from the English-speaking Canada.

The people of Bangladesh are certainly Bangladeshi and theirs is Bangladeshi nationalism. It is by virtue of their national identity and territorial integrity (to be clearly distinguished from Indian, Pakistani, Nepali, Burmese, or Thai nationalism, for example) that theirs is Bangladeshi nationalism. In their national and political identity, they are definitely Bangladeshi, which, needless to say, is already inherently and innately inclusive of their ethnic and racial identity as *Bungalee.* Their valiant freedom fighters fought neither to join and merge with the West Bengal of India nor for Bangladesh to be divided into a number of separate "Balkanized" political entities.[50] As stated by Zoglul Husain, there cannot be any "to be or not to be," or "to exist or not to exist" scenario for Bangladesh army, a patriotically spirited ever vigilant force that represents and stands guard for the independence and sovereignty of Bangladesh. For them the one and only choice is to be and to exist; to defeat any efforts and designs engineered by India to turn Bangladesh into a vassal state.

If Tajuddin's and Sheikh Mujib's unequal 7-point and 12-point agreements, respectively, with India in 1971 and 1972 provide evidence, India never wanted a real army for the independent Bangladesh.[51] According to the agreement/s, there was to be only a National Defense Force, to be called *Jatiyo Rakkhi-Bahini*, which, accordingly, was formed on February 8, 1972 and was trained by Maj Gen Sujan Singh Uban from the Indian RAW (Research and Analysis Wing), while then Lt Col C R Dutta was appointed as the Director-General of the Bangladesh Rifles.[52] While India and its supporters within Bangladesh always advocated that Bangladesh did not really need an army, the overwhelming majority of the people of Bangladesh were and are always proud to have an standing army to safeguard their national sovereignty.[53]

While the people of Bangladesh are mostly *Bungalee*, coming from different religious backgrounds such as Muslim, Hindu, Christian, and Buddhist, the population of Bangladesh also includes people of over two dozens of ethnic and racial tribes (some scholars claim over fifty), mostly of Sino-Tibetan origin. They are Chakmas, Tipras, Khasias, Marmas, Murongs, Mandi-Garos, Saontals, and Manipuri. While ethnically they are not *Bungalee*, they all live within the borders of the independent Bangladesh and, therefore, must be considered as Bangladeshis under the banner of Bangladeshi nationalism. As Syed Haque of the USA points out, "Non-English [people] living in England are not English. They're called British. That's why their nationality is British. Similarly the term Bengali reflects ethnicity whereas Bangladeshi reflects nationality. The nationality of people living in West Bengal is not Bengali; it is Indian. Sylhet was not part of greater Bengal before 1947." This line of argument, perfectly acceptable and appropriate, is based on a clear demarcation, both political and geographical, with the neighboring foreign borders, including West Bengal.

The people of Bangladesh are all Bangladeshis, regardless of what they are in their ethnic, racial, or religious origin. In this, they are no different from the neighboring India, of which the vastly diverse populations of many colors and cultures are all Indians. They are all Indians whether they are of Indo-Iranian-European origin in the north (such as, Persian, Sanskrit, Hindustani, Assamese, Bengali, Gujarati, Marathi, Punjabi, Rajasthani, Sindhi, and Oriya), or the Dravidian origin in the south (Tamil, Telugu, Malayalam, Kannada, and Tulu). Despite their cultural variety which completely separates and segregates the Indian north from the south, they are all Indians whether they are Muslims, Hindus, Christians, Sikhs, Buddhists, and Dalits—all coming together from different faiths and languages. Just as Bangladesh believes in Bangladeshi nationalism, so does India in Indian nationalism to bring together its millions of people of many ethnic origins under the common unifying national ideology—Indian.

An Arab is an Arab in terms of race and ethnicity, and also in terms of what has just been said above as an invalid, untenable, and ineffective Arab nationalism, similar to the loose and fluid *Bungalee* nationalism. However, for all political and practical intents and purposes, both at home and abroad, Arabs have to go by their geographically and politically determined nationality (which subsumes their spirit of nationalism, if any) and the passport they carry with them. Therefore, they are either a Saudi, or a Jordanian, or a Kuwaiti, or an Iraqi, or a Syrian, or an Egyptian, or a Libyan, or an Omani, or a Qatari, or an Emirati, or a Bahraini, or an Yemeni and so on. There may be a Lebanese Arab Muslim or a Lebanese Arab Christian but all are Lebanese under their national identity. There may be a Palestinian Arab Muslim or a Palestinian Arab Christian but all are Palestinians. Those Palestinians who live in Israel proper, not in the Occupied Territories, are Israelis. Similarly, all Americans are American by both nationality and nationalism, be it an ethnic black or an ethnic white, an ethnic Chinese or an ethnic Indian.

Because nationality is defined by politically determined borders along the lines of either language or religion and/or race and ethnicity (with exceptions, of course, for example, the U.S. was not formed on the basis of any of these factors), these borders may keep shifting through future political developments so that any country of today can be broken into more than one nationality tomorrow. For example, there are today's Iraq of Kurds and Arabs, Sunnis and Shiites; Turkey of Turks and Kurds; India of many languages and religions; China of the Communist/Confucian/Buddhist Chinese and Chinese (Hui and Uighur) Muslims; and Russia of the Slavic/Orthodox Christian Russians and Russian (Chechen and

Dagestani) Muslims, etcetera. As Dr Zainul Abedin, who has worked on American racial issues and the New York Times coverage of the Bangladesh liberation war in 1971, puts in his e-post: "Different groups of people with different races, ethnicities, tribes, faiths, cultures, languages make up a nation. Bengalis make up a race, not a nation. Many of us are Bengalis by race, and by nation we are Bangladeshis who include tribal people too."

Bangladesh is one country and one nation with one single political entity under Bangladeshi nationalism. It is this ideological fact that remains the single most unifying factor about the people of various ethnic backgrounds living on the soil of the sovereign and independent geographical territory called Bangladesh. Bangladeshi nationalism does not preclude or exclude the historical linguistic and cultural *Bungalee* roots going back centuries in time. It is inclusive of all those who live within the territory of Bangladesh.

The emergence of Bangladesh as a separate political and geographical entity means there is the logically and politically correct concept of Bangladeshi nationalism of which all Bangladeshis can be proud. This national identity must not exclude the tribal communities in the name of the chauvinistic *Bungalee* nationalism, flawed and misleading as it is. To include all Bangladeshi citizens and avoid any unnecessary confusion with the Indian state of West Bengal in the determination of their identity ("Good fences make good neighbors") is a sound and sensible concept first advocated and articulated as Bangladeshi nationalism by then President Ziaur Rahman in the late 1970s. Here one may find pertinent the words of Austin Peay State University Professor Dr Taj Hashmi:

> Ziaur Rahman […] championed the cause of Islam through his various measures, including "Bangladeshi Nationalism", which is not only appropriate from the viewpoint of political science but it also draws a demarcating line between the Muslim majority Bangladesh and the Hindu majority Indian state of West Bengal.[54]

In other words, President Ziaur Rahman, who as one of the most heroic sons of the soil was the zenith of a high mountain of great prospects and vistas, ensured the independence and sovereignty of Bangladesh on the basis of geographical territory, Bangladeshi nationalism and Bangladesh's Islamic identity. He called for friendly ties with India on the basis of an equal win-win relationship and disapproved of Indian hegemony and encroachment into Bangladesh. While Zia called for unfettered democracy and the determination of the government by free choice, he registered total opposition to Awami/BAKSALi ideology that held the mistaken view that it was solely India that liberated Bangladesh and that Bangladesh was the personal property of only a few families and that the so-called স্বাধীনতার

চেতনা/spirit of independence, regardless of how partial and fragmented it was, was informed by the Awami brand of anti-Islamic secularism.

Notes

1. Delhi University professor of Hindi literature and culture Apurbanand writes about the sectarian and communal Hindu nationalism of India: http://www.dailynayadiganta.com/detail/news/216785
2. Ahmad Safa, বাংলাদেশ: জাতি রাষ্ট্র এবং গন্তব্য/ Bangladesh: nation state and its destination (আজকের কাগজ/Ajker Kagoj, 20 June 1996). Edited by Dr Salimullah Khan on the occasion of the 72nd birthday of Ahmad Safa (June 30, 2014), Republished on the Facebook page: **আহমদ ছফ1 বিদ্যাল**য় or https://www.facebook.com/notes/আহমদ-ছফা-বিদ্যালয়/বাংলাদেশ-জাতি-রাষ্ট্র-এবং-গন্তব্য-আহমদ-ছফা/655818817835706
3. https://www.facebook.com/kai.kaus.31/posts/242621222770160
4. https://www.facebook.com/alm.fazlurrahman/posts/112129336012802
5. http://bangladesh-web.com/new/readers-opinion/4925-2012-12-16-16-21-38; https://sufiborshan.wordpress.com/2016/12/27/অখন্ড-ভারত-বলতে-কিছু-নেই।; https://www.facebook.com/notes/areefur-rahman/ভারতের-সীমান্ত-সম্প্রসারণ-এবং-অখন্ড-ভারত-কায়েমের-অলীক-স্বপ্ন/692542044123098/
6. Quoted by Khodeza Begum in her "United Bengal/United India?" article: https://groups.google.com/forum/#!topic/bangladesh-progressives/mgR24VVOQQI
7. http://www.bbc.com/news/magazine-24159594; Shaikh Mahadi on the Nehru Doctrine and Hyderabad, Sikkim and Bangladesh at http://imbdblog.com/?p=1395#comment-853; Mohammad Mustafizur Rahman on how India annexed Sikkim: http://www.bdface.net/newsdetail/detail/49/247898;
   http://www.bdface.net/newsdetail/detail/34/243956; http://www.bdface.net/newsdetail/detail/49/227068; http://www.muldharabd.com/?p=164; http://www.noyonchatterjee.com/2016/09/blog-post_62.html
8. http://indianexpress.com/article/india/india-others/man-who-got-wendy-doniger-pulped-is-made-must-reading-in-gujarat-schools/99/; http://www.firstpost.com/living/dinananth-batra-to-saffronise-guj-syllabus-birthday-cakes-are-bad-burma-is-in-dia-1633781.html
9. http://www.news18.com/news/india/dinanath-batra-wants-to-remove-tagore-ghalib-mughals-riots-from-ncert-textbooks-1471457.html; http://www.ittefaq.com.bd/world-news/2017/07/25/121565.html
10. (1) http://www.ibnlive.com/news/politics/india-pakistan-and-bangladesh-will-reunite-to-form-akhand-bharat-bjps-ram-madhav-1181205.html;
    (2) http://www.aljazeera.com/news/2015/12/india-bjp-chief-backs-unity-pakistan-bangladesh-151224100753698.html; (3) http://www.ndtv.com/india-news/india-pakistan-bangladesh-will-reunite-says-bjps-ram-madhav-1259184; (4) http://www.

thehindu.com/news/national/akhand-bharat-india-pakistan-bangladesh-will-re-unite-one-day-says-ram-madhav/article8031920.ece; (5) http://www.first-bd.net/crnewsdetail/detail/49/196915; (6) http://www.muldharabd.com/?p=290 and (7) http://www.darjeeling-unlimited.com/losing.html

11. http://m.prothom-alo.com/bangladesh/article/811159/
12. http://www.firstpost.com/india/tathagata-roy-tweets-about-hindu-muslim-civil-war-continues-habit-of-making-communal-remarks-3721071.html
13. http://www.news18.com/news/india/pakistan-will-reunite-with-india-one-day-says-katju-601498.html
14. http://www.old.al-ihsan.net/fulltext.aspx?subid=4&textid=2967
15. http://mzamin.com/article.php?mzamin=4328; http://www.somoyerkonthosor.com/2016/08/14/26394.htm; http://www.news-bd.net/newsdetail/detail/200/235222. For more on Akhand Bharat claims and visions and missions, click http://imbdblog.com/?p=8450; https://youtu.be/XmwjBcUMUCY
16. http://todaysangbad.com/archives/160963
17. https://www.facebook.com/photo.php?fbid=477797765763983&set=gm.1039820156088734&type=3&theater; http://www.bddesh.net/newsdetail/detail/49/215220. Here it is to be pointed out that, in the context of a Muslim majority society, one cannot agree with Farooki's film *Third Person Singular Number* because the main characters "live together" outside of marriage and sexual relationships are discussed freely. That is in conflict with Islam.
18. "The decision to effect the Partition of Bengal was announced in July 1905 by the Viceroy of India, Lord Curzon. The partition took place in October 16, 1905 and separated the largely Muslim eastern areas from the largely Hindu western areas." https://en.wikipedia.org/wiki/Partition_of_Bengal_%281905%29; http://historypak.com/partition-of-bengal-1905-1911/; also see M. Serajul Islam, "Call for Bangladesh and West Bengal to Unite!," Weekly *Holiday* (Bangladesh), February 27, 2015.
19. https://www.facebook.com/photo.php?fbid=973829462648560; https://www.facebook.com/qamrul.islam.bd/posts/1327418603956309
20. http://www.amardeshonline.com/pages/details/2016/02/22/324493
21. http://banews24.com/national2/24-national-2/13497; http://www.dailynayadiganta.com/detail/news/122321. Other books by Abedin include *Chittagong Hill Tracts: A Victim of Indian Intervention* (2003); and *Naga: A Cry for Freedom* (2007).
22. http://en.banglapedia.org/index.php?title=United_Independent_Bengal_Movement
23. The government of British India headed by Viceroy/Governor General Lord Curzon announced the idea for Partition in January 1904 and the decision to implement the Partition in July 1905. The actual partition took place on October 16, 1905. The Partition was, however, opposed by Sir Henry John Stedman Cotton, Chief

Commissioner of Assam 1896–1902, while it led to the formation of All India Muslim League under the Nawab of Dhaka Khwaja Sir Salimullah along the lines of religious divide, as if to counter Indian National Congress, which was considered a representative platform of the Hindus.

24. https://www.facebook.com/alm.f.rahman/posts/10210491286101112
25. In 2016 alone, 31 Bangladeshis have been killed by the Indian BSF at the border: http://www.dailynayadiganta.com/detail/news/196030; http://www.prothom-alo.com/opinion/article/46804/; http://www.dhakatimes24.com/2016/12/26/13598; http://thediplomat.com/2017/02/the-india-bangladesh-wall-lessons-for-trump; http://www.amaderbudhbar.com/2017/02; 1,391 Bangladeshis killed by BSF along border in 45 yrs: http://www.theindependentbd.com/post/82165
26. http://www.banglatribune.com/others/news/142955;
http://newsbd7.com/main/detail/3110; http://banglamail71.info/archives/486
যুদ্ধ শেষে ২৭০০ কোটি টাকার অস্ত্র-সরঞ্জাম লুট করেছিলো ভারতীয় সেনাবাহিনী? (অমৃতবাজার দৈনিক-১২ মে ১৯৭৪) ! ৭৪ সালের চুক্তি সত্বেও ভারত তিন বিঘা করিডোর হস্তান্তর করেনি বাংলাদেশকে ! ৭৫ থেকে বাংলাদেশকে পানির নায্য হিস্যা দেয়নি।পদ্মা শুকিয়ে আজ বাথরুমের টাংকি ! বছরে ২০০ কোটি টাকার ফসল উৎপাদন বন্ধ! সুল্ক জটিলতা সৃষ্টি করে প্রায় ২০ হাজার কোটি টাকার বানিজ্য ঘাটতি তৈরী করেছে ! প্রতিবাদের পরেও টিপাইমুখে বাধ দিচ্ছে সিলেট সহ ১৬ জেলা মরুভূমি হয়ে যাবে ! হিন্দি চ্যানেল প্রচার করতে ৩০০০থেকে ৪৫০০ কোটি টাকা ভারতকে দেয়া হয়। কিন্তু বাংলাদেশী চ্যানেল ভারতে নট অ্যালাউড! গত ৪৪ বছরে ৬১ হাজার বাঙ্গালীকে সীমান্তে হত্যা করেছে !! সাংস্কৃতিক আগ্রাসন,অভ্যন্তরীণ রাজনীতিতে নির্লজ্জ হস্তক্ষেপ, মাথার উপর দাদাগিরিসহ নানাভ1বে বাংলাদেশ আজ ধর্ষিত ভারতের কাছে ! ভারত ৪২ বছর ধরে স্বাধীনতায় সহযোগিতার নামে বাংলাদেশ শোষণ করছে ! এই তো কয়দিন আগে বাংলাদেশী জার্নালিস্টদের বলেছে: ''বাংলাদেশী পাসপোর্ট? নট এলাউড' 'কিউ কি আপ বাংলাদেশকা সিটিজেন হ্যায়! একরকম গলা ধাক্কা দিয়ে হোটেল থেকে বের করে দিয়েছে আপনার বন্ধুরা! তবুও? [সংগৃহীত]

Translated into English: India looted 2,700 crore taka worth of arms and ammunition right after the end of the war in 1971. Despite the 1974 agreement, India did not hand over the Tin Bigha corridor to Bangladesh. It stopped sharing the upstream river water right from 1975. As a result the lower stream Padma is drying out into a toilet tank. Production of about 200 crore taka worth of agricultural produce per year has stopped. There is a trade imbalance of about 20,000 crore taka due to Indian imposed tax/tariff complication. Despite protest, India is building a dam at the tip of the Tipai river that is likely to cause a desertification of 16 districts inside Bangladesh, including Sylhet. Bangladesh gives 3,000–4,500 crore taka to India to let Indian channels air in Bangladesh whereas Bangladeshi channels are not allowed in India. During the last 44 years 61,000 Bangladeshis have been killed at the border. Indian cultural aggression, its unbridled interference in the internal politics of Bangladesh, and its exercise of unnecessary overhead influence have left Bangladesh in a state of nonstop rape by India, which has been exploiting Bangladesh for the last 42 years in the name of helping the latter during its liberation war. Only a few days ago, India kicked out Bangladeshi journalists saying, "Bangladesh passport? Not allowed. Are you Bangladeshi citizens? Get out." Even then the shameless Bangladeshi

Indian-loving politicians, journalists, and intellectuals would continue to slavishly worship India.

27. http://chintaa.com/index.php/chinta/showAerticle/401; http://www.natunbd.net/blog/blogdetail/detail/2601/muhon/81256
28. https://www.linkedin.com/pulse/disputed-heaven-earth-kashmir-syed-idrees; http://primenewsbd.com/index.php?page=details&nc=6&news_id=93556
29. https://groups.google.com/forum/#!topic/bangladesh-progressives/mgR24VVOQQI
30. https://nazmamustafa.wordpress.com/2016/09/14/2246/. Her articles are available at this link: https://nazmamustafa.wordpress.com/2017/02/14
31. The whole relevant passage in the English version of the book stands like this: "The Muslims do not vote for me. Muslims are unfaithful and ungrateful. The Hindus are loyal. I can rely on the Hindus and trust them. But I can't trust the Muslims. Nor can I rely on them. That's why I can contest from three seats in 70% Hindu dominated areas of Gopalganj and Bagerhat, but not even from one seat in Dhaka. Though I had decided to stand from Dhaka, I had to withdraw my nomination after I made queries and came to know that there are not many Hindus in Demra." Mayor of Dhaka Hanif said, that the idea was wrong. If the Muslims did not vote Awami League, how could its candidates win? Bangabandhu's daughter said, basically Awami League had the entire vote bank of the Hindus; the rest is made up by the relatives and sundry groups pressurized to vote in our favor. Had there been no Hindus, my party could not win even in a single seat. I have clinched this caretaker government after so much of movements and fights only to ensure that the Hindus could cast their votes safely and peacefully. Hindus are my strength. Hindus are my hope. The election campaign was progressing fast. Posters, placards, festoons, banners and wall writings were everywhere. There was hardly any empty spot. Meetings and processions were going on all the time." (http://amarfashichai.blogspot.co.uk).
32. Apart from the Rampal Power Plant, Quick Rental Power, and Arms purchase, there are many more, including the use of ports and other devastating and devouring Indian-dominated deals already done or being in the offing, see Dr Rezwan Siddiqui's, Zoglul Husain's, Rezaul Karim's and other relevant articles at: (1) http://www.thedailystar.net/frontpage/indias-proposed-defence-pact-dhaka-uneasy-1376179;

    (2) http://www.dailynayadiganta.com/detail/news/181499; (3) http://bangladesh-worldwide.com/কলাম/1233; http://bit.ly/2msXOlG; (4) http://deshbhabona.com/ফ্যাসিবাদ/2017/03/01/20/28; http://bangladeshworldwide.com/24-প্রচ্ছদ/1299;

    (5) http://deshbhabona.com/স্পটলাইট/2017/03/21/22/40;

    (6) http://www.thedailystar.net/backpage/govt-making-shady-arms-deals-stay-power-1338943;

    (7) http://www.jugantor.com/online/national/2016/12/07/33159; (8) http://www.jugantor.com/last-page/2017/01/04/90342;

    (9) http://rtnbd.net/national/16174;

(10) http://www.facebd.net/newsdetail/detail/49/265507;
(11) http://www.jugantor.com/online/national/2016/12/26/34863;
(12) http://www.jugantor.com/online/national/2017/02/16/39604;
(13) http://www.shokalerkhobor24.com/details.php?id=62579;
(14) http://www.scmp.com/week-asia/geopolitics/article/2075152/keener-arms-china-bangladesh-dithers-defence-pact-india;
(15) http://www.rarenews24.com/2017/02/23; (16) http://www.hindustantimes.com/india-news/new-delhi-eyes-big-defence-pact-with-bangladesh-during-pm-hasnia-s-april-visit/story-jSVUAb63nlFzbHFMzchi6O.html; (17) Hindustan Times report at: http://www.jugantor.com/online/national/2017/03/07/41405; (18) Dr Abdul Moeen Khan at: http://www.jugantor.com/online/politics/2017/03/07/41474; (19) Ahmed Atik at: https://www.dailyinqilab.com/article/68339; (20) Bakhtiar Uddin Chowdhury at: http://www.banglatribune.com/columns/opinion/187375; (21) Dr Tuhin Malik challenging Sheikh Hasina's untruthful claim on transit: http://www.natun-bd.net/newsdetail/detail/49/288977; (22) Ret Major Faruk at: https://wakeupbd.wordpress.com/tag/jumma;(23) Dr Badruddin Umar at: http://www.jugantor.com/sub-editorial/2017/03/19/110240/print; (24) Deepak Acharjee at: http://www.theindependentbd.com/post/85145; (25) Gautama Das at: http://durbiin.com/opinion/104; (26) Dr Asif Nazrul at: http://www.prothom-alo.com/opinion/article/1118965;
http://www.prothom-alo.com/bangladesh/article/1117264;
https://www.youtube.com/watch?v=cG0XGpZ_mp4; (27) Former diplomat Abdul Hannan at: http://www.thedailystar.net/perspective/do-we-really-need-defence-deal-india-1384450; (28) https://www.bdmilitary.com/bdmilitary-blog/defence-pact-india-detrimental-bangladesh;
(29) http://www.newsbangla.net/newsdetail/detail/200/296795; (30) Farhad Mazhar at: http://tazakhobor.net/bd/ltte/92775-2017-04-04-11-30-46; (31) Ebne Golam Samad at: http://www.dailynayadiganta.com/detail/news/209524; (32) Syed Iqram Shafee at: http://www.natunbd.net/blog/blogdetail/detail/11246/Iquram/81616; and (33) Shahid Islam at: http://www.weeklyholiday.net/Homepage/Pages/UserHome.aspx?ID=2&date=04/07/2017

33. http://www.banglatribune.com/business/news/160803
34. newsbd7.com/main/detail/2737;
http://www.facebd.net/newsdetail/detail/49/262949;
http://mynewsbd.net/?p=5989; http://mynewsbd.net/?p=5500; http://www.banglatribune.com/national/news/162323
35. http://rtnbd.net/binodon/18101;
http://www.eurobdnews.com/view/22225/;
http://webcache.googleusercontent.com/search?q=cache:http://bangla.moralnews24.com/archives/38716.html
36. http://bn.southasianmonitor.com/2017/03/13/5335. For Dr Asif Nazrul's comment, see: http://newsorgan24.com/detail/23578

37. http://www.prothom-alo.com/bangladesh/article/1030057/; http://www.banglatribune.com/columns/opinion/156615/; http://bangladeshism.com/tag/tv/; http://bangladeshism.com/2016/11
38. http://rtnbd.net/jati/20098
39. www.newsonbd.net/newsdetail/detail/200/323864
40. http://www.jugantor.com/online/national/2016/10/21/28340/print
41. http://ncbd.org/?author=1
42. http://www.bdmorning.com/desh/149492
43. http://www.jugantor.com/online/politics/2017/04/08/44179
44. Both Alexander the Great and Napoleon Bonaparte were not more than 5'6".
45. http://www.india.com/bengali/world/omg-now-indians-can-join-bangladesh-army/; http://fireservice.portal.gov.bd/sites/default/files/files/fireservice.portal.gov.bd/notices/a8406bdd_2381_4639_b83f_185d6b44d11c/IMG.jpg; http://www.karmakshetra.org/bd-army-sainik-recruitment/; http://www.bd-desh.net/newsdetail/detail/200/216048; http://amardeshonline.com/pages/details/2015/06/06/287350; http://www.rtnn.net/bangla//newsdetail/detail/1/3/111108; https://www.facebook.com/24newsbd/posts/773384342779511; https://www.facebook.com/sobarage/photos/a.144935832326130.31731.144504062369307/482489111904132/?type=3&theater
46. http://www.prothom-alo.com/bangladesh/article/927265
47. Syed Serajul Islam, "Bangladesh: Challenges of Democracy and Good Governance," a paper presented at Southwestern Social Sciences Conference at San Antonio, Texas, April 5, 2014.
48. E-mail, November 23, 2015.
49. http://newagebd.net/158623/did-bengali-nationalism-ever-exist/
50. See Farhan Sadik's report at http://newsorgan24.com/detail/10882, which was separately introduced by Zoglul Husain on another forum with the words: "Like the Balkanization plan of the Middle East and North Africa (MENA), Afghanistan, Pakistan, etc., there are plans for Balkanization of Bangladesh and Myanmar. The US, Israel and India have been working on these […] In Bangladesh, the US wants to carve out a portion in Chittagong division for a new state under its control and leave the entire rest of the country for India to colonize."
51. Mujib's 12-point agreement with India (March 19, 1972), to stay valid for 25 years, was very much like Tajuddin's 7-point agreement the previous year (and Mir Jaffar Ali Khan Bahadur's 12-point agreement with Maj Gen Robert Clive (June 3, 1757). All were unequal to the point of being servile and slavish. See: http://newsbd7.com/main/detail/2765. Also, Rifat-ul-Ahsan's *India-Bangladesh Relations : after 1971* at http://defenceforumindia.com/forum/threads/india-bangladesh-relations.4411/, from which the following is quoted:

There were many secret treaties signed between Indian Govt. and the exiled Bangladeshi Govt. during the liberation war. The points of infamous "Treaty of Subservience" or Seven point agreement are here;

1. Bangladesh government will select only those people for administrative posts who have actively participated in the liberation war and any shortfall therein will be filled by the Indian government officials.
2. A joint force will be formed comprising of the Indian army and the Mukti Bahini and this force will be placed under the command of the chief of staff of the Indian army who will lead the liberation war.
3. Bangladesh will have no standing army.
4. India will help raise a paramilitary force to protect the internal law and order of the country.
5. Open market will be the basis for trade relation between the two nations and this arrangement will be subject to periodical reviews.
6. The Indian army will be stationed in Bangladesh for an indefinite period of time, but the time frame for their gradual withdrawal will be determined through annual meetings between the two governments.
7. Bangladesh will formulate its foreign policy only in consultation with India. Source: Dr Kalidas Baiddya, Bangalir Muktijudher Antoraler Sheikh Mujib, pp. 166–167.

Journalist Oliullah Noman of the now suppressed popular Amar Desh, now living in exile in the UK, wrote about this 7-point agreement and Kalidas Baiddya's views of it: https://www.rbn24.co.uk/?p=6353. Look at the number 7: Tajuddin's 7-point agreement, sadly melancholy Jacques's 7 ages/stages of man in Shakespeare's As You Like It, and the medieval 7 deadly/cardinal sins.

52. For the principles and fundamentals of RAW, visit: http://www.anandabazar.com/photogallery/unknown-facts-about-raw-dgtl-1.368534#. For the bloody and murderous history of the Awami-BAKSALi *Rakkhi-Bahini*, who killed about 30,000 Bangladeshis, please see https://en.wikipedia.org/wiki/Jatiya_Rakkhi_Bahini. They were a reincarnation of Maximilien Robespierre's "Jacobin" Reign of Terror in France, July 1793–July 1794 when he and his henchmen were responsible for the guillotining of many innocent people.
53. https://www.facebook.com/kay.kavus/posts/444012405780649
54. Taj Hashmi, "Ziaur Rahman, Islam and Bangladeshi Nationalism," https://groups.yahoo.com/neo/groups/ saldwr/conversations/messages/710

12

Secularism in Bangladesh

Questions of Politicocultural and Religious Conflict

Following the directly related previous chapter, this chapter, the longest, contends that secularism in the Muslim majority Bangladesh actually means freedom and promotion of all other religions except Islam, which, according to the US-based Pew Research Centre, will be the largest religion in the world by 2070. Muslims in Bangladesh by and large perceive that there is a guiding restraint and a slow demotion of their religion and its gradual displacement educationally, academically, and institutionally. While the dogmatic Muslim-named and Muslim-born secularists cry foul against their own Muslim identity, out of their ignorance and lack of understanding, and their obvious inferiority complex, they are quiet about the rise of Hindu extremism at home and abroad, especially India where, according to Aakar Patel, most extremists are Hindus, not Muslims, and the media has mistakenly identified terrorism with Islam.[1]

Depending on rural or urban areas and family values and orientations, Bangladesh is a conservative to moderate to extremely free, open, and secular (Muslim majority) country. Except a few city quarters (where the bawdy Dhallywood dalliances and deviations are spreading like an infectious disease and the ডানাকাঁটা Shompa Rezas feel proud of having had a background of living with dozens of dogs and puppies in a Hindu household), the people of Bangladesh are generally pious, peace-loving, and God-fearing, feeling the talk of secularism, since 1972 (not before), as a barrier, an impediment, or even an impeachment of their faith. They would not like to descend into a religion without the notion of the existence of one and only God, as Islamically or monotheistically understood.

Secularism has its God-less extreme forms. It is, by all accounts, "Secularism and Its Evil Effects," as goes the title of a booklet by Muhammad Shaker Al-Sharief. A scholarly essay by Dr Firoz Mahboob Kamal of the UK considers the "Terrorism of the Secularist Fascists and the Unending War" in depth and detail.[2] That is the practical reality precipitated by the radical secularist sections of Bangladesh's otherwise religiously practicing harmonious society. As Dr Taj Hashmi of Austin Peay University Tennessee claims, secularism, like socialism,

> [...] was a very remote issue during the Liberation War of 1971, at least among the hoi polloi [the masses, the common people] who supported, helped and fought for Bangladesh [...]. It was like a still-born child, dead before it was even born. Later, many supporters of Mujib turned into "Islam-loving" mainly out of frustration and apprehensions about secularism and socialism, which incidentally did not restore their cherished *Sonar Bangla* or Bengal of Gold.

Hashmi's rhetorical questions themselves imply the answers:

> Are not Bangladeshi politicians, including those belonging to "secular" AL and paradoxically to the Communist Party, raising Islamic slogans and adopting Islamic symbols—"Allah is Most Powerful" being used in the AL banners—to come closer to the average Bangladeshi Muslim voter? The honest answers would be in the affirmative. One may highlight the fact that on the eve of the 1996 Parliamentary Elections, Sheikh Hasina in all her public appearances in rallies, press and TV interviews appeared in a ubiquitous black hijab (never seen before being used by educated Bangladeshi women) and full-sleeved blouse, holding prayer beads in her hand. She successfully used these "Islamic" symbols to get elected as the Prime Minister. Are all these symbolic and socio-politically significant Islamic gestures and regulations [...].[3]

However, the ultra-liberal secularists see Islam and Muslims as "the other," the same way the medieval Christian crusaders did. Calling each such secularist a Donald Trump, film maker Mostafa Sarwar Farooki describes them as fundamentalists of their own kind.[4] That the idea of "fundamentalism" or "a fundamentalist" is highly relative and contextual, to be determined case by case, is demonstrated by the fact that the West Bengal "fundamentalist" Hindu writer Moloy Rai Chowdhury called all Bangladeshi publishers "fundamentalist" just because there were no books by him available at the Ekushey Book Fair (2017) at Bangla Academy Dhaka.[5]

The fantastically liberated ultra-secularists engage in anti-Muslim polemics using their retarded and retrograde intellectualism to establish misconceptions and distortions about the 1,500 years of Islamic civilization. One does not have to renounce one's religious beliefs and degenerate into God-less atheism to become a radical and freethinking being falsely and mistakenly known in Bengali as মুক্তমনা of মুক্তচিন্তা. Weren't the thousands of prophetic guides and preachers of Islam, Judaism, Christianity, and Buddhism, including Socrates, Confucius, and the Dalai Lama, profoundly মুক্তমনা people endowed with the highest kind of মুক্তচিন্তা and মুক্তচেতনা?

Kind, charitable, loving, just, fair, strong, and impartial, didn't those great minds set up or tried to set up a religion-based system and a culture of religious ethos for the emancipation of humankind from the clutches of dark superstitions? Just as all systems and civilizations go through an evolving process—cyclical (spiral or gyre-like), linear or conical—they, as advocates of different religions and beacons of hope, launched different guiding principles and civilizations and had their own evolutionary process. If an atheist or a libertine dislikes a practicing believer and then distorts or misinterprets his religious views and beliefs, how can he be called a freethinking মুক্তমনা? Why does one have to renounce only Islamic religious faith to be included on the list of so-called প্রগতিশীল progressives, while the fanatical and fundamentalist believers in Christianity, Buddhism, Hinduism, and all kinds of sexual (LGBT) orientation be given a clean bill of belonging to the same list without qualms?[6]

Does one have to go back to the time of Prophet Lut/Lot (peace be upon him) and be a male or female homosexual and get involved in the same sex attraction to be named a so-called modern প্রগতিশীল (progressive)? No way. Never. Why to have another Sodom and another Gomorrah only to be turned into another Dead Sea as a retribution for homosexuality? What an inverted and upended definition of a so-called প্রগতিশীল? This is a clear contradiction in inverse proportion, a crab-like crawling through a back channel conduit. Why to do what even the insects and animals do not do? Why to engage in a relationship that no religion—modern or tribal or ancient/aborigines—ever permits? Why can't the gays and lesbians be straight and hetero and normal, attracted to what is heavenly and beautiful and paradisiacal and irresistible to each other? Why not be an Adam to an Eve and vice versa, as natural companions and counterparts to each other? Why to get engaged in self-abuse and be pervert and disgusting and disgraceful only to test HIV positive and get infected with the virus of other incurable diseases, to be shunned by the civilized society, instead of being sympathetic to? God's world belongs to the blessed heterosexuals and so it should stay clean and free of the cursed homos, who are to be discouraged and demotivated and talked out of it.

If a disbeliever attacks the faith and practice of a believer, a believer also, as a human being of flesh and blood, having all kinds of emotions, would be prompted to react the same way, but only to be vilified, unfairly though, as a non-মুক্তমনা. It seems as if discarding everything enlightened, institutionalized, and systematized and being an anarchical epicurean pagan hedonist are preconditions for being a *মুক্তমনা.*, Such a being is in fact very likely to lapse into a stagnant and close minded বদ্ধমনা. Like the terms of "reform" and "reformists," which are not welcome to many in the recent political culture of Bangladesh (depending on who you ask), *মুক্তমনা* also is viewed as and has in fact deteriorated into a term of irritation, allergy, suspicion, and embarrassment, not well-liked by the concerned quarters. Since no human can ever rise above biases and every human has his traditional, cultural and religious prejudices, none can ever claim to be a *মুক্তমনা*, unless one is divinely illumined or endowed with the light of prophethood. However, the minimum a *মুক্তমনা* can do is to believe and engage in a bi- or multilateral সংলাপ (dialogue) with all the representative parties to solve the problems facing the nation today.

In their all-out crusading *jihad* against Islam, the zealous secularists are like the ultra-feminists, who would like to expand the role of women and their persons to the exclusion of men and see everything as a mere tool of male domination or a mechanism for female subordination, just as the Marxists see everything in the frame of class struggle and economic exploitation. Out of their ill-found infatuation with cultural anarchy, the so-called Bangladeshi *মুক্তমনা* secularists are more excited about the controversial aspects of Western and Hindu culture more than their Western cohorts themselves.

For example, they are thrilled about the sensual boyfriend-girlfriend dating relationships, the so-called first and second crushes, the Valentine's Day (February 14, which the pious and religious community calls a বেহায়াপনা Day),[7] the New Year's Eve (December 31st/January 1st), হোলি, মঙ্গল শোভাযাত্রা and similar other occasions in an overwhelmingly mundane and humdrum pleasantry. This areligious and sublunary অপসংস্কৃতি (bad and black culture) "creeps in this petty pace," as Macbeth's tomorrows do and, like his yesterdays, lights "fools/The way to dusty death." This sort of decadent and degenerated culture is being recently promoted, apart from the sexually saturated and phallus-oriented films and the sensually unsocial scenes in some TV serials, by two light, useless, dull, and drab television shows in Bangladesh: Late Night Coffee (LNC) on RTV and আমি এখন কি করবো (AEKK) on Bangla Vision. These shows are as unimpressive as the not so good looking "vision" behind the eye-glasses of the hosts and news casters of some other

TV channels of the "time." Shows like LNC and AEKK are given to encouraging premarital and extramarital relationships with a destructive effect on the family and friends and their religious and moral values.

The secularist charade is a show off of their fetish-like fashionable Bungalee মুক্তচেতনা orientation and their unfounded trepidation about Islam. They should know that their futile "infidel" status will take them nowhere near the unorthodox freethinkers such as Rousseau, Voltaire, Mirabaud, Volney, Tom Paine, Carlyle, Ruskin, Orwell or Russell. On the other hand, they may like to remember what John F Kennedy said in his famous 1961 inaugural speech, in reference to *mortal* man's *power* and the debatable *revolutionary* beliefs, that "the rights of man come not from the generosity of the state, but from the hand of God."

Can Bangladesh, therefore, ensure equal social and economic justice for all, including the minorities, and still be officially and practically a great Muslim country, because secularism is grossly abused by promoting other religions and anti-Islamic forces/elements and demoting and suppressing Islamic culture and values in the Muslim majority Bangladesh? Like the Hindu, Christian, Buddhist, and Jewish countries all over, which bear the broad stamp of their respective religions, can Bangladesh remain mainly an Islamic/Muslim country in its ethos, spirit, and orientation without diluting its Islamic tradition and culture and at the same time properly taking care of its minority interests? Why not? Why should the wrong notion of secularism and its widespread abusive practices replace, displace, and substitute the Islamic environment in a Muslim majority country, religion being the deepest bond and the greatest impulse in the human soul by all means?

Islamic civilization and culture: a brief survey

Spanning from North and West and East Africa to the entire Middle East,[8] Muslim Spain and Sicily, Muslim Constantinople (Istanbul) and Ottoman (Osmanli) Turkey, Safavid Persia, Afghanistan, Pakistan, Mughal India, entire Central Asia, South Asia and South East Asia, Islam is a civilization that immensely contributed during the Middle Ages to the making of the scientific world—astronomical, astrological, mathematical, geographical, medical, legal, architectural, philosophical and cultural. Islamic culture was at the forefront of modernization from the 8th to 15th century when its contributions gave rise to the European Renaissance. Going beyond translating the works of their Greek, Roman, Persian/Iranian, and Indian predecessors, Arabic-speaking Muslim scientists reached new heights in the knowledge of many new disciplines. The first universities of the world were established in

Morocco and Cairo, about a century and a half before there was Oxford in 1096 and two hundred years before there was Cambridge in 1210. Like the themes of the annually held RIS (Reviving Islamic Spirit) conferences in North America, the theme of the 11th annual (2005) Islamic Awareness Week (IAW) in England was *1000 Years of Britain in Islam*. It suggests that Islam's British connections are historically long standing. As recently reported by CNN and the New York Times, a hand written copy of the Qur'an (or at least part of it), thought to belong to the time of Prophet Muhammad in the 7th century and as such perhaps the oldest copy ever, has been discovered at the library of the University of Birmingham.[9]

Abelard of Bath, tutor to Henry II (1154–1189), is known for translating many important Greek and Arabic scientific works from Arabic into Latin, which were then introduced to Western Europe. Salim Al-Hassani's classic *1001 Inventions: The Enduring Legacy of Muslim Civilization* (National Geographic: Washington, D.C., 2012; 1st ed. 2006) chronicles the great contributions of the Muslim Middle Ages. The Arabic and Oriental studies dedicated Dutch publisher Brill's publication of its first Arabic text in 1732—an edition of Ibn Shaddad's 12th century biography of Saladin, its monumental and multigenerational, still ongoing magnum opus, the *Encyclopedia of Islam*, that started at the end of the 19th century, R. P. A Dozy's standard *History of the Spanish/Moorish Muslims* (1861), and the late 19th-century publication of a 16-volume *History of the Prophets and Kings*, which, actually a translation of a 9th century Persian manuscript about the Middle East, took 14 Arabists from six countries to complete, are some of the testimonies to the enduring legacy and impact of Islam.[10]

No one should forget the historical fact that after they retook the Muslim "Moorish" Andalusia (Southern Spain), which had produced hundreds of Muslim scholars, writers, and scientists during hundreds of years, Spanish Christians burnt more than one million books by Muslims in Granada toward the close of the 15th century. It was about the same time that the Europeans led by the Italian poet and "humanist" Petrarch banned all Arabic/Islamic sources of knowledge from their academic courses and threw out all such books from the shelves at the seats of higher learning. However, nearly two hundred years later, Oliver Cromwell and his contemporaries are said to have known the basic tenets of the Qur'an. Arabic texts are thought to have been frequently available at the universities of Oxford and Cambridge since the 17th century. Thomas Jefferson, since his days as a law student, had a copy of the Qur'an in what was the first popular translation (1734) by George Sale, also a lawyer. This speaks a lot about the American president's legacy of religious freedom and pluralism.[11] He found the Qur'an useful as he wanted to broaden the base of his legal studies.

In his attempt to do so, Jefferson also studied the standard work on comparative law of his time, *Of the Law of Nature and Nations* (1672), by Samuel von Pufendorf. The German scholar made numerous references to Islam and the Qur'an, some of course in criticism, expected of a European, but some in approval, especially those related legal precedents. He cited "the Qur'an's emphasis on promoting moral behavior, its proscription of games of chance and its admonition to make peace between warring countries." Keeping with Pufendorf, Sale, in his preface, wrote:

> If the religious and civil Institutions of foreign nations are worth our knowledge, those of Mohammed, the lawgiver of the Arabians, and founder of an empire which in less than a century spread itself over a greater part of the world than the Romans were ever masters of, must needs be so.

Sale described the Prophet of Islam as:

> [...] richly furnished with personal endowments, beautiful in person, of a subtle wit, agreeable behavior, showing liberality to the poor, courtesy to everyone, fortitude against his enemies, and, above all, a high reverence for the name of God. (For the above quotes, see Prange in *SAW*).

The findings of the two scholars, one German and one English, foreshadowed that of the present UN Secretary General Antonio Guterres, of socialist background, who was Prime Minister of Portugal (1995–2002) and the United Nations High Commissioner for Refugees from 2005 to 2015, and who said in his commencement remarks at Naif Arab University, "All the principles embodied in modern international refugee law are to be found in the Shari'ah. Protection of refugees, their property and families, non-refoulement [forced return], the civilian character of asylum, voluntary repatriation—all are referred to in the Holy Koran."[12] Those tolerant, pro-Islamic and friendly findings also foreshadowed those of Edward Gibbon, Johann Wolfgang Goethe, Edmund Burke, Thomas Carlyle, Leo Tolstoy, Ivan Bunin, Jean-Jacques Rousseau, Rainer Maria Rilke, Oswald Spengler, Bernard Shaw, Mahatma Gandhi, Bertrand Russell, and Justin Trudeau. Theirs was an attitude of respect, appreciation, and admiration for the religion of Islam, in contradistinction, of course, with the poets, writers, and philosophers of the deeply held religious (Christian—Catholic, Protestant, Puritan) beliefs such as Gower, Langland, Chaucer, Shakespeare, Spenser, Browne, Jonson, Donne, Descartes, Pascal, Milton, Swift, Dryden, Pope, Wordsworth, Coleridge, Browning, Hopkins, C. S. Lewis, Graham Greene, T. S. Eliot and Claude McKay. However, all of them would metaphorically hold the so-called "liberated" (actually uprooted) ultra-secularists hardly holding any religious faith—falcons who cannot hear the falconer—as perhaps belonging to the category of "hollow and stuffed men," in the language of Eliot.

Although some Western poets, writers, and politicians such as Dante, Spenser, Voltaire, H. G. Wells, Salman Rushdie, Donald Trump, David Duke, Nigel Farage, Marie Le Pen, and Geert Wilders expressed their unfounded dislike of Islam and Muslims, it is the great and glorious aspects of Islam that made countless Western thinkers and public intellectuals write favorably about Islam. In addition to the above (that is, Gibbon, Goethe, Rousseau, Burke, Coleridge, Carlyle, Tolstoy, Bunin, Rilke, Shaw, Gandhi, Russell, Spengler, Trudeau), Edgar Allan Poe, Edward Lane, Jewish-born Leopold Weiss (of Austro-Hungarian-Ukrainian origin), Richard Burton, Harry St. John/Jack Philby, T. E. Lawrence, Marmaduke Pickthall, Martin Lings, French philosopher René Guénon, Malcolm X, A. J. Arberry, T. B. Irving, William Quilliam, Edward Said, film directors (Jack Shaheen, Anglo-American Ovidio Salazar, and Tudor Payne), Swiss-British Charles Gai Eaton, Cat Stevens, Imran Golding, Mark Hanson, Ricky Mitchell, Dennis Bradley Philips, Pierre Vogel, Alexis York Lumbard, Cambridge University Professor Timothy Winter, London University Electrical Engineering Professor Arthur Alison, French medical scientist Dr Maurice Bucaille, Canadian professor and preacher Dr Gary Miller, Leiden University Professor Christiaan Snouck Hurgronje, English explorer and adventurer Sir Wilfred Patrick Thesiger, world famous photographer Peter Sanders, French film director Isabelle Matic, Hollywood actress Lindsay Lohan, Indian poet Kamala Suraiyya Das, prominent Indian Hindu personality and Oxford graduate Mahant Dr Shri Shakti Saroopji Maharaj Adasin Dharmachariya Odai Shakti (who is now known as Dr Islamul Haq), Aminah Assilmi (born Janice Huff and formerly an American Southern Baptist), British ambassador to Saudi Arabia Simon Collis, American woman Lisa Shanklin (originally Catholic Christian), Melvin Abdul Malik Leblanc, Bangladeshi politician Maj (Ret) M A Jalil, and singer Nokul Kumar Biswas, Tony Blair, Lauren Booth (Blair's sister-in-law), and American pop singer Janet Jackson—all either made wonderful remarks, or developed their social and political philosophies, or established Islamic institutions and wrote numerous narratives and scholarly commentaries (including several biographies of the prophet and translations of the Qur'an), praising the religion of Islam and admiring the greatness of its prophet.[13]

Sometimes some Eastern emperors too, such as the 13th century Mongol-Chinese emperor Kubla Khan and his naval chief Admiral Zheng-He expressed a great understanding of Islam with the latter becoming a Muslim indeed. While

Goethe, Tolstoy, Rilke, and Burton, after their awakening experience and realization, were about to embrace Islam and became near-Muslims, Zheng-He, Lane, Weiss, Pickthall, Lings, Guenon, Salazar, Payne, Winter, Hurgronje, Sanders, Philby, Quilliam, Arberry, Irving, Eaton, Stevens, Hanson, Philips, Mitchell, Lumbard, Matic, Alison, Shanklin, Miller, Bucaille, Leblanc, Indian poet Kamala Suraiyya (formerly Kamala Das), Indian guru Shakti Saroopji, Collis, Huff, and Jackson—all reverted/converted to Islam, most of them performing pilgrimages to Mecca, changing to Muslim names and taking Muslim women as their spouses.[14]

Spengler included the great contribution of Islam and Muslim philosophers in his civilizational tables. Burke admired the notion of accountability in the Muhammedan Law. Poe and Rilke were inspired by the Qur'an and the angels of Islamic tradition. Rousseau praised the idea of responsible freedom and social contract as depending upon submission to the general will as enshrined in Islam. Coleridge drew up a failed plan to write an epic about Prophet Muhammad and Carlyle wrote a long essay on Muhammad as a hero in the field of religion. Michael Hurt described the Prophet as "Supremely Successful" in his book, *The Hundred*. In the view of the historian William Montgomary Watt, the Prophet of Islam was the "Best Child of the prophet Adam." According to the liberal Roman Catholic English writer Karen Armstrong, Prophet Mohammad was the best creative genius ever in the world. Visiting Baghdad in 1932 and speaking about the Hindu-Muslim conflict in his own country, poet Rabindranath Tagore called on his Arab hosts to "resend" to India the universalist message of their prophet to rescue the Indian subcontinent from whatever tension it had owing to narrow-minded bigotry there.[15] By the way, "America becomes the country with most conversion rate. Approximately, about 20,000 people embraced Islam after 9/11 due to hate speech against Muslims."

Un-Holi (unholy) and a-*Mangal* অমঙ্গল secularization of Islam and the Muslim-bashing secularist bigots and blockheads in Bangladesh

Not sufficiently educated about their own religion, the fundamentalist Hindus such as the secret group called সনাতন[16] and their cohorts and surrogates in the ultra-liberals in Bangladesh allow their one-sided liberalism and short-sighted secularism to degenerate into atheism or near atheism—itself an expression of extremism. Ignorant about the revealed knowledge of the sacred and the sublime, the secularist morons do not even know how to apply Blaise Pascal's wager that belief in God/*Allah* the Almighty is rational and that "If God does not exist, one will lose nothing by believing in Him, while if He does exist, one will lose everything by not believing." Despite being Muslim themselves either in name or by birth or both, they allow their secularism to translate into an active and loud support for all other religions and religious rituals and celebrations except the Islamic. This is the concern expressed by one of the liberation heroes of Bangladesh, Nur-e-Alam Siddiquee, who is a great nonsectarian political leader.

Citing Siddiquee, former Director-General of the Ministry of Foreign Affairs and Bangladesh Ambassador to Japan, Serajul Islam, wrote about the menacing impact of the rising *Hinduized* secularism and *Hindutva* in the Muslim majority Bangladesh with much ado. He did so with reference to মঙ্গল শোভাযাত্রা *Mangal Shovajatra* (MS) procession of masks and floats that is saturated with Hindu Durga-Devi elements and that coincides with *Chaitra Sankranti*, which is the last day of the year on the Bengali calendar and the পহেলা বৈশাখ *Pahela Baishakh*, the Bengali New Year that falls on April 14.[17] Like the festivals of the Hindu *Holi* (that falls around early March), বসন্তবরণ বসন্তবন্দনা বর্ষবরণ and বৈশাখী বন্দনা (Bengali New Year), all full of wild and rowdy fun and frolic, the *MS* is a secular folk festival in origin, suffused with Hindu elements, in serious conflict with Islam. Cultural programs of বসন্ত and বৈশাখী occasions can be held in a somewhat scaled down manner and need not be overdone and overblown as they currently are, in contradiction with the Muslim milieu of *mahfil* and *mua'melat*.

The tradition of the *MS* symbolizes, in the view of anti-Islamic secularists, the effort of the people to drive away the evil and sinister forces and allow for what they call "progress". It was unfortunately begun by some teachers and students of Dhaka University's hyper Hinduized Fine Arts Faculty in 1989. As if it is already an Indian/Hindustani corner in the independent and sovereign Muslim majority Bangladesh, beef has been forbidden in the said faculty as it was also the case at the last Awami League Council meeting in Dhaka in the excess of reverence for the few Indian Hindu guests attending the Convention. The *MS* has now been recognized, again unfortunately, by the UNESCO in 2016 as an event of cultural heritage of global/international appeal. Also, unfortunately, the Hasina government has shockingly ordered all educational institutions to mark the same on the occasion of the Bengali New Year, to the hurt of the Muslim sentiment.[18] A freedom fighter in 1971 and a great political intellectual, Zoglul Husain of the UK, contends that to force Muslims to take part in the *MS* is to force them to embrace Hinduism.[19] Noyon Chatterjee, Oliullah Noman, and Tarequl Islam not only list the elements of Hindu idolatry that impregnate the *MS*, but also trace the history of its origin in the idolatrous Hindu tradition.[20]

What Muslims believe is that more of those celebrations means more গ্লানি (suffering, insult, harassment), more জরা (stasis and stagnation), more পাপ (sins and crimes), more কঙ্কাল, more কেলেঙ্কারি (rubbish, corruption, scandals), and more জঞ্জাল (chaos, complications, disturbances) and দজ্জাল (deceiving antichrist and false messiah) in a Muslim country. Far from being cleansed, all those dirts and filths are in fact on the rise. In dress and style, all these celebrations belong to Hindu culture and Hindu ritual in a Muslim country, just as the Kolkata-centered Bungalee nationalism means Hindu nationalism, as well argued by M R Akhtar Mukul in his book called, in English, *Kolkata-Centered Intellectuals* (Dhaka: Anonnya Publications, 2014, pp. 29–31). Why not shun the anti-Muslim cultural invasion and infiltration, vulgarly commercialized and extremely secularist (similar to the negative "Islamist," "populist" and "fundamentalist" and different from the positive "secular," "popular" and "Islamic')? Why not avoid such materialistic processions and gatherings, empty of consequential meanings and substance? It is to the same effect that Ranu Chowdhury, in an e-mail post of August 24, 2015, writes:

> I believe in religious freedom for any faith of any denomination. Yet, I cannot reconcile why a country with 90% people belonging to one faith needs to "enshrine" secularism in its constitution. Is there any such example anywhere in the world? … As a layman, I find the use of "secularism" in Bangladesh is for two purposes. First, to give special benefit to a minority group that represents less than 8% of population. We see the evidence lately in the form of its members' presence in the administration, particularly in key sectors, and, of course, at the cost of the majority. The second is for undermining the Islamic values, as well as for "Islam Bashing." […] If an individual prefers to remain secular, or even a non-believer, it is his business. But his personal likes or dislikes should not interfere in state business, nor could he have the license to ridicule one's faith.

Chowdhury thinks (as he put in an e-mail of November 30, 2016) that MS type observances are no more than টিপ্, উলুধ্বনি, ঢোলকড়া, উৎসব উদযাপনের নামে বিভিন্ন বেলেল্লপনা ও অসামাজিক কর্মকান্ড। In yet another e-mail post of June 7, 2016, he says: "Apartheid has been dismantled long time ago. It is reappearing in Bangladesh. A minority of 8% is overtaking the administration of the rest 92%. This is Awami *চেতনা* (spirit) and Secular Unnoti/উন্নতি (development) that the illegal fascist regime never tires of selling and reselling to the bewildered and muted people!" One can take the argument further by saying that the spirit (চেতনা) of liberation has been subject to its politically motivated and increasingly marketed commodification, compartmentalization and commercialization.

When the hibernating Islamic forces (*Huzurs* and *Hefajotes* and *Khelafots* and Imams and *Allamas* and *Qaomis* and *Aliyas* and *Tablighees*) are quiet and idle and passive, complacent with whatever little they are doing, every day will be turned into a day of MS, violating the monotheistic faith, to their defeat, frustration and humiliation. English poet Tennyson imagines that the mighty and mysterious legendary sea monster Kraken sleeping on the floor of the Arctic sea for ages and centuries would become pathetically useless as it would die upon its waking up and coming up to the surface possibly due to the rise in the sea temperature (perhaps foreshadowing today's global warming/climate change).

By virtue of being the last monotheistic religion and having immense and endless amount of literature about it, Islam is obviously a vast field of knowledge and learning, perhaps more than any other religion in the world. Pompous and regressive as they are, the ultra-secularists would outwardly pretend to take a shortcut of separating all worldly affairs from the spiritual and the hereafter but would actually spare no pains to promote any religion (such as Hinduism, Buddhism, Christianity, Judaism, Confucianism and Zoroastrianism) other than Islam, boasting and bragging about their role in advancing the cause of all other religions *sans* Islam. They stop at nothing to stop Islam and go all the way to discourage and disconnect from the practice and propagation of Islam. Humayun Ahmed, the most famous and popular writer of Bangladesh, said it all about the spiritually bottomless baskets of the anti-Islamic infidel আঁতেলs and their domestic animal type bandwagon.[21]

Similarly, by বাঙালী *Bungalee* and/or Bangladeshi culture, the self-declared and free-fall ultras mean all cultures—Indian, Christian, Hindu, Buddhist—except Muslim culture, which is mischievously and deviously eschewed and edged out from the equation. Muslim culture has been a great part of the *Bungalee* and/or Bangladeshi culture and literature. As part of the larger design of secularist suppression, the secularists ignore many writers for their pro-Islamic sympathies. Writers of Islamic bent have been sidelined and marginalized by the secularist forces due to their Muslim/Islamic leanings.

Where is the বাঙালী Muslim culture in today's Bangladesh as represented, in literature alone, by Shah Muhammad Sagir (late 14th/early 15th century), Syed Sultan (1550–1648), Alaol (1607–1673), Abdul Hakim (1620–1690), 18th-century poet Hayat Mamud, Mir Mosharraf Hossain (1847–1912), Kaikobad (1857–1951), Abdul Karim Sahittya Bisharad (1869–1953), Syed Ismail Hossain Siraji (1880–1931), Begum Rokeya (1880–1932), Syed Emdad Ali (1880–1956), Qazi Imdadul Haq (1882–1926), Yakub Ali Chowdhury (1888–1940), Mohammad Lutfur Rahman (1889–1936), S. Wajed Ali (1890–1951), Principal

Ibrahim Kha' (1894–1978), Golam Mostafa (1897–1964), Abul Mansour Ahmad (1898–1979); Jasimuddin (1903–1976), Benazir Ahmed (born 1903), Syed Mujtaba Ali (1904–1974); Bande Ali Mia (1906–1979), Abdul Kadir (1906–1984), Ahsan Habib (1917–1985), Farrukh Ahmad (1918–1974), Kazi Kader Newaz (1909–1983), Shawkat Osman (1917–1998), Talim Hussein (1918–1999), Syed Ali Ahsan (1922–2002), Kazi Din Muhammad (1927–2011), Al Mahmud and many more?[22]

In the un-Islamic secularist culture of a few media and political circles in Bangladesh, Awami Muslim League became Awami League (AL); Jahangirnagar Muslim University, Jahangirnagar University; Fazlul Hoque Muslim Hall, Fazlul Hoque Hall; Salimullah Muslim Hall, Salimullah Hall; Islamic Intermediate College, Kovi Nazrul Islam College and then only Kovi Nazrul College; Law and Muslim Jurisprudence Department, only Law Department; and the national poet Kazi Nazrul Islam, only Kazi Nazrul, with the "problematic" and "troubling" "Muslim" or "Islam" dropped from everywhere. As shown in the links provided in Note #45, there is a systematic attempt to erase, occlude, and obliterate Muslim culture from what is an absolutely Muslim majority Bangladesh.

Even the Arabic/Muslim/Islamic name of God—*Allah*—His best and most proper name, has been secularized, to the embarrassment of the believing and practicing Muslims. Allah the Almighty is called স্রষ্টা সৃষ্টিকর্তা উপরওয়ালা (Creator or one whose abode is above in the skies). Though Muslim themselves (probably only in name, not in faith and practice), the so-called "secularist," "modern" and "liberal" artists and intellectuals would like to avoid calling Allah the Almighty as *Allah*. Their myopic and monolithic secularism makes them suffer from their moral bankruptcy and inferiority complex. It makes them distance from their own Islamic culture and tradition, and come dangerously close to whatever is Hindu and Indian under the leadership of Hindu fundamentalist parties, BJP and RSS, led by PM Narendra Modi, firebrand Hindu priest and Chief Minister of Uttar Pradesh, Yogi Adityanath, and the furious Mohan Madhukar Bhagawat, who are all filled with hatred for Islam and Muslims and are suffused and saturated with the image of *Hinduvta*, to the extent of calling for the rape of dead Muslim women.[23] These Indian Hindu leaders are about to reveal their parties' venomous religious agenda soon.[24]

Referring to the extremist secularists, Zoglul Husain says: "They are against anything Muslim. They use 'secularism' as their mask or mantle to actually propagate their anti-Islamic crusade and false propaganda and to introduce pro-Hindu culture. To them the words, ভগবান ঈশ্বর, are safely secular/ist, whereas the word *Allah* is জঙ্গী (militant) fundamentalist and Islamist!"[25] Many of them are even hired by the Judeo-Christian lobby to write against Islam.[26] As if ashamed of uttering the name of *Allah*, they feel more comfortable to indirectly address or refer to *Allah* in their Bengali vernacular and thereby vandalize and vulgarize the Almighty's most proper name. It is to be mentioned that *Allah* is a name that has the same semantic root as one of the Old Testament words for God, both the Muslim holy scripture of the Qur'an and the Jewish Old Testament being written in the same Semitic family of languages.

By doing what they do, extremist secularist elements let themselves to be pitiably diminished and terribly downgraded.[27] One example is Mita Hoque, who, in an utter hurt and insult to the religious sentiment of the teeming Muslim millions of Bangladesh, expressed her blockheaded bigotry by saying that those (men and women) who either had a beard and a cap or who wore a headscarf could be anything but Bungalee/Bangladeshi. She is still at large without being taken any action against by the Hasina government. And she is only one of a negligible few of her kind in Bangladesh.

Radical secularists and their likes in the Hinduized and Hindu-loving Islamophobes fall short of being pagan and polytheistic in their frigidly frowning ways about Islam, Muslims, and Islamic traditions, rituals, and culture. Theirs is an aggressively regressive and backward looking rationalism, far from being a progressive liberalism. Mask (মুখোশ) and মূর্তি (statue) and অমঙ্গল secularists are tediously tied to the hedonist, idolatrous, hooded and wooded, and primeval wildlife Hindu culture at the expense of their own Islamic identity, which can only be maintained by associating it with the eternally liberating Islamic fundamentals. A great politician like Nur-e-Alam Siddiquee, a great intellectual like Dr Salimullah Khan, a great writer and singer like Mustafa Zaman Abbasi, a great thinker and columnist like Farhad Mazhar, and a great academic and writer like Ebne Golam Samad have expressed their serious reservations and strong oppositions to the মূর্তি and অমঙ্গল culture currently engulfing and billowing out Bangladesh under the Hasina regime.[28] People of a country of 90% Muslims must not fail to understand that all this মূর্তি and অমঙ্গল culture is an encouragement to the Hindus, secularists, atheists, liberals, and ultra-liberals, that displaces and pushes the religion of the majority into the corner, and that has the long term goal of erasing and occluding Islam and paving the way for Bangladesh to turn into a Hindu dominated country, which in some ways it already is under the Hasina regime.

Bengali cultural festivals in the Muslim Bangladesh have all been reduced to idolatrous and primeval fun and frolic suffused and saturated with Hindu elements as if, as pointed out by Dr Rashed Anam of the USA in an e-mail post of April 14, 2017, those festivals have to be celebrated as only Hindu rituals, divorced from and antithetical to Islamic ethos and ethics. Why can't the people of Bangladesh observe those occasions in an Islamically compatible way? There must be a coalescing and convergence of Bangladeshi Muslim forces to exert a concerted effort to thwart the increasing Hinduization of Bangladesh, especially in the form of pagan and polytheistic বন্য অরণ্য অমঙ্গল masks and মূর্তি mantras.

ধিক ধিক Away, away! with the extreme and excessive display and demonstration of the idolatrous Hindu stuff. People of Bangladesh need to come together to do away with (and to say যাক যাক to) the un-and-anti Islamic evil procession in the name of the masked *MS*, which actually invites more jungle অমঙ্গল (more অশুভ in the form of more disunity, more division) than true মঙ্গল (শুভ, good), and which, in the context of a land of monotheistic believers, is actually worse than the Brazilian samba carnival and closer to the ludicrous LGBT parades.

Instead of wearing the Halloween-type animal mask (মুখোশ), the মন্ত্র অমঙ্গল secularists may arrange an animal rights procession—more legit and valid in the context of the broader green, environmental, and ecological movement. When the Sundarbans and its wildlife are facing a demise and destruction due to Hasina-Modi pacts, why to make fun of wild animals with animal masks in a crude corruption and perversion of the sylvan, pastoral, and rural, which are all expansive in spirit? Why to mock at the "locus amoenus" of the idealistic woodlot, timberland, and woodland?

But the secularists are fanatical and fundamentalist in their professed secularism, narrow and partial, and shallow and superficial as it is. Seasonal, opportunist, and not deep-delved, they would come out not only to change the time-honored definition of a historical Muslim Bangladeshi but also hurt the religious sentiment of their own kind—Muslims. Muslim-named and Muslim-born, they are pitifully ashamed of uttering the Muslim word *Allah*, of talking about the timeless fundamentals of Islam and the Muslim greeting of *Salam*, disastrously displacing their religion with the pagan world of Pan and dissociating themselves from the Islamic way of life. Don't they think of their own birth and death, their family and forefathers, or they prefer to be carried away, like the seaweed, by the surface sweep of the secularist ebb and tide, ignoring the deep bottom? Therefore, there should be many more of the likes of singer Mustafa Zaman Abbasi, singer Haider Hussein, Justice Abdur Raouf, Justice Mustafa Kamal, Dr Kazi Motahar Hussein, Hasina government's Religious Affairs Minister Principal Matiur Rahman, (Ret) Air Force Chief Sultan Mahmud, and Moulana Abdul Hamid Khan Bhasani.

The "little learning" of the secularists has made them "a dangerous thing," to take the two phrases from Alexander Pope's *An Essay on Man*. The pitiable secularist souls may be dismissed as "odious vermin," the way the King of Brobdingnag dismisses the English in Jonathan Swift's *Gulliver's Travels*. They think their professed secularism would give them an iota or an aura of knowledge and enlightenment and help them cover their ignorance and intolerance. One knows in no time that the dim-and-dull witted secularists are "secularist" only in terms of their ludicrous Islam-bashing rhetoric. BangoBir Kader Siddiquee's characterization of Abdul Gaffar Chowdhury as an utterly harmful and untrustworthy person says it all about the latter's tu-whit tu-whoo secularist cohorts.[29]

That is why the radical secularists love to champion, in a double standard of convenience and contradiction (and cowardice too), the sectarian and morally decrepit Narendra Modi and love to support his discriminatory Muslim slaughter and his inflammatory ban on beef, food of the people of all religions, except the fanatical and fundamentalist Hindus. That is their lowly height, to use a self-coined oxymoron. The so-called Muslim-named and Muslim-born secularists do not have the courage to accept and embrace their own religion Islam but they would be gluttonously glad to welcome and appreciate other religions.

Believers in the monotheistic Book/s cannot afford to disregard their actions in the temporal here and now, which determine the eternal hereafter and which should therefore be carefully and compatibly arranged and formatted to make sure what they do makes a positive determination toward regaining what John Milton calls "Paradise Lost." Bangladesh needs rightist and right of center patriotic nationalists (such as Mahmudur Rahman, Dr Zafrullah Chowdhury, Dr Asif Nazrul, Maj Akhtaruzzaman, Dr Mina Farah, and Nur-e-Alam Siddiquee), not secularists (like Dr Kamal Hussein), who are lost in the maze of their own confusions and contradictions.

One of the finest media minds, journalist Sanjib Chowdhury of the popular but Hasina-suppressed *Amar Desh*, once said that all should belong and stay attached to their respective religions for the moral, ethical, and, ultimately, lasting upliftment and improvement of the society they are in and that there remains nothing to cling and look forward to if one's religious belongingness is taken away or one becomes empty and bereft of it—the kind described by T S Eliot as a "hollow man." What Chowdhury was driving at translated into the precious saying that "money is lost nothing is lost, health is lost something is lost, character is lost everything is lost." When others choose to revert, convert, and converge to Islam, especially across the West, Bangladeshi Muslim-named and Muslim-born secularists prefer to deviate and diverge. While they are rightly proud of having acquired the independence of their country, it is shocking that they do not mind losing and disengaging with their religion, which is, however, more important than the country, religion being a matter of deeply rooted faith permanently and enduringly related to birth, life, and death and never to be segregated from one's existence, from birth to death.

Controversy over the culture of sculpted statues and idols (মূর্তি)

According to the religious scholars, both the sculptural structure of a statue and the shape and figure of an idol are basically the same, unacceptable, in terms of Islamic dicta and edicts. So they are according to the former judge, Iqtedar Ahmed, a political and cultural analyst.[30] So while in power, can't a practicing Muslim PM be expected to do more to protect and promote Islam, dismiss and denigrate the dangerously indoctrinated secularists (such as the singer Mita Hoque) for their false and propagandistic Islamophobia, and stem the spread of anti-Islamic fundamentalism, fanaticism, and obscenities everywhere? How could a practicing Muslim PM of a Muslim majority country allow the renaming of some roads and structures originally named after great Muslim scholars?[31] How could a practicing Muslim PM of a Muslim majority country allow Muslim দোয়া মুনাজাত (religious prayers and solicitations) in the inauguration of a statue (see below), all such sculpture considered un-and-anti-Islamic and contradictory to Islamic tradition? How could a practicing Muslim PM of a Muslim majority country strangely and illogically support the *MS* at the sacrifice of her religious values to please the Hindus and the Hindu-minded secularists and at the same time, rightly, come to dislike the Supreme Court statue, which must have at first been installed with her approval at the cost of the state money and is now being justly mulled to be removed to please and at the pressure of the *Hefajote*? Isn't it the সর্প এবং ওঝা policy/strategy of biting as a snake and then treating the wound as a rural quack treating the snakebite?

What kind of un-Islamic (secularist?) *Huzur* was he who led that দোয়া মুনাজাত, devotedly deifying the statue of a human in an absolutely absorbed manner? How could a practicing Muslim PM of a Muslim majority country allow the posting of the picture of her father Sheikh Mujib on the front wall facing the devout worshippers in a Muslim prayer hall?[32] How could she allow her surrogate and cohort Rawshon offer Muslim-style দোয়া মুনাজাত for the feline Hindu Suranjit Sen Gupta over his dead body (about to be cremated)? How could she allow the installation of the statue of a pagan female Greek deity in front of the land's highest court? Is it the women empowerment and women enthronement Awami secularist style? Is it the Planet 50–50 gender equality, again Awami style? Is it the secularization and internationalization in the way of "the greatest Bengali ever" *Bangabandhu* Sheikh Mujib's extended family that encompasses Muslims, Christians, and Jews, Asians and Westerners, Bangla and English, so far?

The Supreme Court statue is an illustration of Western secularism and Indian Hindu idolatry (which, the latter, the famous English art critic John Ruskin viciously attacked, see below). Neither of them, naturally, would even pretend to find an example of great and noble justice in the long history of Islam, which is full of the instances of equal, strict, and impartial justice. Similar to the beautiful saree-wearing statue of both local elements and foreign ingredients, the mixed name of the sculptor Mrinal Hoque himself reflects a curious amalgam of cultures. Similarly, it is shocking to see the ignorance and foolishness of Abdul Gaffar Chowdhury, who, as he was defending the Supreme Court statue while he was in Dhaka (on May 21, 2017), said that the holy Black Stone (*al-□ajar al-Aswad*, "Heavenly Stone"), which is just a small piece of rock dating back to the time of Adam and Eve) and the Maqame Ibrahim (preserved and protected real footprint of prophet Abraham/Ibrahim) at the premises of the sacred Ka'abah were also sculptural statues! What a secularist fetid, frigid, and frivolous ignorance and foolishness!

As the ancient mythological sculptor Pygmalion fell in love with his own female ivory statue of Galatea and had her transformed into a living woman with the help of the goddess of love and beauty Aphrodite so that he could have her personally and physically, one only wishes the blind yet attractive Supreme Court statue comes to life, in the statuesque figure of a woman, with a soul injected into it and its vision—its human right—restored to it so that a man can develop a normal phallic and physical attachment with it turned into a living body. The female statue diverts one's attention to the natural male-female relationship rather than direct it to the dispassionate and disenchanted scale of justice the rocky and stony lifeless figure is unnaturally pretending to be holding.

Isn't the statue of the apparently "dead" Queen Hermione miraculously restored to life at the intense sexual desire of the distraught King Leontes in *The Winter's Tale*, one of Shakespeare's last plays in a comedic or romance mode? Italian Renaissance artist Andrea del Sarto (as in Robert Browning's poem) is a technically faultless painter but fails to portray a lively picture by putting forth both body and soul together in the otherwise perfect and flawless sketch of his wife Lucrezia, who, being in love with somebody else, is lacking in love for her own husband Andrea, who thus feels betrayed and uninspired. All fine art and plastic art representations of human figures and deities, from ancient Indian, Greek, Roman, and Renaissance times, often in nude, half-clad, or tightly clad (except perhaps the Asian—Chinese and Japanese), have to do with human libido or its libidinous deification.

W B Yeats contrasts the "silent" sources of Eastern and Western knowledge and civilization in his poem "The Statues." He says the Western rational and intellectual sources originated with the Greek culture/sculpture of statues, which had to do not only with the abstract perfection of a "plummet-measured face" of the nature of Pythagorean numbers at the beginning, but later also the passion of love and individual character and personality of the observer, born of sexual instinct ("casual flesh" and "live lips") and the dreams that the 5th century (BC) Phidias, one of the greatest Greek sculptors, gave to women.

Initially all this is thought, in the poem, to be superior to the multiform "Asiatic vague immensities," but then belittled as "unreality." In the face of what Yeats calls "filthy modern tide" and its destructive "formless spawning fury," he would prefer a return to the ancient original Greek proportions of Pythagorean fixed and perfect types as represented by "The lineaments of a plummet-measured face" and also the "empty eyeballs" of the Buddha, which Yeats finds as the source of true wisdom that comes with divine and spiritual knowledge.

The two real and recent statues in Bangladesh mentioned above have been added to many others of the like across the country, including the strong and stout, and virile and voluptuous অপরাজেয় বাংলা Invincible, Undefeatable, Intrepid Bangla (or Bangladesh) by Syed Abdullah Khalid in front of DU Arts Building. It is great to see that there has been a writ with the High Court seeking removal of the statue of the Greek-Bengali goddess from the Supreme Court premises. Also it is great that the Awami *Ulema* League has wielded a legal protest against the Supreme Court statue, to which all *Ulema*, regardless of their political affiliations, including the elderly Religious Affairs minister Principal Matiur Rahman, should throw their full and complete support.[33] Following the footsteps of the Ulema League, the mild and weak *Hefajote* Islam also has lodged a protest in the form of submitting a petition to the office of the Prime Minister to remove the statue from the Supreme Court premises. Islami Oikkyo-Jote also brought out a procession in protest demanding the removal of the statue as they also protested against the Hindu culture and practice of the MS.[34] They are all too cowardly to have been more forceful from the beginning when the statue was in the process of being installed. However, it is better late than never![35] Likewise, it is better late than never that All Bengal Minority Youth Federation (ABMYF) is demanding removal of the marble statue of Sheikh Mujibur Rahman from the Bekar Hostel (for the unemployed Muslims) in Calcutta.[36]

Along with the state of statue complications, how could a practicing Muslim PM have such a morally and socially compromising and controversial character, reportedly wild and bohemian, as her special assistant?[37] Poet Syed Shamsul Haq, also infamous for his overt obscenities, was one of her great favorites. Fear of God/Allah the Almighty, practice of Islam, and the model political leadership in a Muslim country do not go with this sort of contradictory lapses and deviations, which need to be shunned and discouraged. If the মূর্তি and মঙ্গল culture is encouraged today in the name of the art of mask and sculpture, tomorrow all kinds of nudities, display of the body, sex acts, and pornography also will be encouraged in the name of art, which is what is in the non-Muslim Western society!

The Muslim greeting of *As-salamu-alaikum* (Peace be upon you and with you!) as one of the most misunderstood and politicized one

The doctrinaire secularists, far from being moderate, would neither greet others nor would like to be greeted with what is the noblest and most universal of greetings, *Assalamualaikum* (Peace be upon you and with you!). Lured away by the godless façade of secularism, they have not only exploited the Muslim/Islamic greeting in a socialist and revolutionary context such as লও লও লাল সালাম, but also vulgarly vernacularized and secularized it as only শুভেচ্ছা (Good Wishes), শুভ সকাল (Good Morning), শুভ দুপুর (there being no Good Noon in English), শুভ বিকেল (Good Afternoon), or শুভ সন্ধ্যা (Good Evening).[38] Instead of মরহুম (one seeking God's mercy and forgiveness in death), the secularists, in a diminishment of the profound spirit and fervor, would simply say প্রয়াত (passed), although they would not mind calling the four student leaders as চার খলিফা during the politically exciting times of the late 1960s and early 1970s.

While such expressions are nice and fine in/of/by themselves and may be occasionally used as necessary, these cannot, however, be an equivalent or replacement of the deeply solemn and profound Islamic wishes for the blessings of peace. The Jewish salutation of *Shalom* also means peace and implies that without peace there can be no completion. For all intents and purposes, the Bengali words mentioned above do not even have the same impact or create the same climate of sanctity and gravity as the Western/Christian Good Morning, Good Evening, or Goodbye (deriving from "God be with you"), let alone the higher Muslim greeting of *As-sala-mu-alai-kum*.

However, the Bengali salutations can in fact be used along with the religiously recommended one, which alone exudes a sense of divine peace and helps one to experience a sense of transcendence in the midst of dull and drab mundane routine. Unlike the Bengali or Western expressions of greetings, which, culturally, everybody feels free and comfortable to greet others with, regardless of age and class and gender differences, the Islamic salutation of *Salam*, unfortunately, has been highly stratified and politicized in some Muslim societies where it has become a tradition that only the younger, the lower, and the lesser are expected to greet the older and the higher with this salutation as if it were a sure sign of respect to be duly paid to the deserving seniors. Although the basic protocol of introductions calls for the lesser-ranking (socially, professionally, or by age) to introduce himself/herself to the higher-ranking in any society, introduction with the greeting of *Salam* has become culturally obligatory on the part of the younger or the lesser to the senior in age or rank as a mark of respect for the latter in Muslim countries.

What is worse, with the exception of the whites, if you are a non-Arab (Indian or African) or even an Arab from a poor country working in the affluent part of the Middle East, no matter what you are—a worker or a professional, older or younger, senior or junior—*you* are expected to be the first to offer *Salam* to the rich Gulf Arabs.

If you are an expat of color working in Malaysia, it is implied that you are supposed to be the first to greet the Malays with *Salam*. It is assumed to be beneath the dignity of the proud locals, especially in the Gulf, to greet you with *Salam* first. After all, you are a poor foreign *miskin* (a helpless have-not/ a beggar) making your living in *their* country, already receiving their favors! Unlike the West, morally superior in this respect and treating everybody relatively equally, the Gulf countries by rule do not naturalize you, do not give you immigrant status leading to citizenship, and do not make you one of them, so the question of equal status and equal rights do not arise (in their view).

To digress a little (but by way of expanding on the matter), sometimes if a junior—in age or academically—who always used to greet you with *Salam*—somehow manages to go up the ladder and becomes senior to you administratively, s/he stops greeting you, especially in public, to show that it is s/he who deserves to be greeted and recognized with *Salam* first—an indication of a hierarchically sanctioned respect. On the contrary, there are no such class-and-gender-and-administrative-rank conscious problems with Good Morning, Good Evening, Hi, or Hello, which are class, age, and community neutral. The same is true about the Muslim annual Ramadan Kareem or *Eid* Mubarak, which, unlike the aura of hierarchy falsely associated with *Salam*, everybody is eager and excited to greet others with, regardless of age and class and gender. The as-porous-as-the-puffed-rice (মুড়ি) secularists, on TV and other venues, are impatient to greet each other not with the profound *Assalamualikum* but the fashionable *Eid* Mubarak only (stripped of its solemn and serious religious character), sometimes unnecessarily and ridiculously, for as long as a month and a half after the festive occasion of *Eid* itself.

The true fact is that anybody who is on station (home or work), young or old, high or low, junior or senior, rich or poor, local or expat, is supposed to be greeted first with *Salam* by others who are passing by, have arrived, or have come to see or visit others. Such is the fair, even, and egalitarian principle that Islam prescribes—a principle pretty uniformly adhered to among the Gulf nationals themselves only, who are generally thrifty in extending or according this privilege to others. On the other hand, while the Gulf Arabs abide by this nice equitable principle at least among themselves, other Muslim cultures and communities are so deeply entrenched in class-and-age-ridden consciousness that they are far from living up to it.

Matching with the ubiquitous bowdlerizing female obscenities and nudities encouraged and inspired by ungodly secularism, there is an unacceptable male tendency to wearing bracelets and earrings—in imitation of homosexual desire and same-sex bonding—by actors, artists, dancers, and singers. What a demeaning mockery of what could actually be a refined, elegant, elitist, cultured, dignified, and exalted sense of manliness and masculine style! *Hefajote* and *Khelafot* and *Islami Shashontantro Andolon* and all the rest of the Islamic leaders and preachers and parties, both at the local and the national levels, need to first protest, both on the media and in the society, against this shameful sexual corruption, decadence, and degeneration of Muslim culture in Bangladesh.

The role of the *Hefajote* and the like

Religious Sheikhs, Huzurs, and Imams need to first protest against various other social and moral ills, such as drugs, rape, deadly dowry, child marriage, child labor, child abuse, pre-and-extra marital affairs, poverty, and pornography that are destroying the very fabric of the society from within and without. Instead of remaining confined to the four walls of their Masjids and Madrasas, they need to implement what they say, that Islam is a complete code/way of life. If that is so, they need to get out and hold protest demonstrations every now and then to create a long overdue social awareness about all kinds of moral and political lapses around them. They ought to openly and publicly exercise their moral and religious authority without getting politicized and being bought over. If they cannot resist being politically yielding and compromising, they are useless and hopeless and then they should stop talking about Islam being a complete code/way of life. Let them practice and set examples first of what they say.

Unfortunately, the top Islamic communities are shying and shirking away, as reported on the media, from their commitment, allegedly trying to work out a compromise with the despotic Hasina government from within their own cozy and comfortable corners.[39] It is this position of the Islamic leaders and preachers vis-à-vis the regime, that is, the regime's secularist policy of "displacing" and then "reclaiming" the space of Islam that has been discussed by Bangladeshi Canadian Professor Saidul Islam of Nanyang Technological University Singapore in his article "'Minority' Islam in Muslim Majority Bangladesh: The Violent Road to a New Brand of Secularism."[40] Drawing its strength from the Hasina regime and its backer India, a small minority is dictating its terms to the overwhelming majority, which finds itself forced to digest all the humiliations it is being imposed upon. It is along the same line that the daily Dinkal editor, who is also a well-known media personality, Dr Rezwan Siddiqui, and another political writer Tajuddin superbly articulate their argument about how the present regime intends to train the younger generation of the country in an alarmingly God-less secularist culture without the Islamic knowledge of God/Allah the Almighty and the Prophet of Islam being imparted to them and inculcated by them.[41]

The institutionalized religious communities need to speak up, at the top of their voice and with top priority and urgency, against the repulsive and pugnacious culture of child marriage, child abuse, child labor, discrimination against women, their low wages, deadly anti-women dowry system among the poor masses, rural or urban, and inhuman domestic violence against women. Whatever their finances and other resources are and whatever their orientation is, the religious communities need to rise up at the larger national level against the government. In the past, they were brutally crushed and then silenced, maybe in exchange for a land grant, supposedly made to the seat of the *Hefajote* movement at *Hat-hazari* Chittagong, and recently also for an overdue government recognition of their Qaomi degrees.[42]

Hasina's, Hasanul Hoque Inu's, and Moinuddin Khan Badol's তেঁতুল / *tetul* Huzurs, as savory sour as tamarind, have now become their tastily sweet companions. As Minar Rashid puts it, if they are with them, it is a লীলাখেলা (magical and mysterious show of power in alignment); if they are with the BNP and others, it is a মহাজ্বালা (mega and massive pain, irritation, and frustration).[43] Whatever legitimate gifts received and legitimate goals achieved, *Hefajote* Huzurs must remain committed to standing up to the increasingly Hinduization, secularization, and Rabindraization of Bangladesh. They must rise up the way Ebne Golam Samad has been merciless in exposing the perils of the secularist Rabindra worship (Rabi Puja).[44] They have already proved to be effective, only partly though, against Latif Siddiquee's and other Dhaka-based fanatical secularists' and atheists' anti-Islamic remarks and their secularist introduction of starkly un-Islamic and pro-Hindu/pro-Indian elements in the school curriculum.[45]

Although *Hefajote* suspiciously remained dormant without any protest against the Hindu-stuffed curriculum for three years (2013–2016), they finally came up with their pro-Islamic recommendations which the Hasina government seems to have accepted and accordingly the textbook curriculum has apparently been changed from 2017.[46] In this respect, both the *Hefajote* and the Hasina government deserve to be thanked and congratulated, while the fanatical and fundamentalist secularist support for the pro-Hindu curriculum and their challenge to the newly introduced pro-Islamic works must be successfully opposed and defeated! While the *Hefajote* and all the Islamic forces and all the Islamic-minded Bangladeshis need to stand up against the ultra-secularist obstacles before it is too late, the handful of urban-based groups intoxicated and indoctrinated by their sectarian secularism may wish to listen to a lecture by the Indian scholar and peace activist Ram Puniyani about the conspiracies against Islam and Muslims.[47]

Reportedly, despite being once disparaged and denigrated as তেঁতুল / *tetul* Huzurs, as sour as tamarind, *Hefajote* and other Islamic parties are negotiating about how to enter a compromising and caved-in understanding with the Hasina government, slipping and sliding back from their earlier commitments and letting the memories of one of the worst butcheries in the country on May 5/6, 2013 take a back seat, if not totally forgotten.[48] If the *Hefajote* makes peace with the AL, isn't it like the top religious group selling its conscience—for whatever reasons, political or material—on the very dead bodies of its supporters who got butchered by the AL and who sacrificed their lives for their cause that May at the call of Allama Shafi?

Not only that, any *Hefajote* alignment with the AL only to electorally benefit the latter is a betrayal not only of its own causes but also the popular political opposition, whose leader Begum Khaleda Zia openly made a call for the people to come out in support of the massive and mammoth, yet unforgettably fateful *Hefajote* gathering that May that was mercilessly crushed and cracked down by the Hasina police and the BGB. How could the Allamas, the Moulanas, and the Muftis forget the massacre of their fellow brethren so quickly in their own lifetime?

How could they align with Sheikh Hasina so easily and malign Khaleda Zia, if any, so hastily? It is said that Khaleda also extended them the due recognition they demanded—recognition of their highest degree as equivalent to Master's, back in 2006—which was perhaps in the process of being sealed officially.

It was therefore Khaleda who made the first positive overture toward the overdue recognition of the Qaomi education, although the final "mission accomplished" goal was scored by Hasina with the intention of securing popular Qaomi votes as the need of the moment in terms of electoral politics and greed for power dictated. After killing the *Hefajote* men, Hasina also came forward to lovingly and affectionately take care of them at the end. Although they got their coveted prize from her that they needed for their social dignity and economic establishment, they also had earlier been killed by her. Is not it like গরু মেরে জুতা দান, meaning, "You kill somebody's cow and then try to make peace by gifting the poor man a pair of shoes made of that cowhide." So why would the *Hefajote* be inching away from Khaleda as they tend to be inching toward Hasina? Where are the ideals, and moral values and principles, and the reliability and trustworthiness expected of the religious leaders and preachers, both individually and institutionally?

Even then both Hasina and the *Hefajote* deserve to be congratulated on the matter of the award. There are no reasons for the secularists to cry foul over the recognition of the Qaomi by the government. Studies in the vast subject of divinity, holy books, Islamic revealed knowledge, and religious literature, which are also inclusive of personal, family, collective, social, moral, and economic systems of life, are much higher than the lamentably low quality, shortcut, and one-sided Bangladeshi Master's—a degree getting increasingly partisan and politicized and never making its way on the list of the world rankings.[49] As the British-educated physician of Bangladeshi origin, highly placed in Australia, Dr Fatima Ashrafi, who is into many physical fitness and extracurricular activities, including dancing, says, "Nothing can be more progressive than to understand and follow Islam." She describes the extreme secularists as nothing short of being "misguided humanoids" (E-mail of April 24, 2017). A Muslim should have no qualms to join the first-rate intellectual Farhad Mazhar and the former BGB chief Maj Gen Fazlur Rahman in congratulating both Khaleda and Hasina on their (Khaleda's 2006 and Hasina's 2017) recognition of the Qaomi education, which, as both of them suggested, would need to go through some revision and reformation.[50]

However, one could not quite agree with Farhad Mazhar's statement that "ইতিহাসের প্রহসন হচ্ছে, খালেদা জিয়া হেফাজতের নেতাদের তার ঘরের মধ্যে দীর্ঘকাল পেয়েও যা অর্জন করতে পারেননি, শেখ হাসিনা কয়েক মাসের ব্যবধানে অসাধ্য সাধন করে ফেলেছেন।" The fact is that Khaleda, in and out of power, did what she could do as part of the process that culminated at the hands of Hasina, who also inflicted unforgettable *Jallianwala Bagh* bloodshed on the *Hefajote*. Now the latter (*Hefajote*) decided to accept the prize from Hasina, going back on their earlier declaration that they would not take any laurel from their bloody enemy and also walking over the blood of their own compatriots. It can only be explained away as the competition and conspiracy of both fate and politics that have been playing out to the mutually divergent and exclusive detriment and advantage to the people according to their respective position on the political and temporal wheel of fortune.

Besides their academic specialisms and specialist professions, shouldn't the institutionalized religious community or its individual members also play a role similar to what was played by Shah (Syed Qutubuddin A□mad) Waliullah Dehlavi of Delhi (1703–1773), Faqir Majnu Shah of UP/Dinajpur/Bogra (d. 1787), Syed Ahmad Shaheed Barelvi of Raebareli (1786–1831), Hafiz Moulana Syed Mir Nisar Ali (Titumir) of West Bengal (1782–1831), Haji Shariatullah of Shariatpur, Bangladesh (1781–1840) and his competent son Mohammad Mohsin (or Muhsinuddin Ahmad) alias Dudu Mia, among others?[51] Shouldn't they also act and leave a legacy like the saintly Abdul Sattar Edhi of the Edhi Foundation of Pakistan (a charitable philanthropist and humanitarian organization) or the retired Uttara Bank AGM Pizirul Alam Dulal of Bangladesh, the latter having established a similar organization called "Chandmoni" in Nilphamari for the education of the poor orphans against their possible repugnant and despicable child marriage?[52] All people—government, civil society, civil administration, and the religious community—should follow the example set by Bangladesh's Sharmin Akter, who successfully fought against early or forced marriage at the age of 15 and became known worldwide.

The Islamic scholars and their followers could have registered their disagreement with the education policy and curricular reforms of the Hasina government, perhaps more effectively, through periodic and frequent press conferences, press statements, and newspaper columns and articles, all to be done in the capital city Dhaka, not in the remote provincial areas. That way—Dhaka-based way—they could make themselves more visible and gain more national attention. That way they themselves would have benefitted more, both academically and intellectually, especially in terms of their writing skills and proficiency in the vernacular (Bangla), perhaps even in English.

There cannot be anything wrong with the poor garment girls who work hard to make the bare minimum for a living. The problem lies at the high-level social and colorful screen culture where Muslim women cross the limit in their sexually enticing nudities. Our pious and devout *Ulema* (religious teachers and preaching community) need to protest against such anti-Islamic activities in the form of dirty, filthy, seductive, and sexually provocative and inciting acting, dancing, and nocturnal RainTree fun outing. Rebecca Momen, a ruling party (AL) MP and Chairman of the Women and Children's Welfare parliamentary committee in Bangladesh, said that it was women's open and provocative dress, indecent manners, and sexually inviting conduct that were responsible for rape and abuse of them, including the extramarital (*porokia*) affairs.[53] She said she did not find any fault with men, who were actually drawn in by the exposure of the irresistible female allure of the half-clad women. The same argument was made by the Karnataka Home Minister of India, Dr G. Parameshwara, who said that it was women and their Western style sexually arousing dress that were responsible for their molestations in Bengaluru on the thirty-first night of 2017.

What secularism actually means in Bangladesh: mounds (*maunds*) of "political" flowers by the masses at the foot of the public monuments and memorials on countless occasions, only to be carted and cleared away in no time, but the message and its spirit hardly lasting, cherished, and sustained

Secularism, to the propagators of near to complete atheism, means suppression of Islam (and only Islam) and, hypocritically, promotion of all other religions, including Hinduism, Christianity, Buddhism, animism, paganism, polytheism, and all other folk religions. Fundamentalist Hindu, Muslim, Christian, Jewish, and Buddhist haters of Islam and Muslims are great examples of the so-called *মুক্তমনা মুক্তচিন্তা* (actually বদ্ধমনা) liberalism and secularism in the double standard playing out in today's Bangladesh and India where such haters of Islam and Muslims are promoted whereas peaceful Islamic preachers like Zakir Nayek and Islamic media/TV channels are forbidden. The only criterion of being secular is to hate Islam and love and admire all other religions.

In the name of secularist ideology, many dictators, especially in the Arab and Muslim world (Mubarak, Saddam, Gaddafi, Bashar, Bashir, Ben Ali, Al Sisi), have killed many innocent, God-fearing people. In the context of Bangladesh, secularism, especially the মুরগী অথবা টিপ্ মার্কা Hinduized one, is as partial and fragmented as the spirit (চেতনা) of 1971. It has lost all its positive meanings and connotations as it practically promotes all other religions at the expense of the last and greatest monotheistic religion, Islam, and encourages demotion of Islamic Godliness in the society. To the contrary, Bangladesh as a Muslim majority country needs to strive to maintain its Islamic identity, to be mandated clearly and constitutionally, leaving the minority interests, by no means, neglected and unattended. Secularists' planned and prioritized demotion of Islam and, instead, their promotion of other religions, deviously engineered by them, both are undesirable in a Muslim majority country.

Instead of pleading with and praying to God/*Allah* the Almighty for the reward and forgiveness for the dead in one's own religious way, Bangladeshi brand of extremist secularism has established, like the totem and statue culture, a tradition of laying floral wreaths and lighting candles at the monument and memorial sites and observing a moment of silence in the political meetings and parliaments. Why can't the momentary silence be turned into a soft, clear and fervent offering of Muslim *Fateha* or other offerings in the way of the religious minorities? Those who are not so religious-minded, including the atheists or agnostics, can feel free to remain silent in Yoga-style meditation, but do those who fervently believe in God/ *Allah* the Almighty and their respective religious rituals, both private and public, internal and external, have to confine their responsibility of remembering and commemorating the dead to the laying of the bunches and bouquets of flowers, lighting of candles, and the observance of a minute's silence only? By themselves, do such floral wreaths, candles, and silences, except being more of a saucy and supercilious show and merely secularist extravaganza, mean anything to the dead?

Flowers are of course "superexcellently" fantastic gifts on all other real life and social occasions, providing an opportunity for many working class members to make a living as they do for George Bernard Shaw's flower girl Eliza in the play *Pygmalion* ("My Fair Lady"). Flowers stand for love, purity, simplicity and innocence, in life as well as literature, no doubt. While the love of flowers, buying of flowers for home decoration and giving flowers as a gift to the near and dear ones are excellent practices, the placing and piling of tons of floral wreaths on open structures on national occasions, to be collected and cleared as rubbish in a matter of hours, is a meaningless secularist, atheist and pagan culture, totally un-Islamic and anti-Islamic. No wonder, not a single Islamic party, from the dozens of the kind, participates in this publicly competitive show of floral respects. There may, however, be infrequent, only one-time similar practices in other countries, very occasional in nature, which are far from the regularly held festivals as they are in Bangladesh, pushed too far in their excessive fanfare, as even the highly secular-minded Khoniker Othithee of New York claims.

The spirit and fervor of flowers given at the domestic and friendly level or on the birthdays, anniversaries, and graduation occasions or the flowers meant in the poetical and religious/spiritual verses[54] are entirely different from the completely commercialized and politicized flowers that pile up in some places on 21 February, 26 March, and 16 December and that provide an occasion for nothing more than a redundant and superfluous photo opportunity, however culturally cultivated it is. There is no such (large scale) flower business or hardly any on 4 July (American Independence Day) and 11 November Veterans Day observed at the Vietnam Memorial in the USA. Americans, rightly, mark the occasions by fervent religious (church) services and other formalities, including parades. Nothing happens at the foot of the Washington Monument or Jefferson and Lincoln memorials, except the normal but memorable visits by the members of the public in general.

It is to be made clear that I am not against the memorials and monuments by themselves. However, I am against the excessive fanfare and extravaganza that attends the regularly held mass floral tributes only, almost as a rule or custom. To be more grave and dignified, the ceremony could perhaps be limited, on behalf of the nation, to the head of state or government or his/her representatives and it could also include parades and religious services, among other official functions, as it is in the rest of the world.

Secularism of a very small minority as "a large majority" in Bangladesh

Considering the staggering number of Hindus in high executive positions (in the police, civil admin, education, banking, judiciary, and other sectors) and the excessive fanfare, euphoria and enthusiasm over the widely held Hindu festivals in Bangladesh, it seems the country's Muslim identity is being increasingly compromised, diluted, deflected, and diffused. The minority has become a large "alternative" or "virtual" majority displacing and disadvantaging the real majority. A recent report by Aman Abduhu about the Muslims being discriminated against in their own Muslim majority Bangladesh in favor of the minority Hindus testifies to this fact.[55] On a Channel I TM talk show, Nur-e-Alam Siddiquee expressed his surprise that out of 67 recently promoted additional secretaries, 46 were Hindus, in a country of 91% Muslims.[56] Siddiquee's claims are further corroborated by the *Muldhara* and the daily Inqilab reports providing the statistics about the excessively high number of non-Muslims employed in the government sector of Bangladesh and involved in financial corruption and smuggling.[57] Also interesting is to see how the government gives away a lot of money from the prime minister's relief funds to Hindu religious celebrations committees in different district in Bangladesh.[58]

A Muslim can only raise his eyebrows in shocking disapproval when he sees that the Iftar (breaking of the fast at the sunset) gathering by the Chatro League (student wing of the ruling Awami League) during the holy Ramadan is presided over and conducted by Hindus with the special guest and the special speaker also being Hindu.[59] The same alarming imbalance and discordant note can be noticed in how the basic primary education level also is affected by the recruitment of teachers from the minority whose religious beliefs are different than the Islamic belief of the predominantly Muslim population and who, ironically, do teach Islamic Studies in many junior and secondary schools! (See the links provided in Note #45).

What is even worse is that, under the Hasina regime, hundreds of thousands (about 800,000, as of early 2017) of legal and illegal foreigners, mostly from India, are allowed to stay in Bangladesh leading to the suspicion that many of them are possibly engaged, in cooperation with the native insiders, in illegal and immoral activities.[60] It was reported in an Indian newspaper that as of May 2013 there were as many as 500,000 Indians (from West Bengal, Meghalaya, Assam, Tripura and Mizoram) illegally entering and working in Bangladesh and sending home to India a remittance of over 3.7 billion dollars (to the deprivation of the suffering, starving and struggling locals seeking employment in their own poor-to-developing homeland Bangladesh).[61] Bangladesh's Daily Star confirmed that "Bangladesh happens to be the third largest source of foreign exchange for India – something to the tune of 3.7 billion dollars. And, reportedly, a large number of Indians, many of them in white collared jobs, are working here illegally."[62]

This disproportion is being probably done deliberately with a long term motive. It has become a common phenomenon causing a neo-and-near-and-more-than-partial apartheid to be underway, so that one day the Muslim majority of today would become the minority in Bangladesh. The ominous trend, to the utter pride and pleasure of not only the bordering big brother India but also those within Bangladesh who, in a treacherous and treasonous way, would like to forge a union with India, is likely to create or has already created a physical as well as psychological warfare between the majority and the minority of the population in Bangladesh.

The Hindus are definitely entitled to and may continue to get their fair share, which they have been enjoying in Bangladesh for decades, but for them to undeservedly and excessively get the upper hand and preferential treatment is an ominous and discriminatory sign. It is this politically hidden agenda of

Islam-demoting and Hinduism-promoting partisan secularism that lies behind the "politically correct" but actually misleading and materially commercializing slogan, "Religion belongs to individuals and individual communities while (religious) festivals belong to all."

It is like saying, as Mohamed Nazir of the USA puts it as a sour and bitter protest, "Religion belongs to individuals and individual communities while the Muslim *Eidul Adha Qurbani* beef, Hindu turtle meat, and Christian pork belong to all (ধর্ম যার যার গরুর গোশত শুওরের মাংস কচ্ছপের মাংস সবার । অসাম্প্রদায়িক বাংলাদেশ গড়ার লক্ষ্যে)." If one is not a Hindu, how can one take part in the Puja-*Parvon* celebrations such as *Durga*, *Kali*, Shiva, and Parvati with ardor and candor? How can one do the mingling, interacting, eating, buying, and wearing a matching dress with the devotees and worshippers on different religious occasions without compromising one's fervent faith and piety and their purity and sanctity?

Dr Ahmad Abdul Qader rightly asserts: "ধর্ম যার যার, উৎসব সবার—এ মন্ত্রে উজ্জীবিত হয়ে আমরা সবাই একসাথে উৎসব পালন করব' – প্রধানমন্ত্রীর এ বক্তব্য ইসলাম ধর্মের বিশ্বাসের সম্পূর্ণ বিপরীত ও আপত্তিকর। কাজেই আমরা অনুরোধ করব, দায়িত্বশীল ব্যক্তিরা 'ধর্ম যার যার, উৎসব সবার'- এ জাতীয় বক্তব্য দিয়ে তারা যেন মানুষকে বিভ্রান্ত না করেন। তদুপরি এটি বাস্তবতার সাথে মোটেই সঙ্গতিপূর্ণ নয়। এমনকি রাজনৈতিক উদ্দেশ্যেও এমন বক্তব্য দেয়া যায় না, যা সংশ্লিষ্ট ব্যক্তির ধর্ম বিশ্বাসের সরাসরি পরিপন্থী হয়। কোনো ধর্মাবলম্বীর ধর্মীয় উৎসব অন্য ধর্মাবলম্বীসহ সবাই এক সাথে পালন করতে পারে না। বিশেষত ইসলাম তা অনুমোদন করে না। বস্তুত প্রকৃত সত্যটা হচ্ছে- 'ধর্ম ও ধর্মীয় উৎসব যার যার, রাষ্ট্র ও রাষ্ট্রীয় জাতীয় উৎসব সবার'।[63]

Rendered in English, what Dr Qader means to say is that PM Hasina is utterly wrong to claim that while religion is personal belonging to individuals and individual communities, religious festivals belong to all, regardless. Islamically, what she propagates, Dr Qader argues, is objectionable. He requests the responsible quarters not to mislead the people by saying so. Moreover, this misleading propagation, contrary to the reality of individual faith, should not be put forward even for political purposes. Members of no religious community can observe, especially from Islamic point of view, the religious festival of another religious community.

As mentioned above, 19th century English poet and literary critic Matthew Arnold called religious convictions "the voice of the deepest human experience," not to mention his contemporary social and art critic John Ruskin, who had serious and satirical reservations about the Hindu religion of the Indian colony. Ruskin described it, extremely negatively, as an "irrational," "ignoble and false" custom of idolatry of "inferior race … of vile terror, destitute of thought." He went on to say, in a racist manner:

> […] floating and whirling round any quantity of inconceivable, invisible and, in their symbols, monstrous gods,—gods like cuttle-fish, with uncountable legs; gods like cauliflowers, with inseparably sprouting heads; orbicular gods, with no ends; polygonal gods,

> with any quantity of ends; air-gods, water-gods, mud-gods, vacuum-gods, infinitely ugly abortions of things without origin, infinitely shapeless oddlings of unhatchable egg.[64]

Minorities must be protected and their religious freedom must be upheld but in a way that does not conflict with the majority preferences and priorities, and majority sensitivities and sensibilities that hold Islam as the last and greatest monotheistic religion. Being "politically correct" for the time being only does not mean being timeless and universal, overcoming the hurdles and impediments for the long term, and doing the right and just down the line, both before and after.

In the broader context, secularism describes anything against the blacks or colored people as racist; anything against women as anti-women, anti-feminist, sexist, male chauvinism, gender discrimination and gender inequality; anything against Israel, the Jews and their Judaism as anti-Semitic; anything against the LGBT community as discrimination on the basis of sexual orientation; and, when it is racist secularism, it finds a way to let a white man killing others of color get away with by describing him as mentally deranged and psychologically abnormal with a history of disturbed mental health.

However, it is the same secularism that defends anything against Islam and Muslims as freedom of expression and describes Muslims killing others as terrorists. The fact that secularism de-emphasizes the practice of religion in social and personal life and that it discourages the influence of religion in the community is tantamount to calling for the banishment of religion from the sphere of terrestrial life. Modern brand of secularism practically asks for a pagan society with no place for a monotheistic faith, especially Islam, and makes it possible for the society to lapse into a state of ungodly hedonism. Be they professors, professionals, writers, artists, lawyers, intellectuals or journalists, all should be free to be anything they like—secular, secular-minded or otherwise—but they ought not profess anything at the expense or suppression of Islam, especially when they themselves are Muslims—practicing or not—living in a Muslim-majority society.

Ultra-liberal and excessively liberal secularists consider the role and practice of religion—Islam in particular—unnecessary and out-of-date. They want to keep religion (especially Islam) out of the sphere of life; for them it is something to be expunged, left behind, pushed back, and relegated to the secondary, optional, non-binding status, redundant or addictive. They forget about the enlightening and ennobling influences of religion directly contributing to individual as well as collective moral conduct and character building relatively untainted by mean interests. Islam as the greatest, noblest, and most comprehensive of all religions (of course, to its followers) does include and can never exclude government, governance and politics from the domain of life it prescribes. Islam is inclusive of all humanity, humanism, much more and much beyond, including the life hereafter. In fact, it is a complete code of life and does very well include politics, political participation and political organization to help guide and determine all aspects of life—social, economic, academic, scientific, legal, and so on.

While it is an obligation for all Muslims to try to implement and establish Islam, with logic and reason, of course, they, in doing so, must not violate the law of the land. While they are obliged to conduct themselves in accordance with the Islamic code in their personal and social life, to the best of their knowledge and ability, they must not cause any inconvenience or interruption to the adherents of other religions. It is their sacred duty to ensure and safeguard peace and protection in the community of the people of different religious faiths. There is absolutely no room for hatred and hate crimes in Islam. By contrast, members of the ruling secularist Awami circles take advantage of the social weaknesses of the minority Hindus in Bangladesh and play foul not only with their material possessions but also their women and young daughters.[65]

The Muslim-majority Bangladesh and its Muslim tradition and culture, along with the followers of other (minority) faiths, have not faced, according to Hindu Chief Justice S K Sinha, any sectarian riots in the last fifty years.[66] They should all resist the nation sliding and slipping into ungodly secularism. The so-called secular but actually secularist and fundamentalist neighboring India, which seeks to dominate and subjugate Bangladesh in every aspect/respect, can never be a model for Bangladesh.[67] Mamata Banerjee of India comments on how communal and sectarian India is.[68] Political analyst Goutam Das writes about the Hinduism-based communalism and sectarianism in the Hindu-dominated and Hindu-controlled India.[69] Reputable Indian news magazine *Outlook* writes about the communal riot and plight of minorities in India. Written by Smruti Koppikr and Saba Naqvi, the *Outlook* report, "A Beast Asleep? Ten years after Gujarat 2002," asks if Indians are likely to witness such horror again.[70]

India is a giant "swallowing monster" in the guise of "a friend" that, as Dr Zafrullah Chowdhury claims, was looting and forcing Bangladesh to continue to pay on the long-winding interest even after it had paid off the principal debt long ago for its help during 1971.[71] He also claims that Bangladesh's farcically "elected" Hasina government is being controlled by India and its intelligence RAW (Research and Analysis Wing) that have engulfed the country from all sides.[72] An emancipation from the clutches and tentacles of Indian hegemony, Dr Zafrullah goes on to say, is a must for Bangladesh to be really a free country.[73] It is the Indian hegemonic domination and expansionism, he asserts, that is the cause of terrorism and that breeds terrorism in Bangladesh.[74] Following the terrible abduction of a beautiful intellectual and philosophical mind, Farhad Mazhar, by the shadowy and সন্ত্রাসী / terrorist creatures on July 3, 2017, Home Minister Asaduzzaman Khan admitted that RAW agents were indeed active in Bangladesh.

Animesh Rai and Anwar Mohammad provide an authentic and comprehensive summary of the Indian economic rape of Bangladesh before and after the independence.[75] Professor Badruddin Omar, President of Jatiyo Mukti Council (National Liberation Council) writes about the self-seeking Indian role in the liberation of Bangladesh, saying Indian help was extended at India's own interest of weakening its archenemy Muslim majority Pakistan by breaking it apart and getting rid/relieved of the pressure/influx of the refugees from the emerging Bangladesh, not out of love for an independent country at its eastern border.[76]

As the people of Bangladesh are sure to reject the idea of a joint Bengal under Indian federation, former Ambassador and Secretary, Muhammad Azizul Haque, analyses the question of Bangladesh rejoining "Akhand Bharat" as envisaged by many Indian fundamentalist political parties such as the BJP, RSS, BHP and HM. Observing that it was the Congress's uncompromising and intolerant attitude toward the Muslims that was at the root of the partition of India, Azizul Haque claims: "In every Hindu majority province, the Muslims were victims of serious riots and oppression." He rightly thinks that Muslims were forced to seek separate homelands for themselves. "A separate State was not in the minds of the Muslims at the beginning," asserts the writer—

> But the Congress' intransigent opposition to any measure by the British Government aimed at benefiting the minority Muslim population – like the 1905 partition of Bengal, grant of separate electorate for the Muslims, giving power to the Muslims in those provinces where they were in majority – compelled them to demand a separate homeland. The Congress repudiated all British government plans that stipulated power-sharing with the Muslim League – the party that at those times epitomized the aspirations of almost all Muslims of India.

Azizul Haque concludes saying:

> Until Indian politics truly rises above communal parochialism, until there occurs a paradigm shift in India's politics to ensure politico-economic, socio-religious, cultural and other equity and equality for all religious and ethnic communities regardless of their size, unless India's constitutional secularism truly finds its roots in the society, and until the minority Muslim communities across India are seen to be happily living in honor, prestige and security in India, I do not visualize any reason why the future generations of Bangladeshis should decide to reunite their country with India.[77]

Like Rudyard Kipling's most abstract, impractical, stoical and idealistic poem "If—" (1895), in the form of both parental and military advice, containing more than a dozen first conditionals that are needed to be fulfilled to achieve exemplary and unattainable nobility, glory and greatness, Azizul Haque's series of conditionals in the form of "until" and "unless" makes that political target an utopian dream, never to come true, in a so-called secular but in reality a secularist and congenitally sectarian country—India.

One Zahir Khan provides a good catalogue of the alarming trend how the Muslim majority Bangladesh is inexorably sliding into and being steadily swallowed by pro-Hindu, un-Islamic, God-less secularist elements.[78] One can only agree with Ranu Chowdhury, who nicely enumerates the sucking ills that have been squeezing and engulfing Bangladesh from all around in what amounts to an illustration of Dr Zafrullah Chowdhury's claim mentioned above.[79] In India, Hindu fundamentalism has always been on the rise to the extent that not only the slaughter or sacrifice of cow (for beef) for Muslims has recently been banned, restricted, and prohibited in India under Narendra Modi (leading to the poverty of thousands of cattle-growing Hindu farmers and cattle traders and other deadly instances) but also that Muslims have been systematically discriminated against and killed in hundreds of thousands for ages in India.[80]

If Modi's November 2015 visit to the UK is an indication, he and his BJP have the blood of all Indian minorities on their hands—Muslims, Sikhs, Dalits, Kashmiris, and other non-Hindu victims.[81] Darshana Mitra, a lawyer and researcher at the Alternative Law Forum, Bangalore, has written about Modi's fanatical and fundamentalist discrimination against the Muslims of his own country.[82] The fantastical communalism of Modi's India, far from being secular, is exampled by the fact that the government of the Indian state of Gujarat introduced a bill bolstering the existing laws against the butchering of Hindu-revered animals, that is, cow slaughter is to be punishable by life sentence in Modi's home state of Gujarat.[83] BBC reported how Hindu terrorists raped and killed a family of 14 in Gujarat.[84]

Indian historian Professor Mushirul Hasan has written about the lack or lamentable underrepresentation of Muslims in Indian corporate businesses.[85] U.S. Commission on International Religious Freedom has commissioned a report on the Constitutional and Legal Challenges Faced by Religious Minorities in India that was written by Dr Iqtidar Karamat Cheema, published in early 2017.[86] The previous year (2016), acclaimed Indian writer-journalist Saeed Naqvi published his book, *Being the Other: The Muslim in India*, in addition to his two other earlier ones: *Reflections of an Indian Muslim* (1993) and *The Last Brahmin Prime Minister* (1996).[87] Famed young Indian journalist of Kashmiri origin, Rana Ayyub, recently published *Gujarat Files: Anatomy of a Cover Up*, which is all about the 2002 massacre of Muslims in Gujarat when Modi was its chief minister.[88] Famous Indian writer Arundhati Roy demanded that Modi be brought to trial for his utter irresponsibility and callousness during that horrific bloodshed.

As Zoglul Husain claims, "No one should be fooled by any wolf in sheep's clothing, whatever be the diplomatic or political necessity." Mohammad Abedin (mentioned above) narrates how the Muslims in Bangladesh are being subjected to cultural aggression in the name of secularism from the lackeys of India.[89] Iftekhairun Nisa writes about Indian cultural hegemony in her weekly *Holiday* article, "Cultural Imperialism, neo-colonial style, threatens Bangladesh."[90] Actor-playwright Mamunur Rashid claimed that 80% of the family breakups in Bangladesh were due to the evil impact of Indian serials.[91]

If Bangladesh is a Muslim majority country that as a nation can be proud of many Muslim poets born and brought up in the erstwhile East Pakistan, now Bangladesh, dreaming dreams about their country as a separate geographical and territorial entity of its own, why should Bangladesh have a national anthem different in origin and spirit, incompatible, incongruous, and jarring with the country's unity and emergence? Why should the Presidential or Prime Ministerial Biman Bangladesh Airlines Boeing 777 be called আকাশ প্রদীপ, words taken from a song by Tagore, who had no love lost between him and the Muslims, for whom he had indeed a deep dislike? Isn't it an instance of আকাশ সংস্কৃতি of আকাশ বাণী কলকাতা cultural invasion and infiltration?

On the other hand, Stanford University Professor Audrey Truschke, a leading scholar of South Asian history, argues in her book, *Culture of Encounters: Sanskrit at the Mughal Court*, that

> [...] the heyday of Muslim rule in India from the 16th to 18th centuries was, in fact, one of tremendous cross-cultural respect and fertilisation and not religious or cultural conflict. The divisive interpretation actually developed during the colonial period from 1757 to 1947. The British benefited from pitting Hindus and Muslims against one another and portrayed themselves as neutral saviours who could keep ancient religious conflicts at bay [...]. While colonialism ended in the 1940s, the modern Hindu right has found tremendous political value in continuing to proclaim and create endemic Hindu-Muslim conflict.[92]

According to the *Economist* and *Indian Express* reports, Indian Muslims are increasingly facing anxiety and uncertainty over their bleak future.[93] In their আনন্দবাজার reports in 2014, Avirup Sarker, who teaches Economics at Statistical Institute Kolkata, and Asoka Ghose, general secretary of United Trade Union

Congress, wrote, in the context of the national election of India, that no party/ government did justice to Indian Muslims ever.[94] Indian fundamentalist Viswa Hindu Parishad Joint Secretary Surendra Kumar Jaina said that Indian Muslims, who numbered about 145m, must forget and reject their prophet Muhammad (peace be upon him) and instead follow the path of Sri Rama and that only then they would be given full safety and security in India.[95] No Muslim writers, Noyon Chatterjee claims, find their way into the communal West Bengal's school textbooks, whereas the Hindu writers (starting with Rabindranath, Bankim Chandra, Sarat Chandra, Ishwar Chandra, D L Roy) have their more than fair share of representation in Bangladesh.[96] In fact, the latter densely populate the literary and cultural studies in Bangladesh, just as the fishes abound in water, with, unfortunately, no such luck for any Bangladeshi Muslim writers, including the antebellum ones, in the sectarian West Bengal/India.

The Hindu minority in Bangladesh

By contrast, the Hindus, treated as equally as the Muslims, are far better off in Bangladesh than the Muslims in India, who are being seriously discriminated against. In Bangladesh, the Hindus, who are a very small minority, enjoy more than equal opportunity and are employed everywhere, from top to mid ranking positions, from public service to police service to civil and administrative service to education service to judicial service, from police inspectors to government secretaries to chief justice to college principals to university vice chancellors to members of the parliament to cabinet ministers.[97] For example, as (Ret) Major Akhtaruzzaman claimed, nineteen departments/divisions in the Education Ministry alone are headed by Hindus, who miss no opportunity to introduce Hindu elements in the curriculum.[98] In a country of 90% Muslims, the number of minority Hindus occupying high positions in the government bureaucracy (ministries and different institutions) and other sectors is extraordinarily and alarmingly high.[99] It is this argument that is made by Prof Saidul Islam in his "Minority Islam" article (cited above), of which the abstract reads as follows:

> The [Muslim majority] religion, Islam, is however becoming a "minority" day by day. While Muslims in the West—in spite of being a minority—are enjoying their basic religious freedom, this basic right is increasingly being denied to the Muslims in Bangladesh while it continues to aspire to become a "uniquely secular" society. The study shows that the current regime in Bangladesh has taken on a comprehensive policy of secularization with an aim to emasculate Islamic influence from political and social landscape of

> Bangladesh. Apart from undermining basic religious freedom of Muslims, the policy—which turns out to be both aggressive and violent—is increasingly becoming hostile to democratic principles, rule of law, freedom of movement, and political pluralism.[100]

Islam as the state religion of Bangladesh should have its pristine and peaceful presence, promotion, and practice in the national culture, character, and communities, to be more than merely nominal in the Constitution (as opposed to the extremist and fundamentalist beef-banning Hinduism in the neighboring India)

There are many highly respectable and progressive members of Bangladesh's political and civil society who are open-minded, tolerant, moderate and accommodating, yet great practicing Muslims or Hindus on their own. People like them would never accept an Indian-style secularism that translates into suppression of Islam and gross discrimination against Muslims. Neither would they accept the promotion of other religions over the faith of the majority—, which is Islam, needless to say. There are many civil society entities and political and cultural personalities that are the living examples of the *মুক্তমনা* accommodation of both the practice of religion and moderation in a modern Muslim majority society.[101]

While they do not and should not have any problem with the freedom of all religions, they are, however, unlikely to accept, once it has been included in the Constitution of the country of 90% Muslims on June 7, 1988, the erasure of Islam from it without protest, successful or not. The statement of Islam as the state religion in the Constitution is nothing more than a political gesture toward the majority, as secularism, meaning, freedom of religious beliefs and practices, not curtailing it, is a similar gesture toward the minorities. After all, as Mohammad Abdul Gafur argues, Islam is the historical basis, bedrock, and foundation of the sovereign and independent Bangladesh, which, though a country of successful democratic struggles, Gafur claims in a different article, finds itself at a critical crossroads of the lack of democracy.[102]

Although religious freedom is guaranteed and religious minorities are protected in all or most of the secular countries, that freedom and protection are understandably and legitimately glossed over with the color/flavor of the religion of the majority of those countries—Christian, Hindu, Buddhist, Islamic, so on. However, unlike the other secular countries—developed, democratic, educated and tolerant as they are—, there is an obvious abuse of secularism in Bangladesh, as shown above. Due to the Hindu majority of the surrounding gigantic India and its political, economic and cultural hegemony over its tyrannical protégé and proxy Hasina government in Bangladesh, secularism means a trend toward the domination of Hindus and their religion (Hinduism) at the expense of the devaluation and gradual eclipse of Islam and Islamic culture.[103]

If Islam is taken out of the Constitution, as Ranu Chowdhury argues, then Secularism, alien and threatening to the pious, peace-loving and simple-minded Muslims, should be taken out too. Due to its geopolitical, religious, economic, and educational situation, Bangladesh is not America or the West! The equation or the rationale is more complex than it seems and that is why it makes Qamruddin Chowdhury of the USA comment, in a vein of frustration and desperation, that "the blind pro-Indians should be banned like the Nazis are banned for ever. Bangladesh cannot grow without banning and breaking all relations with India and its supporters. Bangladesh can have relations with all EXCEPT India. This basic foundational truth must be understood and followed with zeal and courage to stand up and live in the world without India's intervention and endless troubles" (E-mail of August 22, 2016).

If one goes, as Ranu Chowdhury does, by the adage that চেনা বামুনের পৈতা লাগেনা (a Brahmin, who is a high caste member of the Hindu religious priest class, does not need to wear a sacred thread around his neck/shoulder to let others know about the identity of his superior status), there is no need for Islam to be officially or constitutionally designated and dictated as the state religion of Bangladesh where a great majority are already Muslims. As the witty and humorous mechanical engineer Mohammad Gani of the USA puts it, it is like asking one to prove that s/he is alive. Gani is not overly excited about Islam being only symbolically and ceremonially recognized as the state religion of Bangladesh, which has now become, for all intents and purposes, a country of "ultra-secularists, corruption, extortion, distortion, grafts, bribery, tortures, murders, goons, denials and denial of denials." Dr Zainul Abedin, a former journalist in Bangladesh and now a mass communication specialist in the USA, says the same, that when the practice is contrary, why to state otherwise on paper? True.

When the state as run by the government is full of violence and bloodshed, distrust, duplicity, and deception and when secularism is up and on the rise trampling down on Islam,[104] what is the point of Islam as merely stated or reinstated as a state religion, twenty eight years after its first introduction? Is it to divide and rule? Is it to play one Islamic party against the other? Can one hope that God/Allah the Almighty is going to be happy with only the declaration of Islam as the state religion with corrupting and contaminating political playfulness behind it and constantly flagrant violations of it in the society? Can the people in general or the faithful in particular be sanguine about Him (God) not punishing them for saying one thing in public and doing another, both publicly and privately?

Words must match and be compatible with actions, and the vice versa. That does not mean Bangladesh needs to be an Islamic state run under the Sharia laws, as Engineer Mohammad Aleem of Montana USA asserts: "State Religion Islam does not mean Bangladesh has to be an Islamic State. It is a representation of people's faith following demographics. State Fruit is jackfruit /কাঁঠাল, which does not mean mango is not a good fruit or not tasty, or, we should eat কাঁঠাল only, not the mango." When the respected *Ulema*, confined to the safe walls of their Masjids and Madrasas, choose to stay away by not doing anything against the hundreds of more serious, harmful, dangerous, and reprehensible social and moral ills, why should they ask for the death of Taslima Nasreen? After all, Bangladesh is not a Sharia state and the country is mostly governed by secular laws. A reprimand served to her by the court according to the existing judicial system would have been more than enough.

(Ret) Sqn Ldr Mohammed Shoaib of the USA takes a correct view in saying (in his March 31, 2016 e-mail post) that:

> Even the self-proclaimed best of secular democracies (USA, UK etc.) practice religion in government affairs. The USA and the UK start new governments and parliamentary sessions by taking the oath of office over the Bible or with the prayers by the chaplain. So, what kind of secularism is this? We don't criticize such gross transgressions because they are "White Masters" but we are quick to blame Bangladesh for having Islam as the state religion when such declaration has no real meaning in the country's law and governance. On the contrary, India is secular by name only. Many of its laws are highly discriminatory against the non-Hindus, especially Muslims. India's law enforcement and justice system is 100% biased against Muslims. To a lesser extent, against other non-Hindu religions. The same is true of Israel, another self-proclaimed secular democracy.

In a similar vein, the UK-based freelancer Isha Khan states: "State religion is not a big deal. It depends on governance and socio-political culture of a country. The Christian Cross is there in the British and many other European national flags. The leaders of these 'secular' countries, including the USA, take oath keeping their hands on the Bible. India is a 'secular' country, but communalism is the order of the day in India."

Fruits and flowers and flags or not, "Religious sensibilities are more intimate and intense." These are the words of one (from the USA, formerly a student politics activist in Bangladesh with an interest in the social sciences), who continues to say, "It is not prudent to impose them on the citizen or even on the tourist." While people are ready to accept many other things foreign and even alien—aspects of culture, clothing style, food, language, education, technology—, they are not and will not be willing to trade and barter their religion. "Position on state religion," he says, "is a testimony of how enlightened and educated we are, especially when it comes to the rights of minority."

Having said all this, the people of Bangladesh must not miss the point that Islam as the religion of the absolute majority of the country was introduced in the Constitution as a popular move by President H M Ershad in 1988 (in the empty slot of Secularism which had earlier been removed from the Constitution). Islam is also the Constitutional state religion of the Muslim-majority Malaysia, just as Buddhism is the state religion of Myanmar. Despite his lopsided lapses in both personal and political life, Ershad seems to have a sincere soft corner for his religion and did one good thing (not to deny the other good things he did) by introducing Islam as the state religion of Bangladesh.

Accordingly, every morning's রবীন্দ্র বন্দনা অর্চনা উপাসনা on the secularist TV Channels, for example, can only follow Islamic programs and lessons, not supplant them. রবীন্দ্র সঙ্গীত (Tagore songs)—perhaps the least preferred and least well-liked (if not most disliked)—is fast declining anyway (except it is in the voice of Kaderi Kibria or Anima Roy, all the rest being dull and boring). Similarly, the increasingly Indianized and Westernized nudities in film and on the screen in the name of the so-called "entertainment"—what is actually a carnal temptation toward a cardinal sin, a deadly sin, a capital vice, called sensual/sexual lust—should be effectively stemmed and censored, curbed and controlled. How could Muslim parents allow their children to slip and slide into the public display and graphic demonstration of their body in a bawdy and bowdlerizing manner? How can they allow their children to commercialize their body, like the marketing of a product, though in a slightly different way from the lower or upper class prostitution?

Such commodification of the human flesh is not the same as the safe, sound, and socially healthy, relaxing, and entertaining art of acting, singing, and performing. There may be even more of musical contests and competitions, and sane and sensible, decent and dignified cultural soirees and evenings, including the solo, duet, folk, modern, patriotic, and band music, live on stage or recorded. However, the Indian/Western concept of body on display as art cannot be a good fit and should never be considered to be allowed in a Muslim culture and community.

Secularism was there in the Constitution at the beginning, dropped in the late 1970s, and reintroduced by the AL in the late 1990s while leaving Islam as it was for fear of losing many Muslim votes. Since then both ideologies—Islam and secularism—have been there in the Constitution as a kind of counter to each other, as much symbolically and ceremonially as realistically. Since Bangladesh is a country of 90% Muslims, there ought to be a reflection of Islamic culture everywhere and in every aspect of life and society, officially and otherwise. Any suppression of Islam would give rise to extremist elements.

In fact, the Indian-influenced and Indian-imposed secularism that was unheard of in Bangladesh until 1972 and that entered Bangladesh with the return of Sheikh Mujibur Rahman via New Delhi to the newly independent Bangladesh should again be pulled out of the Constitution, to be left to live quietly in the hearts and minds of the secularists and their respective rituals, without being politicized and constitutionalized for the purpose of worldly goals and partisan gains only. On the other hand, in addition to Islam remaining undisturbed as the state religion, the main Muslim article of faith that "There is no god but God and Mohammad (pbuh/peace be upon him) is His Prophet-Messenger" needs to be inscribed in Arabic, Bangla, and English in all the government offices across the overwhelmingly Muslim majority Bangladesh. If the American Presidents can officially and publicly stick to their holy Bible, National Cathedral Prayers, "God Bless America," and "In God We Trust," why should the Muslim Bangladesh fall behind in those aspects of life and religion which are positive?

Notes

1. https://scroll.in/article/718458/most-extremists-in-india-are-not-muslim-they-are-hindu
2. http://www.drfirozmahboobkamal.com/english-articles/1190-terrorism-of-the-secularist-fascists-a-the-unending-war.html
3. Taj Hashmi, "Ziaur Rahman, Islam and Bangladeshi Nationalism," https://groups.yahoo.com/neo/groups/saldwr/conversations/messages/710
4. http://www.mzamin.com/article.php?mzamin=18647
5. http://www.banglanews24.com/national/news/bd/554805.details
6. http://insidebd.net/news/2015/02/27/details/12093; http://www.amadershomoys.com/newsite/2015/03/19/240051.htm#.VQvSNLezW1t
7. "Behayapona" means shameless immodesty of sexual nature in dress and manners. Visit http://www.sheershanewsbd.com/2016/02/14/116668
8. For example, the Fatimids and the Mameluks in Egypt, the Umayyads in Damascus, and the Abbasids in Baghdad.
9. http://www.nytimes.com/2015/07/23/world/europe/quran-fragments-university-birmingham.html?_r=0
10. Apart from these, for an idea of Arab/Muslim achievements in the various fields of sciences and their application, see Ahmad Hassan & Donald Hill, *Islamic Technology* (1986); Salim Al-Hassani, *1001 Inventions: Muslim Heritage in Our World* (2006); Mark Graham, *How Islam Created the Modern World* (2006); Victor Katz (ed.), *The Mathematics of Egypt, Mesopotamia, China, India, and Islam* (2007); George Saliba, *Islamic Science and the Making of the European Renaissance* (2007); George G. Joseph,

The Crest of the Peacock: Non-European Roots of Mathematics (1st ed. 1991; 3rd ed. 2011). Charles Singer, an Oxford professor of the history of science and the author of a five-volume survey of technology, was one of the first western scholars to acknowledge Arab scientific primacy in the Middle Ages. Writing nearly 50 years ago, Singer contended that during most of the period from 500 to 1,500, "technologically, the West had little to bring to the East. The technological movement was in the other direction."

11. Sebastian Prange, "Thomas Jefferson's Al-Koran," *Saudi Aramco World*, July/August 2011 (available online).
12. http://www.unhcr.org/uk/news/latest/2009/6/4a42245e9/unhcr-chief-launches-book-islams-contributions-refugee-law.html
13. For Trudeau, watch www.youtube.com/watch?v=ArtiAI52d9M. In this respect one may wish to visit: https://www.youtube.com/watch?v=MuXYjobc-Vo ; http://www.kalamullah.com/Books/Ar-Raheeq%20Al-Makhtum.pdf; and http://investigate-islam.com/pages/who-is-real-terrorist.htm
14. For example, Edward Lane became Mansour Effendi; Leopold Weiss became Muhammad Asad; Marmaduke Pickthall became Muhammad; Martin Lings became Abu Bakr Siraj Ad-din; René Guénon became Shaykh Abdul-Wahid Yahya; T. B. Irving became Talim Ali Abu Nasr; William Quilliam became Abdullah; Malcolm X became Malik El-Shabazz; John Philby became Sheikh Abdullah; Sir Wilfred Thesiger became Mubarak bin London (Arabic for "the blessed one from London"); Charles Gai Eaton became Hassan Abdul Hakeem; Cat Stevens became Yusuf Islam; Timothy Winter became Abdul Hakim Murad; Hurgronje spent a year between 1884 and 1885; Peter Sanders became Abdul Azim; Golding (Director of the Islamic Awareness and Education Project in Wiltshire, England) became Imran; Mark Hanson became Hamza Yusuf; Vogel became Abu Hamza; Dennis Bradley Philips became Abu Ameenah Bilal; Janice Huff became Aminah Assilmi; Melvin Leblanc became Abdul Malik; Shakti Saroopji became Islamul Haq; and Ricky Mitchell became Zaid Shakir. Also see, *Loyal Enemies: British Converts to Islam, 1850–1950* (Oxford U P, 2014) by Jamie Gilham.
15. See the review by Robert Lebling of Harvard Oceanic history professor Sugata Bose's *A Hundred Horizons: The Indian Ocean in the Age of Global Empire* (Harvard U P, 2009) in *Saudi Aramco World* (58:2, March/April 2007, p. 43), also available online.
16. http:/banglamail71.com/religion/news=5216
17. Serajul Islam, "How sharbo-joneen is mangal shovajatra?," Weekly *Holiday*, 29 May 2015.
18. http://www.banglatribune.com/national/news/192887
19. http://deshbhabona.com/2017/03/29/13/06
20. http://www.noyonchatterjee.com/2017/04/blog-post_65.html; http://www.noyonchatterjee.com; https://www.facebook.com/noyonchatterjee5; www.newsbangla.net/newsdetail/detail/49/297047; https://www.rbn24.co.uk/?p=9020

21. https://www.linkedin.com/pulse/বদধজবর-কন-জন-ইসলমক-খব-ছট-কর-দখত-অভযসত-হময়ন-আহমদ-mohammad-reza-azam; http://www.somewhereinblog.net/blog/YusufUnique/30114255
22. See Muhammad Mojlum Khan, *The Muslim Heritage of Bengal: The Lives, Thoughts and Achievements of Great Muslim Scholars, Writers and Reformers of Bangladesh and West Bengal* (UK: KUBE Publishing, 2013); Muhammad Enamul Haq, *Muslim Bengali Literature* (1957); *Contemporary Bengali Writings*: Pre-Bangladesh Period (University Press, 1996). Also, http://www.dailynayadiganta.com/detail/news/153155; http://newagebd.net/137648/fans-pay-tribute-to-al-mahmud/#
23. http://www.first-bd.net/newsdetail/detail/49/201281; http://thelondonpost.net/rape-dead-muslim-women-said-yogi-adityanath-modi-made-chief-minister-india
24. https://www.yahoo.com/finance/news/modi-party-finally-confident-enough-044650396.html
25. Zoglul Husain's e-mail posting of August 24, 2015. Also visit: http://www.bdsangbad.com/details.php?id=21493; Abdul Awal Thakur mentioning Shabana Azmi: http://worldbangla.com/2016/05/24/42291
26. http://dnewsbd.com/english/are-they-hired-intellectuals-for-western-propaganda
27. https://www.youtube.com/watch?v=p1nl5E271Ho. Questions for Mita Hoque: are you a Hindu or a Muslim? Was your late actor-husband Khaled Khan a Muslim or a Hindu? Was there a funeral Janaza prayer when he died? Was he buried or cremated? How do you see the long gray/grey beards along with caps on the heads of many Muslim scholars and intellectuals of Bangladesh, dead or alive? Are/were they Bungalee/Bangladeshi? How do you see the long beard, sometimes with a cap too, of Rabindranath Tagore, Nirmalendu Goon, Asad Choudhury, Shujay Sen, Rahul of Joler Gan, Andrew Kishore, Rinku, Pathik Nabi, Shuvo, freedom fighter Major Kamrul, film maker Subhash Dutta, Bhaskar Bandopaddhya, Mostafa Sarwar Farooki, and Beximco's Salman Rahman? Hindu beard, secular or fundamentalist? Muslim beard is moderate. Can you please show us the picture of your father and grandfather to see if they had cap and beard too? If anyone in Bangladesh is to be arrested, after Latif Siddiquee, for hurting the religious sentiment of Muslims, you should be the next. Why are the police silent about you?
28. http://www.newsbangla.net/newsdetail/detail/200/299981; http://www.sheershakhobor.com/2017/04/15; http://rtnbd.net/opinion/40663; http://www.dailynayadiganta.com/detail/news/215890
29. www.news-bangla.net/newsdetail/detail/200/309258; https://www.youtube.com/watch?v=hCSUa6yyHaM; http://dailybdtimes.com/2017/05/17; www.news-bangla.net/newsdetail/detail/200/309138; According to Siddiquee, Chowdhury once made rude and negative comments about Sheikh Mujib. His role in the Banani RainTree incident has been brought into serious question: www.news-bangla.net/newsdetail/detail/200/310025; http://dailybdtimes.com/2017/05/17/

30. http://www.dailynayadiganta.com/detail/news/212832
31. http://www.natun-bd.net/newsdetail/detail/41/286052
32. http://banglamail71.com/others/news=7054
33. http://www.jugantor.com/online/national/2017/02/02/38449; http://www.newagebd.net/article/13124/writ-seeks-removal-of-greek-goddess-from-sc-premises
34. http://www.dailynayadiganta.com/detail/news/211142
35. http://www.mzamin.com/article.php?mzamin=55012
36. http://www.prothom-alo.com/bangladesh/article/1116100
37. http://dnn.news/post/25597;
http://rtnbd.net/bd/12982;
http://newsbd7.com/main/detail/3205;
https://www.facebook.com/qamrul.islam.bd/posts/1342418069123029
38. The same has been pointed out by Mohammad Zainal Abedin in his piece available at http://banews24.com/feature/13203
39. http://www.banglatribune.com/politics/news/99457/;
http://ournewsbd.com/%E0%A6%B6%E0%A6%AB%E0%A7%80%E0%A6%B0-%E0%A6%9B%E0%A7%
40. Journal of Muslim Minority Affairs (Taylor & Francis) 31:1 (December 2011), pp. 125–141.
41. http://presstime24.com/index.php/details_column/index/57cbcc48db807;
http://newsbd7.com/main/detail/3024
42. http://bn.mtnews24.com/jatio/151617;
http://amar-desh24.com/bangla/index.php/details/nationalnews/7527
43. http://southasiajournal.net/tetul-hujur-now-sour-with-khaleda-sweet-with-hasina;
dnn.news/আ-লীগ-যখন-ইসলামী-ঐক্যজোট-হ;
http://www.eurasiareview.com/21042017-tetul-hujur-now-sour-with-khaleda-sweet-with-hasina-oped;
http://foreignpolicynews.org/2017/04/21/tetul-hujur-now-sour-khaleda-sweet-hasina; http://www.dailynayadiganta.com/detail/news/216176
44. http://blog.bdnews24.com/Habibb/15918/comment-page-1
45. http://www.newsbd7.com/main/detail/3024;
https://www.facebook.com/faraejiandolon/photos/a.435057876549478.109498.433495726705693/997172220338038/?type=3&theater;
https://groups.google.com/forum/#!topic/pfc-friends/bpFP5gPRWuE;
http://newsbd7.com/main/detail/2923;
http://newsbd7.com/main/detail/2962;
http://www.amadershomoys.com/unicode/2016/04/27/102341.htm;
http://www.amardeshonline.com/pages/details/2016/05/24/337209;
http://www.bddesh.net/blog/blogdetail/detail/2662/sottolikhon/60830;
http://www.bdface.net/newsdetail/detail/200/245133
https://www.dailyinqilab.com/details/18421 (Dr Mohammad Issa Shahedi)
46. http://www.prothom-alo.com/education/article/1059823;

http://www.prothom-alo.com/education/article/1060527; http://www.prothom-alo.com/bangladesh/article/1061861;
http://rtnbd.net/national/21147;
http://www.noyonchatterjee.com/2017/03/blog-post_6.html

47. https://youtu.be/WA-oCN7tS64
48. http://www.banglatribune.com/politics/news/99457; http://www.prothom-alo.com/bangladesh/article/849571; http://www.amaderbudhbar.com/2015/12/16. For the graphic images of the brutal massacre of the Hefajote men, visit: http://chairmanbd.blogspot.com.au/2013/05/mass-killing-on-protesters-in-dhaka-at.html
49. http://www.ittefaq.com.bd/print-edition/sub-editorial/2017/05/11/194653.html
50. http://www.jugantor.com/online/opinion/2017/04/22/45340;
https://www.facebook.com/alm.fazlurrahman/posts/1121293360128 02
51. Titumir died of wounds after his bamboo fort (bansher kella) was stormed by the British soldiers. "Syed Ahmad Barelvi and hundreds of his troops and followers were killed by the Sikh army in Balakot, Mansehra District in 1831, but a number of his followers survived and continued to fight on, taking part in tribal uprisings in the North-west province as late as 1897."
52. http://newagebd.net/239317/legendary-pakistani-social-worker-edhi-dies/; for Dulal's Chandmoni, visit: http://www.ittefaq.com.bd/wholecountry/2016/03/27/61308.html
53. http://newagebd.net/190238/362-incidents-of-sexual-assault-in-2015/
54. http://www.dailysangram.com/post/107669
55. http://www.bdfirst.net/newsdetail/detail/49/171254
56. http://www.bd-first.net/newsdetail/detail/200/182657;
https://www.youtube.com/watch?v=SQzReGzAdW0;
http://deshwa.blogspot.com/2013/11/blog-post_4791.html
57. http://www.muldharabd.com/?p=716; https://www.dailyinqilab.com/details/7052
58. http://bit.ly/2dPo9W0; http://bit.ly/2dWXY0f; http://bit.ly/2djqfNa
59. https://www.facebook.com/photo.php?fbid=1001737939880890&set=gm.638851709596503&type=3&theater;
https://www.facebook.com/photo.php?fbid=1001737939880890&set=gm.638851709596503&type=3
60. http://archive.ittefaq.com.bd/index.php?ref=MjBfMDNfMjFfMTRfMV8xXzFfMTE3Mzg2;
http://bangla.samakal.net/2016/03/27/202155
61. https://www.rbn24.co.uk/?p=6036; http://www.siliconindia.com/news/business/15-Nations-Sending-Highest-Remittances-to-India-nid-147515-cid-3.html. Also see, for similar findings, Dr Habib Siddiqui's article of 23 February 2014, "Letter from America: Indian Expats in Bangladesh": http://asiantribune.com/node/71992; http://www.jugantor.com/online/national/2016/08/11/21797/

62. http://www.thedailystar.net/opinion/online-exclusive/20-million-%E2%80%9Cil-legal-bangladeshis-india-%E2%80%93-really-1316185
63. www.dailynayadiganta.com/detail/news/167055
64. *The Works of John Ruskin* 31 (1907), eds. E. T. Cook & Alexander Wedderburn (London: George Allen, 1908), p. 392. This kind of satirical description reminds one of how Ruskin's opposite, the Utilitarian philosopher Jeremy Bentham criticized England in 1828: "priest-ridden, lawyer-ridden, lord-ridden, squire-ridden, soldier-ridden England." Quoted in Javed Majeed, *Ungoverned Imaginings: James Mill's The History of British India and Orientalism* (Oxford: Clarendon Press, 1992), p. 127; and my "Victorian and Pre-Victorian Reaction to (the History and Culture of) British India in the Works of James Mill, Alfred Tennyson, and John Ruskin" in *Readings in Oriental Literature: Arabian, Indian, and Islamic* (Cambridge Scholars Publishing, 2015), p. 229.
65. http://www.amadershomoys.com/newsite/2015/09/11/394975.htm#; http://www.dailysangram.com/news_details.php?news_id=204253
66. http://www.amardeshonline.com/pages/details/2016/01/09/318618#
67. https://goutamdas.com/2016/09/06/. See B. Rajeshwari, *Communal Riots in India: A Chronology (1947–2003)* at: http://www.nagarikmancha.org/images/1242-Documents-Communal_Riots_in_India.pdf; Dr Awatar Singh Sekhon (Machaki) at: http://www.ourbeacon.com/cgi-bin/bbs60x/webbbs_config.pl/md/read/id/314123119205617
68. http://www.somoyerkonthosor.com/2016/07/23/16344.htm
69. For an understanding of communalism and sectarianism, click: http://www.muldharabd.com/?p=1904; https://www.facebook.com/DeswaOfficial/photos/a.1551763671720740.1073741828.1551109385119502/1599914356905671/?type=1&theater
70. http://www.outlookindia.com/magazine/story/a-beast-asleep/280032; http://www.muldharabd.com/?p=1990
71. http://www.amardeshonline.com/pages/details/2015/09/19/302850; https://sathkahonbd.blogspot.co.uk/2016/01/blog-post_946.html; http://www.amadershomoy.biz/beta/2016/12/04/753177/; http://www.amardeshonline.com/pages/details/2016/06/16/340456; Well-documented Indian army's rampant Looting of Bangladesh in 71–74 at: https://groups.google.com/d/topic/soc.culture.bangladesh/NMcDNDC2IpM; https://www.facebook.com/TheIndiaDoctrine/posts/1509001395779735:0
72. http://www.ittefaq.com.bd/politics/2016/04/09/63172.html; http://www.amadershomoys.com/unicode/2016/04/11/96810.htm; http://www.amardeshonline.com/pages/details/2016/06/20/340995
73. http://www.rtnn.net/bangla/newsdetail/detail/1/1/170624

74. http://www.banglatribune.com/others/news/194491
75. For Indian looting of Bangladesh, click: https://animeshrai.wordpress.com/2015/12/17/;
http://www.animeshraiarko.com/2016/10/blog-post_2.html; http://www.muldhar-abd.com/?p=1174
76. http://www.jugantor.com/online/opinion/2016/12/18/34086
77. (1) http://www.thedailystar.net/op-ed/will-we-one-day-reunite-akhand-bharat-576214; (2) http://www.first-bd.net/newsdetail/detail/49/196915; (3) http://www.muldharabd.com/?p=290; and (4) http://www.darjeeling-unlimited.com/losing.html. In the opinion of Zoglul Husain, "Indeed, in the Lucknow Pact of 1916, Jinnah negotiated power sharing between the Congress and the Muslim League, as he was a member of both parties at the time, and the unity of the two parties was established. 'Due to the reconciliation brought about by Jinnah between the Congress and the League, the Nightingale of India, Sarojini Naidu, gave him the title of "the Ambassador of Hindu-Muslim Unity'. Although the Two Nation Theory is attributed to Jinnah, according to some, it was Savarkar of Hindu Mahasabha who used it first. 'He pronounced the two-nation theory, first, in 1923 in his essay Hindutva and next in 1937 in his presidential address to the Mahasabha'."
78. http://www.bddesh.net/blog/blogdetail/detail/2662/sottolikhon/60830;
http://www.bddesh.net/newsdetail/detail/200/216239;
https://www.facebook.com/photo.php?fbid=1550831461906556&set=a.1404130729909964.1073741828.100009391517060&type=3&theater
79. To paraphrase Ranu Chowdhury's enumeration: India has never been a friend of Bangladesh. It has been extracting, one-sidedly, unbelievable amount of benefit from Bangladesh. It has confirmed its role as a hegemon by: 1. cordoning Bangladesh with wire-fencing; 2. strangulating Bangladesh with its crippling control of waters upstream in the 54 rivers that the two countries share; 3. continuing to kill Bangladeshis at the border points; 4. snatching away the island of South Talpotti; 5. flooding the Bangladeshi market with its low quality products; 6. brainwashing the Bangladeshis with a degrading culture; 7. spoiling the Bangladeshi youth with a regular supply of harmful drugs; 8. using Bangladesh territory freely for supply of its goods that includes military wares to its Seven Sisters; 9. letting its hundreds of thousands of nationals (half a million?) live in Bangladesh (legally or illegally), who siphon away billions of dollars ($3.7 billion?) annually from Bangladesh; and 10. establishing its RAW hold on almost all departments, agencies, institutions, and organizations of Bangladesh. The list is never ending. Bangladesh has hardly any debt to India. It fought for its independence in 1971, which India supported not for the love of Bangladesh but to break Pakistan into pieces. Indian PM Indira Gandhi rightly testified it in their parliament by saying, after Pakistan's surrender on 16 December 1971, that they had taken *Hazar saalume ka bodla* on Pakistan. Mrs. Gandhi meant that they had taken a thousand years of accumulated revenge on Pakistan. For India,

Bangladesh was nothing more than a byproduct of her revenge on Pakistan. Yet, she continued to take full credit for the independence of Bangladesh. Nowhere in India's war documents, not even in their movies involving 1971 (such as *Gunday*), the name of Mukti Bahini and its sacrifices were mentioned. India orchestrated the December 16, 1971 surrender ceremony in Dhaka to depict that Mukti Bahini had no role in the war. It is not only a shame on the part of the Bangladesh leadership of the time, but also a deep slur on the *shaheeds* of 1971. It was, however, Moulana Bhasani who reminded the post-independent Awami ruling class that India should be grateful to Bangladesh, not the other way round. What India gained in 1971 far outweighed the material support it provided to Bangladesh during the war. Bangladesh should have its accounting balance sheet fixed and straightened. (E-mail of 19 and 20 September 2015).

80.

- http://economictimes.indiatimes.com/news/politics-and-nation/muslims-constitute-14-of-india-but-just-3-of-india-inc/articleshow/48849266.cms;
- http://www.banglamail24.com/news/151662;
- http://www.mzamin.com/article.php?mzamin=63337;
- http://www.bbc.com/bengali/news/2016/05/160515_india_muslim_youth_who_rented_home_with_hindu_name_gets_govt_job.

For Muslims being killed in large numbers in India for years and being treated as low class citizens there, and then for Indian hate campaign, dangerous propaganda, and hegemonic and expansionist plans against Bangladesh, see the following thirteen links (courtesy of the nationalist and patriotic political activist Zoglul Husain of the UK):

- https://masumse.wordpress.com/2013/12/06/india-is-the-killing-field-for-muslims/;
- http://164.100.24.219/rsq/quest.asp?qref=100652;
- http://www.al-ihsan.net/fulltext.aspx?subid=2&textid=8881;
- http://www.somewhereinblog.net/blog/priyo_bangla/29877905;
- https://www.facebook.com/permalink.php?id=208585302628432&story_fbid=382497445237216;
- https://www.facebook.com/DeswaOfficial/photos/a.1551763671720740.1073741828.1551109385119502/1599914356905671/ ;
- https://en.wikipedia.org/wiki/Sachar_Committee;
- http://indianexpress.com/article/india/india-news-india/ten-years-since-sachar-report-muslims-still-3-in-ias-ips-2982199;
- http://indiatoday.intoday.in/story/rss-mohan-bhagwat-india-pakistan-bangladesh-hindu-nation/1/444241.html;
- https://www.facebook.com/bengalrss;
- http://www.nagarikmancha.org/images/1242-Documents-Communal_Riots_in_India.pdf;

- http://www.amadershomoys.com/newsite/2015/06/23/328592.htm; and
- http://www.bangladeshchronicle.net/index.php/2013/11/kite-flying-by-raw/

81. http://www.kractivist.org/george-galloway-says-narendra-modi-has-blood-on-his-hands-at-protest-as-indian-pm-meets-david-cameron/; http://www.theguardian.com/politics/2015/nov/12/indian-pm-confronted-by-angry-protesters-in-downing-street.
82. https://thewire.in/104236/indians-angry-trumps-new-travel-ban-muslims-look-modi/
83. https://amp.theguardian.com/world/2017/mar/14/indian-state-government-life-sentence-cow-slaughter; https://www.yahoo.com/news/india-state-greenlights-life-sentences-cow-slaughter-005905070.html
84. http://www.times24.net/International/39600/
85. http://www.natunbarta.com/interview/2014/01/28/65932
86. http://www.uscirf.gov/sites/default/files/Constitutional%20and%20Legal%20Challenges%20Faced%20by%20Religious%20Minorities%20in%20India.pdf
87. https://cafedissensusblog.com/2016/11/18/book-review-saeed-naqvis-being-the-other-the-muslim-in-india/
88. http://qshishir.blogspot.ca/2016/06/blog-post.html; "Why Media Blacked Out Rana Ayyub And Her Incisive Book On Gujarat Riots?"
89. http://banews24.com/feature/13203. For Romila Thapar's interesting idea of secularism in the Indian subcontinent, see http://newagebd.net/168302/what-secularism-is-and-where-it-needs-to-be-headed/ and http://newagebd.net/168596/what-secularism-is-and-where-it-needs-to-be-headed-ii/
90. http://www.weeklyholiday.net/homepage/pages/UserHome.aspx?ID=9&date=0
91. https://www.dailyinqilab.com/article/59974; http://bangla.daily-sun.com/post/12956
92. http://zeenews.india.com/entertainment/bookworm/bookworms-trail/hindu-religion-or-culture-was-never-under-attack-during-muslim-rule-in-india_1794893.htm
93. http://www.economist.com/news/asia/21709341-indias-biggest-minority-grows-anxious-about-its-future-uncertain-community; http://indianexpress.com/article/cities/kolkata/status-of-bengal-muslims-still-dismal/
94. http://www.muldharabd.com/?p=1943
95. http://parstoday.com/bn/news/india-i24043
96. http://www.noyonchatterjee.com/2017/02/blog-post_79.html
97. www.muldharabd.com/?p=716; http://deshwa.blogspot.com/2013/11/blog-post_4791.html; http://www.noyonchatterjee.com/2016/06/blog-post_75.html. As of June 2015, out of 22 Additional Secretaries, 14 were from the minority: http://www.bd-desh.net/newsdetail/detail/200/132133; http://www.mopa.gov.bd/uploads/2015/training/local/it1-2015-110.PDF.
98. http://deshwa.blogspot.com/2013/11/blog-post_4791.html; Maj (Ret) Akhtaruzzaman is shocked that 19 departments in the Education ministry of a Muslim majority country are headed by minority Hindus: http://www.desh-bd.net/newsdetail/detail/200/228904; https://www.youtube.com/watch?v=tg-pjDnBmW4. In protest and frustration to the minority Hindu predominance, Engineer Shahadat Hussaini

of the USA reacts in verse in an e-mail post: "পাল, ঘোষ, রায়, আর দত্ত/যদি হয় শিক্ষার বাহক/ আমি পারিনা হাসিতে/বিকশিত করিয়া দন্ত/স্বাধীনতার যুদ্ধে ঝাঁপিয়ে পরেছিলাম/বিলিয়ে দিতে প্রাণ অকাতরে/নহে বিসর্জন দিতে মান/মূল্যবোধ বিজাতীয় সংস্কৃতির উদরে/ওরে তোরা থাম, এখনও আছে সময়/মিথ্যে খেলছিস সতরন্চ /তোদের চালে তোরাই খাবি মার/উল্টে যাবে সাজানো মঞ্চ I"

99. http://deshwa.blogspot.com/2013/11/blog-post_4791.html; Faridpur District Awami League President and his family are Indian Hindus: http://www.u71news.com/?page=-details&article=21.69370; http://bangla.samakal.net/2016/04/27/208698. According one estimate, till 5 November 2013, there were 5 Hindus out of 72 Government Secretaries; 78 out 426 Additional Secretaries; 131 out of 1,241 Joint Secretaries; 125 out of 1,285 Deputy Secretaries; 53 Senior Assistant Secretaries; 96 Assistant Secretaries; 4 District Commissioners (DCs); 5 Deputy DCs; 11 Additional DDCs; and 14 UNOs. Source: http://drhabibsiddiqui.blogspot.com/2014/02/all-those-fuss-about-endangered.html; http://www.noyonchatterjee.com/2016/03/blog-post_64.html; http://archive.is/NzuGN#selection-1129.40-1129.210.
100. http://www.tandfonline.com/doi/abs/10.1080/13602004.2011.556893. For the minority Hindu terrorism and sectarianism in the Muslim majority Bangladesh, click http://www.jugantor.com/bangla-face/2016/09/21/61945; http://bit.ly/2dDlOTa; and the article by Munshi Viswajit at http://www.muldharabd.com/?p=1154
101. For example, *Tamaddun Majlish* (since 1947), President Ziaur Rahman, M. Asafuddowla, Nur-e-Alam Siddiquee, Dr Tuhin Malik, Kazi Zafar Ahmed, Mahmudur Rahman (a national conscience who suffered in jail for too long), Syed Mohammad Ibrahim, Oli Ahmad, Mostafa Zaman Abbasi, Zubaida Rahman, Farhat Qader Chowdhury, Afroza Abbas, Tahsina Rushdir Elias Ali, Dr Shamsher Ali, Syed Ashraf Ali, Water Resources specialist S I Khan, Nokul Kumar Biswas, Sanjib Chowdhury, Sukomol Barua, Farhad Mazhar, Mina Farah, Justice Abdur Raouf, Shahnaz Rahmatullah, Lina Taposhi Khan, Mizanur Rahman Shelly, (late) Bashir Ahmed, Kaderi Kibria, Al Mahmud, Shaheen Samad, Ajmery Nirjhor, Dilara Zaman, Shormila Shaon, (meteorologist) Taslima Imam, Haider Hussein, Andalib and Anmona Partho, Helena Jahangir, Tania Nahid, Mohammad Musa, Shahadat Hussein Selim, Golam Mowla Roni, Fahima Nasrin Munni, M A Latif Khan, Gazi Mohammad Shahjahan, and Sahana Seraj, among others.
102. https://www.dailyinqilab.com/article/54345;http://www.dailyinqilab.com/article/64527
103. For the audacious anti-Islamic statements by Suranjit Sen Gupta, who is a Hindu and whose name came up in association with the Railway "black cat" bribe money, see http://www.prothombangladesh.net/article/14408; http://www.prothombangladesh.net/article/14671
104. For the anti-Islamic activities of some Hindu journalists such as Munni Shaha in Bangladesh, click:
http://www.bdface.net/newsdetail/detail/49/247408; https://www.facebook.com/TheIndiaDoctrine/photos/a.489485057731379.113062.368401646506388/1296918303654713/?type=3&theater

13

Taslima Nasreen

An Ultra-Feminist of Politicocultural and Religious Divide[1]

"I took to bed whoever I wanted. I always refused to sleep with anybody I didn't like"
—TN[2]

After God, English poet John Milton created his evil but amazingly attractive Satan as if he was a parliamentary opposition leader or a rhetorically skilled demagogue in *Paradise Lost* (1667). The other famous versions of Satan in the character of the demonic Mephistopheles were created by Christopher Marlowe in *Doctor Faustus* (1592), Goethe in *Faust* (1808), Thomas Mann in his novel *Doctor Faustus* (1947), and Vaclav Havel in his play *Temptation* (1985), which was influenced by his reading of Mann and Goethe in jail. Salman Rushdie produced his version in his blasphemous *The Satanic Verses* in 1988. In early nineteenth century, English Romantic poets William Blake and Lord Byron had their versions of Satan as an embodiment (or representative) of rebellious energy and freedom against compromise and conventional morality. Their contemporary Robert Southey, in his *A Vision of Judgment* (1821), written in praise of George III, described Byron and Shelley and the like as a Satanic school for their impiety, audacity, atheism, and sexually immoral and scandalous character. They were "men of diseased hearts and depraved imaginations," according to Southey, infecting others with "a moral virus that [ate] into the soul," their works being "lascivious" and "loathsome" in parts, betraying "a wretched spirit of hopelessness."

However, the 52-year old Bangladeshi physician-turned-writer Taslima Nasreen, in her low level of religious literacy, seems to have exceeded all limits in crossing over to the real biblical Belial, Moloch, and Satan. Her actions and words combine the spirit of both what Southey said of Byron-led Satanic school and what Byron said in satirical revenge, more memorably, in his *The Vision of Judgment*: that Southey reading his "mediocre" and "philistine" work as the old and imbecile George III's Poet Laureate (1813–1843) sent the howling devils hurrying back to hell. Nasreen is as averse to Islam and Muslims (in fact, all religious faiths) as Byron was to Southey whom he attacked, in poem after poem (*English Bards* of 1809, the Dedication of *Don Juan* of 1819, and *The Vision* of 1822), as "a dog in the dark," "a scoundrel" and "a renegade."

Himself an atheist, Byron never directly attacked the conventional Christianity or any other religion the way Nasreen has attacked Islam. In fact, Byron had a good opinion about many aspects of Islam and its rituals as he saw them in practice in Ottoman Turkey. In her bawdy barbarism and sexual and impious adventurism, Nasreen seems to have sold her soul to the devil, to the extent of getting intentionally infected by syphilis, as it were, as part of the deal with the evil agent as Mann's fictitious Faustian composer Adrian does. In her extremist fight against religion, Nasreen has actually reduced herself to the level of Havel's limited, uncertain, confused, and self-contradictory Doctor Foustka and the wizard Fistula.

Nasreen is as extreme a secularist and as irrational a jerk as she was/is a hardcore loose libertine completely given to her carnal and fleshly desires, by her own admission.[3] Sometimes the likes of her are hired by Judeo-Christian fundamentalists and atheists to work for their anti-Islamic agenda/propaganda.[4] In her infidel and radical free thought, Nasreen hates and eschews scriptures and sacred revelations. In her extremism she is bent upon hurting people's solemn and profound religious sentiments and creating sensations to grab cheap and easy publicity. She is carried away by her mad and mindless anti-Islamic antipathy and animosity.

As recently as January 2015, Nasreen supported the grossly anti-Islamic *Charlie Hebdo*'s repeated publication (first in 2006) of the satirical cartoon images of Islam's Prophet Muhammad. Muslims and non-Muslims worldwide, including the Pope, Russian President Vladimir Putin and the former British M16 chief Sir John Sawyers, protested that the French weekly was involved in an act of provocation and violation of the limits of freedom. In November 2014, Sanjib Chowdhury, a prominent Hindu journalist of Bangladesh, said that the solution to the ills of the society and in politics lay in a return to the religious values by members of all faiths.

About the same time, Rebecca Momen, a ruling party MP and Chairman of the Women and Children's Welfare parliamentary committee in Bangladesh, said that it was women's open and provocative dress, indecent manners and sexually inviting conduct that were responsible for rape and abuse of them.[5] She said she did not find any fault with men, who were actually drawn in by the exposure of the half-clad irresistible female allure. In response to this, the exiled Nasreen wrote in her Facebook status that an "illiterate," "ineligible," "unqualified" and "rubbish" woman like Rebecca Momen needed to be immediately kicked out by a kick on her "ass." Nasreen took the whole nation to task by saying it was as "dumb" as Momen. It was that mean and nasty that Nasreen's response could take its hue. In July 2015, she threw her satanic support for the pro-Awami and pro-Indian Abdul Gaffar Chowdhury's filthy and foolish remarks, with the help of the Bangladesh Mission in New York, about God/*Allah* the Almighty's 99 names and his other anti-Islam remarks that caused an indignant protest in the social media.[6]

Earlier (in October 2014), Nasreen gleefully threw her self-serving support for her cohort and ruling party (Awami League) member Abdul Latif Siddiquee's ridiculous and ludicrous comments, made abroad (in the USA), defiling Islam, Islam's prophet and Islam's fundamental rituals, especially the annual pilgrimage by Muslims to Mecca.[7] Needless to say, Siddiquee's remarks hurt the sentiments of all believers, not just Muslims, and met with a blizzard of popular protests through different forms and forums, both civil and political, all across Bangladesh. No wonder, he lost his job as a cabinet minister in the Hasina Government and had about a dozen of lawsuits and arrest warrants issued against him. He returned in November, only to be taken behind bars. During October and November, he took shelter in exile in India where Nasreen also has been sheltering for years, probably in political asylum, ousted from Bangladesh long ago for making equally deplorable, despicable, and blasphemous remarks against Islam that did not go without a barrage of protests by the emotionally wounded and offended Muslim community.

In December 2013, there was a controversy, one in a series, over Nasreen, whose Bengali TV serial *Dusahobas* (Difficult Living) was indefinitely postponed by a Bengali channel in Calcutta (Kolkata), India. Despite Nasreen's protestation that the serial had nothing to do with religions and that it was about a Calcutta-based Hindu family and the three daughters facing social evils, the West Bengal Muslims thought it contained scenes that might hurt their religious sentiments and disturb communal peace and harmony. The all-liberated Nasreen is no stranger to creating controversies, especially since 1994 when she was forced to leave her country for a destination in Europe and then in India (Calcutta) in

2004, from where, following a protest in 2007, that time by the West Bengal Hindus, over her other contemporary publications, she had to flee away to take refuge in New Delhi living there ever since.

Early in 2012, after Muslim threats and protests, the Calcutta Book Fair had to cancel the launch of Nasreen's autobiography *Nirbasan* ("Exile") and she was surprised that the cancellation was not challenged by anybody and met with no outcry whatsoever. Interestingly, in September 2012, Nasreen, an outright advocate of sexual liberation, accused the Bangla *Sahittya* (Literature) Academy of India president Sunil Gangopadhyaya of sexually harassing her.[8] Although unlimited sexual freedom and free love can never mean acceptance of rape and sexual humiliation, they however do encourage unwanted advances in the form of sexual violence or molestation as it may have happened in her case.

"A dirty woman called Taslima Nasreen," was the caption of a report by M. H. Faruqi, published in the London-based *Impact International* in July 1994. The report described her as "a woman pornographer," who "advocates what she practices: promiscuity and perversion." It also alleged that she "had been an Indian discovery and recipient of Calcutta's *desi* Booker Prize." Earlier, the monthly's February issue had published a report on her "pornographic life and works." Taj Hashmi, a professor of security studies at Austin Peay State University, Tennessee, exposes the crude vulgarity and ignorance of "this wretched writer," whom he describes as "a bundle of lies" and her admirers as "degenerated self-hating derailed Islamophobes."

All this followed the controversy Nasreen had caused in Bangladesh by openly insulting and castigating, like her predecessor and fellow-countryman, Daud Haider in the 1970s, the most sacred religious beliefs and sanctities of Islam and Muslims. The rubbish that was her 1993 third-rate novella *Lajja* (meaning "Shame," therefore, echoing in its title the work of the same name by her cohort Salman Rushdie) was of course provocative enough to plunge Bangladesh into a violent unrest for a few months next year that saw her books banned one after another and forced her to go into hiding and then secretly run away from the country she could not return to as of today. Even her fellow secular intellectuals, radical progressives and atheists were inclined to taking issue with her and preferred not to come to her rescue. She was violently attacked for defaming Islam in the above mentioned novel in Hyderabad in 2013.[9] The cloud or specter of violent protest may not have yet completely disappeared. The situation may still prove to be potentially explosive if and when she returns from exile abroad (currently India) not only to the stigma she has earned for herself but also the wrath and retaliation of her own people in Bangladesh.

Nasreen was certainly wrong and reckless in the way she conducted herself. Ditched by Paul Gray as a "bad writer" whose work is "stuffed with slack reasoning and prose,"[10] Nasreen had foolishly created a bitter, virulent and vitriolic dispute by hurting the religious sentiment of millions of peace-loving, God-fearing Muslims. "If those mobs in Dhaka howling for Taslima Nasrin's head," continues Gray, "had ever read her books, they might really be angry." What, for example, would they make of (Gray quotes from Nasreen):

When a dog is chasing you, be warned.
That dog has rabies.
When a man is chasing you, be warned.
That man has syphilis.

"This verse may be more nuanced and lyrical in the original Bengali," Gray claims, "but the English translation conveys qualities that even most of Nasrin's supporters in Bangladesh readily concede: she is very angry, not given to nice distinctions, eager to shock and unconcerned with turning fine phrases."

Nasreen has personalized, out of her selfish motive for a publicity stunt, her quarrel with Islam and the Qur'an. She had done the same in "her characterizations of men," says James Walsh, "as insects and rapists, along with the darts she aims at religion."[11] Her statements made to *The Sunday Observer* of India back in 1984; also, a decade later, to the Calcutta-based *The Statesman*, and in an interview with Australian television[12] are absolutely baseless, good as animus-fomenting propaganda as her writings themselves are. Her media statements that the Qur'an should be "revised thoroughly" and that religions are just so out of date that they must be treated as "old archive documents" are certainly all foolish and clownish, ignoble and ignorant, utter nonsense.

There are many sweeping and self-styled proclamations made by Nasreen, such as Islam being "a venomous snake," that must have been intended either to thinly veil or glaringly reveal her own dire desperation born out of personal despair, failures and frustrations. Neither her marriages nor her love affairs nor her writings ever worked to bring her success and happiness. By her anti-Islamic stand, she has been playing into the hands of the Indian Hindu fundamentalist BJP, which, for its own nefarious agenda, was actively involved in promoting her *Lajja* ("Shame"), which gives a completely distorted picture of the traditionally non-existent religious and sectarian tensions and conflicts, if any, in what have largely been cool and quiet and peaceful Hindu-Muslim relations in Bangladesh.[13]

Naturally, the Bangladesh government banned her *Lajja* as it did her other books that followed: the first part of her autobiographical memoir *Amar Meyebela* (translating "Days of My Childhood/Girlhood through Growing Up into Womanhood," 1999); *Utal Hawa* ("Emotionally Exciting/Inspiring/Unsettling Breeze," 2002), *Ka/Dwikhandita* ("Divided/Slashed into Two," 2003) and *Sei Sab Ondhakar* ("Those Darknesses/Dark Times/Dark Days," 2004). Ironically, her Indian West Bengal friends and backers also did not like her nonfiction memoir *Dwikhandita*, a boastful narrative of her sexual stuff and exploits with many a contemporary writer, in part, also her senseless attack on the prophet of Islam, and had it banned there too.

What the former Archbishop of Canterbury, George Carey, said—that *The Satanic Verses* was an "outrageous sneer" on Prophet Muhammad—applies to Nasreen's writings as well. Did she think about the much older Bible and the Torah (the Old Testament and the New) before she passed her imbecile remarks about the much later and, in fact, as the Muslims believe, the last divine revelation, the Qur'an? In her demonic devilish zealotry, she said on May 13, 1994 (to make her May 9 interview on this issue "clear and categorical") that she held "the Koran, the Vedas, the Bible and all such religious texts to be out of place and out of time."[14]

Maybe Nasreen needs an introductory textbook lesson in religion from Prince Charles and Bishop Lord Harris (former Bishop of Oxford and currently Deputy Bishop of Southwark), both of whom are said to have a soft and sympathetic understanding of all religions, including Islam. It was about the same time, that is, about twenty-one years ago when the Nasreen controversy was at its peak, that Prince Charles expressed his wish that he, as the future British monarch, would like to hold a royal title as the Defender of All Religions (not just Christianity) in order to let unity and tolerance prevail among the people.

The liberal minded Harris has recently said that, besides the Bible, a recitation from the Qur'an also should be included during the future inauguration of Prince Charles. While the presidents, prime ministers, and the peacemakers in the Middle East and around the world find it not only morally sound but also politically correct and practically wise to quote from all those ancient and universally valid religious scriptures in the signing-in ceremonies across the Atlantic and the Mediterranean, the tall-talking Nasreen and her pompous, hollow and empty sympathizers, out of their short-sighted visions and mistaken views, find the revered and universal scriptures either "out of place" or to be in need of being "thoroughly revised."

The political leaders in the United States usually conclude their speeches with "God bless America, God bless us all." American presidents go to the church to pray before they take the oath of office by placing their hands on the Bible. Wouldn't Nasreen think it a great idea too that the leaders in her own country should also do the same by noting the role of the most beneficent and most compassionate God/*Allah* the Almighty in the life of the people and the nation/s, thereby the whole creation? The U.S. coins are engraved with "In God we trust." Shouldn't the coins in Nasreen's native country be engraved in the like manner as well?

If she thinks in the negative, she may face the same fate as Lady Hester Stanhope.[15] The most widely used World/Western (both the current Gregorian and the past Julian) calendar in its BCs (Before Christ/before the date on which Christians believe Jesus was born) and ADs (standing for the Latin Anno Domini, meaning *In/After the Year of the Lord*) has been devised according to the date of the birth of Jesus Christ[16] and the Islamic/Muslim calendar started from the date of Prophet Muhammad's migration from Mecca (Makkah) to Medina (Madinah)—in both cases it is the historic religious occasions/events involving the two great religious figures.

Is Nasreen, in her perverted zeal, going to propose a change in the calendar on the basis of the date when a woman would make it to the Guinness Book of Records by having four husbands at a time, as she thinks a woman should as a measure of her equality to/with a man? In one of her newspaper columns, she argues that if a man in Islam is allowed four wives, a woman also should be permitted to have four husbands. What a sick and silly and feverish argument to cause hiccups even to the sourest of celibates in the world! Even Chaucer's Wife of Bath, perhaps the first feminist character in English literature to advocate as many marriages for a woman as necessary, depending on her bodily desire and inner love but only one after another and never two husbands at a time, would hate to buy the haunted Nasreen's hasty talk.

Is Nasreen aware that it is far better for a society to allow a man four wives (polygamy), if necessary, under legal status and protection and a set of circumstances—historical, political, cultural, demographic and, most importantly, economic and physical—than one legal wife and several free girlfriends or mistresses in adulterous extramarital relationships causing violence, divorce, murder? If a woman wishes to sleep with four husbands at a time (polyandry), she would be impregnated with the sperm and child of which husband? Not easy to determine, even at this age of DNA tests, leading only to biological mess and anarchy. Although there may be no truth in the rumor, there was a story that the father of Princess Diana's younger son Prince Harry was her lover James Hewitt (whom the young prince resembled a lot), not her husband Prince Charles.[17] Such questions may be raised in order to direct Nasreen and the slavish Nasreenites (her shortsighted radical and fundamentalist associates), who, like the atheist communists, once made it a fashion not to believe in God/*Allah* the Almighty, to their much-needed therapeutic healing through some eye-opening self-questionings and self-rectification.

Narrowing down the premise at issue, let Nasreen be what she likes—a fanatical atheist, a fundamentalist radical, or a funny feminist. However, as Mahmudul Hasan argues, Nasreen, unlike many other women writers of Bangladesh, "directs her attacks against religion itself, putting almost the entire blame of gender injustice on it," instead of looking for "the emancipatory aspects of Islam and gender egalitarianism in them." She regards Islam as "inherently gender oppressive, castigates it and prefers a western, secular feminist framework to ameliorate women's condition." Critiquing Nasreen's "overtly negative views of Islam," Hasan comments that the "aggressive, anti-religious secularism of the kind pursued by [her]… pours oil into the fire of those who wish to claim, against better knowledge, … that a much-misunderstood label of pluralistic secularism" is what is needed in the specific context of Bangladesh. [18]

It is true others should have no business with her freedom of expression and beliefs—a view supported by Hasan as well. By the same token, however, she should have none either with that of others. From her mean and myopic point of view, religion may have lost its usefulness and universality; from the right and noble and enlightened perspective of the believer, it has always been of supreme importance and greatest significance in life and society. To a believing individual, the importance of religion has only increased, not diminished, especially at a time when the spirit of God-*lessness* has been darkening the world as if "Turning and turning in the widening gyre/ The falcon cannot hear the falconer," paving the way for the brutal and beastly "Second Coming." Nasreen may be let go her way—a way of her own—but she must not be allowed to go unchallenged when she engages, out of her selfish interest, in futile but provocative insinuations and irritating titillations, hurting the deeply cherished religious beliefs of myriads and multitudes. Who is she to pronounce a verdict on the great world religions? Only an uncouth humbug of little knowledge can do so. As Alexander Pope said:

> A little learning is a dangerous thing.
> Drink deep, or taste not the Pierian Spring;
> There shallow draughts intoxicate the brain,
> and drinking largely sobers us again.

No wonder, "in her own country, even liberals have been loath to champion her;" they know she is simply a "deliberately sensational writer" running after a cheap name and notoriety.[19] Her *kamona-bashona*-type (erotically arousing) tabloid pinups got her obscure low-status provincial "literary" prizes from certain self-seeking quarters across the border. The sexually titillating content of her booklets did not escape the notice of Deborah Baker, who wrote from Stockholm (where Nasreen was at the time):

> [Nasreen's] fellow writers were nearly mute during the two months she spent as a fugitive from a Government arrest warrant for blasphemy. Even her fellow feminists in Bangladesh turned on her, accusing her of becoming a patsy for the West ... Many Bangladeshi feminists are particularly discomfited by her writings on sexuality, feeling that there are more important priorities and that by writing about such intimate matters Nasreen exposes women to male titillation and betrays them.[20]

The main contention in Nasreen's case was not how the conservatives or liberals interpreted the meanings of the holy Qur'an—"the jarring point has been less her general case—that traditional interpretations of the Koran have been used to inhibit the emancipation of women—than the provocative methods she has chosen." As it was reported by John Burns, many writers and academics in her own country did not like her aggressive, offensive and hostile methods, "particularly the sexually graphic language she has used in poems and newspaper columns."[21] Eric Weiner quotes *The New Nation*, an English-language daily in Bangladesh, as accusing her of "slow-poisoning the moral and social fiber" of the country.[22] One cannot fail to see how contemptible and shameless she can be when she, in her usual sweeping and shallow generalizations, compares men to dogs and attacks long male hair, beards and dress as concealing "their insatiable lust for wealth and women." Criticizing her "most confrontational" and "most media-savvy" outspokenness, which "has jeopardized not only her life but the lives of many people of conscience," Carolyne Wright, a professor of Sanskrit and Indian Studies at Harvard, thinks Nasreen's campaign endangers "low-profile progressive efforts" of other reformers.[23]

Personally, I strongly believe in freedom of speech, but I also believe in certain restrictions. As we all know, freedoms and responsibilities (implying certain limits) are equal contributions of human civilization and modern democracy. The rule of the majority must not degenerate into the tyranny of the majority. Similarly, while the minority, of any class or kind, must be protected, they must not be allowed to disturb and disrupt the preciously cherished spiritual faiths and values of the great majority; they must be prevented from destabilizing the decently functioning and forward looking relationship of peace and harmony between the two. No one will deny that profusion means confusion, uncurbed freedom means anarchy, and that liberty does not mean license.

In the vein of Robert Frost, one believes in mending the wall for, "good fences make good neighbors." One believes in what Wordsworth described as the proper and desirable dual role of Nature as a moral agent in the upbringing of his little Lucy: "To kindle or restrain." He addressed the difficult question of the spirit of liberty and the spirit of duty again and again in his poetry. In the wake of the violent extremes of the French Revolution (known as the "Reign of Terror" of 1793–1794) and then the excessive aggressions of the French emperor Napoleon, the poet rejected "too much weight of liberty" for the "rich bounties of Constraint" that led to "invigorating transports [...] That choice lacked courage to bestow" (*Ode: The Pass of Kirkstone*). About the same post-Waterloo period, he noted in *Ode to Duty* that "Me this unchartered freedom tires;/ I feel the weight of chance-desires," suggesting a rejection of wayward excesses of both imagination and revolutionary politics.

Nasreen has the right to speak and write whatever she likes. Like a diplomat and a diplomatic compound, the sort of people and places that got increasingly involved in getting her out of the country two decades and a half ago, she must have enjoyed a great degree of immunity in relation to her freedom of expression, as all writers and artists do. Otherwise, given the libidinous and throw-away-religion-and-morality nature of her writings, there would have been a huge hue-and-cry from the time she started publishing. However, by the same token of fairness, frankness and impartiality, she should have been respectful of the dignity of the people's right to religious faiths and beliefs and should never have been as unfair, one-sided and monolithic as she was in trying to displace and distort them.

"If an individual," writes a great Bangladeshi-American and a former army officer in Bangladesh, "prefers to remain secular, or even a non-believer, it is his/her business. But their personal likes or dislikes should not interfere in state business, nor could they have the license to ridicule one's faith." In the name of free speech she must not have made a frontal attack on them. Since she did, and, in doing so, she crossed the commonly denominated and commonly acknowledged boundaries, she has rightly suffered from what Wright calls "perils of free speech" in a rather sympathetic article on her.[24] Put in a different way, actually she did not suffer from "the perils of free speech"—the term "free speech" taken in all its positive expressions and connotations; she just paid the price for her wild, irresponsible and unnecessary excesses.

Whether it is the somewhat confined, polite and formal world of a diplomat or the free and fluid world of a writer, neither side is supposed to provocatively meddle with the deeply held religious faith of a community. In attempting to unseat the deep-seated sacred religious sentiment of the millions of faithful adherents,

Nasreen has foolishly resorted to her dangerously radical liberalism. She has been blanket blinded by her own form of fanaticism, the effect of which has always been disastrous, as the story of human civilization amply shows. Even according to Western ideals, the human right to protect and defend one's religion goes hand in hand with the human right to free speech. As Faruqi says in his *Impact International* piece, "No battle lines need ever be drawn up if the Christians, Jews, Hindus or others respect the right and indeed the desirability of a Muslim to be a *whole* Muslim [not a *half* Muslim as the West has been trying to create] and so do the Muslims regarding the right of others to believe in their religion."

Nasreen's naked attack on the fundamental Muslim faith is uncalled for, since Bangladesh has seen and tolerated, over decades and decades, the communist horde of atheist breed, who did not have to attack and wisely refrained from attacking the religious scriptures of the believers in talking about their leftist ideologies. No one has ever said anything hateful against the communist ideologues and demagogues in spite of the fact that they have been politically active and engaged in a country traditionally dominated by a common bond of Godliness and not by an atheism-tinged secularist bent of non-religious bias, as Sirajul Islam Chowdhury, an intellectual of Marxist orientation, claims.[25] In the absence of some form of watchdog policy, secularism practically lapses into a state of godlessness, just as in the absence of law and order, excess of freedom descends into chaos and lawlessness.

Thank God, with the fall of the Communist regimes in Eastern Europe, the addictive commitment of the opportunist leftists to their all-slogan propagandistic causes has already faded or evaporated, paving the way for their grudgingly falling in love with the rock-solid and dazzling achievements of Western capitalism in the form of free enterprises, democratic reforms and other success stories. Thanks for their waking up! But, again, with the Soviet indoctrination gone, these half-hearted self-deceivers are likely to keep themselves busy by making an issue of a non-issue and exploiting the Nasreen-type situations to please and feed their myopia.

Nasreen did not care to draw a line as to how far she should have gone and, if she did, she went well beyond that line in making her short-sighted comments and statements. The Salman Rushdie of Bangladesh took a cheap shot to advance her egotistical personal ambition to become notoriously famous. Tahar Ben Jelloun, a French writer of Arab origin, is absolutely right when he observes that Nasreen was "jumping on the bandwagon of scandal to sell books that would not sell otherwise." The Belgian orientalist Koenraad Elst says: "The world-famous Moroccan-French author Tahar Ben Jelloun has accused Nasrin of being a careerist, and that Jelloun is displeased by her desire to revise the Koran."[26]

Nasreen claims she wrote fifteen other novels before *Shame*. Obviously, all were ignored owing to their poor quality. Out of desperation she embarked on creating a sensational scandal and grabbing public and media attention at any cost.

One who has neither academically studied religions nor has professionally trained herself in religious matters nor has been a practicing Hindu or Muslim or Christian or Jew automatically forfeits her right to be judgmental on them, especially when that judgment tends to be a negative one. Like any branch of human endeavor with countless areas for academic pursuit and scholarly research, any great religion is a major subject of study. That is why there are Schools of Divinity and Theology, Institutes/Colleges/Faculties of Religious Studies, and Departments of Religion and Comparative Religion in almost all the universities all over the world. That is why there are Judeo-Christian, Islamic, Hindu, Buddhist, Confucian, Manichean, and Zoroastrian laws, traditions and scriptures—all held in veneration.

The whole notion of the institution of the church, the mosque, the synagogue, the temple, and the pagoda is within the scope of this study of religion. A person, whosoever that is, having no knowledge whatsoever of a particular subject, ought to keep quiet, speak only with the intention of understanding that subject, or be cautious and careful in talking about it or give it the benefit of doubt, especially when it is a matter of religion, spirituality and otherworldliness, which together are one of the most deeply rooted sentiments in human beings. The world has seen enough of hatred and strife along religious lines over the centuries since the Middle Ages—in Europe, the Middle East, Indian Subcontinent, Myanmar, Bosnia, Chechnya, Kashmir, Ireland, Sudan, Armenia, Afghanistan, Syria, Crimea, Kenya, Central African Republic, and so on. Nasreen well deserves the price she has been paying for supplying more fuel to the fire; she has owed it to and won it for herself. No one else should be held responsible for her plight. It is she who kicked the ball first, then again and yet again before being kicked by others. In the words of a journalist, she has been shrinking from "the fire storm she had kindled."[27]

Talk about the religious fundamentalists on the streets demanding her death penalty? There will always be some groups, both on the far right and the far left, in every society, who will take a similar stand on the issue of such a heated debate. Like the Los Angeles unrest following the Rodney King verdict in the early 90s, one can understand their deeply stirred religious sentiment that had driven them to the streets, although one cannot support their demand. A radical element was born of another radical element; a radical reaction was begotten of another radical action. Nasreen acted like a dangerous radical liberal; to fight her, there were and still are ultra-orthodox radical elements. In her too blunt and blasphemous statements about the Holy Qur'an, of which she seems to be totally ignorant, one must say—statements that precipitated public demonstrations against her—she hurled extremes only to invite the opposite extremes taking to the streets.

Islam acknowledges, in no uncertain terms, mutual toleration and understanding, individual rights, majority opinion and minority concerns related, first and foremost, to the issues of safety and security, peace and stability. In every system there are some basic rules and regulations, which are not and must not be compromised in dealing with an issue that is likely to tip and threaten the balance of coexistence. Similarly, in each and every case that Islam has to deal with, there is room for possible dialogue, negotiation and adjustment, without violating the basic tenets and principles, so that peace and harmony be maintained and preserved. To quote from a review of *Islam and the Myth of Confrontatio*n by Fred Halliday,

> Islam is not a set menu of moral, political and social behaviour; it offers a pleasingly *a la carte selection.* Fanatic Islamists and *fanatic anti-Islamists*, who conspire together to push the set-menu theory, reinforce the stereotyped belief that there is one binding Islamic answer to all questions of behaviour. This is nonsense: Islam is as variant and flexible as any other great religion.[28]

Variations of the same procedures are in practice in every civilized society. Nurul Kabir, editor of the Bangladesh English language daily *New Age*, writes: "A writer is in hiding today in Bangladesh because certain people do not like what she says. No amount of shuffling and rearranging of legal points can alter this fact."[29] Yes, that is true, but at the same time one could make one's response saying: "You got to start from somewhere at some point. Nothing happens out of nothing." A fanatically liberated individual who, out of her individualistic zeal as well as personal ignorance and vanity, bypassed what could be her sane and sound suggestions for reform in socio-religious matters, caused a nationwide problem by her ultra-smart statements and semi-and-pseudo-and quasi pornographic writings. A solution got to be found under the existing system of law in the country, even if it needs "shuffling and rearranging of legal points" and regardless of that individual's personal plight, for the nation, the country, and the peace-loving pious people must not be taken hostage by the unfounded bubbles of a lone sick individual.

Norway, Sweden, PEN (the international organization of Poets, Essayists, & Novelists) and the British *Article 19* shed crocodile's tears in the name of human rights over the Nasreen phenomenon. They should have extended their offer of refuge to Salman Rushdie first and have taken him out of hiding, ironically, from one of the greatest cradles of democracy—Britain. They actually wanted to take advantage of the poor and small Bangladesh and be credited on the world stage for drumming up the support for the drama of the so-called human rights violation. If human rights could survive in the West with Salman Rushdie still in hiding and with Iran renewing its "fatwa" (religious decree) every year, they would survive in the East too, with Nasreen remaining out of public view for the rest of her life. Deborah Baker precisely hints at the mystery of the West coming to the aid of Nasreen: "She was unwilling or unready to consider why she, alone of all the world's writers in prison, in hiding from their governments, in fear of their lives, had been rescued by the West."[30]

One final note: the furor over the Nasreen stuff died down with her being transported or fleeing away to sanctuaries abroad. After Sweden, France, and the USA, she may now be living in India from where she still keeps writing/making similar blasphemous remarks despite the fact that even the people of the Hindu-majority West Bengal expressed, time and again, their disapproval of her sort of dirt and hurt. However, the case should be resolved, if it still needs to be, to enable her to return, according to the existing law of Bangladesh. She should not be subject to the Islamic law and jurisprudence because the country as a whole is not centrally governed by the *Shari'ah*. Since most of the other legal matters are settled under the existing judicial system, why should she be tried in a religious court or according to the religious law? Therefore, one can never support the demand for her death penalty—neither does Hashmi or Hasan, but I do applaud the Bangladesh High Court ruling that she must stand trial for insulting Islam and hurting Muslim sentiments. Let the existing law take its own course.

In the meantime, let Nasreen and the likes of her (Rushdie, Haider, Syed Shamsul Haq, Imdadul Haq Milon, Rudra Mohammad Shahidullah, Minar Mahmud, and Sunil Gangopaddahaya) awake to a new realization and a sincere repentance by studying hundreds of modern scholarly works on and about Islam and its unique glory and greatness. Let them rise to a new vision by reading only the following few, if not more:

- *The Bible, the Qu'ran and Science: The Holy Scriptures Examined in the Light of Modern Knowledge* by the French scholar, medical scientist and a convert to Islam, Dr Maurice Bucaille (published in French and English in 1970s);
- *The Bible led me to Islam* by Melvin Abdul Malik Leblanc;
- *The Study Qur'an: A New Translation and Commentary* (San Francisco: HarperOne, 2015);[31]

- Robert D Kaplan's 2016 article, "How Islam Created Europe" (http://www.theatlantic.com/magazine/archive/2016/05/how-islam-created-europe/476388);
- Jamie Gilham's *Loyal Enemies: British Converts to Islam, 1850–1950* (Oxford U P, 2014); and
- A few Wikipedia entries such as https://en.wikipedia.org/wiki/Islamic_Golden_Age and https://en.wikipedia.org/wiki/Science_in_the_medieval_Islamic_world

Nasreen and her deviated friends may also like to take a look at *Literary Modernity Between the Middle East and Europe: Textual transactions in nineteenth-century Arabic, English, and Persian literatures* by Kamran Rastegar (Routledge, 2007). God helps those who help themselves. They can help themselves by getting out of their big and blinding bigotry and rising above being in the low and mean status of human expendables and castaways.

Nasreen and the like should not remain suspended in a dark and closed limbo and may instead try to find their way out into the light by being informed about what hundreds of Western (and some Indian) writers, thinkers, and emperors had to say about the religion of Islam and its followers in their eloquently intellectual and philosophical testimony to it, its truth, and the greatness of its prophet.[32] Such personalities would include Napoleon, Thomas Jefferson, Goethe, Rainer Maria Rilke, Leo Tolstoy, Ivan Bunin, Thomas Carlyle, Jean-Jacques Rousseau, Edward Gibbon, Edward Lane, Edmund Burke, Ralph Waldo Emerson, Edgar Allan Poe, Malcolm X, Bernard Shaw, Bertrand Russell, Leopold Weiss, T. E. Lawrence, Marmaduke Pickthall, Martin Lings, George Sale, French philosopher Rene Guenon, Oswald Spengler, Edward Lane, Harry St. John/Jack Philby, William Quilliam, Richard Burton, Alphonse de Lamartine, Mahatma Gandhi, Sarojini Naidu, Annie Besant, Philip Hitti, A. J. Arberry, Washington Irving, Reginald B. Smith, T. B. Irving, Michael Hart, Montgomery Watt, William Draper, Cat Stevens, Swiss-British Gai Eaton, Imran Golding, Mark Hanson, Ricky Martin, Alexis Lumbard, Pierre Vogel, Dennis Philips, Cambridge University professor Timothy Winter, Peter Sanders, Edward Said, English explorer and adventurer Sir Wilfred Patrick Thesiger, film directors (Jack Shaheen, Anglo-American Ovidio Salazar, Tudor Payne, and Isabelle Matic), Michael Jackson's brother and sister American pop artists Jermaine Jackson and Janet Jackson, Canadian Prime Minister Justin Trudeau,[33] UN Secretary General Antonio Guterres,[34] University of London Electrical Engineering Professor Arthur Alison, Hollywood actress Lindsay Lohan, Nollywood (Nigerian) actress Lola Alao Rodiat, Norwegian film maker and journalist Paul Refsdal, Lauren Booth (Tony Blair's sister-in-law), Indian poet Kamala Suraiyya Das, prominent Indian Hindu personality and Oxford graduate Mahant Dr Shri Shakti Saroopji Maharaj Adasin Dharmachariya Odai Shakti (who is now known as Dr Islamul Haq), Aminah Assilmi (formerly American Southern Baptist Janice Huff), French scholar and medical surgeon/scientist Dr Maurice Bucaille, (originally Catholic Christian) Melvin Abdul Malik Leblanc, East Bengal's literary giant Bhai Girish Chandra Sen, Sukohomoy Mukhopaddhaya, Canadian professor and preacher Dr Gary Miller, American Woman Lisa Shanklin, and the Bangladeshi vocal artist Nokul Kumar Biswas, among others (the majority of whom reverted/converted to Islam).[35]

The people and the nation of Bangladesh have got to move on with the other matters of personal, national, and collective importance, contributing to and taking forward their society in particular and the human civilization in general. In the meantime, the Nasreens, the Haiders, and the Rushdies need to ruminate and meditate over the fact that "America becomes the country with most conversion rate. Approximately, about 20,000 people embraced Islam after 9/11 due to hate speech against Muslims." They should know that their saucy, gaudy, and empty rhetoric of "infidelism" will never take them even remotely near the deist freethinkers such as Rousseau, Voltaire, Mirabaud, Volney, Tom Paine, Carlyle, Ruskin, Orwell or Russell. Instead, they may wish to remember what John F. Kennedy said in his famous 1961 inaugural speech, in reference to *mortal* man's *power* and still debatable *revolutionary beliefs*, that "the rights of man come not from the generosity of the state, but from the hand of God." They ought to understand that they, in the context of their vicious intolerance and insolence about religion, can hinder human intellect and delay human progress for a little while only by their narrow and opinionated hatred of others, just like a foggy morning temporarily retards the journey of a traveller until he picks up his pace in the sunshine. They may probably be better off spending, exploiting, redirecting, and tapping into their creative energies in a much more useful, unifying, enlightening, and illuminating way.

Notes

1. An earlier and shorter version published in my *Readings in Oriental Literature: Arabian, Indian, and Islamic*, pp. 305–322. The earliest draft was published in *Asian Thought and Society: An International Review* 23, no. 69 (1998), 237–43. The name "Nasreen" is also written as "Nasrin."
2. http://www.natunbarta.com/opinion/2016/09/16/165266

3. http://bdnews24online.com/2016/03/14/
4. http://dnewsbd.com/english/are-they-hired-intellectuals-for-western-propaganda
5. http://newagebd.net/190238/362-incidents-of-sexual-assault-in-2015/
6. http://newsorgan24.com/detail/10535;
   http://www.dailynayadiganta.com/detail/news/36155; http://www.dailynayadiganta.com/detail/news/36195;
   http://www.dailysangram.com/news_details.php?news_id=195267;
   http://amadersylhet.com/news/9263.
   http://www.dailynayadiganta.com/detail/news/36383;http://www.sheershanewsbd.com/2015/07/06/87673#
7. Notwithstanding his mega corruption scandals as reported by the media, Siddiquee reportedly said that the Muslim *Hajj* was a wastage of time and money—unproductive—and that Prophet Muhammad, son of Abdullah and born in Mecca, found a convenient way to bring affluence and business to the place of his birth through *Hajj*, one of the five pillars of Islam. At the same meeting in New York, Siddiquee is also reported to have criticized Sojib Wajed Joy, son of Prime Minister Sheikh Hasina and, therefore, the Awami "heir apparent," alleging, among other things, that Joy was receiving a monthly salary of US$200,000.00 as information and technology adviser to her PM-mother—which, if true, was of course a terribly filthy and ferocious and outrageous amount in the context of a third-world country. Joy, grandson of Sheikh Mujibur Rahman, one of the greatest Bangladeshis ever, is settled in the USA and married to an American Jewish woman. For further information, visit: https://www.facebook.com/photo.php?fbid=10206542162178389&set=p.10206542162178389&type=3&theater;
   https://www.youtube.com/watch?v=z-IluzvONJA;
   http://newsbd7.com/main/detail/1714;https://www.youtube.com/watch?v=5Na_LpqTeuA;
   http://newsbd7.com/main/detail/2346;http://bdnews24.com/bangladesh/2014/11/23/latif-siddique-returns. For a comparative study of Tarique Rahman and Sajee-Accountability of Public Officials:
   $300m in wild goose chase by social media on http://www.weeklyholiday.net/Homepage/Pages/UserHome.aspx. b Wajed Joy (including the latter's shoddy and felonious behavior and suspicious financial activities) by Shams Mohammad, visit: http://golamami.blogspot.com/2010/02/blog-post.html;
   http://newsbd7.com/main/detail/2346;
   http://www.weeklyholiday.net/Homepage/Pages/UserHome.aspx
8. http://www.youtube.com/watch?v=_DtYOeKcJZw
9. https://youtu.be/8IZY1mt0e-Q
10. Paul Gray, "Jane Austen She's Not," *TIME* Magazine, August 15, 1994.
11. James Walsh, "Death To the Author: As Muslim mobs demand her death, a writer faces government charges," *TIME* Magazine, August 15, 1994.

12. *The Statesman* of May 9 and May 11, 1994; the interview reproduced in *The London Times* (or, *The Times of London*), June 22, 1994.
13. For some of her views, see her interview, "Devil's Advocate: Taslima Nasrin" with Karan Thapar on IBNlive.com, Sunday, 22 April 2007: itv.in/?page=9&&option=com_video&view=list&Itemid=8&v=1;
itv.in/index.php?option=com_video&view=detail&v_id=406&Itemid=8
14. See Ali Riaz, *God Willing: The Politics of Islamism in Bangladesh* (Lanham, MD: Rowman & Littlefield, 2004), 110. Also quoted in the international free speech network of feminist writers called *Women's WORLD: Organization for Rights, Literature and Development*. http://www.wworld.org/archive/archive.asp?lastID=152; Also in *TIME* Magazine, August 15, 1994.
15. Lady Hester, spinster niece of the British Prime Minister William Pitt the Younger, excavated, on the strength of a medieval Italian manuscript copied from the records of a monastery in Syria, the 600 years old ruins of a mosque at the port city of Ashkelon in what was the first archaeological excavation in Palestine in 1815 in the hope of finding a great buried treasure (three million gold coins; instead, she found a seven-foot headless marble statue, which she had smashed into a thousand pieces and thrown onto the sea.
16. Julian calendar was in use from the time of Julius Caesar until it was revised by Pope Gregory XIII in 1582 to correct the errors of time loss according to the former. Due to the Catholic-Protestant antagonism, England did not accept the Gregorian calendar until 1752.
17. http://www.dailymail.co.uk/femail/article-2306021/The-day-Prince-Charles-told-Harry-James-Hewitt-father-end-cruel-gossip.html, 9 April 2013; http://www.showbizspy.com/article/269308/prince-harry-wants-dna-test-he-thinks-his-dad-is-james-hewitt.html, March 27, 2014; http://www.celebdirtylaundry.com/2014/queen-elizabeth-prince-harry-james-hewitt-princess-diana-charles-cressida-bonas-biological-father-wedding-photos/, March 26, 2014.
18. Md Mahmudul Hasan, "Free speech, ban, and 'fatwa': A study of the Taslima Nasrin affair," *Journal of Postcolonial Writing* 46, no. 5 (December 2010), 540–552; also Hasan, "Nasrin Gone Global: A Critique of
Taslima Nastin's Criticism of Islam and Her Feminist Strategy," *South Asia Research*, SAGE Publications, 36, no. 2 (2016): 167–185.
19. *TIME* Magazine, August 15, 1994.
20. Deborah Baker, "Exiled Feminist Writer Tells Her Own Story," *The New York Times* (http://www.nytimes.com/books/97/05/11/reviews/30906.html), August 28, 1994.
21. John Burns, "A Writer Hides. Her Country Winces," *The New York Times* (http://www.nytimes.com/1994/07/31/weekinreview/the-world-a-writer-hides-her-country-winces.html), July 31, 1994.
22. Eric Weiner, "Bangladesh Writer Draws Death Threat," *The Christian Science Monitor*, April 1, 1994.

23. Carolyne Wright, "Taslima Nasreen's Campaign Endangers Other Reformers," *The Christian Science Monitor*, August 18, 1994.
24. Enayetur Rahim & Henry Schwartz, eds. *Contributions to Bengal Studies: An Interdisciplinary and International Approach* (Pustaka, Dhaka: 1998).
25. Quoted in *The New York Times*, July 16, 1994.
26. Helle Merete Brix, a Danish author, who met Nasreen in Denmark, recounts Nasreen's journey in the essay, "An Eternal Exile," https://www.rights.no/2009/11/nasrins-endless-journey/
27. *TIME* Magazine, August 15, 1994.
28. *The Economist* (January 27, 1996), 85.
29. Letter to the editor, *The New York Times*, July 28, 1994.
30. Deborah Baker, "Exiled Feminist Writer Tells Her Own Story," *The New York Times* (http://www.nytimes.com/books/97/05/11/reviews/30906.html), August 28, 1994.
31. This latest work has been edited and translated by Seyyed Hossein Nasr and others. "With an introduction by its general editor, S. H. Nasr, here is a nearly 2,000-page, continuous discussion of the entire Quran that provides a comprehensive picture of how this sacred work has been read by Muslims for over 1,400 years." Other recommended translations of the meaning of the Noble and Glorious Qur'an would include those by George Sale (1734), of which Thomas Jeffersom had a copy to study and benefit from; English convert to Islam, Mohammad Marmaduke Pickthall (1930); Abdullah Yusuf Ali (1930s), which is perhaps the most popular and widely read; A. J. Arberry (1957); Taqui al-Din al-Hilali and Muhammad Muhsin Khan (1977); Austrian-German convert to Islam, Mohammad Asad (1980); American Muslim T. B. Irving (1985); and Egyptian-British SOAS Professor Abdel-Haleem (2014), among many other English translations, mostly by Indian Muslims.
32. http://www.cyberistan.org/islamic/quote1.html
33. For Trudeau, watch www.youtube.com/watch?v=ArtiAI52d9M
34. Antonio Guterres, of socialist orientation, who was Prime Minister of Portugal (1995–2002) and the United Nations High Commissioner for Refugees from 2005 to 2015, said in his commencement speech at Naif Arab University, "All the principles embodied in modern international refugee law are to be found in the Shari'ah. Protection of refugees, their property and families, non-refoulement [forced return], the civilian character of asylum, voluntary repatriation - all are referred to in the Holy Koran." http://www.unhcr.org/uk/news/latest/2009/6/4a42245e9/unhcr-chief-launches-book-islams-contributions-refugee-law.html
35. It is worth-noting that Napoleon (on the testimony of Admiral Lord Horatio Nelson; French bishop, politician, diplomat and Prince Charles Maurice de Talleyrand; and many others), Goethe, Rilke, Lane, Burton, and Tolstoy, among others, are thought to have embraced or were about to embrace Islam, the evidences, though nowadays generally suppressed, being available on the various websites. Among those who adopted the Islamic faith, Napoleon became Ali Bonaparte; Lane, Mansour

Effendi; Weiss, Muhammad Asad; Pickthall, Muhammad; Lings, Abu Bakr Siraj Ad-din; Guénon, Shaykh Abdul-Wahid Yahya; Irving, Talim Ali Abu Nasr; Quilliam, Abdullah; Malcolm X, Malik El-Shabazz; Philby, Sheikh Abdullah; Gai Eaton, Hassan Abdul Hakeem; Clay, Muhammad Ali; Stevens, Yusuf Islam; Winter, Abdul Hakim Murad; Lola Alao, Rodiat; Hurgronje spent a year between 1884 and 1885; Sanders became Abdul Azim; Golding (Director of the Islamic Awareness and Education Project in Wiltshire, England) became Imran; Hanson, Hamza Yusuf; Philips, Abu Ameenah Bilal; Vogel, Abu Hamza; Mitchell, Zaid Shakir; Janice Huff, Aminah Assilmi; Miller, Abdul-Ahad; Melvin Leblanc, Abdul Malik; Shakti Saroopji, Islamul Haq; and Kamala Das, Kamala Suraiyya. Although they converted to Islam, Lauren Booth, Lisa Shanklin, Jermaine Jackson, Janet Jackson, and Arthur Alison did not change their name. The same is true about Refsdal and Bucaille. Nasreen may wish to read the last chapter "Religious Diversity and Islam in America/the West" in my book, *Readings in Oriental Literature: Arabian, Indian, and Islamic*, pp. 410–472. She may also wish to visit: (1) https://www.youtube.com/watch?v=MuXYjobc-Vo; (2) http://www.kalamullah.com/Books/Ar-Raheeq%20Al-Makhtum.pdf; and (3) http://investigate-islam.com/pages/who-is-real-terrorist.htm

14

When Bangladesh Is Divided Over Its National Anthem "Amar Sonar Bangla" (A Tagore Song)

A Politico-Literary Perspective[1]

"O mankind! We have [...] made you into nations and tribes, that you may know one another."

—(*The Qur'an*, Chapter 49: *Al-Hujurat*, Verse 13)

"Patriotism is part of the faith in God/Allah the Almighty."
Traditional Islamic Saying

—(not really a *Hadith* of the Prophet)

"Mother and motherland are more to be proud of than heaven."

—(*The Ramayana* by Valmiki)

Since the early 1990s there has been a dispute, still unresolved, over the naming of the Republic of Macedonia, now independent of the former Yugoslavia. The other party in the dispute is Greece and the bordering Greek province of Macedonia, home of Philip II and his more famous son Alexander the Great. Because of the objection to the name, Republic of Macedonia is known as Former Yugoslav Republic of Macedonia (FYROM) in the international bodies. In a similar case, the Indian State of West Bengal, bordering the independent Bangladesh, has recently been renamed as only "Bangla" or "Bengal" ((the former an endonym or autonym; the latter an Anglicized exonym).[2] "Banga" of Sanskrit *totsomo* origin was another suggestion before the decision was made in favor of "Bangla" or "Bengal." Three or four articles so far, to my knowledge, along with the statement by West Bengal BJP chief Dilip Ghosh, have already generated a debate related to the name change in question.[3] Channel I Trityo Matra devoted its hour-long program on September 22, 2016 to a discussion on the matter between the BNP Vice Chairman Inam Ahmed Chowdhury and Brac University faculty Afsan Chowdhury, with Zillur Rahman, as always, as the moderator.

The debate is about the political, cultural, and economic interests of the two Bengals involved in this name change. Dilip Ghosh said he would prefer to keep the name of West Bengal as it was or rename it as simply "Banga," a word that he argued appeared in the Indian national anthem, "Jana-Gana-Mana-Adhinayaka Jaya Hey" and thus would preserve the cultural ties. Since the word "Bangla" appears in Bangladesh's national anthem "Amar Sonar Bangla," Ghosh finds that there is a conspiracy behind.

"Bangla" is identical with the Awami slogan "Joy Bangla," "Amar Sonar Bangla," DU statue of "*Oporajeyo* Bangla," or even "Bangabandhu." The change to "Bangla" was either silly creating unnecessary confusion about the historical evolution and territorial demarcation in the region or it was a shrewd move of far reaching impact with the long term intention of occupying and merging with Bangladesh and mis/representing the entire Bengal. All the identical terms just mentioned may have been aligned to serve the ultimate and ulterior motif of a larger, united Bangla/Bengal at the expense of the independence and sovereignty of Bangladesh (like Sikkim?).[4] It is to be hastily added here that if West Bengal first separates from India and then joins under the flag of Bangladesh to form a greater Bengal, it is unlikely that any Bangladeshi would ever have any reason to object.

On the other hand, is Bangla now a language or a state? In all three cases (Bangla, Joy Bangla, and "Amar Sonar Bangla"), the term refers to the land, not the language. But Bangla is also the language. It is probably the only instance in the world in which both the land and the language go by the same name as in the Bangla/Bengali mass song *Ami Banglai Gaan Gai Ami Banglar Gan Gai* by Pratul Mukhopaddhaya of West Bengal. It is different from the distinguishing instances all over the world: Bangla Bangladesh, English England, Finnish Finland, French France, German Germany Spanish Spain, Chinese China, Arab Arabia, Hindi Hindustan, Tamil Tamil Nadu, Malay Malaysia, Swedish Sweden, Russian Russia,

Afrikaans Africa, so on. West Bengal could very well remain as it was until recently, obviously implying today's Bangladesh once used to be East Bengal and then became East Pakistan.

If the name change had to be done at all, Banga, Bangla Bhumi, Banga Bhumi, Bangla Pradesh or Banga Pradesh (like Uttar Pradesh or Madhya Pradesh) could perhaps be better and more suitable, rather than merely Bangla.[5] The name change to the unadorned and unembellished "Bangla" has once again sparked off the ongoing debate about the national anthem of Bangladesh that goes into the justification for its long overdue change, which millions, probably the majority of Bangladeshis have been asking for years.

In Western democracies, one can burn their national flags and be critical, humorous, and satirical about their founding fathers and their national anthems—all in the name of their freedom of expression. Hence this criticism of the national anthem of Bangladesh, "Amar Sonar Bangla" (that is, "My Golden Bengal," short of the full and proper name of "Bangladesh"). It is one of the apples of discord tearing the nation apart, far from uniting it. It is unrepresentative of and disuniting about the people of Bangladesh, who find a deep disconnect with it. It is not a fond household name as it should have been as a national anthem.

There are many, in millions, educated either in modern or religious education, all across the country, from the capital to the countryside, who do not like to accept and sing the song as their anthem for a number of reasons. Some of the same reasons, detailed below, have been discussed by Ariful Islam in his own way, who, in addition to the reasons in common, also dwells on the fact that the song contains the language/verses of idol worship and partnership with the concept of one and single God, especially toward the end and is, therefore, religiously inappropriate to the Muslim majority of Bangladesh.[6]

Instead of holding the nation together and binding it as one and single country, the anthem works in reverse to dilute and diffuse the unity of the nation. Despite the fact that Rabindranath Tagore was a poet of great name and fame, Charbak makes a compelling argument about how the song "Amar Sonar Bangla" is an anomaly, a hotchpotch, and a mismatch as the national anthem for Bangladesh not only in view of the song's old-fashioned anachronism but also the bourgeoisie class character and reactionary temperament of the economically advantaged poet it betrays.[7] This chapter argues that the anthem, considered from a number of perspectives, is probably not the best representative of the general opinion and the independence struggle of the people it is supposed to fully or at least adequately represent.

Written for the whole and united (or to be reunited) Bengal, not split into West and East and written about sixty five years before the birth of Bangladesh, the song fails to capture the essential spirit of Bangladesh's struggle for freedom that was won with a great sacrifice. It fails to arrest the essence of the independence of the geographical entity called Bangladesh that came into being after the bloody struggle in 1971. As a decorated freedom fighter, Ranu Chowdhury of the USA, asserts,

> It is for the very respect to our freedom fighters that we need to discard this national anthem of Amar Sonar Bangla that was meant to oppose our very identity as today's Bangladesh. On the one hand, we are hanging those who opposed Bangladesh in 1971; on the other, we are honoring a piece that was opposed to East Bengal, today's Bangladesh. What a logic? What a dichotomy? The poem was composed to oppose the division of Bengal, in effect the making of today's Bangladesh. Its theme was that the "mother Bengal" was one, had to remain one, and could not be sliced. Bangladesh is a country born on March 26, 1971. It is the eastern half of Bengal (which was intended in 1905), not the whole Bengal. The country's name is BANGLADESH, not Bangla or Bengal. (E-mail, April 11 and 15, 2016)

It is exactly in the same vein that Dr Rashed Anam of the USA claims that the present national anthem represents the denial of the very Bangladeshi entity, identity, spirit, ideal, aspiration, advancement, independence, and sovereignty. "It's like Hitler's theme song chosen to commemorate Gandhi's anniversary." In view of the poetical and musical influences on the current national anthem (see below), Anam is also of the correct opinion that "The National Anthem is a very sacred possession. It must be as pure, unvarnished, and original as possible." (E-mail, April 15, 2016).

If the heads of states and governments (presidents, prime ministers, kings, queens, emirs, and sultans) have to be citizens of their countries by birth, it is not far to seek why the writer of the national anthem of a country should also be a citizen of that country, so that it does not have to import one from another country. However, neither was Rabindranath Tagore, the poet of the national anthem of Bangladesh, born in the eastern part of Bengal (now called Bangladesh) nor did he move from West Bengal, out of love or any other ties, attachment, and identification, to settle in East Bengal permanently. Neither did he write the song for the land that was to emerge as the independent Bangladesh in 1971. In fact, he wrote it against the creation/separation of East Bengal from West Bengal in 1905 and would have written it, had he lived on, against the Muslim majority Bangladesh out of his anti-Muslim communalism and sectarianism.[8]

Nor is the song, apart from being an emotionally lacerating cry of vague and vain patriotism, an exciting, arousing, and stimulating one. Nor was the poet one of the Muslim majority of Bangladesh. Millions of Muslims find it hard to connect with the song; they naturally and rightfully expect their national anthem to have at least an idea of an Islamic component, if not completely suffused and saturated with the message and spirit of Islam, which an Islamic song by the national poet Kazi Nazrul Islam is.

Together with the name of a country itself and its national flag, a national anthem is one of the basics by which a nation identifies itself from the time of its birth. The American national anthem is a beautiful combination of both the country's national flag of stars and stripes and its history, from its war of independence with Britain and its gradual acquisition of different states thereafter. A national anthem is among the certain core credentials, of great symbolic, political, and emotional significance, by which a nation binds and unifies itself, crystallizes whatever loose and fluid elements there may exist in the process of cementing its nationhood and establishes the concrete image of its national integrity and identity. Unfortunately, Bangladesh's national anthem is far from meeting those noble and lofty expectations. In fact, it seems to miserably fail and fall short of achieving the fundamental goals and aspirations of national significance—unity, harmony, inspiration and motivation.

A national anthem, like those of all or many other countries across the globe, should reflect the nation's politico-religio-cultural ethos and at the same time be deeply and directly associated with the key turning event in its history, to be widely and popularly acceptable. That is what is with the anthems of India, Pakistan, the USA, the UK, Canada, Russia, Germany, France, South Africa, and Japan, for example. In some cases, the lyrics of the anthems undergo a series of revisions, from short to long, reflecting the changes in the political fortunes of the nation, such as those of Canada, Russia, and Brazil. In some instances, the lyrics are very short and anonymous, as old as more than a thousand years, such as Japan, still retaining, like the UK, the royal/monarchical/imperial associations, but dissociating from the immediate context of WWII. There are anthems that call on God to save the Queen or bless the people, make them happy and prosperous, and answer their prayers, as the British and South African anthems do. Sometimes the same anthem is shared by more than one country. For instance, South Africa, Zambia, and Tanzania enjoy the same song as their national anthem.

Although different surveys and assessments give different lists of top national anthems worldwide or region-wise, all are, however, marked by a patriotic, rousing, victorious, glorious, and historic spirit of peace, pride, liberation and love for the place and its people. As Australia had a national debate, even plebiscite, before adopting its national anthem and Spain had once a competition to write a new national anthem (although no winner was declared and the same on-again off-again national anthem was retained), Bangladesh, too, may follow the precedent to adopt a new national anthem that would unify, not divide, to be infused with an uplifting and arousing spirit of patriotism. After all, the issue is by no means a "settled" one. While a few things are settled in history, many things change to keep pace with the evolving needs and aspirations of the people or the majority.

Forty-five years after the independence, the people of Bangladesh still do not seem to be happy and excited about their national anthem and they seem to continue to feel a considerable degree of unease and discomfort about it. Despite the glory that was Rabindranath Tagore, the winner of the 1913 Nobel Prize in literature, a reflective, patriotic, and rational-minded Bangladeshi, in her/his cool thinking, cannot agree that one of Tagore's songs, "Amar Sonar Bangla," has been chosen as the national anthem of Bangladesh. Neither the song itself nor its writer Tagore has/had any direct or indirect relevance with the emergence of Bangladesh as an independent country in 1971. Neither in theme nor in intention the song qualifies to be the national anthem of Bangladesh. Composed after both the tune and the text of Tagore's older contemporary and Bengali Baul Gagan (Chandra Das) Harkara's "Ami Kothay Pabo Tare," millions of Bangladeshis are deeply dispirited by their national anthem and would therefore agree with the following details of the argument for a possible change.[9]

(According to Dr Zainul Abedin of the USA, who has worked on American racial issues and the coverage of the liberation war of Bangladesh in The New York Times in 1971), Dr Mahbubullah, (late) Dr Aftab Ahmad and (late) Gias Kamal Chowdhury—all noted and influential persons—initiated a "Change National Anthem Movement" when the last two were still alive. There is no doubt that Tagore is/was the greatest Bengali poet-writer ever. He is the pinnacle of Bengali literature of about 250 million people, Bangladesh and the Indian state of West Bengal combined.

That Tagore occupies the most illustrious seat on the Bengali Parnassus does not necessarily justify the high status given to his song "Amar Sonar Bangla" in the independent, sovereign, and Muslim-majority country. Not only can one sincerely question the wisdom and even the political correctness of such a choice but also doubt that any work by Tagore can ever be made Bangladesh's national anthem. Like numerous other songs and/or poems written contemporaneously as well as in the past (by others), this Tagore piece undoubtedly delighted and inspired the people of Bangladesh during their liberation struggle. It did so by virtue of its romantic lyricism and romantic love for Bengali soil and seasonal beauty in general.

However, the song is not a classic of artistic and thematic significance and does not rise to the level of the lofty dignity and sublime gravity expected of a national anthem. There is no unique distinctiveness about its literary merit. Moreover, being remote in its origin from the dream and birth of Bangladesh as an independent nation, the connection of the song with the time and circumstance of Bangladesh's liberation struggle is too thin for it to deserve such a supreme status and distinction.

Additionally, despite his reputation as a great poet, Tagore was not above his sectarian and communal interest against the Muslims of the then East Bengal. There are tons of writings, as many from objective Hindu scholars as dispassionate Muslims, that demonstrate that Tagore's deep anti-Muslim mindset, his discrimination against Muslims, and his often fanatical Hindu fundamentalism were no secret.[10] His strong dislike of Muslims and their prophet and their holy book, having hardly ever composed anything in appreciation or celebration of Muslims or their culture and religion, is widely known. In his inimical detestation and intolerance of Muslims, Tagore was far from his great Muslim friendly older contemporaries such as Kangal Harinath of Kushtia and Bhai Girish Chandra Sen of Narayanganj Dhaka (who also lived for some time in Sherpur Mymensingh), and today's great scholar Prof Sukhomoy Mukhopaddhaya of Santiniketan.[11] Nazma Mustafa, daughter of an once Awami League leader and herself a writer and a poet, describes, in her article on "Santiniketon in the eyes of [poet] Jasimuddin," how the Muslims were neglected and looked down upon by the landholding/landowning Zemindar family of Tagore.[12]

A number of writers, academics and researchers, such as Nirad Chowdhury, Dr Humayun Azad, Dr Ahmad Sharif, Dr Taj Hashmi, Dr Salimullah Khan, Arindam Mukherjee, Bina Biswas, Shakil Sarwar, Noyon Chatterjee, Sohag Ahmad, Muhammad A K Azad, Dr Firoz Mahboob Kamal, Dr Abid Bahar, and Golam Ahamad Mortaja wrote about Tagore's poems, stories and essays that testify to his anti-Muslim bias that amounted to bigotry and hatred. Their criticisms of the incomplete and unwholesome Tagore, who is much less than an idol and more of a fragmentary and contradictory model, demonstrate that the child marriage practicing Tagore was more Hindu than Bengalee, more Hindi-loving than Bangla-loving, and more tribal and colonial-minded "Razakar" of British imperialists than a universalist visionary.[13]

Tagore's enthusiastic support of the Indian *Swadeshi Andolon* (Home Country Movement) or *Swaraj* (Self-rule) leader Bal Gangadhar Tilak and the Maratha Hindu fundamentalist leader Shivaji is well-known.[14] Tilak was known for his fanatical zeal for Hinduism. His inspiration was Shivaji, who, of the time of the Mughal emperor Aurangzeb, was known for his subversive, destructive and anti-social activities. The name of today's Indian Hindu fundamentalist party *Shivasena* (Soldiers of Shiva) derives from the name of Shivaji. Therefore, despite the fact that "Amar Sonar Bangla" does occupy a place, as do many other songs and poems composed during and before the liberation struggle, in the hearts and minds of the people of Bangladesh, an objective and dispassionate mind cannot be convinced that the song deserves the prestige of being the national anthem of the country. It needs to be changed with a befitting one that greatly exudes and imparts the national and patriotic spirit with a sense of lasting unity.

What follows are the further details of the argument:

1. The song is by no means an extraordinarily great one, neither aesthetically nor spiritually. By no account, whether in style or content, it is unique or distinguished. There is no underlying depth of meaning nor is it written in an exalted public voice, as is the case with the national anthems around the world. Like many other Tagore poems, "Amar Sonar Bangla" is simple a reflective nature poem in a conventional style of languorous inward bent. Not surprisingly, the song is sung in the Indian province of West Bengal just as any other song by Tagore without the due respect normally accorded to a country's national anthem. Its images, drawn from the traditional rural Bengal, are trite and hackneyed by virtue of their having been overused in Bengali literature. Even the opening verse ("Amar Sonar Bangla" or "My Golden Bengal") is a cliché, infected with and affected by euphemism.

   The whole poem/song is an exercise in decadent emotionalism. A Bangladeshi-Australian Professor teaching at the University of New England rightly said, "Instead of instilling a patriotic passion, the song lulls one to a spontaneous doze. It lacks the rhythm and the cadence that are normally associated with national anthems, whose lyrics, tune and beat stimulate one's sense of nationalism and patriotism." The same view was expressed by Ranu Chowdhury, that "a national anthem should infuse and enliven our national spirit. Other than being used as a sleep-inducing (*ghum parani*) rhyme and/or an emotional wailing, I don't find anything substantive in 'Amar Sonar Bangla.' What inspiration a student gets from it? What motivation a soldier acquires from it? What idea a national leader finds in it? What creative stimulus a businessman may look for in it? Nothing. A national anthem is supposed to inspire a student, motivate a soldier, be the driving force in a leader and induce encouragement in an entrepreneur."

There may be some who would like to justify "Amar Sonar Bangla" by claiming that it was chosen as one of the ten most beautiful national anthems in the world by a music expert and journalist, Alex Marshall.[15] The same person also claims that one hundred years ago the American poet Ezra Pound heard Tagore sing "Amar Sonar Bangla" in 1912 in London and that Pound liked the song for its soft "baul" tone. The point is, these foreigners had and would have nothing to do with the bloody birth of Bangladesh. Secondly, Pound (who was a poet of "imagism" in modern poetry with a fondness for hard and precise and clear-cut imagery, classical and minimalist economy of language and concentration of meaning, and who lived a nomadic life moving from country to country and would develop a great love for the anti-capitalist and anti-Semitic fascism as embodied in Adolf Hitler) cannot be believed to have liked the facile emotiveness of Tagore's song. If Pound did express any liking at all, it must have been out of courtesy and friendliness for the visiting poet from the British colony of India, whose Bengali language was surely remote and alien to him.

Thirdly, it is slavish and servile, neo/colonial style, to surrender and sacrifice the choice of Bangladesh's national anthem to the taste and temper of the foreigners. Finally, musical excellence alone is at best a secondary criterion in the consideration of the qualities of a national anthem. Had it not been so, one of the myriads of patriotic songs, unsurpassable in their lyricism, could be picked up as the national anthem of Bangladesh. But that would have been crazy and insane. Once a song/poem is decided upon on the basis of its connection with the circumstances of the dream and emergence of the country and its people and on the basis of its simplicity, yet gravity, grandeur, magnitude and comprehensiveness, its lyrics—any lyrics—can be set to music easily by a composer, of whom there is no dearth.

2. The song does not faithfully represent the landscape of today's Bangladesh, of which the images, such as the banyan trees are hardly characteristic and the mango groves also are not as widely seen as it is suggested in the song. Unlike the *Shapla* (water-lily), the rightly chosen national flower of Bangladesh, mango groves and banyan trees do not grow in plenty and are rarely a common sight because they are not widely found all over the country. A few scattered mango groves may be seen only in the north-western part of Bangladesh, extending into India, where the poet's family estate was once headquartered in Shelidah, Kushtia. He composed the song in

the post-partition Bengal (after 1905) when the beautiful Padma used to be in her full tide. It is the region's beautiful and picturesque landscape of the past that finds expression in the poem.

Unfortunately, with the geographical and geological changes over the passage of time, made controversial and complicated by the selfish political agenda of the neighboring countries, the glory of the landscape has been in steady decline to the extent that the once full-flowing and wild Padma, like today's India-caused waterless Teesta and Atrai,[16] is not there any longer. The landscape features which were once a great source of charming beauty are now conspicuous by their absence not only in that part but also the other larger part of Bangladesh. The Padma, probably alluded to in the river-imagery of the song, is now dry and empty of its nourishing waters, running lamentably low owing to the regional geopolitics. At present its beauty and glory are a thing of the past, as thought to have probably been referred to or described in many famous patriotic river songs.[17]

Isn't it better for the Padma and all the rivers to be full and overflowing (and thereby sometimes destructive) than dry and empty and destructive? Unfortunately, about 50 to 80 out of 435 small and big rivers of Bangladesh as sung about in those songs have been dying due to environmental pollution and geopolitical reasons caused by the "friendly fire" of India.[18] Even the Water Resources Minister Anisul Islam Mahmud would not deny the un-neighborly reality created by the "step-brotherly" India.[19]

Since there is no true reflection of the broad spectrum of the natural beauty of Bangladesh in "Amar Sonar Bangla" and since it is not related, immediately or remotely, to the nation's painful emergence, the song cannot be said to have a representative quality about the nation's independence. As a result, the nation as a whole can identify neither with the material particularities nor the remote and abstract generalities of the poem. To put it metaphorically, the people of Bangladesh must not lose the forest for the trees.

A national anthem ought to be characterized by a universalizing and overarching principle suggesting not simply the idea of a free country with its own land and specific and clearly drawn borders but a broad outline of its cherished ideals and farsighted visions. A quick glance at the lyrics of the national anthems of Canada, Australia, the United States, the United Kingdom, India, or Pakistan, for example, is sufficient to understand what I mean by noble and high-spirited generalizations present in a national anthem.

3. Far away from the dream and later the fact of Bangladesh, Tagore wrote "Amar Sonar Bangla," along with "Banglar Mati Banglar Jol," as a campaign for the abolition of the 1905 Partition of Bengal.[20] He meant one and undivided Bengal and that is why he used the word "Bangla," rather than East Bengal (which was to become East Pakistan in 1947 and later Bangladesh in 1971. Tagore's "Bangla" is similar to the Awami League's "Joy Bangla" but dissimilar to the BNP's "Bangladesh Zindabad," which is specific about the Bangladesh as we have it today as an independent country.

   Having chaired the campaign meetings on September 24 and 27, 1905 (as he would also chair the meetings to halt the establishment of Dhaka University in 1912) and having led the *Rakhi Bandhan Utsob* on October 16, 1905, Tagore made it clear in no uncertain terms that he did not want the division (*khandon*) of what he regarded as *BangoMata* (Mother Bengal).[21] In other words, he wrote those songs for the cause of the larger province of the undivided Bengal, consisting of Assam, Bihar, and the greater pre-Partition Bengal itself. The cause of the "reunification" of the divided Bengal was led by the Indian National Congress, the Hindu *Zemindars* (big land owners) of West Bengal and their communal *Swadeshi* (Self-Rule) Movement. The historic Partition of Bengal (*Bango-Vongo*) saw Assam and East Bengal together as a separate Muslim majority province with Dhaka as its capital and a Hindu majority West Bengal together with Bihar and Orissa with Calcutta (Kolkata) as its capital.

   While the elites and the masses of East Bengal supported the Partition, Tagore and his fellow Hindu leaders of West Bengal opposed the Partition for fear of losing influence, labor, and landed estates in the East.[22] As mentioned above, Tagore wrote "Amar Sonar Bangla" and "Banglar Mati Banglar Jol" to rally the supporters of the *Swadeshi* Movement (1905–1911), who in fact used "Amar Sonar Bangla" in their protest meetings in Calcutta. The government of British India, now under Governor General Lord Hardinge, was pressured and prevailed upon into reversing the step it took six years ago, reuniting the two parts of Bengal on December 12, 1911 by the order of King/Emperor George V.

   To appease the Muslim-majority East Bengal and allay the anxieties of its people, the government of British India declared, mainly as a compromise, on February 2, 1912, that a university would be established in Dhaka. To this effect the British government formed a committee consisting of Nawab Sir Salimullah, A K Fazlul Huq, Syed Nawab Ali Chowdhury, and others, who played a pioneering role in establishing the university (see below). So, as Dr Rashed Anam of the USA comments, "Amar Sonar Bangla" symbolizes the rule of dominant Hindu feudalistic system against the aspiration of the people of the then East Bengal for self-determination and as such it was against the independence or advancement of Bangladesh and therefore against the very spirit of both 1905 and 1971.

It was the same people—the Calcutta-based Hindu elites, including Tagore, Calcutta University Vice Chancellor Sir Asutosh Mukherjee, Advocate Sir Dr Ras Bihari Ghose and Girishchandra Banerjee—who also opposed the establishment of Dhaka University (DU) during 1912–1921. The contemporary Calcutta media was full of similar anti-DU sentiment The same people, especially the Hindu lawyers of Calcutta of the time, also opposed the establishment of a High Court in Dhaka. They were all jealous of the educational and professional opportunities to be made available to the Muslims of East Bengal. "Many Hindu leaders were not happy with the government's intention to set up a university at Dhaka [...] The opposition by Hindu intelligentsia was not the only hurdle in the implementation of the plan for the new university ..."[23] Apart from protesting the 1905 Partition, which (the Partition) was done in the interest of the Muslims of East Bengal, Tagore, as mentioned above, strongly opposed the establishment of Dhaka University, having presided over a protest meeting in Calcutta on March 26, 1912, followed by another protest meeting just two days later, 28 March.[24]

"There are two aspects of Tagore," according to the former ambassador Serajul Islam, that we would need to focus seriously. The first is the poem he wrote, "Amar Sonar Bangla" and the second is his role in the move to establish the University of Dhaka. In "Amar Sonar Bangla," Tagore's vision was the whole of undivided Bengal where the majority were Muslims but who lived predominantly in what is now Bangladesh, at that time economically, socially and politically impoverished. The British had, in 1905, partly out of guilt that under their policy of divide and rule, the Muslims had been made into second class citizens and particularly because governing the large province of Bengal from Calcutta had become unwieldy, partitioned Bengal. The hatred of the predominantly Hindus of West Bengal for the Muslims of East Bengal is a historical fact (they disparagingly called our forefathers "bungals"). They were deeply disturbed that the British had decided to assist the Muslims of East Bengal to develop economically, socially and politically. Therefore, they launched the movement for the annulment of the Partition of Bengal. Tagore was very much a part of this anti-East Bengal (Bangladesh) and anti-Muslim movement and the poem "Amar Sonar Bangla" was the theme song of the anti-East Bengal anti-Muslim movement. Imagine, we have adopted this song as our National Anthem! Second, when the British wanted to establish a University in Dhaka, Tagore was one of the signatories on behalf of the "Bhadrolokes" of Calcutta in an application to the British Raj that argued that as Dhaka had a government college, there was no need of a university in Dhaka![25]

It is clear from the above that Ambassador Islam's unambiguous dismissal of "Amar Sonar Bangla" is accounted for on two solid grounds: that the song was a protest against today's Bangladesh and its very nationhood and that the song symbolizes, through Tagore's opposition to the establishment of Dhaka University, an obstacle, a barrier, an impediment to then East Bengalis' intellectual and cultural advancement.

Tagore's role was like that of the Tuscan/Italian poet Petrarch, father of the sonnet form and also, in a way, "father of humanism." In 1345, Petrarch visited Venice, a city with close commercial ties with the Muslim world, when he successfully orchestrated the boycott and banishment of all Arab learning (related to philosophy, astronomy, mathematics and medicine) from European education. He advocated a return to original Greek and Roman sources—a campaign which led, after the Spanish/Christian "reconquest" of the Muslim Iberian Peninsula by the Christian armies, to the burning of more than a million Spanish Arab/Moorish/Persian manuscripts, in original as well as translations of many classical texts, at Granada's public square in 1499.[26]

To summarize, Tagore wrote the song with the thought of the united Bengal under the greater India in mind, not that of an independent Bangladesh. As such, it was not connected with even the dream of the emergence of Bangladesh as a separate political entity with its own geographical boundary—the 55,126 sq. miles area for which thousands and thousands of people had to die. They sacrificed their lives for Bangladesh and its soil, not a bit of the Indian. "Amar Sonar Bangla" is therefore far from suggesting even a remote hint with regard to the political and geographical independence of the country which came into being as Bangladesh. Having nothing to do with the dynamics of a national struggle and its costly build-up over a long period of time, the song fails to evoke a sense of political and cultural history of the geographical area of its own borders called

Bangladesh. It is far from having any relation whatsoever with the defining moment of the language movement of 1952 and the decisive moments of the late sixties and early seventies when the Bangladeshis were fighting for their independent nationhood. As the highly placed Engineer Mohammad Gani of the USA says:

> Tagore's "Amar Sonar Bangla" has absolutely nothing to do with history along the line with the creation of Bangladesh or Hasina's "Own Sonar Bangla." Besides, it does not provide any picture or references of the nine months of brutal bloodshed, mass murders, unspeakable sufferings and painful miseries of then 75 million People of Bangladesh and thus is entirely irrelevant to our freedom struggle as our national anthem. (E-mail of July 22, 2017).[27]

4. A comparison of "Amar Sonar Bangla" with Tagore's "Jana-Gana-Mana-Adhinayaka Jaya Hey" and Bankim Chandra Chatterjee's "Vande (or Bande) Mataram!," which are India's national anthem and national song respectively and which were directly connected with the contemporary Indian politics of Hinduism and Indian nationalism clearly reveals the inferiority of "Amar Sonar Bangla" in terms of gravity and dignity, style and diction as well as its having been against the dream and emergence of Bangladesh. Composed in 1911, "Jana-gana-mana" is not only remarkable in its excellent use of generalizations that embrace the whole of India as a geopolitical existence but also saturated with a spirit of high poetical vision and transcendence, which is lacking in "Amar Sonar Bangla."

   Only the first stanza of the five-stanza "Jana-gana-mana" was adopted as the national anthem of India in 1950. The song was directly connected with the visit of King George V to India in December of 1911 when the British monarch declared, according to the wishes of the Bengali Hindus of West Bengal, the cancellation of the Partition of Bengal. The Indian National Congress, therefore, warmly welcomed the king to Calcutta and had the song "Jana-gana-mana' sung in its December 27 session of that year. It is to be pointed out that the song has recently been criticized by a senior BJP leader and Rajasthan Governor Kallyan Singh for its direct reference to foreign imperialist power as India's supreme guardian.[28]

   However, Tagore, by his own admission, did not write the song as an eulogy to the king as he was asked to do by many members of the Congress, including his good friend Vice Chancellor Sir Asutosh. Instead, he produced something stately and deeply spiritual, keeping in tune with his philosophy of life. As such, the song is a praise of an abstract and metaphysical supreme power or deity (above and beyond the temporal power as represented by King George) for having made India great and beautiful. During the Second World War when Subhas Chandra Bose founded the Free India League in Berlin, it was decided that "Jana-gana-mana," played on the Orchestra for the first time in a ceremony in Hamburg in 1942, should be adopted as the national anthem of India. By contrast, "Amar Sonar Bangla" falls short not only on the matter of direct connectedness with the most important national event, that is, the independence of Bangladesh but also in the power to generate deeper philosophical reflection and forward-looking political dynamism.

5. Bankim's "Vande Mataram!," meaning "Hail to the Mother (Durga)" or "I praise thee, Mother (Durga)" or "Hail to the Motherland" was written in 1876. These were the opening words of a song in his last (1882) novel *Anandamath* ("The Monastery of Joy"), which is full of anti-Muslim themes. The song advocated Indian hegemony and expansionism based on Hindu nationalism and fundamentalism, surreptitiously and indirectly extending to Nehru's *Akhand Bharot* (undivided India) chauvinism. There was also a group called "Vande Mataram," which used to observe the fanatical and fundamentalist "Shivaji" festival.

   Adopted as the national song at the Varanasi session of All India Congress Committee on September 7, 1905, "Vande Mataram" was used to push for the nationalist agenda during the Hindu-dominated *Swadeshi* movement in the wake of the 1905 partition of Bengal. It was the first Bengali nationalist song of note, primarily from the Hindu point of view, to the extent of being regarded as the national anthem of India during the first phase of Indian nationalism. The two Sanskrit words saluting the concept of the earth as the mother of every Indian constituted a memorable lyric chant with the rest of the song forming the powerful driving force in India's struggle for freedom. The first three stanzas describe India's natural beauty and bounty, set to music by Tagore, while the rest is about the rising Indian nationalism of the day with the last two stanzas personifying the country as *Durga*, the terrible ten-armed Hindu goddess worshipped every autumn in Bengal.

   Since the words of the song were thus directly linked to a Hindu deity, they were likely to hurt Muslim sensitivities at a time when there was a need for a nationalist song that would unite all communities in India. No wonder, "Vande Mataram" was not acceptable to Muslims only; it was not acceptable to Christians, Parisis, Sikhs, and other non-Hindus. Muslims have always objected to "Vande Mataram," saying that as a hymn to Durga equating the nation to a deity and calling for the devotee to bow down in respect, it went against the tenets of Islam to sing it. It is from such considerations that Muslims in India, despite a non-binding central government directive, refrained from reciting the song (the first two stanzas) on September 7 this year (2006) to mark the culmination of its year-long centenary celebrations. Even the Indian Sikh community did not obey the government order because it thought the song spread the message of only one religion and did not include the aspirations of the religious minorities in the country.

Moreover, the description of India in the song is more true and appropriate about Bengal than India as a whole. As a result, neither the Muslims nor all Hindus could be expected to be sympathetic to the song. Considering its potential for conflict, "Vande Mataram" was dropped as a candidate for India's national anthem. Tagore, Subash Chandra Bose and Jawaharlal Nehru—all three supported the move (see Tagore's letter to Bose, October 19, 1937). Following the tone of aggressive and reactionary conservatism in religious and social matters in Bankim's later works, the *Vande Mataram* "has been identified with—and sometimes appropriated by—the disturbing religious nationalism manifest in India today … In recent years, it has also found more sinister political use" (Sukanta Chauduri, "History out of Fiction," *New Straits Times*, Kuala Lumpur, October 18, 2000).

6. Although Tagore spent some time in what was then East Bengal (and afterward East Pakistan, now Bangladesh) to take care of his paternal landed property, he was not born in Bangladesh. His birthplace is Calcutta (West Bengal), which has all along been a part of India. He was not a native son of the soil. So, by birth, by nationality and by political identity, he was, still is, and will continue to be an Indian, not a Bangladeshi. Having always believed in the integrity and wholeness of a united and un-fragmented India until his death in 1941, he was never even a dreamer of the political independence of Bengal as a whole, let alone Bangladesh, whereas the people of Bangladesh shed their blood and lost their lives for the very land of Bangladesh as demarcated by its geographic borders.

   It is, therefore, not too much to expect the national anthem to express a sense of the patriotic struggle for the independent nationhood of Bangladesh reflecting a sense of the dream that was behind it. Choice of a national anthem must not depend on the neighborly help of a country during a critical moment. It must not be dictated by the need for the immediate appeasement of a helping neighbor in times of crisis. That need (for reward) can be met by various other political means.

7. In religion, Tagore was not one of the majority of the population of Bangladesh, who are overwhelmingly Muslim. While it may sound somewhat racial, communal and sectarian, the fact of the matter is that the Bangladeshis cannot ignore the larger reality of the religious sentiment of the overwhelming majority. Something which is essentially a matter of national consensus and with which all the people of the nation ought to be able to warmly identify for ages, generations and centuries must not be imposed on a nation from a narrow emotional or political consideration of the moment. To reach a decision about which song/poem should be the national anthem of the country is not to take the advantage of striking the iron while it is hot.

   Instead, it is a matter of cool, informed, detached, and dispassionate judgment keeping the interest of the country and the nation in view so that any unnecessary controversies in the future may be avoided. In the case of such a unifying national symbolism—a priceless gift that a nation earns as a result of its independence and sovereignty—the Bangladeshi nation has to be sensitive to the deeply embedded collective psyche formed by the soil, culture and religion of the land, not necessarily to the partisan interests of certain political elements.

   Religion being one of the most deeply rooted and most powerful human passions, Bangladesh as a nation is not ready and should not be expected to be ready to accept a song by a member of the religious minority who was not even born there as its national anthem. The geography and the demography of the population of Bangladesh give its majority an inviolable natural right to have a national anthem with which they feel highly comfortable and connected. This does not mean that it has to be another "Vande Mataram," a Muslim version of a religious hymn to God. However, the choice should be such that it is justly and naturally expected to express a certain degree of Muslim ethos without alienating the religious minority. After all, a national anthem ought to do with the envisioning of the good for the entire nation united in the common bond of patriotic love and adoration for the native soil under the Almighty Creator and the nurturing of that bond heartily.

   The Indians did not make a work by a member of their minority Muslims, Sikhs or Christians their national anthem. They did not care to be politically correct (to use that overused and unappealing cliché) and they did not commit the folly of being politically correct. They were right not to have done so. Political correctness is a euphemism for the cheap and easy shortcut meant to accommodate the folly of the weak. The Bangladeshis do not have any quarrel with the choice of their wise Indian neighbors. Tagore the poet is certainly not at issue here; the creative artist in him is above the barrier of national borders. However, it is entirely different to use him in the politically and nationalistically sensitive context in which the majority of the people, their religion, their history and the very historic occasion of their independence are indeed the most important determining factors.

Let me give some examples to illustrate the direct relation a national anthem bears either to the key political event or the major religion of a country. France's national anthem was composed in 1792 during the Revolution and the revolutionary army marched on singing it. One unknown patriot, Henry Carey, composed the British national anthem "God Save the King" on the occasion of the birthday of George II in early 1740s. First publicly sung in 1745 during the second Jacobite rebellion of the Catholics in Scotland on behalf of the Stuart claimant of the British throne, "God Save the King" is a prayer to God to grant long life and reign to the protestant George II of German Hanoverian dynasty and to give victory to the forces loyal to him. With its earliest known form slightly differing from the current wording and melody, it is a song of two small stanzas, only the first of which is alive in practice as the national anthem of Britain. The last verses calling for the suppression of the Scots have been entirely forgotten.

Written about the same period, in 1740, another song, "Rule, Britannia" by James Thomson, a minor English poet, was once very popular and used to enjoy the equivalent status of Carey's "God Save the King." Considered contentious in modern times because it fails to address and speak to people of the other parts of the UK (such as the Scots and the Welsh), "Rule, Britannia" is otherwise suffused with the noble sentiments of loyalty, bravery and national glory. It would continue to be "the political hymn of the country," as the poet Robert Southey predicted, "as long as she maintains her political power." The national anthem of the United States, one of the relatively difficult for vocal performance, illustrates the direct relation it bears to that country's war of independence. Francis Scott Key's "The Star-Spangled Banner," composed in 1814 during the Anglo-American War, replaced "America" as its national anthem in 1931 when the US Congress passed the motion.

Singing the praise and victory of his country against the British in impassioned public tone, Key's four-stanza poem of thirty-two lines has the title as a refrain, which is descriptive of the American national flag. Only the first stanza used as the national anthem, the poem ends with the motto, "In God is Our Trust!" Sung to the tune of an old English drinking song, "The Star-Spangled Banner" used to be popular with the US military since it had been written. As far as Key himself is concerned, he was not even a poet, nor a writer; he was just a lawyer in Washington, D.C.

Unfortunately, "The Star-Spangled Banner" has a black history and racially controversial background, so that the African-Americans are not enthusiastic about showing their regard for it, refusing to stand when it is sung.[29] It is as disuniting and divisive as "Amar Sonar Bangla" of Bangladesh, with the Americans offering up a few alternatives in the debate over their national anthem.

In any case, the above-mentioned examples of France, Britain, United States, and India (and to which one can also add Pakistan and many other countries) amply demonstrate how a national anthem is deeply connected with the political aspirations and religious spirit of a people, how it is deeply rooted in the reality of time and place, and yet how it transcends the immediate occasion by virtue of its high, dignified and enlivening manner of expression. When Pakistan became independent on August 14, 1947, the flag-hoisting at the independence ceremony was accompanied by the song, "Pakistan Zindabad, Azadi Paendabad," written in Urdu by a Lahore-based Hindu poet Jagannath Azad (himself son of another renowned Urdu-speaking Hindu poet) on a short notice by Mohammad Ali Jinnah.

This first national anthem (*Qaumi Tarana*) of Pakistan contained the verses meaning, "Each particle of yours/ Is more illuminated than stars/ Today your dust/ Is brighter than the galaxy" or "Oh the land of Pakistan, the stars themselves illuminate each particle of yours/ Rainbows brighten your very dust." The lyrics of the largely Farsi (Persianised) *Pāk sarzamīn shād bād* were written by the little-known Urdu poet Abu Hafeez Jullundhri in 1952. Selected from about 725 entries, *Pāk sarzamīn* was adopted as the national anthem of Pakistan in 1954.

In contrast with the national anthem of Bangladesh, its national flag (originally designed in Iqbal Hall/Sgt Zahurul Haque Hall of Dhaka University in 1970) is an absolutely terrific choice—a nice combination of the green of the land and the bloody struggle of its people for their new-found freedom as symbolized by the sun. (The sun-shape is of course as common and universal a symbol as the stars, the crescent, and the far-and-sharp-sighted eagle, all used by many countries from the ancient Pharaonic and Druid times, politically, culturally, religiously, and militarily). A song/poem which does not rise to a similarly comprehensive and prospective magnitude cannot qualify to be the national anthem of a country. It could be brief but not narrow in compass and canvas. Avoiding subjective personalization and fragmented particularities, a national anthem should employ broad and profound generalizations pertaining to a high and noble vision connected with the very context of the birth and formation of the nation itself.

Francis Scott Key of "The star-spangled banner" (of the USA), Henry Carey of "God save the King/Queen" and James Thomson of "Rule! Britannia" (both of the UK), and Japan's old and anonymous anthem—if all these are a proof, a national anthem need not come from the pen of a great writer-philosopher nor a major poet be necessarily commissioned to compose one unless the situation compels such a procedure. The long history of Canada's national anthem ("O Canada"), originally written in French, is such that initially there was some thought of holding a competition for such a hymn to be performed on the occasion of the national congress of the French Canadians in Quebec, which coincided with the St. Jean-Baptiste Day celebrations in June 1880. But that idea was dropped because of time constraint and finally Judge Adolphe-Basile Routhier was commissioned for the purpose early in the year. Routhier's French original with its several English versions gained steadily in popularity until it was proclaimed Canada's national anthem in 1980 along with its official English version.

In the present case, there must be a rich store of interesting works available to choose from. Once the nation agrees in principle that the current national anthem is not suitable, it should not be a difficult job for a designated representative body of thinkers, writers, intellectuals, and politicians, including Islamic scholars, to unanimously decide on one such work that would meet the desired criteria connected with the eventful past of the emergence of Bangladesh and its democratically diverse yet unified people.[30]

It is said that Sheikh Mujib himself did not like "Amar Sonar Bangla" and that he expressed his frustration and disappointment about it. His choice was Tagore's predecessor D L Roy's ধন ধান্য পুষ্প ভরা আমাদের এই বসুন্ধরা/

Dhana Dhannya Pushpo Bhara.[31] Having been composed on the same occasion (of the division and reunification of Bengal, 1905–1912) and therefore having nothing to do with the bloody and violent emergence of Bangladesh and, like Tagore, Roy also being from India (that is, West Bengal), this song also could not be a right one for the national anthem of Bangladesh.

One suggestion is that there should be an exhaustive survey of national opinion, untainted by any political publicity whatsoever. Australia is a case in point. "Advance Australia Fair," composed in 1878, was proclaimed the Australian national anthem in 1984 following years of debate. There was a national opinion poll of 60,000 people in 1974, followed by a nationwide plebiscite in 1977. On each occasion the song was the preferred choice by them. To date, Australian lawmakers still debate its future, some of them even attacking it as "boring, outdated, and meaningless" and calling for it to be changed. New Zealand wants to change its colonial style national flag marked with British Union Jack and not so distinguishable from the flag of its neighbor Australia. July 16, 2015 was the last date for the submission of new designs, to be followed by a referendum on four selected designs in November and then another referendum later to choose between the current flag and the top one from the four new designs.

History shows national capitals change, national flags change (most recently New Zealand is about to change its flag) and so do national anthems. In fact, such changes are quite common. So why should Bangladesh keep the matter of its national anthem unresolved and should not make a move in quest of a widely acceptable and hopefully permanent solution in the interest of all its sons and daughters, all its generations to come?

As a suggestion, the cute, short and simple 8-line poem, *স্বাধীন বাংলাদেশ* / Independent Bangladesh by Talim Hussein (1918–1999) may very well come into the picture for consideration for a new national anthem of Bangladesh. It is a concise, yet powerful and forceful poem, with the resonant repetition of the name "Bangladesh" in a beautiful refrain. Here are the lyrics/verses of the poem:

বাংলাদেশ—বাংলাদেশ/মৃত্যুবিজয়ী বাংলাদেশ/ যুগ—যুগান্ত পথের প্রান্ত/ অতিক্রান্ত প্রান অশেষ/ বাংলাদেশ/ বহু সংকট পাড়ি দিয়ে আজ/ বিজয়ী বাংলাদেশ / পেয়েছে আপন প্রান—চঞ্চল জীবনের উদ্দেশ/ বাংলাদেশ

Although Gazi Mazharul Anwar's প্রথম বাংলাদেশ আমার শেষ বাংলাদেশ, distinguished for its superb lyrics, could be a great candidate, it will for sure be opposed by the Awami League for the song's association with the BNP. At any rate, glory to our dear homeland, our মাতৃভূমি (Motherland)—our *Pha-yul* (Motherland in Tibetan), our *Patrie* (পিতৃভূমি/fatherland in French), our *Vaterland*/ fatherland and our *Heimat* (আপন দেশ / আমার দেশ / one's own country in German).

Notes

1. This is the up-to-date version of what was published in my book *Readings in Oriental Literature: Arabian, Indian, and Islamic* (2015), pp. 282–304. A shorter version was published in the Weekly *Holiday* (Bangladesh), Forty-Second Anniversary issue (29 December 2006). The earliest drafts appeared in *Asian Thought & Society: An International Review* 25, no. 74 (2000), 157–161 (now inactive); *Politics, Administration and Change* 34 (2000), 68–74 (Australia); *New Quest* 152 (April–June 2003), 29–35 (India); *Studies on Islam* 2, no. 1 (January 2005), 99–108 (India); and the *News From Bangladesh* (NFB) in September 2006.
2. West Bengal used to be known as *Goura* and East Bengal or Bangladesh as *Banga* from the ancient times. From the time of Sultan Shamsuddin Elias Shah around the mid-14th century, both Bengals were joined together as *Banga*, which was divided into two, West Bengal (including Bihar and Orissa) and East Bengal (including Assam), by the British government in 1905, to be reunited again in 1911 at the demand of the elite Hindus and to be separated again in 1947, again according to the wishes of the Hindus, who were then majority in the West and minority (46%) in the two Bengals together.
3. One article in the Times of India, one in Shamprotik, one in The Daily Star, and one in The Daily Naya Diganta: http://www.ntvbd.com/world/75993; http://timesofindia.indiatimes.com/city/kolkata/What-will-Joy-Bangla-now-refer-to/articleshow/53920843.cms; http://www.thedailystar.net/op-ed/politics/bangla-also-ours-1285975; www.dailynayadiganta.com/detail/news/160745; https://youtu.be/_k7bfx5wq0M; http://www.shamprotik.com/পশ্চিমবাংলার-বাংলা-বা-bengal-ন/
4. For details, see "Bangladeshi nationalism and secularism in Bangladesh" chapter.
5. Although Inam Ahmed Chowdhury mentions some of these alternatives in his article, they had come to my mind and I put them in writing before I came across his Daily Star write-up.
6. http://rtn-bd.com/opinion/43747
7. https://lalshongbad.wordpress.com/2016/02/12
8. Historically, West Bengali Hindus always remained pro-All India and pro-Hindi with flip-flops on the issue of a united Bengal, which, in contrast with 1905, they did not want in 1947. However, the majority of Bengali Muslims wanted a united Bengal in 1947. Although the Muslim League leader Muhammad Ali Jinnah did not have any objection to a united Bengal (as proposed in the Suhrawardy-Abul Hashem-Sarat

Chandra Bose plan, which envisioned to revive an independent Nawabi Bengal combining the entire Bengal, Assam, Bihar, and Orissa), the WB Hindus and Congress leaders Jawaharlal Nehru and Sarder Patel opposed it probably in view of their fear of the fact that such a Bengal would/might have a Muslim majority/supremacy. This uncertainty led the Bengal Muslims away from the idea of a united Bengal and pushed them to ultimately side with the prospect of a separate homeland for them that materialized in the form of Pakistan.

9. Dr Rashed Anam points out that Tagore felt obliged to write about the theft, terming it as "drawing inspiration," after he got caught in 1912–1913. He did not reveal his "drawing inspiration," a fine sugar-coated phrase, when he first wrote the song in 1905. For the tune of the song, watch https://www.youtube.com/watch?v=RaFetWNuaoE. Like Anam, there are some who take the issue of Amar Sonar Bangla's derivation from another song very seriously. Given the fact that Tagore was one of the greatest poets ever by virtue of his own merit and talent, perhaps this borrowing, theft or plagiarism need not be exaggerated and treated that grievously. Since Tagore, sooner or later, admitted Gagan Harkara's influence and he knew and wrote about the latter (whom he met in Shelaidah and through whom he may also have discovered Baul Lalon Shah), the matter of the creative imitation, which does not rise to the level of complete cheating or plagiarism, need not be taken seriously. It is a common practice for the poets and the writers, major or minor, from William Shakespeare to T S Eliot, to sometimes imitate, emulate, refashion, revise and recreate other poets' or writers' themes, ideas, form and style in their own works as they struggle to be themselves and to find their own voice. That is why there is the modern literary theory of the burden of the past (Walter Jackson Bate) or the anxiety of influence (Harold Bloom) or the tradition and individual talent (Eliot). If the borrowings are transformed into something new and different by being given a creative treatment to be made the poets' own, integrated in their own way, they need not be taken very negatively.
10. For Tagore's Hindu communalism and sectarianism and his illiberal landowning Zemindari exploitation and discrimination, see:
    1. Amitav Chowdhury's comment and Sharkar Shahabuddin Ahmed's book, ইতিহাসের নিরিখে রবীন্দ্র-নজরুল চরিত (Bangladesh Cooperative Book Society, 1998); http://www.muldharabd.com/?p=1094; http://www.muldharabd.com/?p=840;
    2. https://mukto-mona.com/personalities/rabindranath_alt.htm;
    3. http://www.somewhereinblog.net/blog/FarqueIDB/29382529;
    4. http://www.somewhereinblog.net/blog/lovelyemon/30052506;
    5. https://bn-in.facebook.com/newbasherkella/posts/914509181970380:0;
    6. Nasirul Islam at: https://wakeupbd.wordpress.com/2011/06/10;
    7. Senior academic and established columnist Ebne Golam Samad exposing the secularist perils of increasing Rabindraization and acknowledging the patriotic contribution of Michael M Dutt and Sarat Chandra Chatterjee, at: http://www.

dailynayadiganta.com/detail/news/219324; http://www.somewhereinblog.net/blog/mahmudh4/29377709;
http://blog.bdnews24.com/Habibb/15918;
http://blog.bdnews24.com/Habibb/15918/comment-page-1
8. Munim Siddiquee at: http://www.shodalap.org/munim/20070/;
9. http://www.pipilika.com/site_ajax_calls/show_details/1863628/bn/new_window;
10. http://www.somewhereinblog.net/blog/spark007/29379019; and
11. Dr Salimullah Khan at: http://www.muldharabd.com/?p=414.

11. Sukhomoy Mukhopaddhaya সুখময় মুখোপাধ্যায়ের "বাংলার ইতিহাসের দু'শ বছর : স্বাধীন সুলতানদের আমল". As editor of the weekly Gram Barta, published from Kumarkhali Kushtia, Kangal Harinath made a great contribution to the development of Bengali prose. Critical of the Tagore family's biases and prejudices at the risk of his own life, Harinath was friends with Muslims. The majority of the 42 books by the great genius that was Girish Chandra Sen were about Muslim culture, tradition and religion. First Bengali translator of the meaning of the Qura'an, his translation was published in Kolkata in 1839. See the article by Fahmidur Rahman on Girish Chandra Sen at http://shoncharon.com/2015/06/17 and other materials on Google or Wikipedia search.
12. https://nazmamustafa.wordpress.com/2016/02/29/; https://nazmamustafa.wordpress.com/about/. Her articles are available at this link: https://nazmamustafa.wordpress.com/2017/02/14
13. (1) ইসলাম বিদ্বেষী সাহিত্যের অগ্রদূত রবীন্দ্রনাথ ঠাকুর: http://sohagahmad.blogspot.com/2014/11/blog-post_85.html; (2) Maulana Muhammad A. K. Azad [Abu Arif Al Alawi] at http://docslide.us/documents/the-other-side-of-rabindranath-tagore.html; https://www.scribd.com/doc/105816693/The-Other-Side-of-Rabindranath-Tagore; http://wordsfromsolitude.blogspot.com/2010/06/other-side-of-rabindranath-tagore.html; http://islamicresearchmission.blogspot.co.uk/2012/08/the-other-side-of-rabindranath-tagore.html; (3) http://cybermujahid7.blogspot.co.uk/2015/03/blog-post_65.html; (4) for a slice of their versions of Tagore's plagiarism and his Hindu tribal communalism, see:http://www.openthemagazine.com/article/art-culture/the-forgotten-plagiarism-of-tagore; https://mm-gold.azureedge.net/personalities/rabindranath_alt.html; https://groups.yahoo.com/neo/groups/hOMEOPATHY_bANGLADESH/conversations/messages/469; https://www.facebook.com/newbasherkella/posts/620489624660531; (5) Firoz Mahboob Kamal, "রবীন্দ্রনাথের *পৌত্তলিক* চেতনা এবং বাংলাদেশের জাতীয় সঙ্গিত" at www.drfirozmahboobkamal.com; http://www.drfirozmahboobkamal.com/2010-03-24-10-21-22/1039-belief-dismantling-national-anthem-and-bengali-muslims-surrender.html; and (6) Golam Ahamad Mortaja, *Ei Ek Annyo Itihas: Anonnyo Rabindranath O Thakur Bari* (Bangla Bazar, Dhaka: M. M. Meherullah Research Academy, 2005).
14. For details, see the following three sources: Golam Ahamad Mortaja, *We Will Compose Our Own National Anthem* (*আমাদের জাতীয় সংগীত আমরাই রচনা করিব*), Imprint: Kalakata

: Bisvabangiya Prakasana, 2008. Re: [chottala.com] Anthem, Tagore, Muslims; নয়ন চ্যাটার্জি;

15. As she claims, it was in the newspaper *The Guardian* in 2008 during the Summer Olympics in Beijing.
16. http://bangladeshchronicle.net/2016/02/tista-water/; http://www.amardeshonline.com/pages/details/2016/03/25/328878#; http://www.amardeshonline.com/pages/details/2016/03/25/328880#
17. For example, (1) Manna Dey's *Ei Kule Ami Aar Oi Kule Tumi Majhkhane Nodee Oi Boye Chole Jai*; (2) Kazi Nazrul Islam's *Padmar Dheure Mor Shunno Hridoy Padma*; (3) Abu Zafar's *Ei Padma Ei Meghna Ei Jamuna Surma Nodi Tote*; (4) Bhupen Hazarika's *Padma Amar Ma Ganga Amar Ma*; (5) Hemanta Mukherjee's *O Nodi Re Ekti Katha Sudhai Sudhu Tomare*; (6) Abdul Alim's *Shorbonasha Padma Nodire*; and (7) Humayun Kabir's novel Nadi O Nari (1945). For the present sorry and miserable condition of the Padma and other rivers, see http://www.24livenewspaper.com/site/index.php?url=dailysangram.com/ (13 December 2014); https://youtu.be/QotobyaYNC4; http://www.amadershomoys.com/unicode/2016/03/14/82303.htm#.VuackjFc0mc
18. http://www.bbc.com/bengali/news/2016/04/160309_amarnodi_bangladesh_brahmaputra_siltation; http://www.bbc.com/bengali/news/2016/04/160330_amar_nodi_kapotaksha_siltation.shtml; http://www.bbc.com/bengali/news/2016/04/160409_buriganga_encroach; http://www.bbc.com/bengali/news/2016/04/160229_amar_nodi_shitalakhya_river_pollution_narayanganj_sayala http://www.bbc.com/bengali/news/2016/04/160311_amar_nodi_turag_pollution; http://www.bbc.com/bengali/news/2016/04/160328_amar_nodi_chitra; http://www.bbc.com/bengali/news/2016/04/160313_bangla_amar_nodi_dhaleshwari; http://www.bbc.com/bengali/news/2016/04/160322_bangladesh_amarnodi_fishermen_of_titas; http://www.bbc.com/bengali/news/2016/04/160320_amar_nodi_dharala_stone_excavation; http://www.bbc.com/bengali/news/2016/04/160402_amar_nodi_meghna_river_erosion_chandpur; http://www.bbc.com/bengali/news/2016/04/160409_amar_nodi_dying_river_special_report; http://www.bbc.com/bengali/news/2016/04/160406_amar_nodi_interactive_map;
19. http://www.dailynayadiganta.com/detail/news/182555
20. The government of British India headed by Viceroy/Governor General Lord Curzon announced the idea for the Partition in January 1904 for administrative decentralization as well as for upgrading the eastern part of Bengal and Assam, which lacked in development. (This Partition foreshadowed the 1940 Lahore Resolution of having

separate Muslim majority states). The decision to implement the Partition was made in July 1905. The actual partition took place on 16 October 1905. The Partition was, however, opposed by Sir Henry John Stedman Cotton, Chief Commissioner of Assam 1896–1902, while it led to the formation of All India Muslim League under the Nawab of Dhaka Khwaja Sir Salimullah along the lines of religious divide, as if to counter Indian National Congress, which was considered a representative platform of the Hindus. The lyrics of the second song are as follows: বাংলার মাটি, বাংলার জল, বাংলার বায়ু, বাংলার ফল—পুণ্য হউক, পুণ্য হউক, পুণ্য হউক হে ভগবান॥ বাংলার ঘর, বাংলার হাট, বাংলার বন, বাংলার মাঠ—পূর্ণ হউক, পূর্ণ হউক, পূর্ণ হউক হে ভগবান॥ বাঙালির পণ, বাঙালির আশা, বাঙালির কাজ, বাঙালির ভাষা—সত্য হউক, সত্য হউক, সত্য হউক হে ভগবান॥ বাঙালির প্রাণ, বাঙালির মন, বাঙালির ঘরে যত ভাই বোন—এক হউক, এক হউক, এক হউক হে ভগবান॥

21. "Rakhi" is the abbreviated form of "Raksha" (or Rakkha), meaning protection. "Rakhi Bandhan Utsob" is the Hindu festival that celebrates love and brotherhood on the full moon in the month of Sravana in the Bengali lunar calendar. Here are some examples of the same between the two Bengals today: http://rtnbd.com/bangla/bd/5631; https://www.dailyjanakantha.com/details/article/211527/.
22. http://www.dailynayadiganta.com/detail/news/61828#
23. http://en.wikipedia.org/wiki/History_of_the_University_of_Dhaka, August 3, 2014. Nirad Chaudhuri, Abul Mansour Ahmed, Ahmad Sharif—all mentioned about Tagore's unfortunate role in their writings. See Taj Hashmi, "The Tagore Mania: Identity Crisis and Anti-Bangladesh Syndrome" (2006) at http://www.muktomona.com/Articles/taj_hashmi/tagore110506.htm
24. See Allama Golam Ahamad Mortaja, *Ei Ek Annyo Itihas: Anonnyo Rabindranath O Thakur Bari* (Bangla Bazar, Dhaka: M. M. Meherullah Research Academy, 2005).
25. Serajul Islam was Bangladesh's ambassador to Egypt and Japan. He also served at the Bangladesh Missions in Canberra, New Delhi, Washington, and Beijing. For further details of Tagore's anti-Muslim role, visit http://sohagahmad.blogspot.com/2014/11/blog-post_85.html
26. To follow some important details of history, after the Christian conquest of Cordova earlier and then Granada in 1492, the Nasirid Andalusia decisively fell and the Muslims were expelled from today's Spain and Portugal. In a devastating and horrifying act of treachery by King Ferdinand and Queen Isabella, not only the crops of the Muslim lands were burned to ashes causing famine but also millions of Muslims, mostly women and children, were tricked and fooled to retreat into masjids on April 1, only to be burned alive in fire there. Hence one of the reasons for April 1st to be known as April Fool (http://www.sheershanewsbd.com/2015/04/01/74879#sthash.hD8yZQn3). After the Muslim rebellion of 1499, there were forced conversions in 1502, when there was a royal decree that Muslims wanting to remain in Castile had to convert to Christianity. Those who converted, at least nominally, and their descendants were called Moriscos. They were actually Muslims, forcibly baptized.

27. For Faisal Ahmed's short historical perspective on the song, see: http://newsg24.com/culture-news/511/"আমার%20সোনার%20বাংলা
28. http://www.sheershanewsbd.com/2015/07/09/88067#
29. http://www.cnn.com/2016/08/29/sport/colin-kaepernick-flag-protest-has-history-trnd/index.html
30. It is said that "Amar Sonar Bangla" had already been decided as the national anthem of Bangladesh, in 1970 (as the separation of East Pakistan from West Pakistan was looming large on the horizon) by (the Nagpuri-born Parsi of Mumbai origin) Khusro Faramurz Rustamji-led BSF in the RAW headquarters. Ranu Chowdhury thinks that "'Amar Sonar Bangla' and Secularism are the two 'gifts' Sheikh Mujib received from Indira Gandhi when he stopped over in New Delhi on his way from London to the newly independent Bangladesh on 10 January 1971. These were the first doses toward Indianizing Bangladesh." Ranu Chowdhury also shares what he heard from an insider of the 15 August 1975 changeover that just before the new president Khandoker Mushtaq Ahmed was to address the nation in the morning, newscaster Sarkar Kabiruddin came to check what national anthem would be used to precede the address. President Mushtaq thought for a while and agreed to use the existing one, probably because there was no other anthem readily available on hand.
31. Daily Songram, 12 April 1997/ দৈনিক সংগ্রাম, ১২/০৪/৯৭; Daily Janakantho, 6 August 1996/দৈনিক জনকণ্ঠ, ৬ই আগস্ট, ১৯৯৬

15 Conclusion (Parts A and B)

Today's Bangladesh is reeling and writhing under the yoke of an Awami regime, which is not really a government, but a repressive and reprehensible regime. Its methods and measures, as far as the democratic political opposition is concerned, are neither democratic nor tolerant, neither humane nor moral, neither prudent nor pragmatic. Its ways and means are totally autocratic and authoritarian, and despotic and dictatorial. Democratic character of the country as a battleground for high and noble ideas is completely lost. Its unity in difference and diversity is conspicuous by its absence. Immersed in absolute corruption that absolute power implies, this government-turned-regime is getting away with all its malpractices of partisan politics and policies.

The clutches of the draconian and diabolical regime (described by critics as BAKSAL—II and much worse and more dangerous than BAKSAL-I) allows for no space and respect for the country's democratic political dissent led by the opposition BNP and its allies. As a result, the "topmost burning questions of democracy in Bangladesh," even a radically secular minded Islamophobe, pseudonymous Khoniker Othithee of the USA, does otherwise correctly identify, "are criminalization of politics, influence of black money in politics, undue political influence on supposedly neutral government bodies like Election Commission and law enforcement entities, threat to freedom of speech from the government and its musclemen, and so on" (E-mail, December 4, 2016).

The nation is sharply divided over the issues of its national leaders (both past and present), its ideals of nationalism and secularism, its national anthem, and its being fooled by the pugnacious, ridiculous, repugnant, and reprehensible pseudo elections that were held on January 5, 2014 and afterward (not to speak of the not so highly questionable but still not very free and fair previous ones). Boycotted by the opposition, it is the false and farcical elections of 5 January and those that followed, one after another, equally rigged and stolen, that are the main source of all the problems facing the nation today, including why Prime Minister Sheikh Hasina and her cabinet ministers face protests everywhere they go, receiving more jeers than cheers from the angry crowd of Bangladeshi origin all across Europe, America, Canada, the UN, and so on.[1] Hasina should have been PM of all Bangladeshis, not just the Awamis and Awami supporters and sympathizers. Had she been decidedly so, she would have been received with all cheers and celebration as PM. Instead, she is a bragging, bullying, boastful, bellicose, and belligerent lady, electorally and indignantly frightened by her deep and dark and violent BNP*hobia.*

The enormously talented New York-based columnist Dr Mina Farah, who once mistakenly used to be pro-Awami but then wisely turned into a vehemently anti-Awami figure of boundless courage and energy, has written to this effect, saying it is the same farce and foolishness for the government that came to power by stealing elections to claim that they are running the country "according to the constitution," as it is for the atheists, who would claim they lead their lives "according to the Bible."[2] The nation needs to be united by hard, leader-like, and statesmanlike choices, to be made (according to the pulse of the people and their "unsung" chorus and "unwritten" writing on the wall) by all stakeholders together, not just the neo-fascistically oriented Sheikh Hasina and her party (AL) alone, who are only a few among the many others, all being equally important in light of democratic norms and values and in the process of upholding and upgrading them.

Sheikh Hasina's rule of systematic custodial and judicial torture and persecution, in a spiraling descending order, lost its democratic legitimacy and popular mandate long ago. She is cruelly bent upon prolonging her royal reign, never to be reined in, until the middle of the century, as envisioned by her declared plans in the name of the so-called (one-eyed and corruption-ridden) economic development. All this is at the expense of social justice and rule of law. Her regime is determined to drag on by means of the crafty and crooked Machiavellian, Mephistophelian, Chanakkyan, and Lilliputian (low and mean, nasty and nefarious, divisive and despotic) malpractices and other forms of deadly, destructive, and dreadful state terrorism. The regime's self-created smokescreen of power is being allowed to stay on with the help of the boots and bullets of its politicized and politically criminalized police/RAB and other mechanically, as opposed to dynamically, mechanized muscles and wings.

The entire government machinery, dependent on creating a delusion and a disillusion by force, media propaganda, and party loyalists, is applied against the democratic political opposition, thereby fanning the flames of hatred, exclusion, and intolerance. There is absolutely no space and respect for the political dissent, although it clearly enjoys the mass and majority support—a claim backed by the New York-based Human Rights Watch.[3]

It is strange that PM Hasina's International Affairs advisor Gowher Rizvi, out of uncritical and unquestioning loyalty to his boss, despite being an academic himself, says the prevailing political unrest is not a barrier to economic development—a statement which contains both admission and denial, but which is as strange as the Foreign Ministry's disowning of the twenty-five Bangladeshi casualties in the devastating crane collapse in Makkah, Saudi Arabia.[4] Members of the BNP and the BNP-led opposition, the only viable opposition in the country with the majority of 160 million people supporting them, are arrested every day, in a neo-and-near-and-more-than-partially fascist and পৈশাচিক manner, from their households and indoor meetings and assemblies, preventing them from holding any rallies, gatherings, processions, and demonstrations, either in private or in public.[5]

Over five thousand BNP leaders and activists are now behind bars in dark dungeons across the country. The entire spectrum of the opposition figures and parties are subject to unprecedented forced disappearances, police brutalities, tortuous remands, imprisonments, and all sorts of penal persecutions and harassments on a daily basis under a rule-and-reign of despotism and dictatorship.[6] They are struggling to swim with hands and feet tied. How can Khaleda Zia and all other opposition leaders fight for the people and the country when they are all entangled in a heroically gladiatorial and promethean fight, tethered to the regime's court system, boiling over the police brutalities, tied to bureaucratic discriminations, and burdened with thousands of lawsuits categorically rejected by them as false and fabricated? Can they fight for the country and the people when they are completely preoccupied, from top to bottom, head to toe, fighting court battles they are pitted against so woefully and unjustly on a daily basis?

According to the British news magazine *The Economist*, Bangladesh's standing on the question of democracy is 85th out of 117 countries surveyed.[7] The country's neo-and-near-and-more-than-partially totalitarian regime keeps beating an economic development drum, with an appeal to the party-blind (দলদাস এবং দলকানা) and other dark elements, playing on their worst fears and instincts. Its authoritarian ruler Sheikh Hasina, like George W Bush's false pretext of Saddam Hussein's non-existent WMD (Weapons of Mass Destruction), uses the ghostly specter of Islamic terrorism and anti-independence forces as an overblown and exaggerated excuse to repress the popular opposition, led by Begum Khaleda Zia, the most popular, dignified, and polished leader of the country. Hasina keeps repeating and reiterating her unfounded paranoid and hypochondriac statements regarding the once (and later befriended and reestablished) anti-liberation forces only to consolidate her power and continue her democratically illegitimate and authoritarian rule.

There are no extremist Islamist elements in Bangladesh. That there is a claim by some here and there that there are is in fact a lie and a deception, says Alamgir Mohiuddin, editor of the popular Bengali daily Naya Diganta.[8] If there are any, as suggested by the quotes at the beginning of the book, they are isolated, born and bred of Hasina's ruthless oppression of the people, as also claimed by (Ret) Maj Akhtaruzzaman, or they are planned and planted by the Hasina government as a scarecrow, as claimed by the opposition leader Begum Zia.[9] Saddam Hussein of Iraq fought against Iran for eight years, thinking he was protecting Arab interest and promoting Arab nationalism, but his mistaken cover did not work. He attacked Kuwait for his own interest; that also did not work. Sheikh Hasina's fear of and fight against religious terrorism, either nonexistent or concocted, is a ruse that also would not work, except that it might help her to gain cheap political mileage in the short term. She claims she is a practicing Muslim, which she may be, but she also uses Islam, like her cohort and surrogate Ershad, to bag more and more votes from the God-fearing Muslims.

Ms Hasina's idiosyncratic political bigotry, manifested through her regime's highly humpy, bumpy, quirky, and cliquey rule, has been at the expense of the near-total annihilation and elimination of the majority supported democratic opposition. It is as baseless and unfounded as that of a man who during a campaign event of Donald Trump said that Muslims were a problem in America, that they were running training camps to kill Americans, that Barack Obama was a Muslim, and that he was not even an American. The man's questions, including the comments in response by Trump and his fellow presidential rival Dr Ben Carson, were immediately dismissed as ugly and obnoxious by the American public and the media.

Hasina's fanatical and fundamentalist fight against the democratic freedom of other political parties, secular or Islamic, and their leaders, is like Don Quixote pursuing a self-created, imaginary enemy and fighting a futile and pathetic fight—which he wrongly thought was a noble and chivalric fight—against the windmills, mistakenly taken for giants with long arms. Hasina's jarringly incongruous fight against the democratic political and/or Islamic forces is like the anti-tank bunkers built by the Albanian communist dictator Enver Hoxha (Anwar Hojja) in his unfounded fear of invasion from his fellow communist neighbor Marshal Tito of Yugoslavia.

Sheikh Hasina's international recognition and environment record critiqued

> Baa, baa, black sheep,
> Have you any wool?
> Yes, sir, yes, sir,
> Three bags full;
> One for the master,
> And one for the dame,
> And one for the little boy
> Who lives down the lane.[10]

Dr Mohammad Yunus's Nobel for Peace was never recognized and appreciated by the Awamis and their leader Sheikh Hasina, who never fails and forgets to scornfully detest and criticize Dr Yunus, his record, and his most prestigious international prize. Her one sided criticism of Dr Yunus has been criticized by Dr Asif Nazrul as yet another demonstration of her democratically dangerous and diabolic politically incorrect precedents.[11] She described Dr Yunus as financially corrupt and his Nobel as the result of what she called his "blood-sucking means out of the poor." Her followers said that he managed to get the Nobel by default and that it should have gone to Sheikh Hasina, who they thought was "more eligible."[12]

Logically, one can take the liberty of critiquing the basketful of awards received by Hasina and also perhaps by her allegedly outrageously high-salaried son Sajeeb Wajed Joy. One can question them the way one questions the international awards received by Hasina's Education minister Nurul Islam Nahid as allegedly fake and false.[13] Despite building "Towers of London," "Bastilles" of Paris, "Berlin Walls," "Abu Ghraibs" of Baghdad, "Guantanamo Bays," North Korean Kim's Walls, Syrian Bashar's Walls, and Venezuelan Maduro's Walls (if not Trump's Mexican Walls)—to refer to those historically infamous symbols of barrier, bondage, division, detention, torture, and incarceration—to divide the nation and destroy its previously growing democracy, Ms Hasina and her son continue to receive international awards, including many honorary doctorates for the former. It is certainly a matter of pride for them to annually receive as many awards as to make their baskets full, faster than a race can be run.

Had the mother and the son led a democratically elected government, recognized by all concerned, paving the way for a vigorous and vibrant democracy in the interest of the people, the whole nation would have been wholeheartedly proud to see its prime minister and her son receive such international awards. Had there been nationwide collective consensus and bipartisan peace, unity, amity, and prosperity, their laurels would have shone brighter and looked worthier. Had Hasina and her son Sajib Wajed Joy built patriotic walls like the ancient Roman Servian Wall and Hadrian's Wall to be inclusive of all and wall in, not wall out, the political opposition of the country, they would have been pleased to share the international recognition they received with the whole nation together as one single, not segregated, nation. Had they mended the (political) wall that required repair, as does the speaker in Robert Frost's poem, to maintain good rapport with their political rivals, all the people of different democratic hues and views could have basked in the limelight of the international attention Hasina and her son received.

In 2016, Sheikh Hasina was proud to obtain Planet 50–50 award, despite the fact that gender inequalities and gender insecurities in terms of abuse, rape, murder, torture, child labor, and teen marriage remain the order of the day, over 80%, in a country of 160m, most of them being the poor masses. The same year she received the Agent for Change award, despite the fact that it is a country of vast social and political injustice, oppression, repression, and persecution, changing for the worse, where there is not a single thing that is not questionable, controversial, strange, mysterious, and conspiratorial. Hasina's son was proud to receive the ICT for Development award. Only God knows what the heck all these high-sounding and headline-making global awards mean, how big and coveted they are, how appeasing, pandering, patronizing, or aspired for, and how consolatory or competitive they are.

Why are the top leaders of the world deprived of or not selected for those bombastic awards? Are they reserved only for a "chosen" and "selected" few from the third world countries? Why do the majority of seats in the UN General Assembly Hall go empty when such third world leaders speak as if they are there only to address the inanimate objects—chairs and tables—rather than a living audience of humans? In the context of the fact that the Bangladeshis are deeply divided and poles apart and that there is no let up on the daily special operations by the police/RAB rounding up scores and scores of fellow citizens belonging to the opposition or otherwise (many of them getting killed every day) and turning the whole country into a dark prison and a killing field, what do these awards really mean and what do they bring to the nation as a whole?

The same year American business magazine Forbes ranked Sheikh Hasina as the 36th most powerful woman in the world. She also received the UN environmental "Champion of the Earth" award (for which the UN was reportedly given a large sum).[14] She received the award despite the fact that there is a tremendous environmental and industrial pollution, both in the capital and the countryside, all around the country. Dhaka is one of the dirtiest, stinkiest, crowded, congested, and most polluted cities in the world. The rivers and the drains, both in the capital city as well as all other cities of the country, are blocked and clogged, being piled high with mountains of rotten rubbish, similar to the smelly, junk-filled ancient river Tiber in Rome during the last BCs and early ADs.[15]

All opposition parties, civil societies, environmentalists of the country, and the UN World Heritage Committee are of the view that while the prime minister was receiving international environment awards, she was going to destroy the Sunderbans, one of the largest mangroves and ecological treasures in the world in the southwest of the country. She was doing so as a result of her India-Bangladesh joint venture—construction of a 1,320 MW coal-fired power plant in Rampal on the Indian side of the border, according to a losing, unequal rip-off treaty with India.[16] In January 2017, in Davos, former Vice President and Nobel laureate Al Gore advised Sheikh Hasina not to proceed with the construction of the plant that was going to be harmful to the rare and precious natural species all around the site.[17] Local and International bodies and media widely protested against haughty and hot-headed Hasina's ongoing move with the plant.[18]

Satirically dismissing the critics, Hasina, however, argues that those very animal species need to be asked if they would have any problem with the new power plant that is underway. The brave and brilliant Dr Tuhin Malik, journalist/columnist Minar Rashid, India People Science Forum National General Secretary and Energy and Environment Specialist Shoummyo Dutta, Farzana Kabir Khan of Germany, Save the Sunderbans Foundation Chairman Dr Sheikh Faridul Islam, as well as Bangladesh's national committee for the protection of oil, gas, mineral resources, power and ports have separately given befitting replies that incontrovertibly refute the obstinate PM's insistence on the plant.[19] Civil Society leader and former Government Adviser Advocate Sultana Kamal says the Rampal air pollution would mortally affect the whole area, from Narsingdi to Kolkata, causing many deaths every year.[20] The controversial Rampal plant would cause 6,000 early deaths, according to the Greenpeace leader Lauri Myllyvirta.[21]

The project having the potential to cause a great harm to the nearby natural treasure has been warned against by the green activist, Nobel laureate and former US Vice President Al Gore. It is also against the wishes of Hasina's great father

Sheikh Mujib, who was determined to save the Sunderbans at any cost.[22] In the face of her arrogantly going forward with the project, UNESCO has urged a halt to the joint Indo-Bangla plan for the coal plant in the Delta.[23]

Dr Rezwan Siddiqui, editor of the daily Dinkal, writes about the environmental hazards that would cause a havoc to the Sunderbans.[24] A civic forum of green campaigners called All For Sunderbans called on the government to explore an alternative location for the Rampal power plant, observing that the project will have an adverse impact on the biodiversity of the Sunderbans, the largest mangrove forest in the world, and that the country needed no power plant at the cost of the Sunderbans as it was a home to rare species that were already on the verge of extinction.[25] Doesn't Hasina care for the geologically and geographically "green" fact that Mother Nature does not need people, but that it is the people who need her for their survival?

People of Bangladesh need to save not only the Sunderbans but also Bangladesh from keeping sliding into the dark hole of authoritarian rule! Is UNESCO contributing to that sliding by now withdrawing its earlier objections to the construction of the plant nearby its heritage site, just as the World Bank may be contributing to the possible continuing corruption by withdrawing its reservations concerning the funding of the construction of the Padma Bridge? Have these world bodies been lobbied hard to yield and give in, some way or another?

According to critics such as Dr Farah and many other political watchers and observers, many international awards were and can be bought and the awarding organizations are alleged to have been "donated" (to use an euphemism for "bribe") a large sum in exchange for which they are pleased to return the favor to their donor clients (who, suggestively, often hail from the third world) and honor them with equally large (yet, ironically, lank and lin and thin) recognitions of immediate political and media mileage, which is definitely devoid of real and lasting significance. *Prothom* Bangladesh and Newsbd7 report critiques of such awards, the latter even bringing into the scene the former Ugandan dictator Idi Amin to compare with Sheikh Hasina in terms of his style of winning and buying medals.[26] As if in a dramatic aside or soliloquy, one may reflect that (like Bashar Al-Assad of Syria, Hosni Mubarak and Abdul Fattah Al-Sisi of Egypt, Nicolas Maduro of Venezuela, Robert Mugabe of Zimbabwe, and Hun Sen of Cambodia), Hasina seems to be lucky to have been anointed and enunciated, while Khaleda Zia, like the hapless people of those countries, including the vast majority of her own country, seems to be unlucky to have been deserted and abandoned by God.

Similarly, as reported on the media, the role of Chevron, the largest producer of natural gas in Bangladesh, behind Sheikh Hasina being ranked 13th on the list of the world's 100 thinking personalities, has come to surface through the role that her son Sajeeb Wajed Joy is thought to have played behind the scene. As shown by the investigative writings such as the one called "$300m in wild goose chase by social media" by Toronto-based practitioner of international law Shahid Islam, published in the weekly Holiday of Bangladesh, Joy is said to have been involved in playing a role in connection with Chevron and other entities.[27] In April 2016, an exclusive write-up by David Bergman in the Indian website, The Wire, revealed that a "Suspicious Activity Report" (SAR) covering a transaction of US$300 million recorded in a memo of the FBI was linked to Wajed. But the court documents did not provide any further information about the reference to US$300 million.[28] CNN, Barrister Rafiqul Hoque, and Advocate Syeda Ashrafi Papia touched on a number of issues connected with Joy's questionable activities and financial dealings, the latter being alleged to have amassed as much money from suspicious sources as to be enough to construct as many as 20 Padma bridges.[29] Joy, however, denied bagging 300m in black money.[30]

In any case, it is as if it does not matter any longer to the commercially driven international community as to which country is being run how, by who, or what form of government, and how polluted it is, morally, politically, and environmentally.[31] Comparing Dhaka's state to that of an ailing patient in the intensive care unit of a hospital, Mayor Anisul Huq of Hasina's own party said, "Dhaka is now the second worst livable city in the world. Besides the agonizing traffic conditions and hazardous environment, the last monsoon revealed its vulnerability in drainage system. Alongside traffic congestion, another Mayor, Sayeed Khokon, also of Hasina's party, mentioned water-logging as another major problem of Dhaka."[32] Notwithstanding, Sheikh Hasina has been "recognized" as "a champion of the earth" or one of the Foreign Policy magazine's sole and fast—not democratically consultative—decision makers, as all dictators of absolute powers are.

The same criticism could be directed at the American Fortune magazine, which placed a great democratic political leader, Angela Merkel, together with Sheikh Hasina, who rules as undemocratically and tyrannically as one can imagine in the context of Bangladesh. Like the unpredictable Greek goddess Fortune and the medieval Wheel of Fortune symbolizing fate or destiny and ever turning the highs low and the lows high, was it to maintain some kind of balance by the Fortune magazine between the different levels and categories of political leaders? If Hasina could be there, what could have been wrong with the other dictators of the world? These recognitions are being questioned by many.[33] True, many dictators—old and modern—were and are among the great global thinkers too. Fascist Hitler's autobiographical manifesto *Mein Kampf* (My Struggle), originally published in 1925/1926, has been recently republished in Germany, seventy years after his death, in view of his exceptional thinking that found its way into his book.

However, would the UN or the *Foreign Policy* journal one day regret their extending recognition to certain people just as some Nobel committee members have regretted awarding the "politicized" peace prize to Barack Obama, Shimon Peres, and Henry Kissinger?[34] Were there any "politically correct" factors behind Sheikh Hasina having been awarded international prizes just as there may have been political considerations in selecting many Nobel laureates when the coveted prize went to some obscure, controversial, or undeserving people?[35]

Here it is to be mentioned that the cruel, cowardly, and communal Aung San Suu Kyi of Myanmar's Nobel for Peace has become highly controversial in view of her stony silence, inexcusable inaction, and remorselessness on the issue of the widespread and indiscriminate slaughter of the Muslim Rohiyngas of her Buddhist majority country. The innocent and poverty-stricken stateless Rohiyngas are facing the most heinous and horrendous ethnic and religious cleansing, to the extent of total extinction and extermination, worse than what happened in Bosnia and Herzegovina in the 1990s.[36] Millions are signing off an online petition asking the Nobel Committee to revoke Suu Kyi's inglorious and infamous Nobel.[37]

Imran H Shorkar of GanaJagaran Mancha made a blistering attack on Suu Kyi, saying she was the worst and most detested and undeserving name among all the Nobel awardees.[38] However, Suu Kyi is not alone; Winston Churchill, who made millions of Bengalis die of hunger in 1943 but was awarded a Nobel for literature in 1953, should also be included among the infamous (see Note #6 in "Bangladesh: A Trial Separation"). Shouldn't his political Nobel too be posthumously reconsidered?

One (that is, Buddhist Suu Kyi) who was herself under house arrest under the Burmese Buddhist junta for many years and tasted the pleasures of confinement should understand the value of freedom and liberation more than anybody else. Nobel laureate and Buddhist Pontiff Dalai Lama also, who dwells in the mountains of Dharmasala India, is totally silent about the inhuman torture his Burmese Buddhist followers are inflicting on the fellow Burmese people simply because they connect with a different religious faith other than theirs. Next door neighbor and Nobel winner Dr Yunus too should have spoken out, early on, against the inhuman plight and predicament the Rakhaine Rohingyas have been suffering from for years.[39] Have these regional septuagenarian and octogenarian Nobel winners become morally shrunk, slimmer, and smaller than their much younger and granddaughter-like Malala Yusofzai, who has spoken out, though late in time? If the young Nobel winner Malala can speak out, why would they remain in the self-imposed confinement of their cozy bower and ivy and ivory tower? Peace laureates doing nothing for peace to return and prevail and to give peace a chance?[40] What a moral reversal of values like the way it is in Hasina's Bangladesh?

The Hasina loyalists are lamenting that she did not yet get the Nobel for which they think she is eligible. They are forming human chains to demand that she be given a Nobel for peace.[41] Jealous of Dr Yunus, badly treated by them in a step-brotherly way, they think it was Ms Hasina, who should have been given the prize for peace.[42] Neutral and fair-minded watchers and human rights observers shy away from such a claim when they see that there is so much horror and terror and torture under the Hasina administration that the country is completely immersed in them. Journalist Masud Mazumder gives an accurate picture of why Hasina is still short of deserving a Nobel for peace.[43] When many Indian writers and artists have renounced their honors and titles in protest of the violent social ills in their questionably free and democratic India,[44] their counterparts in the police state of Bangladesh frantically run after such rewards and recognitions from the democratically illegitimate Hasina government.

No sooner the journalist-writer Svetlana Alexievich of Belarus had gotten the Nobel prize in literature for 2015, there started a wave of disappointment because she "has flattered smug imbeciles with tales of the new Evil Empire of Russia and of its bloodthirsty Tsar Vladimir the Terrible [Putin] … This year's Nobel Prize for Literature honors an age of intellectual dishonesty, dullness, and a lethally bathetic intellectual age."[45] No sooner Colombian President Juan Manuel Santos had disputably gotten the 2016 Nobel for Peace, there started a protest by human rights activists in Bogota on the reason that there was no peace, which was still far from being achieved and that simply an agreement with the FARC rebels was not enough for Santos to receive a Nobel. "The Nobel committee saw peace where others didn't."[46] So, who knows, if that is the checkered history of the Nobel, Hasina may get one soon too. When the purely Western creation Malala got one in 2014, the youngest ever to receive the prize at the age of seventeen only, critics with their eyebrows raised started quoting Shakespeare: "Some are born great, some achieve greatness, and *some have greatness thrust upon them*" (my emphasis). Would Hasina also have greatness thrust upon her?[47]

The free world may be helpless against Benjamin Netanyahu of Israel, Bashar Al-Assad of Syria, Kim Jong-Un of North Korea, Abdul Fattah Al-Sisi of Egypt, and Robert Mugabe of Zimbabwe—as helpless against the Indian occupation of Kashmir, the Israeli occupation of Palestine, the Chinese occupation of the Tibet, Chinese communism and their control of the South China Sea through their artificially built militarized islands, Iraqi Shiite-Sunni conflict, Al-Qaeda, IS (Islamic

State), CS (Christian State), Boko Haram, Al-Shabab, Yemeni Houthi, Christian neocons and, finally, the LGBT community.[48] Apparently, the world is also helpless against the despotic and dogmatic regime in Bangladesh, which is stringently closed to all possibilities. Does the free world prefer to overlook and connive at the cruel ruthlessness with which the Hasina regime is terrorizing the popular political opposition of the country? Is the free world helpless against forcing her to practice democracy, upgrade democratic process, and promote democratic culture? Is it too weak to make her pay the cost of freedom, and serve the nation with transparency and accountability? Is it because she and her small Bangladesh are sheltered and shielded by the larger India,[49] like Assad and his small Syria by the larger Iran and Russia, and Netanyahu and his small Israel by the larger West?

Ms Hasina mourns for Indian flood victims, fine, but shouldn't she feel and care to feel for the hundreds and thousands of her own people, who, due to her partisan and authoritarian rule, are living behind bars for years and are systematically getting arrested, imprisoned, remanded, killed, kidnapped, and disappear every day, every other day, or every now and then, their mothers and daughters and wives shedding tears in cusecs at home and at Dhaka Press Club?[50] Is the world morally regressing or progressing? Has it come to a stagnant, pernicious, and pugnacious standstill by compartmentalizing the ills and pushing them aside, on the one hand, and the economic and strategic interests, on the other.

Huntington versus Fukuyama

Free market capitalism may be expanding and spreading everywhere, but liberal democracies? Not really. Starting from the Crusades of the Middle Ages to the redrawing and reorganization of the Arab World and the rolling back of the Turkish Ottoman Empire during WWI to the creation of Israel and its deadly conflict with and occupation of Palestine in the aftermath of WWII to the "controlled demolition" of the two WTC towers in New York on 9/11/2001, to the Western creation of ISIS and Malala, followed by the bloody involvement of the Western powers in the Muslim countries killing millions of Muslims since 2001, clashes of faiths, cultures, civilizations, and ideologies are on the fast track, far from abating and receding.[51]

Left, Right, and Center are still unfolding, adapting, and adjusting to each other in different ways. The geo-political and religious scenarios are so complex that there seems to be neither an end to history nor an end to human sociological development nor is there a last man. Samuel Huntington, then, rings truer than Francis Fukuyama. It is the same as Vladimir Putin seems to be more over-powering than Barack Obama, Donald Trump, David Cameron, Theresa May, Stephen Harper, Francois Hollande, and Tony Abbott, all combined! Putin has demonstrated his power in aggressively siding with the tyrant Bashar Al-Assad, who slaughtered hundreds of thousands of his own people and terrorized millions to make them to run away triggering an unprecedented refugee crisis in history. Putin has demonstrated his power by annexing Crimea and threatening to annex parts of the Baltics and Ukraine. Trump is riding the high tide of white nationalism, white supremacy, and Islam-bashing rhetoric.

However, all of them, together with the Shiite Iran and the Lebanese Shiite Hezbollah, are on the same track in viewing the Shiite-allied brutal Bashar as "softer," "more moderate" and "more acceptable" than the ISIS, which is no more than a secretive, clandestine group, not even a government and far less than a government. What an irony!

Who is worse and more vicious—Bashar or the ISIS? One is an open mass murderer with a track record of unleashing terror and bloodshed of catastrophic proportions with the help of his deadly and beastly army of cluster and barrel bombs and chemical weapons, leaving millions dead, under siege, dying of hunger and starvation, forced to flee and be displaced, but still enjoying power and privilege under an umbrella of international protection. The other is an internationally squeezed and severely punished underdog bearing only a Sunni Muslim/Islamic name, brutally terrifying though it is, no doubt. What a moral cowardice in the face of the powerful windmill of the butcher Bashar and what a chivalrous "Quioxotic" feat in the face of the weaker and self-created enemy giant of the ISIS?

While both of them are devils, of unequal scale though, and while both need to be bombed equally and uniformly, with equal force and priority, to be completely eliminated, it is probably the ISIS that has been one-sidedly demonized in turn, more than Bashar, by the international community. The geostrategic fight, however geopolitically and religiously sensitive it may be, should be taken to both Bashar and the ISIS on equal footing. Had the butcher Bashar himself been butchered early on, a few years ago, and had the ISIS, like the butcher Bashar, been left alone, to itself, both the recent influx of refugees and the international (Russian, French, Lebanese, Turkish, Saudi, Iraqi, and Syrian) disasters could have probably been avoided. As a corollary, the Western powers should leave Putin to take the Baltics and build his old Soviet empire, rather than allowing him to boost and bolster the butcher Bashar with a formidable military force right under their nose.

The AL and the BNP: differences deepening, gravitating, pivoting

Getting back to the point in focus, it seems one of the most politically motivated interests of Hasina's extremely loyalist and slavish police/RAB is to go after and come down hard on the members of the BNP-led alliance, perhaps sometimes due to their anti-BNP and pro-AL zealotry and sometimes their being instructed by the fiercely and fanatically anti-BNP Hasina government, as if no one had any right to engage in opposition politics and as if there was no place for anybody else except the Awami-Baksali group to get together and discuss politics, indoors as well as outdoors.

The atmosphere of fear, fright, fraud, fabrications, prosecutions, persecution, endemic bribery, extortions, underhand deals and behind the scene ballot stamping has surpassed all past records.[52] Joshua Kurlantzick, a senior fellow for Southeast Asia at the Council on Foreign Relations, gives an account of Bangladesh's gradual descent into chaos, comparing it with countries such as Thailand, Malaysia, Cambodia, Venezuela, Syria, Libya, Egypt and others.[53] The Hasina regime justifies its actions by saying that the people (who are only nominally and not actually) the ultimate source of power are not there on the street to protest against her police boots and bullets and thereby launch a movement, implying that people are happy with the way the regime functions and handles the affairs of the state as they are.

Nothing is farther from truth than this unsound and mistaken fallacy. The great majority of the people are in support of the opposition but they are not allowed to gather on the street, bring out processions, stage demonstrations, and hold public meetings. They stay away for their well-founded fear for life. When almost all the opposition leaders, from national to district to *Upazela* (County) to more local (village) levels, are regularly facing police remands of corporeal punishment, confinements of tortures and tribulations and jail sentences on a daily basis for years, the prospect of their supporters getting out on the street, only to get either forcibly prevented and arrested or mortally hit by police bullets and batons, flying at the slightest stir, evaporates to the extent of being nil and nonexistent.[54] To justify its actions, now more than eight year old oppressive regime cites only a couple of small and stray examples about how it was forced to scrap its airport plan in Munshiganj and its defense forces housing plan in Rupganj in the face of the local opposition, which was actually allowed to go ahead by the mercy of the government and its police.

The irony is, in these two matters—non-political as they were—, the regime did not want to stop the local villagers from coming out by using its baton-wielding police and did not want to create an unnecessary nuisance. An airport or a military residential area can easily be planned and developed in another part of the country. Neither the remotely local and isolated instances as above nor the withdrawal of the more recently imposed non-political VAT (value added tax) on students tuition in the face of their vital and viral collective opposition can validate the regime's eight years of bloody and violent authoritarianism and cannot legitimize or substantiate its claim that the people, long frightened by its fearful and ferocious policies of regimentation and containment, do not pay heed to the call of the political opposition to take to the streets nationwide.

In the midst of the endless violence resulting from the sluttish Awami misrule and misdeeds,[55] it is always good to see the BNP leaders raising hopes about a national election every now and then. However, as the ruling AL dictatorially keeps repeating and reiterating, there is absolutely no sign, even a specter of it, on the horizon, no possibility of an election to be held any time soon or before 2019. People's aspirations about a meaningful election in the sense of being free, fair, inclusive and participatory, and about a representative government have been raised and dashed again and again like a boat tossed and floundered around the waves of a stormy sea. The BNP's is only a soft and harmless political deduction about the possibility of a parliamentary election from what is actually an insignificant and inconsequential tug of war within the AL and the AL-led coalition that includes what (the late) Kazi Shiraj termed as the parasitical JSD (Hasanul Hoque Inu) with its inflammatory anti-Awami past. [56]

Any war of words is to be calmed and put to rest in no time, if necessary, by the AL's sole and single leader Sheikh Hasina. She has already instructed the coalition members under her thumb to immediately stop their intra-party খোঁচা খুঁচি (infighting, internecine friction)—a substandard expression by her, in keeping with her often distasteful style of Bangla.[57] The BNP-led opposition has been asking for election since the one-sided "nonelection" of January 5, 2014, which it boycotted for the reasons of the lack of democratic equality and transparency. It claims that not only the 5 January election but also the one before (in 2008, though to a lesser extent) was basically a ballot-box stuffing with pre-determined results in defiance of all the rules and practices of freeness and fairness.

The opposition call for free and fair elections, made repeatedly, came to no effect as it fell on the deaf ears of the murderous Awami regime, politically sheltered and financed by India.[58] No amount of bickering within the Awami rank and file is enough to force their sole and supreme leader Hasina to declare a mid-term election or whatever. For example, (Ret) General Shafiullah, part of the spat with Sheikh Fazlul Karim Selim, threw his challenges to the critics, reiterating the reality that he, as then chief of army, had no loyal troops to carry out his orders on August 15, 1975 to move against the victorious rebels, let alone saving the life of the assassinated Sheikh Mujibur Rahman. The troops were all supportive of the coup with both Gen Shafiullah and then Air Chief A K Khandoker (also under attack by Selim and others) publicly accepting the changeover and announcing their allegiance to the new government of Khandoker Mushtaque Ahmed.[59]

Ironically, there being no ethics, no morality, no standards, and no last words in politics that, as the saying goes, makes strange bedfellows, both Shafiullah and Khandoker became in no time top associates (if not close cronies) of Mujib's daughter Hasina. She cared the least to draw them into her coterie together with the once vehemently anti-Mujib Motia Chowdhury and Hasanul Hoque Inu, who, strangely, enjoy especially reserved seats in Hasina's inner circle. It follows that the outcome of the salvos and skirmishes among the allies, for instance, the currently near-and-more-than Awami Inu, on the one hand, and Sheikh Selim, Syed Ashraful Islam, Kazi Firoz Rashid, and Nur-e-Alam Siddiquee, on the other, would also amount to nothing under the hard, intransigent, obstinate and belligerent guardianship of Sheikh Hasina, who, with the help of her police and intelligence apparatus and Indian agents, is determined not to yield to any acceptable or reasonable standards of democracy and transparency.

PM Hasina's steamroller rope-less and rein-less reign has left the political opposition in a state of continuous writhing, reeling, twisting, and recoiling since 2009. A literary analogy can be drawn with T S Eliot's Prufrock, who is left fixed in "a formulated phrase … sprawling on a pin … wriggling on the wall." Hasina's bulldozer sway made most of the opposition leaders—young and old—suffer inordinately and excessively.[60] Consequently, they have now become a dead horse or lame duck—useless and ineffective—a situation detrimental to the already dying and dwindling democracy in Bangladesh. In the present situation of torture and persecution, top pro-opposition journalists such as the exceptionally talented but long-imprisoned Mahmudur Rahman, Shaukat Mahmood, and Shafik Rehman—all three of sturdy and steely character—were taken to police custody for purely politically vengeful allegations and, without bail, were tortuously police-remanded again and again, for a number of times, each time for days, as if they were low class robbers, serial killers, or mean reptiles.[61]

Like Tarique Rahman and his late brother Arafat Rahman Koko and then M K Anwar, Mirza Fakhrul Islam Alamgir, Ruhul Kabir Rizvi, Gayeshwar Chandra Roy, Salahuddin Ahmad, Rafiqul Islam Mia, Mahmudur Rahman,

Shafik Rehman, Shawkat Mahmud, Mahmudur Rahman Manna, and Amanullah Aman,—thousands and thousands of politicians and political activists have been captured and incarcerated to the point of being rendered disabled and incapacitated physically. Unlike the democratic West, where the opposition does not have to call for the government to step down before its term expires (except in exceptional circumstances) because the opposition knows it has its freedom to assert and exercise its democratic rights during the term of any government without any constraint and restriction, the situation is completely different in Bangladesh where the opposition is being deprived of all its freedom at every step along the way on a daily basis!

The AL loyalists and activists, be they in the police/RAB, civil administration, press, education, or any other areas, out of their immoral and illegitimate intolerance and vindictiveness, deliberately misread into the democratic anti-Awami or anti-Hasina criticism. Everybody should have the right to say whatever they wish to say. Patriotic Bangladeshis, in their exercise of freedom of speech, whatever that means in the harsh and hardline Hasina regime, point to her political excesses so that she could easily evade and avoid any repetition of the 15 August 1975, which marked a sharp and steep reversal of the wheel of fortune. It is she who also reminds herself that she is at the top of the terrorists' hit list. By doing so, doesn't she succumb to the Bengali saying, চোরের মনে পুলিশ পুলিশ (thieves and miscreants have always the fear of the law enforcing police on their mind)?

By contrast, the Westerners engage in a vital and vibrant debate in the freedom of speech they all enjoy. Where is such productive and fruitful dialogue in Bangladesh except the (Donald) Trump-like low and mean name-calling against the political opposition by the Awami League?[62] Like Trump, only the ruling AL is free to say whatever it likes to say, in an unrestrained and unbridled way, in its authoritarian and totalitarian interest. If the BNP says even one hundredth of what the AL says (and that also in the way of legitimate reaction only, not as the initial action), it faces খবর আছে—meaning, jail and জুলুম (oppression and persecution) and হামলা ও মামলা (attacks and penal lawsuits). In its despotic grip on power (which may never slip away), the Awami government-turned-regime continues to calumniate and make negative, defamatory, and controversial statements not only against the popular opposition led by Khaleda Zia but also her very own person.

The national institutions of Bangladesh, charged with polarization, are on the brink of collapse, one after another, following their being completely politicized and criminalized. Cabinet ministers, though found guilty by the court, are allowed to stay on in their posts. Institutions—political, economic, judicial, administrative, law enforcement, educational, and media—are not allowed to function freely on their own but are forced to act according to the unscrupulous wishes of the Awami leadership and their followers. The various wings of the AL such as their student and youth wings are up to terrorizing the people through their different cells operating all over the country. There are unrest, disruptions, interruptions, and interregnums everywhere. There are hardly any classes at Government colleges and universities with millions of students without being properly taught in face-to-face classroom instruction and without being regularly given midterms and finals!

Dawson College Montreal Professor Abid Bahar's visual and graphic presentation at Harvard, based on authentic media images, illustrates the lamentable situation of different institutions of Bangladesh.[63] The regime's development drum has been satirically dubbed as উন্নয়নের নমুনা ঢাকা হলো যমুনা, referring to the capital city (and all other towns) getting submerged when it rains and are turned into an underwater metropolis to be crisscrossed by boat, which is, ironically, the symbol of the regime. The Daily Star reports to the same effect that Dhaka and other cities easily get inundated when it rains, be it in season or out of season.[64]

Along with the জল জট (clogged and scanty drainage) and জন জট (overcrowded congestion), there are innumerable other problems such as যানজট (traffic jam), session জট (jamming batches of graduating students), জোট জট (inter-alliance tension), বিদ্যুৎ বিভ্রাট (power outage), যান্ত্রিক গোলযোগ (mechanical/technical malfunctioning or communication failures), পরিবেশ দূষণ (environmental pollution), widespread commodification and distribution of education at the expense of quality, আমলাতান্ত্রিক জটিলতা (bureaucratic red tape interference), মানবাধিকার লংঘন (human rights violations), নিরাপত্তার অভাব (lack of security), দায়বদ্ধতার অভাব (lack of accountability), নিয়োগ বাণিজ্য (immoral and illegal commercialization and profiteering in recruitment), মনোনয়ন বাণিজ্য (election nomination profiteering), coaching বাণিজ্য (selective private tuition and admission profiteering), ghoulish ঘুষ (rampant bribery) everywhere, tender বাণিজ্য (profiteering in tender trade), নিত্য প্রয়োজনীয় দ্রব্য মূল্যের উর্ধগতি (daily necessities and commodities getting pricier), favoritism, nepotism, flattery, sycophancy, dishonesty, double standard, discrimination on the basis of (opposition) political profiling, personal and political invectives and vindictiveness, forced disappearances, extremely high rate of indiscriminate murders ("easier than killing flies"),[65] সর্বত্র অস্থিরতা (pervasive mayhem and restlessness), widespread violence against women, সর্বদা প্রশ্নপত্র ফাঁস (exams getting leaked out every now and then), সর্বত্র সীমাহীন নির্লজ্জ বেহায়াপনা অশ্লীলতা বেঈমানি and দুর্নীতি (shameless nudity and obscenity, intellectual and political prostitution and hypocrisy, and financial corruption scandals everywhere[66]), tyranny of the made-up and concocted majority in the parliament, quasi-judicial tyranny, সর্বত্র হিংসা প্রতিশোধ পরশ্রীকাতরতা (hatred, jealousy, vindictiveness, and revenge everywhere), রুগ্ন ও অসুস্থ রাজনীতি (sick and sickening politics of lawlessness, duplicity, and unaccountability), the Awami student wing Chatro League's ever unbridled সন্ত্রাস (terrorism), Awami রাষ্ট্রীয় সন্ত্রাস (state terrorism) in different forms, police brutalities, and, above all, one-and-single party rule and its despotic politicization, teetering polarization and evil and cruel otherization.[67]

Also, Bangladesh, born of a bloodbath, cannot afford to descend and devolve into a less than fully and completely independent state of its own integrity and sovereignty. It must not allow itself to be victimized by the hegemonic designs of India and its un-neighborly selfish self-interest. Examples are too many to count:

(1) New Delhi being Sheikh Hasina's mainstay and main power base (at least according to the aggressive, audacious, threatening and fundamentalist BJP/RSS; (Ret) Gen Shankar Roychowdhury, former Chief of Army Staff and a former Member of Indian Parliament; and the fine, noted journalist and columnist Kuldip Nayar);[68]
(2) The Felanis at the border;
(3) Barbaric BDR massacre mysteries/conspiracies (an insider-outsider job?);
(4) Low-flowing-to-drying Padma-Teesta-Atrai waters;[69]
(5) Anti-Bangladesh agreements with India, such as power plants, nuclear projects, military pacts, and access to ports and roads;[70]
(6) Indian goods flooding Bangladesh markets;
(7) Huge trade imbalance with India; and
(8) Cultural invasion and political interference by India.

In Nayar's words, "Sheikh Hasina's main strength is New Delhi which has put all eggs in her basket [...] Hasina has even damaged India's image because of her authoritarian rule. She brooks no criticism and [...] she and India have become synonymous." Bangladesh must not let itself to be colonized by a new East India Company under the auspices of any government—present or future.

Bangladesh must emerge and evolve into a truly independent and sovereign country of its own, remaining, however, on friendly, neighborly, equal, and balanced terms with India. The relationship between Bangladesh and India ought to be similar to the relationship between the economically and militarily smaller Canada and the more powerful and much stronger America.[71] More analogies may be Taiwan in relation to China; Singapore in relation to Malaysia and Indonesia; Kuwait, Qatar, Bahrain, and Israel in relation to the bordering bigger (Arabian and Persian) Gulf countries; the Baltics (Lithuania, Latvia, and Estonia) in relation to the huge Russia; and the different European countries in relation to their common European Union. Bangladesh should aspire to become a democratic country of free and fair elections like, in addition to Western democracies, the neighboring India, Taiwan, Israel, and South Korea, and not an undemocratic and authoritarian country in relation to its own opposition parties.

Both in internal and external affairs, Bangladesh should stay a strong and free country with an aim to becoming a model Muslim democratic country of transparency, accountability, and good governance so that the Bangladeshis do not have to longingly and painfully look for what freedom means so many years after the 1971 independence. Bangladesh separated from Pakistan not to become slavish and servile to any other country in turn. It is that kind of Bangladesh that was envisaged and dreamed about in the political thought of Suhrawardy, Sher-e-Bangla, Moulana Bhashani, Sheikh Mujib, and the great President Zia, the last having not only been the modern maker of Bangladesh but also the as হাজার বছরের শ্রেষ্ঠ বাংলাদেশী (the greatest Bangladeshi ever, of a thousand years). It is that kind of Bangladesh that has been drawn in the political vision of the following bold, heroic, eminent citizens and political leaders—all critical of the totalitarian one party regime of Sheikh Hasina, called "Lady Hitler" and "Lady Mir Jaffar" by the highly popular leader of the country's democratic movement, Khaleda Zia, and New York's Bangladeshi-origin darling daughter Dr Farah, respectively.[72]

Who's who in the opposition, political, and/or otherwise

The major part of the existing political atmosphere of Bangladesh, under the Hasina regime, is one of bitter baloney and malafide malarkey—as vicious, vituperous, vitriolic, malignant, and malevolent as it could be. In this context, one may like to make an evaluative roll call of the great champions of bonafide democracy and benevolent democratic balance and harmony the way W B Yeats does of the Irish Easter Uprising heroes in 1916. These champions would include the exiled steadfast and determined Tarique Rahman, a victim of the *Uddins*-and-Hasina era physical and judicial torture and, by all accounts, the rightful future leader of the opposition BNP. Hopefully already feeling sorry for being rude to anybody prior to 2006, Tarique is likely to prove to be an able, agile, competent, and charismatic leader like his noble and nimble father, who has left a great legacy for his son and his people to build on.

Tarique's party Secretary General Mirza Fakhrul is a polite, soft-spoken, and much sacrificing man of clean conduct and good image, no doubt, much beaten up and repeatedly imprisoned by the Hasina men. Unfortunately, he is cooler than cucumber, lighter than newcomer. In terms of demeanor and outward bearing, Mirza Fakhrul does not seem to be one to be able to create and leave a lasting impact or impression, as the senior Shah Muazzem Hussein is. His words do not seem to carry much weight and curry favor with the people. He is not as big and ballistic, and as large and long-range in his tone, talk, and style as his party deserves. Mechanical Engineer Mohammad Gani of the USA is right to point out that many BNP supporters and followers were "quietly voicing their frustration" against Mirza Fakhrul, who, lacking the "crucial components necessary for delivering credible and effective leadership at the national level, was enmeshed in controversy inside the BNP itself" (E-mail of April 28, 2017).

Apparently not having enough steam and stamina, Mirza Fakhrul is not as active, assertive, effective, and efficient as he should be (his Awami counterpart Syed Ashraf was not any better, perhaps even worse; Obaidul Quader is boring, monolithic, myopic, and monotonous). Mirza Fakhrul is not as loud, bold, clear, appealing, motivating, and inspiring as the others, for example, the venerable veteran Shah Muazzem Hussein, Gayeshwar Chandra Roy, Mahmudur Rahman, Mahfuzullah, Dr Tuhin Malik, (Ret) Maj Akhtaruzzaman, the two *DeshKonnyas*/দেশকন্যাs Syeda Ashrafi Papia and Barrister Rumin Farhana,[73] (late) Shafiul Alam Prodhan, and Barrister Andalib Partho.

Seemingly weak in organizational capacity and rhetorical oratory, Mirza Fakhrul only visits his own constituency in Thakurgaon, outside Dhaka. His নিরুত্তাপ (subdued and lukewarm) comments and statements do not fly, lying low, if not falling totally flat. He is like the slow-and-dull speaking Sakhawat Hussein Khan of Narayanganj, who was lamentably fading beside the well-known and charismatic Dr Selina Hayat Ivy and who had no warmth, no fluency of speech and no exciting enthusiasm, thus handing in a crushing and devastating defeat to the party he was fielded by—BNP.

Mirza Fakhrul is also comparable to the low-key and low energy US Presidential candidates, such as Jeb Bush, Ben Carson, Ted Cruz, and Chris Christie. Following the Brexit from the EU, Labor MP and shadow foreign secretary Hilary Benn said that his party leader Jeremy Corbyn was "a good and decent man but he is not a leader, and that's the problem." The same was echoed by the shadow health secretary Heidi Alexander, who said: "As much as I respect you (Corbyn) as a man of principle, I do not believe you have the capacity to shape the answers our country is demanding." Mirza Fakhrul seems to be no different than Corbyn. The BNP needs to find a better replacement for its current Secretary General.

Regarding Mirza Fakhrul's weeping at a Reporters' Unity meeting, Ranu Chowdhury commented: "I saw it on TV. Didn't like it. Why would a top leader of a major party cry like a woman? It certainly raises question about Fakhrul's suitability as SG of the BNP. He was supposed to be a role model to his party men. What message he tries to covey to them by displaying such emotional expression and shedding tears in public gathering? I am sure the Awamis will soon gleefully say, 'Look where we pushed the BNP to. They can only wail. Nothing else.'" One would definitely agree with the point made by Chowdhury, while one could also differ on a different ground. Critics dismissed America's Commander-in-Chief Barack Obama as a Mourner-in-Chief for his emotional singing at the condolence of the blacks shot dead, although to others it was a very powerful and memorable moment.

As has been said above, Mirza Fakhrul is a soft and polite man, who should try to transform himself into a commanding and charismatic personality. However, given the uninterrupted Awami butchery, bulldozer and steamroller on the BNP for years (which, in 2010s, can only be compared to the victimization of the Jews by Hitler in 1940s) and the way Fakhrul contextualized the situation in his speech (with respect to the unbearably painful and pitiful condition of his party men and women, some of them hiding as *Rickshawalas*), his breaking into tears may be viewed with sympathy and justification. Apart from being a top leader, expected to be tough, he is also human, which made him betray his emotions while speaking on that occasion. The particular occasion made the radiation physicist Dr Muazzam Kazi of the USA reflect that "People are living under occupation, there being no breathing ground in Bangladesh. The spirit of the liberation war is completely chocked to death." Anyway, the reality is, cry or no cry, nothing has made and nothing is going to make any difference to the despotic Awami lords and ladies, not any time soon.

Other champions of democracy and fair play are the following: M K Anwar, one of the finest politicians, but suffering from the repression of the ruthless Hasina regime; Dr Osman Farooque, a man of weight and dignity with persuasive arguments; Gayeshwar Chandra Roy, who is one of the bold and courageous voices in the BNP, known for being deeply committed with pithy and axiomatic statements; former Deputy Prime Minister Shah Muazzem Hussein, who is a class by himself, a sharp-spoken and strong-willed personality with an amazing ability to make stimulating and arousing comments in a clear and commanding style; diehard and determined Abdullah al-Noman and Amir Khusru Mahmud Chowdhury; Tarikul Islam, physically unfit but forcefully assertive; courteous and polite Inam Ahmed Chowdhury; Ehsanul Hoque Milon, a fluently speaking man of action with a difference; and Ruhul Kabir Rizvi, a politician of great sacrifice and unflinching commitment with cool and catchy comments (yet, unfortunately, not as admirably charismatic though).

Both (Ret) Col Oli Ahmad and (Ret) Maj Gen Syed Mohammad Ibrahim are men of principles and commitments in their own ways. However, as the latter's unclear, if not doubtful, role in the 1996 failed coup by the pro-Awami Gen Nasim and some of his write-ups indicate, Gen Ibrahim, though firmly and appreciably in the BNP alliance at present, seems to cherish a very soft corner for the top Awami leaders.[74] (Late) Shafiul Alam Prodhan was a man of uncommon courage and confidence. Shaukat Mahmood, Amanullah Aman, Taimur Alam Khandoker, and Muazzem Hussein Alal, Dr Sakhawat Hussein Shayanta, Barrister Sarwar Hussein, and Sheikh Rabiul Alam—all are patriotically passionate and heroically sacrificing. There are (Ret) Major Hafizuddin Ahmad, one of the most articulate, exciting, and well-spoken; forcefully assertive Dr Asaduzzaman Ripon; and the long suffering Lutfuzzaman Babar, who had a distinct and dashing style of his own, no matter what his savage নিন্দুক critics claim him to be by way of their destructive নিন্দা criticism of him. Let millions send him a message of condolence on the loss of his mother while he is still a long victim of jail and জুলুম (injustice and discrimination) of this government.

There are countless others, all at the top of their respective professions, who are/were moderately or highly critical of the destructive policies of the Awami government and its misrule and misdeeds. Such intellectuals and politicians included former Prime Minister Kazi Zafar Ahmed and former opposition leader Maj (Ret) M A Jalil, especially in the later stage of their lives; celebrated journalist Ataus Samad; (Bhasha) Matin; Dr Piash Karim, Professor Nur Mohammad Mian; great journalist, columnist, language movement hero, and freedom fighter Sadeq Khan; and even the pro-Awami ABM Musa, all gone.

Others of the kind include the elderly but still formidably assertive former Secretary M Asafuddowla; Mahmudur Rahman, a heroic and indefatigable personality of national conscience, a unique national treasure, put behind bars for years and suffering for too long under the tyrant regime; sound and sensible former President Dr Badrudduza Chowdhury (despite his tendency to be slightly oscillating between the AL and the BNP at times); firm, intrepid and heroically outspoken Barrister Mainul Hussein often lashing out at the disreputable Hasina regime's credibility deficit; Dr Zafrullah Chowdhury, one of the boldest and finest political commentators ever, with competence and confidence, though everything he says could not be agreed upon;[75] Mahmudur Rahman Manna (one of the most assertively spoken and patriotically sacrificing politicians, who (or somebody else like him such as Mahmudur Rahman and the veteran Shah Muazzem Hussein) should be made or inducted as the BNP's Secretary General or any other high profile position; Dr Tuhin Malik, a rising political hero and a golden boy of Bangladesh whose words are among the best and brightest and as such deserve to be bound in gold;[76] highly knowledgeable and articulately spoken TV personality Mahfuzullah; his elder brother Dr Mahbubullah, one of the most honest and perceptive political observers; and the fair-and-neutral-minded Dr Debopryio Bhattacharya. All of the above are like-minded and far-flying birds of a feather and therefore on anybody's list they can trust and rely on.

There are many more: Nur-e-Alam Siddiquee (a thumping and thundering voice of justice, morality, and neutrality, though some of his BNP-related suggestions are unfair and impractical under the dangerous Hasina regime);[77] ASM Abdur Rob; Sanjib Chowdhury of Amar Desh (one of the finest media minds); Advocate Subrata Chowdhury (who lashes out at the Hasina regime in a crystal clear voice); outstanding political commentary and talk show personalities, such as Dr Rezwan Siddiqui of the daily Dinkal; daily Naya Diganta editor Alamgir Mohiuddin; Dr Mina Farah (who is as tall and erect as a minaret in her intellectual capacity and as far sighted as a fighter jet in her imaginative vision); brave and brilliant Dr Asif Nazrul;[78] Lawyer Shahid Islam of Toronto; blogger Kai Kaus; blogger Noyon Chatterjee; senior academic and columnist Ebne Golam Samad; columnists Abdul Auwal Thakur; Minar Rashid; Jiblu Rahman; Stalin Shorkar; Qamrul Islam; blogger Nazma Mustafa;[79] and Farhad Mazhar, who, though was a writer and thinker of guts and grit, heroically moving from his once left-wing and anti-Islamic past to right-wing pro-Islamic present, has fallen silent after his terrifying abduction on 3 July 2017. All of them are committed and forceful against the Awami excesses, abuses, aberrations, abnormalities, and irregularities. Their comments and columns deserve to be carved in stone.

Other remarkably impressive figures would include Dr Hussein Zillur Rahman, Adilur Rahman Khan (a hall of fame human rights figure), *News Today* editor Reazuddin Ahmed, journalist Ashraf Kaiser (one of the smartest political analysts), political analyst Goutam Das, Barrister Pervez Ahmed, Channel I *TM* Zillur Rahman, Badiul Alam Majumder, Nurul Kabir (despite being too intellectual to be clear and effective, like Zahiruddin Shopon of the BNP, and despite being disrespectfully unresponsive to the inquirers to him as the editor of an English daily), Dr Salimullah Khan (a formidable intellectual of clear and concrete vision with an amazing command of clearly stated facts and figures), and Junaid Saki (one of the most neutral and impressive political commentators)—all of whom are highly critical of numerous Awami policies—some of them being more critical than others and some being equally critical of the opposition BNP, while being supportive of both parties on certain issues.

Among the other patriotic fighters for a democratic Bangladesh are the former DU VC Professor Emajuddin Ahmed, a man of pluck and brass with honesty and integrity; noted columnist and journalist Shafik Rehman (despite his some stances considered incongruous and incompatible with Islam); loud and clear Barrister Andalib Partho; strong and assertive Barrister Mahbubuddin Khokon and Advocate Ahmad Azam Khan; fierce and forceful Major (Ret) Akhtaruzzaman; former Secretary Ali Imam Mazumder; former Ambassadors Mir Mohammad Nasir Uddin, Serajul Islam, Mufazzal Karim, and Humayun Kabir; strong and steadfast Selima Rahman; former MPs Shamsuzzaman Dudu, Sarder Sakhawat Hussein Bokul, Zahiruddin Shawpon, Kalim Uddin Ahmed Milon, and Zainul Abedin Farook; former Secretary and CTG Advisor Dr Akbar Ali Khan; former Cabinet Minister Dr Mizanur Rahman Shelley; former Bangladesh Bank Governor Dr Salahuddin Ahmed, (Ret) Justice Abdur Raouf; (Ret) Justice M A Aziz (who was way better than the other CECs after him, especially Rakibuddin Ahmed), Ebne Golam Samad; and columnist Mohammad Abdul Gafur.

The list can go on to include, among others, the former BDR chief (Ret) Maj Gen ALM Fazlur Rahman, Dr Shahadat Hussain of Chittagong, Siddikur Rahman Khan, Dr Mustafizur Rahman of Bangladesh Development Studies, business entrepreneur Selima Ahmed, Professor Sukomol Barua, Professor Abul Kashem Fazlul Haque, former Islamic Foundation DG Syed Ashraf Ali, M A Latif Khan, Gazi Mohammad Shahjahan, Khaliquzzaman of BSD, and Shahadat Hussein Selim,— all incredibly sane and sensible men of inexhaustible energy and enthusiasm. Finally, there is the Awami Golam Mowla Roni, once jailed by the his own Awamis for being critical of some other fellow Awamis, who is, however, said to have said that his leader Hasina would have to be born again to learn the modesty, manners, and courtesy of Khaleda and acquire the popularity of the latter.[80]

Apart from those powerful men and women mentioned above, there are many others of note, fighting on with fire and force for a free and fair democratic Bangladesh. They would include: fluent, fervent and articulate *DeshKonnya* দেশকন্যা Syeda Ashrafi Papia, a marvelous woman of meteoric mettle and temerity; and the "like father like daughter," admirably eloquent, another *DeshKonnya* দেশকন্যা Barrister Rumin Farhana, a woman of cool, convincing and compelling arguments. It is a shame for the BNP high command not to put these two women in high profile positions.

Other women of tireless tenacity and stamina would include Mayor Dr Selina Hayat Ivy (an incredibly strong and ebullient woman, who, though of Awami stock, is quite fair and independent minded);[81] "like father like daughter," tough, tenacious and vivacious *DeshKonnya* দেশকন্যা Shama Obaid; former MPs Nilufar Chowdhury Moni, সেরা/superb Shammi Akhter, and রণজয়ী/battle-reigning Rehana Ranu, all three admirably persistent and persevering; Advocate Fahima Nasrin Munni, Ferdous Akhtar Wahida, and Shirin Sultana, all remarkable in their resilience and spiritedness; "like husband like wife" DeshKonnya দেশকন্যা Dr Dilara Chowdhury; Dr Amina Mohsin (though not so strong); *DeshKonnya* দেশকন্যা Afroza Abbas (a good addition to the BNP—strong, active and capable); Farhat Quader Chowdhury; Farjeet Quader Chowdhury; and Tahsina Rushdir (whose kidnapped husband Elias Ali, a BNP leader, is believed to be long dead as Monnujan Sufian, a former AL state minister, claimed long ago, even addressing Tahsina as an widow[82])—all women of exemplary courage and constancy, all daring and dauntless and steady and steadfast in the face of all-consuming Awami horror and terror.

There are many other public intellectuals, academics, journalists, and lawyers, critical in different degrees of the sluttish Awami bad governance, from being absolutely clear to "academically" modest and moderate to "politically correct." The following deserve a mention, some of them being neutral to pro-AL and some, neutral to pro-BNP, while some are completely neutral and some are mincing and mumbling in an effort to sound neutral, either for fear of Awami reprisal or being only half committed to the cause, balancing with this or that side.

Nonetheless, the democratic-minded personalities would include veteran political thinker and prolific writer Professor Badruddin Umar (despite his unacceptable left background), Dr Shahdin Malik, Dr Tofael Ahmed (local government academic), Professor Abdullah Abu Sayeed, Professor Abu Sayyid, Professor Abdul Latif Masum, Professor Nasim Akhter Hussain, Professor Ferdous Hussein, Professor Abdus Sattar, Professor Imtiaz Ahmed, Sultan Mohammad Mansur (one of the finest and most fair-minded), and Professor Shafique Siddiq (who would like to see a separation of the government from the party, his wife Sheikh Rehana, though somewhat reluctant at the moment, as the next AL chief and Joy as the next head of the government, and who would pungently laugh at the Hasina crony Ershad and his JP as being utterly unreliable, and who would credit both the BNP and the AL as enjoying equal popular support of at least 30% each with the people's voting rights to be ensured side by side with whatever economic development may have been achieved out there).

Other fair or foul weather birds of more or less similar feather are: Dr Manzur Ahmed Chowdhury, Dr Sharmin Murshed, Advocate Manzil Murshed, journalist Matiur Rahman Chowdhury (his sickness probably hastened by his lost freedom of speech under the regime), Zahir Uddin Shopon, M A Aziz of New Age, Sohrab

Hasan of Prothom Alo, Syed Ashik Rahman, Hasan Ahmed Chowdhury Kiron, Dr Mamun Ahmed, Dr Iftekharuzzaman, former judge and now a columnist Iqtedar Ahmed, Mujahidul Islam Selim of CPB, former Election Commissioner Brig Gen Sakhawat Hussein, Dr Naznin Ahmed, Dr Borhan Uddin Khan, Kazi Shiraz, Mohammad Shahjahan, Professor Raunak Jahan, Barrister Shamim Haider Patwary, Professor Ataur Rahman, Professor Shahiduzzaman, Human Rights figure Nur Khan Litton of Ain O Shalish Kendro, Advocate Elina Khan, (Maj) Zillur Rahman, Mahmud Bin Feisal of SATV (a journalist of fair and fine talk), Ashish Shoikat, pro-Awami Golam Murtoza and Syed Ishtiaq Reza, Afsan Chowdhury (minus his anti-Islam stand), Selim Omrao Khan, Tushar Abdullah, Kazi Abdul Hannan, Rubayyat Ferdous, journalists Munir Haider and Oliullah Noman (in exile due to the threat on them because of their freedom of speech), Saleh Uddin of Ittefaq, Kamrul Hasan Darpon, Amanullah Kabir, Mahfuz Anam, Abu Sayyid Khan, Saiful Haq of Biplobi Workers Party, Munira Khan of FEMA, Syed Abul Moksud, Mustafa Firoz (a cool and caring Bangla Vision journalist), Dr Tarek Shamsur Rahman and, lastly, senior Barrister Rafiqul Hoque (despite his off-and-on flips and flops), who was once disparagingly and distastefully referred to by Hasina as মুই কার খালুরে and who would still be inclined to be well by her side, notwithstanding his occasional support for Khaleda as well.

In other words, the Bangladesh that was dreamed about by the literary, cultural and political organization called *Tamaddun Majlish* (since 1947/1948),[83] the pro-BNP Freedom Fighters of 1971, and the members and supporters of the শত নাগরিক (Citizens in Hundreds) of today, along with thousands of unknown and unsung stars, is the Bangladesh one would like to see to evolve and emerge and last and leave a lasting legacy in its trail as it chalks out its future course of action. All of the above need to be acknowledged and appreciated for their strong to balanced critical view of the neo-and-near-and-more-than-partially totalitarian Awami regime under which the country is endlessly suffering, literally reeling and writhing.

A similarly ideal Bangladesh was envisioned in the literary and/or poetical creations of Alaol, Shah Muhammad Sagir, Abdul Hakim, Bhai Girish Chandra Sen (1835–1910), Mir Mosharraf Hossain (1847–1912), Mohammad Kazem alias Kaikobad (1854/1857–1951), Syed Nawab Ali Chowdhury (1863–1929), Abdul Karim Sahittya Bisharad (1869–1953), Syed Ismail Hossain Siraji (1880–1931), Begum Rokeya (1880–1932), Syed Emdad Ali (1880–1956), Yakub Ali Chowdhury (1888–1940), Mohammad Nasiruddin (1888–1994), Mohammad Lutfur Rahman (1889–1936), S. Wajed Ali (1890–1951), Principal Ibrahim Khan (1894–1978), Golam Mostafa (1897–1964), Jasimuddin (1903–1976), Benazir Ahmed (born 1903), Farrukh Ahmad (1918–1974), Kazi Kader Newaz

(1909–1983), Shawkat Osman (1917–1998), Talim Hussein (1918–1999), Syed Ali Ahsan (1922–2002), Shahed Ali (1925–2001), Kazi Din Muhammad (1927–2011), Al Mahmud and many more.[84]

A similarly unified and glorious Bangladesh was dreamt about in the artistic and religious thoughts of Kazi Nazrul Islam (as expressed in his Islamic songs), and George Harrison and Ravi Shankar in August 1971 when they organized the Concert for Bangladesh, described as "the historic fundraising concert for charity, the first of its kind [...] to relieve the humanitarian crisis unfolding in Bangladesh in its struggle for independence from Pakistan." The same would apply to the late film maker Chashi Nazrul Islam.

A similar Bangladesh has been longed for in the artistic and religious thoughts of the poet and essayist Abdul Hye Sikder; legendary lyricist and songwriter Gazi Mazharul Anwar; top vocal artists such as Shahnaz Rahmatullah, Mustafa Zaman Abbasi, Baby Naznin; Apel Mahmud, Rizia Pervin, Konok Chapa, Asif Akbar (of the song খালেদা জিয়া তোমার নেই তুলনা);[85] band singers Shafin Ahmed and Hamin Ahmed of Miles; singers like Ayyub Bacchuu and S I Tutul (for their exemplary love of their parents); Qaderi Kibria (for his deep faith in Allah the Almighty, Who he insists saved his life in 1971 from the Pakistani gunpoint); poet Al Mahmud, lyricist Abu Zafar, singers Samina Chowdhury, Ajmery Hoque Nirjhor, BinduKona, and Dolly Shayontini (also for their deep faith in Allah the Almighty); Dilruba Khan; Nancy (who suffered, under this despotic Hasina regime, simply because of her pro-BNP Facebook status); Bari Siddiquee; poets Abu Shahriar, Hasan Hafiz, and Abu Saleh (as versified in Saleh's nursery rhyme);[86] actress Dilara Zaman; actors Helal Khan, Ashrafuddin Ujjol, and Ilias Kanchan; filmmaker Mostafa Sarwar Farooki (in terms of his anti-secularist and anti-Indian position); famed singers Monir Khan (of the song স্বাধীনতা স্বাধীনতা স্বপ্নের স্বাধীনতা/the freedom that was being dreamt of), Dr Lina Taposhi Khan (as in her Islamic songs), Nokul Kumar Biswas (for his Islamic songs and his deep love and affection for his lost parents), Shayan (whose আমার মুক্তিযোদ্ধা being about those notorious freedom fighters who are/were involved in corruption and criminal activities); and, of course, Haider Hussein as in his patriotic songs such as, আমি স্বপ্ন দেখি ("I dream dreams"), কতটুকু অশ্রু গড়ালে রিদয় জলে সিক্ত ("How much tears need to flow to soften the heart with water"), and কি দেখার কথা কি দেখছি কি শোনার কথা কি শুনছি … ("I'm not supposed to see what I see, I'm not supposed to hear what I hear, I'm not supposed to think what I think, I'm still searching for freedom so many years after the independence").

Those lyric cries grew out of the lacerating frustration that in Bangladesh there is too much of suffering and deprivation, inequalities and disparities, criminal mismanagement, and mischiefs and misappropriations. At the same time it is a country of religious fervor with an unnecessary excess and abundance of Eid hugs and greetings, religious meetings and preachings, মিলাদ মাহফিলস and ritualistic prayers, and the observances of কুলখানি ওরশ মাজার পূজা ইত্যাদি etc. It is full of homilies, platitudes, high talks, and high hopes on countless political and cultural occasions, festivals, receptions, celebrations and performances. This whole bunch of stuff is being seen, heard of, and reported about only in Bangladesh, like nowhere in the rest of the world, which is far more clean and caring.

Unfortunately, the political and religious vows and promises made in Bangladesh do not seem to count, hardly materialize into reality, and rarely translate into commitment. They never find their way into the hearts and minds of the people. All this is mainly due to the dirty, un-Islamic, and unholy business and showoff in the name of Islam. The consequence is that the country remains full of negative, subversive, corrupt, greedy, backdoor, and under the table temptations and influences. Development, yes, but must not be in an authoritarian manner, not along the dark and narrow passage or corridor of only one party (which is the Hasina party), not by silencing the majority, not at the expense of national unity and solidarity, not by pushing aside democratic tolerance and openness, and not by twisting and treading and tilting and trampling down on credible and participatory elections.[87]

A fully compatible and congenial Bangladesh was/has been drawn in the political and green/environmental thoughts of, for example, (the late) Abul Mansour Ahmad (as in his 1982 book, বেশি দামে কেনা কম দামে বেচা আমাদের স্বাধীনতা (Our Freedom: Bought at High Price But Sold Cheap); Syeda Rizwana Hassan of BELA (Bangladesh Environmental Lawyers' Association), a beautiful woman of rare breed; Bangladesh Environment Movement leader and architect Iqbal Habib; road transport and communications specialist Dr Shamsul Hoque of BUET; scientific and religious scholar Dr Shamsher Ali; pro-Awami but firmly fair-minded political commentator architect Mubasshyer Hussein; anti-Islamic and pro-Awami writer Anisul Hoque (as his seemingly neutral prose cartoon story of "The Country of the Lying Shepherd" and "এ কী করলেন দুই ব্যাংক-ডাকাত!"/What these two bank dacoits have done! suggest); once pro-Awami, yet the Awami-rebuffed Imran H Shorkar of GanaJagaran Mancha (who has learnt to distance himself from his earlier deep Awami bias, long after his Shahbugee days).

A solution suggested

Eliot ends his 1922 masterpiece *The Waste Land* (which uses a variety of both Indian [Hindu/Buddhist] and Western sources and which metaphorically describes the dull and dry boredom, vacuity, monotony, and meaninglessness of modern life) with triple benediction from ancient Sanskrit/Pali scriptures: "Datta Dayadhvama Damyata/ Shantih Shantih Shantih," meaning "Give Sympathize Control/ Peace Peace Peace," as opposed to arrogance, viciousness and selfishness. The word "Shantih" is a formal ending to a Hindu Upanishad in the context of which it means peace and tranquility that transcend understanding.

Let this conclusion be concluded, in a similar manner, with a statement on what is needed most in the politics of today's Bangladesh: dialogue, dialogue, dialogue, not mass detaining the fellow citizens every single day and turning the whole country into an open prison in the most despotic and unpatriotic manner. Despite all the nasty and pejorative comments by Trump, the beauty of the American politics and democracy is that there are always free and open bipartisan talks, debates, meetings, discussions, and handshakes with equal opportunity for all in a level plain (playing) field. Many Republicans are against the Republican candidate Trump and the vice versa. When the Republican Party office in North Carolina was firebombed around the middle of October 2016, Democrats came forward to raise funds to help rebuild it immediately. This should be the spirit of the Hasina-led Awami politics and this is the spirit for which the liberation war was fought. It was not fought to lock its spirit up in particular party slogans and confine it to its increasing commodification, compartmentalization and commercialization. There needs to be a space for accommodation and compromise with all and for being inclusive of all aimed at establishing national unity and harmony.

There needs to be an environment for a return to the culture of democratic rules and principles that would see the burial of the blinding and blistering power-crazy differences and that would see both Mujib and Zia respected and recognized as much as they deserve, not more nor less.[88] Measures of trust and tolerance need to be taken by unconditionally releasing all political prisoners and ensuring that free and fair elections would be held by all means and at any cost with the president and the prime minister coming from the opposition and the ruling party respectively. That would be to strike a political balance and stop the tyranny of any kind of majority—real or prearranged, true or preplanned, actual or predetermined.

The president should be the president of the country, not a partisan president of any particular party only, simply advancing the cause of the party s/he belongs to by conniving at the political disasters and catastrophes his/her party is involved in causing and pushing along. However titular and ceremonial his/her role may be, s/he can still play a significant role through the morally symbolic value his/her office holds. Similarly, the prime minister should be the prime minister of the entire nation, not one to solely pursue and look after the interest of his/her party, while despotically and dictatorially crushing and cornering and crippling the popular opposition by the state police-turned-party-and-partisan-apparatchiks under her/his neo-and-near-fascist control.

The Hasina regime must stop the conflicting খেঁচা খুঁচি (ugly and peevish and crabbed spars and tugs of war) in vicious and murderous rivalries with Khaleda and the BNP. As early as early seventeenth century, Queen Elizabeth I's Lord Chancellor (equivalent to Prime Minister), Sir Francis Bacon, also a philosopher of practical wisdom, said:

> Revenge is a kind of wild justice. It is the glory of man to pass by an offense. That which is past is gone and irrevocable: wise men have enough to do with things present and to come: therefore, they do but trifle with themselves that labor in past matters.

In other words, revenge, especially when it is excessive, is a beastly nature. Those who are morally superior should be forward looking and forget the past to plan about the present and the future. Bacon's words foreshadow those on revenge and forgiveness by the Harvard Professor Kanter, quoted at the end of "Let's follow the example of Mujib's clemency" chapter. While the United Nations should take more and more of soldiers from Bangladesh for its peace keeping missions abroad, it should also exert its leverage to pressure Hasina into returning to peace through democratic rule at home.

The very last word

The Hasina-led Awami Bangladesh must do away with its policy of sluttish bifurcation of the nation, and the ruthless otherization and reckless victimization of dissent, and its own supremacy narrative. This wrong-headed policy only creates more confrontation, more enemies, and more extremists. Can there be a greeting of hearty "Salam," a very "Good Morning," a true "Happy New Year" and a sincere "Eid Mubarak" among all the Bangladeshis? Can there be a new dawn in politics, as fresh and hopeful and awakening as the dawn in nature, a new clear horizon to be welcomed with warmth from the heart's core? Can there be a new spreading tree of rich and luxuriant foliage to give people a nice and cool shade? Can the hundreds of beautiful patriotic songs and poems about the independence, the mother, and the motherland have a real meaning with a true justice system, rule of law, social justice, and freedom and emancipation for all?

Unlike the ever old, yet ever new and liberating "*Assalamualikum*" and "I love you," everything in Bangladesh seems to be weary, wearied, worn out, tiring, tormenting, squeaky, sneaky, squinty, and quirky, being more and more of the same, merely and morbidly "a kind" of new, not going far enough in freeing the nation from the partisan bondage of the police and the party. Echoing Tennyson's New Year poem, "Ring Out, Wild Bells," the people of Bangladesh wish to ring out the tyranny of the regime and ring in a new era of democratic freedom and harmony when the crippled and cornered BNP would be able to pre-empt its ever-on-hold (in the name of thirteen excuses during the twelve months of the year/ বারো মাসে তেরো পার্বন), ebbing and receding, hopeless, helpless and useless call for movement/agitation against Hasina and the despotic and dictatorial Hasina-AL also can stop prolonging its stay in power in the name of its so-called hoodwinking partisan development visions.

Until that kind of political situation comes to prevail in which elections after elections, polls after polls, local as well as national, would NOT be rigged and ripped and raped and bought over and stolen away and trampled down, what is the point of having fraud after fraud in the name of election? Until that kind of political environment returns in which the rights and liberties of the people of Bangladesh would NOT be slit and snapped, torn and tattered, curtailed and short circuited, and abrogated and violated, what is the point of holding yet another and then another farce in the name of this or that election? The Hasina regime cannot go on posing as a (fake) democracy and playing gimmicks with democracy and disowning the majority belonging to the political opposition by force, arresting, remanding, and imprisoning them day in and day out.

Nothing, no effort, no measure, no amount of internal reorganization and democratization of this or that party, especially in the opposition alliance, will work under the all-consuming horror and terror and torture and boots and bullets of the present Hasina regime. Only free and fair elections, especially a parliamentary one under a new and neutral care taker government, can make a real difference. Inclusive and impartial elections are the elixir, bread and butter, and the lifeline of the democratic system. In a beautiful, brilliant and comprehensive article that dwells on a number issues, from the harmful Rampal power plant to the servile and slavish Election Commission to the fantastical Election Commission Search to the lack of free and fair elections, Jamaluddin Bari writes about how dangerous it is to kill and cripple the state/national institutions leading to intolerably dire circumstances for the nation.[89]

Let the people decide who they want to govern them through credible and participatory elections, not by pleasing India all the way down and up. They will be happy to get back their voting rights stolen from them, the billions looted from their banks and businesses and share markets, and the guarantee that they are safe, free from the violence and uncertainty of everyday life in the form of disappearances, abductions, assassinations, and road/traffic accidents.[90] Otherwise, the nation would have to wait for a miracle or an act of God to happen (similar to the survival stories of the Nobel Malala, Rana Plaza Reshma, and Sylheti Khadija). It may also need to be reset and restarted by a political pied piper, who would have the magic not only to rescue it, at least gradually and incrementally, slowly but surely, from the nuisance of the political rats and insects of all sizes and colors, but also, if necessary, make it pay a heavy price over a certain loss as a retaliation for the violations of and by the adult criminals.

Only then there could be a way to discern and distinguish between leadership and dictatorship, statesmanship and despotism; a way to indict and not to endorse the neo-and-near-authoritarian autocrats; to stop umpteen citizens from being blindly arrested every single day and every other day; and to eventually re-launch a newly branded democratic Bangladesh, free from its political Zika, Ebola, and Chikunguniya viruses! If that is still far to seek and is unlikely to happen in the near future, let an interim/caretaker government in the form of an enlightened and benevolent civilian and/or military dictatorship take over and run the country for a few years to fix it once and for all!

May God lead the people of Bangladesh "from the depths of darkness [...] into light," to invoke the verse after the key Throne verses in the holy Qura'an (II.257), as He delivered many other nations, old and modern, throughout the human, political, religious, sociological, and anthropological history of the world! May He save and protect and keep Bangladesh away from all kinds of extremism, fanaticism, and radicalism, especially the present neo-despotism, neo-fascism, neo-authoritarianism, and neo-monarchism, Awami style! Aameen!

Notes

1. http://www.sheershanewsbd.com/2016/05/16/127894;
   http://mynewsbd.com/?p=7081;
   http://www.bdface.net/blog/blogdetail/detail/9759/abdulmatin/79288;
   http://www.prothom-alo.com/bangladesh/article/643696/;
   http://www.mzamin.com/details.php?mzamin=OTQwNDA=&s=MQ==;
   http://www.amardeshonline.com/pages/details/2015/09/24/303715;
   http://www.amardeshonline.com/pages/details/2015/09/22/303441;
   https://www.youtube.com/watch?v=847N1b5clHU
2. http://www.dailynayadiganta.com/detail/news/56232#; http://www.dainikamadershomoy.com/2015/09/14/48310.php

3. http://www.mzamin.com/details.php?mzamin=OTM5MjA=&sOA==; http://www.mzamin.com/details.php?mzamin=OTQwMTE=&s=MQ==
4. http://www.amadershomoys.com/newsite/2015/09/13/396169.htm#;
5. For the Awami politics of revenge with about 20,000 lawsuits against 500,000 BNP men and women, visit http://www.bd-pratidin.com/lead-news/2015/09/23/108126; http://www.bd-pratidin.com/lead-news/2015/09/24/108315
6. http://newagebd.net/182036/enforced-disappearances-reminiscent-of-dictatorial-rules/
7. http://www.amadershomoys.com/newsite/2015/09/15/397724.htm#
8. http://www.dailynayadiganta.com/detail/news/200232
9. http://www.bd-pratidin.com/editorial/2017/01/25/202697; http://www.bd-pratidin.com/home/printnews/110049; http://www.prothom-alo.com/bangladesh/article/643825/; http://www.amardeshonline.com/pages/details/2015/09/20/302995; http://newagebd.net/175894/bangladesh-to-turn-into-militant-state-if-democracy-not-restored-bnp/;
   http://newagebd.net/175925/no-existence-of-is-in-bangladesh-ershad/
10. It is a nursery rhyme which, like many other rhymes for children, is full of historical meaning with a sense of pain and sorrow behind it. In 1275 the king of England imposed a tax on all wool exported out of the kingdom. The rhyme expresses the farmers' and wool merchants' resentment at having to pay a bag's worth of wool in taxes. The song later came to be associated with modern slavery.
11. www.amadershomoy.biz/unicode/2017/01/28/217840.htm
12. http://www.ittefaq.com.bd/national/2017/01/26/101244.html. If Dr Yunus has problems with his tax return and other economic issues, according to some media reports, he should come forward to clear his name:
    http://www.kalerkantho.com/print-edition/first-page/2017/01/31/458198;
    http://www.bd-pratidin.com/first-page/2017/02/14/207721;
    http://www.bd-pratidin.com/first-page/2017/01/31/204248;
    http://www.rtnn.net/bangla/newsdetail/detail/1/2/167610;
    https://www.dailyjanakantha.com/details/article/246566;
    http://www.bbc.com/bengali/news/2016/08/160824_clinton_foundation_muhammad_yunus_donation
13. https://www.bdnetwork24.com/2017/07/19/শিক্ষামন্ত্রী-নাহিদের-আ/;
    http://banglamail71.info/archives/1114;
    http://www.newsonbd.net/newsdetail/detail/41/324249
14. http://www.prothombangladesh.net/news/14396
15. http://www.prothom-alo.com/bangladesh/article/1082457; http://www.dailybartoman.com/details.php?id=37029
16. http://www.thebengalitimes.com/politics/2016/11/26/21836;
    http://bdexpress.uodoo.com/detail/3922736346367256/tags_bangladesh/tag_technology/1474451585298

17. https://www.youtube.com/watch?v=ohx14rDJUnY&feature=youtu.be; http://bdnews24.com/bangladesh/2017/01/19/hasina-faces-question-on-rampal-power-plant-at-davos
18. https://www.washingtonpost.com/news/energy-environment/wp/2016/07/18/a-new-power-plant-could-devastate-the-worlds-largest-mangrove-forest/?utm_term=.2d313d1ed323;
https://www.theguardian.com/environment/2016/oct/19/un-tells-bangladesh-to-halt-mangrove-threatening-coal-plant;
http://www.dhakatribune.com/bangladesh/2017/05/05/greenpeace-rampal-plant-cause-6000-early-deaths/
19. http://m.dailynayadiganta.com/detail/news/194001; http://www.prothom-alo.com/opinion/article/1069151; http://www.ntvbd.com/bangladesh/108665; http://amardesh24.com/bangla/index.php/details/focus/3883;
http://www.amadershomoy.biz/unicode/2017/01/31/218762.htm;
http://www.dailynayadiganta.com/detail/news/193372;
http://deshbhabona.com/%E0%A6%AB%E0%A6%BF%E0%A6%AB%E0%A6%A5-%E0%A6%B7%E0%A7%8D%E0%A6%9F%E0%A7%87%E0%A6%9F/2017/01/28/18/56/
20. http://www.prothom-alo.com/bangladesh/article/1169601
21. http://www.newagebd.net/article/14948
22. "আমরা গাছ লাগাইয়া সুন্দরবন পয়দা করি নাই। স্বাভাবিক অবস্থায় প্রকৃতি এটাকে করে দিয়েছে বাংলাদেশকে রক্ষা করার জন্য। বঙ্গোপসাগরের পাশে দিয়ে যে সুন্দরবনটা রয়েছে এইটা হলো বেরিয়ার। এটা যদি রক্ষা করা না হয় তাহলে একদিন খুলনা, বরিশাল, পটুয়াখালী, কুমিল্লার কিছু অংশ, ঢাকার কিছু অংশ এ পর্যন্ত সমস্ত এরিয়া সমুদ্রের মধ্যে চলে যাবে এবং এগুলো হাতিয়া, সন্দ্বীপের মতো আইল্যান্ড হয়ে যাবে। একবার যদি সুন্দরবন শেষ হয়ে যায়—তো সমুদ্র যে ভাঙন সৃষ্টি করবে সেই ভাঙন থেকে রক্ষা করার কোনও উপায় আর নাই।" https://soundcloud.com/nirzhar-noishabdya/16-july-1972
23. http://www.nytimes.com/aponline/2016/10/20/world/asia/ap-as-bangladesh-coal-plant-criticized.html?mwrsm=Facebook&_r=0
24. http://www.dailynayadiganta.com/detail/news/157649
25. http://www.newagebd.net/article/13123/greens-say-no-power-plant-at-cost-of-sunderbans
26. http://www.prothombangladesh.net/news/14396; http://newsbd7.com/main/detail/3144
27. http://www.weeklyholiday.net/homepage/pages/UserHome.aspx?ID=2&date=05/06/2016;
https://www.justice.gov/sites/default/files/usao-sdny/legacy/2015/03/25/Lustyik%20Et%20Al.Indictment.pdf;
http://newsbd7.com/main/detail/3021. See David Bergman at:
http://southasianmonitor.com/2017/02/17/canada-court-really-clear-bangladesh-officials-corruption;

https://thewire.in/109388/did-a-canada-court-really-clear-bangladesh-officials-of-corruption

28. For details, see: https://en.wikipedia.org/wiki/Sajeeb_Wazed; http://thewire.in/30447/exclusive-us-court-dismissed-claim-of-plot-to-injure-bangladesh-pm-son/
29. http://ireport.cnn.com/docs/DOC-1060321; https://www.youtube.com/watch?v=52SLsywK7AE; http://bhoreralap.com/?p=4050; http://bbc-bangla-vs-bangladesh.tumblr.com/post/127384714408; http://nncworld.tv/2016/05/02/;https://www.facebook.com/qamrulpage/photos/a.707572235933287.1073741828.707513919272452/1300199296670575/?-type=3&theater
30. https://www.dailyinqilab.com/details/16589/
31. BNP Vice Chairman Shah Muazzem Hussain described Hasina being awarded the environment prize as ludicrous and ridiculous: http://www.amadershomoys.com/newsite/2015/09/18/400205.htm
32. http://www.thedailystar.net/city/dhaka-icu-patient-annisul-146059
33. http://www.prothom-alo.com/bangladesh/article/644521; http://www.sheershanewsbd.com/2015/10/02/98501; http://www.sheershanewsbd.com/2015/09/18/97040
34. http://www.commondreams.org/news/2016/12/07/groups-demand-arrest-war-mastermind-kissinger-nobel-peace-prize-forum?utm_campaign=shareaholic&utm_medium=email_this&utm_source=email
35. Mahatma Gandhi never won the Nobel. In literature, Leo Tolstoy, Graham Greene, James Joyce, Vladimir Nabokov, Saul Bellow, Robert Frost, William Somerset Maugham, George Orwell, Anton Chekhov, Henry James, W. H. Auden, and Jorge Luis Borges, among many other great writers, never got the prize. Visit https://eyeoflynx.wordpress.com/2014/03/05/great-authors-who-didnt-win-a-nobel-prize-for-unlikely-reasons/; https://www.quora.com/Who-are-the-greatest-writers-to-never-have-won-the-Nobel-Prize-for-Literature
36. http://edition.cnn.com/2016/11/17/asia/myanmar-rohingya-aung-san-suu-kyi/index.html
37. Chor Monai Pir of Bangladesh deserves appreciation for his protest plan against the barbaric massacre of the Rakhaine Rohingyas by the Burmese government. But where is Dr Mohammad Yunus? Why is he so silent too? He got a Nobel for peace, but why did he have to remain silent? As a neighbor, why didn't he raise his voice and call on Suu Kyi to stop this senseless madness?
38. http://www.amadershomoy.biz/beta/2016/11/29/749591; http://www.rtnn.net/bangla/newsdetail/detail/1/3/162710
39. Dr Yunus has, however, spoken out quite late, together with many other Nobel Laureates (at his initiative), around the very turn of the year (2016). As the saying goes, "Better late than never."

40. Ranu Chowdhury of the USA's e-mail (of November 26, 2016) reads: "Someone suggested that Bangladesh should lay a claim on Rakhaine because historically this part belonged to Bengal until the British ceded it illegally, illogically and unreasonably to Burmah in 1948. I think the proposal has merit and deserve consideration by our historians, strategists, think tanks and writers." I think Bangladesh should go even further. Bangladesh should immediately declare war and invade Myanmar. That's the only way to attract the world attention and force the world powers to come up with a permanent solution—either for the Burmese Suu Kyi to accept the Rohingyas as bonafide citizens of Myanmar or to give them an independent state in Rakhaine.
41. http://www.kalerkantho.com/online/Politics/2016/04/26/351831. Recently Awami student wing, Chatro League, demanded that Hasina be given a Nobel.
42. http://www.prothom-alo.com/bangladesh/article/864427/
43. http://www.dailynayadiganta.com/detail/news/160961
44. http://www.prothom-alo.com/international/article/655636/
45 For those who rejected coveted awards, visit http://newagebd.net/166508/where-are-you-when-we-need-you-jean-paul-sartre/#; http://www.thedailystar.net/op-ed/award-couldnt-be-rewarding-enough-1199137
46. http://edition.cnn.com/2016/10/07/opinions/nobel-peace-prize-win-without-peace-ghitis/index.html
47. See how Malala's story of 2012 was preplanned by the West: http://www.prothom-alo.com/international/article/1190351; For more on the controversial Nobel peace prize winners, visit http://www.sheershanewsbd.com/2015/11/16/104009
48. In this respect see Dan Glazebrook's report on Boko Haram: http://newagebd.net/180633/deadliest-terror-in-the-world-the-wests-latest-gift-to-africa/; and Uri Avnery's article at http://newagebd.net/180607/there-is-no-such-thing-as-international-terrorism/
49. http://www.uniindia.com/india-backs-hasina-govt-over-war-crime-trials-in-bangladesh/india/news/283217.html;
http://timesofindia.indiatimes.com/city/delhi/Indiaappreciative-of-Bangladesh-action-against-war-crime-accused/articleshow/49910886.cms;
https://www.facebooKcom/qamrulpage/posts/1126063257417514:0; http://www.dailyinqilab.com/details/48548/
50. http://newagebd.net/181381/pm-shocked-at-loss-of-lives-property-in-chennai/; http://www.prothom-alo.com/bangladesh/article/702499/; http://www.thedailystar.net/country/families-disappeared-19-demand-govt-intervention-182302;
http://www.dailynayadiganta.com/detail/news/74731#;
http://www.sheershanewsbd.com/2015/12/04/106367
51. http://www.revolutions2040.com/15-years-later-physics-journal-concludes-3-wtc-towers-collapsed-due-controlled-demolition/;
http://www.globalresearch.ca/going-after-the-islamic-state/5401439
52. http://newagebd.net/115485/al-allies-deny-people-rights-to-vote-again/#

53. http://www.thenational.ae/arts-lifestyle/the-review/a-look-at-bangladeshs-steady-descent-into-chaos#full
54. http://www.sheershanewsbd.com/2015/09/25/97847
55. http://www.thedailystar.net/frontpage/top-quote-135328
56. http://www.amadershomoys.com/newsite/2015/09/13/396005.htm#
57. The BNP has always criticized Sheikh Hasina for her offensive style: http://www.sheershanewsbd.com/2015/10/04/98778
58. http://www.amadershomoys.com/newsite/2015/09/09/393104.htm#. According to a source, India provided TK 300 crore to Awami League to win the 1996 election(*Weekly Shugondha*, April 26, 1996). Shah Mohammad Saifuddin claims that India's clandestine support for a particular party is a testament to the fact that India had a strategic reason to help Bangladesh in 1971. See http://bangladesh-web.com/view.php?hidRecord=173793
59. In Shafiullah's own admission, he could not do anything despite receiving the rescue call from Sheikh Mujibur Rahman on the morning of August 15, 1975 because he found that almost the entire army was supportive of the coup. http://newsorgan24.com/detail/11823; https://www.youtube.com/watch?feature=player_embedded&v=WKZ7PicCC3Y
60. http://www.thedailystar.net/backpage/37-bnp-men-charged-murder-135481; http://newagebd.net/153258/govt-obstructs-bnps-founding-anniversary-celebration-bnp/#sthash.BOUNdHRH.dpbs; http://www.thedailystar.net/backpage/khaleda-un-probe-disappearances-135466
61. http://thewire.in/30447/exclusive-us-court-dismissed-claim-of-plot-to-injure-bangladesh-pm-son/; http://www.dailynayadiganta.com/detail/news/55402#; http://www.dailynayadiganta.com/detail/news/56496#
62. Trump kept being on the offensive saying that the Americans were being led by "foolish," "stupid" and "most incompetent" people," who, in his view, were destroying his/their country, referring to the entire Obama administration, including Obama himself. He always had doubt about Obama being a US citizen by birth and never refrained from calling Hillary Clinton a "crooked" woman, a liar and a falsifier. A political outsider or first time politician, who never held any elected office but remained politically active in indirect ways, Trump was notorious for his offensive, sexist, nasty and anti-women rhetoric with reference to their looks and menstrual periods, his own genitals, and his anti-Muslim and anti-Hispanic comments. Similarly, the evangelical Carson, a retired black neurologist of religious transformation but religious discrimination against the Muslims, was also not a professional politician in the sense of having never had any political experience but he also was active in writing and speaking about various social and political issues. Both were diametrically opposed to each other, Carson being cold, dry, boring, conservative, once violent-then-turned strangely soft-spoken, low-energy, and anti-Muslim, to the point of being denigrated as a "buffoon," and Trump being derided as controversial, high-energy and inflammatory, who, in the free America, was criticized as no better

than "The Apprentice" reality show host, flamboyant Miss Universe entertainer, a comic book villain, a national disgrace, an international pariah, a spoiled brat and a human leech. Trump represents a mix of politics and pop culture. Bill Clinton made fun of Trump as being "fact-free" (if not "fat-free"). Trump, himself dubbed as "Dumb Dump Trump" and "Trash Trump," who was as rich in hypocrisy as money, called another Republican Presidential hopeful, Senator Marco Rubio, "a clown" and "sweaty" and went so far as playing prank on the latter.

63. Powerpoint (Bangladesh's Collasping Institutions: A Sociological Understanding of Sheikh Hasina's Rule of Bangladesh)
64. http://www.thedailystar.net/country/unusual-rain-climate-change-blame-136609; http://www.thedailystar.net/video-stories/hour%E2%80%99s-rain-brings-dhaka-its-knees-video-136528;
    http://www.thedailystar.net/city/dhaka-drainage-struggles-deal-unusual-rain-levels-136621; http://www.thedailystar.net/frontpage/dhaka-deluged-136426
65. http://www.dailynayadiganta.com/detail/news/56473#;
    http://www.sheershanewsbd.com/2015/09/19/97125#;
    http://www.sheershanewsbd.com/2015/09/27/97990
66. http://www.thedailystar.net/bangladesh-14th-most-corrupt-country-53165;
    http://www.banglanews24.com/fullnews/bn/471976.html;
    http://www.bbc.com/bengali/news/2016/03/160307_bangladesh_bank_hacking;
    http://www.ittefaq.coMbd/national/2016/03/07/58620.html; http://banglamail24.com/news/137962;
    http://www.sheershanewsbd.com/2015/09/18/97054#
67. http://newagebd.net/172061/khaleda-blames-hasina-al-police-rab-for-killings/;
    http://www.amardeshonline.com/pages/details/2015/11/02/309031#;
    http://www.jugantor.com/sub-editorial/2015/10/31/345311
68. http://www.thestatesman.com/news/opinion/has-bangladesh-lost-its-focus/122729.html;
    http://bangladeshwatchdog.blogspot.com/2009/03/delhi-cant-afford-to-let-dhaka-slip-off.html; http://newsorgan24.com/detail/15197;
    http://www.telegraphindia.com/1160303/jsp/frontpage/story_72530.jsp;
    http://mzamin.com/article.php?mzamin=984&cat=8/;
    http://www.ittefaq.coMbd/national/2016/03/05/58173.html;http://www.amardeshonline.com/pages/details/2016/03/05/326152#; http://www.amardeshonline.com/pages/details/2016/03/05/326144
69. http://bangladeshchronicle.net/2016/02/tista-water/;
    http://www.amardeshonline.com/pages/details/2016/03/25/328878
    http://www.amardeshonline.com/pages/details/2016/03/25/328880
70. http://ncbd.org/?author=1;
    https://mail.google.com/mail/u/0/#inbox/154b6124a0b14637;

http://newagebd.net/234052/another-pointer-incumbents-india-appeasement/; http://www.amardeshonline.com/pages/details/2016/04/20/332633; http://online-bangla.com.bd/post/17134/

71. The former prime minster of Canada, Pierre Trudeau (father of the new Prime Minister Justin Trudeau) famously referred to Canada's relationship with the United States as akin to sleeping with an elephant. "One is affected by every twitch and grunt," he said in a speech in Washington when Richard Nixon was the president. They did not like each other very much just as President Barack Obama and the immediate past prime minister of Canada, Stephen Harper, did not get along very well. Although the relationship between Obama and the younger Trudeau (Justin) seems to be warm and cozy, at least at this initial stage, Obama would not budge on the concessions expected by Canada from America neither would Trudeau turn back on his decision of withdrawing the Canadian fighter jets from Iraq/Syria, to the displeasure of the USA. http://www.cbc.ca/news/politics/justin-trudeau-barack-obama-apec-chris-hall-1.3326179
72. http://newagebd.net/172061/khaleda-blames-hasina-al-police-rab-for-killings/; http://bangladeshchronicle.net/2015/11/lady-hitler-hasina-running-bangladesh-bnp-chief-khaleda-tells-london-meeting/; http://www.bd-desh.net/newsdetail/detail/49/224502; https://www.facebook.com/Mina-Farah-486760374674596/
73. The term or the title means "Daughter of the Land," my self-coined, which occurs throughout the book whenever the names of Farhana or Papia come up.
74. http://www.newsofbd.net/columndetail/detail/71/6785
75. Despite his excessive and unfounded praise of Sheikh Hasina, Dr Chowdhury is an eminent public figure. He is one of the national heroes along with Mahmudur Rahman and Mahmudur Rahman Manna. His critical remarks are in the positive and constructive criticism of the BNP, which are the same as those of many BNP supporters. Dr Chowdhury also points out on every occasion the sufferings inflicted upon the BNP by the Hasina regime. His criticism of the BNP is perfectly acceptable for the good of the BNP. For his excellent remarks, see: www.poriborton.com/interview/21122; http://www.dhakatimes24.com/2017/04/11/28000; http://www.poriborton.com/interview/21230;http://www.rtnn.net/bangla/news-detail/detail/1/3/172371; http://bangla.bdnews24.com/politics/article1318213.bdnews; http://bangla.bdnews24.com/politics/article1157451.bdnews;and http://www.jugantor.com/online/politics/2017/04/11/44526. However, I don't agree with Dr Chowdhury's view that the BNP made a mistake by not joining the crowd to pay its last respects to the highly controversial writer Syed Shamsul Haq. Did the AL do its share in regards to Brig Gen Hannan Shah and Dr Piash Karim? Neither do I agree with a few of the suggestions Dr Chowdhury made in his খোলা চিঠি (Open Letter) to the BNP Chair on the occasion of the party's council in March 2016 (http://www.mzamin.com/article.php?mzamin=6093). I find some of the suggestions impractical and too idealistic in the context of the brutal and horrendous political reality of Bangladesh. Is he not aware of the bitter realities, acrimonies, and animosities in the politics of Bangladesh? Why would he expect only

the BNP to play the role of the Good Samaritan? Why would he not write a similar *Khola Chiti* to PM Hasina too? Dr Chowdhury says the BNP should celebrate January 10 to mark the release and return of Sheikh Mujib in 1972. With great respects to him, how can he say that when the AL is out to destroy and eliminate all the memory of Zia and the largest political party of Bangladesh, the BNP? Does the Hasina -AL celebrate in gratitude to Zia the day he allowed Sheikh Hasina to return and revive the AL and launch multi-party democracy and political pluralism? The BNP needs full and complete and unconditional support in this critical juncture and should not be expected to achieve unrealistic and impossibly idealistic goals in the face of the iron rule of the AL and its torture and terror, boots and bullets and jail and জুলুম (persecution and discrimination) and remand and ডাণ্ডাবেড়ি (chains and shackles) and kidnappings and abductions and disappearances.

76. One of Dr Tuhin Malik's golden statements was that he said that there was a godmother behind all godfathers, presumably referring to Sheikh Hasina and Shamim Osman and the like: https://www.facebooKcom/photo.php?fbid=1735421156680012&set=p.1735421156680012&type=3&theater
    For his other golden statements, visit http://www.bd-pratidin.com/editorial/2015/11/05/107710; http://www.bdfirst.net/columndetail/detail/124/5133
77. Siddiquee's suggestions that Khaleda Zia should go for voluntary imprisonment and that Tarique Rahman should return home (only to get his backbone cracked and crushed and broken again) are totally unacceptable and impractical. His rejection of Khaleda's demand for the deployment of army with magistracy power during the elections is biased and unfair. Does he live in Hasina's Bangladesh or Obama's America?
78. I couldn't be one, though, with Dr Nazrul when said he would prefer the AL to the BNP coming to power through free and fair elections. Is he then more for the dangerous AL than the popular BNP? Did he really mean it or it was not to antagonize the AL too much?
79. The articles of the last mentioned are available at this link: https://nazmamustafa.wordpress.com/2017/02/14
80. For a discussion of democracy going down the drains in Bangladesh, see http://www.dailynayadiganta.com/detail/news/60102; http://www.dailynayadiganta.com/detail/news/59818;
81. Ivy is believed to have once said that no patriotic citizen could actually support the AL): https://www.facebook.com/photo.php?fbid=180274572373541&set=p.180274572373541&type=3&theater.
82. https://www.youtube.com/watch?v=p8ykkomN4OQ; https://www.youtube.com/watch?v=4kVDEiaB-aQ. There was a story sometime after Elias's abduction that two decomposed bodies were discovered in water near the Goalando Ghat Faridpur, suspected to be of Elias and his driver. The BNP Senior Joint Secretary Ruhul Kabir Rizvi claimed on April 18, 2016 that four years on, Elias was still held by the Hasina-AL intelligence.

83. Tamaddun Majlish leaders/founders (Principal Abul Kashem of Physics DU, Principal Dewan Mohammad Azraf, Prof ASM Nurul Hoque Bhuiyan of DU, politician Abul Hashim, writer & politician Shahed Ali, Prof Abdul Gafur, Prof Ghulam Azam, Prof Badrudin Umar, Prof Hasan Iqbal, A. K. M. Ahsan, S. Ahmed, Farid Ahmed, Shawkat Ali, M. A. N Shahidullah Shahittyoratno, Sanaullah Nuri, Prof Kazi Motahar Hossain, journalist Abul Mansur Ahmed, Prof Munir Chowdhury, Abdur Rahman, and Sulaiman Khan, among others) played a uniquely illustrious and historic role in the language movement in late 1940s and early 1950s. Unfortunately, they, now completely sunk in oblivion, are not remembered by the ungrateful in the month of February. Their vision of a Muslim Bangladesh has receded and withdrawn into the far and distant background, like the waves of the ebbing tide, in the present Bangladesh, affected by and infected with its own secularist fanaticism and fundamentalism. See: http://www.thedailystar.net/in-focus/the-origins-the-language-movement-574846; http://thedailynewnation.com/news/51438/the-historic-language-movement.html; http://www.bdnow.net/blog/blogdetail/detail/2601/muhon/74424; https://en.wikipedia.org/wiki/Tamaddun_Majlish; http://en.banglapedia.org/index.php?title=Tamaddun_Majlish
84. Besides Note #44 in the "Secularism" Chapter, see Sukhomoy Mukhopaddhaya সুখময় মুখোপাধ্যায়ের "বাংলার ইতিহাসের দু'শ বছর : স্বাধীন সুলতানদের আমল"; Hussain Imon, *Muslim Contribution to Bengali Literature* (in three installments): http://imbdblog.com/?p=8259; http://imbdblog.com/?p=8278; http://imbdblog.com/?p=8477; Muhammad Mojlum Khan, *The Muslim Heritage of Bengal: The Lives, Thoughts and Achievements of Great Muslim Scholars, Writers and Reformers of Bangladesh and West Bengal* (UK: KUBE Publishing, 2013); Muhammad Enamul Haq, *Muslim Bengali Literature* (1957); *Contemporary Bengali Writings*: Pre-Bangladesh Period (University Press, 1996). Also, http://newagebd.net/137648/fans-pay-tribute-to-al-mahmud/
85. https://www.youtube.com/watch?v=IDt2qJdnfy8
86. "ধরা যাবে না ছোঁয়া যাবে না বলা যাবে না কথা / রক্ত দিয়ে পেলাম শালার এমন স্বাধীনতা!/ যার পিছনে জানটা দিলাম যার পিছনে রক্ত/ সেই রক্তের বদল দেখো বাঁচাই কেমন শক্ত, / ধরা যাবে না ছোঁয়া যাবে না বলা যাবে না কথা /রক্ত দিয়ে পেলাম শালার মরার স্বাধীনতা!/ বাঁচতে চেয়ে খুন হয়েছি বুলেট শুধু খেলাম/ উঠতে এবং বসতে ঠুঁকি দাদার পায়ে সেলাম, / ধরা যাবে না ছোঁয়া যাবে না বলা যাবে না কথা / রক্ত দিয়ে পেলাম শালার আজব স্বাধীনতা!" Shakera Akhter, winner of national awards in singing and dancing and a graduate in Bangla from The National University of Bangladesh, who now lives in the USA, rhymes it in verse in her own way: "ধরা যাবে না, ছোয়া যাবে না / কোন কথা বলা যাবে না / পেলাম খাচায় বন্দী / এমন স্বাধীনতা".
87. http://www.dailynayadiganta.com/detail/news/60097
88. http://newagebd.net/156976/honouring-mujib-zia-may-pave-way-for-natl-unity-bnp/
89. https://www.dailyinqilab.com/article/61738
90. http://bangla.moralnews24.com/?p=50972

Afterword

Given the despotic and dictatorial one-party rule in Bangladesh,[1] the entire spectra of the country's political opposition believe that there can be no free and fair election under Sheikh Hasina, that she would never allow herself to be defeated so long as she was in power, and that she would do everything possible to make sure the outcome of the elections, be they general or local, went in her favor. The opposition demand that there be a neutral government at the time of the national polls has been supported, time and again, by the civil society, intelligentsia, critics, columnists, and the commentators, all alike, including the former President Badrudduza Chowdhury and the former minister (as a CTG member) and prominent lawyer Barrister Mainul Hussein. The blunt, candid, and outspoken Barrister Hussein, on Channel I TM of December 30, 2016, was clear and unequivocal about the impossibility of clean and credible elections under Hasina. All the fair and neutral minds of the country have been dismissing the pro-Awami hue and cry about the need for only a so-called "strong" Election Commission (EC) as a foul and false alarm, an eyewash, misplaced, if not totally mistaken.

They stress the fact that in the context of Bangladesh, no EC can ever be strong if the central government remains partisan and prejudiced with the entire bureaucracy, civil administration, law enforcement agents, and the media polarized and politicized, deeply entrenched in their partisanship and embedded with the government. If the nominally independent EC is already soft to the extent of being servile, slavish, and spineless, with no guts and gear and personality of its own, as has been the case since 2008, especially 2012, it is all the better for the biased and jaundiced government at the front and center, which maliciously and mischievously uses the deceptive name-and-paper-and-frame-only independence of the EC as a cover for its election-related ill deeds and misdeeds. Even if it is assumed that the EC is going to consist of tough and strong individuals, it would, however, still fail to stay strong and would hardly be able to do anything neutrally and independently under the ominous watch, threatening stare, veiled yet must-follow guidance, and covert yet commanding instructions of the all-controlling and all-powerful Hasina-led sitting government.

When this government did not and does not keep any electoral promises, did not dissolve the parliament before January 5, 2014 election (in violation of all democratic rules and norms), did not care to form a neutral government to earn the trust and confidence of the opposition, did not hold another election soon after the questionable 5 January as it promised it would, and does not allow the BNP to hold meetings and rallies, it can never be trusted or expected to hold free and fair, credible and inclusive elections. It exploits the issue of *khichuri* constitutional continuity when it suits it; it tramples it down when doing so favors it.

The Awami Hasina regime is again preparing, in its old phony and farcical tricks and tactics, its domesticated and subservient Ershad-cum-Rawshon team as the next con and consecutive opposition in the parliament, allowing the couple to hold their meetings and rallies in the Awami-owned Suhrawardy Uddyan, which, though a state-owned public venue, is off-limits to the BNP. A Bangladeshi-Canadian academic, based in the USA (that is, Dr Taj Hashmi of Austin Peay State University Tennessee) is critical of both the BNP and the Awami League (but certainly more of the latter). He believes, according to an August 2017 group e-post, that while "Ziaur Rahman was most definitely the most honest leader that Bangladesh has ever seen after Khwaja Nazimuddin, Hussein Shaheed Suhrawardy, and several other dedicated leaders involved in our politics during the 1930–1960s,"

> No political parties and no elections can overthrow this [Awami] regime. The whole bureaucracy, including the police, RAB, and other law-enforcers are [allegedly] jointly plundering the nation, along with bankers, industrialists, traders, professionals, so-called civil society members, and the NGOs. On top of that, Modi and Trump also are with the regime. BNP alone can't do anything and the average age of BNP leaders is 70++, and they are not all that honest either.

> I am a die-hard anti-Bakshal, and always prefer BNP to Awami League. But I have been extremely disillusioned with BNP's top and mid-level leadership. As I mentioned earlier, this is a totalitarian regime with bureaucrats and police and RAB and BGB as plundering buddies. It can't be removed through a peaceful, democratic process. NO WAY!
>
> What history tells us is that no brutal/fascist/quasi-fascist regime anywhere in the world was ever overthrown through elections. The Russian, Polish, Romanian, and East German communist regimes had to go because of mass insurrections. Conversely, some of those regimes were sometimes somewhat tolerant. For example, the Polish one allowed Lech Walesa to mobilize support for his Solidarity Movement. Hasina regime even doesn't tolerate a very mild, not-so-obedient Chief Justice's dissent.

The Narayanganj election between Dr Selina Hayat Ivy and Advocate Sakhawat Hussein was an eyewash, a hoodwink throwing dust in the eyes. It was allowed to run on a seemingly free and fair platform because the Hasina-led Awami League knew it was the pretty and popular and well-spoken Ivy who was going to win landslide, no matter what, so why not take the credit of allowing a relatively clean and credible election to cite an example of to be gladly and gleefully manipulated as necessary, for example, holding the next general election with Hasina at the helm. Mind the BNP, that prospect is a far cry, an illusion, a will-o'-the-wisp, a jack-o'-lantern, a hinkypunk![2] A strong EC, even if that is partially possible, is just a small step, but the real big and decisive and determining step is the formation of an acceptable interim neutral government during the time of the election.

Can the political opposition as represented by Khaleda Zia and her BNP-led alliance do more than what she/they have been doing?

The answer is both no and yes.

Khaleda Zia tried hard but to no avail. She is old and infirm and weak, both physically and mentally. She is completely alone living a lonely life, confined to her complete isolation and having lost both her sons, one literally and one half-literally, the former's death abroad (Malaysia) hastened by years of political, physical, and mental torture, both at home and away from home, and the latter living in exile (in London) with the burden of a bundle of politically cooked lawsuits and also the burden of his broken bones—most cruelly broken by his political foes in the *Uddins* years ago.

Despite all this, Khaleda tried to face and overcome the sand-and-cement trucks around her but to no success, due to the Awami police blocking her way.

Her own people could not come out in her support and rescue her from her bondage because they were already terrified by the relentless Awami terror coming down hard on them. Khaleda tried to protest by homelessly staying in her office premises for months but again to no avail and again her people proved to be hopelessly useless, mainly for the reason of the fear of the all-swallowing Awami police.

Time and again Khaleda tried to hold public meetings but failed. She was prevented from doing so by the Awami government and the Awami police. Anything and everything she says, from the EC reforms to the CTG formation suggestions, are immediately ruled out by the despotic and dictatorial Awami regime. Anything Khaleda says is hastily and impatiently dismissed right away without giving it an iota of thought; if she does not say anything, the regime hastens to say she did not care and did not have any regard for the people and the nation. What a doubling down on the Awami culture of denial and destruction!

Khaleda herself and her entire team are up to their neck fighting, like the Prometheus of ancient Greek myth and ancient Roman heroic gladiators, thousands of vindictive lawsuits on a daily basis. The politically motivated court cases are a preemptive strike against their potential to launch a political agitation for a democratic Bangladesh through a free and fair election. Khaleda and her men and women, despite almost insurmountable police odds and obstacles and bars and barricades, called for peaceful and democratic অবরোধ (siege), time and again, but all went in vain, due to the extremely hard and harsh Awami obstinacy and obduracy.

As Mohiuddin Anwar of the USA puts it,

> When opposition leaders cannot even conduct a public meeting in Bangladesh, especially in the capital Dhaka, how can a mass movement be carried out by Khaleda Zia to unseat the fascist Hasina regime? Sheikh Hasina is utilizing the brutal Police/RAB/BGB forces to stop any mass movement against her government. Hasina won't return democratic rights of the people as long as she remains in power. Opposition BNP will capture power only over the dead body of Sheikh Hasina as it happened during her father's rule. Awami League does not believe in handing over power to any opposition party to save their own lives. Mass movement won't be possible at this moment because of the brutal Police/RAB of Sheikh Hasina. People want to remove the tyrant ruler Hasina but do not want to sacrifice their own precious lives. (E-mail: July 13, 2017)

A similar idea was expressed by Dr Rashed Anam, also of the USA, when he said, "When there is no shred of democratic rights in the country, what good is it for us to talk about political integrity of different groups? Where one cannot exercise his political choice, what good is it to talk about political choices?" (E-mail: July 15, 2017).

In other words, there can be no wider and more serious protest or movement against the awful Awami autocracy and authoritarianism so long as there are the following existing:

1. Sheikh Hasina's tricky and tactical application of formalin to let the BNP merely survive as a crippled and cornered and crawling entity, as opposed to creating a democratically and electorally level-playing field for the opposition to succeed as a viable and effective opposition and compete with her AL;
2. Awami police/RAB boots and bullets and batons and remands and ডান্ডাবেড়ি and jail and জুলুম and হামলা ও মামলা and গুম ও খুন;
3. A certain percentage of the youth and the students working as Awami hoodlums and hooligans with live guns, pistols, *ramda*, and machetes;
4. All sectors, from the police/RAB to the civil bureaucracy/administration to the judiciary to the military, enjoying politically prompted promotion, empowerment, and salary hikes and therefore choosing to remain passive, pacifist, and peaceful, quietly or vehemently loyal to Hasina;
5. Rigged, farcical, staged, arranged, and theatrical elections, all tilted and twisted in/to her favor;
6. An EC that loves to be slavishly loyal to the Hasina government, delivering the results accordingly without caring in the least to be strong and neutral and above bias;
7. Corruption-ridden development projects, accompanied by scams and schemes, letting all the big fishes and businesses involved to be financially fat with both black and white money;
8. All the existing mass media tailored to promote the Hasina government agenda and act like a surrogate mouthpiece, while closing down the other media that try to be objective and independent or just different;
9. (Big fish) Indian hegemonic control and containment of the small fish Bangladesh, from top to bottom, right to left, all around and all over, so much so that Anwar Mohammad compares it to the ancient German Faust legend, that is, English dramatist Christopher Marlowe's story of Dr Faustus in which Faustus, a great scholar, sells his soul to Satan/Lucifer/Mephistopheles, out of evil temptations, for 24 years of black magic that brings him worldly joy, power, and privilege by the end of which period Faustus dies a Pharaoh-like death of intolerable pain and suffering only to face eternal damnation.[3] Animesh Rai too provides an authentic and comprehensive summary of Indian economic rape of Bangladesh before and

after the independence.[4] It is the same hostile and selfish India that refuses to change Bangladesh's currency notes for 50 crore rupee in Indian money following India's invalidation of its 500 and 1,000 rupee bills.[5]

Things should not have been the way they currently are, in the first place, forty-six years after independence. They are being run in a neo-and-near-and-more-than-partially fascist and totalitarian way. One freedom fighter, Ranu Chowdhury of the USA, was prompted by his sense of frustration to say: "But watching the state of Bangladesh today, the soldier himself sadly ponders: Was it worth? I believe, the soldier is not alone to think so. What a historical freak!"

Noting the futility and ineffectiveness of the political parties' discussion on the matter of the formation of the EC with President Abdul Hamid, who formed the same "jei lau shei kodu" committee—Awami saturated, Awami affiliated, and Awami loyalist—as his predecessor Zillur Rahman did, Chowdhury opined:

> And we shall have a replay of January 5. Let the opposition keep sucking its thumb. Shouldn't one feel sorry for the pitiable state the party (BNP) has been reduced to? Shouldn't its leadership feel ashamed of facing the public when it fails to lead them? The rank and file surely ask: where is the Khaleda Zia of the 1980s and 1990s? Why doesn't she come out of her comfort zone, face the BAKSALi fascism in open, if need be, and be a martyr? (E-mail of 25 January 2017)

I say I'm one of those who think so. I should also like to add that all the weak, ineffective, old and feeble-minded BNP leaders should resign. They utterly failed to rise up to the call of Khaleda to come out to the street in support of the Hefajote on May 5. Had they gotten out and thronged the streets of Dhaka alongside the Hefajote, the Hasina-Awami government would have fallen that very day. Shame on the BNP leaders, activists, and supporters!

The cold to lukewarm Mirza Fakhrul Islam Alamgir's performance (though much better than Awami Syed Ashraf and Obaidul Quader), should be as appealing as that of Shah Muazzem Hussein, Gayeshwar Chandra Roy, Amir Khusru Mahmud Chowdhury, *DeshKonnya* Advocate Ashifa Ashrafi Papia, *DeshKonnya* Barrister Rumin Farhana, *DeshKonnya* Shama Obaid, Maj Hafiz, Maj Akhtaruzzaman, (late) Shafiul Alam Prodhan, Barrister Andalib Partho, Dr Osman Farooque (although he is not very active for the reason of Awami witch-hunting and Awami vindictive politics), and Ehsanul Huq Milon, all of whom should be or should have been in the upper echelons of the party. It is long overdue that there be an overhaul and a restructuring of the BNP leadership. Similarly, Barrister Mainul Hussein, Dr Zafrullah Chowdhury, Mahmudur Rahman, Mahmudur

Rahman Manna, writer-journalist and media personality Mahfuzullah, Dr Tuhin Malik, ASM Rob, and journalist Ashraf Kaiser should all be invited and inducted into the top positions of the party to take it forward and inject and instill a fresh life into it.

The fuss and fanfare about the EC Search Committee was an eyewash, a theatrical farce, like January 5. Any dialogue on the EC or the Search Committee by President Abdul and PM Hasina with the political parties was just unnecessary, if only the President and the PM had the honesty, goodwill, and integrity at all. There was/is no need for the Search Committee because they know the people out there who are quite neutral and can make a strong EC. If they had the good intention, they could go ahead on their own, with discussion only with the BNP, to directly form an EC to the satisfaction of all. Don't they know there are many good and fair-minded people even within the Awami and the BNP camps, in addition to those who do not necessarily belong or subscribe to the views of either party? They pretend to be sleeping but they are actually awake.

To expect something different or neutral from President Abdul was to hope against hope, to chase a wild goose. Although he seemed to be a bit more of his own person than the last President, he failed to do his bit in consultation with his real boss Hasina, just as the latter who was distantly hoped to give a bit of semblance of fairness to the elections miserably failed to do her bit. Once again President Abdul, like his predecessor Zillur, proved to be partisan and failed to rise above the pure and sole party interest, not befitting the President of the people, the nation, and the country.

Given the theatrical staging of the endless Search Committee talks and its formation under both President Zillur and President Abdul, all this was as unnecessary as wearing glasses over the clear-sighted eyes when lying on bed and then putting a handkerchief over the glasses and then setting up a curtain over the bed, all to hide and cover up the ulterior motives. As the ugly heads ultimately creep up though the cover-ups to glaringly reveal themselves with gaping holes in them, such talks and tales are like annoying extra growths on the body needing a surgical operation to do away with, to return back to sound health with sound mind.

In view of all what is happening in Bangladesh and then looking back, the soldier in Ranu Chowdhury and the freedom fighters sacrificed for nothing or hardly anything. It wasn't worth their while. It wasn't worth the risk they took. They made all that sacrifice not to see the ruthless and repressive Hasina regime arresting hundreds every day and making the country empty of freedom and bereft of democracy. Since 2009, I've increasingly grown to be a pessimist, a frustrated idealist. One could be hopeful from 1971 through 2008, but not since.

One can be hopeful about God's endless mercy though. One can be hopeful about the expected return, as a pattern, on one's work, on the field, or in the office, at regular intervals; one can be hopeful about the regular diurnal, nocturnal, seasonal, lunar, and solar cycles; about the universal sunset and the sunrise, rain or shine, clear or cloudy skies; but not Bangladesh under the steamroller of the Hasina police/RAB and their pet and domestic hoodlums and hooligans.

I'm one with the fantastically firm and clear former Secretary Asafuddowla, a respected elder, who is one of the rare living pessimists in Bangladesh, because he could see nothing dawning on the horizon. If nothing positive and decisive happened for the Palestinians, Syrians, Iraqis, and the Rohingyas for ages, what can one hope for Bangladesh? One can only hope against hope about a divinely sanctioned miracle or an act of God to happen for the betterment of Bangladesh and its people. As the strong and intrepid Barrister Mainul Hussein said, if there was no democracy, no freedom of speech, and no free and fair elections, if there was a blockage here and blockade there, alternative forces would find their way to come forward to take over.

At the same time, one would like to ask, why should Bangladesh slide into becoming like Nawab Sirajuddowla's Bengal betrayed to the British by local and foreign agents, Lhendup Dorji's Sikkim surrendered to India by himself, Tipu Sultan's Mysore and the Nawabs' Hyderabad, both gone to India? Why should Bangladesh slide into becoming a one-party country like Sudan, Zimbabwe, Venezuela, Indochina, Egypt, Yemen, other countries of the Middle East, Central Asian countries, and the Communist/Socialist countries? Why are Khaleda/BNP alone expected to swim with their hands and feet tied? If they do with them and their supporters confronting the repressive regime in the street, won't Bangladesh become like Syria, Iraq, and Afghanistan, as pointed out by Mohiuddin Anwar, a freelance writer for a news agency in Washington, DC? Why shouldn't the AL play its part and why should it continue to fool the people and forcibly hang on to power without participatory and credible elections?

The only option that remains to be explored is the one suggested by Dr Zafrullah Chowdhury again and again—a united opposition movement with all the opposition figures and parties to take to the street together to express their anathema and opprobrium against the semi-and-near-fascist Hasina government. Why are still Dr Badrudduza Chowdhury, Dr Yunus, ASM Abdur Rob, Nur-e-Alam Siddiquee, Kader Siddiquee, Kamal Hussein, Mahmudur Rahman Manna, Junaid Saki, CPB, BSD, *Hefajote*, and Chor Monai Pir isolated loners, distanced and disengaged from each other? Along with the BNP-led 20-Party Alliance, all the lone wolves should unite, at least on a short term, to form an effective and strong pack of wolves to drive away or at least scare the autocratic and authoritarian incumbent to yield to the popular demand of the day—free and fair and participatory elections—from national down to local.

While some of my like-minded friends and freelancers are supportive of my above views, some would like to take a sour and serious note of dissent finding them as "kinder and gentler" and allowing that it is the BNP and its organizational and leadership weaknesses that are largely, if not solely and squarely, responsible for the problems and failures they face today. A section of those freelancing anti-Awami and pro-opposition watchers and observers would argue that the BNP and its oddly formed and detrimentally dysfunctional leadership lost many chances to fire and seize upon. Their arguments are not without merit. Like Dr Zafrullah Chowdhury, representative of them is Ranu Chowdhury's comment (May 5, 2017): "I wonder when would the opposition come to its sense that the more it remains inactive the sharper will be the attacks of the fascist government. There is a Chinese saying: in every disaster or desperate situation, there is an opportunity. BNP has been failing to avail itself of those opportunities. And, BNP's loss is AL's gain."

However, it's also true, it's easier said than done from within a fantastically and frighteningly controlled country, starting all the way from the BDR massacre on, when even the country's powerful military had to keep quiet and lie low over the loss of its own officers during those long fateful hours of bloody operation at Pilkhana.

While I do not have any intention of erupting into friendly fire or family feud, especially in a situation where not just the BNP but all Bangladeshis have become local political Rohingyas, I have always maintained that in the face of the ongoing and all devouring control of Bangladesh in the 21st century under which all opposition rights have been snatched away and all opposition leaders, from top to bottom, both sick and old, are each shouldering the burden of dozens of lawsuits and are constantly running away for fear of their lives every day and are living a virtual jail-and-remand-and-exile life, the BNP cannot be expected to do more than what it has been doing.

One third of the nation is all predatory in nature, character, and practice, all enjoying their wild freedoms and well protected from all sides, for whom all the rest are an easy prey, at the cruel "mercy" of the former, which is both omnivorous and carnivorous. How timid or courageous we all are, living abroad, can be determined when we all walk in the same shoes (of the political victims) in the same native homeland. Why should there be an overwhelming and all-controlling despotism for the majority and a wild and overflowing freedom for the ruling minority from 2009 onward, as of today, which should not and must not have been in the first place? Putting aside the matter of changing one or two faces in the leadership of the BNP (much suffering, much sacrificing, yet unimpressive Mirza Fakhrul being one of them), one cannot switch from the BNP to the (B)AL to jump into the Bay of Bengal and transform one's timidity into temerity and one's cowardice into courage. Why should only the BNP fight and die for others if the people accept the way it is under Sheikh Hasina, who faces popular protest wherever she goes (abroad) but who would suppress such popular outburst of dissent at home with the help of her "she-owned" police/RAB/BGB?

Let the political situation in Bangladesh evolve without any blood and violence but with all freedom and fairness, regardless of how long it takes. Unless and until there is a change of heart in Sheikh Hasina for peace, unity, equality, and social justice or there is a divine propeople miracle descending from the sky and miraculously transforming the situation, there may not be anything new and different any time soon in the political wilderness and the electoral map of Bangladesh. I believe people can only pray for Sheikh Hasina to live up to the composite and comprehensive spirit of liberation and its whole and holistic totality, not dissect and dismantle it, piece by piece, part by part, only to suit her purpose and manipulate it in her favor the way she dumped and ditched the otherwise fair and fine neutral CTG system that was in place for a few terms for the good of all, including herself and her party.

In the meantime, let me reiterate, reaffirm, and reconfirm my support for the BNP under Khaleda and Tarique, no matter how lonely and long suffering they are, despite their party's weaknesses in the Awami-caused dire circumstances. Under the AL's high and hot and hostile steamroller, I cannot think of any opportunity to qualify and tone down my pure, unmixed, unconditional, and unequivocal support for the BNP, despite its organizational weaknesses under the soft-spoken Mirza Fakhrul. In the absence of the young, competent, and charismatic Tarique and in the event of the great and glorious Khaleda going to Awami jail, the remarkably radiant and resplendent Dr Zubaidah Rahman should take over. In fact, she should do so soon at her earliest convenience, although she is also a victim of Awami vandalism of many a lawsuit against her.

Bangladesh Zindabad BNP Zindabad
President Zia Khaleda Zia Tarique Rahman Zindabad

Notes

1. https://indianseye.wordpress.com/2014/11/22/sheikh-hasina-bangladesh-the-worst-dictator-in-history/
2. "[…] An atmospheric ghost light seen by travellers at night, especially over bogs, swamps or marshes. It resembles a flickering lamp and is said to recede if approached, drawing travellers from the safe paths."—from the Wikipedia.
3. http://www.muldharabd.com/?p=1174
4. For Indian looting of Bangladesh, click: https://animeshrai.wordpress.com/2015/12/17/; http://www.animeshraiarko.com/2016/10/blog-post_2.html
5. http://www.kalerkantho.com/print-edition/first-page/2017/01/18/453250